Frame Analysis

FRAME
ANALYSIS

An Essay on the Organization of Experience

Erving Goffman

HARPER COLOPHON BOOKS
Harper & Row, Publishers
New York, Hagerstown, San Francisco, London

FRAME ANALYSIS: AN ESSAY ON THE ORGANIZATION OF EXPERIENCE
Copyright © 1974 by Erving Goffman

First HARPER COLOPHON edition published 1974

LIBRARY OF CONGRESS CATALOG CARD NUMBER: 74–4644

STANDARD BOOK NUMBER: 06–090372–4

79 80   12 11 10 9 8 7 6 5 4 3

Contents

Acknowledgments

Parts of this book were presented in lectures at Brandeis and the Universities of Tennessee, Manchester, and Edinburgh. A version of the whole was given as the Fenton Lectures, State University of New York at Buffalo, Spring 1970. I have drawn from papers done by students in my class on "frame analysis" over the last decade. I am grateful once again to Lee Ann Draud for her editorial and colleagial help in all phases of the book. Michael Delaney provided a very detailed critical reading; without specific recognition, I have incorporated a great number of his suggestions. Dell Hymes, William Labov, and Joel Sherzer provided a sociolinguistic environment. Mike Robinson, of Harper & Row, gave much-needed editorial assistance.

From *The Blacks: A Clown Show* by Jean Genet. Reprinted by permission of Grove Press, Inc. and Rosica Colin Limited.

From the *Boston Traveler*. Reprinted by permission of the Hearst Corp., Boston Herald American–Sunday Herald Advertiser Division.

From *The Connection* by Jack Gelber. Copyright © 1957 by Jack Gelber. Reprinted by permission of Grove Press, Inc. and the author.

From *Dear Abby* by Abigail Van Buren. Reprinted by permission of the Chicago Tribune–New York News Syndicate, Inc.

From *The Evening Bulletin*, Philadelphia. Reprinted by permission of The Philadelphia Evening and Sunday Bulletin.

From *Film Technique and Film Acting* by V. I. Pudovkin, translated by Ivor Montague, Memorial Edition, 1958. All rights reserved. Reprinted by permission of Grove Press, Inc., New York, and Vision Press Ltd., London.

From Kenneth Macgowan and William Melnitz, *Golden Ages of the Theater*, © 1959. Reprinted by permission of Prentice-Hall, Inc., Englewood Cliffs, N.J.

From Tom Prideaux, *Life* Magazine, Copyright © 1968 Time Inc. Reprinted with permission.

From *Lives of the Gamesters* by Theophilus Lucas, in *Games and Gamesters of the Restoration*. Reprinted by permission of Routledge & Kegan Paul Ltd.

From Los Angeles Times/Washington Post News Service dispatches, © The Washington Post. Reprinted by permission.

From Alan F. Blum, "Lower-Class Negro Television Spectators: The Concept of Pseudo-Jovial Scepticism," in Arthur B. Shostak and William Gomberg, eds., *Blue-Collar World: Studies of the American Worker*, © 1964. Reprinted by permission of Prentice-Hall, Inc., Englewood Cliffs, N.J.

From *Mutt and Jeff* by Al Smith, © 1972 McNaught Syndicate Inc. Reprinted by permission of the McNaught Syndicate.

From *The New York Times*. Copyright © 1962, 1966, 1967, 1968, 1970 by The New York Times Company. Reprinted by permission.

From *Peace* by Aristophanes, in *The Complete Greek Drama,* vol. 2, edited by Whitney J. Oates and Eugene O'Neill, Jr. Copyright 1938, renewed 1966 by Random House, Inc. Reprinted by permission of Random House, Inc.

From the *Philadelphia Inquirer.* Reprinted by permission.

From *The Observer,* London. Reprinted by permission.

From Reuters dispatches. Reprinted by permission.

From the *San Francisco Chronicle,* © 1954, 1962, 1963, 1964, 1965, 1966, 1967, 1968 by Chronicle Publishing Co. Reprinted by permission.

From *Theory of the Film* by Béla Balázs. Copyright © 1952 by Dobson Books, Ltd. Reprinted by permission of Dover Publications, Inc., New York, and Dobson Books, Ltd., London.

From *Time.* Reprinted by permission of *Time,* The Weekly Newsmagazine; Copyright Time Inc.

From *The Times,* London. Reproduced from *The Times* by permission.

From United Press International dispatches. Reprinted by permission.

from *Victims of Duty* by Eugène Ionesco. Reprinted by permission of Grove Press, Inc., New York, and Calder & Boyars Ltd, London.

From *We Bombed in New Haven,* by Joseph Heller. Copyright © 1967 by Scapegoat Productions, Inc. Reprinted by permission of Alfred A. Knopf, Inc. and Candida Donadio & Associates, Inc.

In this book a number of references are made to others I've written, for which the following abbreviations are used:

B.P.   *Behavior in Public Places: Notes on the Social Organization of Gatherings*
(Glencoe, Ill.: The Free Press of Glencoe, 1963)

E.   *Encounters: Two Studies in the Sociology of Interaction*
(Indianapolis: The Bobbs-Merrill Company, 1961)

I.R.   *Interaction Ritual: Essays on Face-to-Face Behavior*
(Garden City, N.Y.: Doubleday & Company, Anchor Books, 1967)

R.P.   *Relations in Public: Microstudies of the Public Order*
(New York: Basic Books, 1971; Harper & Row, Publishers, Harper Colophon Books, 1972)

S.   *Stigma: Notes on the Management of Spoiled Identity*
(Englewood Cliffs, N.J.: Prentice-Hall, 1964)

S.I.   *Strategic Interaction*
(Philadelphia: University of Pennsylvania Press, 1969; New York: Ballantine Books, 1972)

Frame Analysis

1

Introduction

There is a venerable tradition in philosophy that argues that what
the reader assumes to be real is but a shadow, and that by attending to what the writer says about perception, thought, the brain,
language, culture, a new methodology, or novel social forces, the
veil can be lifted. That sort of line, of course, gives as much
a role to the writer and his writings as is possible to imagine and
for that reason is pathetic. (What can better push a book than
the claim that it will change what the reader thinks is going on?)
A current example of this tradition can be found in some of the
doctrines of social psychology and the W. I. Thomas dictum: "If
men define situations as real, they are real in their consequences."
This statement is true as it reads but false as it is taken. Defining
situations as real certainly has consequences, but these may
contribute very marginally to the events in progress; in some
cases only a slight embarrassment flits across the scene in mild
concern for those who tried to define the situation wrongly. All
the world is not a stage—certainly the theater isn't entirely.
(Whether you organize a theater or an aircraft factory, you need
to find places for cars to park and coats to be checked, and these
had better be real places, which, incidentally, had better carry
real insurance against theft.) Presumably, a "definition of the
situation" is almost always to be found, but those who are in the
situation ordinarily do not *create* this definition, even though
their society often can be said to do so; ordinarily, all they do is to

1

assess correctly what the situation ought to be for them and then act accordingly. True, we personally negotiate aspects of all the arrangements under which we live, but often once these are negotiated, we continue on mechanically as though the matter had always been settled. So, too, there are occasions when we must wait until things are almost over before discovering what has been occurring and occasions of our own activity when we can considerably put off deciding what to claim we have been doing. But surely these are not the only principles of organization. Social life is dubious enough and ludicrous enough without having to wish it further into unreality.

Within the terms, then, of the bad name that the analysis of social reality has, this book presents another analysis of social reality. I try to follow a tradition established by William James in his famous chapter "The Perception of Reality,"[1] first published as an article in *Mind* in 1869. Instead of asking what reality is, he gave matters a subversive phenomenological twist, italicizing the following question: *Under what circumstances do we think things are real?* The important thing about reality, he implied, is our sense of its realness in contrast to our feeling that some things lack this quality. One can then ask under what conditions such a feeling is generated, and this question speaks to a small, manageable problem having to do with the camera and not what it is the camera takes pictures of.

In his answer, James stressed the factors of selective attention, intimate involvement, and noncontradiction by what is otherwise known. More important, he made a stab at differentiating the several different "worlds" that our attention and interest can make real for us, the possible subuniverses, the "orders of existence" (to use Aron Gurwitsch's phrase), in each of which an object of a given kind can have its proper being: the world of the senses, the world of scientific objects, the world of abstract philosophical truths, the worlds of myth and supernatural beliefs, the madman's world, etc. Each of these subworlds, according to James, has "its own special and separate style of existence,"[2] and "each world, *whilst it is attended to,* is real after its own fashion;

---

1. William James, *Principles of Psychology*, vol. 2 (New York: Dover Publications, 1950), chap. 21, pp. 283–324. Here, as throughout, italics in quoted materials are as in the original.
2. *Ibid.*, p. 291.

only the reality lapses with the attention."[3] Then, after taking this radical stand, James copped out; he allowed that the world of the senses has a special status, being the one we judge to be the realest reality, the one that retains our liveliest belief, the one before which the other worlds must give way.[4] James in all this agreed with Husserl's teacher, Brentano, and implied, as phenomenology came to do, the need to distinguish between the content of a current perception and the reality status we give to what is thus enclosed or bracketed within perception.[5]

James' crucial device, of course, was a rather scandalous play on the word "world" (or "reality"). What he meant was not *the* world but a particular person's current world—and, in fact, as will be argued, not even that. There was no good reason to use such billowy words. James opened a door; it let in wind as well as light.

In 1945 Alfred Schutz took up James' theme again in a paper called "On Multiple Realities."[6] His argument followed James' surprisingly closely, but more attention was given to the possibility of uncovering the conditions that must be fulfilled if we are to generate one realm of "reality," one "finite province of meaning,"

---

3. *Ibid.*, p. 293.

4. James' interest in the varieties-of-worlds problem was not fleeting. In his *Varieties of Religious Experience* (New York: Longmans, Green & Co., 1902) he approached the same question but through a different route.

5. "But who does not see that in a disbelieved or doubted or interrogative or conditional proposition, the ideas are combined in the same identical way in which they are in a proposition which is solidly believed" (James, *Principles of Psychology*, 2:286). Aron Gurwitsch in his *The Field of Consciousness* (Pittsburgh: Duquesne University Press, 1964) makes a similar comment in a discussion of Husserl:

Among such characters we mentioned those concerning modes of presentation, as when a thing is one time perceived, another time remembered or merely imagined) or when a certain state of affairs (the identical matter of a proposition) is asserted or denied, doubted, questioned, or deemed probable. [p. 327]

6. First appearing in *Philosophy and Phenomenological Research*, V (1945): 533–576; reprinted in his *Collected Papers*, 3 vols. (The Hague: Martinus Nijhoff, 1962), 1:207–259.) A later version is "The Stratification of the Life-World," in Alfred Schutz and Thomas Luckmann, *The Structures of the Life-World*, trans. Richard M. Zaner and H. Tristram Engelhardt, Jr. (Evanston, Ill.: Northwestern University Press, 1973), pp. 21–98. An influential treatment of Schutz's ideas is Peter L. Berger and Thomas Luckmann, *The Social Construction of Reality* (Garden City, N.Y.: Doubleday & Company, Anchor Books, 1966).

as opposed to another. Schutz added the notion, interesting but
not entirely convincing, that we experience a special kind of
"shock" when suddenly thrust from one "world," say, that of
dreams, to another, such as that of the theater:

> There are as many innumerable kinds of different shock experi-
> ences as there are different finite provinces of meaning upon which
> I may bestow the accent of reality. Some instances are: the shock
> of falling asleep as the leap into the world of dreams; the inner
> transformation we endure if the curtain in the theater rises as the
> transition into the world of the stageplay; the radical change in our
> attitude if, before a painting, we permit our visual field to be lim-
> ited by what is within the frame as the passage into the pictorial
> world; our quandary, relaxing into laughter, if, in listening to a
> joke, we are for a short time ready to accept the fictitious world of
> the jest as a reality in relation to which the world of our daily life
> takes on the character of foolishness; the child's turning toward his
> toy as the transition into the play-world; and so on. But also the
> religious experiences in all their varieties—for instance, Kierke-
> gaard's experience of the "instant" as the leap into the religious
> sphere—are examples of such a shock, as well as the decision of
> the scientist to replace all passionate participation in the affairs of
> "this world" by a disinterested contemplative attitude.[7]

And although, like James, he assumed that one realm—the
"working world"—had a preferential status, he was apparently
more reserved than James about its objective character:

> We speak of provinces of *meaning* and not of subuniverses be-
> cause it is the meaning of our experience and not the ontological
> structure of the objects which constitute reality,[8]

attributing its priority to ourselves, not the world:

> For we will find that the world of everyday life, the common-sense
> world, has a paramount position among the various provinces of
> reality, since only within it does communication with our fellow-
> men become possible. But the common-sense world is from the
> outset a sociocultural world, and the many questions connected

---

7. Schutz, *Collected Papers*, 1:231.

8. *Ibid.*, p. 230. See also Alfred Schutz, *Reflections on the Problem of
Relevance,* ed. Richard M. Zaner (New Haven, Conn.: Yale University
Press, 1970), p. 125. On matters Schutzian I am indebted to Richard
Grathoff.

with the intersubjectivity of the symbolic relations originate within it, are determined by it, and find their solution within it.[9]

and to the fact that our bodies always participate in the everyday world whatever our interest at the time, this participation implying a capacity to affect and be affected by the everyday world.[10] So instead of saying of a subuniverse that it is generated in accordance with certain structural principles, one says it has a certain "cognitive style."

Schutz's paper (and Schutz in general) was brought to the attention of ethnographic sociologists by Harold Garfinkel, who further extended the argument about multiple realities by going on (at least in his early comments) to look for rules which, when followed, allow us to generate a "world" of a given kind. Presumably a machine designed according to the proper specifications could grind out the reality of our choice. The conceptual attraction here is obvious. A game such as chess generates a habitable universe for those who can follow it, a plane of being, a cast of characters with a seemingly unlimited number of different situations and acts through which to realize their natures and destinies. Yet much of this is reducible to a small set of interdependent rules and practices. If the meaningfulness of everyday activity is similarly dependent on a closed, finite set of rules, then explication of them would give one a powerful means of analyzing social life. For example, one could then see (following Garfinkel) that the significance of certain deviant acts is that they undermine the intelligibility of everything else we had thought was going on around us, including all next acts, thus generating diffuse disorder. To uncover the informing, constitutive rules of everyday behavior would be to perform the sociologist's alchemy —the transmutation of any patch of ordinary social activity into an illuminating publication. It might be added that although James and Schutz are convincing in arguing that something like the "world" of dreams is differently organized from the world of everyday experience, they are quite unconvincing in providing any kind of account as to how many different "worlds" there are and whether everyday, wide-awake life can actually be seen as but one rule-produced plane of being, if so seen at all. Nor has

---

9. From "Symbol, Reality, and Society," Schutz, *Collected Papers*, 1:294.
10. *Ibid.*, p. 342.

there been much success in describing constitutive rules of everyday activity.[11] One is faced with the embarrassing methodological fact that the announcement of constitutive rules seems an
open-ended game that any number can play forever. Players
usually come up with five or ten rules (as I will), but there are no
grounds for thinking that a thousand additional assumptions
might not be listed by others. Moreover, these students neglect to
make clear that what they are often concerned with is not an
individual's sense of what is real, but rather what it is he can get
caught up in, engrossed in, carried away by; and this can be
something he can claim is really going on and yet claim is not
real. One is left, then, with the structural similarity between
everyday life—neglecting for a moment the possibility that no
satisfactory catalog might be possible of what to include therein
—and the various "worlds" of make-believe but no way of knowing how this relationship should modify our view of everyday
life.

Interest in the James-Schutz line of thought has become active
recently among persons whose initial stimulus came from
sources not much connected historically with the phenomenological tradition: The work of those who created what has come to be
called "the theater of the absurd," most fully exhibited in the

---

11. Schutz's various pronouncements seem to have hypnotized some
students into treating them as definitive rather than suggestive. His version of the "cognitive style" of everyday life he states as follows:

1. a specific tension of consciousness, namely, wide-awakeness, originating in full attention to life;
2. a specific *epoché*, namely suspension of doubt;
3. a prevalent form of spontaneity, namely working (a meaningful
spontaneity based upon a project and characterized by the intention
of bringing about the projected state of affairs by bodily movements
gearing into the outer world);
4. a specific form of experiencing one's self (the working self as the
total self);
5. a specific form of sociality (the common intersubjective world of communication and social action);
6. a specific time-perspective (the standard time originating in an
interaction between *durée* and cosmic time as the universal temporal
structure of the intersubjective world).

These are at least some of the features of the cognitive style belonging
to this particular province of meaning. As long as our experiences of this
world—the valid as well as the invalidated ones—partake of this style we
may consider this province of meaning as real, we may bestow upon it
the accent of reality. [*Ibid.*, pp. 230–231.]

analytical dramas of Luigi Pirandello. The very useful paper by Gregory Bateson, "A Theory of Play and Phantasy,"[12] in which he directly raised the question of unseriousness and seriousness, allowing us to see what a startling thing experience is, such that a bit of serious activity can be used as a model for putting together unserious versions of the same activity, and that, on occasion, we may not know whether it is play or the real thing that is occurring. (Bateson introduced his own version of the notion of "bracketing," a usable one, and also the argument that individuals can intentionally produce framing confusion in those with whom they are dealing; it is in Bateson's paper that the term "frame" was proposed in roughly the sense in which I want to employ it.)[13] The work of John Austin, who, following Wittgenstein,[14] suggested again that what we mean by "really happening" is complicated, and that although an individual may dream unrealities, it is still proper to say of him on that occasion that he is really dreaming.[15] (I have also drawn on the work of a student of Austin, D. S. Schwayder, and his fine book, *The Stratification of Behavior.*)[16] The efforts of those who study (or at least publish on) fraud, deceit, misidentification, and other "optical" effects, and the work of those who study "strategic interaction," including the way in which concealing and revealing bear upon definitions of the situation. The useful paper by Barney Glaser and Anselm Strauss, "Awareness Contexts and Social Interaction."[17] Finally, the modern effort in linguistically oriented disciplines to employ the notion of a "code" as a device which informs

12. *Psychiatric Research Reports* 2, American Psychiatric Association (December 1955), pp. 39–51. Now reprinted in his *Steps to an Ecology of Mind* (New York: Ballantine Books, 1972), pp. 177–193. A useful exegesis is William F. Fry, Jr., *Sweet Madness: A Study of Humor* (Palo Alto, Calif.: Pacific Books, 1968).

13. Edward T. Cone, in the first chapter of his *Musical Form and Musical Performance* (New York: W. W. Norton & Company, 1968), quite explicitly uses the term "frame" in much the same way that Bateson does and suggests some of the same lines of inquiry, but I think quite independently.

14. See, for example, Ludwig Wittgenstein, *Philosophical Investigations,* trans. G. E. M. Anscombe (Oxford: Basil Blackwell, 1958), pt. 2, sec. 7.

15. See, for example, chap. 7 in his *Sense and Sensibilia* (Oxford: Oxford University Press, 1962).

16. London: Routledge & Kegan Paul, 1965.

17. *American Sociological Review,* XXIX (1964): 669–679.

and patterns all events that fall within the boundaries of its application.

I have borrowed extensively from all these sources, claiming really only the bringing of them together. My perspective is situational, meaning here a concern for what one individual can be alive to at a particular moment, this often involving a few other particular individuals and not necessarily restricted to the mutually monitored arena of a face-to-face gathering. I assume that when individuals attend to any current situation, they face the question: "What is it that's going on here?" Whether asked explicitly, as in times of confusion and doubt, or tacitly, during occasions of usual certitude, the question is put and the answer to it is presumed by the way the individuals then proceed to get on with the affairs at hand. Starting, then, with that question, this volume attempts to limn out a framework that could be appealed to for the answer.

Let me say at once that the question "What is it that's going on here?" is considerably suspect. Any event can be described in terms of a focus that includes a wide swath or a narrow one and—as a related but not identical matter—in terms of a focus that is close-up or distant. And no one has a theory as to what particular span and level will come to be the ones employed. To begin with, I must be allowed to proceed by picking my span and level arbitrarily, without special justification.[18]

A similar issue is found in connection with perspective. When participant roles in an activity are differentiated—a common circumstance—the view that one person has of what is going on is likely to be quite different from that of another. There is a sense in which what is play for the golfer is work for the caddy. Different interests will—in Schutz's phrasing—generate different motivational relevancies. (Moreover, variability is complicated here by the fact that those who bring different perspectives to the "same" events are likely to employ different spans and levels of focus.) Of course, in many cases some of those who are committed to differing points of view and focus may still be willing to acknowledge that theirs is not the official or "real" one. Caddies

---

18. See the discussion by Emanuel A. Schegloff, "Notes on a Conversational Practice: Formulating Place," in David Sudnow, ed., *Studies in Social Interaction* (New York: The Free Press, 1972), pp. 75–119. There is a standard criticism of "role" as a concept which presents the same argument.

work at golf, as do instructors, but both appreciate that their job
is special, since it has to do with servicing persons engaged in
play. In any case, again I will initially assume the right to pick
my point of view, my motivational relevancies, only limiting this
choice of perspective to one that participants would easily recognize to be valid.

Further, it is obvious that in most "situations" many different
things are happening simultaneously—things that are likely to
have begun at different moments and may terminate dissynchro-
nously.[19] To ask the question "What is *it* that's going on here?"
biases matters in the direction of unitary exposition and simplic-
ity. This bias, too, I must be temporarily allowed.

So, too, to speak of the "current" situation (just as to speak of
something going on "here") is to allow reader and writer to continue along easily in their impression that they clearly know and
agree on what they are thinking about. The amount of time
covered by "current" (just as the amount of space covered by
"here") obviously can vary greatly from one occasion to the next
and from one participant to another; and the fact that participants seem to have no trouble in quickly coming to the same
apparent understanding in this matter does not deny the intellectual importance of our trying to find out what this apparent
consensus consists of and how it is established. To speak of
something happening before the eyes of observers is to be on
firmer ground than usual in the social sciences; but the ground is
still shaky, and the crucial question of how a seeming agreement
was reached concerning the identity of the "something" and the
inclusiveness of "before the eyes" still remains.

Finally, it is plain that retrospective characterization of the
"same" event or social occasion may differ very widely, that an
individual's role in an undertaking can provide him with a distinctive evaluative assessment of what sort of an instance of the
type the particular undertaking was. In that sense it has been
argued, for example, that opposing rooters at a football game do
not experience the "same" game,[20] and that what makes a party

19. Nicely described by Roger G. Barker and Herbert F. Wright, *Mid-
west and Its Children* (Evanston, Ill.: Row, Peterson & Company, 1964),
chap. 7, "Dividing the Behavior Stream," pp. 225–273.

20. Presented perhaps overstrongly in a well-known early paper by Albert H. Hastorf and Hadley Cantril, "They Saw a Game: A Case Study,"
Journal of Abnormal and Social Psychology, XLIX (1954): 129–234.

a good one for a participant who is made much of is just what makes it a bad one for a participant who thereby is made little of.

All of which suggests that one should even be uneasy about the easy way in which it is assumed that participants in an activity can be terminologically identified and referred to without issue. For surely, a "couple" kissing can also be a "man" greeting his "wife" or "John" being careful with "Mary's" makeup.

I only want to claim that although these questions are very important, they are not the only ones, and that their treatment is not necessarily required before one can proceed. So here, too, I will let sleeping sentences lie.

My aim is to try to isolate some of the basic frameworks of understanding available in our society for making sense out of events and to analyze the special vulnerabilities to which these frames of reference are subject. I start with the fact that from an individual's particular point of view, while one thing may momentarily appear to be what is really going on, in fact what is actually happening is plainly a joke, or a dream, or an accident, or a mistake, or a misunderstanding, or a deception, or a theatrical performance, and so forth. And attention will be directed to what it is about our sense of what is going on that makes it so vulnerable to the need for these various rereadings.

Elementary terms required by the subject matter to be dealt with are provided first. My treatment of these initial terms is abstract, and I am afraid the formulations provided are crude indeed by the standards of modern philosophy. The reader must initially bestow the benefit of mere doubt in order for us both to get to matters that (I feel) are less dubious.

The term "strip" will be used to refer to any arbitrary slice or cut from the stream of ongoing activity, including here sequences of happenings, real or fictive, as seen from the perspective of those subjectively involved in sustaining an interest in them. A strip is not meant to reflect a natural division made by the subjects of inquiry or an analytical division made by students who inquire; it will be used only to refer to any raw batch of occurrences (of whatever status in reality) that one wants to draw attention to as a starting point for analysis.

And of course much use will be made of Bateson's use of the term "frame." I assume that definitions of a situation are built up in accordance with principles of organization which govern events—at least social ones—and our subjective involvement in them; frame is the word I use to refer to such of these basic elements as I am able to identify. That is my definition of frame. My phrase "frame analysis" is a slogan to refer to the examination in these terms of the organization of experience.

In dealing with conventional topics, it is usually practical to develop concepts and themes in some sort of logical sequence: nothing coming earlier depends on something coming later, and, hopefully, terms developed at any one point are actually used in what comes thereafter. Often the complaint of the writer is that linear presentation constrains what is actually a circular affair, ideally requiring simultaneous introduction of terms, and the complaint of the reader is that concepts elaborately defined are not much used beyond the point at which the fuss is made about their meaning. In the analysis of frames, linear presentation is no great embarrassment. Nor is the defining of terms not used thereafter. The problem, in fact, is that once a term is introduced (this occurring at the point at which it is first needed), it begins to have too much bearing, not merely applying to what comes later, but reapplying in each chapter to what it has already applied to. Thus each succeeding section of the study becomes more entangled, until a step can hardly be made because of what must be carried along with it. The process closely follows the horrors of repetition songs, as if—in the case of frame analysis—what Old MacDonald had on his farm were partridge and juniper trees.

Discussions about frame inevitably lead to questions concerning the status of the discussion itself, because here terms applying to what is analyzed ought to apply to the analysis also. I proceed on the commonsense assumption that ordinary language and ordinary writing practices are sufficiently flexible to allow anything that one wants to express to get expressed.[21] Here I follow Carnap's position:

> The sentences, definitions, and rules of the syntax of a language are concerned with the forms of that language. But, now, how are these sentences, definitions, and rules themselves to be correctly expressed? Is a kind of super-language necessary for the purpose? And, again, a third language to explain the syntax of this super-language, and so on to infinity? Or is it possible to formulate the syntax of a language within that language itself? The obvious fear will arise that in the latter case, owing to certain reflexive defini-

---

21. *Wovan man nicht sprechen kann, ist nicht der satz, "Wovan man nicht sprechen kann, darüber muss man schweigen."*

tions, contradictions of a nature seemingly similar to those which are familiar both in Cantor's theory of transfinite aggregates and in the pre-Russellian logic might make their appearance. But we shall see later that without any danger of contradictions or antinomies emerging it is possible to express the syntax of a language in that language itself, to an extent which is conditioned by the wealth of means of expression of the language in question.[22]

Thus, even if one took as one's task the examination of the use made in the humanities and the less robust sciences of "examples," "illustrations," and "cases in point," the object being to uncover the folk theories of evidence which underlie resort to these devices, it would still be the case that examples and illustrations would probably have to be used, and they probably could be without entirely vitiating the analysis.

In turning to the issue of reflexivity and in arguing that ordinary language is an adequate resource for discussing it, I do not mean that these particular linguistic matters should block all other concerns. Methodological self-consciousness that is full, immediate, and persistent sets aside all study and analysis except that of the reflexive problem itself, thereby displacing fields of inquiry instead of contributing to them. Thus, I will throughout use quotation marks to suggest a special sense of the word so marked and not concern myself systematically with the fact that this device is routinely used in a variety of quite different ways,[23]

22. Rudolf Carnap, *The Logical Syntax of Language,* trans. Amethe Smeaton (London: Kegan Paul, Trench, Trubner & Co., 1937), p. 3.

23. I. A. Richards, for example, has a version in his *How to Read a Page* (New York: W. W. Norton & Company, 1942):

We all recognize—more or less unsystematically—that quotation marks serve varied purposes:

1. Sometimes they show merely that we are quoting and where our quotation begins and ends.
2. Sometimes they imply that the word or words within them are in some way open to question and are only to be taken in some special sense with reference to some special definition.
3. Sometimes they suggest further that what is quoted is nonsense or that there is really no such thing as the thing they profess to name.
4. Sometimes they suggest that the words are improperly used. The quotation marks are equivalent to *the so-called*.
5. Sometimes they only indicate that we are talking of the words as distinguished from their meanings. "Is" and "at" are shorter than "above." "Chien" means what "dog" means, and so forth.

There are many other uses. . . . [p. 66]

that these seem to bear closely on the question of frame, and that I must assume that the context of use will automatically lead my readers and me to have the same understanding, although neither I nor they might be able to explicate the matter further. So, too, with the warning and the lead that ordinary language philosophers have given us. I know that the crucial term "real" may have been permanently Wittgensteined into a blur of slightly different uses, but proceed on the assumption that carefulness can gradually bring us to an understanding of basic themes informing diversity, a diversity which carefulness itself initially establishes, and that what is taken for granted concerning the meaning of this word can safely so be done until it is convenient to attend to what one has been doing.

A further caveat. There are lots of good grounds for doubting the kind of analysis about to be presented. I would do so myself if it weren't my own. It is too bookish, too general, too removed from fieldwork to have a good chance of being anything more than another mentalistic adumbration. And, as will be noted throughout, there are certainly things that cannot be nicely dealt with in the arguments that follow. (I coin a series of terms—some "basic"; but writers have been doing that to not much avail for years.) Nonetheless, some of the things in this world seem to urge the analysis I am here attempting, and the compulsion is strong to try to outline the framework that will perform this job, even if this means some other tasks get handled badly.

Another disclaimer. This book is about the organization of experience—something that an individual actor can take into his mind—and not the organization of society. I make no claim whatsoever to be talking about the core matters of sociology—social organization and social structure. Those matters have been and can continue to be quite nicely studied without reference to frame at all. I am not addressing the structure of social life but the structure of experience individuals have at any moment of their social lives. I personally hold society to be first in every way and any individual's current involvements to be second; this report deals only with matters that are second. This book will have weaknesses enough in the areas it claims to deal with; there is no need to find limitations in regard to what it does not set about to cover. Of course, it can be argued that to focus on the nature of personal experiencing—with the implication this can have for giving equally serious consideration to all matters that might momentarily concern the individual—is itself a standpoint with marked political implications, and that these are conservative ones. The analysis developed does not catch at the differences between the advantaged and disadvantaged classes and can be said to direct attention away from such matters. I think that is true. I can only suggest that he who would combat false consciousness and awaken people to their true interests has much to do, because the sleep is very deep. And I do not intend here to provide a lullaby but merely to sneak in and watch the way the people snore.

Finally, a note about the materials used. First, there is the fact that I deal again in this book with what I have dealt with in others—another go at analyzing fraud, deceit, con games, shows of various kinds, and the like. There are many footnotes to and much repetition of other things I've written.[24] I am trying to order my thoughts on these topics, trying to construct a general statement. That is the excuse.

Second, throughout the book very considerable use is made of anecdotes cited from the press and from popular books in the biographical genre.[25] There could hardly be data with less face value. Obviously, passing events that are typical or representative don't make news just for that reason; only extraordinary ones do, and even these are subject to the editorial violence routinely employed by gentle writers. Our understanding of the world precedes these stories, determining which ones reporters will select and how the ones that are selected will be told. Human interest stories are a caricature of evidence in the very degree of their interest, providing a unity, coherence, pointedness, self-completeness, and drama only crudely sustained, if at all, by everyday living. Each is a cross between an *experimentum crucim* and a sideshow. That is their point. The design of these reported events is fully responsive to our demands—which are not for facts but for typifications. Their telling demonstrates the power of our

---

24. So much so that I use source abbreviations, a list of which can be found on p. xi.

25. An analysis of incidentally published stories—"fillers"—is provided by Roland Barthes along with an exhibition of literary license in "Structure of *Fait-Divers*," in his *Critical Essays*, trans. Richard Howard (Evanston, Ill.: Northwestern University Press, 1972), pp. 185–195.

conventional understandings to cope with the bizarre potentials of social life, the furthest reaches of experience. What appears, then, to be a threat to our way of making sense of the world turns out to be an ingeniously selected defense of it. We press these stories to the wind; they keep the world from unsettling us. By and large, I do not present these anecdotes, therefore, as evidence or proof, but as clarifying depictions, as frame fantasies which manage, through the hundred liberties taken by their tellers, to celebrate our beliefs about the workings of the world. What was put into these tales is thus what I would like to get out of them.

These data have another weakness. I have culled them over the years on a hit-or-miss basis using principles of selection mysterious to me which, furthermore, changed from year to year and which I could not recover if I wanted to. Here, too, a caricature of systematic sampling is involved.

In addition to clippings as a source of materials, I draw on another, one as questionable as the first. Since this study attempts to deal with the organization of experience as such, whether "actual" or of the other kinds, I will have recourse to the following: cartoons, comics, novels, the cinema, and especially, it turns out, the legitimate stage. I am here involved in no horrors of bias different from the ones already exhibited in the selection of bits of human interest news. But I am led to draw on materials that writers in other traditions use, whether in literary and dramatic criticism of current "high" culture or in the sort of sociological journalism which attempts to read from surface changes in commercially available vicarious experience to the nature of our society at large. In consequence, many of the things I have to say about these materials will have already been said many times and better by fashionable writers. My excuse for brazenly dipping into this preempted domain is that I have a special interest, one that does not recognize a difference in value between a good novel and a bad one, a contemporary play or an ancient one, a comic strip or an opera. All are equally useful in explicating the character of strips of experienced activity. I end up quoting from well-known works recognized as setting standards, and from minor works current at the time of writing, but not because I think these examples of their genre have special cultural worth and warrant endorsement. Critics and reviewers

cite the classics of a genre in dealing with current works in order
to explicate what if anything is significant and artful in them. I
draw clumsily on the same materials—as well as critiques of
them—simply because that is what is easy to hand. Indeed, these
materials are easy to everyone's hand, providing something of a
common fund of familiar experience, something that writers can
assume readers know about.

* * * * * *

That is the introduction. Writing one allows a writer to try to
set the terms of what he will write about. Accounts, excuses,
apologies designed to reframe what follows after them, designed
to draw a line between deficiencies in what the author writes and
deficiencies in himself, leaving him, he hopes, a little better defended than he might otherwise be.[26] This sort of ritual work

---

26. There is a useful article by Jacob Brackman called "The Put-On"
(*The New Yorker*, June 24, 1967, pp. 34–73). In his twelve-page introduction to the paperback edition he writes:

Updating. If "updating" this essay were to mean exchanging more current jokes and performers for ones since disappeared, and appending
how there came to be "put-on" head boutiques, and TV game shows, and
a Sears Put-On clothing shop, and publishers crowing "This is the novel
that makes you ask: *Is the author putting me on?*", and thousands of
winkful commercials that seemed to say, "I know that you know that
I'm trying to sell you. Let's you and me both goof on the product
together."—if I were to "update" along these lines, and if I were to add
little exegeses of Tiny Tim's wedding, Paul Morrissey's movies, Paul
McCartney's death, then the piece would begin to stink of inauthenticity.
. . .

I think you must let a piece like this stand—not in its syntax, necessarily, but within the limits of its original awareness—as a fragment of
cultural history. It may have been valid to the precise present for a
matter of months, or days; who will quibble now that time is so short?
Once the vision's devoured, mulched and incorporated, unless it has been
frozen somewhere, its moment—when only so much had happened,
when only so much had been revealed—is lost forever. All we have left
are "updated" reports, grotesquely stretched, debased and freshened up,
as what played itself out between haircuts is made to seem the rage of
a decade. If I were to do this piece today (which would itself be impossible) hardly anything in it would stay the same. Of things in the real
world about which one can try to write, sensibility may be the slipperiest.
If I won't write the new piece now, how can I go back and meddle with
the old one? [*The Put-On* (New York: Bantam Books, 1972), pp. 10–11.]

Brackman also argues that current items of cultural interest date very
rapidly and fully, and, by implication, that writings concerned with these
items will date quickly, too. He also suggests that the point of such writings

can certainly disconnect a hurried pedestrian from a minor inconvenience he might cause a passing stranger. Just as certainly, such efforts are optimistic when their purpose is to recast the way in which a long book is to be taken. (And more optimistic still in the case of a second edition's preface to an already prefaced edition, this being an attempt to recast a recasting.)

* * * * * *

But what about comments on prefaces? Where does such a topic taken up at such a point leave the writer and the reader (or a speaker and an audience)? Does that sort of talk strike at the inclination of the reader to discount or criticize prefacing as an activity? And if it turns out that the preface was written in bad faith, tailored from the beginning to exemplify this use that will have come to be made of it? Will the preface then be retrospectively reframed by the reader into something that really isn't a preface at all but an inappropriately inserted illustration of one? Or if an admission of bad faith is made unconvincingly, leaving open the possibility that the disclosure was an afterthought? What then?

* * * * * *

And does the last comment excuse me in any degree from having been puerile and obvious in commenting on prefaces, as when, in a book analyzing jokes, the writer is excused the badness of the cited jokes but not the badness of the analysis of them? (A novelist who nowadays injects direct address in the body of his work—"Dear Reader, if you've gone this far, you'll know I hate that character . . ."—easily fails to change the foot-

---

is to bring the not quite consciously appreciated to awareness, and to do this first, and that once again a restatement or republication will sound stale. All of this I think has some truth and correctly describes the contingencies of that kind of subject matter, there being inevitably an unstated element of the reader's interest that derives from the current interest of the item. This element will decline rather quickly, leaving the writer having written something that can no longer be read with interest. In fact, every analyst of jokes has faced this problem, since the current version of a basic joke which he writes about today will sound very dated tomorrow. But given what Brackman is stuck with reprinting, his introduction does the framing work that introductions can do to segregate the producer from his product, in this case arguing that the piece was an expression of his sensibility *then,* not now.

ing we allow him; but what if he writes that he would like to succeed in such a device but knows we will not let him?)

*   *   *   *   *   *

And what about discussions about being puerile and obvious? A word incorrectly spelled can, I think, be successfully used by the misspeller as an illustration of incorrect spelling and ana-lyzed as such. But can a writer posture in his writing and then effectively claim that all along he was only providing an illustra-tion of bad taste and lack of sophistication? Would it be neces-sary for him to show, and if so, how would he, that his claims were not merely a device hit upon after the fact to make the best out of what he was not able to prevent from being a bad thing?

*   *   *   *   *   *

And if in the first pages after acknowledging colleagues who had helped, I had said: "Richard C. Jeffrey, on the other hand, did not help." And if I had gone on here (in these later pages) to suggest that the aim had been to make a little joke and inciden-tally bring awareness to a tacit constraint on acknowledgment writing? Then the explication of this aim could be seen as bad faith—either a post-hoc effort to hedge on having tried to be witty or an admission of having entrapped the reader into accepting a plant, that is, a statement whose reason for inclusion would later be shown to have not been apparent. But if, as is in fact the case, the whole matter is enclosed as a question within a section of the introduction dealing with a consideration of introductions and is therefore not to be seen as having an initial character as a simple, straightforward introduction, what then?

And after all of this, can I get the point across that Richard C. Jeffrey in fact didn't help? Does this last sentence do it? And if so, had a conditional been used, as in: "And after all of this, could I get the point across . . . etc." What then? And would this last comment transform an assertion into an illustration and so once again cast the matter of Richard C. Jeffrey in doubt?

*   *   *   *   *   *

And if the preface and the comments on the preface and the comments on the comments on the preface are put in question, what about the asterisks which divide up and divide off the various sections in which this is managed? And if the orthog-raphy had still been intact, would this last question itself have undermined these framing devices, including the ones which bracket this sentence with the prior one?

*   *   *   *   *   *

And if above I had said: "What about the * * * * * * which divide up and divide off . . ."; would this be a proper use of print, and can an easy rule be formulated? Given the motivational relevancies of orthographers, a book on orthography can properly use a batch of print to illustrate print, to the neglect of saying something with its meaning. Similarly, a geography book can properly switch from words to maps. But when a mystery writer has his hero find a coded message on a torn bit of paper and then shows the clue to the reader by insetting it in the center of the page as though it were a map in a geography book, so that the reader sees the tear as well as the message, what sort of shift to a nonfictional frame has the writer asked the reader to make, and was he quite within his rights to ask it? Is it overly cute for an anthropologist reporting on the role of metaphor (with special reference to animal sources) to write, "One always feels a bit sheepish, of course, about bringing the metaphor concept into the social sciences and perhaps that is because one always feels there is something soft and wooly about it"?[27] Similarly, if I try to get dodgy with prefaces, is this not different from writing about tricks done with prefaces (which characteristically need not be undertaken at the beginning of a study)? Is this not the difference between doing and writing about the doing? And in considering all of these matters, can I properly draw on my own text ("And if above I had said: 'What about the * * * * * * that divide up and divide off . . .'; would this be . . .") as an illustration? And in this last sentence has not all need to be hesitant about the right to use actual asterisks disappeared, for after all, a doubtful usage cited as an example of doubtful usage ceases to be something that is doubtful to print?

*   *   *   *   *   *

And if I wanted to comment on the next to last sentence, the one containing a parenthesized quoted sentence and questionably real asterisks, could I quote *that* sentence effectively, that is,

---

27. James W. Fernandez, "Persuasions and Performances: Of the Beast in Every Body . . . And the Metaphors of Everyman," *Daedalus*, Winter 1972, p. 41.

employ the apparently required punctuation marks and yet allow the reader an easy comprehension of what was being said about what? Would the limits of doing things in print have been reached?

*   *   *   *   *   *

That is what frame analysis is about.

2

Primary Frameworks

I

When the individual in our Western society recognizes a particular event, he tends, whatever else he does, to imply in this response (and in effect employ) one or more frameworks or schemata of interpretation of a kind that can be called primary. I say primary because application of such a framework or perspective is seen by those who apply it as not depending on or harking back to some prior or "original" interpretation; indeed a primary framework is one that is seen as rendering what would otherwise be a meaningless aspect of the scene into something that is meaningful.

Primary frameworks vary in degree of organization. Some are neatly presentable as a system of entities, postulates, and rules; others—indeed, most others—appear to have no apparent articulated shape, providing only a lore of understanding, an approach, a perspective. Whatever the degree of organization, however, each primary framework allows its user to locate, perceive, identify, and label a seemingly infinite number of concrete occurrences defined in its terms. He is likely to be unaware of such organized features as the framework has and unable to describe the framework with any completeness if asked, yet these handicaps are no bar to his easily and fully applying it.

In daily life in our society a tolerably clear distinction is

21

sensed, if not made, between two broad classes of primary frame-works: natural and social. Natural frameworks identify occur-rences seen as undirected, unoriented, unanimated, unguided, "purely physical." Such unguided events are ones understood to be due totally, from start to finish, to "natural" determinants. It is seen that no willful agency causally and intentionally interferes, that no actor continuously guides the outcome. Success or failure in regard to these events is not imaginable; no negative or posi-tive sanctions are involved. Full determinism and determinate-ness prevail. There is some understanding that events perceived in one such schema can be reductively translated into ones perceived in a more "fundamental" framework and that some premises, such as the notion of the conservation of energy or that of a single, irreversible time, will be shared by all. Elegant versions of these natural frameworks are found, of course, in the physical and biological sciences.[1] An ordinary example would be the state of the weather as given in a report.

Social frameworks, on the other hand, provide background understanding for events that incorporate the will, aim, and controlling effort of an intelligence, a live agency, the chief one being the human being. Such an agency is anything but implac-able; it can be coaxed, flattered, affronted, and threatened. What it does can be described as "guided doings." These doings subject the doer to "standards," to social appraisal of his action based on its honesty, efficiency, economy, safety, elegance, tactfulness, good taste, and so forth. A serial management of consequentiality is sustained, that is, continuous corrective control, becoming most apparent when action is unexpectedly blocked or deflected and special compensatory effort is required. Motive and intent are involved, and their imputation helps select which of the various social frameworks of understanding is to be applied. An example

---

1. Edward Shils, in a suggestive paper on the sociopolitical aspects of the moral order, "Charisma, Order and Status," *American Sociological Review*, XXX (1965): 199–213, argues:

  The fundamental discoveries of modern science in cosmology, astron-omy, medicine, neurology, geology, genetics, are significant as disclosures of the basic order of the cosmos. Scientific order, like the order disclosed by theology, has its imperatives. Being in "regular relations" with the truths of science, doing things the "scientific way," having a "scientific attitude" are as much responses to the imperatives of the order disclosed by scientific research as pious godfearingness is a response to the im-peratives of the theologically disclosed religious order. [p. 204]

of a guided doing would be the newscast reporting of the weather. So one deals here with deeds, not mere events. (We support some perceivedly basic distinctions within the social sphere, such as that between human and animal purposiveness, but more of this later.) We use the same term, "causality," to refer to the blind effect of nature and the intended effect of man, the first seen as an infinitely extended chain of caused and causing effects and the second something that somehow begins with a mental decision.[2]

In our society we feel that intelligent agents have the capacity to gear into the ongoing natural world and exploit its determinacy, providing only that natural design is respected. Moreover, it is felt that, with the possible exception of pure fantasy or thought, whatever an agent seeks to do will be continuously conditioned by natural constraints, and that effective doing will require the exploitation, not the neglect, of this condition. Even when two persons play checkers by keeping the board in their heads, they will still have to convey information concerning moves, this exchange requiring physically competent, willful use of the voice in speech or the hand in writing. The assumption is, then, that although natural events occur without intelligent intervention, intelligent doings cannot be accomplished effectively without entrance into the natural order. Thus any segment of a socially guided doing can be partly analyzed within a natural schema.

Guided doings appear, then, to allow for two kinds of understanding. One, more or less common to all doings, pertains to the patent manipulation of the natural world in accordance with the special constraints that natural occurrings impose; the other understanding pertains to the special worlds in which the actor can become involved, which, of course, vary considerably. Thus each play in checkers involves two radically different bases for guidance: one pertains to quite physical matters—to the physical management of the vehicle, not the sign; the other pertains to the very social world of opposing positions that the play

---

2. Refinements provided by philosophers unintentionally express the murkiness of our ideas here. See, for example, Arthur C. Danto, "What We Can Do," *Journal of Philosophy*, LX (1963): 435–445, and "Basic Actions," *American Philosophical Quarterly*, II (1965): 141–148; and Donald Davidson, "Agency," in Robert Binkley et al., eds., *Agent, Action and Reason* (Toronto: University of Toronto Press, 1971), pp. 3–25.

has generated, wherein a move can equally well be made by voice, gesture, or the mails, or by physically shifting a checker by the fist, any combination of fingers, or the right elbow. Behavior at the board can easily be separated into making moves and shifting checkers. And an easy distinction can be drawn between a clumsy move, one that ill considers the strategic positions of the two players, and a move made clumsily, one that has been badly executed according to local social standards for accomplishing physical acts. Observe that although an adult with a newly acquired prosthetic device might play checkers fully mindful of the physical task involved, ordinary players do not. Decisions as to which move to make are problematic and significant; pushing the checker once the decision is made is neither. On the other hand, there are guided doings such as fixing a sink or clearing a sidewalk in which sustained, conscious effort is given to manipulating the physical world, the doing itself taking on the identity of an "instrumental procedure," a task, a "purely utilitarian" activity—a doing the purpose of which cannot be easily separated from the physical means employed to accomplish it.

All social frameworks involve rules, but differently. For example, a checker move is informed by rules of the game, most of which will be applied in any one complete playing through of the game; the physical manipulation of a checker, on the other hand, involves a framework informing small bodily movements, and this framework, if indeed it is possible to speak in terms of *a* or *one* framework, might well be manifest only partially during the playing of a game. So, too, although the rules for checkers and the rules of vehicular traffic can be (and are) well enough explicated within the confines of a small booklet, there is a difference: the game of checkers incorporates an understanding of the governing purpose of the participants, whereas the traffic code does not establish where we are to travel or why we should want to, but merely the restraints we are to observe in getting there.

In sum, then, we tend to perceive events in terms of primary frameworks, and the type of framework we employ provides a way of describing the event to which it is applied. When the sun comes up, a natural event; when the blind is pulled down in order to avoid what has come up, a guided doing. When a coroner asks the *cause* of death, he wants an answer phrased in the natural schema of physiology; when he asks the *manner* of death, he wants a dramatically social answer, one that describes what is quite possibly part of an intent.[3]

The idea of a primary framework is, then, the first concept that is needed: I wish it were more satisfactory. For example, there is the embarrassing fact that during any one moment of activity, an individual is likely to apply several frameworks. ("We waited till the rain stopped and then started the game again.") Of course, sometimes a particular framework is chiefly relevant and provides a first answer to the question "What is it that's going on here?" The answer: an event or deed described within some primary framework. Then one can begin to worry about the microanalytic issues of what is meant by "we," "it," and "here" and how the implied consensus is accomplished.

Now a further consideration is necessary. When an x and y axis can be located as the framework within which to identify a given point, or a checkerboard is brought to mind as a matrix within which to locate a move, the notion of a primary framework is clear enough, although even here there is the issue of the dependency of a particular framework upon our understanding of frameworks of that type. When one looks at some ordinary happening in daily life, say, a passing greeting or a customer's request for the price of an article, an identification of the primary

---

3. Marshall Houts, *Where Death Delights* (New York: Coward-McCann, 1967), pp. 135–136. Guy E. Swanson, "On Explanations of Social Interaction," *Sociometry*, XXVIII (1965), presents the same argument and then warns that this observation itself does not carry us far enough:

We understand or explain an empirical event by showing that it is an instance, an aspect, a phase, a consequence, or a cause of other events. Conceptualization is the symbolic formulation of such relationships. In translation, one provides more than one conceptualization for a given event. Thus a wave of the hand might be conceptualized in physical terms as a discharge of energy, in biological terms as a neuro-muscular process, in psychological terms as a symptom of anxiety, and in social terms as a gesture of greeting.

The special danger for our purposes is that translation, the multiple conceptualization of an event, is made a substitute for an identification of the steps by which events of one order, that is, behavioral interaction, become events of another order, that is, social interaction. To show that a wave of the hand may fruitfully be considered both as a symptom of anxiety and a greeting tells us nothing of how it came to be either or how it might become merely one and not the other. Translation is a matter of *multiple classification*. What we require are interrelated *implications*. [p. 110]

framework is, as already suggested, very considerably more problematic. Here indeed is where the writers in the tradition I am employing have quietly fallen down. To speak here of "everyday life" or, as Schutz does, of the "world of wide-awake practical realities" is merely to take a shot in the dark. As suggested, a multitude of frameworks may be involved or none at all. To proceed, however, an operating fiction might be accepted, at least temporarily, namely, that acts of daily living are understandable because of some primary framework (or frameworks) that informs them and that getting at this schema will not be a trivial task or, hopefully, an impossible one.

In describing primary frameworks so far I have limited attention to those that are assumed (explicitly or in effect) by the individual in deciding what it is that is going on, given, of course, his particular interests. The individual, it is true, can be "wrong" in his interpretations, that is, misguided, out of touch, inappropriate, and so forth. "Wrong" interpretations will be considered throughout. Here I want only to mention the belief that in many cases the individual in our society is effective in his use of particular frameworks. The elements and processes he assumes in his reading of the activity often *are* ones that the activity itself manifests—and why not, since social life itself is often organized as something that individuals will be able to understand and deal with. A correspondence or isomorphism is thus claimed between perception and the organization of what is perceived, in spite of the fact that there are likely to be many valid principles of organization that could but don't inform perception. And just as others in our society find this an effective claim, so do I.[4]

---

4. Some students would have it, of course, that the belief I express here is unnecessary and misplaced and that one ought to restrict oneself totally to analyzing a subject's conceptions without drawing on the issue of their validity, except when this issue is itself treated as merely another matter to examine ethnographically. Else one confound subject matter with the means of studying it. Such a position introduces a famous problem of its own, the requirement that readers exempt the writer's generalizations from the treatment he advocates for everyone else's. (I believe writers should be indulged in this requirement, since they often succeed in illuminating matters through this indulgence.) More important, it can be argued that although all interpretive responses ought to be treated as a subject matter, *some* happen to provide useful beginnings *of*, not merely *for*, analysis.

II

Taken all together, the primary frameworks of a particular social group constitute a central element of its culture, especially insofar as understandings emerge concerning principal classes of schemata, the relations of these classes to one another, and the sum total of forces and agents that these interpretive designs acknowledge to be loose in the world. One must try to form an image of a group's framework of frameworks—its belief system, its "cosmology"—even though this is a domain that close students of contemporary social life have usually been happy to give over to others. And note that across a territory like the United States there is an incomplete sharing of these cognitive resources. Persons otherwise quite similar in their beliefs may yet differ in regard to a few assumptions, such as the existence of second sight, divine intervention, and the like.[5] (Belief in God and in the

---

5. According to an AP report (*San Francisco Chronicle*, March 4, 1968), Marine Colonel David E. Lownds authorized Lance Corporal D. E. Isgris to use brass divining rods to search for suspected North Vietnamese buried tunnels in Khe Sanh:

"No matter how stupid anything is, and I don't say the brass rods are stupid, we use it," said the base commander. . . .
Wells' [commander of the sector where an underground tunnel was found] men—from C Company, First Battalion of the 26th Regiment—are using divining rods. Over a tunnel the rods are supposed to either cross or spread apart, depending on the individual.

The military is not alone in manifesting this sort of open-mindedness. As a last resort, the then assistant attorney general of Massachusetts, John S. Bottomly, apparently authorized use of the Dutch seer Peter Hurkos in an effort to identify the Boston Strangler. See Gerold Frank, *The Boston Strangler* (New York: New American Library, 1966), pp. 87–120. The widely publicized (and televised) efforts of the late Bishop James A. Pike to reach his son who had departed to the other side is another case in point. (See, for example, *Time*, October 6, 1967; Hans Holzer, *The Psychic World of Bishop Pike* [New York: Crown Publishers, 1970]; and James A. Pike [with Diane Kennedy], *The Other Side* [New York: Dell Publishing Co., 1969]. An historical treatment of late Victorian spiritualism in England is provided by Ronald Pearsall, *The Table-Rappers* [London: Michael Joseph, Ltd., 1972].) I might add that often those who hold these occult beliefs feel they are supporting a scientific view, merely one that has not yet been accepted by the authorities in charge of our sciences. Here see Marcello Truzzi, "Towards a Sociology of the Occult: Notes on Modern Witchcraft" (unpublished paper, 1971).

sacredness of His local representatives seems to constitute currently one of the largest bases of dissensus in our society concerning ultimate forces. Tact ordinarily prevents social scientists
from discussing the matter.)

III

The notion of primary framework, unsatisfactory as it is, does
allow one immediately to consider five distinctive matters and to
appreciate something of their bearing on our overall understanding of the workings of the world.

1. First, the "astounding complex." An event occurs, or is
made to occur, that leads observers to doubt their overall approach to events, for it seems that to account for the occurrence,
new kinds of natural forces will have to be allowed or new kinds
of guiding capacities, the latter involving, perhaps, new kinds of
active agents. Here are included what appear to be visitations and
communications from outer space, religious healing miracles,
sightings of monsters from the deep, levitations, horses that are
mathematically inclined, fortune-telling, contacting the dead, and
so forth. As suggested, these astonishing occurrences imply the
existence of extraordinary natural forces and guidance capacities: for example, astrological influences, second sight, extrasen-
sory perception, and so on. Believe-it-or-not books are available
detailing events that are "still unexplained." Occasionally scientists themselves make news by giving what is defined as serious
attention to ESP, UFOs, influences deriving from the phases of
the moon,[6] and the like. Many private persons can call to mind at
least one event which they themselves have never quite been able
to account for reasonably. Yet in general, when an astounding
event occurs, individuals in our society expect that a "simple" or
"natural" explanation will soon be discovered, one that will clear
up the mystery and restore them to the range of forces and
agents that they are accustomed to and to the line they ordinarily
draw between natural phenomena and guided doings. Certainly
individuals exhibit considerable resistance to changing their

---

6. See, for example, *Time*, January 10, 1972, a story entitled "Moon-
struck Scientists."

framework of frameworks. A public stir—or at least a ripple—is caused by any event that apparently cannot be managed within the traditional cosmology. An example from the press might be cited:

> Alamasco, Colo.—An autopsy on a horse believed by its owners to have been killed by inhabitants of a flying saucer has revealed that its abdominal, brain and spinal cavities were empty.
>
> The pathologist, a Denver specialist who wished to remain anonymous, said the absence of organs in the abdominal cavity was unexplainable.
>
> Witnessing the autopsy Sunday night at the ranch where the carcass was found were four members of the Denver team of the National Members Investigating Committee on Aerial Phenomena.
> . . . .
> When the pathologist sawed into the horse's brain cavity he found it empty. "There definitely should have been a good bit of fluid in the brain cavity," the pathologist said.
> . . . .
> The Appaloosa's owners said they believe the horse was killed by occupants of a flying saucer. Several others in the San Luis Valley, where as many as eight sightings of unidentified flying objects have been reported in one evening recently, had said they agree. . . .[7]

And we expect a resolution as follows:

> Moscow (AP)—A Russian housewife who startled the world seven years ago with her claims of "finger vision" has been exposed as a fraud, a Soviet newspaper said.
>
> Five scientists who tested Mrs. Rosa Kuleshova concluded that she had been peeking through holes in her blindfold.
>
> Mrs. Kuleshova, a celebrity in her home town, gained an international reputation when her alleged powers to see with her fingertips were publicized in the Soviet press in 1963.
>
> The commission wrote that Mrs. Kuleshova's claims were given credence erroneously in 1963 when she was tested by Soviet scientists who shined a beam of color on her hands while her eyes were covered by various means.
>
> But the color machine made "squeaking and rustling noises," the commissioners wrote and helped tip her off as to what color came next. . . .[8]

---

7. *San Francisco Chronicle*, October 10, 1967.
8. *The New York Times*, October 11, 1970.

Let me repeat: in our society the very significant assumption is generally made that all events—without exception—can be contained and managed within the conventional system of beliefs. We tolerate the unexplained but not the inexplicable.

2. Cosmological interests, in some ways the largest we can have, support a humble entertainment: the exhibition of stunts, that is, the maintenance of guidance and control by some willed agency under what are seen as nearly impossible conditions. Here is found the doings of jugglers, tightrope walkers, equestrians, surfers, trick skiers, knife throwers, high divers, daredevil drivers, and, currently, astronauts, these last having the greatest act of all, albeit one for which they must share credits with American technology. One might also include the stunts that individuals can learn to perform with their physiology, as when a function like blood pressure or pain response is brought under voluntary control. Note that "animal acts" play an important role in regard to stunting. Trained seals, sociable porpoises, dancing elephants, and acrobatic lions all exemplify the possibility of ordinary guided doings done by alien agents, thus drawing attention to the cosmological line drawn in our society between human agents and animal ones. So, too, when animals are shown to have been pressed into doing the sort of utilitarian tasks that are felt to be the exclusive province of man, as when a chimp causes deep consternation on the highway because her trainer has taught her to steer an open sports car while he appears to be asleep in the next seat, or a troop of chimps is employed by a farmer in Australia to help with the harvesting.[9] It might be added that some academic research is supported by the same interest, the object being to establish with precision just where the line ought to be drawn between animals and man in regard to capacity for guided doings.[10]

---

9. Some comments on apes at work are available in Geoffrey H. Bourne, *The Ape People* (New York: New American Library, Signet Books, 1971), esp. pp. 140–141.

10. The leading illustrations here are the efforts to establish communication with dolphins and to test the effects of human socialization upon monkeys. Academicians are also, of course, employed to critically test claims regarding animals that, if established, would necessitate a modification in our primary beliefs. See, for example, O. Hobart Mowrer, "On the Psychology of 'Talking Birds': A Contribution to Language and Personality Theory," in his *Learning Theory and Personality Dynamics* (New York:

It is worth noting that both the astounding complex (in the form of human freaks) and stunts are closely associated with circus sideshows, as if a social function of circuses (and latterly, marine museums) were to clarify for patrons what the ordering and limits of their basic frameworks are.[11] Stunts also figure in vaudevillelike nightclub acts (now much in decline), as do the talents of trained dogs, acrobatic teams, jugglers, magicians, and, as will be considered later, "mentalists." Whatever the viewers obtain from such exhibits, it is clear that interest in cosmologically grounded issues is an everyday concern of the layman and by no means restricted to laboratory and field researchers.

3. Consider now "muffings," namely, occasions when the body, or some other object assumed to be under assured guidance, unexpectedly breaks free, deviates from course, or otherwise slips from control, becoming totally subject to—not merely conditioned by—natural forces, with consequent disruption of orderly

---

The Ronald Press, 1950), pp. 688–726. Of course, no traditional philosophical system was complete without a thumping statement on the "essential" difference between man and animals; it is only recently that this responsibility has been taken over by students in the social and biological sciences.

11. The monstrosities that were exhibited in sideshows to country folk and townspeople in our society seem cousin to the ones used in some preliterate initiation ceremonies, or so Victor Turner suggests in "Betwixt and Between: The Liminal Period in *Rites de Passage*," in his *The Forest of Symbols* (Ithaca, N.Y.: Cornell University Press, 1967):

> Earlier writers . . . are inclined to regard bizarre and monstrous masks and figures, such as frequently appear in the liminal period of initiations, as the product of "hallucinations, night-terrors and dreams." McCulloch goes on to argue that "as man drew little distinction (in primitive society) between himself and animals, as he thought that transformation from one to the other was possible, so he easily ran human and animal together. . . ." My own view is the opposite one: that monsters are manufactured precisely to teach neophytes to distinguish clearly between the different factors of reality, as it is conceived in their culture. . . .
>
> From this standpoint, much of the grotesqueness and monstrosity of liminal *sacra* may be seen to be aimed not so much at terrorizing or bemusing neophytes into submission or out of their wits as at making them vividly and rapidly aware of what may be called the "factors" of their culture. I have myself seen Ndembu and Luvale masks that combine features of both sexes, have both animal and human attributes, and unite in a single representation human characteristics with those of the natural landscape. . . . Monsters startle neophytes into thinking about objects, persons, relationships, and features of their environment they have hitherto taken for granted. [pp. 104–105]

life. Thus, "flubs," "goofs," and—when the guidance of meaning in talk should have occurred—"gaffes." (The limiting case would be where no blame whatsoever attaches, as when an earthquake is given full responsibility for a person's having spilled a cup of tea.) The body here retains its capacity as a natural, causal force, but not as an intentioned, social one. An example might be cited:

> Five persons were injured—two seriously—yesterday when a car went out of control and ran them down on a crowded Haight-Ashbury sidewalk.
>
> The driver of the car, 23-year-old Ed Hess of 615 Cole Street, was taken in a near hysterical condition to Park Station, where he was booked on charges of carrying a concealed weapon and suspicion of possessing dangerous drugs.
>
> "I couldn't stop the car," he cried. "There were people all over—four, six, eight people—but oh, God, it wasn't my fault."
>
> . . . .
>
> Witnesses said the car was westbound on Haight Street just past the Masonic Avenue intersection when it jumped the curb, plowed into the windows of the New Lite Supermarket and swept 50 feet farther down the sidewalk.
>
> . . . .
>
> "I didn't mean to hurt them," he [Hess] sobbed, "but they were all around me—on my left, right, all around."[12]

Note, a stunt occurs when we might well expect and even condone a loss of control, a muffing when exemplary effort is not felt to be needed to maintain control, but nonetheless control is lost.[13]

---

12. Reported in the *San Francisco Chronicle,* April 19, 1968.

13. Learning-to-do almost always involves a period of frequent muffings, and performance will occasionally involve muffings on the part of the fully competent. Here an awesome example is the work that captains do on the bridge of big ships. When a ship is docking or approaching another ship, the swath it cuts provides an elegant demonstration of the skill with which it is guided, a demonstration which can be directly witnessed from anywhere within a monstrously large sphere. And yet that which the captain must direct is clumsy and not very responsive, and distances on water are very hard to judge. Further, the port may be unfamiliar, or "highlining" may be required between two other ships. Add to this the lives aboard and the value of the vessel and its cargo, and some idea can be obtained of the horror the captain lives with in regard to the possibility of suddenly "losing the picture," of not knowing precisely where he is and what is happening. Naval discipline, a rigid circus in its own right, has been accounted for by this anxiety in regard to muffings. (On matters nautical I draw on an unpublished paper by David L. Cook, "Public Order in the U.S. Navy" [University of Pennsylvania, 1969].)

The apparent locus of control exerted in guiding an act provides a perspective on failures to control and indeed a suggestion of how we distinguish among types of doing. Some acts are seen as being implemented by the limbs alone, as when we rub an eye, light a match, tie a shoe, balance a tray. Some are seen as located in an extension of limbs, as in driving a car, raking a lawn, or turning a screw driver. Finally, there are doings which seem to begin with the body or an extension of it and end up guiding something that is palpably separated from the initial control, as when a golf ball, a tobacco quid, or a missile ends up where it was aimed. Early socialization presumably assures competence in the first; adult socialization—specifically job training—competence in the other two. Observe that one of the consequences of this learning program is the transformation of the world into a place that is appreciably governed by, and understandable in terms of, social frameworks. Indeed, adults in urban communities may move about through months of their days without once finding themselves out of control of their bodies or unprepared for the impingement of the environment—the whole of the natural world having been subjugated by public and private means of control. In any case, attention is directed anew to sports, such as skating, skiing, surfing, and riding, which allow youths and adults to reaccomplish guided control of their bodies through uneasily managed extensions of them. A recapitulation of early achievement results, accompanied (as of old) by many muffings, but now in a special context, play—a case of counterphobia for the leisure classes. To be noted, too, is the obvious appeal of the Laurel and Hardy type of comedy which presents incompetence and bungling on a massive scale, and the "vertigo" rides at fun fairs which allow individuals to lose control of themselves in carefully controlled circumstances.

4. Next to consider is "fortuitousness," meaning here that a significant event can come to be seen as incidentally produced. An individual, properly guiding his doings, meets with the natural workings of the world in a way he could not be expected to anticipate, with consequential results. Or two or more unconnected and mutually unoriented individuals, each properly guiding his own doings, jointly bring about an unanticipated event that is significant—and these actors have this effect even though their contributed doings remain fully under control. We speak here of happenstance, coincidence, good and bad luck, accident, and so

forth. Because no responsibility is imputed, one has something like a natural framework, except that the ingredients upon which the natural forces operate are here socially guided doings. Note, too, fortuitous consequences may be felt to be desirable or undesirable. I cite an instance of the latter:

> Amman, Jordan—A ceremonial salvo was fatal to a Palestinian commando yesterday. He was killed by a stray bullet as guerrilla units fired their rifles in the air at burial services for casualties of an Israeli air raid Sunday.[14]

The notion of fortuitous connection is obviously delicate, as though those who put it forward as an account had some doubts about using so pat a solution or were concerned that another might have these doubts. This precariousness becomes especially evident when a particular kind of happenstance occurs a second or third time to the same object or individual or category of individuals.[15] So, too, meaningfulness will be hard to avoid when the beneficiary or victim of the fortuitousness is in a prominent class of persons containing only one member.

The concepts of muffings and fortuitousness have considerable

---

14. *San Francisco Chronicle,* August 6, 1968.

15. Roland Barthes, in "Structure of the *Fait-Divers,*" in his *Critical Essays,* trans. Richard Howard (Evanston, Ill.: Northwestern University Press, 1972), suggests:

> Here we encounter the second type of relation which can articulate the structure of the *fait-divers:* the relation of coincidence. It is chiefly the repetition of an event, however anodyne, which marks it out for the notion of coincidence: *the same diamond brooch is stolen three times; a hotelkeeper wins the lottery whenever he buys a ticket,* etc.: why? Repetition always commits us to imagining an unknown cause, so true is it that in the popular consciousness, the aleatory is always distributive, never repetitive: chance is supposed to vary events; if it repeats them, it does so in order to signify something through them; to repeat is to signify. . . . [p. 191]

Some empirical evidence is provided in a useful paper by Rue Bucher, "Blame and Hostility in Disaster," *American Journal of Sociology,* LXII (1957): 469.

A general vulnerability of social organization seems to be involved here. All of us belong to many cross-cutting categories, membership in which is determined by one or more shared attributes. If good or bad fortune is visited upon a few identified individuals, we and they will seek for an understanding by examining the attributes they share, especially the ones that appear to be exclusive to them. If the category which results is broad —as it was, for example, in regard to the persons apparently of interest to the Boston Strangler—then diffuse unsettlement of the population can occur.

cosmological significance. Given our belief that the world can be totally perceived in terms of either natural events or guided doings and that every event can be comfortably lodged in one or the other category, it becomes apparent that a means must be at hand to deal with slippage and looseness. The cultural notions of muffing and fortuitousness serve in this way, enabling the citizenry to come to terms with events that would otherwise be an embarrassment to its system of analysis.

5. The final matter to consider bears upon the segregation issue expressed in "tension" and joking. As will be argued throughout, individuals can rather fully constitute what they see in accordance with the framework that officially applies. But there is a limit to this capacity. Certain effects carry over from one perspective in which events could easily be seen to a radically different one, the latter the one which officially applies. The best documented case, perhaps, is the slow development of the easy right of medical people to approach the human naked body with a natural instead of a social perspective. Thus, it was only at the end of the eighteenth century in Britain that childbirth could benefit from an obstetric examination, an undarkened operating room, and delivery—if a male physician was to do it—unencumbered by its having to be performed under covers.[16] The gyneco-

---

16. Peter Fryer, *Mrs. Grundy: Studies in English Prudery* (London: Dennis Dobson, 1963), chap. 17, "The Creeping Obstetrician," pp. 167–170. It should not be assumed that in the West individuals have shown a continuously increasing capacity to suffer examination in a naturalistic perspective and treatment in a purely instrumental, "physicalistic" one. We no longer have slaves, and therefore, presumably, no longer do individuals have to suffer the kind of impersonal testing described by Harold Nicolson in *Good Behaviour* (London: Constable & Co., 1955):

> The slave dealers, whether those of Delos or the *mangones* who ran the slave-market by the Temple of Castor in Rome, would display their wares in the manner of horse-copers, allowing prospective purchasers to examine the teeth and muscles of the animals, taking them for little runs on a string to show their paces. Slaves were exhibited for sale in a wooden cage, their feet being smeared with white-wash, and tablets stating price and qualifications hung around their necks. [p. 63]

In any case, one should see that allowing ourselves to be treated as objects is a form of conduct, if only a passive one. Persons being made up by stage cosmeticians, measured by their tailors, and palpated by their physicians conduct themselves in much the same way. They respond to requests to assume various positions, may engage in desultory side talk, but the rest follows a widespread understanding as to how to act when we are supposed to be merely bodies.

logical examination is even today a matter of some concern, special effort being taken to infuse the procedure with terms and actions that keep sexual readings in check.[17] Another example is the difficulty faced by those who would promote the practice of rescue breathing; mouth-to-mouth contact apparently cannot easily be dissociated from its ritual implications.[18] Similarly, we manage to let orthopedists and shoe salesmen touch our feet, but first we make sure to clean what might ritually contaminate. Or consider the Sensei, the instructor at karate, who, when his students take up a proper position, ordinarily can touch crucial points of their bodies instrumentally, as might a physician, to determine directly whether the appropriate tension is present. Consider the question of limits to this sort of physicalistic framing that is introduced by the admission of female students:

> When Sensei makes the rounds to test our "stance," by touching the "butt" and thigh muscles, he just doesn't touch ours. After three months he finally did touch the fifteen-year-old's "butt," but he still avoids us older women like the plague. It seems clear that twenty-five-year-old Sensei cannot see us as other than females who can be touched for one purpose and one purpose only.[19]

It should be obvious that the human body and touchings of it will figure in the issue of frame maintenance, just as the body's various waste products and involuntary movements will figure in

17. The staging of the gynecological examination so as to sustain non-sexual interpretations is nicely detailed in James M. Henslin and Mae A. Biggs, "Dramaturgical Desexualization: The Sociology of the Vaginal Examination," in James M. Henslin, ed., *Studies in the Sociology of Sex* (New York: Appleton-Century-Crofts, 1971), pp. 243–272. A useful treatment is also available in Joan P. Emerson, "Behavior in Private Places: Sustaining Definitions of Reality in Gynecological Examinations," in Hans Peter Dreitzel, ed., *Recent Sociology No. 2* (New York: Macmillan, 1970), pp. 74–97. Emerson argues that although joking during a gynecological examination may provide too open a reference to what must be inhibited, other more subtle means will allow (and oblige) participants to give nonmedical matters (such as "feminine" modesty) their due. Here see also "A Simultaneous Multiplicity of Selves," in *E.*, pp. 132–143. Emerson's paper provides a useful reminder that when one schema applies, its tenure may shift from moment to moment and may never totally exclude alien readings— and (it is felt) properly so.

18. See, for example, Maurice E. Linden, "Some Psychological Aspects of Rescue Breathing," *American Journal of Nursing*, LX (1960): 971–974.

19. Susan Pascalé et al., "Self-Defense for Women," in Robin Morgan, ed., *Sisterhood Is Powerful* (New York: Random House, Vintage Books, 1970), p. 474.

tensions regarding boundaries.[20] For it seems that the body is too constantly present as a resource to be managed in accordance with only one primary framework. It seems inevitable that our interpretive competency will allow us to come to distinguish, say, between an arm waved to signal a car on and an arm waved to greet a friend, and that both wavings will be distinguished from what we are seen as doing when we dispel flies or increase circulation. These discernments in turn seem linked to the fact that each kind of event is but one element in a whole idiom of events, each idiom being part of a distinctive framework. And here what is true of Western society is probably also true of all other societies.[21]

---

20. Mary Douglas, *Purity and Danger* (London: Routledge & Kegan Paul, 1966), provides a text:

But now we are ready to broach the central question. Why should bodily refuse be a symbol of danger and of power? Why should sorcerers be thought to qualify for initiation by shedding blood or committing incest or anthropophagy? Why, when initiated, should their art consist largely of manipulating powers thought to inhere in the margins of the human body? Why should bodily margins be thought to be specially invested with power and danger?

. . . .

Second, all margins are dangerous. If they are pulled this way or that the shape of fundamental experience is altered. Any structure of ideas is vulnerable at its margins. We should expect the orifices of the body to symbolise its specially vulnerable points. Matters issuing from them is marginal stuff of the most obvious kind. Spittle, blood, milk, urine, faeces or tears by simply issuing forth have traversed the boundary of the body. So also have bodily parings, skin, nail, hair clippings and sweat. The mistake is to treat bodily margins in isolation from all other margins. There is no reason to assume any primacy for the individual's attitude to his own bodily and emotional experience, any more than for his cultural and social experience. This is the clue which explains the unevenness with which different aspects of the body are treated in the rituals of the world. In some, menstrual pollution is feared as a lethal danger; in others not at all. . . . In some, death pollution is a daily preoccupation; in others not at all. In some, excreta is dangerous, in others it is only a joke. In India cooked food and saliva are pollution-prone, but Bushmen collect melon seeds from their mouths for later roasting and eating. [pp. 120–121]

21. A Borneo society might serve to provide an illustration:

The clasping of hands, or throwing an arm about the neck of a friend of the same sex, or a relative beyond the range of defined incestuous relationships, serves to establish boundaries of permitted tactile contacts in social action situations. Lovers regularly denote their status by mutually clasping waists while walking in public. Community members not related, or in the status of special friends, or lovers, are not permitted the

IV

One general point should be stressed here. The primary perspectives, natural and social, available to members of a society such
as ours, affect more than merely the participants in an activity;
bystanders who merely look are deeply involved, too. It seems
that we can hardly glance at anything without applying a primary framework, thereby forming conjectures as to what occurred before and expectations of what is likely to happen now. A
readiness *merely* to glance at something and then to shift attention to other things apparently is not produced solely by a lack of
concern; glancing itself seems to be made possible by the quick
confirmation that viewers can obtain, thus ensuring that anticipated perspectives apply. For surely we have as an important
motivational relevance the discovery of the motivational relevance of the event for the other persons present. Mere perceiving,
then, is a much more active penetration of the world than at first
might be thought.

Bergson approaches this argument in his fine essay *Laughter:*

> *Any arrangement of acts and events is comic which gives us, in
> a single combination, the illusion of life and the distinct impres-
> sion of a mechanical arrangement.*[22]

> Rigidity, automatism, absent-mindedness and unsociability are
> all inextricably entwined; and all serve as ingredients to the
> making up of the comic in character.[23]

---

familiarity of such forms, since each denotes a meaning of opening
another close level of tactile experience. Touching or holding contacts
are permitted among non-married adults of opposite sex only during
instances of divination and curing relationships between a female ritual
specialist and seriously ill persons. In the course of both divination and
curing rituals a female specialist in the supernatural seeks out the site
of illness through gross palpation of trunk and limb areas. In most instances, areas of sexual meaning are avoided. There is no practice of
generational transfer of political power through tactile contact, although
ritual and magical formula and associated power passage between an
aged female ritual specialist and a girl pupil may involve clasping of
hands as a symbolic transfer is effected. [Thomas R. Williams, "Cultural
Structuring of Tactile Experience in a Borneo Society," *American Anthropologist*, LXVIII (1966): 33–34.]

22. Henri Bergson, *Laughter,* trans. Cloudesley Brereton and Fred Rothwell (London: Macmillan & Co., 1911), p. 69.
23. *Ibid.*, p. 147.

We laugh every time a person gives us the impression of being a thing.[24]

In pointing out that individuals often laugh when confronted by a person who does not sustain in every way an image of human guidedness, Bergson only fails to go on and draw the implied conclusion, namely, that if individuals are ready to laugh during occurrences of ineffectively guided behavior, then all along they apparently must have been fully assessing the conformance of the normally behaved, finding it to be no laughing matter. In sum, observers actively project their frames of reference into the world immediately around them, and one fails to see their so doing only because events ordinarily confirm these projections, causing the assumptions to disappear into the smooth flow of activity. Thus, a properly dressed woman who closely examines the frame of a mirror on sale at an auction house and then stands back to check on the trueness of the mirror's reflection can well be seen by others present as someone who hasn't really been seen. But if she uses the mirror to adjust her hat, *then* others present can become aware that only a certain sort of looking had all along been what was expected and that the object on the wall was not so much a mirror as a mirror-for-sale; and this experience can be reversed should she appraisingly examine a mirror in a dressing room instead of examining herself in the mirror.[25]

---

24. *Ibid.*, p. 58.

25. I do not mean to imply that no stable meaning is built socially into artifacts, merely that circumstances can enforce an additional meaning. Cannon shells, five-gallon jars, and bits of disused plumbing can be transformed from utilitarian goods into decorative lamps, but their value as the latter depends on their never quite ceasing to be the former. At best the result is not a lamp but an interesting lamp. In fact, a certain amount of sport can be found in subordinating an official use to an irreverently alien one, as when pranksters manage to play pushbutton phones for tunes, not numbers, a possibility opened up by the fact that each button, when pushed, produces its own distinctive tone (*Time*, March 6, 1972).

Here again I argue that the meaning of an object (or act) is a product of social definition and that this definition emerges from the object's role in the society at large, which role then becomes for smaller circles a given, something that can be modified but not totally re-created. The meaning of an object, no doubt, is generated through its use, as pragmatists say, but ordinarily not by particular users. In brief, all things used for hammering in nails are not hammers.

3

Keys and Keyings

I

1. During visits to the Fleishacker Zoo beginning in 1952, Gregory Bateson observed that otters not only fight with each other but also play at fighting.[1] Interest in animal play has a clear source in Karl Groos' still useful book, *The Play of Animals*,[2] but Bateson pointedly raised the questions that gave the issue its wider current relevance.

Bateson noted that on some signal or other, the otters would begin playfully to stalk, chase, and attack each other, and on some other signal would stop the play. An obvious point about this play behavior is that the actions of the animals are not ones that are, as it were, meaningful in themselves; the framework of these actions does not make meaningless events meaningful, there being a contrast here to primary understandings, which do. Rather, this play activity is closely patterned after something that already has a meaning in its own terms—in this case fighting, a

---

1. "The Message 'This Is Play,'" in Bertram Schaffner, ed., *Group Processes* (New York: Josiah Macy, Jr., Foundation Proceedings, 1955), p. 175. The entire discussion of play by Bateson and the conferees (pp. 145–242) is useful. See also the treatment by William F. Fry, Jr., *Sweet Madness: A Study of Humor* (Palo Alto, Calif.: Pacific Books, 1968), pp. 123 ff.

2. Trans. Elizabeth L. Baldwin (New York: D. Appleton & Company, 1896).

well-known type of guided doing. Real fighting here serves as a model,[3] a detailed pattern to follow, a foundation for form.[4] Just as obviously, the pattern for fighting is not followed fully, but rather is systematically altered in certain respects. Bitinglike behavior occurs, but no one is seriously bitten. In brief, there is a transcription or transposition—a *transformation* in the geometrical, not the Chomskyan, sense—of a strip of fighting behavior into a strip of play. Another point about play is that all those involved in it seem to have a clear appreciation that it is play that is going on. Barring a few troublesome cases, it can be taken that both professional observers and the lay public have no trouble in seeing that a strip of animal behavior is play and, furthermore, that it is play in a sense similar to what one thinks of as play among humans.[5] Indeed, play is possible *between* humans and many species, a fact not to be dwelt upon when we sustain our usual congratulatory versions of the difference between us and them.

Since Bateson's discussions of animals at play, considerable work has been done on the subject, allowing one to attempt to state in some detail the rules to follow and the premises to sustain in order to transform serious, real action into something playful.[6]

a. The playful act is so performed that its ordinary function is not realized. The stronger and more competent participant restrains himself sufficiently to be a match for the weaker and less competent.

b. There is an exaggeration of the expansiveness of some acts.

c. The sequence of activity that serves as a pattern is neither followed faithfully nor completed fully, but is subject to starting

---

3. "Model" is a tricky word. I shall mean throughout a design that something *else* is patterned after, leaving open the question of whether or not this design is an ideal one; in brief, a model for, not a model of.

4. Fry, *Sweet Madness*, p. 126, uses the term "foundation behavior" here.

5. P. A. Jewell and Caroline Loizos, eds., *Play, Exploration and Territory in Mammals* (London: Academic Press for the Zoological Society of London, 1966), p. 2.

6. Here I follow in part Caroline Loizos, "Play in Mammals," *ibid.*, p. 7; and in the same volume, T. B. Poole, "Aggressive Play in Polecats," pp. 23–24. See also W. H. Thorpe, "Ritualization in Ontogeny: I. Animal Play," in *Philosophical Transactions of the Royal Society of London* (being "A Discussion on Ritualization of Behaviour in Animals and Man," organized by Julian Huxley, December 1966), pp. 311–319.

and stopping, to redoing, to discontinuation for a brief period of time, and to mixing with sequences from other routines.[7]

d. A great deal of repetitiveness occurs.[8]

e. When more than one participant is to be involved, all must be freely willing to play, and anyone has the power to refuse an invitation to play or (if he is a participant) to terminate the play once it has begun.

f. Frequent role switching occurs during play, resulting in a mixing-up of the dominance order found among the players during occasions of literal activity.[9]

---

7. Konrad Lorenz, "Play and Vacuum Activities," in *L'Instinct dans le comportement des animaux et de l'homme* (Paris: Masson et Cie, 1956):

It [a kitten] will suddenly crouch, lift the hind legs alternately and make a very interesting aiming movement with its head, all of which is photographically identical with what the adult Cat does in stalking a Mouse. The kitten, however, thus "stalks" one of its siblings, rushes at it, clasps it with both front paws and performs rhythmical thrusts at the other with the hind legs. This, again, is a movement performed in a serious fight between adult Cats. Alternately the kitten, jumping at the other, may suddenly stop, stand broadside to its opponent, hunch its back and ruffle the hair of its tail, in other words, assume an attitude characteristic of the serious defense against a dangerous predator. It is only in play that these movements can follow each other in such quick succession. The autochthonous readiness for hunting, rival fighting and defense against predators are mutually exclusive or at least inhibitive. [p. 635]

A version for the highest primate may also be cited:

Most of the rough-and-tumble play consists of behaviour which on the surface looks very hostile: violent pursuit, assault, and fast, evasive retreat. However, the roles of the participants rapidly alternate and the behaviour does not lead to spacing out or capture of objects; the participants stay together even after the chasing ends. Also the movements involved are quite different from those in fights over property. The facial expressions and vocalizations, and motor patterns involved separate out into two quite different clusters. Thus beating with clenched fist occurs with fixating, frowning, shouting, and not with laughing and jumping. Wrestling and open-handed beats occur with jumping and laughing and not with frown, fixate and closed beat. So although rough and tumble looks like hostile behaviour it is quite separate from behaviour which I call hostile because of its efforts, i.e., involving property ownership and separation of individuals. [N. G. Blurton-Jones, "An Ethological Study of Some Aspects of Social Behaviour of Children in Nursery School," in Desmond Morris, ed., *Primate Ethology* (London: George Weidenfeld & Nicolson, 1967), p. 358.]

8. Suggested in Stephen Miller, "Ends, Means, and Galumphing: Some Leitmotifs of Play," *American Anthropologist*, LXXV (1973): 89.

9. On dominance reversal in pigs, see Glen McBride, "A General Theory of Social Organization and Behaviour," *University of Queensland Papers*, Faculty of Veterinary Science, I, no. 2 (June 1964): 96.

g. The play seems to be independent of any external needs of the participants, often continuing longer than would the actual behavior it is patterned after.

h. Although playfulness can certainly be sustained by a solitary individual toward a surrogate of some kind, solitary playfulness will give way to sociable playfulness when a usable other appears, which, in many cases, can be a member of another species.[10]

i. Signs presumably are available to mark the beginning and termination of playfulness.[11]

The transformational power of play is nicely seen in the way certain objects are prone to be selected for play or prone to evoke play. These often will be ones that, like balls and balloons, tend to sustain initial impact through movement, thus producing the appearance of current guidedness. Thorpe provides a statement:

> Play is often related to an object, a "play-thing," which is not one of the normal objects of serious behaviour. These objects may include the body as a whole, or its parts.[12]

A plaything while in play provides some sort of ideal evidence of the manner in which a playful definition of the situation can utterly suppress the ordinary meanings of the world.

2. By keeping in mind these comments on animal play, one can easily turn to a central concept in frame analysis: the key. I refer here to the set of conventions by which a given activity, one

---

10. See, for example, Thorpe, "Ritualization in Ontogeny," p. 317.

11. McBride, "A General Theory of Social Organization": "For example, in pigs, the initiator will usually scamper around the pen before running up to another animal, often a socially dominant pig, and biting the latter on the neck. . . . In dogs, play is initiated by a wagging of the tails after normal recognition formalities" (p. 96).

Miller, "Ends, Means, and Galumphing":

. . . baboon social play seems to be invariably demarcated by a metamessage "this is play." A loping, bouncy gait is often seen when an infant or juvenile invites a chase or fight, etc.; the face, however, seems the most important communicative area. Wide-open and quickly moving eyes and open mouth with teeth not bared are two components of the "this is play" signal. All the social play interactions observed involved the participants constantly looking at each other's faces. Eye-contacts were brief and frequent, often occurring throughout the interaction and *always* occurring at a start, stop, of change of activity. The face-to-face encounter appeared to be the only necessary component of all the play observed. [p. 90]

12. Thorpe, "Ritualization in Ontogeny," p. 313.

already meaningful in terms of some primary framework, is
transformed into something patterned on this activity but seen by
the participants to be something quite else.[13] The process of
transcription can be called keying. A rough musical analogy is
intended.[14]

---

13. J. L. Austin, in discussing his notion of "performative utterances,"
that is, statements which function as deeds, in *How to Do Things with
Words* (New York: Oxford University Press, 1965), presents a version:

> (ii) Secondly, as *utterances* our performatives are *also* heir to certain
> other kinds of ill which infect *all* utterances. And these likewise, though
> again they might be brought into a more general account, we are delib-
> erately at present excluding. I mean, for example, the following: a per-
> formative utterance will, for example, be *in a peculiar way* hollow or
> void if said by an actor on the stage, or if introduced in a poem, or
> spoken in soliloquy. This applies in a similar manner to any and every
> utterance—a sea-change in special circumstances. Language in such
> circumstances is in special ways—intelligibly—used not seriously, but in
> ways *parasitic* upon its normal use—ways which fall under the doctrine
> of the *etiolations* of language. All this we are *excluding* from considera-
> tion. Our performative utterances, felicitous or not, are to be understood
> as issued in ordinary circumstances. [pp. 21–22]

Leonard Bloomfield in *Language* (New York: Henry Holt & Company,
1946), pp. 141–142, concerned himself with much the same issue under
the title "displaced speech." The point is to try to apply to all social behavior something of what linguists and logicians have considered in regard
to statements.

14. In linguistics, the term "code" is sometimes used to refer to just the
sort of transcription practices I have in mind, but so also are "variety" and
"register," the first sometimes used to refer to the linguistic practices of a
particular social group and the second to the linguistic requirements of a
particular kind of social occasion. (Here see Dell Hymes, "Toward Linguistic Competence" [unpublished paper].) Linguists also use "code" to refer to what I here call primary framework. In law, "code" is used to refer to
sets of norms—such as traffic laws. Biologists have still another use for the
term. In everyday usage, "code" carries the connotation of secret communication, as it does only incidentally in cryptography, where technical use of
the term seems to have originated. Interestingly, the term from cryptography that comes closest to the linguistic and biological referent is cipher,
not code.

My choice of term—"key"—has drawbacks, too, the musical reference not
being entirely apt, since the musical term "mode" is perhaps closer to the
transformations I will deal with. Note, in reference to key I use the term
"convention," not merely "rule," because here it is probably best to leave
open the question of necessity, obligation, and interdependence. Hymes, it
might be added, uses the term "key" somewhat as I do. See his "Socio-
linguistics and the Ethnography of Speaking," in E. Ardener, ed., *Social
Anthropology and Language* (London: Tavistock Publications, 1971),
pp. 47–93.

Now if one is restricted to a look at otters or monkeys one won't find many things like play, even though play seems to be the sort of thing that leads one to think of things like it. Bateson suggests threat, deceit, and ritual. In all three cases, presumably, what appears to be something isn't quite that, being merely modeled on it. When attention is turned to man, however, many different kinds of monkey business can be found. Keys abound. In addition to what an otter can do, we can *stage* a fight in accordance with a script, or *fantasize* one, or describe one *retrospectively*, or *analyze* one, and so forth.

A full definition of keying can now be suggested:

a. A systematic transformation is involved across materials already meaningful in accordance with a schema of interpretation, and without which the keying would be meaningless.

b. Participants in the activity are meant to know and to openly acknowledge that a systematic alteration is involved, one that will radically reconstitute what it is for them that is going on.

c. Cues will be available for establishing when the transformation is to begin and when it is to end, namely, brackets in time, within which and to which the transformation is to be restricted. Similarly, spatial brackets will commonly indicate everywhere within which and nowhere outside of which the keying applies on that occasion.

d. Keying is not restricted to events perceived within any particular class of perspectives. Just as it is possible to play at quite instrumentally oriented activities, such as carpentry, so it is also possible to play at rituals such as marriage ceremonies, or even, in the snow, to play at being a falling tree, although admittedly events perceived within a natural schema seem less susceptible to keying than do those perceived within a social one.

e. For participants, playing, say, at fighting and playing around at checkers feels to be much the same sort of thing—radically more so than when these two activities are performed in earnest, that is, seriously. Thus, the systematic transformation that a particular keying introduces may alter only slightly the activity thus transformed, but it utterly changes what it is a participant would say was going on. In this case, fighting and checker playing would appear to be going on, but really, all along, the participants might say, the only thing really going on is play. A keying, then, when there is one, performs a crucial role in determining what it is we think is really going on.

3. Because our individual can now answer the question "What is it that's going on here?" with "They're only playing," one has a means of distinguishing types of answers to that question that was not quite available before. More is involved than merely a matter of variation in focus.

One answer speaks to the fact that the individual may be confronted by "engrossables," a set of materials whose concatenations and interactions he can become caught up in or carried away by, as might warrant the answer: "King Arthur has just unsheathed his sword and is about to defend Guenevere," or "The little otter is about to attack his mother," or "His bishop is about to threaten my knight," this last answer being the one he could give a sympathetic kibitzer or—with the pronouns changed—a forgetful opponent. These answers have an inward-looking experiential finality. They go as far as participants might feel it possible into the meaningful universe sustained by the activity—into what one might call a *realm*. (Only some realms ought to be thought of as *worlds*, since only some can be thought of as "real" or "actual.")

The other possibility is to provide a commonsense version of what is here being attempted, namely, frame analysis: "In the Scott novel, the writer has the character Ivanhoe do all kinds of strange things," "The otters are not really fighting," "The men seem to be playing some kind of board game."

When no keying is involved, when, that is, only primary perspectives apply, response in frame terms is not likely unless doubt needs combating, as in the reply: "No, they're not merely playing; it's a real fight." Indeed, when activity that is untransformed is occurring, definitions in terms of frame suggest alienation, irony, and distance. When the key in question is that of play, we tend to refer to the less transformed counterpart as "serious" activity; as will be seen, however, not all serious activity is unkeyed, and not all untransformed activity can be called serious.

When response is made in terms of the innermost engrossable realm of an activity, time plays an important role, since dramatically relevant events unfold over time and involve suspense, namely, a concerned awaiting of the outcome—even in the case, perhaps, of chess by mail. When response is made in terms of frame, however, time often seems to drop out or collapse because the same designation can equally cover a short or long period of some activity, and developments within it may be discounted, not qualifying as something to take special note of. Thus, a statement such as "They're playing checkers" may override what it is that is happening now in regard to the strategic situations of the two players, dropping these details from what is perceived.

All of which allows another go at reality terms. Actions framed entirely in terms of a primary framework are said to be real or actual, to be really or actually or literally occurring. A keying of these actions performed, say, onstage provides us with something that is not literal or real or actually occurring. Nonetheless, we would say that the *staging* of these actions was really or actually occurring. Nonliteral activity is *literally* that, or is if everyday usage is to be followed. Indeed, the real or the actually happening seems to be very much a mixed class containing events perceived within a primary perspective and also transformed events when these are identified in terms of their status as transformations. And to this must be added the real that is construed retrospectively—brought to mind because of our way of defining something as not qualifying in that way.

But that is too simple, too. For there are strips of doing which patently involve a keying but which are not much seen in these terms. Thus, as often remarked, our interpersonal greeting rituals involve questions about health which are not put or taken as literal requests for information. On these occasions kissing can also occur, the gesture following a form that is manifest in the more sexualized version, but here considerably disembodied. And between males, blows can be exchanged, but obviously ones not given or received as serious attacks. Yet upon observing any of these ceremonies we would say that a real greeting was occurring. A literal act can then have figurative components within it not actively seen as such. And for a keying of a greeting one would presumably have to look to the stage or, say, a training school for the polite arts. In order to be careful, then, perhaps the terms "real," "actual," and "literal" ought merely to be taken to imply that the activity under consideration is no more transformed than is felt to be usual and typical for such doings.

II

Although the characterization of types of primary framework that has been suggested is not itself particularly satisfactory, a categorization and itemization of keys and their transposition conventions seems more promising. In what follows, an attempt is made to review some of the basic keys employed in our society. They are treated under five headings: make-believe, contests, ceremonials, technical redoings, and regroundings. And in distinguishing between the original and the copy, I leave quite unconsidered the question of how the copy can come to affect the original, as when crime films establish language and style for actual criminals.

1. *Make-believe:* By this term I mean to refer to activity that participants treat as an avowed, ostensible imitation or running through of less transformed activity, this being done with the knowledge that nothing practical will come of the doing. The "reason" for engaging in such fantasies is said to come from the immediate satisfaction that the doing offers. A "pastime" or "entertainment" is provided. Typically participants might be expected to be free of pressing needs before so indulging themselves and to abandon these enjoyments unceremoniously should basic needs or urges become acute—a dour philosophy not particularly borne out by animal experimentation. Further, the engrossment of the participants in the dramatic discourse of the activity—the innermost plane of being—is required, else the whole enterprise falls flat and becomes unstable. Finally, when an individual signals that what he is about to do is make-believe and "only" fun, this definition tends to take precedence; he may fail to induce the others to follow along in the fun, or even to believe that his motives are innocent, but he obliges them to accept his act as something not to be taken at face value.

a. The central kind of make-believe is playfulness, meaning here the relatively brief intrusion of unserious mimicry during interaction between one individual and others or surrogates of others. The practices to follow in transforming a strip of actual activity into playfulness have already been considered in regard to animal play and will not be fully reconsidered here. However, some amplification is required.

The function of play has been commented on for many centuries, to little avail. However, it is probably possible to say something about the location of playfulness in the flow of activity, since playfulness is favored at certain junctures in social intercourse.[15] In any case, brief switchings into playfulness are everywhere found in society, so much so that it is hard to become conscious of their widespread occurrence. (In this study, the situational study of playfulness is not attempted.)

When particular animal species are examined, one finds that not all aggressive behavior can be keyed as play. Thus among polecats, apparently, sustained neck biting, "sideways" attack, defensive threat, and screaming are found in actual set-to but not in play.[16] Presumably a polecat that tried to perform these acts unseriously would be ineffective in its aim. What is observable here is a limit to the content of play, and, in a way, a limit to this particular kind of keying. Of course there will be other limits. Allowable play, obviously, can get out of hand:

> A polecat which does not wish to indulge in play or has already had enough, threatens its opponent by hissing and baring the teeth; this results in the attacker desisting. If one of the animals is smaller or weaker than its opponent which is being too rough, it cries plaintively until it is released.[17]

It is apparent, then, that although individuals can playfully engage in an extremely broad range of activity, limits on playfulness are established in various groups—*limits* being a factor to be attended to throughout frame analysis. Among familiars, for example, there will be appeals to "taste"; it is not nice to make light of certain aspects of the lives of friends. In the game of

---

15. Playfulness seems to be facilitated where there is special evidence that the activity could not be meant literally, as when a betrothed girl is jokingly bussed by a close friend of her fiancé in his immediate presence, or when boxers, weighing in, exchange a joking gesture of blows for the camera. If a serious playing through of the act is physically impossible, playfulness may also be favored, as when unacquainted persons wave at each other, each going in the opposite direction in his respective train. (Sophia Loren, on her arrival at Kennedy International Airport, kissed an employee through a plate glass window in response to his greeting [*San Francisco Chronicle*, May 26, 1966].) Where seriously spoken words might expose opposition, especially in the matter of overlapping jurisdiction, playful unseriousness may be employed—as implied in the classic analysis of joking relationships. Where one essential faction of participants is present in a setting containing elaborate equipment for a social event that is soon to be staged with the help of the now absent faction, joking use of the setting may occur.

16. Poole, "Aggressive Play in Polecats," pp. 28–29.

17. *Ibid.*, p. 27.

"dozens" played by black urban youths, statements made about a player's parent are seen as displaying the wit of the insulter, not the features of the parent, and so can be wondrously obscene. A mild-sounding insult that happened to refer to known features of the particular parent would be given a different relevance and cease to be unserious.[18] Similarly, jests by an individual about his having a bomb in his bag are not tolerated by air hostesses,[19] just as mock robberies are not by bank tellers, and certain jokes using certain words told by certain nightclub performers are not tolerated by certain local police. In Las Vegas a man in a cocktail lounge who complied with his girl's request to scare her out of her hiccups by pulling a .38 from his waistband and sticking it into her tummy was arrested for his gallantry.[20]

The issue of limits can hardly be considered without looking at another, namely, changes over time and place in regard to them.

---

18. A full analysis is available in William Labov, "Rules for Ritual Insults," in David Sudnow, ed., *Studies in Social Interaction* (New York: The Free Press, 1972), pp. 120–169; and William Labov, *Language in the Inner City* (Philadelphia: University of Pennsylvania Press, 1973), pp. 297–353.

19. Would-be jokesters presumably now know that kidding an airline stewardess about having a bomb in their briefcase is no longer excusable, but this leaves open frame ploys that are more complicated, such as: "It's not permissible, is it, Miss, for me to jokingly say that this bulge in my briefcase is a small bomb?" In any case, these limits themselves have unstated limits which experience occasionally explicates:

A pretty United Air Lines stewardess halted a trembling, wild-eyed man who was trying to enter the pilot's cabin yesterday 33,000 feet over Oregon countryside.

"I've got a bomb in my hand," he told Mary Lou Luedtke, 27, "and I want to see the captain."

Miss Luedtke shot a horrified glance at the man's hand and saw that he was carrying a simple, yellow piece of wood with metal straps dangling from each end.

"I got it from God," the man said.

Miss Luedtke invited him to sit down, but he refused.

A male passenger noticed the commotion and grabbed the man by his coat lapel. He forced the "bomber" to a seat and talked quietly with him for the rest of the trip.

When the DC-8 jet from Seattle landed at San Francisco International Airport at 1:05 P.M. authorities took the man into custody. [*San Francisco Chronicle*, February 18, 1966]

Working in a very delicate situation, the " 'bomber' " managed somehow to hit upon the pattern of behavior that would allow him (apparently) to feel he was serious but not allow others to so respond.

20. Reported by Paul Price, *Las Vegas Sun*, October 27, 1965.

As an example, take this bit of fooling around just after the French Revolution:

> Outside, Heindreicht and his men were erecting the guillotine. One or two of the Director's friends strolled out to watch the work; caught up in the prevailing mood of geniality, the *bourreau* invited them to come onto the platform and inspect things at close quarters; the guests were charmed; affable Heindreicht explained the mechanism, pointed out little features with modest pride; M. Sardou was among the group; in a final spasm of hilarity, he insisted on being placed on the *bascule*. The headsman entered into the spirit of the thing, seized the humorous author, pushed him onto the plank. One of the bales of straw used to test the blade before each execution was laid where his neck should have been. The blade flashed down, sliced through the straw an inch or so away from M. Sardou's head. It was irresistible! Everyone was in splendid humour by the time Troppmann was led out past the cordon of troops, their swords lifted in the traditional salute, to replace the man of letters.[21]

That sort of thing may have been acceptable then, but it wouldn't be now; indeed, the ceremony of execution itself is coming to be thought no longer acceptable. Or consider the decline of sacrilegious mockery. What today could be equivalent to the most famous of the eighteenth-century Hell Fire Clubs, Sir Francis Dashwood's sturdy little group of Restoration Rakes, which enjoyed a semiannual, week-long retreat in buildings surrounding the ruins of Medmenham Abbey? These remains had been rebuilt and furnished to provide the setting for a serious camping of Catholic rituals, and on so extensive a scale that there could be few settings for real worship in America today to match it. Indeed, it is said that servants were not to be trusted as witnesses, lest stories spread and cause violent offense to the populace, this at a time when it was not easy to violently offend Londoners.[22] Contemporary society seems to oblige less flare at its playfulness, at least playfulness of the private kind, although one ought not to

---

21. Alister Kershaw, *A History of the Guillotine* (London: John Calder, 1958), p. 72.

22. See E. Beresford Chancellor, *The Lives of the Rakes*, vol. 4, *The Hell Fire Club* (London: Philip Allan and Company, 1925); Burgo Partridge, *A History of Orgies* (New York: Bonanza Books, 1960), chap. 5, "The Medmenhamites and the Georgian Rakes," pp. 133–166.

underestimate the continued capacity of the English for irreverence in their staged fun.

b. Playfulness, then, is one form of make-believe. A second is fantasy or "daydreaming." Although children jointly act out spurts of free-form make-believe, the typical arrangement is a one-person production, often solitarily sustained. The individual imagines some strip of activity, all the while knowingly managing the development and outcome to his own liking or disliking. Daydreams involve reveries of an acutely cautionary or pleasant kind,[23] whether cast in the past or the future. Interestingly, daydreams are not merely not shared in the act, but, unlike dreams, are not even seen to be a subject matter for retelling later. These flights are characteristically short and not very well organized, although, of course, an individual may spend a great deal of time thus engaged. (Surely the total number of man-hours a population spends per day in privately pursued fantasy constitutes one of the least examined and most underestimated commitments of its resources.) Note, daydreaming presumably occurs in the mind, there being little outward behavioral accompaniment, overt signs of talking to oneself being the principal exception.

Although daydreams are ordinarily seen as private matters, a post-Freudian variant ought to be mentioned, namely, the sort of reporting about self that clinicians feel it worthwhile to elicit and clients are willing to engage in. An industrialized version is promoted by the so-called projective techniques. The Thematic Aperception Test, for example, is designed to evoke fantasy responses to test materials, which responses, presumably, the subject thinks are evoked by the materials and not by his predispositions. Thus responses are thought to escape usual censorship.

In fact, of course, responses to projective tests provide something more than, or rather something different from, merely a set of fantasies delivered on request around specific pictorial themes. For example, TAT subjects commonly decline in whole or part the request to take the materials "seriously" as a seeding for the

---

23. J. Richard Woodworth, "On Faking Reality: The Lying Production of Social Cooperation" (Ph.D. diss., Department of Sociology, University of California, Berkeley, 1970), p. 26. Woodworth suggests: "A principal characteristic of fantasy is the *concentrated* relation it bears to matters of pleasure and pain."

production of thinly disguised, self-referential daydreams. Subjects sometimes burst out laughing nervously, or comment on the scene from the perspective of art criticism, or identify the characters as kinsmen or famous persons, or revert to supernatural stories, or guy a stereotyped response (with accompanied singsong voice), or place the scene as an illustration from a popular magazine. Some effort is made by interpreters to treat *these* responses as symptomatic, but on the face of it, at least, what has occurred is that the task set before the subject has been denied and other frames have been brought to bear. One can find here, I want to add, a hint of the flexibility that keying brings to the management of participation—in this case participation in a clinical task.[24]

c. Consider now <u>dramatic scriptings</u>. Include all strips of depicted personal experience made available for vicarious participation to an audience or readership, especially the standard productions offered commercially to the public through the medium of television, radio, newspapers, magazines, books, and the legitimate (live) stage. This corpus of transcriptions is of special interest, not merely because of its social importance in our recreational life, or, as already suggested, because of the availability of so much explicit analysis of these materials, or because the materials themselves are easily accessible for purposes of close study; their deepest significance is that they provide a mock-up of everyday life, a put-together script of unscripted social doings, and thus are a source of broad hints concerning the structure of this domain. So examples drawn from dramatic productions will be used throughout this study.

The issue of framing limits can be illustrated especially well by reference to dramatic scriptings. For example, the following news report shortly after John Kennedy's assassination:

> "Manchurian Candidate," the movie about a madman who attempts to assassinate the President with a scope-equipped rifle, has been yanked out of all theaters in the area and is being withdrawn nationally; ditto an earlier Sinatra film, "Suddenly," about a similar attempt on the President's life.[25]

---

24. Erving Goffman, "Some Characteristics of Response to Depicted Experience" (Master's thesis, Department of Sociology, University of Chicago, 1949), chap. 10, "The Indirect Response," pp. 57–65.

25. Herb Caen, *San Francisco Chronicle*, December 2, 1963.

So, too, frame change through time:

> Under foreign domination the Greeks had indeed produced New
> Comedy; the Romans, overwhelmed under their own Empire, gave
> themselves up to a merely sensual existence. In their theatres
> pantomime took the place of tragedy, while comedy gave way to
> farce. Since the sole aim was to tickle the jaded palate of the
> public, producers not only lavished all the resources of wealth and
> technique on their extravagant productions, but also descended to
> the lowest depths of the disgusting and the obscene. Even Livy
> regarded the theatre of his day as a danger to public morals and
> the existence of the State; soon sexual displays were visibly pre-
> sented on the stage, and stage "executions" were carried out in
> reality (by substituting for the actor a condemned criminal).[26]

It might be added that most of these changes have been sufficiently slow and separate, one from another, so that during any
one occasion participants could feel that a particular frame
prevailed and would be sustained.

The obvious moral limit associated with scripted productions in
our society is sexual, the general argument being that certain
activities of a lewd and lascivious kind are not to be depicted in
print, onstage, or on the screen. For example:

> Sacramento—The Senate approved and sent to the Assembly
> yesterday a bill by Senator Lawrence E. Walsh (Dem–Los Angeles)
> making it a misdemeanor to perform such productions as "The
> Beard" on any state college campus.
>
> The bill would make it a misdemeanor for any person to engage
> in "any simulated act of sexual intercourse or deviate sexual
> conduct during a play, motion picture, television production, spon-
> sorship, or control of any State college."
>
> Teachers or school officials who "knowingly" permit, procure,
> assist or counsel a person to engage in such acts would be equally
> responsible and subject to misdemeanor penalties.[27]

---

26. W. Beare, *The Roman Stage* (London: Methuen & Co., 1964),
p. 238, partly cited in Elizabeth Burns, *Theatricality: A Study of Convention in the Theatre and in Social Life* (London: Longman Group, 1972;
New York: Harper & Row, 1973), p. 15.

27. *San Francisco Chronicle*, May 10, 1968. There seems to be, incidentally, a tricky frame difference between kissing and screwing. The first
can be done onstage as a simulated act, with lips not touching, or,
posturally, as a "real" kiss, with lips touching, but in either case the kiss
is presumably not "really" felt and is therefore a keyed kiss. ("Social" or

A considerable literature, legal and otherwise, exists on this matter of pornography. Not too much attention, however, seems to have been directed to the fact that rulings do not attach to "indecent" acts alone, but also to the presentation of these acts in particular frames. As might be expected, sentiment varies considerably according to the particular key in question. Obviously, what is offensive in a movie might not be offensive in a novel.[28] In attempting to judge the suitability of a given presentation, reasons are very hard to provide, I think, partly because we look to the original model for an explanation instead of looking to the character of a frame involving a particular kind of keying.

Pornography itself, that is, the scripting of sexuality that is "improperly" explicit for the frame in question, can be considered along with other "obscenities." A recent study provides a statement and an analysis:

> These reflections suggest two preliminary definitions of obscenity: (1) obscenity consists in making public that which is private; it consists in an intrusion upon intimate physical processes and acts or physical-emotional states; and (2) it consists in a degradation of the human dimensions of life to a sub-human or merely physical level. According to these definitions, obscenity is a certain way of treating or viewing the physical aspects of human existence and their relation to the rest of human existence. Thus, there can be an obscene view of sex; there can also be obscene views of death, of birth, of illness, and of acts such as that of eating or

---

cousinly kisses are not meant to be "felt," and the difference here between a staged version and the real thing would presumably have to be referred back to the wider facts, for the simulation of perfunctoriness is all too perfectly managed.) Here the stage context and the play frame can dominate (and hence restructure) the event. The second seems to fall somewhat beyond the power of dramaturgic framing: physically real screwing onstage seems to be treated by audiences more as a literal sexual act than as a dramaturgically keyed one. According to our current belief system, actual penetration defies theatrical transcription. This is ceasing to be true of the cinematic frame, although here, too, framing limits obtain, as will be considered later.

28. A difference which can itself change. In the late sixties, movies seemed to have considerably narrowed the gap; for example, *Midnight Cowboy* was as raunchy on screen as in the text. In the early seventies, novels seemed to have somewhat regained their difference, once again moving ahead (or back, depending on one's perspective); Cynthia Buchanan's *Thinking Girl* is an example. More recently still, the influence deriving from the increasing acceptability of hard-core pornographic films seems to foretell a new round in the competition.

defecating. Obscenity makes a public exhibition of these phenomena and does so in such a way that their larger human context is
lost or depreciated. Thus, there is a connection between our two
preliminary definitions of obscenity: when the intimacies of life are
exposed to public view their value may be depreciated, *or* they may
be exposed to public view in order to depreciate them and to
depreciate man.[29]

In brief, the issue is frame limits, the limits concerning what can
be permissibly transcribed from actual events to scriptings
thereof. And the details are particularly interesting. Whatever
the body can become involved in can be touched upon, but the
view must be veiled and distanced so that our presumed beliefs
about the ultimate social quality of man will not be discredited.
The body as the embodiment of the self must make its peace with
its biological functioning, but this peace is achieved by ensuring
that these functions will be seen in "context," meaning here as
incidental to human social experience, not the focus of attention.
Stories can call for persons to eat, make love, and be tortured, but
as part of an inclusive human drama, not as an isolated display
or a matter of interest to examine closely in its own right.

  2. *Contests:* Consider sports such as boxing, horse racing,
jousting, fox hunting, and the like. The literal model seems to be
fighting (or hunting or fleeing from) of some kind, and the rules
of the sport supply restrictions of degree and mode of aggression.
(Examine what occurs during ritualized sparring contests over
troop dominance by rival male animals, or when solicitous elders
separate two brawling youths and license them only for a "fair
fight" with rules, an informal umpire, and a circle of earnest
watchers.)

  Framing limits regarding combatlike contests are very well
marked, with considerable change through time and, what is ·
more, fairly well documented. Typically these changes have been
seen as signs of the decline of toleration for cruelty and performer risk, at least in the recreational sphere. Just as cats are no
longer "burnt alive in baskets at Lewes on Guy Fawkes Day, their
agonized shrieks drowned by the delighted shouts of the onlookers,"[30] so cock fighting, bearbaiting, ratting, and other blood

---

29. Harry M. Clor, *Obscenity and Public Morality* (Chicago: University
of Chicago Press, 1970), p. 225.

30. Christina Hole, *English Sports and Pastimes* (London: B. T. Bats-
ford, 1949), p. 5.

sports have been prohibited. The changing frame of organized boxing can be followed from its bare-handed beginnings at the turn of the eighteenth century, to the introduction of skin gloves some decades later, to the Broughton Code in 1743 and the Queensbury rules circa 1867.

Some sports, then, can be identified as keyings of elementary combative activity—ritualizations, in ethological terms. But obviously this view has limited use. There are lots of sports, such as hockey and tennis, which bring competing sides into structured opposition, but the specific equipment employed and specific goal enjoined can only suggest a primary framework. This embarrassment to the analysis I am recommending is even more marked in the case of games. In the little game "King of the Castle" played by small children and by lambs,[31] the reference to everyday dominance is clear. In developed adult games this reference is attenuated and no great value seems to remain to uncovering possible mythic or historic roots in specific life activity; one deals, in effect, with primary frameworks.

There seems to be a continuum between playfulness, whereby some utilitarian act is caught up and employed in a transformed way for fun, and both sports and games. In any case, whereas in playfulness the playful reconstitution of some object or individual into a "plaything" is quite temporary, never fully established, in organized games and sports this reconstitution is institutionalized—stabilized, as it were—just as the arena of action is fixed by the formal rules of the activity. (That presumably is what we mean by "organized.") And as this formalization progresses, the content of play seems to become further and further removed from any particular replication of day-to-day activity and more and more a primary framework unto itself.

A final note. I have stressed the changing limits in regard to dramatic productions and sports, arguing that here historical documentation is very rich. The value of these materials for us is apparent. Above all else, dramas and contests provide engrossables—engrossing materials which observers can get carried away with, materials which generate a realm of being. The limits placed on this activity are limits placed on activities that can become engaging and entrancing. The history of these limits is

---

31. Thorpe, "Ritualization in Ontogeny," p. 316.

the history of what can become alive for us. And if keyings have a history, then perhaps primary frameworks do, too.

3. *Ceremonials:* Social ritual such as marriage ceremonies, funerals, and investitures are examples. Something unlike ordinary activity goes on in them, but what goes on in them is difficult to be sure of. Like scripted productions, a whole mesh of acts are plotted in advance, rehearsal of what is to unfold can occur, and an easy distinction can be drawn between rehearsal and "real" performance. But whereas in stage plays this preformulation allows for a broad simulation of ordinary life, in ceremonials it functions to constrict, allowing one deed, one doing, to be stripped from the usual texture of events and choreographed to fill out a whole occasion. In brief, a play keys life, a ceremony keys an event. Also, unlike stage productions, ceremonials often provide for a clear division between professional officiators, who work at this sort of thing and can expect to perform it many times, and the officiated, who have the right and the duty to participate a few times at most. And for them, a few times are all that are needed, for on the occasion of these "performative displays" something gets accomplished once and for all which has important connections and ramifications in their wider world. Finally, observe that in plays a performer appears as a character other than himself; in ceremonials, on the other hand, the performer takes on the task of representing and epitomizing himself in some one of his central social roles—parent, spouse, national, and so forth. (In everyday life the individual is himself, too, but not in so clearly a self-symbolizing way.)

Once it is seen that ceremonials have a consequence that scripted dramas and even contests do not, it is necessary to admit that the engrossment and awe generated by these occasions vary greatly among participants, more so, perhaps, than is true in general for nonceremonial activity. Furthermore, through time, the same script may be retained but widely different weight imputed to the doings, so one can move from a full-blooded ritual to a mere or empty one. A good example here is the coronation of Queen Elizabeth. The Queen and Mr. Shils no doubt had a view of the proceedings that differed somewhat from that of skeptics.[32]

4. *Technical redoings:* Strips of what could have been ordi-

---

32. Nicely argued in Burns, *Theatricality,* pp. 19–20.

nary activity can be performed, out of their usual context, for utilitarian purposes openly different from those of the original performance, the understanding being that the original outcome of the activity will not occur. These run-throughs are an important part of modern life yet have not been much discussed as something in their own right by students of society. Consider briefly some varieties of these doings.

a. In our society, and probably in all others, capacity to bring off an activity as one wants to—ordinarily defined as the possession of skills—is very often developed through a kind of utilitarian make-believe. The purpose of this practicing is to give the neophyte experience in performing under conditions in which (it is felt) no actual engagement with the world is allowed, events having been "decoupled" from their usual embedment in consequentiality. Presumably muffing or failure can occur both economically and instructively.[33] What one has here are dry runs, trial sessions, run-throughs—in short, "practicings." When an instrumental task is at issue, we speak of a mock trial or exercise, of which one up-to-date illustration is provided:

> Simulation is a newly developing area of medical education which provides lifelike clinical experience without actually involving living patients, and indeed where the participation of a living patient would be undesirable or impractical. Simulation techniques may involve very simple manikins for practicing mouth-to-mouth resuscitation or very complex computer-operated automatons capable of recreating many essential life functions. Denson and Abrahamson have been evaluating a manikin, "SIM-One," which reproduces all essential cardiorespiratory and nervous system functions associated with the administration of general anesthesia. The manikin responds "appropriately" to both correct and incorrect treatment, mechanical and pharmacologic, and is quite capable of regurgitating or simulating cardiac arrest. The unit may be halted at any time during "induction" or "maintenance" of general anes-

---

33. There are some data to suggest that even in the animal world practicing, as distinct from play, is a possibility. See Rudolf Schenkel, "Play, Exploration and Territoriality in the Wild Lion," in Jewell and Loizos, eds., *Play, Exploration and Territory,* esp. p. 18. Note, practicing has one irreversible, unkeyed element. The number of run-throughs required for an individual or a team to acquire proficiency with a task or script can be taken as an indication of learning capacity, flexibility, motivation, and so on.

thesia for instruction and revision of therapy before the "patient dies" or is harmed.[34]

When a social ritual or a theatrical play or a musical score is to be mastered, we speak of rehearsals. The distinctive thing about rehearsals is that all the parts are eventually practiced together, and this final practice, in conjunction with a script, allows for more or less full anticipation of what will be done in the live circumstances.[35] Lots of activities that are run through cannot be scripted closely, because not all the main participants of what will be the live action are part of the same team. An individual may "rehearse" in his mind what he is going to say on a particular occasion, but unless his speech is a long one to which a passive response can be anticipated, "rehearsal" here is a figurative use of the term, and the rehearser is partly kidding himself. Similarly, television stories concerning undercover agents (e.g., *Mission Impossible*) involve the heroes in designing and executing a detailed scenario that ought not to be counted on in real life, because continuous response is required from those not on the team, and this response, of course, cannot be scripted, only induced and anticipated more or less. Even when all participants *are* basically on the same side, as in military field exercises, the planned course of action, the scenario, may require controllers to periodically reestablish and redirect what it is that is "happen-

---

34. Daniel O. Levinson, M.D., "Bedside Teaching," *The New Physician*, XIX (1970): 733.

35. Indeed, when the end product of a performing effort is a tape and not a live show, the final version can be an edited composite of strips taken from several run-throughs. During these tries the performers will rightfully feel that they are not obliged to "stay in frame" throughout, as they would in a "real" performance, and yet they are proving to be producing what will come to be treated as bits of the final show.

All of which again raises the issue of reality. A political speech may have little value as a reliable indication of what the speaker will actually do, but it can be said to be a real speech. A TV audience (and certainly a radio audience) obtains a version of the talk that is slightly different from the one obtained by a live audience, but the difference doesn't much signify, perhaps. But what if an ailing president waits for a moment of good feeling and then tapes his talk before a cheering assemblage of his own staff, a talk that has been built up from small, self-sufficient passages ("preclips") which allow for the editing out of ineffective bits, and then releases the tape to the networks for later broadcast? Is the result a show or a speech? And is the notion of keying sufficient to deal with the matter?

ing"; forces that have gone too far ahead for the scenario will
have to be held up and slow forces advanced.

When an elaborate action is plotted closely in advance, the
sequence of steps covertly played out in the mind or on paper in
order to check on timing and the like, we speak of planning. As
suggested, task trials, rehearsals, and plannings together can be
seen as varieties of practicing, all these variations together to be
distinguished from "real experience," this presumably providing
for learning, too, but differently.

The places where practicing occurs are a wonder to behold.
Here Dickens has informed our orientation; Fagan teaching his
young charges how to steal hankies, using simulated conditions,
is part of our tradition. So, too, are "caper" movies, such as *Rafifi,*
which focus on execution of a planned, timed, and rehearsed
operation. In any case, of smugglers one can read:

> One group has even gone to the trouble to buy three regular,
> upholstered VC-10 airliner seats from BOAC so that they can train
> their couriers, bowed down with gold, to sit in them for hours on
> end without getting cramped and to be able to get up without ap-
> pearing a cripple at the end of the journey.[36]

Dulles provides similar comments regarding his line of work:

> The "live" situations in the training school are intended to
> achieve somewhat the same end as combat training with live
> ammunition. Pioneer work along these lines was done during
> World War II in the Army schools which trained prisoner-of-war
> interrogators. The interrogator-trainee was put up against a man
> who was dressed like an enemy officer or soldier, acted like one
> who had just been captured and spoke perfect German or Japa-
> nese. The latter, who had to be a good actor and was carefully
> chosen for his job, did everything possible to trick or mislead the
> interrogator in any of the hundred ways which we had experienced
> in real interrogation situations in Europe and the Far East. He
> refused to talk or he deluged the interrogator with a flood of incon-
> sequential or confusing information. He was sullen or insolent or
> cringing. He might even threaten the interrogator. After a few
> sessions of this sort, the interrogator was a little better prepared to

---

36. Timothy Green, *The Smugglers* (New York: Walker and Company,
1969), p. 217.

take on a real-life POW or pseudo defector and was not likely to be surprised by one.[37]

And Scandinavian Airlines, to advertise its good work, shows pictures of air hostesses-to-be practicing the serving of liquor in a flight simulator filled with company customers and trainers at the "Air Hostess College, Sandefjord."[38] And in a broadcasting studio, the warm-up of the live audience may require the practicing of clapping.[39]

Practicing provides us with a meaning for "real thing," namely, that which is no longer mere practicing. But, of course, this is only one meaning of real. A battle is to a war game as a piano recital is to a finger exercise; but this tells us nothing about the sense in which warfare and music are different orders of being.

What are the limits of practice? We are accustomed, for example, to wedding rehearsals, but little knowledge is available as to how far up the ritual ladder this sort of practicing goes. We would probably be surprised about the ins and outs of rehearsal for a coronation or a papal investiture, the assumption being that the personages involved are so high in ritual status that they ought to be too unbending to rehearse at all, although, of course, even more than lesser folk, they have to bend this way. Pictures of the president of the United States rehearsing for his daughter's wedding are news, although perhaps barely.[40] Perhaps we also have some conception of how much participants ought to be willing to invest of themselves in practicing. This might be too little betimes, too little enough, that is, to make news:

> Hinkley Point, England (UPI)—A sergeant major in the British Army Cadets thought it was downright un-British when, with a simulated war exercise about to take place, the "enemy" refused to participate because it was raining.
>
> Sgt. Maj. Roy Blackmore of the West Somerset Cadets said: "An officer told me his unit would not take part because it was raining and they didn't want to get wet."[41]

---

37. Allen Dulles, *The Craft of Intelligence* (New York: New American Library, Signet Books, 1965), p. 167.

38. *Newsweek*, September 7, 1970.

39. See Gerald Nachman, "Now a Word from the Audience," *Daily News* (New York), September 11, 1973.

40. *Life*, June 18, 1971.

41. *The New York Times*, December 29, 1968.

And so much might be involved as to provide notable autobiography, as Lillian Gish illustrates in her description of filming *Way Down East* under D. W. Griffith:

> The scenes on and around the ice were filmed at White River Junction, Vermont, where the White River and the Connecticut flowed side by side. The ice was thick; it had to be either sawed or dynamited, so that there would be floes for each day's filming. The temperature never rose above zero during the three weeks we worked there.
>
> For the scene in which Anna faints on the ice floe, I thought of a piece of business and suggested it to Mr. Griffith, who agreed it was a fine idea. . . . I suggested that my hand and my hair trail in the water as I lay on the floe that was drifting towards the falls. Mr. Griffith was delighted with the effect.
>
> After awhile, my hair froze, and I felt as if my hand were in a flame. To this day, it aches if I am out in the cold for very long. When the sequence was finally finished, I had been on a slab of ice at least twenty times a day for three weeks. In between takes, one of the men would throw a coat around me, and I would warm myself briefly at a fire.[42]

The question of too little or too much investment is an obvious aspect of framing limits. Less obvious is the issue of the propriety of practicing itself. Something of a joke is made about young people practicing smoking in front of a mirror in order to acquire a sophisticated look. But behind the joke seems to be an understanding that "expressive" behavior, as found, for example, in greetings, statements of love, facial gestures, and the like, ought never to have been practiced, is rather always to be a by-product of action, never its end. And to sustain this theory of behavior, we must refrain from teaching and practicing such conduct or at least teach and learn disavowably.

The organization of practicing provides a good example of how individuals can recognize that in reality a keying is involved even though for them matters are quite serious. Thus, hairdressing and barber colleges train their students on live heads provided by subjects who are willing to accept semitrained work because the price is so good. Such customers devotedly hope for standard

---

42. Lillian Gish, *The Movies, Mr. Griffith and Me* (New York: Avon Books, 1969), pp. 233–234.

competence (and will have prideful stories to tell when they get it) but are not in a position to demand it.

An interesting feature of practicing is that instructor and student are likely to find it useful to focus conscious attention on an aspect of the practiced task with which competent performers no longer concern themselves. Thus, when children are being taught to read aloud, word pronunciation can become something that is continuously oriented to, as if the meaning of the words were temporarily of little account.[43] Indeed, the same text can be used as a source of quite different abstractable issues: in the above case, spelling, phrasing, and so forth. Similarly during stage rehearsals, proficiency with lines may come first, movement and timing later. In all of this one sees again that a strip of activity is merely a starting point; all sorts of perspectives and uses can be brought to it, all sorts of "motivational relevancies" can be found in it.

Practicing has another developmental feature. In a performer's acquisition of a particular competence, the first step attempted is often easier and simpler than any he will take in the serious world, whereas the last practice session before he goes forth is likely to involve a higher concentration of varied difficulties and emergencies than he is ever likely to face in real life.[44] The first

---

43. A useful treatment is available in an unpublished paper by John J. Gumperz and Eleanor Herasimchuck, "The Conversational Analysis of Social Meaning: A Study of Classroom Interaction."

44. For example:

Simulators are expensive to build and operate but hold tremendous promise. Significant phases of acute, subacute, and chronic disease could be compressed into a few minutes' time and operant techniques used to develop diagnostic and therapeutic skills. Cardiac arrest, anaphylactic shock, diabetic acidosis, congestive failure, myocardial infarction, and other common major illnesses could be "diagnosed" and "treated" repeatedly until proficiency is second nature. [Levinson, "Bedside Teaching," p. 733.]

Nevertheless, there is a view among some students of the legal process that most rules are inherently uncertain and that most legal concepts are flexible and variable in meaning. In the United States, habits of thought inculcated during the course of legal training may encourage this point of view. Law students learn by debating the application of doctrine to extremely difficult borderline situations derived from cases reviewed by appellate courts. One object of this exercise is to train the students' minds in legal thought and develop skills of advocacy, and this object, it is believed, is best accomplished through the examination of difficult

phase of training thus affords the learner some protection from the anxiety produced by incompetent performances, and the last phase provides an arrangement in which the attention and interest of the performer can be held at a time when he can probably handle live conditions. In any case, the world of practice is both simpler and more complex than that of actual, "live" conditions.

Note that these extremes must miss some of the point. Insofar as real performance depends on how the performer manages himself under fateful conditions, a dry run can only approach "real" conditions, never achieve them. This dilemma is seen most clearly perhaps in war games, where participants must take seriously that which can ultimately be made serious only by what can't be employed: "live" ammunition lethally directed.[45]

---

questions, rather than easy questions and well-settled law. [Lawrence M. Friedman, "Legal Rules and the Process of Social Change," *Stanford Law Review*, XIX (1967): 791.]

Another example is found in the training of craps dealers. As might be expected, the terminal phases of dead table training involve dealing to a vastly complicated layout, the "bets" large and varied beyond what is likely to be met in real play.

45. Novelistic versions of field exercises and maneuvers present another issue. If a manageable exercise is to be accomplished, both "sides" must abide by all the conventions of real warfare and some special ones in addition: for example, a scoring device of some kind must be relied upon to determine who has been injured and how severely and what damage has been done to what equipment; private property and other areas out of bounds must be avoided; stopping and starting signals must be allowed to govern. And of course, to ensure all of this, umpires and controllers must be respected. But if the exercise is to test the capacity to infiltrate, to employ surprises, to outwit traditionally inclined opposition, in short, to win in any way and at any price, then it is just these ground rules of the war game that may have to be breached. Thus, cheating becomes the right way because it is the wrong way. See, for example, E. M. Nathanson, *The Dirty Dozen* (New York: Random House, 1965), pp. 425–434; William Crawford Woods, *The Killing Zone* (New York: Harper's Magazine Press, 1970), pp. 117–167.

Military presentation of field exercises suggests a less dramatic framing problem. Apparently the great restriction on war games is not bullets but nature. In actual warfare a vast confusion of uncertain factors is present: the weather, the "friendliness" of the natives, shortwave reception, the clogging of roadways with prisoners, fleeing householders, disrepaired vehicles, and so forth. For killing, like speaking, occurs in a context. In actual exercises, these factors in the main can at best be painted in by the umpire through verbal announcements, a simulation that seems even more academic than the use of color-coded equipment and personnel tags to distinguish slight damage, severe damage, destruction, and contamina-

b. So there is practicing. A second class of redoings consists of "demonstrations" (or exhibitions), that is, performances of a tasklike activity out of its usual functional context in order to allow someone who is not the performer to obtain a close picture of the doing of the activity. This is what happens when a salesman shows how a vacuum cleaner works to pick up the dirt he has instructively dropped on a housewife's floor, or when a visiting public health nurse shows an unwashed mother how to wash a baby, or when field commanders are shown what a piece of artillery will do, or when a pilot at full altitude shows his passengers what the sound and sensation will be like when air flaps are lowered:

> In our descent I may extend the air brakes to slow up our speed. This is what it will be like [extends air brakes, plane shudders]. The shudder in the cabin is quite normal [retracts brakes].

thus using a closely predicted demonstration as a means of ensuring that later what might be taken as a sign for alarm, an unguided doing, will be seen as an intended, instrumental act. Observe that demonstrating, unlike practicing, is typically done by someone who can perform proficiently, and typically only one or two run-throughs occur. Of course, the two types of redoings may be employed together, as when a teacher provides a demonstration and a student replies with a practice trial. And an aspirant for a job may be tested for proficiency by being obliged to perform one or two run-throughs before critical eyes, creating circumstances in which a performance has a significance unusual for it but (at least for the performer) one that is no less consequential. More complicated still, we have execution sports, such as figure skating, fancy diving, and gymnastics, which allow for presented competitions involving run-throughs that are at once indications of amount of skill and demonstrations of ideal form.

The limits of demonstration have some interest. First is the limit, already suggested, regarding bedside teaching, namely, the use of patients to illustrate (for students) treatment even while actual treatment is being given. The implication is that at least at

---

tion. See, for example, Department of the Army Field Manual (FM 105–5), *Maneuver Control* (Washington, D.C.: Department of the Army, 1967), pp. 51–130.

certain junctures, this particular duality of perspective should not be allowed.

Second is the limit regarding substance. It is felt that no single demonstration should entail too much cost, certainly in many cases not the cost involved in actual activity. Here too much dramaturgy might be thought inappropriate. Even Abbie Hoffman thinks so, as implied in his citation of the following news report:

> Fort Belvoir, Va., Oct 4 (AP)—The Army demonstrated today its latest riot control tactics and equipment.
>
> The setting was Riotsville, U.S.A., a mockup of a city area swept by disorder.
>
> While about 3,000 persons observed from bleachers, a Riotsville mob made up of soldiers dressed as hippies set fire to buildings, overturned two cars and looted stores.
>
> Then, with bayonets fixed, troops wearing black rubber gas masks arrived on the scene and controlled the "mob" with tear gas.[46]

Again something similar can be said about practicing. Thus, the use of outdated though seaworthy ships either for target practice or as demonstration materials for new bomb capabilities of aircraft can press the limits. Similarly, in the training of race horses, practice runs and trial heats must be managed so as not to damage the beast, that contingency being reserved for actual races.

Finally, most interesting of all, there is a version of the segregation problem. Although the demonstrating of something can be radically different from the doing of that something, there is still some carry-over—especially if "real" equipment is used—and this carry-over can be sufficient to prohibit demonstration. At the same time, one must expect historical changes regarding these limits, as this news release suggests:

> Toronto, Aug. 4 (Canadian Press)—The Canadian Broadcasting Corporation has lifted its ban on commercials that had been regarded as too intimate for television.
>
> Advertisements for girdles, deodorants, brassieres, health clubs, hair removers, and bathroom tissues may now be seen on the network.

---

46. Photographically cited in his *Revolution for the Hell of It* (New York: Dial Press, 1968), p. 192.

"Subjects that were not considered polite in mixed company a number of years ago now are considered acceptable," said Charles Spraggett, supervisor of press publicity for the C.B.C.

A ban on panties remains.[47]

I would like to add that a treacherous distinction is sometimes attempted between demonstrations for theory and demonstrations for practice—a nice framing issue bearing directly on the matter of limits. Thus, a course on guerrilla warfare at San Francisco State College (in the student-run experimental program) apparently pressed the limits, at least as the press reported:

> "This is an important speech," the barrel-chested, welterweight instructor of the Experimental College course in guerrilla warfare explained. "This is where Carmichael sets a new direction for the Black Power movement—calling on blacks to organize themselves, become nationalistic, almost racist."
>
> After the speech, recorded at Huey Newton's birthday party rally in Oakland, a panel of "combat veterans" took the stage and reviewed, historically, the tactics and practice of urban warfare, discussing sabotage, espionage, counter-intelligence and weaponry, with emphasis on the Battle of Algiers.
>
> This unusual college class, a subject of controversy off campus, is being investigated by the state attorney general's office.
>
> "If it is a classroom discussion on guerrilla warfare," says Charles O'Brien, chief deputy attorney general here, "that is one thing; if it is an exercise in guerrilla warfare, if they are training guerrillas, that is quite another thing."[48]

And in fact a detailed course in sabotage could hardly escape providing instruction as well as enlightenment. The concept of "demonstration" thus has embarrassing ambiguities.[49]

c. In our society there is considerable (and growing) use of replicative records of events, that is, replays of a recording of a strip of actual activity for the purpose of establishing as fact, as having occurred, something that happened in the past. Whereas

---

47. *The New York Times*, August 5, 1957.

48. Dexter Waugh reporting in the *San Francisco Sunday Examiner and Chronicle,* April 21, 1968.

49. A further example: exhibition ball games. They aren't "serious," since the outcome does not affect a series or the players' individual records. But an exciting contest can occur.

a demonstration provides an ideal running through of an activity for learning or evidential purposes, documentation employs the actual remains of something that once appeared in the actual (in the sense of less transformed) world without, it is claimed, a documentary intent. Written and photographic records are standard examples, as are artifacts from an actual strip of activity, now tagged as "exhibits." Recently tape and video recordings have enormously expanded the use of documentation. In any case, the variety of documentation is great: courtroom evidence, industrial stroboscopic examinations, X rays for medical use, time-and-motion studies, linguistic use of taped speech, replays in sportscasting, news shots of historic events, camera coverage of battlegrounds, and so on.

The power of the documentary key to inhibit original meanings is impressive. Take, for example, one of the Lenny Bruce obscenity trials:

> The task of reaching a verdict was handed to the jury after Bruce's unprintable word and unprintable story were related in his own words in an 18-minute excerpt taped from his October 4 [1961] show.
>
> "This show is high comedy," Bendich [Bruce's lawyer] announced before pulling the switch to start the performance. "I am going to ask that the audience be allowed to respond to the humor. It wouldn't be human not to."
>
> Judge Horn stopped Bendich in mid-argument.
>
> "This is not a theater and not a show. I am not going to allow any such thing," the Judge replied.
>
> Judge Horn then turned to the spectators in the crowded courtroom and said, "I am going to admonish you to control yourselves in regard to any emotions you may feel."
>
> The warning was taken solemnly—and so, it developed, was the performance.
>
> No one laughed, and very few in the room showed the trace of a smile during the sampling of the humor of Lenny Bruce.[50]

An experimental illustration is provided by Richard Lazarus' research on stress. A film on primitive subincision rites was shown to selected audiences wired for the metering of heart rate

---

50. From a longer report by Michael Harris, "Lenny Bruce Acquitted in Smut Case," *San Francisco Chronicle,* March 9, 1962.

and palmar skin resistance.[51] By altering the soundtrack, the experimenter could partly determine the perspective the audience employed. One of these perspectives, "intellectualization," offered an anthropological line, in part transforming the scene into documentation—a keying which appreciably reduced stress response for college students.

But, of course, there are limits to the documentary frame, and they have special interest. There is a normative question as to whether recordings of any kind should be used as evidence against a person whose unwitting action provided the source of the material. Correspondingly, it is believed that the individual ought to have protection against recordings of his voice and actions at times when he is unaware that documentation is being created. Further, there is the issue of a document's permissible use even after its subjects have freely given their consent; educational television's use of filmed family psychotherapy is an example.[52] In these cases, the concern is not with the document per se but with the rights of the persons documented, and behind this a concern for their interests on occasions when they might be tempted unwisely to consent to publicity.

Another limitation is even more instructive in its way, namely, the limit on the dissociation between the action documented and the document itself, the concern being that if a reprehensible or horrible or improper action is represented, whether this be an unkeyed action or itself a keying, how free can the documentation be of the original sin? At first blush, of course, one might think there would be no limits, since everyone clearly appreciates that a documentation of a past event is not that past event. But, nonetheless, connection is felt, and connection is honored:

> Fort Lauderdale, Fla. (AP)—The City Commission's new ordinance to ban obscenity in books, magazines and records for those under 17 is so specific in describing anatomical features and acts

---

51. Partly reported in Joseph C. Speisman et al., "Experimental Reduction of Stress Based on Ego-Defense Theory," *Journal of Abnormal and Social Psychology*, LXVIII, no. 4 (April 1964): 367–380; Richard S. Lazarus and Elizabeth Alfert, "Short-Circuiting of Threat by Experimentally Altering Cognitive Appraisal," *Journal of Abnormal and Social Psychology*, LXIX, no. 2 (August 1964): 195–205.

52. See Edward A. Mason, M.D., "Safe to Be Touched; How Safe to Be Exposed?" film review in *Community Mental Health Journal*, II (1966): 93–96.

KEYS AND KEYINGS 71

which may not be portrayed that The Miami Herald reported the definition is unprintable.[53]

> Winchester, Ind., Dec. 29 (UPI)—Winchester's new antipornography ordinance may not take effect because the local newspaper says its language is not in good taste.
>
> In an article explaining the position, Richard Wise, publisher of the Winchester News Gazette and Journal Herald, said:
>
> "We are not questioning the wisdom of the ordinance itself or the constitutional right of persons to buy or sell such material. Rather, we are simply exercising our right to print only matter which we feel is reasonable or tasteful and we do not believe the language with definitions is in good taste."
>
> Winchester ordinances must be printed in a Winchester newspaper of general circulation in order to take effect, and Mr. Wise has the only one.[54]

Lenny Bruce, reporting on one of his New York obscenity trials, suggests another illustration:

> The *New York Law Journal* pleaded guilty to not publishing the lower court's statement, with an explanation: "The majority opinion, of necessity, cited in detail the language used by Bruce in his night-club act, and also described gestures and routines which the majority found to be obscene and indecent. *The Law Journal* decided against publication, even edited, on the grounds that deletions would destroy the opinion, and without the deletions publication was impossible with the *Law Journal* standards."[55]

Reportings of pornographic content are not the only instances for which documentary limits exist. The "Moors" murder trial pressed matters to another kind of limit:

> Chester, England—The tape-recorded screams of a little girl pierced the stillness of the courtroom at Britain's "bodies on the moors" trial yesterday.

---

53. *The Evening Bulletin* (Philadelphia), November 1, 1968.

54. *The New York Times,* December 30, 1973. For this and other help I am grateful to Millie Owen.

55. Lenny Bruce, *How to Talk Dirty and Influence People* (Chicago: Playboy Press, 1966), p. 195. Mr. Bruce, in the lines that follow, can go on to provide an illustration of what it was the *Law Journal* could not apparently print, since the framing restrictions that apply to the *Journal*'s business do not apply to Mr. Hefner's. Observe that I have not cited what Mr. Bruce goes on to cite, because restrictions of my frame allow me to do that only if something would be lost in not doing so, which is not the case, although *now*, in the light of this comment on the frame of academic books, I might have warrant for repeating Bruce's illustration.

Women in the public galleries wept. Others covered their ears as the 16-minute recording was played.

Prosecutor Sir Elwyn Jones told the court they were the sounds made by 10-year-old Lesley Ann Downey as she was tortured and pornographic photos taken of her just before she was slain.

Jones alleged that the recording was made by Ian Brady, 27-year-old stock clerk, and his 23-year-old mistress, Myra Hindley.

. . . .

Lesley Ann disappeared after going to a fairground the day after Christmas 1964. Police later dug her nude body from a shallow peat grave on the wild Pennine moor.

As the child's screams sounded in the oak court, Miss Hindley and Brady stared impassively at the bullet-proof glass surrounding them.[56]

It is apparent that dramatic presentation, illustration, and documentation all share some issues regarding limits of a somewhat moral kind, especially in connection with what is sexually tabooed. And it is apparent that whenever an exercise in license is examined closely, various limits will still be found. Take, for example, a book specifically concerned with sexual matters, as reported in a review:

This book, copyright Copenhagen 1968, is presumably one of the first fruits of Denmark's abolition of sexual censorship. It consists of 42 black-and-white photos of a couple making love in as many positions, with a shortish blurb on the facing pages setting out the main pros and cons of each. The photos have a specifically disturbing quality in that (obviously by design) they neither show us organs nor the facial expressions of the participants.

The lack of the first seems relatively natural and is accounted for by the topography of the bodies, but the preservation of the models' facial anonymity leads to a few bizarre effects. One position, for instance, "is one of the few . . . where the union of the sexual organs and movements is visible for both" and "the purely mental effect of this may in turn contribute significantly to an increase of sexual excitement." Well and good. But the models in the illustration virtually eschew this excitement; their eyes and

---

56. *San Francisco Chronicle*, April 27, 1966. The issue of courtroom documentation leads into another, that of limits of newspaper reportings of courtroom documentation. For comments on the Moors trial reporting and the problem of "imitative crime," see Louis Blom-Cooper, "Murder: How Much Should Be Reported?" *The Observer* (London), May 1, 1966, p. 11.

heads averted from us and from each other, they appear to be watching a telly somewhere in the middle-distance.[57]

That such limits should be discernible is hardly news. However, what does seem to be newly demonstrated in the last five or ten years is how changeable these limits are. The rightness of existing limits can arouse deep feelings of support, and yet next year these limits can be quietly breached and the year thereafter the breach can be ratified. Apparently in matters of frame, rulings can change very rapidly—if contemporary experience is a fair measure.

d. Group psychotherapy and other role-playing sessions ought to be mentioned, if only because the vast literature in the area provides a ready opportunity for formalization of the transformational practices employed.[58] Here, presumably, the reliving of experience under the director's guidance serves not only to illustrate themes but also to alter the actor's attitude to them.

e. No matter what sort of routine, keyed or unkeyed, is considered, there is the possibility that someone will want to run through it as an "experiment," not to achieve its ordinary end but for purposes of study, a playing out under circumstances in which an hypothesis can be tested and disinterested examination, measurement, and analysis can occur. "Natural" conditions may be maintained as much as possible, except that natural reasons don't exist for the performance. Note, in order for the term "key" to be unreservedly applied here it must be assumed that the participants in the activity—experimenter, subjects (when there are any), and the scientific audience—all share the same appreciation of what it is that is happening while it is happening, namely, an experiment of a particular kind.

Again, of course, the question of limits arises. The antivivisection movement is one expression of this concern, reaction to medical study within German concentration camps another. A further example is the unease shown about experimentation with the centers of the brain—electrical and chemical stimulation

---

57. Review by Christopher Williams in *New Society*, October 2, 1969, p. 365, of *Sexual Techniques*, by Mogens Toft, with photographs by John Fowlie (Souvenir Press).

58. An interesting effort at formalization (with full aliveness to similarities and differences) is provided by Eric Bentley, "Theater and Therapy," in *New American Review*, no. 8 (New York: New American Library, 1970), pp. 131–152.

resulting in emotional and behavioral changes produced at the experimenter's will. In all of this, desecration of something felt to be sacred is involved, namely, the mind. Desecration of experience also figures. Here a leading contemporary incident is the Masters and Johnson research on the female orgasm.[59]

5. *Regroundings:* Major types of keys have been reviewed: make-believe, contests, ceremonials, and technical redoings. A further general class needs be mentioned, it being conceptually the most troublesome of the lot. What is involved is the performance of an activity more or less openly for reasons or motives felt to be radically different from those that govern ordinary actors. The notion of regroundings, then, rests on the assumption that some motives for a deed are ones that leave the performer within the normal range of participation, and other motives, especially when stabilized and institutionalized, leave the performer outside the ordinary domain of the activity.

One example of regrounding is found in charity work, as when an upper-middle-class matron serves as a salesperson at a salvage sale, or when the following social impossibility occurs:

> When she [Princess Margaret] was about 25, she stood behind a counter selling nylon stockings and nightgowns at a church bazaar in Ballater, Scotland, on a Saturday night. A young man edged through the crowd of women and asked for a pair of nylons. "What size?" asked Princess Margaret. The man blushed, then said: "I don't know, but they're for a young lady about your size." "Oh," smiled Margaret, "then you'll want eights."[60]

Given the rather strict rules regarding talk with a member of the Family, there could hardly be anything better to indicate the strength of a key to reconstitute what it keyed—although not so

59. The first published report was William H. Masters, M.D., "The Sexual Response Cycle of the Human Female," *Western Journal of Surgery, Obstetrics and Gynecology*, LXVIII (1960): 57–72. The researchers brought a wide variety of research controls into the activity held in our society to be the most private and delicate, causing individuals to be subjects in new ways. Not merely were the limits extended in regard to doing things for experimental purposes, but it is hard to imagine how these limits could be pressed any further in this particular direction. A version of the negative reaction was well stated in Leslie H. Farber's "I'm Sorry, Dear," *Commentary*, November 1964, pp. 47–54, a piece that is almost as funny as the research it criticizes.

60. Reported in the *San Francisco Chronicle*, November 5, 1965.

strong as to prevent the boy from blushing or the event from acquiring news status. (Nor need one restrict oneself to the good works of the better classes. In crofter communities in Shetland, where Sunday is defined as a day for clean clothes and the right to recess from croft work, a recently bereaved woman may be given a few hours of Sunday labor by her neighbors; the labor is the same, but now it has become the work of the Lord.) A woodsman's labor undertaken as recreation[61] or as medical prescription is another example. Still another: lowly tasks performed as penance by exalted sinners. Mountain climbing is yet a further example, the election of which to undertake—and not Everest—being a seventh wonder of the world:

> Shipton had invited me to accompany him on an exploratory trip to the southeast of Everest. . . . For ten days we climbed and explored in country that men had never seen. We crossed difficult passes and visited great glaciers. And at the end of it, it wasn't so much our achievements I remembered, exciting as they had been, but more the character of Eric Shipton; his ability to be calm and comfortable in any circumstances; his insatiable curiosity to know what lay over the next hill or around the next corner; and, above all, his remarkable power to transform the discomfort and pain and misery of high-altitude life into a great adventure.[62]

Also, there is the arrangement, now in considerable disfavor, whereby a neophyte attaches himself to a craftsman, shopkeeper, or professional and does the work of an assistant, doing this job with little or no pay in exchange for an opportunity to learn the trade. (Here, what for the professional is literally work is for the apprentice an opportunity to practice.) And, of course, there is participant-observation, at least when done with prior self-disclosure.

Relatively broad and obvious regroundings have been cited, although certainly more subtle versions also exist. Thus, in the law it is often possible to mark a clear difference between ordinary cases, brought primarily on the instigation of a plaintiff, and "test" cases, the latter chosen because they clearly engage a prin-

---

61. See Gregory Prentice Stone and Marvin J. Taves, "Research into the Human Element in Wilderness Use," Society of American Foresters *Proceedings* (Memphis, Tenn., 1956), pp. 26–32.

62. Edmund Hillary, *High Adventure* (New York: E. P. Dutton & Co., 1955), p. 50.

ciple, one that the participating lawyers and judges want to see
resolved even if it means the nominal opponents will be carried
into something beyond their resources or concern.

Now examine one example of regrounding in detail, namely,
shilling Nevada style. This particular example is apt because the
regrounding involved is of a well-formalized game—twenty-one
or blackjack—and because the keying itself is sometimes explicated and formalized by casinos. In any case, a shill nicely patterns his playing after the game in question, yet there is a
systematic alteration at every point in play to distinguish shilling
from playing.

Legitimate shilling is a device officially employed to keep
games going when no "live" players, or an insufficient number of
them, are present. The current argument in the industry is that
many players do not like to enter a game that is not in play, so
shills provide an appearance of action. (Thus, in the trade, shills
are sometimes called "starters.") Further, some players do not
like to play "head on" against a dealer, and here, too, shills may
be called on. (Management, of course, can use shills for less
presentable purposes, the least dubious of which is to prevent the
sort of head-on play in twenty-one that card counters favor.)[63]
The following, then, are rules for legitimate shilling:

  a. The play in general:
    1. Don't address customers unless addressed, then before they
       get the wrong idea, quietly tell them that you are a game
       starter.[64]
    2. Leave whenever the dealer or pit boss tells you to.
    3. Give attention to the play, but do not become involved in it.
    4. Cut the cards, change seats, or leave on request of the dealer.

---

63. In earlier decades of Nevada gambling, shills were used in many
ways; one, for example, was to help the dealer cheat a customer by "taking"
a good card otherwise destined for the player or "leaving" a card that was
bad for him. Currently shills are "put in" to "break up" a run of player
"luck," a practice the full implication of which introduces a topic ordinarily restricted to descriptions of primitive society.

64. There is an interesting parallel here provided by telephone answering
services. A standard tack is for the service to respond as though the intended recipient's secretary were answering but to correct this tacitly induced wrong impression should the caller ask for information or help that
the answering service can't supply. Here see Julius A. Roth and Mary Ellen
Robbins Lepionka, "The Telephone Answering Service as a Communication
Barrier: A Research Note," *Urban Life and Culture*, II (1973): 108.

    5. Don't draw attention to any mistake made by the dealer.

    6. Play fast.

  b. Money:

    1. Bet one chip each play and one and a half on the play after a blackjack.

    2. Stack the chips in piles which the "eye" can read easily, and give back to the dealer any that accumulate over a specified amount.

    3. Don't toy with money or touch it unnecessarily.

    4. When coming into a game, exchange your shill "button" for ten chips (minimal table value but not less than a dollar), and on "being taken out," hand back all your chips and retrieve your shill button.

  c. Rules of play:

    1. Do not split or double down or take "insurance."

    2. Hit all soft hands except soft 17 and stay on all stiffs.

These rules[65] systematically alter the character of play; follow them and you will have transformed table play into what can be mistaken for play but isn't.

III

In discussing primary frameworks it was argued that an issue regarding segregation could arise when two different perspectives were applicable to a matter but only one was meant to apply, and that often some tension and joking would there be found. As suggested, one must expect the same issue to occur in regard to keyings and, by the very nature of the case, to occur frequently. A nude female model, for example, is not in one sense literally naked; she is serving as a model, a nude, a human statue as it were, a lending of a person to an inanimate act, in short, the

---

65. Use here of the term "rule" presents an interesting problem. Generically one might prefer to say that conventions were involved, not rules; after all, shilling could quite nicely be done with a somewhat different set of guidelines, and in fact there is some variation from casino to casino. But casino management tends itself to here employ the term "rules." Instructions to beginners are presented as rules, the breaking of which will result in negative sanctions. Some casinos actually have written outlines of these practices and use the term "rules" in the description. Here one sees, of course, some of the trouble that can be caused by making technical use of terms that are used in an allied way by one's subjects.

embodiment of a body. Here, as in the medical cases earlier cited,
care will often be exerted to pointedly bracket the modeling activity, ensuring clear-cut before-and-after boundaries. And rules
may obtain prohibiting catching the eye of the model during
work, the assumption being that any mutually ratified exchange
may weaken the hold of the artistic frame and its capacity to
preclude other readings, specifically the kind available to participants in an informal conversational encounter.

Keyings seem to vary according to the degree of transformation they produce. When a novel is made into a play, the transformation can be said to vary all the way from loose (or distant)
to faithful (or close), depending on how much liberty has been
taken with the original text. In general, in the matter of the
faithfulness of a replication, one issue will be the number of
keyings away the copy is from the original. When a novel is made
into a movie and then the movie is "adapted" as a musical
comedy, we assume the second effort will be further away from
the original text than the first. A second issue will be the frame
itself: a story presented in a novel seems more likely to appear in
fuller form than when scripted as a puppet show.

The set of practices available for transforming a strip of activity into a particular keying can presumably operate in both directions. As a novel is made into a movie, so, alas, a movie can be
made into a novel. Another example here is the set of equiva-
lences for punctuation, allowing us to pass between typescript
and print. Clearly, underlining is in the first what italics is in the
second, and the translation can be made in either direction, that
is, in the typing of print or the printing of typescript.

But this view of transformation is more geometrical than
might be desirable. Our purpose often will not be to learn how
one strip *could* be generated from another by the application of
translation rules, but rather how two similar strips *were* both
generated from a common model and differ from each other in
certain systematic ways. One might find it reasonable to speak of
two performances of a play given by the same company on two
successive nights, or two readings of the same part given by two
different actors, or two varieties of American speech—male and
female—and feel it awkward to speak of one version being a
keying of another. In each example both versions are keyings of a
common model, and although rules might be written in each case

for transposing one version into another, the student engaging in
this exercise might be the only one with any interest in doing so.
There is the further fact that a copy made from a model may
omit certain elements of the original, as, for example, in a line-
drawing caricature of a human figure, or the integration of a
mathematical expression containing a constant, so that although
one could always move from original to copy, the copy alone
might not provide enough information to allow full translation in
the other direction. In any case, the possibility of comparing two
transformations of the same text and that of deriving one transformation from another should be left open. Thus, a translation
of a play from French into English might be viewed either as a
second version of an underlying text or as an English keying of a
French pattern of expression.

There is a deeper issue concerning reversibility. The reporting
of an event and its documentation are not only seen as reductions
of or abstractions from the original, but are also understood to
possibly influence later occurrences of the real thing. Thus, for
example, there is a concern that the detailed reporting of a crime
may lead to further crimes modeled after the report. But although this sort of circularity may be imagined and presumably
occurs, we seem to have a strong feeling that reportings and
documentation ought not to be the cause of the actual event they
record; the causality should all be in the other direction. Further,
we sometimes act now with the sole intent to provide the hard
evidence that can be called on later as documentary proof of our
having (or not having) acted in the manner that comes to be
questioned. We have charity balls so that the next day news
coverage will appear, the coverage and not the ball serving to
advertise the charity. And, of course, when a minor social occasion is graced by an important political speaker, the transcription
given out to the major news media is likely to be the reason for
the original performance, not merely its consequence.

Now a general theme, albeit in particular form: keyings are
themselves obviously vulnerable to rekeying. This has already
been implied in various ways. Although it is possible to rehearse
something that will become a real doing, such as a robbery, it is
much more likely that what will be rehearsed is the staging of
something in a play, which, of course, is already a copy. Routinely, those who draw up plans for a building first make rough

sketches of the plans, and routinely, apparently, the military
rehearses rehearsals:

> The officer preparing the exercise rehearses the exercise as a
> final check on his plan. He conducts the rehearsal well in advance
> of the scheduled exercise so that he will have time to correct any
> errors and readjust the time schedule. He rehearses the umpires
> and aggressor detail first, repeating the rehearsal as necessary so
> that everyone is thoroughly familiar with his duties. He follows this
> with a full-scale rehearsal, using a practice unit. The individual
> who originally directed that the exercise be prepared should be
> present at the rehearsal to make any changes that he deems neces-
> sary or to give his approval of the field exercise.[66]

So we must deal with retransformations as well as transformations. Nor can any obvious limit be seen to the number of rekeyings to which a particular strip of activity can be subject; clearly,
multiple rekeyings are possible. Hal and Falstaff, when brought
alive in Shakespeare's play, can rehearse the forthcoming interview with Henry IV, this being a staged keying.[67] A *New Yorker*
cartoon can depict two male models posing (under the direction
of a photographer) at a chess board for a liquor ad, apparently
deep in play, one saying to another, "I wish I had learned to play
the game."[68] (Three bounded spaces will be present: the space
made available on the page by the absence of print, this marking
the limits of the print-on-page frame; the area covered by the
cartoonist's wash or coloring, this marking where the realm
depicted in the cartoon begins; the boundary drawn *within* this
particular example of the cartoon realm to show what the depicted photographer will restrict his depicted shot to, and thus
where the cartooned keying of a posing session begins.)[69] And, of

---

66. Department of the Army Field Manual (FM 105–5), p. 26.

67. *Henry IV, Part I*, Act II, Scene 4.

68. January 30, 1965, by B. Tobey.

69. The punch lines provided by one of the cartooned models are,
syntactically speaking, clearly part of the nonposing part of the cartoon,
the part that includes the preoccupied photographer, the part that is to be
thought of as not turning up in the picture the photographer is taking. But
the physical placement of the words—in this case below the cartoonist's
wash—need not comply with the conventions that govern the portrayal of
scenic space. These words could appear in a "balloon" *inside* the "photographed" space and still cause no confusion. For we treat space one way
for scenic presentations and another way for textual presentation, this dual

course, not only can a particular stage play be presented in various versions or styles, from classical to modern dress, but also one of these versions can be satirized, guyed, camped, or played broad, the persistent purpose being to use a traditional presentation as a substance in its own right, as something in itself to work upon. (Thus, one function of referees and umpires during contests is to prevent the players from making a game of a game, that is, treating the contest unseriously, rekeying what was meant to have a less complex frame structure.)

Earlier it was argued that a key can translate only what is already meaningful in terms of a primary framework. That definition must now be qualified. As suggested, a *re*keying does its work not simply on something defined in terms of a primary framework, but rather on a keying of these definitions. The primary framework must still be there, else there would be no content to the rekeying; but it is the keying of that framework that is the material that is transposed.

IV

At the beginning of this chapter a distinction was drawn between actual, untransformed activity and keyings, and it was argued that in the latter case description could be either in frame terms or in terms of the innermost or modeled-after activity. Now terms must be found that will allow us to address rekeyings and to maintain some kind of control over complications.

---

treatment being one of the basic conventions of the cartoon frame. (Here I draw on David S. Marshall, "A Frame Analysis of the Cartoon" [unpublished paper, University of Pennsylvania, 1971].) Fry has an interesting footnote on the boundary between print and cartoon:

> Cartoons have their own special frame establishers—some verbal, some nonverbal. In the first place, they appear in magazines and newspapers. This fact, in itself, causes the specimen to acquire a particular complexion. Then, they are always set off from the rest of the material by a little lined box or a wide blank border. And they are frequently captioned to indicate their genus, but this is not essential. The point is: cartoons are recognizable as such by reason of the communication that "this picture is not of real life," or "is not a real advertisement," by means of conventional message-cues. It is awesome, when one thinks objectively about it, how few mistakes are made in cartoon recognition. [*Sweet Madness*, p. 143.]

Given the possibility of a frame that incorporates rekeyings, it becomes convenient to think of each transformation as adding a *layer or lamination* to the activity. And one can address two features of the activity. One is the innermost layering, wherein dramatic activity can be at play to engross the participant. The other is the outermost lamination, the *rim* of the frame, as it were, which tells us just what sort of status in the real world the activity has, whatever the complexity of the inner laminations. Thus, a description in a novel of a game of twenty-one has as its rim the special make-believe that was called a dramatic scripting, and innermost is the realm that can become alive for persons involved in blackjack. The rehearsal of a play is a rekeying, just as is a rehearsal staged within a play as part of its scripted content; but in the two cases, the rim of the activity is quite different, the first being a rehearsal and the second a play. Obviously, the two rehearsals have radically different statuses as parts of the real world. Note, in the case of activity defined entirely within the terms of a primary framework, one can think of the rim and the innermost core as being the same. And when an individual speaks of another not taking something seriously or making a joke of it, what the speaker has in mind is that the activity, whether laminated or not, was improperly cast by this other into a playful key. Indeed, it is quite possible to joke with another's telling of a joke, in which case one is not taking seriously his effort to establish a frame—one involving an unserious keying. Finally, it is convenient to refer to a particular frame by the label we give its rim; thus, "the rehearsal frame," "the theatrical frame," and so forth. However, one ought to keep in mind that often what is being described is not the frame as a whole but the keying it sustains.

4

Designs and Fabrications

Keying provides one basic way in which a strip of activity can be transformed, that is, serve as an item-by-item model for something else. Differently put, keyings represent a basic way in which activity is vulnerable. A second transformational vulnerability is now considered: fabrication. I refer to the intentional effort of one or more individuals to manage activity so that a party of one or more others will be induced to have a false belief about what it is that is going on. A nefarious design is involved, a plot or treacherous plan leading—when realized—to a falsification of some part of the world. So it would appear that a strip of activity can litter the world in two ways, can serve as a model from whose design two types of reworking can be produced: a keying or a fabrication.

A few terms immediately become necessary. Those who engineer the deception can be called the operatives, fabricators, deceivers. Those intendedly taken in can be said to be contained —contained in a construction or fabrication. They can be called the dupes, marks, pigeons, suckers, butts, victims, gulls. When two or more individuals cooperate in presenting a deception, covert communication among them is likely to be required, and even when not required, the grounds for indulging it are there.

This is collusive communication; those in on it constitute a collusive net and those the net operates against, the excolluded.[1]

As suggested, fabrications, like keyings, require the use of a model, the use of something already meaningful in terms of primary frameworks. But whereas a keying intendedly leads all participants to have the same view of what it is that is going on, a fabrication requires differences. (Satires and takeoffs are meant to be seen as copies and make no sense without this common recognition; and certainly Beethoven meant to avow his source when he rang up changes on "God Save the King." Plagiarists, on the other hand, are necessarily committed to keeping their copying in the dark.)

Observe that for those in on a deception, what is going on *is* fabrication; for those contained, what is going on is *what* is being fabricated. The rim of the frame is a construction, but only the fabricators so see it.

Fabrications, unlike keyings, are subject to a special kind of discrediting. When the contained party discovers what is up, what was real for him a moment ago is now seen as a deception

---

1. Collusion is managed through framing cues, some of which are standardized and have a social history. A comment on one is recorded:

. . . winking? No doubt it continues in private, in remote unexplored northern valleys, in old farces performed by tired touring companies; but as a major feature of the British Way of Life it seems to have died out. The sly wink of the diplomat, often accompanied by the laying of a finger to the nose, the confiding wink of the comic, the jolly wink of the gay young curate boldly stretching the limits of the permissible at parochial parties, the meaning wink of the bookies' hanger-on, the insulting wink of the reveller at the unprotected female, the wink which, between financiers, is as good as a nod—they have all vanished from fiction and all but vanished from life, which has become, in consequence, less colourful and dangerous and much more prim. [*Punch,* March 28, 1962, for the finding of which I am indebted to Dawn Brett.]

Once collusive channels have been established, they can, of course, be used for all kinds of frame-relevant purposes, for example, the transmission of warning that what a third party has been saying is to be understood as his effort to deceive and thus is not to be taken at its face value. Thus:

Sometimes an underworld person, speaking to another about some third person also present, will use a word like "ship," "Binnie," "hill," or "daily." In each case he is indicating that the third person is telling lies, telling the tale. "Ship under sail," "Binnie Hale," "hill and dale," "Daily Mail"—these are all rhyming-slang for "The Tale," and are shortened, for greater concealment to the first word. [Jim Phelan, *The Underworld* (London: George G. Harrap & Co., 1954), p. 161.]

and is totally destroyed. It collapses. Here "real," as James suggested, consists of that understanding of what is going on that drives out, that "dominates," all other understandings.

A slight reshuffling of terminology is now required. If deceptions are placed on one side, on the other will be untransformed activity, along with keyings and rekeyings—in a collective word, "straight" activity. On one side a frame whose rim is by design beyond the awareness of categories of participants; on the other side, one whose rim is apparent to all relevant parties.

Let me repeat that since frame incorporates both the participant's response and the world he is responding to, a reflexive element must necessarily be present in any participant's clearheaded view of events; a correct view of a scene must include the viewing of it as part of it.

The notion of discreditation raises some issues. Definitions of the situation inevitably terminate as new ones take hold; it can be correctly said of two men that they finished their checker game and began to cut the grass. In brief, understandings have natural endings. Situations can also be violently disrupted, as when, say, a checker game is stopped in order to put out a fire, or a summer theatrical audience dismissed because the generator has broken down. So, too, the mood of a pleasant occasion, the sense in which the participants have been drawn out of themselves into a jointly sustained enjoyable state, can be abruptly dispelled and destined not to be re-created during that occasion. The memoirs of a gentleman spy provide an example:

> The Gulf of Riga in the summer was dotted with the yachts and launches of prosperous citizens and I spent many happy days sailing around the Gulf. One of these outings remains imprinted on my memory. Together with several other English people I was week-ending on a magnificent launch owned by a generous and wealthy member of the Schwartzhaeupter. As the craft sailed down the River Dvina we drank copious draughts of vodka; by the time we reached the rolling Baltic most of the passengers were rolling as well. All through the cruise a good-looking young man, Niki Balinski, sat on the cabin roof and played to us gay, wild and abandoned songs on the balaleika. He had a club-foot and wore a heavy iron attachment, but with his instrument and his melodious voice he was always the life and soul of the party. One of those sudden squalls for which the Baltic is well known struck the boat, causing it to heel violently over and Niki, in the middle of a gypsy lovesong,

was thrown from the cabin roof into the sea, his heavy iron boot dragging him immediately beneath the white-crested waves. He never surfaced and was not seen again. The ship's company, aghast at the appalling accident, searched for several hours, but in vain; it was a much subdued party that returned to shore to report the incident to the police.[2]

But in both routine (or "natural") terminations and unanticipated ones, the capacity of the same performers to restage the disrupted show at another time is ordinarily not threatened. The current definition of the situation is disrupted, but the possibility of defining things this way with these participants remains. Fabrications introduce the possibility of a different kind of disruption, one in which discovery can sharply alter the capacity for those involved to participate together in that kind of activity again.

Fabrications can be classified in many ways for purposes of analysis. They can be ordered according to how long they last or the number of persons contained by them. They can be ordered according to the materials that are manipulated. Thus a motive can be made to deceive, as can an intent, a gesture, a show of resolve or a show of a lack of it, a statement, an artifact, a personal identity, a setting and its gathering, a conversation, an extensive physical plant, a gust of wind, an accident, a happenstance, a company of Israeli commandos dressed as Arab prisoners and airline mechanics to surprise skyjackers,[3] a Trojan horse. Indeed, even what a safari gets to see of the jungle can be fabricated—as when a hunting guide arranges to have a pride of lions learn to look for food at a particular place (on hearing a whistle pitched higher than man can hear), and then, after a two-week buildup through the forest with his party, bagging everything but lions by good woodsmanship, brings them to the point where a lion kill will assuredly occur, leaving his clients deeply satisfied with what they have been able to wrest from an alien and antagonistic world of raw nature.[4] The classification and analysis I propose is one based upon the end served by the fabrication.

---

2. John Whitwell, *British Agent* (London: William Kimber & Co., 1966), pp. 66–67.

3. Reported in *Time,* May 22, 1972.

4. Alexander Lake, *Killers in Africa* (New York: Doubleday & Company, 1953), pp. 40–43.

II

First to consider are *benign* fabrications, those claimed to be engineered in the interest of the person contained by them, or, if not quite in his interest and for his benefit, then at least not done against his interest. Here inadvertent disclosure collapses the disclosed design and can make the erstwhile dupe somewhat suspicious of the operation in the future, but no great damage to the operator's moral character need result. Benign fabrications themselves come in varieties.

1. In all societies there exists, I believe, the practice of what can be called "playful deceit," namely, the containment of one or more individuals for the avowed purpose of fun—harmless, unserious, typically brief entertainment. The understanding is that the victim will soon be let in on the joke and that he can be relied on to take it "in good spirit" or "like a sport," in other words, that he will sustain the notion that his interests have not been harmed, that he himself might have played such a joke, and that, in a sense, he has just been waiting for this moment of disclosure to join those in on the joke in laughing at a part of himself he has now cut himself off from.[5] To ensure that matters will come to

5. Playful joking must be distinguished from its less innocent brethren, the various forms of the "put-on." Given the working assumption in informal conversation that a speaker will build his knowledgeability on a particular topic into each statement—howsoever modestly and tactfully—a trapping of one's opponent is possible by making an unsophisticated statement that will evoke a ready correction, and only then a realization on the part of the corrector that he has been led into showing his willingness for minor triumphs, since it soon becomes clear that the speaker was merely acting naïve and wanted his act to become gradually apparent. More damaging, a jokester can build up a false conversational world around a victim so that the victim feels he has obtained a full expression of the other's position and character; then the jokester gradually increases the dimensions of his arguments and feelings in the direction of a stereotype, perhaps beyond credibility, and departs, leaving the victim to slowly realize that he has been the butt of a joke. Similarly, the victim can be given praise and assurances, a "buildup," until he realizes he is being toyed with. And, of course, these short flights can be pushed into the domain of the short con. It is said, for example, that currently inner-city blacks are much oriented to "playing game," "working game," and "getting someone in a bag," involving short-run verbal persuasion and the "hyping" or conning of those in their more or less immediate circle, and that this approach to persons present comes to be a prevailing mode of adaptation. See Boone Ham-

be taken in the right frame, a jokester may well seek out a third-party witness who can be brought into the joke from the beginning by means of frolicksomeness or half-hidden collusive looks; if needs be, there then will be independent evidence that all along a joke was being attempted. (When no such anchor is available, the trickster may find himself going too far, perhaps forced to continue with his fabrication in an attempt to perpetuate it as a piece of actual reality.) It might be added that in genteel kidding, witnesses keep the secret, keep "a straight face," but often feel it would be a little harsh to otherwise join in to support the construction, as though the active collaboration of two or more individuals in playfully containing a butt would imply fairly deep disrespect.[6]

Playful deceits differ internally in the degree of their organization and in the nature of the target. At the most informal level is "kidding," whereby the perpetrator merely contains the victim for the duration of a phrase, or sentence, or turn at talking, and lets him in on the joke before the utterance is over. Somewhat more organized is what was called "leg-pulling," whereby the victim is caused to commit more than his momentary belief, being caused to perform some act under false auspices, as when he is sent on a fool's errand to buy something on a day when the stores are closed or told to borrow a left-handed monkey wrench. A contemporary example is the practice enjoyed by ghetto youths of teasing cruiser cops by acting as if a fight is in progress, thus twisting the man's tail.

Although leg-pulls are officially seen as harmless and therefore

mond, "The Contest System: A Survival Technique" (Master's thesis, Department of Sociology-Anthropology, Washington University, 1965). On put-on's in general see Jacob Brackman, The Put-On (New York: Bantam Books, 1972).

6. At a dinner party in Rome, Kirk Douglas, seeing Princess Margaret compliment Sam Spiegel on his Fabergé gold cigar case, challenged him to present it to her as a gift to "help strengthen Anglo-American relations." It is reported that Spiegel paled but offered the case up and that the Princess graciously accepted. Some ten minutes later (it is reported) the Princess tried to bring the joke to a close, only to find that the case had been lifted from her bag and passed from hand to hand around the table, thereby, of course, consolidating the whole party into the gag. That sort of joke in that sort of company is a sufficient savagery to merit three-picture, four-column newspaper treatment and to raise the question of limits. See San Francisco Chronicle, October 17, 1965, report by Roderick Mann from the London Express.

something that "any" member of a social circle ought to be ready to suffer, a profanation of some kind is still involved, marking a limit to transformational power. The victim need not take the joke seriously, in fact, is obliged not to, but he must take seriously the fact that those who played him the fool thought it allowable and even appropriate to do so. In any case, it seems that within any small social circle some members will be thought to be eminently available for this kind of teasing, and one or two others (often the most dominant) will be defined as off limits for such foolery.

Consider, too, the "practical joke," namely, a more or less elaborate fabrication of a bit of the victim's nonverbal environment in order to lead him into a misconception of what is happening, often at a moment when the perpetrator is not present to see the result. (Often, as Bergson nicely argues,[7] the trickster's technique is to alter a slice of the victim's world so that even though he takes his usually effective precautions to "shape conduct in accordance with the reality which is present," he ends up displaying a "mechanical inelasticity." He fails to sustain guided doings.)

Next consider surprise parties, the ritualized fabrication arranged in the American middle classes. The butt is led into visiting a friend, only to find that celebrants and gifts await. Unlike leg-pulls, a considerable amount of organization is necessary. Unlike practical jokes, no hostile undertone is patently present— the butt can illustrate the pure case of retrospective acceptance of a plot, and why not, since it enriches him in several ways?[8]

However broadly organized, surprise parties tend to be held in honor of only one person. Playful fabrications can involve wider targets, a collectivity of some kind, even when the aim is purely prankish. Thus what used to be called a lark or a rag:

> Cambridge, Mass.—Harvard University students awoke yesterday to the shocking "news" that Harvard was giving up intercollegiate football.
>
> The lead article in what appeared to be an extra edition of the

---

7. Henri Bergson, *Laughter*, trans. Cloudesley Brereton and Fred Rothwell (London: Macmillan & Co., 1911), pp. 10–11.

8. The TV show *This Is Your Life* provides a commercial version, wherein preselected guests are "surprised" by the materialization of beloved figures from their distant past.

Harvard Crimson, the campus newspaper, quoted Harvard President Nathan M. Pusey as saying the board of overseers had approved a decision to discontinue football as an intercollegiate sport after the current season.

But it was all a carefully planned and executed hoax.

The single-sheet "extra" was published by The Dartmouth, the campus newspaper of Harvard's sister Ivy League college which Saturday handed Harvard a 14–0 defeat on the football field.

Nelson Lichtenstein, associated editor of The Dartmouth, disclosed that staff members delivered the Sunday morning "extra" to Harvard and Radcliffe dormitories during the night.[9]

Another playful deception to consider is "corrective hoaxing." A very broad audience is usually involved, often the public at large, and the object frequently is to make a moral point as well as to have some fun. The gullibility of audiences is typically at issue, and behind this the argument that those who manage the public interest have become frozen in their roles, cut off from functioning properly. Thus it is sometimes expected by the tricksters that society will forgive any illegality on their part because of the lesson to be learned and because no profit is apparent for the tricksters. It might be added that often the immediate targets for the hoax, that is, those directly taken in, will not much see the event in a benign way. In any case, there are many examples of the following:

> A make-believe crime was staged at Powell and Sutter streets yesterday—and it showed what a cinch it is to get away with strongarm robbery in broad daylight.
>
> Designed to alert the public to the dangerously high rate of crime in San Francisco's streets, the stunt was conducted by the Optimist Club.
>
> . . . .
>
> The plan was for Miss McKinnie to walk around the corner of Sutter into Powell street where Cresalia [of the Optimist Club] would come up behind her, snatch her borrowed $185 dyed French rabbit coat and $285 gold bracelet, then flee toward Union square.
>
> Police had been alerted.[10]

Corrective hoaxing seems eminently suitable for chronicling, and an appreciable literature in the area is available, much of it

---

9. *San Francisco Chronicle,* October 25, 1965.
10. From a fuller report by Maitland Zane, *ibid.,* July 13, 1966.

incidental to biographies and the like, but some of it specialized.[11] I believe the most glorious instance of this sort of fabrication in modern times was the "Dreadnought Hoax," in which the
professional practical jokester Horace Cole, along with Virginia
Woolf and friends, caused the admiral of the British flagship to
receive at tea a royal party purportedly containing two princes of
Abyssinia.[12] Note that whereas in leg-pulls available colluders
are employed as guarantors that a joke was meant all along, in
elaborate hoaxes this device is often insufficient, necessitating the
employment of legalistic measures (the depositing of a time-
stamped confession with a reputable agent, the spelling of a
giveaway name backwards), so that when the clue is pointed out
full evidence will thus be provided.[13] For even more than in one-
victim play, once corrective hoaxes have been launched and once
public agencies and the media become involved, it is difficult to
bring matters to an end.[14]

Playful fabrications have an obvious limit, the breaching of
which may lead to a questioning of the culprit's moral and mental
character, the accusation being that he has shown "very bad
judgment"; in any case, the law ordinarily is specifically to be
excluded in drawing the line and in penalizing those who fall on

---

11. Notably Curtis D. MacDougall, *Hoaxes* (New York: Dover Publications, 1958).

12. Joseph M. Hone, "The Abyssinian Princes Who Outwitted the British
Navy," in Alexander Klein, ed., *Grand Deception* (New York: Ballantine
Books, 1955), pp. 112–115.

13. For example:

To put an end to, or at least expose the promiscuity with which the
Rhode Island Senate granted one-hundred-dollar bonuses to World War
veterans who failed to apply for them during the specified period which
ended in 1923, a Republican member in 1936 introduced in the Demo-
cratic-controlled legislative chamber a bill to pay a bonus to Sergeant
Evael O. W. Tnesba of the Twelfth Machine Gun Battalion. Unanimous
consent for its immediate consideration was granted, a Democratic sena-
tor seconded it and the bill was passed. It was reconsidered after someone read the machine gunner's name backwards. [MacDougall, *Hoaxes*,
p. 280.]

Similarly, when Barbara Whitner (*Time*, October 5, 1970) organized eleven
fellow conspirators to prove that anyone could get welfare relief in California, and hence that the wrong persons were getting it, she apparently
arranged the following control: "To protect themselves from fraud proceedings the group defaced all checks, food stamps and free medical cards by
writing on them 'Not for deposit at any time—Cheaters, Inc.'"

14. MacDougall, *Hoaxes*, pp. 285 ff.

the wrong side of it. Leg-pulls are not supposed to be overly elaborate, nor are they to cause the butt to begin adjusting to what he has been led to take as significant changes in his social situation, whether these expectations have been induced by giving him ego-expanding hopes that will soon prove false or bad news (regarding, say, loss of position or loved ones) that will shortly prove ill-founded.

2. Here to be considered is "experimental hoaxing," namely, the practice of conducting human experiments which require on methodological grounds (as almost all human experiments do) that the subject be unaware of what it is that is being tested and even unaware that an experiment of any kind is in progress. Presumably ignorance on the subject's part is a safeguard against his consciously influencing his response, his aim being, for example, to produce a self-approving effect or to help the experimenters obtain the results they seem to desire. After the experiment is over, it is customary to tell the subject what was "really" happening and to enlist his retrospective support of the experiment.[15] He is to accept in good spirit what has been done to him—accepting this because of the value placed upon the advancement of science, and because, after all, no real harm has been done. Often some of the apparent subjects will "really" be part of the experimental control; they are called shills, ringers, or confederates. It can probably be safely said that almost all college students who majored in psychology have been used as experiment dupes, and, of course, not a few have been used as confederates.

It will be noted that very commonly what the subjects are

---

15. A standard statement, fresh because early, was provided by Asch in 1951 in connection with his group pressure experiment involving seven shills and one patsy:

Toward the conclusion of the interview each subject was informed fully of the purpose of the experiment, of his role and of that of the majority. . . . It should be added that it is not justified or advisable to allow the subject to leave without giving him a full explanation of the experimental conditions. The experimenter has a responsibility to the subject to clarify his doubts and to state the reasons for placing him in the experimental situation. [S. E. Asch, "Effects of Group Pressure upon the Modification and Distortion of Judgments," in Eleanor E. Maccoby et al., eds., Readings in Social Psychology, 3d ed. (New York: Henry Holt & Company, 1958), pp. 175–176.]

tricked into doing is itself an apparent experiment. In such cases experimental hoaxing clearly involves a fabrication of what is already a keying of activity, namely, the activity performed as an experiment.[16] Just as rekeyings can occur, so, of course, can fabrications of keyings, resulting in something that is two laminations removed from untransformed events, albeit only one from straight activity.

Recently, experimental hoaxing has been attempted in natural settings, in streets and public establishments. The experimenter initiates brief contact encounters with sequences of subjects who are induced into a false impression of what is happening and allowed to continue for a time in it. Here the subject is typically not enlightened at the end of his performance, because, perhaps, of the understanding that the deceit is so temporary and so trivial in its demands that the good will of the subject can be assumed.[17] One example may be cited, the work of a very fine linguist, who, in correcting for nonresponse in his language survey, used the following dodge to inveigle response *and* to make sure that the respondents would not know that it was their pronunciation that was being studied—for, of course, if they knew, they would be likely to modify their speech accordingly:

The ALS [American Language Survey] television interview was designed to obtain information on the use of the five variables by

16. In order, as is said, to isolate the effect of particular factors, experimentalists often put the subject up against what he thinks to be part of an ordinary world when in fact a rigorously randomized selection is what he is to come up against. A subject thinks he is attempting to shoot effectively a pinball machine, when in fact the little ball is being secretly guided to a hole that will produce controlled results, so that his response to standardized situations can be assessed. He thinks he is dealing with another subject, but the other is a thoroughly instructed collaborator whose response will cover the required possibilities. And in fact, the subject may be led to think he is responding to a subject like himself in the next room, while all the time the response he receives to his own act has been randomly programmed beforehand, so that the interaction he ends up having is with a research design, not a person. (On this last, see Richard and S. Lynne Ofshe, "Choice Behavior in Coalition Games," *Behavioral Science*, XV [1970]: 337–349.) Although experimentalists have shown a certain respect for the human body, they have shown little regard for the experience of subjects, something that might well indeed be worth respecting.

17. Public order experiments are quite similar to the hoaxes that Allen Funt and his *Candid Camera* program appeared to present, except that Funt was obliged to obtain legal consent for use from the victim.

non-respondents. It was originally designed for those who refused the regular ALS interview, and was afterward applied to give information on the speech of those who could not be reached within the time allotted for field work.

In the case of those subjects who did not have telephones, or whose telephones were not listed, the ALS television interview was conducted in person. If the subject had refused previously a request for an interview by one interviewer, the ALS television interview was conducted by the other interviewer. For those subjects whose telephones were listed, the television interview was conducted by telephone. . . . In the first half of the interview, we asked the subject questions about the quality of the television picture he was receiving for various channels. This subject was chosen as the one likely to obtain the maximum percentage of response from those who had refused the regular ALS interview. Each of the questions was designed to elicit at least one example of a particular variable.

Which channels give you the best reception? the worst? which do you watch the most often? the least often?

From these questions, we obtained examples of (r) in *four*, (th) in *thirteen*, and two auxiliary variables to be discussed in Chapter X: the vowel of *nine*, and the first vowel of *thirteen*.

For the variable (eh), which frequently does not occur in short observations, we elicited the word *bad*.

Would you say that this condition was *very* bad or *not so* bad?

It was necessary to use the word *bad* in our question in order to obtain a uniform response. The effects of influencing the respondent were minimized by laying heavy stress on *very* and *not so*, and slurring over the word *bad* so that it was not clear which value of the variable the interviewer was using.[18]

The experiments so far mentioned are characteristically short-lasting and, of course, well circumscribed in place. There are other possibilities. Evaluation studies of "therapeutic" approaches which have a residential base can give rise to manipulations that are considerably more embracing than the ones so far mentioned,

---

18. William Labov, *The Social Stratification of English in New York City* (Washington, D.C.: Center for Applied Linguistics, 1966), pp. 182–183.

and because of this have more pointedly raised the issue of frame limits.[19]

It is interesting to compare experimental hoaxing with another social science technique, secret participant-observation.[20] Here the activity under observation is not itself created merely for the purpose of study, as is true in the case of experiments, and uncovering of the subterfuge typically deflates not the activity as a whole but only the social relation of its bona-fide participants to the observer, the latter now being seen to be not what he had been thought to be. And here the postexposure plea that the observer's intent was scientific very often fails to right matters, and a period of time may follow when the subjects continue to have strong feelings about what was done to them. As they should.

The propriety of engaging in any experimental hoaxing, especially on so large a scale as is found in colleges, has not been much pressed yet, although it is quite conceivable that it might be.[21] However, the moral limits have recently been given public attention through questions raised concerning medical ethics. One issue deals with the simple fact of deception, namely, the right of the experimenter to conceal from his subjects that that is what they are, or (when they know this) what the experiment is about. A second issue has to do with the kinds of risks and

19. Here sociologists as well as psychologists qualify as perpetrators. See, for example, La Mar Empy and Jerome Rabow, "The Provo Experiment in Delinquency Rehabilitation," *American Sociological Review*, XXVI (1961): 679–695.

20. Case reports are available in Kai T. Erikson, "A Comment on Disguised Participant Observation in Sociology," *Social Problems*, XIV (1967): 357–366.

21. What has been pressed is that the hoax is not quite a hoax, since the experimental frame does not so much create an environment in which subjects can be tested as it does create one in which they actively attempt to discover what it is the experimenter wants of them, what it is that will make the undertaking successful for all concerned, what, in brief, is being demanded of them. Here see, for example, Martin T. Orne, "On the Social Psychology of the Psychological Experiment: With Particular Reference to Demand Characteristics and Their Implications," *American Psychologist*, XVII (1962): 776–783; Robert Rosenthal, "On the Social Psychology of the Psychological Experiment: The Experimenter's Hypothesis as Unintended Determinant of Experimental Results," *American Scientist*, LI (1963): 268–283; and Neil Friedman, *The Social Nature of Psychological Research: The Psychological Experiment as a Social Interaction* (New York: Basic Books, 1967).

dangers subjects should be exposed to without their knowledge and hence without their consent. In the medical field the cancer studies of Dr. Chester Southam provided a leading case,[22] and in the psychological field, perhaps the studies of Stanley Milgram on obedience to authority.[23] Behind these concerns, of course, is found a lingering anxiousness regarding the model of medical experimentation established in the German concentration camps.

3. As an adjunct to job training, the use of "training hoaxes" is emerging. The neophyte is treated as though he were engaged in the real thing, and only later is he let in on the secret that all along his activity was occurring in protective insulation from the world he thought he had in view. (The pretty case here is the stagecraft the British are said to employ to give their intelligence agents firsthand experience with the cold-hunger-beating-interrogation treatment.)[24] Or the trainees are in on the secret and perform their training on unsuspecting members of the public at large. In some cases the dupes are let in on the secret after the exercise is terminated, as when intelligence teams practice document stealing in a local establishment and then report on the lack of security. But sometimes not. Third-year medical students may engage in training on a hospital floor while allowing patients to continue to misidentify them as doctors. A handbook for investigators recommends the following as a training procedure:

> The investigator will find there is no substitute for experience. When not on actual assignment, the investigator should practice

---

22. A report is available by John Lear, "Do We Need New Rules for Experiments on People?" *Saturday Review*, February 5, 1966, esp. pp. 65–70. The particular issue concerned the injection of presumably harmless cancer cells into a sample of aging patients in order to study rejection, the patients not being informed about what they were getting. A very full collection of relevant documents bearing on the general issue is now available: Jay Katz et al., *Experimentation with Human Beings* (New York: Russell Sage Foundation, 1972).

23. See Stanley Milgram, "Behavioral Study of Obedience," *Journal of Abnormal and Social Psychology*, LXVII, no. 4 (1963): 371–378; and "Some Conditions of Obedience and Disobedience to Authority," *Human Relations*, XVIII (1965): 57–76. Subjects were led under command of the experimenter to give what they thought were dangerous electrical shocks to a shill posing as another subject, experiencing some stress as a consequence.

24. One description is provided by Greville Wynne, *The Man from Moscow* (London: Hutchinson & Co., 1967), pp. 92–95.

shadowing or tailing in order to get the feel of such work. It is easy, when driving a car, to see how long a strange car can be kept in sight. When out for a stroll, it becomes an interesting game to see how far a pedestrian can be followed undetected. If the pedestrian realizes he is being followed, nothing is lost.[25]

And in a description of British underworld characters one reads of a professional who, in order to make sure that a plan to rob a payroll official in daylight on a public street was sound, apparently tested out the timing of his plan by binding and gagging practice persons in different locales, the subjects not knowing what was happening, or, after being left trussed in the street, why.[26]

4. There is a class of fabrications much like training hoaxes through which an unsuspecting individual is deceived, the aim being to test his loyalty and character. The classic instance of these "vital tests" is the stiffish one God allowed Satan to run on Job ("Behold, all that he hath is in thy power; only upon himself put not forth thine hand"), wherein the subject, in spite of the calamities that were made to befall him, stood firm in his faith, and at the end of the test, when nothing more could be done to his kin, his chattel, and his real estate, was declared worthy and rewarded with twice his original investment, a long-term gain on capital for not selling Him short. This is something like a demonstration, but the equipment whose operation is run through is a person, and for the test to tell he must not be told that it is on.

Vital tests are perhaps best known in the matter of information control: individuals doubtful of the loyalty of a teammate may purposely give him strategic information and then wait to see if indeed it comes to pass that the information has been divulged. Intelligence people have been known to test personnel in this manner, sometimes, it is said, with tests that cost lives, as when a doubted agent is given information of an impending raid and evidence of his loyalty or disloyalty is derived from whether or not the installation raided seemed to have anticipated it. (The

---

25. Jacob Fisher, *The Art of Detection* (New York: Sterling Publishing Co., 1961), p. 96. Fisher does not address himself to the interesting question of what happens to the ease of mind of the haphazardly selected subject who finds out he is being followed and looks into his life to find a reason why.

26. Phelan, *The Underworld*, pp. 81–82.

hypothetical strategic counter to this sort of test has acquired a certain status in gossip among intelligence commentators, the question being how far a government has gone in not alerting its own people to an uncovered enemy plan, the purpose being to protect secret channels of communication.) Local law enforcement provides examples, too:

> Scotland Yard [the popular name for the intelligence unit of the Chicago Police] police had often suspected that some Municipal Court clerks warned racketeers of impending raids through information they picked up when police officers made applications for search warrants. On one occasion, members of Scotland Yard placed a wiretap on the judge's phone and then sent a police officer to the judge's chambers to apply for a search warrant. Within a few minutes, the judge's clerk was overheard calling the downtown office of the syndicate and warning them that a raid was to be made.[27]

Vital tests are also employed by large organizations in order to check up on the honesty, speed, and courtesy of their employees and as such make news only when a novel organization is involved:

> Porto Alegre, Brazil, Sept. 14 (AP)—Police were surprised that the suspect in a stolen car was their superintendent, Lt. Col. Pedro Americo Leal, until he explained he was testing the alertness of two policemen who apprehended him.
>
> While congratulating them he suggested they could have reacted quicker instead of having to chase him two blocks. This pair fared better than two other policemen whom Leal locked in a room when he caught them sleeping on duty.[28]

Nor should we expect that impersonal organizations alone are involved. Consider a homely application:

> *Dear Abby:* Roy and I have been going around together for three years. We're not kids—we're both in our fifties.
>
> Roy has mentioned marriage several times, but nothing definite was said about "when."
>
> I always suspected that Roy could still be interested in other women, although he kept telling me I was wrong. Well, I decided

---

27. Samuel Dash et al., *The Eavesdroppers* (New Brunswick, N.J.: Rutgers University Press, 1959), p. 221.
28. *Philadelphia Inquirer*, September 15, 1968.

to put him to the test, so I wrote him a note saying I had seen him somewhere and I asked him to meet me at a certain place at a certain time. Then I signed another woman's name. I went to the "meeting place" at the appointed time and hid, and sure enough, there was Roy all spruced up and waiting!

Isn't this a sign that he would go to meet another woman if he had the chance?[29]

What seems special about complex organizations is not that they employ vital tests, but that they can often manage to legitimate such activity.

Whatever their significance in actual life, vital tests have a role in our fantasies. When a novel event occurs, especially one with disappointing consequences, the individual can to some extent remove himself from its effects by defining it as a vital test imposed upon him and hence not at all what it appears to be. Here (as will later be considered) a fundamental looseness in the hard facts of the world is introduced. The husband of a hospitalized mental patient, upon being asked how his wife felt about the hospital, told a sociologist the following story:

> Well, she feels that putting her in that first ward wasn't right—that there should have been more segregation of the patients at first. I tried to tell her it's part of the treatment. That during the first week or ten days they want the patients to be irritated, to see how they react. Like that clanking radiator. (With a knowing smile) I'm sure that was a planned thing—it wasn't just accident. It's planned that way to see how the patients react. I'm sure that's part of their diagnostic program up there. Of course I could be wrong—it could be that there was actually something wrong with the heat—but I doubt it very much.[30]

5. Consider "paternal constructions," the rather large class of deceits and fabrications that is performed in what is felt to be the dupe's best interests, but which he might reject, at least at the beginning, were he to discover what was really happening. The falsity is calculated to give him comfort and render him tractable and is constructed for those reasons. No doubt the most common, the most basic, example is that of ordinary tact: we routinely

withhold evidence from another that might make him feel bad unnecessarily. Although constructions are involved here, they are not very elaborate and are often as short-lived as the phases in conversation upon which they can be based. There are many other deceits practiced *for* the person they are practiced *on* that are only somewhat more elaborate:

> For 40 minutes late yesterday a United Air Lines jetliner with 93 persons aboard circled over San Francisco with its nose wheel retracted and unable to go down.
> "We're going to have a little rough landing," the pilot told his 85 passengers. "Nothing to worry about."
> . . . .
> Just before 7 p.m. the jet roared down into the airport, landed safely on its main wheels and—for an agonizing 800 feet—shot sparks as the nose scraped along the runway.
> . . . .
> "It was eerie," said stewardess Sugimoto. "We knew about it all the way from Seattle and couldn't tell anyone."
> The pilot of the plane, 56-year-old Virgil Vaughan of Denver, sipped black coffee and explained, "We knew the nose gear wasn't working as soon as we left Seattle but we decided to fly in. It could have started to function during the flight. And why tell the passengers—they'd only worry."[31]

In recent years a pretty form of paternal deceit has developed in connection with the management of secure research projects under arrangements with organizations such as the (U.S.) National Security Agency. Obliged to keep secret all aspects of a particular undertaking, professionals of various kinds will have to operate with a degree of cover even in regard to their loved ones. They can be obliged to conceal the source of funds for the project, the identity of the participants, the place of work, the time worked, and the material utilized. In consequence, they will have to black out a piece of many of their days. But they can do this with the knowledge that were their everyday associates to know what in fact was actually happening, no umbrage would be taken; retrospectively, the secrecy would be forgiven as having been in everyone's interests.

The standard forms of paternal fabrication are found, of

---

31. *San Francisco Chronicle*, November 6, 1964.

course, in the treatment situation, medical and psychiatric. In the medical world, there is the classic practice of withholding bad news from patients who are soon to die or whose condition is dire. The patient's definition of the situation, of course, is for the most part composed of his reading of the meaning of what is being done to and for him. In this context, therefore, information that is incorrect or even inadequate produces a considerably false world. The how and when of disclosure, of course, is a much discussed medical topic. Professional counseling on the management of lying by laymen has become a standard practice of up-to-date medicine, of which a somewhat extreme example may be cited:

> The mishap occurred when the circumcision was being performed by means of electrocautery. The electric current was too powerful and burnt the entire tissue of the penis which necrosed and sloughed off.
>
> The parents were . . . understandably desperate to know what could be done and suffered through a long saga of finding no answer. Then a consultant plastic surgeon, familiar with the principles of sex reassignment, recommended reassignment as a girl. . . .
>
> At the time of surgery, when we saw the parents in person for the first time in the psychohormonal research unit at Johns Hopkins, we gave them advice and counselling on the future prognosis and management of their new daughter based on experience with similar reassignments in hermaphroditic babies. In particular they were given confidence that their child can be expected to differentiate a female gender identity, in agreement with her sex of rearing. They were broadly informed about the future medical program for their child and how to integrate it with her sex education as she grows older. They were guided in how to give the child information about herself to the extent that the need arises in the future; and they were helped with what to explain to friends and relatives, including their other child. Eventually, they would inform their daughter that she would become a mother by adoption one day, when she married and wanted to have a family.[32]

Psychiatric treatment provides paternalistic fabrications of much greater dramatic scope, I think, than that found in medi-

---

32. John Money and Anke A. Ehrhardt, *Man and Woman, Boy and Girl* (Baltimore: Johns Hopkins University Press, 1972), pp. 118–119.

cally inspired fabrications, the latter tending to a certain amount
of repetitiveness and stereotyping. Consider the treatment trap,
whereby the next-of-relation manages under false pretenses to
maneuver the patient-to-be into the hands of a practitioner, an
institution, or the law. A kind of surprise party may be involved.
Or, in effect, an ambush:

> The son of Turlock's mayor was overpowered and booked for
> assault with a deadly weapon yesterday after firing three shots
> from a high-powered rifle in front of the family home.
> Police Chief John Viarengo said Enoch Christoffersen, Jr., 21,
> held five officers and ten Stanislaus county deputies at bay with the
> rifle and a pistol.
> The mayor's son, a former patient at Modesto State Hospital,
> had been brooding about injuries sustained by a former girl friend
> in an auto accident.
> Eventually, Christoffersen was persuaded by a friend, Paul
> Carlson, 20, to "go fishing."
> The two got into Christoffersen's auto and headed for Oakdale.
> Three plain clothesmen followed in an unmarked car.
> When the two men stopped and got out at Oakdale, Chief
> Viarengo said, the detectives overpowered Christoffersen and
> lodged him in the county jail.[33]

6. There remains to look at a limiting case, fabrications that
are purely strategic. By definition he who engineers a benign
fabrication is not contaminated morally by his deceiving, and the
basic interests of the dupe are not denied. The implication is that
fabrication involves two elements: a moral one pertaining to the
reputability of the deceiver and a strategic one pertaining to
misdirectings of the dupe's perception and (consequently) his
response. It is apparent, for example, that contests often allow
and even require the use of misdirection, the use of feints, bluffs,
and hidden moves, that these actions depend upon the formulation of a design that is kept secret, and that these secrets are
purely "strategic," in the sense that the viability of the misdirection is alone at stake, not the moral character of the misdirector.
(Indeed, as will later be illustrated, misdirection in games is

---

33. *San Francisco Chronicle*, February 26, 1965. Note in the text above
that reference to fishing is in quotes, meaning that no "real" fishing was
intended; the term "friend," however, is printed straight.

usually a right, the violation of which can be grounds for legal action, civil if not criminal.) It is also apparent that although the game-defined interests of a player can certainly be thwarted by these permissible deceptions, this loss itself is part of the game realm and not to be taken seriously. Righteous indignation can be evoked, but only if framed jokingly. When one turns to competition between business organizations or between nation states, the same analysis can apply but now less surely. Obviously, there are many matters we feel a corporation or a state has a right to hide from competitors, either by close silence regarding actual plans or through falsely indicated courses of action. And yet, of course, the parties thereby kept in the dark will have serious interests seriously threatened. Interestingly, as sweeping as these consequences can become, those involved may still exhibit the tendency (as will be illustrated later) to fall into the language of games and to draw upon the distancing and irony which games allow.

III

I have considered various fabrications that can be claimed to be benign, essentially harmless for those who are contained by them—and if not harmless, then at least not injurious to fundamental rights: playful fabrication, experimental hoaxing, training hoaxes, vital tests, paternal constructions, and strategic fabrications. The category as a whole was meant to be responsive to distinctions made by persons in our society, not to distinctions which I think are otherwise indicated. Here, obviously, the structure and organization of framed activity is not all that is in question; also involved is the moral attitude of the citizenry to these undertakings.

A second class of fabrications, the *exploitive* kind, is now to be considered: one party containing others in a construction that is clearly inimical to their private interests, here defining "private interests" as the community might.

1. The great exemplar in the matter of exploitive fabrication is nature herself, and the great devices are the ones this questionable lady has led organisms to employ (through the workings of natural selection) for protection and for predation, these devices

involving camouflage, mimicry, and intimidation.[34] The pointed source in social life is the con game.

I do not propose to dwell here at length on the varieties of exploitive fabrication. The literature on these constructions is both large and well known. I want only to mention in passing some of the differentiating features among members of this class. Obviously a distinction can be made between those fabrications whose perpetrators are acting within, and even *for,* the law (as when police interrogation teams cook up a line to take that is calculated to produce a confession), and those who are operating outside the law, the victim being an eventual complainant. (The complication here, as suggested, is espionage plots, which have a mixed status, being considered legitimate from the point of view of the employer of the agent and illegitimate from the point of view of the persons taken in.) And as in the case of the more benign fabrications, a distinction can be drawn between those deceits meant to delude one or two individuals and those designed to delude a wide public, the stock swindles perpetrated through the South Sea Company being an impressive example of the latter.[35]

Unlike benign fabrications, the exploitive kind, as suggested, can evoke suppressive legal action, criminal or civil, of the kind brought against certain forms of confidence game, false advertising, mislabeling, and cheating at cards. The intellectual problem, of course, is to try to explicate why some commercial activity falls under such a ban and other such activity, equally misrepresentative, does not, but this consideration leads to complex legal issues which I cannot hope to develop. Some of what the Better Business Bureau acts against, the Federal Trade Commission does, too; some not. Many activities that are not condoned are not actively prosecuted. For example, the art of "skip tracing," designed to obtain the home address, place of employment, or banking location of uncommunicative debtors calls for contact fabrications: the debtor may be approached through a questionnaire attached to a letter from a government-sounding agency,

---

34. See, for example, H. B. Cott, *Adaptive Colouration in Animals* (London: Methuen & Co., 1940); Adolf Portmann, *Animal Camouflage* (Ann Arbor: University of Michigan Press, 1959); and Roger Caillois, *The Mask of Medusa,* trans. George Orish (New York: Clarkson N. Potter, 1960).

35. See, for example, Virginia Cowles, *The Great Swindle* (New York: Harper & Brothers, 1960).

the letter bearing an American Eagle emblem and a Washington, D.C., address, the whole calculated to cause the recipient to mistakenly accord the document official status.[36] If a complaint is made, this sort of trickery clearly can be grounds for legal action and a swindle charge. Similarly, skip tracers who use the telephone to say they represent a government agency perform an illegal act. However, skip tracers who try to get information on the phone by claiming to be lining up contestants for a TV show or conducting a market research survey or checking on details of insurance policies can probably argue that they are engaged in innocent tricks of their trade, which trade, after all, is to support the justice of debt collection. All these mail and phone practices clearly involve fabrications, but only some are outside legal limits.

2. It is clear that containment bears upon, and is taken to bear upon, the relationships of the persons involved. Take, for example, the following domestic text:

> *Dear Abby:* I have been badly shaken at times, but not quite so much as when I discovered birth control pills in the purses of both my daughters. One is 21 and engaged and the other is 19 and going steady.
>
> I did not cause a scene, nor have I told their father. He would probably throw them both out. I feel as though I have been completely wrung out.
>
> I told the girls of my discovery and they were both embarrassed. I didn't give them a sermon, I simply told them they were both fools. Of course they said it was common practice these days. Is it Abby?
>
> I cannot punish them by disconnecting their telephones or grounding them from dating any more. What can I do?[37]

Here, right at home, one can find a tangle of containment, a tangle characteristic of this process. When an individual confronts others with discrediting discoveries made about them, he often ends up exposing how his intelligence was obtained, and this can discredit assumptions about his relation to the discredited. In the story, after all, mother has to admit that she went through other people's purses. Further, when an individual con-

---

36. For skip tracing, I draw on the discussion by Myron Brenton in *The Privacy Invaders* (New York: Crest Reprints, 1964), pp. 29–30.

37. *The Evening Bulletin* (Philadelphia), July 22, 1971.

fronts others with the facts, he is forced into a deception coalition with them—at least in effect—unless he also relays the news to all interested parties. In our story the parental solidarity which the girls' father had with their mother has been secretly somewhat undercut.

There is still another point to the story. Discovery of the pill is reasonably taken to mean discovery of premarital sexual relations, and this demonstrates that the show the girls had presumably been giving of virginity was false. But today this assumption regarding self may have very little informed the various presentations the daughters made to their mother, in which case nothing very fundamental has been discredited—except, of course, the image the mother had of her girls. But if the mother assumes that her daughters are direct and honest with her in all matters which she is likely to see as important, then indeed the discovery demonstrates the dealings she has had with them were part of their containment of her, were, in brief, discreditable.

All of which recommends that another look be taken at the notion of falseness.

A young man with a family, a profession, a good house location takes to weekend coke snorting and somehow or other is caught and brought to trial. His social credentials are not something created to cover, say, dealing in dope; his front was there before he took up with the drug, at a time when this moral garb would have been judged a sound indicator of his character, a proper warrant for reading from the manner to the man. Nonetheless, at the moment of arrest he may correctly feel that the law views his respectable appearances as a mere pretense, a counterfeit, a disguise, radically incompatible with the act of which he is accused, incompatible with what his essential self must have been all along. And, indeed, he himself may entertain this view. Thus arrest can throw him into confusion, deeply undercutting the style of presentation he usually maintains. Here, note, falsity is a state fairly far removed from something meretricious in detail; it is geared, rather, to our beliefs concerning the nature of persons and the meaning of arrest. And it is in part these beliefs which render any individual's past vulnerable to arbitrary rereading and him to being revealed as someone who has been a deceiver all along. Were we to come to the belief that an individual could be false in one regard and quite respectable in all others, then such purely dramatistic bases of discreditation and social control would be weakened.

3. It is an assumption about constructions, never really made explicit, that there are two essential parties: a fabricator who does the manipulation and a dupe whose world is fabricated and who is misled in consequence. But in fact a further class of constructions is possible, one that typically, but not necessarily, has an exploitive element. A fabricator can engineer a definition of a second party in order to be in a position to dupe a third party into certain false beliefs concerning the second. The second party—the victim—need not be taken in and indeed is unlikely to be. What is required is that the person who has been misrepresented be unable for some reason to convince the third party of the facts. One might speak here of "indirect" fabrications as opposed to "direct" ones.

The classic example of indirect fabrication is the plant or frame-up involving the creation of compromising false evidence:

> London—The cases of a number of men serving prison terms and the careers of more than 20 Scotland Yard detectives were being investigated yesterday after a court declared one of London's toughest crime-busters legally insane.
>
> Detective-sergeant Harry Challenor was certified insane last week by a court looking into charges that he and three junior policemen planted evidence on people they arrested last summer.[38]

Which can be matched from an observational study carried out in 1966 in three major American cities:

> Our observers also found that some policemen even carry pistols and knives that they have confiscated while searching citizens; they carry them so they may be placed at a scene should it be necessary to establish a case of self-defense.[39]

Another example is the engaging practice of sending enemy spies large payments for services they haven't rendered, so that upon

---

38. *San Francisco Sunday Chronicle*, June 7, 1964. There is a cognate use of the term "plant" in reference to a person, namely, someone who has been placed in an organization to serve as an "inside man."

39. Albert J. Reiss, Jr., "Police Brutality: Answers to Key Questions," *Trans-action*, July–August 1968, p. 10. A term the police sometimes use for this technique is "farming," on which see Jonathan Rubinstein, *City Police* (New York: Farrar, Straus & Giroux, 1973), pp. 388–390.

discovery it will appear that the spies are in the employ of those who should be the enemy.

Planting evidence, then, is one means to indirect fabrication. Another is to engineer the special circumstances in which the victim, on his own, will behave in a manner that is discreditable (or in a way that can be presented to him as being discreditable), the behavior having been fully recorded.

A third method, the most economical of all, is merely to avow discreditable facts; for it is not essential that the victim be established in a discrediting act, only that the fabricators be in a position to make discrediting imputations stick. The model here— indeed, the scenario in detail—is provided by the story of Susanna and the Elders, the latter being two dirty old men (the first in Judeo-Christian history) who responded to Susanna's rejection of their advances by making a full-scale try at falsely accusing her—a respectable married woman—of consorting with a lover. The false witnessing itself only failed because Daniel happened by and was able to reverse the evidence by means of the split-witness ploy, and this without ever having gone to a police academy. I might add that if it is given to young women to be vulnerable to false accusations made by old men, old men, in turn, are apparently vulnerable to young girls:

> Six Torresdale girls who told police they were given apples and candy containing razor blades by a neighbor on Halloween were arrested today after they admitted their stories were false.
> Based on their stories, police had arrested Jack Thomas, 52, of Ditman st. near Megargee, in the Liddonfield housing project in Torresdale. He was charged with intent to maim and cruelty to minors and was remanded to the city Detention Center in lieu of $10,000 bail.[40]

In consequence, certain accusations, such as that of rape, can become routinely problematic; the accuser and the accused can be confident that they will both be doubted.[41]

Once the difference between direct and indirect fabrication becomes evident, it should be possible to admit to the latter class a possibility that first seems not to belong there: bearing false

---

40. *The Evening Bulletin* (Philadelphia), November 5, 1969.
41. See, for example, Gail Sheehy, "Nice Girls Don't Get into Trouble," *New York Magazine*, February 15, 1971, pp. 26–30.

witness against oneself. Here the individual functions in two different capacities simultaneously: as fabricator of the false besmirching picture and as person who is defamed by it. The purpose, presumably, is the notoriety, the public identity, obtained through the false confession. In any case, it is known that widely publicized crimes bring forth false confessions, that war establishes the conditions for effectively drawing attention to oneself through admissions of spying,[42] that the claims women make to the police of having been attacked and raped can prove upon occasion to lead newspapers to report the claim with quotation marks (these marks being one of the less gentle framing devices available to the press), and that neglected functionaries such as nightwatchmen sometimes stage what is designed to be taken as the remnants of an armed attack.[43] A limiting, marginal case is the "insurance fire," for here, obviously, the flames the individual sets to his own situation have a silver lining. Note, the use of any self-enhancing social front is also a means of bearing false witness in regard to the self, but we differently perceive such fabrication because self-interest as conventionally defined is being served, not something that looks like victimization.

It has been argued that indirect fabrication, whether based on evidence that is planted, engineered, or avowed, empowers the fabricator to discredit the victim before others. This is exactly like the power possessed by one who uncovers, through research, secret recording, or another's confidences, facts about the victim that discredit him. It is apparent, then, that false facts as well as valid ones can allow their knower to blackmail the victim, that is, to *threaten* to discredit him before important audiences unless he agrees to do something he would ordinarily never do (such as give up money, disclose his employer's secrets, participate as the inside man in a theft, and so forth) or agrees not to do something he ordinarily would do (such as expose the blackmailer).[44] And

42. For example, during World War II, a Mrs. O'Grady of the Isle of Wight managed to get herself arrested as a Nazi spy on the basis of evidence she manufactured. See Vernon Hinchley, *Spies Who Never Were* (London: George G. Harrap & Co., 1965), chap. 4, "The Trial of Mrs. O'Grady," pp. 70–84.

43. A case is reported in the *San Francisco Chronicle*, December 17, 1964.

44. On blackmail see S., pp. 75–77; and S.I., pp. 73–74. Blackmail, note, has a particular social, almost moral, quality: there is a good reason why

this coercion (unlike the kind exerted by one who holds a gun) can be effective even when the victim is not in the presence of the coercer, this being one of its special strategic values.

I have dwelt at length on indirect fabrications because they provide a bridge from the houses of cards erected by con men to the lives of ordinary people. In the everyday case, the social front that an individual presents to his various associates during his daily round allows them to make some assumptions about his social worth and moral standards, the latter including, importantly, the practice of candor and openness regarding failures in these matters. If it can be demonstrated that one of these premises is false, the individual can be seen as maintaining a false position, allowing, if not encouraging, those around him to live in a false world, at least insofar as their view of him forms a part of their world. Thus, he does not have to fabricate a construction—he does not have to *do* anything—merely fail to embody the attributes and standards of conduct expected of him. Blackmail stories tend to rely on the uncovering (or manufacture)[45] of

---

the victim should want to suppress what the blackmailer acts as though he knows, but if the victim refuses to give in to the threat, the blackmailer has nothing to gain from that particular victim by going through with the disclosure. A discredited, stubborn victim is good only for maintaining the value of blackmail in general, and the particular blackmailer may not be much moved by this contribution to the reputation of his trade, although he should be. The Elders went ahead with their threat out of spite, but spite has no place in a well-conducted business—although the impression that one is spiteful does. In brief, to make blackmail work, the blackmailers must act as if they will tell unless obeyed, but *after* they have not been obeyed, there is little reason to tell. To make blackmail work *well*, then, the blackmailers must convincingly act as if they do not appreciate their dilemma.

As recently suggested (Mike Hepworth, "Deviants in Disguise: Blackmail and Social Acceptance," in Stanley Cohen, ed., *Images of Deviance* [London: Pelican Books, 1971], pp. 198–199), one's accomplice in a discrediting act is nicely situated to become one's blackmailer, providing, of course, he has less to lose from disreputability than oneself. (The moral of the story is that if one must sin, 'tis best done with one's betters.) In all of this, observe, blackmail is to be distinguished from extortion, where what is at stake is life and property, not reputation. The great informant system maintained by the police and the FBI is an interesting marginal case: threat of disclosure of past deeds presumably helps to motivate information giving, but here the agency making the threat is also the agency that will begin to inflict the price of defiance.

45. In the creation of willing agents, intelligence people have manufactured single-issue newspapers which tell of the death of someone with whom the victim had fought. See Pawel Monat, *Spy in the U.S.* (New York: Berkley Publishing Corporation, Berkley Medallion Books, 1963), p. 177.

spectacular secrets, ones whose disclosure would bring the law against the victim and turn some of the persons closest to him against him. But, of course, unspectacular embarrassments have some blackmail power, too. And given the ease of engineering unworthy behavior, planting false evidence, or bearing false witness, real secrets are not necessary; secrets-in-effect can be created, with the result that although the victim has not in any way contained those around him, he is in danger of appearing to have done so. So the reason why the individual can confidently continue to assume that others will feel he is playing matters straight is not that he is—even if he is—but that no one has been motivated to organize information in order to render him discreditable.

IV

So far but one way has been considered in which the individual can be caused to be out of touch with what it is that is really going on: he can be deceived, whether with benign or exploitive intent. Moreover, we allow that a person who is hoodwinked can be understandably gulled, he himself contributing to his containment only what would ordinarily bring him to a realistic alignment to the world.

Common sense allows for another possibility: "understandable error." We feel that the sense perceptions of an individual can work against his acquiring a realistic view of what it is that is going on, and excusably so, providing only that something special in the circumstances accounts for his error and that he is reasonably alive to the corrective information the world (we think) will soon provide him. (Indeed, a belief that the truth will out is a fundamental element in the cosmology of Western man.) One can speak here of "illusion." So there are deceptions and illusions.

In thinking about fabrications, whether of the benign or exploitive kind, it seems natural and obvious to see deceivers and the deceived as different persons, else, of course, strategic information could not be withheld, false facts could not be put forth, and a fabrication could hardly be sustained against discreditation. But one must press beyond this point if the class to which illusion and deception belong is to be fully developed.

For we have the understanding, vague, undeveloped, but nonetheless there, that in various ways the individual may actively work against his own capacity for effective framing, setting himself against his own ability to realistically orient himself in the world. In some cases he may obtain help in his misconstruings from persons teamed up with or against him, and in some cases they themselves may not be deluded about what is going on, having intentionally laid the groundwork for it. But still, without the very active cooperation of the dupe, here at least, it is unlikely he would be taken in. Note, self-induced misalignment is likely to involve mainly perception, not action, for the latter must soon face corrective action from others.[46]

If, then, one thinks of *deception* as falsehood intendedly produced by persons not taken in by their own fabrication and one thinks of *illusion* as error resulting from a misconstruing that no one induced purposely and that is understandable in the circumstances, then one can think of *self-deception* (or delusion) as wrongheadedness actively aided, if not solely produced, by the head that is wrong.[47]

With delusion one has defects in what is taken to be the fundamental character of normal actors. An individual equipped and geared with one of these eccentric features grinds out a stream of behavior whose frame he, and often he alone, is blind to. In the case of some of these defects, a pass can be made at stating the transformations which they perform on ordinary conduct; in other cases, only a gloss is possible.

1. An interesting form of self-deception is the dream.[48] Here, surely, the individual all on his own is his own deceiver. Dreams are special in that only the dreamer can have any appreciation of what is going on while it is going on and any memory thereof— even though others can figure as protagonists in the dream, be fairly sure that dreaming is occurring, and be told of the dream after it is over. Dreams have other interesting features. The dreamer himself must in some sense take all the dramatic parts,

---

46. An argument recommended by Lee Ann Draud.

47. A useful statement is provided by Amelie O. Rorty, "Belief and Self-Deception," *Inquiry*, XV (1972): 387–410, to whom I am grateful for help in this and other matters philosophical.

48. On the dream as a type of experience to be analyzed by looking at its similarities and differences to other modes of experience, see Norman Malcolm, *Dreaming* (New York: Humanities Press, 1959).

and apparently he does so remarkably well, the significance of which has never been adequately developed. Also the fabrication conventions are notoriously liberal: presumably any liberty can be taken with the original models in the dream in that any character can turn into any other character and simultaneously can be in many different places; in any case, it is hard to think of principled limitations, dreaming being something of a limiting case. Yet some of the conditions for dreaming are very strict: the dreamer must first be genuinely asleep, and the dream can be collapsed and shown to be merely a dream by waking up the dreamer—a waking he is vastly vulnerable to. (In this easy vulnerability, dreams are somewhat like leg-pulls.)

The question arises as to the relation between the world dreamed, that is, the innermost drama of the dreamed events, and the unfabricated environment of the dreaming—the room, the dreamer, and so forth.

It is plain that even when the dreamer, in his dream, represents the room in which he is dreaming, the representation is of an entirely different domain than the room itself. The room in the dream is being dreamed; it does not exist in space, although the room in which the dreaming occurs does.[49]

Presumably the dreamer cannot put into his dream anything that is not in some sense already in him; he must make do with traces stored up from the past. Some of this material, apparently, is likely to be recently acquired. And, of course, some of what is used will be quite current; for there is the reasonable belief that dreaming in part protects the dreamer from being awakened by local disturbances. It can be argued that this dreamwork consists of the reframing of disruptive events—as when the sharp closing of the bedroom door is presented as a gunshot in the dream. (Here, in miniature, is a nice illustration of the whole role of framing in the reconstitution of events.)

Finally, the controversial issue of the active role the dreamer may take in his dreaming apart from generating the content of the dream. There are reasons for suggesting that when a dream is particularly unpleasant, the dreamer may discount its reality

---

49. See Margaret Macdonald, "Sleeping and Waking," in Donald F. Gustafson, ed., *Essays in Philosophical Psychology* (Garden City, N.Y.: Doubleday & Company, 1964), pp. 250–251.

while dreaming, on the grounds of its being only a dream, and he may even be able to wake himself up in order to stop the dream. It seems also the case, incidentally, that dreams are forgotten very soon after the dreamer awakens, even when he does so "in the middle of a dream." (Frame analysis urges us to clearly distinguish these possibilities from a radically different set, for it is possible that the individual could *dream* he is being awakened from his dream or that he is waking himself up from it. In fact, some students of dreams claim that it is in this way only that dreams are penetrated.)[50]

2. A consideration of dreaming leads directly to a consideration of "dissociated states"—fugues, somnambulistic acts, and the like. It is believed that when so transported, the individual may act with an intent that is cut off from his general awareness and his critical faculties; consequently he cannot be held "responsible" for what he may do. (Here the leading case, apparently, is that of murder accomplished while the doer is asleep and acting under a delusion.)[51] As in the case of dreaming, the delusion presumably can be terminated by waking the individual. The current image is that the dissociated actor has practical access to certain physical competencies, and that the dreamwork is performed in such a fashion that use can be made of the real world without embarrassment to the transformation that has been performed upon it.

3. Consider now a form of self-delusion that is considerably different from dreaming: so-called psychotic fabrications. Here the individual presumably deludes himself, but he does his delusioning not within a dream but within the world sustained by other persons. Indeed, as in the case of so-called paranoid responses, he can convince others of his beliefs, at least tempo-

---

50. *Ibid.*, p. 262.

51. *King* v. *Cogdon*. See Richard C. Donnelly, Joseph Goldstein, and Richard D. Schwartz, *Criminal Law* (New York: The Free Press, 1962), pp. 551–552. In the psychiatric literature, amnesias of various sorts are often considered along with dissociated states. The amnesiac, presumably, is cut off from some part of his biography (for psychodynamic reasons) but retains his competencies in all other regards and presumably could be held responsible for his actions. The social importance of the amnesias is as an essential ingredient of TV soap serials and other operatic scripts; it is here one can be certain they will occur and certain that they *can* occur.

rarily.[52] He cannot—in the ordinary sense—be wakened from his construction because he has not gone to sleep to produce it. However, with psychotic beliefs, as with dreams, a coming to is possible. This coming to is called getting insight, and it is said that psychotherapy can bring it about. A point to note, however, is that it is part of our belief regarding insanity that this coming to need never occur. The individual can remain locked in his "illness" forever.

It is possible to try to describe the sense in which an individual defined as insane is seen as an incompetent, faulty actor. One could also try to write the rules for transforming ordinary behavior into the kind that would evoke the feeling from witnesses that the actor was insane. Here again frame analysis has some application. Thus, it is argued that one of the upsetting things "psychotics" do is to treat literally what ordinarily is treated as metaphor, or at least to seem to do so.[53] (I have seen patients approach a friendly staff person and, apparently as a put-on, direct a hostile gesture toward him, this gesture proving, upon further examination, to be in quotes, part of a storytelling, an illustration performed on the staff person of an interaction that had occurred to the patient in the past.)

4. Psychotic propensities can place the subject in the world of social frameworks and the real-life doings performed within these frames, but do so on radically disqualifying terms. An interesting contrast is with another form of self-delusion: so-called hysterical symptoms. Here (in theory) the individual simulates a

52. The classic study here, of course, is C. Lasègue and J. Falret, "La Folie à deux ou folie communiquée," *Ann. Méd. Psychol.*, XVIII (1877): 321–355, available in translation by Richard Michaud in *American Journal of Psychiatry*, supp. to no. 4 (1964), pp. 2–23. One of the great illustrative sagas is D. H. Ropschitz, "Folie à Deux," *Journal of Mental Science*, CIII (1957): 589–596, wherein is recounted how an M.D. patient in a mental hospital succeeded temporarily in taking over the management of the establishment by enlisting the love of the head matron.

53. See, for example, Harold Searles, "The Differentiation between Concrete and Metaphorical Thinking in the Recovering Schizophrenic Patient," *Journal of the American Psychoanalytical Association*, X (1962): 22–49. (Also in his *Collected Papers on Schizophrenia and Related Subjects* [New York: New York University Press, 1965], pp. 560–589.) See also Gregory Bateson, "A Theory of Play and Phantasy," *Psychiatric Research Reports* 2, American Psychiatric Association (December 1955), pp. 39–51; reprinted in Bateson's *Steps to an Ecology of Mind* (New York: Ballantine Books, 1972), pp. 177–193.

physical disorder, an act to be defined within a natural (in this case the physical-medical) framework, but one part of himself is kidding another. Genuine regression, if there is such a thing, is another case in point.

5. Finally consider hypnotism. Here the active intervention of the hypnotist is presumably necessary, but nonetheless a degree of self-deception would seem to be implied. It is of special interest that the rules for behaving as though hypnotized and the formula for producing and terminating the state are fairly well articulated, providing a sort of model of framing conventions. Martin Orne's version may be cited:

> The common characteristics of these various [hypnotic] states that bring them all under the heading of "hypnosis" would appear to include: posthypnotic amnesia, apparent inability to use a given motor system when a functional paralysis is suggested, various sensory illusions including positive and negative hallucinations of all sensory modalities, apparent memory disturbances or improvements as well as reported increased control over autonomic nervous system functions.[54]

The implication of these behavioral features for our conception of the character of the person in trance will be considered later.

V

After distinguishing between benign and exploitive fabrications, a different division has now been suggested: other-induced (whether benign or exploitive) and self-imposed. Consider now the bearing of fabrication on social structures. What is the relation of a particular fabrication to the ongoing stream of wider social activity in which it occurs?

If one starts with a social activity for which there is a prescribed involvement, a prescribed spirit and depth of participation, it is simple enough to consider the types of alternate involvement that may occur. First, as already suggested, is the understanding that persons such as janitors, stagehands, newspapermen, waiters, and servants may be involved in only a very

---

54. Martin T. Orne, "The Nature of Hypnosis: Artifact and Essence," *Journal of Abnormal and Social Psychology*, LVIII (1959): 278.

narrow aspect of a given undertaking, since often they have a right to treat the whole activity as merely one more instance of the type, something to be handled without becoming vicariously involved in the drama of the main events. But, of course, these marginal persons are likely to know what is "really" going on and appreciate that this is merely not going on for them.

Second, it is often understood that although a particular degree of involvement is preferred, considerable variation in intensity is acceptable, boredom marking one boundary and "overinvolvement" the other. There is hardly an encounter in which at least one participant doesn't exercise momentary tact in his treatment of the other, acting, in fact, as if he more approved of the other than is the case—which action is likely to require him to withdraw for the moment from easy involvement in the proceedings.

Also, there is no doubt that each individual brings a personal style to each occasion of his participation (and not necessarily the same style) which can be seen in frame terms as a rendition, a mini-keying of a prescribed form; similarly, it must be seen that a participant's passing mood can for its duration transform slightly everything he does. Yet these imprints on normal participation can usually be accepted as permissible.

So, too, a fairly large number of "bad" reasons for participation will be tolerated and thus, perforce, a range of motives for involvement, for it is common during routine social occasions for legitimate participants to have a complex of reasons for participation, some of which might embarrass the trust of other participants were these reasons to be fully disclosed. When we learn that an enthusiastic meeting-goer is not motivated by public spirit but is an insurance agent (or mortician, or politician, or dentist) making himself available to the circumstances in which "contacts" might incidentally occur, we are merely saddened a little about meetings and life, but probably neither is discredited.

Golf, for example, in American folklore was a sport that a young man might indulge in to show his occupational seniors that he was on the move in the right direction, and when he got to play a foursome with his social betters, he might well have managed his own participation more to prove likability than skill. This sort of making a convenience of the game is, I believe, more or less understood to be part of what can be expected in golf, part of a normal distribution of intent, a normal use of the game as

cover. We might even be ready to accept the interests of a
severely handicapped person to prove that someone with his
disability could still somehow manage to play golf, or the interest
of a social inferior to integrate a club—just to break symbolically
the rule of total exclusion theretofore applied to members of his
kind. It requires a Penkovskiy to really make an utter convenience of the game:

> Most athletic clubs are open to the public, including foreigners.
> Golf is the most popular sport among the well-to-do. Agent meet-
> ings can be held at golf courses as easily as in other athletic clubs.
> During the week there are very few people at the golf courses. On
> these days the intelligence officer and his agent can arrive at the
> golf course (preferably at different times, twenty to thirty minutes
> apart), each can begin to play alone, and at a previously desig-
> nated time can meet at, let us say, the sixteenth hole or at some
> other hole (there is a total of eighteen holes). Saturdays and
> Sundays are less suitable days for holding agent meetings at golf
> courses because on these days many players gather, tournaments
> are held, and single play is not permitted. Golf courses are found
> on the edges of wooded areas or parks in broken terrain where
> there are many hidden areas. These hidden areas are the best
> places for holding meetings. In some cases, meetings can be held
> in clubhouse restaurants.
>
> To hold successful meetings at golf courses, one should learn
> the conditions there ahead of time. A basic requirement is to know
> the game and how to play it. Therefore students should learn this
> game while still at the academy.[55]

When one turns to various occupational settings in which a
server has special reasons for holding and controlling the customer, then, of course, the line between ordinary activity and
fabrications becomes still harder to draw.

For example, the role of a pit boss in Nevada casinos is to keep
an eye on dealers and players while giving the appearance of

---

55. Oleg Penkovskiy, *The Penkovskiy Papers,* trans. Peter Deriabin
(Garden City, N.Y.: Doubleday & Company, 1965), pp. 116–117. Mr. Penkovskiy also describes the use that can be made of motels as clandestine
meeting places, this by virtue of the special in-and-out features of these
establishments (pp. 118–119). However, motels have come to be identified with such a wide range of activities in addition to sleeping through
the night that it might be difficult to establish exactly what might constitute a false, discrediting use.

merely kibitzing, of jocular disinterest, a kind of public relations style. Similarly, while a dealer is giving the impression of being a friendly functionary who doesn't care whether the player loses or wins, often he is, in fact (if he is experienced), keeping close watch out for cheaters, the level of play, the distribution of the largest denomination of chips, the "drop" currently "put down" at his table during the shift, potential ambiguities in the customer's actions, the view of his own actions that the "eye" in the ceiling above him obtains, and so forth. Yet it seems an understanding of this wariness does not establish the activity of boss or dealer as something discreditable. (On the other hand, if the dealer is even more wary because he is trying to collaborate with a player in "sluffing off" money under the eyes of the eye, or if the boss, while smiling to a suspect player, is phoning to have a photographer come out and pretend to snap the man next to the suspect while, in fact, obtaining a picture that will be used in the gallery in the eye, then one has a clear-cut collusive net in operation and a clear-cut case of fabrication, subject, like all constructions, to discreditation.)

Similarly, in urban settings, grocery stores currently sometimes employ the following devices to combat shoplifting:

> Hiring plainclothes detectives to roam their aisles and follow suspicious-looking shoppers;
> Installing a variety of mechanical detective devices—such as round-the-corner mirrors and "honesty towers" with two-way mirrors through which detectives can watch what's going on in the store;
> Moving higher-priced grocery items to the front of the store where employees can keep close watch over them.[56]

This makes plain the fact that the sociable smile the manager gives his customers can conceal some unsmiling concerns. However, it seems that legitimate shoppers get used to this sort of invigilation (as do casino employees who come to appreciate that the place is wired, enabling management to overhear them talking anywhere on the premises) and accept the arrangement as not discrediting their relationship to management.

In all of this, note, there is a relationship between the power of

---

56. Reported by Sylvia Porter, *San Francisco Chronicle*, February 8, 1965.

an individual to disrupt and discredit and the number of persons participating in the activity. One individual member of the audience uninvolved in a stage production need not discredit the show; one participant uninvolved in lovemaking can.

There is another issue here. When an individual is unmasked, the discrediting that occurs may be narrowly circumscribed to something that is seen as falling within some larger whole, and it is this larger whole—itself not necessarily threatened—that we may have in mind when we consider what is really going on. When a casino twenty-one player learns that the dealer, underneath it all, really has his eyes peeled for cheating, a bit of the relationship with the dealer may be discredited, but the game itself is ordinarily not threatened. When a player finally learns that the fellow player he had been commiserating with is really a shill, his incipient relation to someone whom he now knows to be a house employee is discredited, but the game itself is not. When, however, a shill is brought in so that the dealer can use that hand as a convenient dumping ground for cards he does not want to deal to the customer, that is, to facilitate "second carding," then what was the shill keying becomes subtly but profoundly transformed into a shill construction. Similarly, when invitees at a wedding party discover that the fellow guest with whom they had struck up a conversation at the gift table is really a private detective in party drag hired by the insurance company, they will find that the conversation has suddenly become untenable and will reperceive the guard's dinner jacket as a uniform or a disguise; but the wedding as a legal fact and a social occasion need not be undermined. When the Queen of England discovers that the man over whose wheelchair she had been graciously leaning (in order to convey to him a few words of encouragement during ceremonies in Hyde Park for Victoria Cross holders) is an undecorated car parker, in quite good health and of no military experience, on "a lark,"[57] one can see that *that* particular act of sovereignty would surely be discredited, but it is uncertain whether or not the incident would cast a pall over the entire garden party.

However, just as the collapse of a reality can leave undisturbed

---

57. Picture of car parker, wheelchair, and Queen leaning available in *The Washington Post,* June 28, 1956.

the social occasion in which it occurs, so one finds that something longer standing than a ceremonial affair may be involved. The discrediting that occurs may retrospectively and prospectively undermine a linked series of prior occasions and anticipated ones. When a mark tumbles to what has been happening in the Big Con and sees things for what they are, he sees that a whole sequence of past meetings and planned future ones involve a concerted fabrication. When an expert embezzler suddenly disappears with a firm's $200,000, a firm in which for two years he functioned as a promising bookkeeper-treasurer, a firm which now after 113 years of business will have to declare bankruptcy, a two-year standing set of relationships is collapsed, a work record, a career, a personal identity, and, of course, a business.[58] When a resistance worker is arrested by a Nazi officer who had succeeded in passing himself off as someone desiring to change sides, and the resister's response to the German is, "My congratulations, *mon colonel*. You played your game well!"[59] game here presumably refers to something that is at once artificial and encompassing, and the point is that it includes more than the interaction in which the arrest occurred; it also includes all the interactions through which misplaced confidence was established. When a Nevada casino player finds that the dealer has shortchanged him in paying a win, he may merely move to another table; when, however, he finds that his winning streak has caused management to bring in a new dealer long before a scheduled change, he can begin to doubt the house and to consider moving to another casino, or even, upon the repetition of such an experience, to consider giving up playing in the state. Indeed, in the United States, the so-called Stalin Trials tend to be seen as a collective whole, a use of a nation's basic legal institutions for the sole purpose of staging a show, a systematic translation of a judicial process into a political display, and this whole is read as discrediting evidence regarding an entire political system.

Plainly, then, a deceiving design can generate a continuing organization of activity that will become subject to discrediting. And whenever a discrediting occurs, it will have a backward and

<hr />

58. *San Francisco Sunday Examiner and Chronicle*, October 31, 1965, and *San Francisco Chronicle*, April 28, 1966.

59. E. H. Cookridge, *Inside S.O.E.* (London: Arthur Barker, 1966), p. 180.

forward reach, sometimes long, sometimes short, but a reach nonetheless.

It is here in regard to this reach that one can locate a basic concept: *suspicion.* It is what a person feels who begins, rightly or not, to think that the strip of activity he is involved in has been constructed beyond his ken, and that he has not been allowed a sustainable view of what frames him. Suspicion must be distinguished from another important feeling, *doubt,* this being generated not by concern about being contained but concern about the framework or key that applies, these being elements that ordinarily function innocently in activity. Suspicion and doubt are to be seen, then, as two very central affects generated by the very way in which experience is framed. Insofar as it is hard to imagine a citizenry without suspicion or doubt, it is hard to imagine experience that is not organized in terms of framing.

A final point about the issues that bear on system of reference. There are some fabrications that possess the features we think of as inhering in the Big Con: small strips of thoroughly simulated activity patched together into a single scenario. With that image in mind, it can be seen that fabricators might on occasion employ a straight bit of activity as one element in the whole, thus increasing verisimilitude. A con man who meets his marks in a genuine bank and ushers them into a private room that he knows will not be in demand during their presence has lifted a genuine scene (and one costly to fabricate) into his design, the scene being genuine at one level and false at another. Similarly the following:

> London—Actress Vanessa Redgrave, 30, stunned a packed theater here by ripping away the top of her stage costume and dancing around half naked.
>
> Movie cameras rolled, recording Miss Redgrave's dance and the embarrassed reactions of the richly-dressed audience—all paid film extras who had no previous hint of what would happen.
>
> It happened Wednesday as one scene in her new picture "Isadora." . . .[60]

Description here would have to be careful. The movie *Isadora* is a "real" movie, not a faked one, except for one bit in it which is not genuine cinema, having been produced by a real set producing

---

60. *San Francisco Chronicle,* December 8, 1967.

not scripted response but the real thing. Indeed, a further twist can occur: it has been argued by poker players that the best bluff is an unintentional one, that is, an individual's playing conduct following upon his misidentifying his own holdings. Here, again, is straight activity which functions in the scene as a bluff.[61]

61. Examples of "naturalism" in intelligence plots are considered in S.I., p. 43.

5

The Theatrical Frame

Because the language of the theater has become deeply embedded in the sociology from which this study derives, there is value in attempting from the start to address the matter of the stage. There is value, too, because all kinds of embarrassments are to be found. All the word *is* like a stage, we *do* strut and fret our hour on it, and that is all the time we have. But what's the stage like, and what are those figures that people it?

I

A performance, in the restricted sense in which I shall now use the term, is that arrangement which transforms an individual into a stage performer, the latter, in turn, being an object that can be looked at in the round and at length without offense, and looked to for engaging behavior, by persons in an "audience" role.[1] (It is contrariwise the obligation to show visual respect which characterizes the frame of ordinary face-to-face interaction.) A line is ordinarily maintained between a staging area where the performance proper occurs and an audience region

---

1. A different definition of performance is recommended in Dell Hymes, "Toward Linguistic Competence" (unpublished paper, 1973): "And there is a sense in which *performance* is an attribute of any behavior, if the doer accepts or has imputed to him responsibility for being evaluated in regard to it."

where the watchers are located. The central understanding is that the audience has neither the right nor the obligation to participate directly in the dramatic action occurring on the stage, although it may express appreciation throughout in a manner that can be treated as not occurring by the beings which the stage performers present onstage. At certain junctures the audience can openly give applause to the performers, receiving bows or the equivalent in return. And a special condition obtains in regard to number of participants: the performance as such is very little dependent on either the size of the cast or the size of the audience, although there are maxima set by the physical facts of sight and sound transmission.

Performances can be distinguished according to their purity, that is, according to the exclusiveness of the claim of the watchers on the activity they watch.

Dramatic scriptings, nightclub acts, personal appearances of various sorts, the ballet, and much of orchestral music are pure. No audience, no performance. The limiting cases here are ad hoc performances, those that occur within a domestic circle when a party guest does a turn at the piano or guitar for the optional beguilement of other guests who happen to be close by, or a raconteur tells a longish story to friends, or a parent reads at bedtime to his children. The term "personal" is used here because the performer typically supplies his own scenery and props, and no prior agenda need be present to obligate the individual to perform.

Contests or matches when presented for viewing come next. Although the social occasion in which the set-to occurs is crucial, and behind this the gate that is collected at the door, the whole affair depends upon the contestants' acting as if the score outcome itself is what drives them. The players, then, must convincingly act as though something were at stake beyond the entertainment of those who are watching them. League rankings, personal performance records, and prize money all help to stabilize these nonperformance features, pointing to something that is significant in its own right which could not be resolved without actually playing the match through. (Thus it is thinkable that a series match might be played for the record in the absence of any audience.) And, of course, the action will take place in a ring or grounds, not on a stage. As might be expected, there seems to be

no type of sport or game that does not provide a full continuum
from matches that no one is expected to bother to watch,
through those that acquire a few temporary watchers, to championship matches whose audiences can achieve a respectable
Nielsen rating.

A little less pure are personal ceremonies such as weddings
and funerals. These occasions typically contain watchers, but the
latter function as witnesses and as guests and usually come by
invitation, not fee. I might add that whereas the wider significance of a contest outcome is often seen as part of recreational
life and in one sense unserious, ceremonials tend to provide a
ritual ratification of something that is itself defined as part of the
serious world.

Lectures and talks provide a very mixed class in regard to
performance purity, in brief, a variable mixture of instruction
(for which the listener may well be held responsible) and entertainment. At one extreme are the briefing sessions which staff
officers hold for pilots before a raid or the demonstrations that
visiting specialists provide medical students in a surgical theater;
at the other, the political analysis provided by stand-up comics of
the educated school. (The interesting mix is somewhere between,
namely, the capacity of "gifted" speakers to conceal from those
whom they amuse that that is almost all that is occurring.)

Most impure of all, I suppose, are work performances, those
that occur, for example, at construction sites or rehearsals, where
viewers openly watch persons at work who openly show no
regard or concern for the dramatic elements of their labor.[2] On-
the-spot TV news coverage now offers up the world, including its
battles, as work performances, this, incidentally, inclining the
citizenry to accept the role of audience in connection with any
and all events.

These distinctions among performances refer to the official
face of activity, not to its underlying character and intent. A
political trial may be presented as a straight contest when, in
fact, it is a scripted dramatic fabrication, a more domestic version
being the transformation that television and its timing have
brought to some boxing matches and practically all professional

---

2. Commercial recordings of orchestral rehearsals are now available,
presumably to allow audiences an intimate glimpse of the conductor at
work. One wonders how these strips differ from the real thing.

wrestling. Similarly, when we say pejoratively of a person that he has given a "real performance," we can mean that he has taken more than usual care and employed more than usual design and continuity in the presentation of what is ostensibly not a performance at all. In any case, some terminological help is required here to relieve the burden carried by the word "performance," especially in discussions about contests. In order to be particularly clear about frame, one might say that a bridge game that is televised or otherwise placed before an audience is a presented match; as part of a scripted movie, a dramatized match; as something a cheater arranges, a rigged match. And presumably a play about cheating at bridge would provide viewers with a dramatized rigged match; and a news clip of a roller derby, a re-presented rigged match.

One point bears repeating. In considering legitimate stage performances it is all too common to speak of interaction between performer and audience. That easy conclusion conceals the analysis that would be required to make sense out of this interaction, conceals the fact that participants in a conversation can be said to interact, too, conceals, indeed, the fact that the term "interaction" equally applies to everything one might want to distinguish. The first issue is not interaction but frame. In a conversation, the content of one speaker's statement can call forth a direct replying response from another participant, both responses being part of the same plane of being. During a performance it is only fellow performers who respond to each other in this direct way as inhabitants of the same realm; the audience responds indirectly, glancingly, following alongside, as it were, cheering on but not intercepting. But more of that presently.

II

Consider now one subspecies of performance, the kind that presents a dramatic scripting live onstage. Reserve the term "play" for the author's written text, the term "playing" for one go-through from beginning to end of the play before a particular audience. The term "production" can refer to the effort of a particular cast on the occasion of any one run of the play, here defining "run" as the full series of playings presented by one cast on the basis of one continuous period of preparation. A run may involve but one playing, but the economics of production dictate otherwise.[3] For the iron laws of stagecraft apply: the audience can only be asked for their attention, considerateness, and a fee, and the actors have a right to stage the whole thing again before a next night's audience.

The theater seems to provide—at least for Western society—an ideal version of a basic conceptual distinction, that between a performer or individual actor who appears on stage and the part or character he assumes whilst employed thereon. Nothing could be more natural and clear than to speak of an actor like John Gielgud taking a part like Hamlet.

In thinking about unstaged, actual social life, theatrical imagery seems to guide us toward a distinction between an individual or person and a capacity, namely, a specialized function which the person may perform during a given series of occasions. A simple matter. We say that John Smith is a good plumber, bad father, loyal friend, and so forth.

If we sense a difference between what a Gielgud does onstage and what a Smith does in his shop (or with his family, or at a political rally), we can express it by saying that Hamlet's jabbing away is not real, is make-believe, but that a repaired pipe (or a vote cast) is. We use the same word, "role," to cover both onstage and offstage activity and apparently find no difficulty in understanding whether a real role is in question or the mere stage presentation of one.

But, of course, none of these formulations is adequate, and especially inadequate is the term "role." What Smith possesses as a person or individual is a personal identity: he is a concrete organism with distinctively identifying marks, a niche in life. He is a selfsame object perduring over time and possessing an accumulating memory of the voyage.[4] He has a biography. As

---

3. Kabuki theater, for example, sometimes has a one-night run, but apparently not for the reasons we occasionally do.

4. Partly in response to the transplant fashion in surgery, some philosophers have recently refocused attention and doubts regarding this body-continuity assumption. See, for example, D. Parfit, "Personal Identity," *Philosophical Review*, LXXX (1971): 3–27; Amelie O. Rorty, "Persons, Policies, and Bodies," *International Philosophical Quarterly*, XIII (1973): 63–80; David Wiggins, *Identity and Spatio-Temporal Continuity* (Oxford: Basil Blackwell, 1967).

part of this personal identity, he claims a multitude of capacities or functions—occupational, domestic, and so forth. When Gielgud does Hamlet he is presenting a fictive or scripted identity exhibited through Hamlet's fictive capacities as son, lover, prince, friend, and so forth, all of which capacities are tied together by a single biographical thread—albeit a fictive one. But what Gielgud is literally doing, of course, is making an appearance in the capacity of stage actor, this being merely one of his capacities— albeit his best-known one. It is the same capacity he employs when he arrives in time for rehearsal or attends a meeting of Equity.

And the problem is that we tend to use the term "role" to refer to Gielgud's professional occupation, to the character Hamlet (being a part available to Gielgud), and even to the special capacity of Hamlet as son or as Prince. The difference between actual and scripted becomes confused with the difference between personal identity and specialized function, or (on the stage) the difference between part and capacity. I shall use the term "role" as an equivalent to specialized capacity or function, understanding this to occur both in offstage, real life and in its staged version; the term "person" will refer to the subject of a biography, the term "part" or "character" to a staged version thereof. Interestingly, in everyday affairs, one is not always aware of a particular individual's part in life, that is, his biography, awareness often focusing more on the role he performs in some particular connection—political, domestic, or whatever. Contrariwise, part is the common concern in drama, much less attention being given to a character's special roles.

There is further trouble. As suggested, it is quite clear that an individual employed in stage acting will demonstrate at least a dual self, a stage actor (who seeks help from the prompter, cooperation from other members of the cast, response from the audience) and a staged character. But what about the individual who is part of the "theatrical audience"? What elements does he possess?

One is the role of theatergoer. He is the one who makes the reservations and pays for the tickets, comes late or on time, and is responsive to the curtain call after the performance. He, too, is the person who takes the intermission break. He has untheatrical activity to sustain; it is real money he must spend and real time he must use up—just as the performer earns real money and adds or detracts from his reputation through each performance. The theatergoer may have little "real" reason for having come, his motives being ones he would not like to see exposed. The theatergoer is the stage actor's opposite number.

Each person who is a theatergoer is something else, too. He collaborates in the unreality onstage. He sympathetically and vicariously participates in the unreal world generated by the dramatic interplay of the scripted characters. He gives himself over. He is raised (or lowered) to the cultural level of the playwright's characters and themes, appreciating allusions for which he doesn't quite have the background, marital adjustments for which he doesn't quite have the stomach, varieties in style of life for which he is not quite ready, and repartee which gives to speaking a role he could not quite accept for it were he to find such finery in the real world. One might speak here of the onlooker role, keeping in mind that that term seems also and better to cover brief, open, yet unratified vicarious participation in offstage, real activities. It is important to see that the onlooking aspect of the audience activity is not something that is a staged or simulated replica of a real thing, as is the action onstage. The offstage version of onlooking is not a model for the theatrical kind; if anything the reverse is true. Onlooking belongs from the start to the theatrical frame.

The difference between theatergoer and onlooker is nicely illustrated in regard to laughter, demonstrating again the need to be very clear about the syntax of response. Laughter by members of the audience in sympathetic response to an effective bit of buffoonery by a staged character is clearly distinguished on both sides of the stage line from audience laughter that can greet an actor who flubs, trips, or breaks up in some unscripted way.[5] In the first case the individual laughs as onlooker, in the second as theatergoer. Moreover, although both kinds of laughter are officially unheard by the characters projected on the stage—these creatures being ostensibly in another plane of being—the effect of the two kinds of responsive laughter on the performer is presumably quite different; the sympathetic kind may cause him

---

5. Suggested by Susanne K. Langer, *Feeling and Form* (New York: Charles Scribner's Sons, 1953), p. 341.

to pause in his performance so as to accommodate the response, whereas the other kind of laughter may cause him to move forward with his lines as fast as is practicable. And, of course, both kinds of laughter are radically different from the kind enacted by a character; *that* kind of laughter *is* heard officially by the other characters. Note, there is no embarrassment when the sympathetic laughter of one member of the audience contagiously causes other members to take up the response, but should a character's laugh cause the onlookers to take up the *same* response, something deeply ungrammatical would have occurred.

One might argue, then, that theatrical audiences incorporate two elements: theatergoer and onlooker. If one shifts to other audiences, say, the kind which attends to a written text, the kind that could equally well be called a readership, the same twofold distinction is found, and moreover some additional reason provided for drawing it. The onlooking side of matters remains somewhat the same; viewing a play and reading its text involve something of the same experience. The other element of the audience role, however, differs sharply according to type of audience. Not much is common between going to the theater and taking up a book.

III

It is an obvious feature of stage productions that the final applause wipes the make-believe away.[6] The characters that were

6. On just coming onstage, a well-known actor may be applauded, the applause being addressed not to the character he will project but to himself qua actor. He responds in that role by a show of pleasure or by holding up the action for a moment while freezing in his part, the latter tack providing an exquisite illustration of the conventional nature of theatrical strips. During the production a particularly deft piece of work may also be applauded, the theatergoers addressing themselves not to the unfolding inner drama but to the skill of the actors. Opera institutionalizes much more of this "breaking" of frame by audiences. Interestingly, here, too, there have been marked changes in conventions through time, as suggested by Kenneth Macgowan and William Melnitz in *Golden Ages of the Theater* (Englewood Cliffs, N.J.: Prentice-Hall, 1959):

Until the triumph of realism in the last decade of the nineteenth century, acting was essentially and almost everywhere a bravura display of individual talent. Today we still clap a player when he has made an exit after a particularly fine effort, but audiences used to interrupt an actor

projected are cast aside, as are those aspects of the viewers that entered sympathetically into the unfolding drama, and persons in the capacity of players or performers greet persons in the capacity of theatergoers. And on both sides of the stage line the same admission is achieved as to what indeed had been going on, this being especially marked in the case of a puppet performance when the appearance out front of the puppeteers totally undermines the illusion that had been carefully fostered until then.[7] Whatever had been portrayed onstage is now seen as not the real thing at all but only a representation, one made benignly to provide vicarious involvement for the onlooker. (Indeed, at curtain calls actors routinely maintain the costume they wore when the curtain came down, but now the costumes are worn by individuals who do not fill them characterologically but slackly serve as mere hangers, a hat off or a scarf missing, as though to make a point that nothing real is to be attributed to the guise.) In brief, make-believe is abandoned.

Of course, if one watches curtain calls closely, one can easily see that they are patterned almost as much as any stage *character* performance, but different orders of patterning are involved; we are slightly embarrassed by knowledge of the first but not of the second. (Similarly, the informal chatter a popular singer may offer between songs is likely to be scripted, yet is clearly received

---

to applaud the delivery of an emotional speech. Like an operatic aria, the scene was sometimes repeated if the applause was loud enough. Consequently, there was a lack of ensemble in most theaters, and of both an inner and an outer resemblance to life. [p. 119]

Obviously, then, even apart from the suspension of the staged realm that we readily accept for the moments between scenes and acts, it is impossible to break the illusion before the play is over and still maintain it. And the "we" here probably includes most of the world. Thus, one can read of a Kabuki play:

After this monologue he [the hero] struts onto the stage and, wielding a long sword, kills the ruffians who attempt to strike at him. In this pompous manner he rescues the worthy but helpless man. The fighting over, the hero approaches the *hanamichi*, and the curtain falls on the stage behind him. On a narrow ledge in front of the curtain he speaks to the audience by way of salutation, as an actor and not as the hero of the play. After this, he resumes his role in the play and goes off the stage, sword on shoulder, along the *hanamichi*. [Shūtarō Miyake, *Kabuki Drama* (Tokyo: Japan Travel Bureau, 1964), p. 88.]

7. Gerold L. Hanck, "A Frame Analysis of the Puppet Theater" (unpublished paper, University of Pennsylvania, 1970).

as outside the song frame, thus unofficial, informal, directly communicated.) Furthermore, in accordance with the fundamental principle that anything mentionable can be retransformed, one should expect that quite convincing curtain calls can be scripted and acted in a movie about the legitimate stage—of which there are surely as many as we need. And one should note the frame sophistication involved in the Kabuki takeoff on *Shibaraku*, a traditional Kabuki play, the satire being designed as a female version of the original. A female impersonator (an *omnagata*) of course takes the part using a male costume, but in the finale, when greeting the audience, he reverts to delicate female response.[8]

None of the above requires particularly careful thinking. But when one tries to get some picture of the character of events *during* and *within* a performance, when the inner realm of the drama is being sustained, conventional understandings are less helpful. A painstaking approach is required.

IV

To understand the organization of the inner world of a stage play (or any other dramatic scripting), one must try to get a clear view of the relation an individual can have to other kinds of doings. In the world of real, everyday activity, the individual can predict some natural events with a fair amount of certainty, but interpersonal outcomes are necessarily more problematic. In any case, in matters affecting himself he must await fate, await something that will unfold but hasn't yet. In the case of make-believe the individual can arrange to script what is to come, unwinding his own reel. With fabrications it is apparent that the fabricators have some opportunity to "play the world backwards," that is, to arrange now for some things to work out later that ordinarily would be out of anyone's control and a matter of fate or chance.[9]

Corresponding to these various arrangements will be various information states. By an "information state" I mean the knowledge an individual has of why events have happened as they

8. Miyake, *Kabuki Drama*, pp. 88–89.

9. See the chapter on "Normal Appearances" in *R.P.*

have, what the current forces are, what the properties and
intents of the relevant persons are, and what the outcome is
likely to be.[10] In brief, each character at each moment is accorded an orientation, a temporal perspective, a "horizon." In the
con operation, for example, the dupe does not know that he is
going to happen upon someone who will become his confederate
and that they both will happen upon someone who seems to be a
dupe. The con men, however, are somewhat more God-like; they
know about their "real" personal and social identity and, barring
some quite unforeseen event, know what it is that is going to
seem to happen to them and the prospective mark. Of course, the
dupe is likely to know some things about his own situation which
he does not divulge to his newly acquired associates.

Turn back now to the inner realm of a stage play in progress.
Obviously the playwright, the producer, the prompter, and the
players all share a single information state concerning the inner
events of the play; they all know what will prove to be involved in
the happenings and how the happenings will turn out. Rehearsals make this all too clear. Further, this knowing is much
more appreciable than real persons ordinarily share about *their*
world, since the playwright has decided in advance just how
everything will work out. Just as obviously, during a performance
the characters projected by the performers act as if they possess
different information states, different from one another and, of
course, less complete than the one the actors and the production
crew possess. Note, the make-believe acceptance of different
information states, different from one's fellow characters and
different from the production staff, is an absolute essential if any
sense is to be made out of the inner drama on the stage. Any
utterance offered in character on the stage makes sense only if
the maker is ignorant of the outcome of the drama and ignorant
about some features of the situation "known" to the other characters.[11]

If one is willing to restrict oneself to a consideration of the
players themselves in their scripted and performed duties, one

---

10. Modified from John von Neumann and Oskar Morgenstern, *The
Theory of Games and Economic Behavior* (Princeton, N.J.: Princeton University Press, 1944), pp. 51–58.

11. In von Neumann's language, in plays, as in poker, "anteriority" does
not imply "preliminarity."

could speak of the play as a keying and the acting as a form of make-believe. In brief, *during* the play, the person playing the hero acts as if he doesn't know what the villain is going to do, and the person playing the villain acts as if he can hide his intent from the hero, although both these individuals have a common and full knowledge of the play and of the distribution of this knowledge. This means that at least some of the characters will be hoodwinking the other characters, that all will be "ignorant" of certain problematic outcomes, and that the play will therefore be, given only the actors and their real information states, a keying of a fabrication.

So, taken by themselves, the performers can be seen to be playing at containing each other. But when one adds the audience to the picture, matters become somewhat more complicated. It is, of course, perfectly possible and not at all rare for a theater-goer to know how the play he is watching comes out, because he either has read it or has seen it on another occasion. But that is not the first fact to look at. The first thing to see is that members of the audience in their capacity as onlookers, as official eaves-droppers, are accorded by the playwright a specific information state relative to the inner events of the drama, and this state necessarily is different from the playwright's and in all likelihood different from that of various characters in the play—although one or more play characters may be accorded the same informa-tion state as the audience, a bridging function which may pass from one set of characters to another.[12]

Being part of the audience in a theater obliges us to act as if our own knowledge, as well as that of some of the characters, is partial. As onlookers we are good sports and act as if we are ignorant of outcomes—which we may be. But this is not ordinary ignorance, since we do not make an ordinary effort to dispel it.

---

12. Indeed, whenever a producer provides a strip of represented material for consumers, a moving point of development is likely to be maintained for the consumer, the point moving along from one instance of consump-tion to the next, this requiring that the producer tactfully set aside *his* current view of the material. As Charles Fillmore argues in a useful paper on point of view in narrative ("Pragmatics and the Description of Dis-course" [unpublished paper]), the practice even in nonfiction book writing is to say: "This subject will be treated at length in a later chapter," even though the person writing that statement actually stands to his book so as to warrant him saying, "This subject was treated. . . ."

We willingly sought out the circumstances in which we could be temporarily deceived or at least kept in the dark, in brief, transformed into collaborators in unreality. And we actively collaborate in sustaining this playful unknowingness. Those who have already read or seen the play carry this cooperativeness one step further; they put themselves as much as possible back into a state of ignorance, the ultimate triumph of onlooker over theatergoer. (Note the journalistic convention obliging reviewers to stop short of giving the ending away.) After the curtain comes down, of course, the joke is over, and everyone knows the same what-has-been-happening.

It might be said, then, that a stage production was some sort of voluntarily supported benign fabrication, for the audience treats disclosure somewhat as they would that which terminates a leg-pull executed in good taste and all in fun. But leg-pulls involve the faking of real activity, whereas the stage uses materials that are frankly keyings—open mock-ups of dramatic human actions —and at no time is the audience convinced that real life is going on up there. It also might be claimed that plays are like card games in the matter of suspense. In games the players voluntarily place themselves in circumstances of ignorance concerning each other's holdings and then wait in suspense as the facts gradually come to light. In the theater, if the cast, the critics, and the audience all play according to the rules, *real* suspense and *real* disclosure can result. But there is a difference. The materials in the realm of card play are not mock-ups of life but events in their own right, albeit trivial in certain ways. More important, unless cheating is occurring, each player not only *can* be ignorant of the holdings of the opponents and the final outcome of the game but *must* be. The player cannot say, "I enjoyed that hand so much that I'm going to come back tomorrow night and play it again." And something similar can be said of sports contests. Here the whole design, including handicapping techniques, assures that outcomes will not be known in advance, in fact, will be unknowable in advance. Through very careful manipulation of a model-like environment, suspensefulness is given a real basis.

To repeat, it is perfectly obvious to everyone on and off the stage that the characters and their actions are unreal, but it is also true that the audience holds this understanding to one side and in the capacity of onlookers allows its interest and sympathy

to respect the apparent ignorance of the characters as to what
will come of them and to wait in felt suspense to see how matters
will unfold.[13]

I do not mean to argue here that every play is merely a

---

13. Ionesco, in a play, makes the point:

CHOUBERT: You're right. Yes, you're right. All the plays that have ever
              been written, from Ancient Greece to the present day,
              have never really been anything but thrillers. Drama's al-
              ways been realistic and there's always been a detective
              about. Every play's an investigation brought to a success-
              ful conclusion. There's a riddle, and it's solved in the final
              scene. Sometimes earlier. You seek, and then you find.
              Might as well give the game away at the start.
MADELEINE: You ought to quote examples, you know.
CHOUBERT: I was thinking of the Miracle Play about the woman Our
              Lady saved from being burned alive. If you forget that bit
              of divine intervention, which really has nothing to do
              with it, what's left is a newspaper story about a woman
              who has her son-in-law murdered by a couple of stray
              killers for reasons that are unmentioned . . .
MADELEINE: And unmentionable . . .
CHOUBERT: The police arrive, there's an investigation and the crimi-
              nal is unmasked. It's a thriller. A naturalistic drama, fit
              for the theatre of Antoine.
                   . . .
MADELEINE: What about the classics?
CHOUBERT: Refined detective drama. Just like naturalism.
              [Eugène Ionesco, *Victims of Duty*, in his *Three Plays*, trans.
              Donald Watson (New York: Grove Press, 1958), pp. 119–120.]

A more serious version is to be found in Bertrand Evans' detailed in-
formation-state analysis in *Shakespeare's Comedies* (Oxford: Oxford Uni-
versity Press, 1960). He takes as central the playwright's control of awareness—of the characters' and of the audience's. He argues that a dramatist
has three courses: to cause the audience to be less informed about the
relevant facts than the characters, equally informed, or more informed.
And that detective story writers take the first course, Shakespeare in his
comedies the third. He states:

   . . . if a comedy requires two hours and a half to perform, attention is
   centered for nearly two hours on persons whose vision is less complete
   than ours, whose sense of the facts of situations most pertinent to themselves is either quite mistaken or quite lacking, and whose words and
   actions would be very different if the truth known to us were known to
   them. [p. viii]

It should be added that when the audience is given more information than
is one (or more) of the characters, this knowing must still be incomplete;
for in the very degree that the focus shifts from what the audience is to
discover to what a character is to discover, the audience must be kept in
ignorance of the *response* of the character to eventual discovery.

whodunit. Even whodunits have to be more than that. For temporary concealment of eventual outcome itself serves a purpose, that of showing that fate or destiny will work itself out and visit meaningful if not just deserts upon the play's characters. As Langer suggests:

> Dramatic action is a semblance of action so constructed that a whole, indivisible piece of virtual history is implicit in it, as a yet unrealized form, long before the presentation is completed. The constant illusion of an imminent future, this vivid appearance of a growing situation before anything startling has occurred, is "form in suspense." It is a human destiny that unfolds before us, its unity is apparent from the opening words or even silent action, because on the stage we see acts in their entirety, as we do not see them in the real world except in retrospect, that is, by constructive reflection. In the theatre they occur in simplified and completed form, with visible motives, directions, and ends. Since stage action is not, like genuine action, embedded in a welter of irrelevant doings and divided interests, and characters on the stage have no unknown complexities (however complex they may be), it is possible there to see a person's feelings grow into passions, and those passions issue in words and deeds.[14]

V

The argument, then, is that the theatrical frame is something less than a benign construction and something more than a simple keying. In any case, a corpus of transcription practices must be involved for transforming a strip of offstage, real activity into a strip of staged being. Now I want to consider in some detail one bundle of these conventions, those which mark the difference between actual face-to-face interaction and that kind of interaction when staged as part of a play.

---

14. Langer, *Feeling and Form*, p. 310.

Even news stories can be written to maintain narrative suspense until the last paragraph, although readers surely understand that the event reported on has already finished occurring. And even news stories often manage, with the unfolding of the punch ending, to illustrate a theme of morality or fate. More to the point, when the lead neatly encapsulates the story line, giving the show away, as it were, the story can still be written in the gradual disclosure form, as though the reader could be counted on to dissociate his capacity for suspenseful involvement from disclosive information he has been given a moment ago.

1. The spatial boundaries of the stage sharply and arbitrarily cut off the depicted world from what lies beyond the stage line. (Many other social activities are, of course, restricted to a particular roped-off or elevated space, but with the possible exception of ritual, these activities are conducted as though events outside the boundary were of the same general order of being as those within. Not so in theatrical staging.) Further, the endings of a drama can follow somewhat the possible endings in real life; the beginnings of a play don't seem to have much of a parallel in unstaged activity. For typically the curtains open on an episode in progress, with no attention given by the characters to the fact that they have suddenly come into view. Movies, incidentally, can effect a more gradual introduction of the realm the onlookers will enter.

2. As a means of injecting the audience into the staged activity we employ the convention of opening up rooms so that they have no ceiling and one wall missing—an incredible arrangement if examined naïvely.[15] The point here is not that the doings of the characters are exposed—after all, there are lots of doings that

---

15. And not, of course, a necessity:

The modern convention which enables our theatre-going audience to see into the interior of a house would have startled the Greeks and Romans. Their basic convention was quite different. The stage represented for them an open street, or some other open place; they were the general public assembled on the other side of the street or in the open country, and looking at the buildings which fronted on the street or open space. Every scene, in order to be shown on the stage, had to be thought of as taking place in the open air. In Mediterranean countries much does take place in the open which in our latitude would occur indoors; but the real and sufficient reason for staging a banquet, a toilet-scene or a confidential conversation on the street was that otherwise such a scene could not be staged at all. [W. Beare, *The Roman Stage* (London: Methuen & Co., 1964), p. 178.]

Beare goes on to make the following comment in regard to disclosive practices:

The expedients to which the dramatists are forced to resort by this convention are evidence of the validity of the convention itself. If it is necessary to disclose what is supposed to be taking place within the house, a character on the stage may be asked to peep inside the door and report what he sees. [pp. 178–179]

In Western drama, in contrast, it is events happening outside the room which must be disclosed by this heraldic device.

are—but that no apparent protective and compensative adjustment is made by the characters for this exposure.

3. Spoken interaction is opened up ecologically; the participants do not face each other directly or (when more than two) through the best available circle, but rather stand at an open angle to the front so that the audience can literally see into the encounter.

4. One person at a time tends to be given the focus of the stage, front and center. (He will often rise from a chair to take it.) The others onstage, especially those not engaged in talk with the current central person, tend to be arranged out of focus, their actions muted, the result being that the attention of the audience is led to the speaker.

5. Turns at talking tend to be respected to the end, and audience response is awaited before a replying turn is taken. A version by a member of the trade illustrates:

INTERVIEWER: What sort of regimen do you put yourself through? Well, let us say in *Dear Liar*, which I'm sure was a very taxing part.

CORNELL: One of the most taxing ones I've ever done. You were listening, if you were not speaking. I would say that the person who does a solo performance, such as, perhaps, John Gielgud does in his *Ages of Man*, would be less tired than the person who did Brian's-and mine—Brian Aherne's and mine—because, if you're talking yourself, as I am talking at the present moment, I can make pauses. I can take my time. I can think it over. If I want to walk across the stage and back after a particular scene, I can do it. With dialogue, or two people, shall I say, on the stage—not a dialogue, but with two people working together—there wasn't a moment when I had not to listen to Brian, and vice versa, and always be aware that we must not respond before the audience responded. It's so easy for you to go off in your timing—for him to say something funny, and I would feel like smiling or laughing, and yet I knew that if I did smile or laugh, somehow the focus of the audience would move for a second past him to me and, consequently, I might break up a laugh that was coming. I had to wait till they began to respond, before I could. So it took constant effort. And if you were tired, you might naturally smile at something, or laugh at something, or take your handkerchief—I had to because I had a cold—but you knew all the time that you might do something that would distract just that second. And so you never could be at ease, at all.[16]

It is thus that the audience response is systematically built into the interaction on stage.[17]

---

16. Katharine Cornell, in Lewis Funke and John E. Booth, *Actors Talk about Acting* (New York: Random House, 1961), pp. 203–204.

17. Of course, given this interposition convention, the way is clear for a pair of actors to make dramaturgical news:

INTERVIEWER: What is the secret of your teamwork?

LUNT: I don't know. I guess each of us is interested in the other. That's one thing. And, of course, there is our way of speaking together. We started it in *The Guardsman*. We would speak to each other as people do in real life. I would, for instance, start a speech, and in the middle, on our own cue, which we would agree on in advance, Lynn would cut in and start talking. I would continue on a bit, you see. You can't do it in Shakespeare, of course. But in drawing-room comedies, in realistic plays, it is most effective. How can I make that clear? We what is known as overlapped . . .

INTERVIEWER: Without waiting . . .

LUNT: Yes, in the middle of a sentence. That is exactly what I mean, what we are doing right now. We are talking together, aren't we? You heard what I said, and I heard what you said. Well, to do that on the stage, you see, you have to work it very, very carefully, because you overlap lines. So that once I say the line, "Come into the next room and I will get ready," your cue really is "the next room," and you say, "All right," and I continue and say, "and I will get ready," underneath, as it were. Of course, I must lower my voice so that she is still heard. Is that clear?

INTERVIEWER: This interaction is presumably what every actor dreams of.

LUNT: They thought it couldn't be done. They said you will never do it. And when we first played *Caprice* in London, they were outraged because we talked together. Really outraged, the press was. But it was a great success. And I think it was the first time it was ever done. I don't know. It just happened because we knew each other so well and trusted each other. Although sometimes I have been accused, and I accuse her, of stepping

6. A fundamental transcription practice of "disclosive compensation" is sustained throughout the interaction. The assumption is that in unstaged, actual interaction the speaker achieves a joint spontaneity of involvement between himself and all his hearers. This apparently is done by his omitting from the conversation topics that would be grossly unsuitable for any of his hearers to share with him, or topics that are shared in widely different degrees by his hearers, as well, of course, as topics of "no interest." He then commonly proceeds by means of a maximum of laconicity, that is, by truncating his explication as much as is consistent with providing hearers adequate cognitive orientation. In the case of newcomers or persons who can well be somewhat left out of the talk, he may provide initial, pointed, orienting comments, but perhaps more as a courtesy than anything else—a courtesy that allows the outsider to act as though he isn't. Eavesdroppers are thus destined to hear fragments of meaningful talk, not streams of it. (Indeed, when participants sense they are being audited, they may employ a self-conscious hyperlaconicity approaching a secret code.) The theater, however, stages interaction systematically designed to be exposed to large audiences that can only be expected to have very general knowledge in common with the play characters performing this interaction. Were the persons onstage to orient to the audience as persons to adjust the conversation to—by filling in, censoring, and so forth—the dramatic illusion would be entirely lost. One character could say to another character only what could be said to a roomful of strangers. The audience would be "in" nothing. On the other hand, if the audience were not filled in somehow, it would soon become entirely lost. What is done, and done systematically, is that the audience is given the information it needs covertly, so the fiction can be sustained that it has indeed entered into a world not its own. (In fact, special devices are available,

---

on a line or a laugh or a bit of business. "Why do you come in so quickly?" "Why don't you . . ."
[Lynn Fontanne and Alfred Lunt, *ibid.*, pp. 45–46.]

The rule of one-at-a-time is especially marked in radio drama, where almost everything depends on verbally imparted information, and therefore no interference therewith is tolerable. (See the unpublished paper by John Carey, "Framing Mechanisms in Radio Drama" [University of Pennsylvania, 1970].)

such as asides, soliloquies, a more than normal amount of inter-rogation, self-confession, and confidence giving—all to ease the task of incidentally providing information needed by the on-lookers.)[18] Thus, staged interaction must be systematically man-aged in this incidentally informing manner.

7. Utterances tend to be much longer and more grandiloquent than in ordinary conversation; there is an elevation of tone and elocutionary manner, owing, perhaps, in part to the actor's obli-gation to project to the audience and be heard. Also, of course, playwrights presumably have more than average competence with expression, more than average literary education, and they certainly have more time to contrive apt, pithy, colorful, and rounded statements than do individuals engaged in natural, un-staged talk. And while ordinary interactants can attempt to set up an utterance that they have already prepared, playwrights achieve this control constantly as a matter of course.

8. In actual face-to-face talk between persons who have a settled relation to each other, there will often be occasions when the relationship is not in jeopardy and little new information bearing on the relationship is being conveyed. What is problem-atic between the two will currently not be at issue. Further, it is possible and even likely that nothing else of import or weight will be occurring. So, too, if a conversation between the two is occur-ring in the immediate presence of others who are not partici-pants, then these others are likely to be disattending much of what is occurring between the pair, providing only that the two are "behaving natural," that is, unfurtively and in accordance with the setting. Thus, from the point of view of matters external to the particular conversation, nothing much will be getting done through the conversation. In dramatic interaction this style is adhered to more or less but as a cover for high significance, on the assumption that nothing that occurs will be unportentous or insignificant. Which implies, incidentally, that the audience need not select what to attend to: whatever is made available can be taken as present for a good reason. As Langer suggests:

---

18. Considered in Elizabeth Burns, *Theatricality: A Study of Convention in the Theatre and in Social Life* (London: Longman Group, 1972; New York: Harper & Row, 1973), chap. 5, "Rhetorical Conventions: Defining the Situation," pp. 40–65. Note the contrast here with the filmwriter who can use flashbacks and flash forwards.

We know, in fact, so little about the personalities before us at the opening of a play that their every move and word, even their dress and walk, are distinct items for our perception. Because we are not involved with them as with real people, we can view each smallest act in its context, as a symptom of character and condition. We do not have to find what is significant; the selection has been made—whatever is there is significant, and it is not too much to be surveyed *in toto*. A character stands before us as a coherent whole. It is with characters as with their situations: both become visible on the stage, transparent and complete, as their analogues in the world are not.[19]

It is assumed, then, that the audience will take in the whole stage and not disattend any action occurring onstage. (After all, it takes something as large as a three-ring circus to be a three-ring circus.) Yet while the audience is reading the whole stage, characters onstage will act at times as though they themselves are disattending one another.

Here, incidentally, is an interesting contrast between stage and screen. Stage design allows one individual to take the center and claim the audience's prime attention; but *all* of him more or less will thus be put before the viewers. In movies, the spatial frame boundaries are much more flexible; there are long shots, mid-shots, and close-ups. By varying the angle and the closeness of the camera, a small gesture involving a small part of the actor's body can be blown up to fill momentarily the whole of the visual field, thereby assuring that the expressive implications of the gesture are not missed.

VI

I have described some eight transcription practices which render stage interaction systematically different from its real-life model.

19. Langer, *Feeling and Form*, p. 310. Burns provides another statement:

Moreover the audience is supposed to attend to everything that happens on the stage. In ordinary life the spectator selects the characters and events to which he will pay attention. But for the theatre audience the selection is of course made by dramatist, producer and performers. The spectator responds to their sign language and accepts their version of reality. [*Theatricality*, p. 228.]

Still other such conventions will be considered later. In any case, here is the first illustration of what will be stressed throughout: the very remarkable capacity of viewers to engross themselves in a transcription that departs radically and systematically from an imaginable original. An automatic and systematic correction is involved, and it seems to be made without its makers' consciously appreciating the transformation conventions they have employed.

As a further illustration of our ability to employ transformations, look for a moment at the dramatic scriptings presented on the radio stage—the radio drama frame.[20] Obviously, there are media restrictions that must be accepted: for example, in the early days, soprano high notes could blow out transmitter tubes, so crooning came into vogue;[21] and since a sharp increase in volume when volume was already high could not be handled, many sound effects (for example, gunshots) could not be employed.[22]

A basic feature of radio as the source of a strip of dramatic interaction is that transmitted sounds cannot be selectively disattended. For example, at a real cocktail party, an intimate conversation can be sustained completely surrounded by a babble of extraneous sound. A radio listener, however, cannot carve out his own area of attention. What the participant does in real life, the director has to do in radio and (to almost the same degree) on the stage. Therefore the following convention has arisen:

> In radio drama, spatial information is characteristically introduced at the beginning of a scene, then faded down or eliminated entirely. Unlike the everyday experience of reverberation in a kitchen, we cannot disattend reverberation running under the dialogue on radio. It is therefore introduced in the first few lines and faded out. The same rule operates for spatial transitions. Moving the scene from the city out to the country might be signaled by:
>
> MAN: I'll bet Joe and Doris aren't so hot out there in the country. (Music fades in, SFX [sound effects] birds chirping, fade out music, birds chirping runs under dialogue)
> JOE: Well, Doris, this country weather sure is pleasant.

20. Here I draw extensively on the previously cited unpublished paper by John Carey, "Framing Mechanisms in Radio Drama."

21. *Ibid.*

22. *Ibid.*

Within three lines, the birds will be faded out, though they might
return just before the transition back to the city.[23]

Similarly, there is the convention of allowing one or two low
sounds to stand for what would ordinarily be the stream of
accompanying sound. Again in both these examples the power of
automatic correction is evident: the audience is not upset by
listening in on a world in which many sounds are not sounded
and a few are made to stand out momentarily; yet if these conditions suddenly appeared in the offstage world, consternation
would abound.

Behind the need for these conventions is something worth
examining in more detail, something that might be called the
"multiple-channel effect." When an individual is an immediate
witness to an actual scene, events tend to present themselves
through multiple channels, the focus of the participant shifting
from moment to moment from one channel to another. Further,
these channels can function as they do because of the special role
of sight. What is heard, felt, or smelled attracts the eye, and it is
the seeing of the source of these stimuli that allows for a quick
identification and definition—a quick framing—of what has occurred. The *staging* of someone's situation as an immediate
participant therefore requires some replication of this multiplicity, yet very often replication cannot be fully managed. A protagonist in a radio drama will be in a realm in which things are
presumably seen, and in which things that are heard, felt, and
smelled can be located by sight; yet obviously the audience can
only hear.

As might be expected, conventions became established in radio
to provide functional equivalents of what could not otherwise be
transmitted. Sound substitutes become conventionalized for what
would ordinarily be conveyed visually. For example, the impression of distance from the center of the stage is attained by a
combination of volume control and angle and distance of speaker
to microphone. Also:

> By establishing a near sound, distant sounds, and intermediate
> sounds within a given scene, the production director can fairly
> accurately tell an audience the size of the scene they are hearing.
> If in a dramatic scene you hear a door open and a man's footsteps

———————
23. *Ibid.*

on a hollow wood porch, and then you hear him "Hellooo" a loud call which comes echoing back after a few seconds, the routine says that the scene is taking place in a large space.[24]

A second solution has been to anchor by verbal accompaniment such sounds as are employed, this assuring that what might otherwise be an isolated sound is identified as to character and source. ("Well, Pete [sound of key turning], let them try to open that lock.") However, ordinarily, natural talk does not proceed in this manner. During broadcasts, then, comments that have been chosen, or at least tailored, to lock a sound into a context must therefore be dissembled as "mere" talk; and again, this dissembling is systematically overlooked by the audience.

In addition to the "multiple channel effect," another element in the organization of experience can be nicely seen in the radio frame: syntactically different functions are accorded to phenomenally similar events. The question is that of the realm status of an event; and some sort of frame-analytical perspective is required in order for this question to be put. Two examples.

First. Music in actual, everyday life can function as part of the background, as when an individual works while records play or suffers Muzak in its ever increasing locations. Music can be accorded this in-frame background role in radio transcriptions of social activity—staged Muzak. (As might be expected, because in-frame music can also serve to set the scene for listeners, its first occurrence is likely to have foreground loudness; as the scene proceeds, however, the music will have to be progressively muted so that conversation can be heard.) But music can also be used as part of the radio drama frame to serve as a "bridge," a signal that the scene is changing, music being to radio drama in part what curtain drops are to staged drama. Such music does not fit *into* a scene but fits *between* scenes, connecting one whole episode with another—part of the punctuation symbolism for managing material in this frame—and therefore at an entirely different level of application than music within a context. Furthermore, still another kind of music will be recognized: the kind that serves to foretell, then mark, the dramatic action, a sort of aural version of subtitles. This music pertains to particular events that are devel-

24. Albert Crews, *Radio Production Directory* (New York: Houghton Mifflin Company, 1944), p. 67, cited in Carey, "Framing Mechanisms in Radio Drama."

oping in a scene, and even though it may terminate at the same time as the kind serving to link scenes or close the stage, its reference is much less holistic. Unlike background music, however, the protagonists "cannot," of course, hear it.[25] So syntactically there are at least three radically different kinds of music in radio drama; and yet, in fact, the same musical composition could be used in all three cases.[26] It would be correct to say here that the same piece of music is heard differently or defined differently or has different "motivational relevancies," but this would be an *unnecessarily* vague answer. A specification in terms of frame function says more.[27]

The second example involves consideration of sound volume. The attenuation of sound is used in the radio frame as a means of signaling the termination of a scene or episode, leading to the reestablishment of the drama at what is taken to be a different

---

25. Eileen Hsü, "Conflicting Frames in Soap Opera" (unpublished paper, University of Pennsylvania, 1970). Carey, "Framing Mechanisms in Radio Drama," provides a comment on the mechanics of this multiple level of use:

The board fade also told the listener if music was a vehicle for transition; if it was to act as mood lighting; or if it was part of the action on stage. For example, by establishing a perspective between music and a microphone, the director suggests that the music is on stage; by keeping mike distance constant and board fading, in the context of a cross fade between two characters, the director suggests that music is helping to make the transition; and by keeping mike distance constant while board fading in and out of a scene, the director suggests that the music indicates how the people in the scene feel or how you should feel about them.

26. The form of scripted drama called a musical provides a fourth role for music. A character may not only enact a performance of song or music (this having the same realm status as background music, merely a more prominent place), but may also "break into" musical expression as though this could be interposed in the flow of action without requiring a formal shift into the performer role. The lyrics and especially the mood of these songs will have something to do with the drama in progress, but how much is an awesomely open question. What the remaining characters do during these musical flights is itself complex and no less a departure from dramatic action than the offering itself. Here, then, is the Nelson Eddy syndrome. That we can suffer it (or almost) attests again to the immense flexibility of framing practices. Observe that the same suspension-of-action arrangement allows for the interposition of other delights—a dance turn, an instrumental rendition—accompanied or unaccompanied by voice.

27. There is an instructive parallel here in the organization of cartoons. As already suggested, the space enclosed in a response balloon is taken to be radically different from the space employed in depicting a scene, and the former can be enclosed in the latter without taking up any scenically real space.

time or place, or an "installment" termination—again, something handled on the stage by means of a curtain drop. This is done by a "board fade," that is, a reduction of transmission power. But reduction in sound level can also be achieved by having an actor or other sound source move away from the microphone. Attenuation of sound created by moving away from the microphone can be aurally distinguished from a board fade and is used *within* a scene to indicate that an actor is leaving the scene.

Note, in both the fading out of background music (to eliminate interference with the speakers) and the attenuation of sound owing to someone's going off-mike (to express leave-taking), the auditor is meant to assume that the frame is still operative, still generating a stream of hopefully engrossing events—events that are part of the unfolding story. Music bridges and board fades, however, are not meant to be heard as part of the "province of meaning" generated within a scene but rather as the beginning of what will be heard as between-scenes and out of frame.

VII

There are, then, systematic differences between the theatrical and the radio frame. Each is only one lamination away from an imaginably real model, but the transformations involve somewhat different conventions. As a second contrast to theater, look for a moment at the version of events provided in a novel.

First, novels and plays share important properties, indeed, do so along with other types of dramatic scripting. Whereas in real life each participant brings to an activity a unique store of relevant personal knowledge, attends to a slightly different range of detail, and presumably remains unaware of much that could be available to his perception, this is not so in the realm of dramatic scriptings. As already suggested, that which appears is preselected as what the audience must select out. In effect, then, all members of the audience are given the same amount of information.

Further, in plays and fiction, the audience assumes that what the writer chooses to inform them about up to any one point is all that they need in order to place themselves properly in regard to the unfolding events. It is assumed that nothing that ought to be known has been skipped; a full portrayal of the scene has been provided.[28] Of course, during any scene but the last, the audience may not be seeing what one or more of the characters are presumably seeing, but this ignorance is proper to the perspective the audience is meant to have at the moment. At the end the audience will be shown all it needs in order to arrive at a full understanding that the story intends. And as with unfolding events, so with unfolding characterization:

> When we read a novel, whatever we need to know about a character is revealed to us in the work. By the end of the work our awareness of the character has come to some kind of resting point. We know by then all that we wish to know. All the questions or problems that are raised by the character are resolved. If they are not, if the novel deliberately leaves the character ambiguous, the very ambiguity is a resting point. This is where we are meant to be left, the point of what we have read. It is ambiguity to be taken as ultimate, not one such as in actual life we seek to get beyond. In that sense one can say that characters exist for the sake of novels rather than novels for the sake of character.[29]

Along with this assumption of sufficiency goes another. It has already been suggested that lines uttered in plays provide required background information in the guise of otherwise determined talk. A similar conspiracy in the text of plays and novels allows for events to occur incidentally now that will be crucial later. Thus, a character who exhibits a capacity to draw resourcefully on such means as are at hand in order to solve a problem is drawing on what was earlier provided surreptitiously just so that this resourcefulness would be demonstrable now.[30] The same

28. Wayne C. Booth, *The Rhetoric of Fiction* (Chicago: University of Chicago Press, 1961), pp. 52–53. I have drawn considerably from Booth's very useful study and have much profited from sources that he cites.

29. Martin Price, "The Other Self: Thoughts about Character in the Novel," in Elizabeth and Tom Burns, eds., *Sociology of Literature and Drama* (London: Penguin Books, 1973), pp. 269–270.

30. One example from a spy story, Michael Gilbert's *Game without Rules* (New York: Harper & Row, 1967). The heavies (Cotter et al.) have dismembered the heroine's (Paula's) dog so that they can remind her father of their blackmail hold on him. Then the following "background" on Paula and her friend Richard, who have been sent to the country to induce an attack by Cotter:

One of the pleasantest features of their stay, thought Richard Redmayne, had been the efforts they had made to bring the place back to

can be said about other personal qualities, such as bravery, decisiveness, and so forth. Here in order to simulate what (it is taken) can be expressed about personal qualities in real life, a very central feature of real life must be completely abrogated, namely, that the individual will have to meet a developing situation with materials that were not assembled with the meeting of that situation in mind, since he could not possibly know at the time of assembly what would later prove to have been useful to assemble.

Consider now some differences between the novelistic and theatrical frames. It might seem theoretically possible to transform a play into a novel by the application of one rule: everything heard or seen by the audience could be simply rendered in printed words in an impersonal, authorial voice. Differently put, it would seem theoretically possible to write a novel, all of which

---

life. For a fortnight he and Paula and the dour Mrs. Mason had washed and scrubbed and scoured and sandpapered and painted. Paula had revealed several unexpected skills. First she had dismantled and cleaned the engine and dynamo which supplied them with electricity. Then, with the aid of a carload of technical stores from Norwich, she had stepped up the output, so that bulbs which had previously shone dimly now glowed as brightly as though they were on mains.

"My father taught me not to be afraid of electricity," she said. "It's just like water. You see water coming out of a tap. A nice steady flow. Halve the outlet, and you double the power. Like this." She was holding a length of hosepipe in her hand, swilling down the choked gutters in the yard. As she pinched the end of the hose, a thin jet of water hissed out.

"All right," said Richard ducking. "You needn't demonstrate it. I understand the principle. I didn't know it applied to electricity, that's all."

"Tomorrow," said Paula, "I'm going to get Mrs. Mason to stoke up the boiler, and I'm going to run a hose into the big barn. I'll use a proper stopcock, and we'll build up the pressure. Then you'll see what steam can do. Did you know that if you get a fine enough jet and sufficient pressure you could cut metal with steam?" [pp. 74–75]

required, of course, to set up the climax of the story:

Paula saw the danger out of the corner of her eye. She swung round and fired both barrels. The first missed altogether. The second hit the driver full in the chest. As she fired, she dropped the gun, put out a hand without hurry, laid hold of the steam hosepipe and flicked open the faucet.

A jet of scalding steam, thin and sharp as a needle, hissed from the nozzle and seemed to hang in the air for a moment, then hit Cotter full in the face as he stooped for his gun. He went forward onto his knees. The hose followed him down, searing and stripping. [Ibid., p. 79.]

could be staged by causing the characters to speak lines and to bear witness with the audience to audible effects offstage and audible and/or visible effects onstage. (Of course, there would be a complication: onlookers can directly see an actor's expressive behavior and do their own interpreting; readers must be told about this expressive behavior, and the describing of it cannot really be done without stating what the interpretation is to be.) Apparently, however, no novelist has thus restricted himself, although short-story writers have made an attempt. For the fiction frame presents the writer with fundamental privileges not available to the playwright; and at best these have been selectively forsworn.

Onstage, one character's interpretive response to another character's deeds, that is, one character's reading of another character, is presented to the audience and taken by them to be no less partial and fallible than a real individual's reading of another's conduct in ordinary offstage interaction would be. But authors of novels and short stories assume and are granted definitiveness; what they say about the meaning of a protagonist's action is accepted as fully adequate and true. That is a ground rule for the game of reading. Interestingly, a reader can spend his adult years writing about the imputational or constructive nature of personal characterizations and yet, when reading fiction, never once give pause to what he is letting the author get away with.

Furthermore, playwrights are obliged to tell their story through the words and bodily actions of all of their characters, these occurring currently, moment to moment, as the play progresses. Fiction writers enjoy two basic privileges in that connection. First, they can choose a "point of view," telling their story as someone outside of the characters or through the eyes of one of them, sometimes constructing a special character for this purpose.[31] Moreover, they can change this point of view from one

---

31. Here see Booth, *Rhetoric of Fiction*, esp. chap. 6, "Types of Narration," pp. 149–165; Norman Friedman, "Point of View in Fiction: The Development of a Critical Concept," *PMLA*, LXX (1955): 1160–1184; Michel Butor, "The Second Case," *New Left Review*, no. 34 (1965), pp. 60–68. Butor states:

If the character knew his own story entirely, if he had no objection to telling it, to others or to himself, the first person would be obligatory: he would be giving his evidence. But as a general rule, it is a question of forcing it from him, either because he is lying, because he is hiding

chapter or section to another or even employ multiple points of view in the same strip of action. Point of view itself can have, for example, spatial aspects, as when the narrator describes the physical scene from the perspective of a particular character, following the character as he moves along; a "temporal" aspect, whereby the author limits what he says to what a particular character could know at the time concerning what is then going on and what is going to happen—as suggested, a horizon or information state that the author can change, even to the point of "stepping into" the future of the character in question and alluding to what he is going to have to see as having been happening; and a "cultural" aspect, as when the writer casts his comments in the style and tone a particular character would presumably employ.[32]

Second, fiction writers, unlike playwrights, have the privilege of access to sources of information not derived from the perceivable scene in progress. Relevant past events and foretellings of future events can be introduced without going through the spoken words or current physical deeds of a character. A character's unexpressed thoughts and feelings can be directly told without makeshift devices such as the soliloquy. By the simple process of scripting a character to think about the part of his past that is contextually relevant for the current situation, and by surreptitiously taking over from him at that point and extending the job, fiction writers can add vast amounts to a story. In fact, anyone can:

> It looked like the dockworker was going to reach for his knife. John knew what to do. As a boy he had always been fascinated by knives and had managed to gather a large collection of them. He used to practice making passes and throwing them and had learned all about all the best holding positions. Six blocks from where he had

something from us or from himself or does not possess all its elements, or because, even if he does possess them, he is incapable of putting them together in the right way. The words spoken by the witness will take the form of islands in the first person within a story told in the second person which provokes them. [p. 64]

32. Here I draw on Boris A. Uspensky's "Study of Point of View: Spatial and Temporal Form," a preprint from his *The Poetics of Composition: Structure of the Artistic Text and the Typology of Compositional Form*, trans. Valentina Zavarin and Susan Wittig (Berkeley: University of California Press, 1974).

lived was Spanish Harlem and a gang on the border had adopted him, taught him what they knew when they saw how good he was. And he had come to be able to tell just by watching another's first move how much experience he was going to be up against. So now he felt no concern for himself. And he thought wryly that Mary must know something was wrong but not know what.

Think what a dramatist must do to get *that* in—assuming, of course, he wanted to. It might be added that novelists are in a position to refer explicitly to someone else's real or fictive text while writing it into their own (like reading someone's speech into the *Congressional Record*), thus providing readers a sense that they are in knowledgeable hands:

> Major Smythe remembered the rising flight of the scorpionfish, and he said aloud, with awe in his voice, but without animosity, "You got me, you bastard! By God, you got me!"
>
> He sat very still, looking down at his body and remembering what it said about scorpionfish stings in the book he had borrowed from the Institute and had never returned—*Dangerous Marine Animals*, an American publication. He delicately touched and then prodded the white area around the punctures. Yes, the skin had gone totally numb, and now a pulse of pain began to throb beneath it. Very soon this would become a shooting pain. Then the pain would begin to lance all over his body and become so intense that he would throw himself on the sand, screaming and thrashing about, to rid himself of it. He would vomit and foam at the mouth, and then delirium and convulsions would take over until he lost consciousness. Then, inevitably in his case, there would ensue cardiac failure and death. According to the book the whole cycle would be complete in about a quarter of an hour—that was all he had left—fifteen minutes of hideous agony! There were cures, of course—procaine, antibiotics and antihistamines—if his weak heart would stand them. But they had to be near at hand. Even if he could climb the steps up to the house, and supposing Dr. Cahusac had these modern drugs, the doctor couldn't possibly get to Wavelets in under an hour.[33]

So, too, a writer can editorialize by open authorial comment on what his characters are doing, or, more subtly and quite inevitably, by the "tone" he conveys in providing narrative continuity.

---

33. Ian Fleming, *Octopussy* (New York: New American Library, Signet Books, 1967), p. 53.

I have suggested how staged interaction differs from what it copies and how, in turn, radio and the novel differ from the stage. Observe that this argument is compatible with the folk notion that everyday life is to be placed on one side and the fanciful realms on the other. However, terms were introduced which begin to provide what will be needed in order to question this division.

6

Structural Issues
in Fabrications

I. *Retransformations*

The notion of primary framework has been defined, and it was argued that a strip of activity correctly perceivable as organized in terms of these frameworks is subject to two basic types of transformation, two basic replicating processes, each capable of littering the world with a multitude of copies: keyings and fabrications. Whatever the "actual" is, it is something that is subject to these two modes of recasting. Further, keyings themselves are subject to rekeying, a transformation of transformations. Now one must consider that, of course, fabrications, too, may enter in various ways into this process of retransformation. Indeed, examples of constructions have already been employed without the point being made that *re*transformations were involved.

According to the definitions so far employed, the innermost part of a framed activity must be something that does or could have status as untransformed reality. When this activity is not actually occurring but only serving as a model for a keying, then one can think of the strip that results as exhibiting one transformation and two layers or laminations—the modeled after and the modeled, the copied and the copy—and can see the outer layer, the rim of the frame, as establishing the status in reality of the activity. Together these two layers—untransformed events and their keyings—constitute a relatively simple "layering," one with two layers, not many: in a word, a layering that is shallow, not deep. Obviously, the layering of a frame, whether shallow or deep, will constitute an important element of its structure. Indeed, it is because of such layering that there is some warrant for using a term such as structure.

Every possible kind of layering must be expected. The sawing of a log in two is an untransformed, instrumental act; the doing of this to a woman before an audience is a fabrication of the event; the magician, alone, trying out his new equipment, is keying a construction, as is he who provides direction for the trick in a book of magic, as am I in discussing the matter in terms of frame analysis. An Avis girl serving a customer generates a simple bit of actual social reality; when a company agent is sent around incognito to see if service standards are being maintained (if indeed this spying happens), a vital test occurs, a transformation of what others contribute to her straight activity into a fabrication. And when we are faced with the following full-page ad:

> "Look, sister, I asked you for a red Plymouth convertible. Don't hand me any jazz about a reservation and don't tell me all you've got left are sedans. Just you get a wiggle on and try harder like your ads say. Or I'll find somebody who will."
>
> That's how our Mr. X carves out a living: bugging Avis girls. Just to see if he can wipe the smiles off their faces.
>
> . . . .
>
> Company spies aren't nice. But neither is being No. 2.
>
> The names of some Avis employees are reported to our president. Some will get his personal check for ten dollars for trying harder.
>
> Some won't.[1]

we are looking at a keying of a fabrication. So, too, the taking of drugs is an untransformed, instrumental act. And experiment in regard to drug taking is a keying. But, of course, if scientific control is to be sustained, it is likely that subjects will have to be split in two in a manner unbeknownst to themselves so that one set can take the drug and the other a placebo, just as it is likely that the specific hypotheses tested will have to be concealed from

---

1. *San Francisco Chronicle*, February 14, 1966.

them. So it will be necessary to have a fabrication of the keying. But yet another lamination is possible. The experimentalist Martin T. Orne, who has helped establish the argument that subjects in an experiment tend to provide the results they assume the experimenter is concerned to demonstrate, has attempted to prove his point (I think with great effect) by keying experiments in the following manner:

> A group of persons, representing the same population from which the actual experimental subjects will eventually be selected, are asked to imagine that they are the subjects themselves. They are shown the equipment that is to be used and the room in which the experiment is to be conducted. The procedures are explained in such a way as to provide them with information equivalent to that which would be available to an experimental subject. However, they do not actually go through the experimental procedure; it is only explained. In a non-experiment on a certain drug, for example, the participant would be told that subjects are given a pill. He would be shown the pill. The instructions destined for the experimental subjects would be read to him. The participant would then be asked to produce data as if he actually had been subjected to the experimental treatment. He could be given posttests, or asked to fill out rating scales or requested to carry out any behavior that might be relevant for the actual experimental group.[2]

Which provides us with a keying of a fabrication of a keying.

Just as one can have keyed fabrications, so also there can be fabricated keys, this time the rim of the frame lodged in a fabrication, not a keying. On Forty-second Street in New York, it is said, there are hustlers whose schtick is to dress and act shady, dart out from the shadows furtively, and offer a watch or ring very cheap, no questions asked, in apparent collusion with the prospect against law and order; but in fact, the goods offered are bought legitimately at a price which reflects their true worth, which is very little. Or the following: Escaping prisoners of war, wanting to make a dash across an open space between two prison buildings and needing to time their run to coincide with a particular phase of the sentry's round, used the stop-and-start feature of practicing in this way:

---

2. Martin T. Orne, "Demand Characteristics and the Concept of Quasi-Controls," in Robert Rosenthal and Ralph Rosnow, eds., *Artifact in Behavioral Research* (New York: Academic Press, 1969), pp. 155–156.

For several days we had arranged music practices in the evenings in the senior officers' quarters (the theatre block). The music was to be used for signalling, and we had to accustom the sentry in front of us to a certain amount of noise. . . . Douglas Bader, keeping watch from a window, acted as conductor. Their room was on the third floor, overlooking the German courtyard. Bader could see our sentry for the whole length of his beat. He was to start the practice at 7:30 P.M., when the traffic in the courtyard had died down. From 8 P.M. onwards he was to keep a rigid control on the players so that they only stopped their music when the sentry was in a suitable position for us to cross his path. It was not imperative that they stopped playing every time the sentry turned his back, but when they stopped playing that meant we could move. We arranged this signalling system because, once on the ground, we would have little concealment, and what little there was, provided by an angle in the wall of the outbuildings, prevented us from seeing the sentry.[3]

And it is not hard to find examples that add a layer to this frame structure but do not change the status of the rim. Thus, if a card game such as poker involves the license to bluff—a benign fabrication—then dealing "seconds" is obviously a transformation of this benign fabrication into the exploitive kind, since the whole of the game comes to be something in which the player is contained. The dealer at home, practicing his seconds—as professional dealers are wont to do whether they deal seconds or not—is keying an exploitive fabrication of a benign fabrication, as he is when he privately demonstrates his "action" to a prospective employer.

It should be noted that because a keying is already a mock-up of untransformed activity—a version often accomplished by one hand and a few bold strokes—the *retransformation* of this result into a rekeying or fabrication would seem to require less work than that entailed in the original transformation. Whatever it is that makes untransformed activity vulnerable to transformation makes transformations even more vulnerable to retransformations; and when the first is found, the second seems likely to follow. For example, if it is in the nature of vacuum cleaning that a salesman may engage in this act to sell a machine, thereby transforming a utilitarian doing into a demonstration, so it is in

---

3. P. R. Reid, *Escape from Colditz* (New York: Berkley Publishing Corp., 1956), p. 165.

the nature of such a transformation that it can be retransformed, as when a man employs this doing as a device to gain access to a house for improper purposes, or when a housewife allows the demonstration in bona-fide cases to proceed solely in order to get her carpet cleaned. Here, incidentally, the medical world figures strongly. There is some concern that someone not a physician might improperly enjoy himself in the role:

> Oklahoma City (UPI)—Police identified a 21-year-old Oklahoma City bill collector last week as the man who has been posing as a doctor to trick housewives into submitting to his advances.
>
> . . . .
>
> The suspect was arrested in Guthrie trying to persuade a 26-year-old mother to undress as a part of a health examination.
>
> Three other Oklahoma City area housewives have reported similar incidents to police in recent weeks. A typical case was that of a young woman who said the man told her he was a doctor and was checking for encephalitis, a mosquito-borne disease. All three said they undressed before they became suspicious.[4]

And, of course, there is some concern that properly qualified physicians might abuse the powerful license of their perspective, the power to transform what appears to be a nonmedical activity into a prescription:

> Los Angeles—A housewife has filed a $100,000 malpractice suit against a psychiatrist. She claimed he prescribed sexual relations with himself as therapy and then charged her for the "treatments."
>
> . . . .
>
> In the suit the 33-year-old mother of two said she had held the doctor in "complete confidence and trust." He persuaded her, she said, that her problems stemmed from a lack of sexual activity and suggested himself as a sexual partner.
>
> She said she agreed to the "treatments" for several months and then became "worried and remorseful" because he had stopped charging for the visits.
>
> Mrs. Keene said that when she implored him to stop the treatments, he criticized her sexual abilities and told her he was intimate only because she "was so available."
>
> Then he billed her for $225.[5]

---

4. *Las Vegas Sun*, November 26, 1964.
5. *San Francisco Chronicle*, May 25, 1966. As might be expected, the issue of where therapy leaves off and the real thing begins is the subject matter of a recent study by a psychiatrist, the monographic result of which

More important than occurrences, I think, is the framework tension associated with the subject, as exhibited in jokes, cartoons, stories, and the like. Terry Southern's *Candy* is a good example, a takeoff on regroundings as such, depicting how the most sexual of all activity might be encouraged as part of a yoga exercise, the avowed purpose of which was to achieve mastery over bodily functions and perfection of sensory control. Southern's use of a comic device to send up such faked regroundings is itself a device for providing readers with a disguise *they* will accept for pornography, since the reader is allowed to frame the text as a satire on the use of literary covers for dirty books.

When an ostensible key is used to cover deception, the persons taken in—contained—may not be present, may, indeed, be "society at large" or some other nebulous watchdog agency. Thus, a standard device for scouting pornography laws is to provide nudity shows under the guise of an art class. Recently New York's Forty-second Street strip provided a further twist:

> This year, simulated sex shows came to New York. Imported from the West Coast, performances in New York are presented in the guise of an educational experience. Patrons, so the signs say, do

---

might be seen as having what is sometimes called "a wider audience." (See Martin Shepard, M.D., *The Love Treatment: Sexual Intimacy between Patients and Psychotherapists* [New York: Peter H. Wyden, 1971].)

All of this provides examples of fabricated keyings. Medical action, of course, opens up the possibility of (and concern about) using *ordinary* medical procedures as a front for improper action, that is, as a fabrication. A line, therefore, must be drawn between actions that just get by—for example, not quite necessary operations because the hospital has a surgical program—and the following, an out-and-out fabrication.

> Tacoma, Wash.—A jury of eight men and four women convicted Dr. Robert E. Boehme last night on a charge that he tried to kill his wife by giving her an injection while she was in the hospital.
> . . . .
> He is accused of giving his wife, Mary, 33, a toxic injection last June 30 while she was hospitalized here for a head injury. [*San Francisco Chronicle*, February 7, 1966.]

Injection of extermination camp prisoners fits the same frame structure, except that in those cases only the patients were kept in the dark as to what was really happening.

May I add that children who play doctor for naughty reasons are sustaining a frame structure no less complicated than the ones described above. The medicine that is practiced during this play is very childish, but the competency exhibited in regard to framing is already fully adult.

not come to see a sex show; they come to find out how one is filmed. The M.C. circles a fake movie set with a home movie camera, occasionally stopping to bark directions.[6]

Just as keyings can be transformed into fabrications, so, too, of course, fabrications can be transformed into still other fabrications; in brief, containment can be recontained. So, too, fabrications seem particularly subject to this proliferation. Exploitive constructions provide the obvious examples. A tidy one is provided in the technique apparently employed by an accused rapist:

> Jack Payton, 48, of N. Wilton St. near Arch, was sentenced after pleading guilty to assaulting, raping, and robbing a 35-year-old nurse last Feb. 14. He also was sentenced to concurrent prison terms on charges of assaulting three other women.
>
> . . . .
>
> Several victims complained the rapist had approached them, wearing a ski-mask and carrying a knife. He told them, they said, that he had just committed a robbery—and then forced them to walk with him as "cover" to throw off police.
>
> Instead, the women said, they were pulled into alleys or led into vacant houses and raped.[7]

And everyday examples can be found. When a member of a domestic or work organization decides on an action that will be considered disloyal (such as leaving), he is likely to continue as if nothing were up until the right moment. He thus contains those with whom he lives or works. Discovering this disloyalty, the discoverers need only do nothing overt about it and they have made a charade of his charade.

Exploitive fabrications are not, however, the only beginnings for refabrication. Benign fabrications can be exploitively fabricated: some patients who feel they have been railroaded into the

---

6. *Time*, October 19, 1970. It might be noted that apparently when Ken Kesey's Merry Pranksters drove across the country in their school bus, they managed, on occasion, to deal with the local law and local citizenry by taking movies of efforts to control and inspect the troupe, thus causing the locals to be uncertain regarding frame, that is, uncertain as to whether actual activity was occurring or a sort of movie-making. Responses to the Pranksters were thus expropriated and made part of the movie, even if this involved "Breaking up the cop movie," that is, the one put on by their competitors. See Tom Wolfe's impressive treatment, *The Electric Kool-Aid Acid Test* (New York: Farrar, Straus & Giroux, 1968), esp. pp. 68–104.

7. *Philadelphia Inquirer*, January 23, 1969.

mental hospital for improper reasons have been right. Self-deception can also be fabricated. If the affectation of a medical symptom is the fabrication of a natural event purportedly to be perceived within a natural framework, so the simulation of delusion in order to obtain a psychiatric diagnosis—as when an effort is made to avoid military service by feigning mental illness—is a fabrication of a fabrication. Incidentally, an interesting contrast here is provided in what its practitioners label "direct analysis":

> The patient's delusion is a deception practiced for the purpose of gaining a remote or unobtainable object. His unconscious invents, lies, connives, disguises, and does magic to this end. When the delusion is finally organized, it may or may not be accompanied by anxiety. The absence of anxiety attests to a diabolic efficiency. So long as the delusional system remains so efficient, it interferes with movement toward the resolution of the psychosis. In this situation, as soon as possible, I employ a device called the trick against the trick.
>
> The procedure must be carried out with assistants who are drilled in their parts. A patient believed her father was condemned to death in the state capital. I had the family foregather and produced a spurious reprieve from the governor. . . .
>
> Certain paranoid patients think they are current political figures, great historical figures or divine religious figures. In order to have the patient who is always suspicious of you encouraged to abandon this suspicion, you act as though there is no doubt that they are who they say they are. Before Christ and the Holy Trinity you bend your knee and cross yourself. For Moses, Abraham and others, you become reverential in the tradition of the Old Testament.[8]

Of course, therapy is not the only reason for entering and guiding delusional systems. The chief of Hitler's secret service apparently had other reasons:

> However, it was relatively easy to discover that Mussolini was held prisoner on the small island of Maddalena; the real difficulty was to convince Himmler of the fact. As he had confidence only in his

---

8. John N. Rosen, M.D., *Direct Analysis* (New York: Grune & Stratton, 1953), p. 22. Compare the staged containment in Luigi Pirandello's *Henry IV*, wherein the hero, disappointed in the loyalty of his loved ones, feigns madness, feigns he is a medieval king, then gets his erstwhile loved ones to perform corresponding parts to him in his private asylum. They think they are entering his delusion in order to pacify him; he is containing them in order to enjoy his disgust.

magicians, a seance had to be carefully prepared; and the Reich-fuhrer finally had Mussolini's place of detention revealed to him by a pot-bellied, bald old medium in an impressive trance.

This incident was by no means exceptional. More than once Schellenberg had to produce some frightened fortune-teller in order to overcome Himmler's reluctance to take a decision.[9]

The focus can be narrowed to the everyday. For example, some service trades (and not merely that of professional medium) owe a portion of their income to "taking cases" deriving from palpably unsound projects. An indictable example from the private investigator field is given:

> Private detective Irv Kohn was arrested yesterday and charged with bilking $24,000 from a heartbroken mother who asked him to find her dead son.
>
> The son of 70-year-old Elizabeth Stevens, William, 38, shot himself to death here in October, 1961—some two years before she engaged Kohn to find him, the District Attorney's office said.
> . . . .
> "She has difficulty accepting the fact of her son's death," said one of Kohn's attorneys, James Purcell.
>
> "Kohn promptly found out her son was dead and told her to stop wasting her money," Purcell added.
>
> But witnesses told the Grand Jury, Mrs. Stevens, who resides at a hotel at 41 Jones Street, paid $24,000 to Kohn during the period from October, 1963, to August of 1965.[10]

And a generalization from the trade:

> An electronics company president told senators yesterday his firm does a flourishing business in selling [bugging] devices to "the man who wants to act his daydreams of being a flesh-and-blood James Bond."[11]

Also shopkeepers who allow a customer to state his wishes and then encourage him to satisfy them by complimenting his choice

---

9. Gilles Perrault, *The Secrets of D-Day,* trans. Len Ortzen (London: Arthur Barker, 1965), p. 133.

10. *San Francisco Chronicle,* June 11, 1966. Here I am grateful to Howard S. Becker. Private detectives are the unsung heroes of the psycho-therapeutic professions, being willing to take upset persons seriously when no available therapist is, and although interest in a fee seems to be in-volved, this is, after all, an interest known to physicians.

11. *Ibid.,* June 10, 1966.

are not considered to be entering and sustaining a delusional belief, although it is difficult to say why this particular form of containment should be exempt from blame. And policemen who take an easy and perceivedly humane way out with psychotics are similarly seen as only doing their job:

> In direct dealings with the patient the policeman tries to establish and maintain the pretense of a normal conversational situation. All of the patient's remarks, allegations, or complaints are treated in a matter-of-fact manner. Policemen do not attempt to suppress or eliminate the absurd and bizarre, but rather leave them aside while concentrating verbal exchanges on the ordinary aspects of things. By this method every situation acquires a certain sense of normalcy. For example, in one observed instance a middle-aged lady complained, in highly agitated panic, that she was pursued by neighbors with an unheard-of weapon. Without questioning the lady's beliefs about what is possible in the domain of weaponry, or what might be reasonably assumed about the motives of angry neighbors, the officers went through the motions of dealing with the situation as if it involved a bona fide complaint. They searched the premises for nonexistent traces of impossible projectiles. They carefully took note of mundane particulars of events that could not have happened and advised the lady to be on the alert for suspicious occurrences in the future.[12]

II. *The Nature of Recontainment*

There is a popular view that the fabrication of fabrication can be typified by the Big Con; the dupes are innocents who have allowed avarice to misguide them into helping (they think) with a financial conspiracy, and the operators are criminals who play characters utterly alien and false for them, doing so by means of elaborate props temporarily assembled for the occasion. If this view were valid, the world would be a less treacherous place than it is.

---

12. Egon Bittner, "Police Discretion in Emergency Apprehension of Mentally Ill Persons," *Social Problems*, XIV (1967): 288–289. There is an interesting line to draw between this kind of charade (setting aside the issue of how frequently it actually occurs) and the mild, tactful support that fellow conversationalists give to someone with a strong pet peeve.

1. Consider the standard forms of recontainment in our society.

a. First "secret monitoring." When an individual maintains a position that can be discredited (and thus sustains a fabrication of some kind), it is very likely that there will be some place and occasion in which his actions provide the evidence that could accomplish this. His position is saved, of course, by his controlling who it is who witnesses this discrediting behavior.[13] In this context, to hear or to see is to acquire the power to destroy—not, of course, the act that is witnessed but the act the performer puts on at other times. Insofar as the monitor does not immediately allow the monitored to know that monitoring is occurring—and that, of course, is entirely the usual procedure—then what occurs is a species of recontainment wherein the current conduct of the person who monitors sets a trap for the later conduct of the monitored.

The standard example here is wiretapping by police and other government agencies of those suspected of crimes. Insurance agencies also provide exemplary cases:

> Mervin Clayton sat rigidly in the chair, carefully swiveling his entire upper torso rather than his neck if he needed to look in another direction.
>
> He told the City Retirement Board yesterday that the neck injury he suffered last December fighting a fire still prevented him from moving his neck from side to side, or turning his head "without excruciating pain" in his back and arms.
>
> Enter Detective Richard Rasmussen and his home movies.
>
> The flicks showed a five-minute sequence of Clayton, 49, at a cabin in Squaw Valley gracefully shoveling snow, lifting logs and stacking them, working in his garden, and driving his car.
>
> "That's the kind of work a housewife would do," protested the fireman—still rigid in both his posture and diagnosis. "It is not the equivalent of a fireman's duty."

---

13. Here again ordinary language is ambiguous. When we say an act is discreditable we mean either that it can be discredited by some available bit of information or that it itself can destroy some other show, in short, either that it is vulnerable to discreditation or productive of discrediting. In this study I lean to the first usage. Thus, a *discrediting* act becomes one that can give the lie to a *discreditable* one.

The Board didn't agree, revoked Clayton's $542.03-a-month pension, and sent him back to work.[14]

Discreditable testimonials are of interest to the law. The secret monitoring of what discredits them can therefore be given legal warrant. The secret monitoring of what is discrediting to shows that are outside the province of the law is often seen as having no warrant at all:

> *Dear Abby:* I know it was wrong, but I read some letters my daughter received from her boy friend and I've been crushed, frustrated and heartsick ever since. She is 22, works in a university town and has been dating a student there. She's brought him home for weekends and he seemed so fine. She has repeatedly condemned girls who have had to get married, but her sin is worse because we are Catholics and do not believe in birth control, which she apparently has been practicing. She goes to church and confession, yet she continues in this behavior, which the boy's letters reveal.[15]

And from here there is a natural transition to monitoring which would very widely be defined as improper, namely, the kind that nullifies the right of those in the appropriate context to maintain purely strategic secrets, as opposed, that is, to the "dark" ones which undercut character, not merely plans. Take, for example, the secrets that card games are designed to allow players to keep from one another and upon which false shows regarding one's hand are allowably constructed:

> An eye in the ceiling may have cost some of the world's best gin rummy players a million dollars.
>
> Behind the windowless walls of Beverly Hills' exclusive Friars Club, checks for huge gambling losses have been changing hands since 1961.
>
> . . . .
>
> A Federal Grand Jury has been investigating reports of crooked gambling for more than a month, and—although there have been

---

14. *San Francisco Chronicle*, September 7, 1967. It is difficult to keep up with technological developments in the field of surveillance. A glimpse of the art up to 1967 is provided by Alan F. Westin, *Privacy and Freedom* (New York: Atheneum Publishers, 1970), chap. 4, "The Listening and Watching Devices: New Techniques of Physical Surveillance," pp. 69–89.

15. *San Francisco Chronicle*, November 4, 1965.

no indictments and much of the inquiry is still secret—a pattern now emerges.

In two different card rooms at the club, peepholes were installed in attic spaces above the gaming tables. From these vantage points a hidden observer, using optical devices, could read cards held by players.

In the observer's hand was an electronic sending device similar to a Morse Code transmitter.

Strapped to the arm or leg of the observer's confederate in the card room below was a receiving device called a tapper, which gave silent taps as the key was pressed on the sending set.[16]

It could be argued that a basic assumption about social life is violated by these various forms of monitoring. We expect that some places will exist where privacy is ensured, where only a known number of persons will be present, and where such persons will be only those of a given category. Here, presumably, the individual can conduct himself in a manner that would discredit his standard poses were the facts known; and, of course, it is just these places that are the best ones to bug. This is the principle behind the notion of putting a one-way mirror in the school toilet,[17] for it is there that drug negotiations are likely to occur if any do occur on the premises. (In brief, bug the backstage.) It is only one step further to provide suspects with what looks like a private room so that they can then and there feel inclined to discuss strategic secrets.[18] Similarly, in card games, the arrangement by which a player is allowed and even obliged to shield his cards (that is, prevent the identification of his holdings) allows him to commit himself to secrets thus hidden, which, in turn, generates the circumstances in which improper monitoring becomes useful—and practicable.

The final transition, of course, is to quite ordinary proper behavior. For in everyday life it seems routine that howsoever the individual presents himself on any occasion before any audience, there will be other places, times, and audiences when he quite

---

16. *Ibid.*, July 4, 1967.

17. See Bill Cooney's article, " 'Spy' Mirrors in School Washrooms," *ibid.*, November 19, 1963.

18. A review of the use of secret monitoring to provide uncensored data for those who would improve sales, services, servers, and so on, is given by Westin, *Privacy and Freedom*, pp. 112–113.

properly conducts himself in a manner that would discredit this first performance were his other conduct to be vividly brought to light. Barriers to communications such as walls and distance, along with audience segregation, ensure that such discrediting will not occur. *Any* monitoring of *any* individual's behavior that he does not know about will then have a discrediting power; all forms of secret surveillance function to undermine later activity, transforming it into a discreditable performance.[19]

I have argued that one who is vulnerable to secret monitoring is engaging in a false show that can be discredited by what has been monitored, and that, analytically, the main focus of concern is not upon the activity that is monitored but upon the later activity that is discredited by what has been monitored. Two qualifications must now be mentioned.

First, if the monitoring has been done by someone in a personal relationship to the one who is monitored, then, of course, this relationship is discredited, for adult relationships are likely to be defined in terms that exclude this sort of spying.

Second, consider the scene that is monitored. It seems almost inevitable that should the unsuspecting performers find they are giving themselves away, that is, giving the lie to some other show they will attempt to maintain, then they can hardly help but engage in some hasty effort to cover what is exposed. Flusterings, clumsy movements, and self-consciousness result; in short, behavioral disorganization, a vain effort to push the scene backward in time so that it can be replayed guardedly. A woman claims to have been crippled grievously by a car accident. In order to attack her insurance claim, company-employed investigators spy on her until they can get a picture of her, say, bowling a strike.[20] In which case, not only will her courtroom appearance

---

19. Suggested in "Normal Appearances" in *R.P.*, pp. 286–303. An interesting example is found in the contingencies established by television coverage, especially coverage of an event that has been accorded little of this treatment in the past. At the state funeral of President Kennedy participants who were away from the immediate bereaved and the center of ritual did what is quite standard in these circumstances: they got caught up in little conversations or "aways" and drifted from the official ethos of the occasion; they smiled, laughed, became animated, bemused, distracted, and the like. The transmission of this behavior by the roving camera discredited their expression of piety otherwise displayed and no doubt initiated a shift to greater carefulness by officials at official occasions.

20. Case reported in *The Boston Globe*, November 24, 1966.

be discredited, but also, should she, in the middle of a bowling match, spot the investigator at work, her game will likely be thrown off, too. As would, similarly, a crime-planning session at the moment the planners discover their quarters have been bugged and that continuation of the session can hardly be fruitful. In this way one can begin to account for the furor created when a teacher discovers that a pupil, with the moral support of his father, is secretly taping her classes to collect evidence of her political persuasion; relations with parents and the conduct of *current* classes both become unsettled.[21]

b. Secret monitoring, then, can constitute one form of recontainment. Another can be produced by penetration—the process whereby an agent who is disloyal to a team exploits legitimate (as opposed to clandestine) access to social settings in which the team's strategic or dark secrets are unguarded or their discrediting conduct is observable. Penetration may occur either by "turning" a member who had been in good standing or by infiltration.[22] Recent developments in drug use and political radicalism have focused attention on the practice of penetrating organizations, groups, and milieus:

> Pretty coed, Mrs. Linda Hobbie, who was enrolled as a special student in film art at Fairleigh Dickinson University, Madison, N.J., was uncovered as an undercover narcotics agent spying on students. She was planted after officials noticed an abnormal amount of drugs being used.[23]

---

21. Reported in *Life*, April 26, 1963, in an article entitled, "Hell Breaks Loose in Paradise." A similar furor, leading to a teacher's resignation, occurred when the mother of three of the teacher's pupils posed as a teen-age student and then reported very critically on the quality of the teaching. (*San Francisco Chronicle*, October 9 and 12, 1963.)

22. The history of infiltration has yet to be written. Torquemada and Richelieu were certainly innovators in the use of variously stationed spies. The Sûreté, founded in 1810, was the first police organization to make systematic use of infiltration and informing in the criminal (as opposed to political) realm, and under its founder, Eugène Vidocq, provided the world with a model for criminal intelligence organization. Pinkerton was the first in America to develop the practice of infiltrating criminal gangs—from the mid-nineteenth century—and his organization was, of course, employed by the Union to spy during the Civil War, thus reversing the usual move from political spying practices to domestic ones. (Here see Jürgen Thorwald, *The Marks of Cain* [London: Thames & Hudson, 1965], p. 130.) The czarist Ochrana was also an innovator in infiltration practices.

23. *Boston Record American*, March 17, 1967.

> Atlantic City, Aug. 17—The work of a youthful-looking state police officer, who posed as a high school senior, led today to a series of narcotics raids in which 37 persons were arrested here and in surrounding communities.
>
> . . . .
>
> The raids, which started at 5 o'clock this morning, followed nine months of investigation, during which the 25-year-old policeman attended classes daily as an enrolled student at Atlantic City High School.
>
> Only William Faunce, the school principal, knew his identity, which is still being kept secret. "He blended right in with the other students and they accepted him," Mr. Faunce said.[24]

It should be added that public interest in "inside stories" has led journalists to penetrate organizations and social movements, a practice that is illustrated, for example, by an article subtitled "A *Life* Reporter Who Joined a 'Committee' Incognito Tells an Inside Story."

> In September, *Life* Reporter Sam Angeloff, using his middle name, Tony, joined up incognito with the antiwar Vietnam Day Committee at the University of California (Berkeley). To learn how marches like those shown here happen, he spent four weeks helping organize them.[25]

The sociological technique of participant-observation ordinarily involves a degree of infiltration, too, for even when the student informs his subjects that he is engaged in studying them, they are unlikely to appreciate in detail what sorts of facts he is collecting and which of the appearances they maintain will be discredited by these facts.

As a process, penetration tends to be attributed to the world of political, criminal, and industrial intrigue, and the whole matter has a storybook air. This should not, however, lead one to overlook the importance of penetration in everyday life. Firsthand gossip, the kind told by an actual witness, tends to entail betrayal and what is in effect the penetration of the betrayed circle. Whatever a wife tells her lover about her husband, the lover has learned by virtue of having penetrated the family circle—only in effect, of course, because presumably the guiding intent of the

---

24. *The New York Times,* August 18, 1967.
25. *Life,* December 10, 1965.

lover is not to acquire this sort of information, its acquisition
being an incidental gain or cost of the relationship.[26]

   c. A consideration of penetration leads easily to another
process: "entrapment." This is the activity through which a discrediting act is called forth by a *provocateur* on the grounds that
he is a proper person with whom to share the secret world. Entrapment thus is an active form of penetration; instead of waiting
for incriminating events (or ones otherwise usable against the
dupe), the vulnerable activity is induced:

> Reno (UPI)—Attorney Harry Busscher, arrested in a dramatic
> courtroom incident last February by district attorney's officers, was
> found guilty last night of subornation of perjury.
>
> . . . .
>
> Busscher was arrested during a recess of the divorce case he was
> trying in district court after a witness allegedly perjured himself
> when he testified that one of Busscher's clients met Nevada resi-
> dency requirements for divorce.
>
> The client, Ben Wood of Oakland, Calif., testified at Busscher's
> trial that he was actually an undercover agent for the district
> attorney and that he had been in California during the period he
> was to have met the residency regulation.
>
> Wood said Busscher told him it could "be arranged" for him to
> meet the requirements so he could obtain a six-week Nevada
> divorce.[27]

----

26. The lover's strategic position has some interest here. He (to employ
the grammatical sex) not only receives information he should not have,
but he also can divulge information about himself in comparative security
since the recipient cannot relay these facts without endangering the position she is trying to maintain, namely, that of someone who could not possibly be in a position to acquire this sort of information. Thus, the strategic
weakness of legitimate relationships is that facts divulged or witnessed in
them are subject to easy betrayal. Of course, the lover's position has some
strategic weaknesses, too. Over time, the errant spouse is likely to find
reason to goad her husband with what she has done, or, perhaps more
commonly, to confess in order to provide evidence that a sincere effort is
now being made to give the marital relationship another chance. This
betrayal of the betrayal is sometimes not betrayed, in which case it is the
lover, not his loved one's spouse, who ends up in the dark, not knowing
who knows what. There are two other possibilities. The errant spouse may
secretly confess that she has confessed, thus restoring a little of the lover's
prior edge. Or the reestablished marital couple can agree to inform the
lover that the affair has been confessed (and is presumably over) and that
this informing has been jointly sanctioned. All in all, then, your seducer
often ends up having no say in what is said.

27. *Las Vegas Sun*, December 12, 1964.

A common form of entrapment is the one employed by journalists and better business bureaus in response to those who extend exploitive offers, whether offers of an intrinsically dubious kind or dubious of their kind. Thus, agencies that hard-sell land in Florida might want to anticipate being set upon by a journalist and his wife who pose as an interested couple, go through the whole hard-sell process, including bugged closing room, and then depart with a salable commodity that isn't land.[28] Dancing schools, matchmaking agencies, income tax services,[29] and door-to-door magazine salesmen have also had cause for suspicion. Psychiatric hospitals, purporting to be psychiatric and hospitals, have been misused in this fashion.[30] TV repairmen have reason for care also, for the Law can appear in many guises:

> New York (AP)—Teresa Heath and Joan Stephroe made sure their television sets were in perfect working order, then they made separate calls to Phillip's TV Rental and Repair Service.
>
> Miss Heath said Phillip Schwartz, operator of the service, took her set and later returned it with a bill for $50.30. In addition, she claimed, he had replaced some new parts with secondhand parts.
>
> Miss Stephroe reported Schwartz presented her with a $46 bill for unneeded repairs. Schwartz was charged yesterday with petty larceny, false advertising and conspiracy.
>
> Housewives Heath and Stephroe were detectives assigned to the Manhattan district attorney's office, which had received complaints about Schwartz' operation.[31]

Three techniques of recontainment have been reviewed: secret monitoring, penetration, and entrapment. All three are subject to much moral and legal concern, to strict limits of various kinds, and to attendant disputes about the enforcement of these limits. These recontainments are thought not nice; although the legality

---

28. See Al Hirshberg, "Hard Sell in Boom Land," *Life*, November 13, 1964. The subtitle of the article is "A House-Hunting Couple Gets the Full Treatment at Florida's Cape Coral." Perhaps a more accurate description would be "An Article-Hunting Couple Gives the Full Treatment at Florida's Cape Coral."

29. See Owen Edwards, "Many Happy Returns," *New York Magazine*, March 15, 1971.

30. Recently, for example, by Ann Barry, as reported in her *Belleview Is a State of Mind* (New York: Harcourt Brace Jovanovich, 1971).

31. *The Evening Bulletin* (Philadelphia), December 30, 1971.

of engaging in them varies considerably, a question of ethics always exists.

Secret monitoring is currently a matter of active controversy. For example, in 1965 senatorial investigation disclosed that Internal Revenue offices in various cities had apparently been using "surveillance rooms," not only so that citizens could secretly identify racketeers, but also so that officials could learn about the secrets ordinary taxpayers might be sharing with their lawyers; after disclosure of this collection practice, corrective action was promised by the IRS commissioner.[32] A similar issue has arisen as a consequence of the miniaturization of radio transmitters. These devices allow for concealed placement on a willing informant who thus becomes transformed into a fully mobile human microphone who can secretly retransmit to a distant receiver any conversation he can manage to join. The legitimacy of fighting crime in this way became a legal case carried all the way to the Supreme Court—which in 1971 ruled in favor of allowing the procedure.[33]

Entrapment, even more than secret monitoring, is restricted by law[34] and morality. In some cases this restriction appears to be due to the deep understanding that a potential offender should

---

32. See *San Francisco Chronicle*, July 14, 1965.

33. *Time*, April 19, 1971.

34. Which from the perspective of law enforcement agents can be seen as quite strict, as Wayne R. LaFave, *Arrest* (Boston: Little, Brown and Company, 1965), suggests in his discussion of the work plainclothesmen do with prostitutes:

Not only is the experienced prostitute often able to identify plainclothes officers, but she may routinely avoid making any statements encompassing all three elements [of legal evidence].

As a consequence, the police have considerable difficulty obtaining convictions in accosting cases. Judges frequently dismiss such prosecutions, giving as a reason the defense of entrapment, or "enticement" in situations where it is doubtful whether the doctrine of entrapment, as defined in appellate opinions, is applicable. According to the police, dismissals have been granted in accosting cases where the officer used a Cadillac, because "everyone knows that the police officers use cheap cars"; where the officer disguised himself as a taxi driver or uniformed laborer; where the officer made a telephone call to a number which he had obtained and which he was told belonged to a prostitute; where the officer stopped his car beside a prostitute on a street corner when she had not beckoned to him; and where the officer bought the girl a few drinks or otherwise spent some time with her before the accosting. [p. 458]

not be unduly tempted into offense; certainly (it is felt) an undercover agent should not himself initiate the indictable offense, as appears to have been done, for example, by such practiced police spies as "Tommy the Traveler."[35]

These restrictions on recontainment, however, should not blind us to the fact that persons so engaged are overwhelmingly associated in one way or another with law enforcement agencies. Indeed, it is one of the conceits of the age that at a time when stage actors are generally suspected of being effete, the real acting is being staged by the very best representatives of the stolid masculine classes, sturdy dress-up artists who take on parts under circumstances of risk that trained actors might never accept. No doubt the arm of the law provides some assurance for these amateur-professionals. How else to account for the willingness, say, of a high school teacher, who, acting on the request of the police, drifts into a student conversation about weed and lets it be known that he is in short supply, later making half a dozen buys from campus pushers, this leading in due course to the arrest of the ring, consisting of four students.[36] Of course, more than legal license is involved. Behind an undercover agent is some unit of government, and apparently we feel that disguise on behalf of such an agency is usually acceptable, even praiseworthy, however differently the dupes may feel. This profound license is a framing convention; it transforms self-interest into selflessness and insulates a misrepresenter from the immorality of misrepresentation. Insulates as might a game. But here the game engulfs the world and is played against persons who may fail to recognize that they have become players.

The restrictions on recontainment mentioned so far bear on the person betrayed, the issue being that the potential offender ought to be given a reasonable chance of restraining himself and not be guilty unless he acts on his own instigation. But another limit is placed on entrapment, this one as interesting from the perspective of frame analysis as the last: to wit, what role behav-

---

35. Whose extensive work at various universities is reported in *Time*, June 22, 1970.

36. Reported in *San Francisco Chronicle*, June 6, 1965, under the banner, "How Galileo [High School] 'Dope Ring' Was Broken." The news report provides no comment concerning the relationship this fine actor had thereafter to the student community.

ior ought a *provocateur* abjure because of the contaminating character of the behavior itself? For behind some restrictions on recontainment is an appreciation of the limits of transformation. For example, some indecent acts done to trick individuals into betraying themselves are acts that cannot be performed without somehow polluting their doer in something of the way he would be polluted were he to perform the act straight, not as a construction:

> Tallahassee, Fla.—A disclosure that college boys are being used as bait to trap homosexuals brought protests yesterday from Florida State University officials and the Governor.
>
> "As great as the need may be to expose sexual deviates, the procedure of involving college students in the process seems altogether wrong," said Dr. Harry Day, dean of students. "It is hoped the practice will not be continued."
>
> Police Chief Frank Stoutamire and assistant chief Robert Maige confirmed reports circulating for weeks that students are paid $10 each for part-time work as informers against sex offenders.[37]

2. Secret monitoring, penetration, and entrapment as forms of recontainment are different from the classic con game kind in one particular: little by way of extensive props are required for the job, even though the trickster may need to assume a part not his own. Now one should go on to see that those who would contain others, expose themselves not only to the somewhat disguised or the somewhat concealed, but also to those who can do the job merely by persisting to be themselves.

When individuals plan illegal acts or have salable secrets, they run the risk of team-member defection. So, too, when individuals attempt to deal in contraband, or bribe someone into betraying an organization, or engage in various forms of extortion, they open themselves up to being set up, as they do when they attempt a con; the person put upon need only complain to the police and he is likely to be asked to play along until the right time. Here, note, the person who thus contains the would-be aggressor need not wear a disguise or acquire props; and certainly he need not assume a false biographical identity. He need only go on doing what he ordinarily would be doing—he is cast correctly, already

---

37. *San Francisco Chronicle*, December 29, 1965.

has the props, knows the lines.[38] All of which directs attention from the vulnerability of those subject to secret monitoring, penetration, and entrapment, to the vulnerability of those who would engineer these recontainments.

It is perfectly clear that when one individual is contained by another, the fabricator has power over the contained. Disclosure negates this power. However, when one party discovers he is contained, obviously denouncement of the other is not the only possibility. Ordinarily a strategically sounder one, as already suggested, is for the discovering party to continue temporarily to act as if no discovery has been made, thus radically transforming the situation into one in which containment is itself contained. An opportunity to bring everyone to the same footing has been temporarily forgone, inevitably resulting in the creation of another layering to the frame. Although often what has occurred is merely cognitive, something subjectively located within the mind of the one who makes the discovery he does not disclose having made, still a fundamental strategic event has taken place, one with objective import for the flow of events, as will be seen when the discoverer springs the trap that his inaction has baited. Indeed, here "acting as though nothing were wrong," concealing everything in one's head, becomes a very real strategic move, a juncture in the flow of events where a behavioristic, objective view quite misses the fundamental facts.

It follows that the professional monitor, infiltrator, or entrapper is made vulnerable by the vulnerability he produces in others. All that is required to bring about his downfall is for his dupes to discover what is happening and do nothing about disclosing their discovery. Continuing on with what they would otherwise be doing but now taking special care to lead the opponent astray, the duped can easily dupe, and amateurs can defeat the professionals. As one might say, the frame can be reversed.[39] Of

_____

38. An argument developed in "Normal Appearances," in *R.P.*, esp. pp. 270–277.

39. Sometimes called "turning the tables" and the "switch." The act need not always be passive, as the following example from a spy novel suggests:

The operation we were now engaged in was known as the switch. When an operator starts out to shadow another, the outcome will be found among five main possibilities. One: the tag is never noticed, and the shadowed man leads the adverse party to his destination, unknowing. (It seldom happens. An operator who doesn't even notice a tag isn't

course, the innocent who here engineers a switch is often not himself a stranger to guile; for if he were not engaged in activity discrediting to his public show he might not have been subjected to monitoring or infiltration or entrapment in the first place. So, in fact, one deals here with the containing of recontainment and something more layered than the Big Con.

However uncommon actual frame reversals may be, they are commonly reported. The use of discovered recording devices to convey exonerating privacies is a stereotype, as is the use of a discovered agent to convey false intelligence unknowingly or (if he has been turned) knowingly. The setting up of would-be entrappers is also recorded, and not merely in the exemplary tales told by ghosted prostitutes. Witness what has been attributed to a great modern French rogue, Pierre Aunay:

> Posing on another occasion as a heroin pusher, he conned two U.S. Narcotics Bureau agents into laying a trap for him, and slipped the noose with $12,000 in exchange for several bags of what proved to be merely powdered sugar.[40]

And, of course, the espionage literature recommends that aspiring infiltrators are prime targets for frame reversal. For example, if a foreign agent has applied for a job in an intelligence agency in an attempt to infiltrate it, he must be prepared to return for successive interviews and to rely on these interviews for evidence that he is being processed in the ordinary way. If he is suspected, he has made it easy for his interviewer to string him along while full evidence is being collected:

> Three times, at the request of the FBI, I called him to the office and interviewed him while his contacts were checked out, keeping him available until the FBI could move in on him with a tight case. I

---

allowed to stay in the business very long.) Two: the tag is noticed but can't be flushed, in which case the operator must simply lead him a dance and leave his original destination unexposed. Three: the tag is noticed and then flushed, and the operator can then make for his original destination unaccompanied. Four: the tag is noticed, flushed and challenged. (I did this with young Hengel. In that case my tag was not an adverse party, but it makes little difference: there's always a temptation to challenge after flushing, if only to see their face go red.) Five: the tag is noticed, flushed and followed. The switch has been made, and the tag is now tagged. [Adam Hall, *The Quiller Memorandum* (New York: Simon and Schuster, 1965), pp. 147–148.]

40. *Time*, January 26, 1968.

felt like a Judas the last time I shook hands with him and told him we'd be in touch with him if a need for his services arose, knowing that he was walking out of my office into the custody of federal agents. I don't know what happened to him.[41]

Interestingly, it is reported that the task of sustaining such a reversal can be extended deeply into domestic organization. For example, the following anecdote about the situation of British officialdom in Stockholm during World War II, a group which, incidentally, functioned as part of the London–Europe underground:

> One escaped prisoner, whom I shall call Wells, although that was not his name, presented a very much less pleasant problem. He arrived in Sweden by the usual route, and his account of his escape was suspiciously circumstantial.
> . . . .
> Our vague doubts were more than justified. Wells, London told us, was strongly suspected of being a traitor, who had been allowed to escape by the Germans in order that he might serve them in England as an agent. . . .
> Unfortunately Wells's stay in Stockholm was prolonged by the fact that for several days after we received this ominous signal no aircraft was available to fly him to Scotland. For more than a week those who knew the man's secret were forced to treat him with a show of hollow friendship and approbation which it was very difficult and unpleasant to maintain. It was particularly difficult for Mr. Wright [the military attaché's confidential clerk], with whom Wells stayed, and who had, of course, seen the sinister telegram from London. As it happened, Mrs. Wright was at the time producing a little entertainment in aid of one of the many war charities in which she was interested. Wells offered to do a conjuring act, and Mrs. Wright, who knew nothing of the shadow which hung over him, accepted the offer with gratitude. It was really horrible to see Wells, arrayed in a hired dress suit, take the stage and give a polished performance of standard conjuring tricks. One felt rather like a prison officer on duty in the condemned cell. We were deeply relieved when we could at last put the man aboard an aircraft and wish him good luck. He would need it.[42]

41. Robert Hayden Alcorn, *No Bugles for Spies* (New York: Popular Library, 1964), p. 34.

42. Ewan Butler, *Amateur Agent* (London: George G. Harrap & Co., 1963), pp. 125–127.

3. I have so far considered some obvious forms of recontainment (including what can be accomplished by secret monitoring, penetration, or entrapment) and the special vulnerability of these designs. *Serial containment* is sometimes involved, the original plotter being taken in by parties other than those whom he plotted against: "In Ciudad Juarez, Mex., two pickpockets kneeling in a church robbed Andres Quinonez of his wallet and $13 while he was praying, were arrested by a policeman kneeling behind them."[43] And a second structure was considered. *frame reversal:* he who attempts to take in others is discovered, unbeknownst to himself, in his attempt, and his erstwhile dupes elect to conceal the discovery and control the person discovered. Other arrangements can be mentioned. *Mutual containment* ought to be possible—it certainly is within the plays of Shakespeare. And no doubt a kind of *containment competition* can occur, with two sides each trying to con the other, knowing that the other is trying to con it, but each trying to outcon the other.[44] Containment competition is somewhat similar to what occurs in bluff games such as poker. It also seems possible in the "real" world, as a student of shoplifting reminds us:

---

43. *Time,* April 20, 1953. A second example. During the early sixties in Nevada when computer strategy for twenty-one had become available and casinos had not yet taken effective countermeasures, it was possible to beat the game. Since the strategy was an extremely academic matter, it was largely graduate students and college teachers who acquired the skill, and these persons were largely unsocialized in the manner and style of play affected by "rounders" and other serious players. Thus, twenty-one players with skill never before attained by man found themselves being treated as tourists by dealers, and were either helped out, coached, or derided. Many such experts felt it to be wise to encourage the dealer in this error so as to avoid countermeasures against "counters." In brief, these new experts fell into character as squares and tried, often successfully, to put the dealer on. Since such players found themselves almost invariably lasting much longer than anyone else around them—if not actually winning—the nearest pit boss often ended up unobtrusively casing the player. Not uncommonly, then, a dealer found himself cajoling a player while in fact being contained by him, even as the pit boss contained the container.

44. Herbert Asbury, in his history of American gambling, *Sucker's Progress* (New York: Dodd, Mead & Co., 1938), describes the heroic model: ". . . a lame gambler named James Ashby, who exercised his talents in a field wherein there was comparatively little competition—he preyed almost entirely upon his fellow sharpers" (pp. 205–206). Pool hustlers, at least in novels, have acquired the same reputation. An extended stage and movie example of containment competition is Anthony Shaffer's *Sleuth.*

A man, for example, was observed by the writer and a store detective pocketing a snakeskin billfold valued at $24.00. The store detective, who observed the man acting very suspiciously and conspicuously, did not arrest him. . . . She assumed, correctly it appeared later, that the thief's motivation was to be arrested after having "thrown" the merchandise (kicked the billfold into an inconspicuous corner). Perhaps he would have resisted arrest and forced the detective to injure him (such cases have occurred before) in the arrest proceedings. He might even have stationed seemingly reputable witnesses in strategic locations to observe the damage inflicted upon him. He could therefore become the plaintiff in a suit for large damages from the store. In this particular case, at least, the store detective pointed out that the thief had indeed "thrown" the stolen billfold by the simple expedient of placing it between his sets of his pockets and allowing it to fall to the floor. If captured, there would be no evidence of stolen merchandise on his person: he would have seemed to be an innocent victim of an overenthusiastic store detective and the store would have been the victim of a cleverly arranged suit for false arrest.[45]

There are, then, varieties of recontainment reminding us that the classical con game involves a variety of its own—one team containing another by splitting into two subteams, one ostensibly uniting with the dupe to ostensibly contain the other. I want to mention a final retransformation, one which will be of concern to us later, to wit, *sequential containment*. In this arrangement, the dupe is let in on the secret of his containment even while this exposure process is managed so as to further contain him. As an example I cite a favorable review of a well-received monographic report on a psychological experiment:

For the specific study each of the S's (22 normal Harvard undergraduates being studied intensively at the [Harvard Psychological] clinic) spent several weeks writing an essay on his personal philosophy of life. He was then told he would meet another S for a discussion in which they would challenge and defend their respective philosophies. The other S was actually a skilled lawyer who met with each of the S's under special instructions to attack S, challenge his philosophy, pointing out inconsistencies, and make him alter or withdraw his statements. Twelve minutes of this dyad were recorded on sound movies which constituted the self confrontation

---

45. Mary Owen Cameron, *The Booster and the Snitch* (New York: The Free Press, 1964), pp. 28–29.

when S viewed the playback; once ostensibly by himself (he was being observed all the time); once with E who interrupted the film at critical points, asking S the significance of certain movements, gestures and speech habits, how he actually felt at that moment, and having him free associate to similar events in his childhood history; and once, a year and a half later, when he tried to recapture his feelings at the time of the stressful interchange.[46]

III. *Transformational Depth*

Starting with untransformed activity (whether defined within a natural or social framework), two basic transformations were identified—keyings and fabrications—and consideration was given to retransformations, being multiple laminations of experience. Some types of recontainment were also examined. I want now to consider a specific issue: How many laminations can a strip of activity sustain? How far can things go? How complex can a frame structure be and still be effective in setting the terms for experience?

Consider first the potential complexity of experience whose outermost lamination—whose rim—involves serious exploitive fabrication. An extreme here, no doubt, is found in espionage, especially in connection with the management of agents suspected of having been turned. As remarked, an agent can be discovered by those he is attempting to contain and, to save his skin, be obliged to sell out his first employers, whose efforts now to contain the enemy will themselves be contained; later he can admit to his erstwhile employers that he has been turned (or be discovered by them), be obliged to continue to act as though he were duping his original masters, and then be discovered by those who had thought they had turned him, this latter discovery leading to an attempt at a further switch.[47]

The limits here are fairly evident. After a certain number of turnings, no one can trust anyone, and the effort to assess what weight to give to events reported by the agent can come to out-

---

46. Review by Leonard D. Eron in *Contemporary Psychology*, November 1963, of Gerhard Nielsen, *Studies in Self Confrontation* (Copenhagen: Munksgaard, 1962).

47. The contingencies of turning are considered in *S.I.*, pp. 56–58.

weigh whatever value the agent has either as a source of possibly valid information about the enemy or as a conduit for transmitting misleading information to them.

Now consider cases of transformation in which the rim of the frame is either a keying or at worst a playful and quite temporary fabrication. Shakespeare provides a suitable beginning. The "play within a play" which Hamlet uses to catch the conscience of the king is, starting from the innermost point, a strip of possible past happening—the murder of Gonzago—and the sort of strip that could be keyed for drama were Hamlet real. So we have a threatrical framing of reality. The staged audience for this inner play, including the King, ought to be able to sustain an open agreement with the performers, the visiting troupe familiar of old to Hamlet, that a "mere" play is in progress: the staged audience need not know the outcome of the play but need only be willing to give itself over to the unfolding drama as if it could be real, yet do this in such a way that it will withdraw its involvement after the curtain comes down, clearly having seen from moment to moment all along that of course only a play was being presented. However, Hamlet's particular choice of play under the circumstances, and especially his quiet change of some dozen or sixteen lines in the script, transforms the theatrical keying into an exploitive fabrication, into something the King would have denounced were he to have known in advance what he was getting in for. So we have a fabricated theatrical framing. But this, of course, is all in itself part of the play that Shakespeare wrote, a play that persons who are actors stage before persons who are really members of an audience. The actors who play the staged audience and the actors who play the parts of stage actors equally share the information state that the producer possesses. And since the play in question is *Hamlet*, no actual audience is likely to be much ignorant of the play's development and outcome. However, the individuals on the stage will be obliged to manage and conceal their knowledge of the play's development and outcome in a different way from the way the real audience manages theirs. So one has, starting from the innermost point, a strip of events which could have actually occurred, transformed for dramatic production, retransformed as a construction to entrap the King, transformed once again, since all this plotting actually happens in a play, not merely by means of a play. And of course, the mountain of literary comment on the play is a keying of all this.

Comedy designed to make a comic point about multiple layering of activity can carry things considerably further than Shakespeare did. For example, in the film *Love and Larceny,* the hero, an ex-criminal retired on full civil pension—a legitimate job, a wife, and a nice new apartment—opens his door to a suspicious-looking man who wants to sell a candlestick cheap. The seller and the couple sustain a tacit coalition against the legitimate order by bargaining over what is obviously a stolen article. The innermost kernel, then, is a sales discussion, but one that has been systematically reframed, so that while the bargaining appears to be just that, it is actually so transformed as to tacitly allow both parties to know that it is known between them that a stolen article is being sold. The couple retires to another room to get the money, returns, and pays for the candlestick. But the old short-con operation has been performed—the substitution of a cheap article for the good one, a contained containment. The hero, being a pro himself, is on to the ruse and exposes the seller. So once again all three characters apparently share a single frame of reference; divisive fabrications have been discredited. After the exposure the hero draws the seller into talk about places and persons they know in common, being as they are members of the same community. In this discussion the hero exposes discrediting facts about himself. The seller then shows his true colors, arresting the hero. For the seller all along was a detective, and the trick-selling was itself a ruse. So in apparently being caught out and returning to unfeigned or "straight" activity, the seller was really entrapping the hero and, of course, his wife. The dropping of pretenses was part of the pretense. But now, with this second admission on the seller's part, the deception is really over and the two men depart, the hero, with a tearful farewell, in handcuffs. Once downstairs in a car, however, the two men show us that all along the seller was a teammate of the hero's, and the whole plot was a device the hero could use as a means of getting away from his legitimate fixtures. So the second exposure of deception was a fabrication, too, but this time only the wife was contained. And, of course, the whole thing is a movie, so it is all a playful fabrication. Rehearsals during the movie production will have generated still another lamination.

So here is another basis of limits on depth of transformation. One does not ask how many laminations can be reached before generalized suspicion occurs or discrediting becomes likely, but rather, if the purpose of the audience is merely to follow the charade and enjoy the cognitive complexity and the purpose of the performing characters is to cooperate in performing such a show, how far can matters be pushed before confusion occurs?

Two arguments then become relevant. First, the intrigue itself can become very complex. By virtue of the fact that the whole interaction is scripted, each party can count on producing precisely the effect it desires and obtaining precisely the response it planned for. In turn, this response can be produced by someone who is scripted to be fully alive to the intent of the instigator and fully competent to give the appearance of falling into the trap when indeed, "in fact" he hasn't. And so forth. This sort of thing cannot be accomplished when only one of the parties can be counted on to follow a script, this being the situation in real life.[48] Second, the onlookers become dependent on framing cues

---

48. A qualification is required. Frame complexity can apparently develop in two ways, intensively and extensively. The intensive mode turns on one action-decision—as in the question of when Sherlock Holmes ought to get off the train to avoid meeting up with Moriarty—and involves the mirror problem: If he thinks that I think that he thinks, and so on: This is the kind of complexity that game theory seems to have been chiefly concerned with, and here real strategic situations may indeed become as complicated as scripted ones. The extensive aspect of complexity turns on the issue of sequence or chaining. The fabricators plan an action against a party, anticipate the party's response, prepare an elaborate replying action to that predicted response, predict the party's response to *that* action, and so forth. Although this sort of horizontal design can be employed if the whole interaction is scripted—as it is in frame comedies and spy novels—the same sequence length is not possible when only one of the parties can be trusted to conduct itself as planned. Obviously, a small deviation from expectation early in the sequence can unhinge later steps in the plan. "Serious" strategic thinking tries to solve this problem by contingency planning, that is, working out a reply at any one decision point for all imaginable opponent responses, but that sort of matrix design would seem to have strict sequence limits.

In dramatic scriptings, the contingencies of fabrication are often linked with the contingencies of resorting to force, thereby producing executed plans the real world would never allow. The plotters must approach their goal by getting past a series of checkpoints, encumbered, moreover, with various pieces of heavy equipment. Some points they will manage by misrepresentation, some by "neutralization" through force, in either case not without having to face what ought to be quite unpredictable response. In

to keep matters clear, and the producers of the show become
dependent on the capacity of onlookers to respond to intentionally planted signals; which, of course, onlookers seem remarkably able to do.

In general, then, the deepest layering can be expected to occur
in scripted presentation of a novelistic, theatrical, or cinematic
kind, and to be, therefore, in some sense unreal.[49] But this
unreality should not conceal from us the fact that while watching
the show, the audience can follow along and read off what is
happening by attending to the relevant framing cues. *That* is the
great lesson, and it tells us about a crucial human capacity exercised in regard to actual events as well as fictive ones.[50] A good
example is provided by the film critic Béla Balázs:

> Asta Nielsen [a German actress] once played a woman hired to
> seduce a rich young man. The man who hired her is watching the
> results from behind a curtain. Knowing that she is under observa-

---

addition, the team may have to be split up into groups, each approaching
from a different direction and a different series of checkpoints, thereby requiring not only a sequence of successful maneuverings but also the close
synchronization of these overcomings.

49. Literary treatment of dreams allows a similar complexity. An illustration:

> An example of such a transformation as part of the fool's inner life is
> provided by a gag by Hanswurst, a reincarnation of Harlequin in the
> eighteenth-century Viennese theater. The gag explores a state of con-
> sciousness in which "I" and something that might or might not be "I"
> but is separated from it by a kind of "nothing" are hopelessly confused
> and in which life goes on in accordance with intentions that Hanswurst's
> "I" has trouble in understanding. Hanswurst lies down to sleep, dreams
> that he is dreaming, and in this second dream dreams again that he is
> dreaming; in this dream-within-a-dream-within-a-dream he dreams that
> he has awakened, goes to sleep again, and dreams that he is awake and
> must force himself to sleep so that he can dream; he dreams that he
> again goes to sleep and is in his sleep so angry about not dreaming that
> he awakens and lies the rest of the night without dreaming in a kind of
> sleeping wakefulness that is at the same time a dream. [William Wille-
> ford, *The Fool and His Scepter* (Evanston, Ill.: Northwestern University
> Press, 1969), pp. 62–63.]

50. Human because presumably we are best at it; but natural in fact.
Animals not only provide Gregory Bateson with the message "This is play,"
but also are very competent in determining when an act is play or is not.
As often said, a dog can very nicely distinguish between being kicked
and being tripped over, although the physical effect may be the same.
H. Hediger, in *Studies of the Psychology and Behaviour of Captive Animals*

tion, Asta Nielsen feigns love. She does it convincingly: the whole gamut of appropriate emotion is displayed in her face. Nevertheless we are aware that it is only play-acting, that it is a sham, a mask. But in the course of the scene Asta Nielsen really falls in love with the young man. Her facial expression shows little change; she had been "registering" love all the time and done it well. How else could she now show that this time she was really in love? Her expression changes only by a scarcely perceptible and yet immediately obvious nuance—and what a few minutes before was a sham is now the sincere expression of a deep emotion. Then Asta Nielsen suddenly remembers that she is under observation. The man behind the curtain must not be allowed to read her face and learn that she is now no longer feigning, but really feeling love. So Asta now pretends to be pretending. Her face shows a new, by this time threefold, change. First she feigns love, then she genuinely shows love, and as she is not permitted to be in love in good earnest, her face again registers a sham, a pretence of love. But now it is this pretence that is a lie. Now she is lying that she is lying. And we can see all this clearly in her face, over which she has drawn two different masks. At such times an invisible face appears in front of the real one, just as spoken words can by association of ideas conjure up things unspoken and unseen, perceived only by those to whom they are addressed.[51]

But, of course, the whole scene is part of a movie, and the persons playing in it have no intention or expectation of tricking the audience into any misunderstanding; so Miss Nielsen is conducting herself so as to make it evident to the audience that

in *Zoos and Circuses* (London: Butterworth's Scientific Publications, 1955), provides a text:

In respect of its ability to interpret expression and the training signals connected with emotional stimuli, the animal is often far superior to man, at least in so far as it can distinguish between true and false straight off. In the majority of cases therefore, human play-acting and make-believe misfire with the animal during training. In order to obtain a satisfactory performance, the appropriate expression and the training signals directly connected with it must be genuine; these signals must really relate to the emotional content which the animals originally had. As a rule, the animal will not respond to empty gestures and shallow mimicry. [p. 125]

51. Béla Balázs, *Theory of the Film*, trans. Edith Bone (New York: Roy Publishers, 1953), p. 64. The passage was drawn to my attention by Kaye Miller.

she is staging lying that she is lying, and somehow the viewers receive enough signs to easily peel apart the layers.

IV. *Actor Transforms*

A central difference between natural and social frameworks is the role accorded actors, specifically individuals. In the case of natural perspectives, individuals have no special status, being subject to the same deterministic, will-less, nonmoral way of being as any other part of the scene. In the case of social frameworks, individuals figure differently. They are defined as self-determined agencies, legally competent to act and morally responsible for doing so properly. In this latter connection, then, individuals have an entirely special role in activity. Moreover, this role is diffusely relevant. The properties we attribute to normal actors, such as correct perception, personal will, a range of adult competencies, access to memory, a measure of empathy regarding others present, honesty, reliability, fixed social and personal identity, and the like are counted on in a multitude of ways whenever interpersonal dealings occur.

It follows that any apparent need to redefine an actor as possessing other than these conventional attributes can have a very pervasive effect upon the activity in which the altered person participates.

In the everyday business of living, the individual routinely treats others from within both social and natural perspectives and does so, moreover, with a close, effortless interweaving of the two types of frameworks. Thus, traditionally, medical practitioners have felt they obtain two kinds of information from a patient, signs and symptoms, the first involving objective biological indicators, the second subjective reports. Similarly, in the manufacture of coin-operated weighing machines, the printed directions and the coin slot are designed for full-fledged actors, the springs for weighted things, animate or inanimate.

Given this conventional division, however, there are occasions when we anticipate treating an individual within a social framework but find that he is perceivedly disqualified, or partly so, thus inducing the application of a natural perspective: he appears dead, or drunk, or in the process of having a fit, or insane, or too young to know better, or sleepwalking in a dream, or simply asleep.[52] There are also, as will be considered later, occasions when disagreement may occur as to whether to apply a natural or social perspective. This disagreement itself may not be due to some sort of error, but to inadequacy of the frameworks themselves, including the decision rules for establishing or excluding application.[53]

Questions of actor status arise in other contexts. First, there exists what must be a universal practice, that of openly playing at some major disqualification, as when a man jokes drunkenness or insanity or a snoring sleep, or a child plays the game of "statue" involving spinning into a freeze. (A recent switch has been the take-me-to-your-leader robot theme in which an individual enacts a guided object, not a guiding agent.) It is this sort of play that is institutionalized in the circus clown's display of a wide range of fundamental incompetencies.[54] From this sort of

---

52. Sleeping is a marginal disqualification. It renders the sleeper incapable of social intercourse only if the stimuli are insufficiently disturbing to awaken him.

53. Perhaps the best-known example of these cosmological difficulties is our Western treatment of mental disorder as a claim to a natural, not social, understanding of events. Put simply, at one extreme, say the organic brain defects, there is wide agreement that it would be wrong to apply a social framework involving the imputation of fully qualified actor status; and at the other extreme, perhaps the mild psychoneuroses, so-called, there might be fairly wide agreement that ordinary social standards could be applied. However, the many cases in between lead to considerable difference of opinion. Moreover, the same person viewing the same dubious actor will not be consistent and will not restrict himself to a natural or to a social perspective. Various legal rulings, such as the McNaghten and the Durham, express the difficulty and do not resolve it. For an illustration of both the cure and the disease, see Thomas S. Szasz, "Some Observations on the Relationship between Psychiatry and the Law," *AMA Archives of Neurology and Psychiatry*, LXXV (1956): 297–315; "Psychiatry, Ethics, and the Criminal Law," *Columbia Law Review*, LVIII (1958): 183–198; "The Insanity Plea and the Insanity Verdict," in Thomas S. Szasz, ed., *Ideology and Insanity: Essays on the Psychiatric Dehumanization of Man* (New York: Doubleday & Company, Anchor Books, 1970), pp. 98–112. A useful collection of excerpts on the insanity defense can be found in Richard C. Donnelly, Joseph Goldstein, and Richard D. Schwartz, *Criminal Law* (New York: The Free Press, 1962), pt. 6, pp. 734–854.

54. For example, Sidney Tarachow, "Circuses and Clowns," in Géza Róheim, ed., *Psychoanalysis and the Social Sciences*, vol. 3 (New York: International Universities Press, 1951):

The clown does incredibly stupid things and never seems to learn; even in the judgment of the child he is stupid. Equipped with a broom,

open play it is only a step to that sort of jest which requires the individual to act, say, as though asleep, his anticipation being that he will shortly expose the deception in a note of joking, and that those who were taken in will take this taking in in good spirit as though not having been seriously taken in at all.

From here matters that will more concern us can be taken up: the use by an individual of some disqualification of his status as a full-fledged actor to delude himself or to deceive others, in either case for the purpose of achieving an end otherwise unobtainable to him. The product is not something destined to be resolved and wiped away in a joke that brings all participants to the same view of matters. Rather exploitive fabrication is involved, an effort that can have quite substantial consequences for participants. By noting the deep-seated ramifications in the definition of the situation produced by this sort of actor transform, the central role that our conception of actors plays in the framing of events can be better appreciated.

Begin the consideration by looking at an extreme case: the act of playing dead. The standard version comes from the animal world;[55] thus the phrase "playing possum." The human version is a source of news:

> Placerville—A Placerville skin diver told last night how he lay in the jaws of a white shark in Bodega Bay, Saturday, and played dead.
>
> . . . .

---

he tries to sweep away a circle of light cast by a spotlight, but never succeeds. He follows a bauble suspended from his own headdress. He engages in endless bickering or problems with another clown, problems and quarrels that could be settled in a moment if either clown showed an ounce of intelligence. Other clowns act out the most fantastic childish indulgences. One might endlessly break dishes, another eat enormous amounts of pie. Another is abysmally dirty. Sometimes the dirty clown creates a comic situation in which the superego is gratified. The clown removes a fantastic number of dirty shirts and finally arrives at a spotlessly clean one. They are absolutely undisciplined, in a childish way. There is a good deal of aggression as well as masochism. They strike each other, quarrel, fall, trip. The slapstick and bladder are prominent. They make fun of authorities, they imitate the ringmaster, they ape policemen, boxers, firemen. [p. 179]

55. See, for example, Hediger, *Studies of the Psychology and Behaviour of Captive Animals*, pp. 52–53. He also argues that foxes sham sleep as a predatory ploy (p. 150). Indeed, stories have been told of wolves feigning crazy behavior to entice ducks into taking a closer view. (See Farley Mowat, *Never Cry Wolf* [New York: Dell Publishing Co., 1971], pp. 75–76.)

Logan told authorities he was hunting for abalone in about 18 feet of water when he felt something grab his leg. He turned in time to see the shark seize him.

. . . .

"I could see it was a shark so I just went limp and played dead and it finally let go," Logan recalled. When the shark did let go, Logan floated quickly to the surface and shouted to three companions in a nearby boat.[56]

Ascom City, South Korea—The only reason I'm [Pfc. David L. Bibee] alive now is because I didn't move when a North Korean yanked my watch off my wrist. I just played like I was dead.

. . . .

The first thing I knew a hand grenade hit right beside me.

It rolled me over and I slid down the (50 foot) hill. . . .

I heard the North Koreans talking. They were getting our (ammunition) magazines and our rifles.

One of them came up and shined a light in my face—a red light.

He shined it down on my wrist and he jerked my watch off.

. . . .

I was the only one left alive. Several of my buddies got killed.

And the only reason I'm alive now is that I played like I was dead.[57]

To play dead seriously is to render oneself totally disqualified as an actor. The useful contrast here is with the fabrication of physical incapacity. In our society two forms are identified.

The first is "malingering," namely, the shamming of a physical disorder in order to avoid undesired events—again, a process well known in the animal world.[58] What is involved, presumably, is

---

56. *San Francisco Chronicle,* July 29, 1968.

57. Reported in *The Boston Traveler,* November 3, 1966.

58. Raising afresh the issue of intentionality. An individual feigning physical incapacity presumably is (1) aware of what he is doing, and (2) will stop doing it the moment the relevant audience is gone. Animals that feign incapacity (as when a golden plover shams lameness) stop their show when prey or predator have left the scene but ordinarily cannot be said to be aware of the deception-in-effect which natural selection has made available to them. Hediger, however, argues that animals tainted by continuous contact with man do fake incapacity in the double sense found in man:

One of the countless tricks that the four-year-old gorilla ["Achille," a resident in the Basel Zoo] used for procuring human contact was to push

the actor's presentation of symptoms which have a demand function, obliging others to suppress social frameworks and allow a
purely naturalistic reading of some special segment of the simulator's activity. A healthy hand that doesn't salute causes its
possessor to be judged within a social schema; a bandaged hand
that is similarly remiss is treated as properly displacing social
niceties, obliging an interpretation along medical lines. Malingering (or "goldbricking," as its lesser varieties have sometimes been
called) is an adaptive technique that seems to be found in every
severely subordinated group and in America has a noble history
going back to plantation life.[59]

The second form of feigned incapacity is what is called "hysterical illness" or "conversion reaction." Through this the individual presumably deludes himself about his malfunctioning,
even in the face of skeptical witnesses or, of course, no witnesses
at all. Apparently this kind of maneuver is not nearly as common
as it was in Freud's time (when he studied the "disease" and
formulated the bizarre notion of psychosexual trauma as the root
cause), but insofar as hysterical reactions are (or were) found,
one is given support for the notion of the individual being able to
con himself.[60] It might be added that those obliged to make a

---

its arm out through the top of the wire mesh of his air-conditioned cage
and pretend that he couldn't get it back again. Several times Head Keeper
Carl Stemmler, before he realized that it was all a humbug to try to get
some human company, hurried to help the gorilla out of its plight.
[*Studies of the Psychology and Behaviour of Captive Animals*, p. 150.]

59. Raymond A. and Alice H. Bauer, "Day to Day Resistance to Slavery,"
The Journal of Negro History, XXVII (1942): 406–410.

60. The primal sources are Joseph Breuer and Sigmund Freud, *Studies
in Hysteria*, trans. A. A. Brill (1895; Boston: Beacon Press, 1950), and
Sigmund Freud, "Some Points in a Comparative Study of Organic and
Hysterical Paralyses," in *Collected Papers*, 5 vols. (London: International
Psycho-Analytic Press, 1924), 1:42–58; "Fragment of an Analysis of a
Case of Hysteria," in *Collected Papers*, 3:13–146; *The Problem of Anxiety*
(New York: W. W. Norton & Company, 1938). A current statement is
Frederick J. Ziegler and John B. Imboden, "Contemporary Conversion
Reactions," *Archives of General Psychiatry*, VI (1962): 279–287. A thump-
ing psychoanalytical statement is provided at the beginning of the Breuer-
Freud monograph:

Our experiences have shown us *that the most varied symptoms which
pass as spontaneous, or, as it were, as idiopathic attainments of hysteria,
stand in just as stringent connection with the causal trauma as the transparent phenomena mentioned.* To such causal factors we are able to refer

differential diagnosis between malingering and hysteria do not have a task that can very satisfactorily be performed.[61] Note that when death or illness is simulated, the simulator is drawing on our frame understanding, our cosmological belief, that at any moment a social framework may have to give way in the face of accident or incident, leaving the field temporarily dominated by interpretations within a natural perspective.

It seems characteristic that disqualification of some of an individual's capacities on medical grounds leaves others of his capacities uncontaminated, and that a split between questioned and unquestioned functioning results. This possibility is to be contrasted with what occurs with some other major actor transforms, namely, hypnotic trance, drunkenness, and insanity, in which *all* the actor's social competencies (it is felt) are reduced or eliminated.

It is tempting to try to describe the rules or premises of an actor transform as it is conventionally represented and perceived. For example: hypnosis. Individuals are felt to have a variable capacity to be subject to it. Bracketing practices are clear-cut, a longish introduction under the direction of the hypnotist at the beginning and a less protracted release (a snap of the fingers sometimes sufficing) by the same person at the end. The subject once "under" becomes will-less, ready to accept very loose reidentification of the various objects around him, including himself, in accordance with the specifications of the hypnotist. The behavior style is that of somnambulism, the speech to have a colorless, dead quality. The subject (it is often felt) will not do things that are radically alien to his moral standards. Some sort of time limit is envisaged for any one trance. There will be a hallucinatory capacity in all sensory modalities and memory alteration, in that some things will be unrecallable that are accessible under normal conditions. Finally, upon coming out of the spell, the subject will

---

neuralgias as well as the different kind of anesthesias, often of years' duration, contractures and paralyses, hysterical attacks and epileptiform convulsions, which every observer has taken for real epilepsy, *petit mal* and tic-like affections, persisting vomiting and anorexia, even up to the refusal of nourishment, all kinds of visual disturbances, constantly recurring visual hallucinations, and similar affections. [pp. 1–2]

61. See, for example, David J. Flicker, "Malingering: A Symptom," *The Journal of Nervous and Mental Disease*, CXXIII (1956): 26–27.

have amnesia regarding the period during the spell. Upon occurrence of the proper instruction during the spell and the proper
signal after it has been ostensibly terminated, there can be
posthypnotic suggested action. With these rules it should be
possible to churn out hypnoticlike behavior; and indeed (as will
be considered), it is through the use of such rules, I believe, that
this behavior is churned out.

A comment now about another actor transform, homosexuality, specifically the male variety. The practice of certain acts of a
direct sexual kind and participation as a member in the gay
community are both called homosexuality. What is to be attended
here is something else, a style of male behavior that is called
swish, campy, or effeminate, especially when this occurs in conjunction with evidence concerning the above two mentioned
forms of homosexuality. For homosexual style, as here defined,
constitutes a transformation of ordinary male behavior, the
transforming pattern drawn from current stereotypes of female
behavior. (An uneasy balance seems to be maintained here,
allowing this transformation to be clearly distinguished from
what an individual does who is "medically reassigned" a sex and
acquires a new behavioral style as a serious lifelong undertaking,
and from what jokesters do who momentarily mock-up an age,
class, or ethnic style not their "own.") It is this transformation,
along with attendant admissions, that has served as a fabrication,
a means by which the performer can intentionally disqualify
himself for such displeasures as military duty.

Actor transforms raise the question of frame limits and tell us
something about their character. Within informal circles in our
society there seems to be no great disapproval of the open, playful imitation of insane, drunken, or homosexual behavior, providing only that these sallies are of brief duration and occur in
circles where everyone qualifies or no one qualifies. Such play
counts as one means by which individuals exhibit the great
flexibility of commitment found in informal interaction, allowing
them to be momentarily not themselves, sometimes in order to
say things that might not be permissible coming from themselves.
Of course, such frivolity can meet with a degree of disapproval
from those who are concerned about the dignity of the mimicked
group; indeed, the passing into a racial or ethnic style (unless the

performer has a birthright to it) is less appreciated today than a decade ago, and homosexual shticks currently are thought questionable by some—and differently from the way the same behavior is disapproved when performed by someone presenting himself as a real homosexual. In any case, even when these bits are disapproved of, disapproval is on the grounds of fairness and good taste; there is no immediate concern lest the imitator be seen to be contaminated personally by his imitation.

When one turns from playfulness to the theatrical frame, the issue of limits becomes touchier. Until recently, both in plays and in movies, homosexual characterization was somewhat taboo, since it was apparently felt that the actor could not insulate himself from the reputation of the part he played, that to act a homosexual was to invite suspicion of being one.

It is in regard to exploitive fabrications, however, that limits regarding actor transforms become most striking. Under very special circumstances, as when a prisoner of war affects linguistic incapacity or insanity, no depreciation is shown by his home audiences; indeed, applause is the result. But in other cases, the character performed is felt to be grossly improper for a person of no defect to portray, and various penalties and psychiatric interpretations are applied to reinforce an "intrinsic" connection between performing and the part performed. In brief, an individual is allowed to portray someone who is crazy or sick or dumb or queer for unserious, recreational reasons, but to do so in a serious context, in which exploitive fabrication, not fun and games, is involved, is to invite serious discrediting. It is significant that here, apparently, change has recently occurred, for it seems that views of the indelibility of certain simulations are now changing rapidly, and that (for example) young men today are more prepared than of old to affect a maladjusted or homosexual style to avoid military service and more likely to be unashamed before their friends and associates about having done so.

Another matter. If indeed there is no actor transform that cannot be simulated, the question arises as to how much simulation routinely enters various kinds of transforms. Obviously, most dead-looking people are literally dead, and are not, in some sense, behaving at all, although live persons certainly are behaving to them, and as soon as the corpse can be got to by the undertaker, it will be styled to play its role.[62] Perhaps something the same can be said about persons who appear to be asleep or give the impression of being grossly retarded mentally. But when this argument is extended to other transforms, answers get shaky. It is known that insanity has been simulated for various purposes,[63] but what is uncertain is how routinely such simulation enters into the behavior of most persons designated insane. To what degree are the insane adhering to a style they have in mind as to how insane people behave; that is, to what degree are they conducting themselves as opposed to merely being? Surely, when members of a subordinated social group (such as American Indians) are seen as nonadult, as children not to be trusted, they are engaging in a strategic alignment, an exploitation of common stereotypes concerning irresponsibility and sometimes simply the playacting of irresponsibility for what can be gained thereby.[64] And children themselves? How early in life could they cease to act childlike?

Nor is the matter of conscious simulation the final issue. Men often treat women as faulted actors with respect to "normal" capacity for various forms of physical exertion. Women so treated often respond by affirming this assessment. On both sides there

---

62. Clearly the timing of a death can be a matter of debate, and there is no *full* agreement by the medical as to the definition of death; it is even the case that modern medical technology has considerably complicated these issues. Obviously these matters are very relevant for the ethnography of hospital work and very useful in explicating the need for, and fallibility of, decision rules for the application of any frame whatsoever, but to subordinate all sociological interests to this one—the issue of frame definition—is a bit much. It is a useful methodological device to assume that social inquiry has no concern with what a physical or biological event might be "in itself," but only interest in what the members of society make of it. However, it is also necessary to ask what the event makes society make of it, and how it conditions social life in ways not appreciated as such by participants.

63. Ernest Jones, "Simulated Foolishness in Hysteria," in his *Papers on Psycho-analysis* (Toronto: Macmillan Co. of Canada, 1913), pp. 141–153; A. C. Cain, "On the Meaning of 'Playing Crazy' in Borderline Children," *Psychiatry*, XXVII (1964): 278–279; Benjamin M. Braginsky, Martin Grosse, and Kenneth Ring, "Controlling Outcomes through Impression-Management," *Journal of Consulting Psychology*, XXX (1966): 295–300.

64. Niels Winther Braroe, "Reciprocal Exploitation in an Indian-White Community," *Southwestern Journal of Anthropology*, XXI (1965): 166–178, more fully reported in his useful Ph.D. dissertation, "Change and Identity: Patterns of Interaction in an Indian-White Community" (Department of Anthropology, University of Illinois, 1970).

may be unquestioning belief and a long-acquired capacity to act accordingly without guile or self-consciousness. Nonetheless, cannot the question be put as to whether "real" incapacities are involved or merely institutionally sustained belief?

V. *Fabricated Frameworks*

In almost all that has been considered so far about fabrication in general and actor transforms in particular, the assumption holds that although the particular activity in question is managed as a fabrication, still, activity of that kind could actually occur. There are claimed actions, however, such as the various forms of second sight, humanoid visitations from outer space, astrological influence, and the like, that might be impossible, and therefore what is being fabricated is not merely one occasion of the activity but also the *possibility* of that activity itself. And since these possibilities involve arcane powers, forces radically incompatible with our whole system of empirical knowledge about the workings of the physical world, one can say (as I would) that what is being fabricated are frameworks themselves. Thus, one can take the position that a person who is taken to be possessed and involuntarily responsive to the will and force of otherworldly personages who have taken residence in him must be deceiving either himself and his audience or only the audience; but surely someone is being deceived on every occasion when possession is felt to occur.[65] An argument can be made that all hypnosis is of this order[66]

---

65. On the conventions for framing behavior as possession, see T. K. Oesterreich, *Possession*, trans. D. Ibberson (New York: New York University Press, 1966); also Alfred Métraux, *Voodoo in Haiti*, trans. Hugo Charteris (New York: Oxford University Press, 1959). Once the visitors take up residence they empower the host to contact the dead, see into the future, cure diseases, and exhibit other unnatural competencies. Like a dream, the person in a trance is expected to "come out of it," and signs are available for marking this transition. Unlike dreaming (and hypnosis) a coming to does not mean a disbelief regarding what seemed to be going on during the trance.

66. The argument (which I believe) is that the subject is gradually led into a social situation in which he feels obliged to maintain the view that the hypnotizer appears to have committed himself to, namely, that there is such a thing as hypnosis and that the subject is falling under it. Certainly show-biz hypnosis is of this order. The standard statements of the "role-playing" theory of hypnosis can be found in T. R. Sarbin, "Contributions to

and all insane behavior, too.[67] So, too, it can be argued
that drunken comportment is, first off, social behavior that ad-
heres to one's sober understanding of how drunken people comport themselves, and that in so conducting oneself certain license
and nonresponsibility can be obtained.[68]

There are interesting issues here. For example, according to
psychoanalytical doctrine it is quite possible for an individual
under certain forms of psychic stress to regress and act like a
child. Papers on the subject thus provide descriptions of what it is
like to act like a child:

> When one tried to test his [a fifteen-year-old patient's] reflexes he
> resented it like a timorous child who does not understand what is
> being done. After a while he began to blubber and cry, and tear-
> fully clung to his mother's skirt. This culminated in his bellowing
> "Want to doe home; Tum home with me." He absolutely refused to
> be soothed by either his mother or me, and behaved like an incon-
> solable baby, so that finally she had to take him home. The speech
> alteration accorded well with his babyish behavior, for it is well
> known how characteristic of early childhood speech is the replace-
> ment of posterior linguo-palatals by the corresponding anterior
> ones.[69]

> The foolishness showed all the characteristics of childishness,
> namely complete irresponsibility, apparent purposeless naughti-
> ness for its own sake, absurdity, silliness and almost imbecile
> ignorance.[70]

Role-Taking Theory: I. Hypnotic Behavior," *Psychological Review*, LVII
(1950): 255–270; Martin T. Orne, "The Nature of Hypnosis: Artifact and
Essence," *Journal of Abnormal and Social Psychology*, LVIII (1959): 277–
299; J. P. Sutcliffe, " 'Credulous' and 'Skeptical' Views of Hypnotic Phenomena: Experiments on Esthesia, Hallucination, and Delusion," *ibid.*,
LXII (1961): 189–200. In a recent article ("Goal Directed Fantasy and
Hypnotic Performance," *Psychiatry*, XXXIV [1971]: 86–96), Nicholas P.
Spanos has suggested in something close to frame terms that hypnotic subjects may be collaborating with the hypnotist not so much in terms of
voluntarily playing at the part of hypnotic subject, but voluntarily agreeing
to mentally seek out the kind of fantasy scenario in terms of which the
demanded action would make sense.

67. For example, see Thomas J. Scheff, *Being Mentally Ill: A Sociological
Theory* (Chicago: Aldine Publishing Company, 1966), esp. chap. 3, "The
Social Institution of Insanity."

68. Craig MacAndrew and Robert B. Edgerton, *Drunken Comportment*
(Chicago: Aldine Publishing Company, 1969).

69. Ernest Jones, "Simulated Foolishness in Hysteria," pp. 145–146.

70. *Ibid.*, p. 150.

But of course this behavior can be seen not as that of an aged child but rather that of a competent adult attempting to act as he thinks a child might—much as he would were he admittedly and openly attempting to perform a brief strip of childlike behavior in jest and play. Ernest Jones goes further and argues for the similarity of this conduct not to a child's behavior but to a child's version of a child's behavior:

> Following Freud, I have elsewhere pointed out that the occurrence of this particular form of foolishness sometimes seen in hysterical adults has its exact counterpart in the fits of exaggerated childishness at times indulged in by some children. These fits when pronounced are often the prelude to nervous giggling, uncontrollable laughing or outbursts of weeping. The motive actuating the behavior of these children is to delude their elders into regarding them as being "too young to understand," and into, therefore, ignoring their presence.[71]

Whether regression is seen as actual childlike behavior or the simulation of what the actor takes to be childlike behavior, the conventional argument is the same, namely, the actor is not in some sense or other acting purposely, mindfully, and with guile in order to create a false impression; he himself actually is not aware of his simulating. The question, however, is whether this self-deception is ever actually present. Regression in all its claimed occurrences may be by way of a knowing deception.

Some further considerations. It seems that in our society when a fabricated framework comes to be questioned on rational grounds a special kind of entertainment can occur, one in which supernatural frameworks are simulated but with no clear-cut claim that they are literally in dominion. That appears to be the state that "mind shows," as well as other magic displays, have reached today.[72] A decade ago, of course, the magician or mentalist was presented as engaging in the real thing—much as today's nightclub hypnotists still profess to be exhibiting actual hypnosis.

---

71. *Ibid.*, pp. 150–151.

72. Correspondingly, there has apparently been a shift among mentalists from the term "supernatural" to terms such as "paranormal." Here again I draw on Marcello Truzzi, "Towards a Sociology of the Occult: Notes on Modern Witchcraft" (unpublished paper, 1971).

Finally, the obvious question. What if most of the members of an alien society believe in the validity of a framework that we, or at least some of us, might think must be necessarily invalid? Could one, and should one, speak of fabrication in effect?

Communication with the dead, this constituting a special belief concerning the nature of them and the powers of some of us, provides an illustration and a possible answer. No doubt there are communities in which a respectable number of persons believe in this possibility. Here it is perfectly possible for the student to show that this belief has real social functions and that the individuals seen as having special gifts for this sort of contacting acquire a real social role, the practicing of which has real consequences for those for whom (or upon whom) it is practiced. But it must still remain that those seen as effecting this communication are not really doing so; for whatever goes on when live persons communicate with each other certainly does not go on when one of them is dead. Moreover, however well entrenched in a particular society this belief in dial-the-dead might be, it is probably still the case that the belief is subject, even in local terms, to discreditings, which belief in ordinary communication is not.[73] The delicate issue, it seems, is that in certain matters, often socially important ones, no very effective check may be available in the society regarding the validity or invalidity of a framework. A specific belief may not be crucial and a specific confrontation of competing frames of reference not possible. Or there may be little interest in pressing such alternative accountings as exist, or little attention paid to such as are presented.

---

73. This argument, of course, could be seen as an ethnocentric, naïve extension of our own belief in Western science to societies with their own quite different systems of belief. But *that* kind of relativism might be naïve, too. For Western science can be seen as but one expression of a general empiricism and rationality that every society must have a good bit of in various sectors of its undertakings, else the reproductive continuity of its members could never have been achieved.

7

Out-of-Frame Activity

Given a spate of activity that is framed in a particular way and that provides an official main focus of attention for ratified participants, it seems inevitable that other modes and lines of activity (including communication narrowly defined) will simultaneously occur in the same locale, segregated from what officially dominates, and will be treated, when treated at all, as something apart. In other words, participants pursue a line of activity—a story line—across a range of events that are treated as out of frame, subordinated in this particular way to what has come to be defined as the main action.

Of course, individuals can give the appearance of respectful involvement in their declared concern when, in fact, their central attention is elsewhere. And, indeed, the management of these appearances can itself distract from the obligatory focus of attention, producing a specifically interactional tension.[1] But although all of this is of interest, it is not the main one here. My primary concern is to examine what it is that persons are allowed (or obliged) to treat as their official chief concern, not whether or not they actually do so.

Here adopt an imagery. Say that in every circumstance in which an individual finds himself he will be able to sustain a main story line of activity, and that the range of matters so treatable will vary from one setting to another. From the perspective

---

1. An argument developed in "Fun and Games," *E.*, pp. 41–45.

of the participants one might refer here to a capacity; from the perspective of the situation itself, a channel or "track." And using the same metaphor, one could go on to consider some of the channels of subordinated activity—deeds or events managed in what (at least) appears to be a dissociated way.

I

A significant feature of any strip of activity is the capacity of its participants to "disattend" competing events—both in fact and in appearance—here using "disattend" to refer to the withdrawal of all attention and awareness. This capacity of participants, this channel in the situation, covers a range of potentially distracting events, some a threat to appropriate involvement because they are immediately present, others a threat in spite of having their prime location elsewhere.

Some sense of this arrangement can be obtained by examining extreme cases of disattention. For example, this occasion of disattending a significant distal event:

> Peking—President Kwame Nkrumah of Ghana last night publicly ignored the coup which had toppled his regime and announced his intention of going ahead with his Vietnam peace mission.
>
> Appearing tense and grim, Nkrumah addressed a Chinese Communist state banquet given in his honor here as if nothing had happened in his home country, where the army has seized power.
>
> His Chinese hosts also politely refrained from making any public comment on the coup, which took place as Nkrumah was flying here from Burma. . . .
>
> Nkrumah, wearing his usual dark tunic suit, similar to the style worn by Chinese leaders, mounted a stage after dinner to speak, mainly on the need to strengthen Afro-Asian solidarity.
>
> . . . .
>
> The deposed President was politely but not enthusiastically applauded after his speech.
>
> . . . .
>
> The whole evening was pervaded with a strained, abnormal and almost unreal atmosphere caused by a situation unprecedented in the normally rigid protocol of official visits to Peking.[2]

---

2. *San Francisco Chronicle*, February 25, 1966.

And now an event occurring close to the location from which it must be disattended:

Mark Rudd rose from his aisle seat and walked slowly, deliberately, to the front of St. Paul's Chapel. Several hundred members of the Columbia University community shifted decorously in their seats as Vice President David B. Truman prepared to deliver a five-minute eulogy to Martin Luther King, assassinated in Memphis five days before. Veering to his right, Rudd stepped up into the choir, cut in front of the vice president and placed himself in front of the microphone. Truman stopped; the microphone went dead.

"Dr. Truman and President Kirk are committing a moral outrage against the memory of Dr. King," Rudd said quietly, leaning over the lectern. How, he demanded, can the leaders of the University eulogize a man who died while trying to unionize sanitation workers when they have, for years, fought the unionization of the University's own black and Puerto Rican workers? How can these administrators praise a man who fought for human dignity when they have stolen land from the people of Harlem? And how, Rudd asked, can Columbia laud a man who preached non-violent disobedience when it is disciplining its own students for peaceful protest? "Dr. Truman and President Kirk are committing a moral outrage against the memory of Dr. King," Rudd repeated. "We will therefore protest this obscenity." He stepped down from the stage and walked, shoulders hunched slightly forward, down the center aisle and out the main chapel door into the April sun. Forty others followed him. Truman continued on his way to the microphone and delivered his eulogy as if nothing had happened.[3]

Of course, the classic example here occurs in response to parade-ground military discipline:

London—A woman visitor to London let out a shriek yesterday as she stood watching the rock-steady guards outside St. James' Palace.

Blood was flowing from the hand of one of the sentries, where he had cut himself on his bayonet. The sentry stood immobile, eyes straight ahead, and upper lip stiff.

The woman who shrieked and another woman ran forward to bandage the guard's hand with a handkerchief.

But he did not move until a police constable had told the orderly

3. Jerry L. Avorn et al., *Up against the Ivy Wall* (New York: Atheneum Publishers, 1969), p. 28.

officer. A replacement was marched on, and the wounded guard marched off—head high, lip still stiff.[4]

Incidentally, from this anecdote one can deduce that if the individual is to be quite fully assimilated to a uniform element in an overall design—as in choreography in general—then a mechanism will be required for removing failures, and in such a fashion that the removal process itself can be assimilated to the pattern—as though these scenes occurred in submarines and a special lock were required to allow something inside to get outside without flooding everything. Thus, to remove a dancer who has been forced out of frame by cramps, make an unscheduled momentary dropping of the curtain. Or among the more fully costumed:

> The first time she saw a novice faint in the chapel, she broke every rule and stared. No nun or novice so much as glanced at the white form that had keeled over from the knees, though the novice fell sideways into their midst and her Little Office shot from her hands as if thrown. For a few moments while the prayers continued, the surrounding sisters seemed to be monsters of indifference, as removed from the plight of the unconscious one as though she were not sprawled out blenched before them on the carpet. Then Gabrielle saw the nun in charge of the health of the community come down the aisle. The nursing nun plucked the sleeve of the nearest sister, who arose at once and helped carry the collapsed novice back down the aisle, past a hundred heads that never turned, past two hundred eyes that never swerved from the altar.[5]

Parade-ground decorum raises a general issue about disattention. The regrettable fact (it is believed) is that whenever individuals are incorporated into an activity in roles of some kind, they will, as performers, as human machines, always be faced with their physiology—exhibited in a desire to shift slightly, scratch, yawn, cough, and engage in other side involvements affording "creature release." There are four general means of coming to terms with these little exigencies. One is to suppress them. In middle-class society suppression occurs in almost all social circumstances in regard to flatus. The second is to treat such releases as do occur as though they had not occurred at all.

---

4. *San Francisco Chronicle,* June 17, 1962.
5. Kathryn Hulme, *The Nun's Story* (London: Frederick Muller, 1957), pp. 37–38.

(These are the two solutions employed in parade-ground manners. They may be linked with a formal device by which a performer, in role, can ask permission to step out of ranks to perform his release, becoming, when he does so, altogether out of frame, this being a version of the mechanism already considered in connection with incapacitated uniformed performers who cannot themselves perform a proper exit ceremony.)[6] The third is for the performer to shield his lapse from the perception of others by twists and contortions of various kinds or by restricting his impropriety to a part of his body that is already shielded from view. The fourth is for him to assume liberties, openly attending to his comfort or openly asking permission to do so or sufferances for having done so, the assumption being that the requirements of his role are not so strict as to disallow momentary withdrawal. In these last cases, the actor attends to his creature concerns and the others present disattend his attendance. (In this way, a speaker at the beginning of a talk may momentarily go out of frame in order to greet silently a familiar member of the audience or exchange a nicety with the chairman, and during the talk pause at an appropriate juncture to take a sip of water, clean his glasses, or arrange his notes. Correspondingly, he will be able to sustain certain out-of-frame side involvements, such as toying with his pen or squaring off the objects on the lectern.)

In contrast to parade-ground practices, where very little by way of diversionary side involvement is allowed, there are formal board games such as checkers in which very little by way of discipline is required of performers and diversionary interruptions are easily dissociated from the play in progress. The performer in his capacity as opponent or protagonist is obliged to be mindful of the state of the game and to manage, with more or less physical aplomb, to get his piece to the intended square at the right time; but outside of that, he as a person will be allowed a wide range of side and subordinate activities. Perhaps, as will be argued, because board games are so well designed to generate involvement they do not need formal help in this regard. More to the point, the entities that board games set into play are not persons but pieces, and so perhaps the individuals who direct a set of them can be allowed all manner of lapses—after all, the

---

6. The basic example is the traditional schoolroom signal of a few generations ago, whereby a child indicated by holding up one or two fingers what he wanted to be excused for.

pieces themselves don't sniffle or scratch or clean their pipes, being indeed as disciplined as tin soldiers.

These two extremes—parade grounds and board games—are themselves to be contrasted with the staging of a drama. The theater even more than the parade ground obliges the performer to refrain from all momentarily motivated creature releases and other side involvements, but it does this in connection with the fact that in the theater these disruptions have a special syntactical value. On the stage a whole "natural" person is projected, a full identity whatever the special role requirements of a particular scene. As such, the performer will have to enact appropriate creature releases, for obviously the typical discrepancies between performer and role are ones the actor must put into his part if he is to perform a seemingly genuine, fully rounded person. But, of course, these little movements and expressions will be judiciously scripted into the preformulated flow of interaction on the stage and thus will not constitute genuine side involvements at all. When an actor literally fails to contain himself during performance of his part he can, of course, attempt to assimilate this disruption to the character he is projecting, as if, in fact, the discrepancy had been part of the script; and fellow performers may attempt to cooperate in this covering, adjusting their own lines and actions to contain the event "naturally." But if this remedy fails, then embarrassment will be very deep, deeper, perhaps, than can occur on the parade ground or any other place of great formality; for what is embarrassed is an identity, not a role, and beyond this the plane of action in which the other characters have their being, too.[7]

---

7. Similarly, when the audience witnesses an actor forgetting his lines and hears the prompter providing them, the whole dramatic illusion can be threatened, not merely the flubber's contribution to it. Again the issue is the syntactical level at which the error occurs. We may speak metaphorically of an actor in literal life forgetting his lines and having to be prompted, but it is hard to think of an everyday flub that cuts as deeply into unstaged reality as a missed line does in a dramatized event. Something like a man forgetting the first name of his wife when introducing her would have to be drawn upon. Of course, children who put on a play for a school audience can survive all manner of breakdown, as can their audience, but that is because no one expects to become much encaptured by the play, attention focusing on the effort of the little actors, not their efficacy. For the same reason children make, and are suffered in making, many gaffes in offstage interaction. That, in part, is what it means to be treated as—to "be"—a child.

It is clear that on many occasions, not only certain events but also certain persons will be disattended. Guards, janitors, and technicians all routinely function as nonpersons, present in a relevant way but treated as though not present. (At business, governmental, and academic meetings, a young female will sometimes be present to fetch coffee and paper, relay messages from outside the room to persons inside, place calls, and so forth, while expressing by her entire manner—walk, talk, and seating posture—that she is claiming as little space as possible and that what she does is to be disattended.) Of course, there are limits. During the Oakland antiwar demonstrations of 1967, doctors and ministers, labeled as such, expected to be treated as noncombatants, as outside the fray, but were apparently put upon by the police. They later formally complained that their rights—rights of being nonplayers in the events—were not respected.[8]

When one examines transformed interaction, such as that presented onstage, one finds, of course, that matters are, as it were, formalized with a rigorous line drawn around the official realm of activity and its characters and relatively great capacity to disattend events not cast as part of this domain. Something of an extreme can be found in non-Western drama:

> The Japanese Bunraku puppet tradition provides the most extreme example of such a channeling of audience perception because it asks the audience to ignore the visible presence of all three puppeteers in the act of manipulating a single puppet. It is quite clear here that without reliance on the anchoring power of such selective disattention it would be impossible for the audience to enjoy the performance.[9]

> European spectators at Chinese plays always find it surprising and offensive that attendants in ordinary dress come and go on the stage; but to the initiated audience the stagehand's untheatrical dress seems to be enough to make his presence as irrelevant as to us the intrusion of an usher who leads people to a seat in our line of vision.[10]

---

8. See Terence Cannon, "Barricades in Oakland," *The Movement,* November 1967, p. 3.

9. Gerold L. Hanck, "A Frame Analysis of the Puppet Theater" (unpublished paper, University of Pennsylvania, 1970).

10. Susanne K. Langer, *Feeling and Form* (New York: Charles Scribner's Sons, 1953), p. 324. Of course, since Langer wrote these words playwrights and directors in search of new gimmicks have employed precisely

The audience, of course, is not alone in exhibiting a willingness to disattend. The characters projected by the performers systematically disattend the individuals on the other side of the stage, both as playgoers (in that fidgeting, latecoming, and the like can be disattended) and as onlookers (as when riotous cheers and booing are systematically disattended during a boxing match or baseball game).

The scope of disattention varies in pretty ways. It is said that soldiers in the heat of battle can sustain injuries without feeling pain and never sense that anything is wrong with them until they are back at a base camp. I once was present when a fire broke out in a downtown Las Vegas casino. From the second floor smoke and smell began to pour down, fire sirens were heard, firemen rushed in and ran upstairs with equipment, more smoke came down, eventually the firemen left, and all the while on the first floor the dealers continued to deal and the players continued to play. In the same establishment on another night I saw a cocktail waitress get into a fight with a customer, tear the shirt off his back, and have him ejected—all without anyone's much looking up. On the other hand, those who have worked the fields near a road in rural Scotland know that the slightest distraction—a bird, a dog, a tourist walking by—will be reason enough to stop for a moment and examine what is happening. On the theatrical stage, actors projecting play characters may be prepared to treat as not occurring the disturbance caused by latecomers or persons who shake bracelets, cough, sneeze, crinkle candy wrappings, clap prematurely, churn in their seats, and so forth, but will often be unwilling to tolerate being photographed. So, too, sometimes concert artists:

> But the crowning stupidity occurred during Andres Segovia's recital, when a nut in the audience actually stood up and tried to photograph him—at which The Master stopped playing and called out in a touching misuse of the language: "Impossible, please!"[11]

Further, in theater, as suggested, there is a marked tendency to focus on one speaker at a time, but still others onstage can

---

these stage practices. Nor can one think of a practice no longer employed that might not come to be employed for the novelty to be derived from it. In general, then, there is reason here for speaking of theatrical practices or conventions, not hard and fast rules.

11. Reported by Herb Caen, *San Francisco Chronicle*, March 24, 1968.

engage in some activity meant to be witnessed simultaneously. In radio drama, on the other hand, no such complexity is allowable, for, as suggested, we appear to have less capacity to single out sounds than to single out sights.

Capacities regarding the management of distraction vary quite considerably across time and place. Today the minor adjustment noises that are just tolerated from theater audiences are apparently relatively slight compared to eighteenth-century practice. For in general, playgoer discipline is much stricter now than in most other periods of the Western stage:

> The insistence that all plays must have an uninterrupted mood and increasing suspense is something which has yet to be proved, although it is undoubtedly a requirement of most western drama. Confusion in the auditorium, the coming and going of characters, eating and drinking, have characterized the whole history of the European theatre to within a very recent period. To give one instance, the English Restoration theatres were accustomed not only to eating, drinking and card-playing but to duels and assignations as well.[12]

There are, of course, historic records of too much distraction leading to riots, to a collapse of the theatrical frame, but that too much was very much indeed by our standards:

> But what provided the biggest incitement to rioting were the stage seats, those "twelve penny stools" of Johnson's time that had become a luxury for titled young bloods to indulge in. The stage gallants not only exchanged greetings between themselves and harangued the audience whenever they felt inclined, they often directly interfered with the performers. On one occasion, for instance, Peg Woffington played the entire part of Cordelia clasped round the waist by an overamorous seat-holder. Mrs. Cibber, too, in the tomb scene in *Romeo and Juliet* frequently thrilled the audience to enthusiasm—including the hundred or so who were with her in the tomb.[13]

One should also consider whether or not some sounds are themselves harder to disattend than others, apart from absolute

---

12. Mordecai Gorelik, *New Theatres for Old* (New York: Samuel French, 1955), p. 62.

13. Stephen Tait, "English Theatre Riots," *Theatre Arts*, XXIV (1940): 97.

volume.[14] Apparently in our culture irregularly timed sounds are more distracting than regular ones. More to the point (as will be considered later), sounds that produce an ambiguity as to what frame they are to be heard in seem to produce distraction.

II

It has been suggested that during the occurrence of any activity framed in a particular way one is likely to find another flow of other activity that is systematically disattended and treated as out of frame, something not to be given any concern or attention. Drawing loosely on a particular imagery, it was said that the main track carrying the story line was associated with a disattend track, the two tracks playing simultaneously. Now a second stream of out-of-frame activity must be considered, this one even more consequential, perhaps, for the main activity than the first, yet nonetheless—to a degree—kept out of focus.

In doings involving joint participation, there is to be found a stream of signs which is itself excluded from the content of the activity but which serves as a means of regulating it, bounding, articulating, and qualifying its various components and phases. One might speak here of directional signals and, by metaphorical extension, the track that contains them.[15]

The most obvious illustration of directional cues is, of course, literary punctuation, for it comprises one corpus of conventions, one code, that is learned consciously, often all too consciously. In any case, these marks nicely illustrate the special character of

---

14. Suggested in John Carey, "Framing Mechanisms in Radio Drama" (unpublished paper, University of Pennsylvania, 1970).

15. This notion derives from Gregory Bateson. See particularly the comments on "metacommunication" scattered throughout his chapters in Jurgen Ruesch and Gregory Bateson, *Communication* (New York: W. W. Norton & Company, 1951), and the following:

> It would also be important to identify among animals any signals of the following types: (a) signals whose only meaning would be the acknowledgment of a signal emitted by another; (b) signals asking for a signal to be repeated; (c) signals indicating failure to receive a signal; (d) signals which punctuate the stream of signals; and so on. [p. 209]

Bateson thus restricts the directional track to communicative activity (and also relation management), but there seems to be no reason not to generalize the notion to activity as such.

the directional stream—the quality of not being attended focally yet closely organizing what is attended.[16]

An interesting part of the directional stream is what might be called *connectives*.[17] In all activity, especially spoken activity, it is crucial to be able to locate who is doing what at the moment it is being done. In face-to-face talk, location is usually established for the hearer by judgments of relative intensity of sound as between his two ears, by his identifying the personal style of the speaker, and by seeing the speaker's lip movements. In telephone contact, on those occasions when unfamiliarity prevents voice identification, social categorization (sex, age, class, and so on) usually occurs, names are often given quickly, and it is assumed that only one person at one end will be speaking, all of which, of course, sharply limits the problem. In novels, connectives again occur, namely, tags such as "he said," "he replied," "he answered," coming after a sentence, or somewhat similar ones coming before. (Interestingly, readers demonstrate a nice capacity to wait for a line to be finished before demanding a connective.) And as an alternative to these standard connectives, there is occasional use of mere spatial arrangement, especially when the sense of what is being said makes it very evident who is speaking.

Connectives will be further considered later. The point here is that although in written dialogue connectives are everywhere and very stereotyped, they are very little seen, and if seen, not seen as something to judge closely for stereotyping—as would be the text itself.

---

16. The modern linguistic approach to the syntax of a sentence provides the most developed example available of frame analysis—if a slogan be allowed to wag the dog. Serial position of the words establishes two main sections, noun phrase and verb phrase, and whatever falls within one of these slots is applied to whatever falls within the other. Each segment thus provides a reading across everything within the other segment. And it is a matter of indifference whether a segment contains a noun, a phrase, a clause, a sentence, a paragraph, or the whole of the world. And serial position which provides directions for how to organize the content of the sentence is not itself a matter of direct attention, merely establishing where the dividing bracket is to go. Similarly, within each major segment, the same mode of analysis can be applied until minimal constituent elements are reached.

17. In a useful paper, "Shifters, Verbal Categories, and the Russian Verb," Russian Language Project, Department of Slavic Languages and Literature, Harvard University (1957), Roman Jakobson used the term "connector" in much the same way, for which information I am grateful to Dell Hymes.

In addition to connectives for linking acts to actors, there are devices for linking statements by one actor to replies by another in pairs meant to be seen as linked. In ordinary talk, temporal sequence largely solves this problem, as it does onstage and in the cinema. Such distant cousins to ordinary talk as puppet inter-action also share this temporal linkage feature. In the novel and in printed plays, a functional equivalent of temporal sequence is provided, namely, spatial sequence—in the West, starting at the top left side of the page and going to the bottom, one line at a time, each line taken from left to right. Thus, sequence in reading is taken as sequence in action. In comic strips, two func-tional equivalents to temporal sequence are found. First, the boxes (or "frames" as they are called) are to be read left to right. Within a box, the character to the left, namely, the character one would ordinarily attend to first if one were moving left to right, is taken as having spoken first, and thus the other character's words or actions are taken as a reply (or "in response") to the first. In actuality, however, all the speeches and actions of all the figures are simultaneously available.

It might seem that our willingness to employ a spatial equiva-lent for temporal sequence is an appreciable accomplishment, but the temporal sequencing that is inherent in the spoken narra-tion of an event is itself already a transformational accomp-lishment of note—so notable, in fact, that students as well as their subjects typically remain unaware of the achievement. A spoken or written representation of a strip of interaction strongly encourages the use of temporal sequence and its functional sub-stitutes, a first actor's move being described in full before the disclosure of a second actor's responsive move. In effect, then, transcription practices favor a first actor's finishing before a second actor begins. That finishing is what printed or spoken narration needs. But *real* interaction does not need that waiting in the same degree. While a first actor is still making his move, a second actor begins his reply. (This last sentence is itself a good illustration. Before coming to say "a second actor begins his reply," I had to *finish* saying, "While a first actor is still making his move." And if I had reversed the clauses, to wit: "A second actor begins his reply while a first actor is still making his move," I could make the same point, but I would be relying on the same transformational practice. For I would have *finished* saying, "A second actor begins his reply" *before* saying what it began dur-ing.)[18] These misplaced finishings are, of course, read out of our understanding of what we read, but that surely is what our capacity to accept transformations is about. Note, students of interaction have apparently been better at recording the aspects of statement-reply complexes that are temporally sequenced, that is, spread out, first one move, then the answer to it, than the aspects of the complex that occur simultaneously.

In talk a central element in the directional track is the broad class of behaviors which provides what are sometimes called qualifiers, markers, and the like, these sustained across a strip of discourse by means of paralinguistic and kinesic cues. Hand gestures can function in this way. More central still (as Bateson argued) are the signs which inform about the working of the communication system. A current version under the term "regu-lators" can be cited:

> The next category of nonverbal behavior is what we are calling REGULATORS. These are acts which maintain and regulate the back-and-forth nature of speaking and listening between two or more interactants. They tell the speaker to continue, repeat, elaborate, hurry up, become more interesting, less salacious, give the other a chance to talk, *etc.* They can tell the listener to pay special atten-tion, to wait just a minute more, to talk, *etc.* Regulators, like illus-trators, are related to the conversation, but while the illustrators are specifically interlaced with the moment-to-moment fluctuations in speech, the regulators are instead related to the conversational

---

18. Understandably, then, we are able to shift easily from temporal to spatial sequencing, for after all, something of a transformation is required in both cases. As Boris A. Uspensky suggests:

An analogous manifestation of the reordering of simultaneous actions into sequential actions may be observed, in film, in connection with the use of montage: for example, the face of a man telling a joke is shown in a close-up shot, and then the face of the listener, who begins to smile, is shown; the smile does not appear simultaneously with the telling of the joke but after the joke is told, even though the reaction is meant to be a simultaneous one. ["Study of Point of View: Spatial and Temporal Form," a preprint from his *The Poetics of Composition: Structure of the Artistic Text and the Typology of Compositional Form*, trans. Valentina Zavarin and Susan Wittig (Berkeley: University of California Press, 1974), p. 26.]

And just as understandably, we can shift from face-to-face conversation to the telephonic kind, a shift that necessitates a sudden increase in tem-poral sequencing, a sudden diminution of overlapping.

flow, the pacing of the exchange. The most common regulator is the head nod, the equivalent of the verbal *mm-hmm;* other regulators include eye contacts, slight movements forward, small postural shifts, eyebrow raises, and a whole host of other small nonverbal acts.[19]

Here, then, are the cues which tell a speaker that he is or isn't being listened to. Here the listener can warn that he is getting ready to try to take over the floor or that he inclines to decline the speaker's invitation to do so. And it follows that the directional stream includes cues from the done-to as well as the doers, cues which help regulate activity, although they themselves are not to be examined full face. In Yngve's phrase, a "back channel" is employed.[20]

Observe that what is carried in the disattend track can be blotted out, in fact as well as appearance, but not so directional cues, for these must be kept in mind enough so that they can do their work. And because what they do has a framing effect, structuring (or dramatically restructuring) what came before or comes after, the quietest impropriety here can be heard as very noisy. What might ordinarily be handled with ease as something to disattend becomes precarious when it can be read as part of the directional flow. Thus, at an outdoor political rally a dog

19. Paul Ekman and Wallace V. Friesen, "The Repertoire of Nonverbal Behavior: Categories, Origins, Usage, and Coding," *Semiotica*, I (1969): 82. See also *I.R.*, pp. 34–36.

20. Victor H. Yngve, "On Getting a Word in Edgewise," Papers from the Sixth Regional Meeting of the Chicago Linguistic Society (Department of Linguistics, University of Chicago, 1970):

In fact, both the person who has the turn and his partner are simultaneously engaged in both speaking and listening. This is because of the existence of what I call the back channel, over which the person who has the turn receives short messages such as "yes" and "uh-huh" without relinquishing the turn. The partner, of course, is not only listening, but speaking occasionally as he sends the short messages in the back channel. The back channel appears to be very important in providing for monitoring of the quality of communication. [p. 568]

Here see also the useful study by Adam Kendon, "Some Functions of Gaze-Direction in Social Interaction," *Acta Psychologica*, XXVI (1967), esp. pp. 42–47. It might be added that the more one applies videotape and other microanalytical analyses to spoken interaction, the more one finds that wide arrays of listeners' apparently incidental side involvements regulate, and are regulated by, current speaker's action.

barking at random can often be disattended more or less effectively; but if the dog happens to chime in so that his bark can be taken as a comment upon something being said, the chime occurring precisely at a response juncture in the saying, it will be hard indeed to manage the difficulty. Laughter or its suppression can become general. A similar disarray occurs—as will be considered later—when directional statements are unwittingly incorporated into the story line.

III

Consider now the capacity of individuals to be given messages designed to be read or heard, understood, but yet not distract unduly from attention given the story line. Highway advertising is one example. Another is the stream of print that is flashed across the very bottom or the very top of a television or movie screen when, say, an important announcement must be made immediately. One might speak here of the overlay channel. As with directional cues, these messages are to be managed in a dissociated way; unlike directional cues, however, they bear no reference to the story line and thus provide as clear as possible an illustration of how attention (and cognition) can be split in two.

IV

Whenever an individual participates in an activity, he will be situated in regard to it, this entailing exposure over a given range to direct witness, and an opportunity, over much the same range, to acquire direct observations. These latter implications of "sitedness," in conjunction with his auditing capacities, generate a series of points beyond which he cannot obtain evidence as to what is going on. He will find barriers to his perception, a sort of *evidential boundary*. Everything beyond this boundary will be concealed from him. Just as one can think of an activity as affording possibilities for disattending events and directional cues, so one can think of an activity as affording the possibility of concealment, this embracing the sum of matters that can occur beyond the evidential boundaries of its participants. Note, directional cues and overlayed communication are treated *as if* out of frame; what is beyond the evidential boundary is *actually* out of frame, at least as a sensible stimulus.

If one takes a particular scene of face-to-face interaction as a point of reference, standard evidential boundaries can be suggested. First is what is sometimes called backstage activity, namely, action occurring before and after the scene or behind it that is relevant to it and at the same time (in likelihood) incompatible with it.

Second is the actor himself. Minimally he figures in two ways. His thoughts and feelings can be seen as coming from some source within his body, especially within his skull. And these "internal states" make their appearance through intended and unintended bodily expression, especially through his face and words. His epidermis can thus be seen as a screen, allowing some evidence of inner state to pass through, but also some concealment, as when the individual maintains a "straight" face or tactfully chooses his words. The same epidermal screen allows him to receive secret signals from offstage or onstage without allowing this reception to be perceived by others. In addition to functioning as a screen relative to what is presumably inside him, his body also functions as a barrier which prevents those on one side of him from seeing what is directly on the other side or those in back of him from seeing his facial expression. It is from behind such a shield—it is because of such an interposition of self—that he can secretly signal confederates within the scene or conspirators behind it. I shall speak here of the concealment channel.

It is not difficult to see that exploitive fabrications are likely to rely on the capacity of some of the participants in a setting to act (and communicate) in a manner not perceptible to some of the others. One must ask, however, whether activities that are less divisive depend on secrecy arrangements, too.

An easy step from outright deception is stage performances. It is from here, of course, that our root imagery for behind-the-scenes derives. The point, however, is that howsoever unreal we know a stage performance to be, we are still embarrassed by hearing the prompter; he provides directional cues but not ones that can be treated *as though* they were out of frame—they must be out of frame objectively. Similarly, although we know that a commercial in some sense is not believed by the announcer and that certainly he is reading a script, not talking extemporaneously, we still find our involvement disrupted when a sudden view of the teleprompter is obtained.[21] So, too, it is obviously apparent that a puppet cannot perform on its own, yet in some traditions, puppeteers go to considerable lengths to reduce the visibility of the wires in order, as is said, to heighten the illusion.[22]

Actual informal face-to-face conversation ("natural talk") would seem to provide a sharp contrast both to dramatic scriptings and fabrications, yet here, too, the concealment channel plays a part. Participants will almost always be obliged to exert some tact, and this work, of course, relies on an evidential boundary—in this case whatever it is that "real" thoughts and feelings are hidden behind. Audience segregation is also assumed, since many of the responses that occur could be discredited were the inappropriate others suddenly to appear. That such discreditings do not always occur is not the point; the discrepancies are nonetheless there and open up discrediting as a possibility. In brief, even ordinary talk is something of a construction.

Given the stage as one of the best-appreciated evidential boundaries, excluding from almost all angles of perception everything that happens before the curtain rises and after it falls as well as what occurs in back of the stage during a performance, and given the view of informal conversation (and more so, its broadcasted versions) as an arrangement wherein the gestural configuration and surface of the body function as a screen and shield in regard to evidence about inward thoughts and feelings, one should go on to examine the evidential boundaries sustained in other kinds of activity. A simple example is the telephone. Here, for obvious reasons, sound alone must be relied on, which means that silent collusive signs between a talker and someone standing next to

21. The evolution of this device is of special interest, involving a special combination of engineering and interaction know-how. Early versions required off-angle glances, with disclosive results. The current one employs clear glass plates that can be placed in front of the camera lens (or directly between speaker and live audience) and is perceptible only to the performer. He appears to be looking at the viewer (or the audience) but is actually seeing the script. (For this and many unacknowledged suggestions regarding the mass media I am much indebted to John Carey.)

22. Hanck, "A Frame Analysis of the Puppet Theater." For example, some puppeteers employ a fine wire mesh in front of the stage to obscure sight of control wires.

him can be as broad and open as the colluder wishes to make them.[23]

Formal card and board games provide further arrangements to consider. Chess and checkers, defined as games of "full information," oblige the player to keep his intent in his head and hope that his play will not be read for the strategy determining it. And since words need not be spoken, only bodily gesture must be inhibited. Feigning, however, is possible, that is, the making of a play that is itself not the most useful, solely so the implications drawn from it will throw the opponent off the scent. Card games, however, typically allow a player to know his own holdings while concealing some or all of them from others by the opaque back of the cards—as a right from opponents, as a duty from partners. The body as a screen is thus extended to the cards, body and cards ostensibly functioning as a single whole in establishing an evidential barrier.[24]

It is apparent that the capacity of an activity to afford a screen—the concealment track—is very much related to the capacity of the receptors of the participants. A seeing person's conversation with the blind allows him a license of deviation not available to him during ordinary face-to-face interaction. When standards must be maintained only before specialized agents, such as schoolteachers, parents, and the like, then, of course, the concealment area broadens considerably. It is thus that a motorist may glance around him at an isolated crossway, see no police in sight, and "run a light," transforming the whole highway around him momentarily into a concealment track.[25]

V

I have suggested that in addition to sustaining a story line in any stream of interaction, the individual is also capable of sustaining

---

23. See "Tie-Signs," in *R.P.*, pp. 220–222.

24. Ostensibly only. In fact, in bridge, although exposure of own cards to partner is a rare and deadly sin likely to remove the practitioner from respectable circles, improperly giving partner information through the *manner* in which one states one's bid or plays a card is rather common and commonly tolerated.

25. Rules differently impinge on systems of action. In checkers, for example, it is thoroughly expected that no infraction of the rules will occur whatsoever. In the order maintained in classrooms, infractions will be anticipated.

subordinate channels of activity, of which four were discussed. This implies that individuals possess a nice capacity to give no outward sign of attention and little, if any, inward concern to something that is, after all, within cognitive reach—and in the case of regulative cues, must be. The issue, I think, is not that the individual at any one moment will be merely simulating interest in the story line but that he establishes himself in the setting and manages himself so that at any juncture, should the need arise, he smoothly carries on his official involvement in the face of something distracting that has begun to occur, including the need to convey furtive signals through the concealment channel. This capacity to cope with a range of disruptions—anticipated and unanticipated—while giving them the minimal apparent attention is, of course, a basic feature of interaction competency, one seen to develop with "experience."

The most natural and convincing involvement in a story line, then, is always something more disciplined than might appear. It should not surprise us, therefore, to see how effectively a political speaker can treat as not occurring the chairman's effort to adjust the microphone or a press photographer's series of flash shots from front and center. Nor that a talk show performer can give the appearance of participating "naturally" in talk while in fact he is keeping very close continuous track of time, camera target, upcoming topic shifts, the potential trouble that other performers might be getting into, and the like. Nor that when individuals speak before a tape recorder, they can, when a spool has to be changed, stop the flow of talk that seemed theretofore to be directed solely to the live members of the audience.[26] Nor that when media technicians ask an official to repeat an act (such as signing a bill, greeting a notable visitor, laying a cornerstone, and so on) he will generally oblige, even though his ability and willingness to do this may reflect ironically on the real act, suggesting that all along it was something that could be repeated at will, and therefore itself a "mere" act.[27]

---

26. In *The Maltese Falcon*, Dashiell Hammett provides an early example, or rather a keying of one. Sam Spade is hotly replying to the importuning D.A., and at the end of an impassioned speech, "he rose and turned his head over his shoulder to address the stenographer: 'Getting that all right son? Or am I going too fast for you?'"

27. Because these shots have come to be treated as symbolic of the whole event, and because those who manage such events are increasingly alive to the importance of media coverage, there is no want of these portraits. Here,

VI

1. The discriminations that have been made among subordinate tracks perhaps provide a beginning, but—like everything else associated with framing—the structuring that is implied is itself transformed in various ways, reused, indeed, made several kinds of convenience of. Channels established to deal with one kind of activity are, for the very reason that they have been so established, exploited to deal with a different kind of material.

Some examples. As suggested there seems to be hardly any unstaged activity in which participants are not allowed some out-of-frame side involvements. For example, minor adjustments in the interests of comfort are almost always allowable and dis-attendable by others. At the same time, these acts can also serve as subtle directional cues and very generally do. But note that they have strategic properties; they are more or less under the control of the individual who evinces them and at the same time provide something of an understanding that no intent is involved. Understandably, then, the actor can draw upon these minor side involvements in order to establish an alignment in the situation that he will be able to disclaim if necessary and to which the recipient will be able to act blind—if *he* chooses. In this way the actor can express a wide range of disaffection: rejection of responsibility for what is happening, disdain for fellow participants, desire to leave or to terminate a conversation, "boredom," and so forth. Indeed, through the use of these apparently innocent devices, an individual can effectively "attack the situation," forcing others present to give their attention to something about which they are obliged to appear unconcerned. And, contrariwise, he can also express enthusiastic support that might not be warranted by his relationship to the recipient. Here, then, are "takes," "burns," "fishy looks," blushes, glowerings, and various expressions of sympathy and agreement. Here are the cues which tell a

perhaps, familiarity breeds insufficient contempt, for we often fail to note the number of removes these pictures are from untransformed reality. The greeting between two heads of state is but a ceremonial token of the relation between two states, the important matter in question. A candid photograph of the meeting is a keying of this token. A press photograph is likely to be a transformation of this transformation, since the subjects are likely to position themselves—if not oblige with retakes—in accordance with the need of the camera.

speaker how he is being received so that he can strategically tailor his remarks even while he is making them—or strategically decide (and be free to decide) not to do so.

In sum, in ordinary social interaction recipients of another's behavior—witnesses to his acts—provide some sort of gestural display of their alignment or position relative to the implications of his behavior. Even when no words are allowed them, they manage to externalize a portrait of their attitude toward the event. They respond editorially to what their neighbor does even while he is doing it. (It is thus, it could be argued, that Darwin accounts for gestures of threat or submission—for portraiture— and beyond this the capacity which animals and men have for keying and fabrication.) And they provide this back-channel response through disattendable expressions such as minor side involvements. Thus, if we did not have an animal nature demanding occasional creature release, we might have to invent something like it; and no doubt whatever beastliness we actually do have is here encouraged because of what can be accomplished with it.

2. The possibility of exploiting the disattend track directs attention to a further issue. As already remarked, the ongoing alignment response of witnesses to a deed allows the doer to modify his doings accordingly, even while he is doing them. When these back-channel alignment displays are carried in the concealment track instead of the directional track, a second function emerges. For, managed in this manner, they allow their maker to stand up to adversity in a way that suggests to him or to third parties who might be watching him that he is not to be trifled with, not to be discounted, and yet the individual who called forth the display has no reason to feel that insubordination has occurred and that a response is required.

It is in this context of self-saving, half-empty gestures that evidential boundaries play a particularly significant role. For when an adversary's back is turned, subordinated individuals may then provide a broad display of their alignment to him. Indeed, we have gestures specialized for this purpose—gestures felt to be never performed to a person's face but only behind his back. Thumb-to-nose and sticking-out-tongue are examples, ones identified with youthful users who presumably employ these dissociated devices more frequently than do adults.

But, of course, evidential boundaries need not wait for a wall to loom or a back to be turned before they can come into being. The arrangements which allow an individual to draw back-channel directional cues from what he is attending to peripherally also allow him to act as though he has not seen something (or heard something) when indeed he has—and moreover to perform this act of nonperception without exposing himself to any utterly convincing argument that he is merely acting. In consequence, face-to-face interaction can be seen to have in its very structure a "mixed motive" quality involving close but tacit collaboration between opponents.

3. Now glance at another complication. It was suggested that one special channel or track in the organization of experience is the disattend track, encompassing locally occurring events to be treated as not relevantly occurring. Side involvements of various kinds are illustrations of what may be carried in this channel; background features of the scene are others. Given this, it is understandable that the disattend track would be exploited to carry secret communication. Thus, the "high signs" employed by confederates, that is, secret teammates, typically draw upon those behaviors that properly have nothing to do with matters of current concern. An early American example can be given:

> River gamblers seldom operated alone; usually they traveled in groups of from three to six, adopting various disguises and pretending never to have met until they boarded the steamboat. They capped and roped for one another's banking games, and when one succeeded in enticing a sucker or two into a short card session, the others were always on hand to help make up a table. If a sharper obtained a seat in an honest game of experienced players, where the usual methods of trickery were dangerous, "his confederates would seat themselves in such a position that they could see the cards held by his adversaries, and 'item' the strength of their hands to him by signs." These were made by hand, by twirling the head of a cane in a certain manner, by puffs of cigar smoke, by shifting a quid of tobacco in the cheeks, and in almost every other conceivable fashion.[28]

Nor is the body required for these signs. A bank will do:

> The guard walks through the entire bank, checking the vault area especially closely. If everything is satisfactory, he then sets up a signal to alert the rest of the employees that it's safe to enter the

28. Herbert Asbury, *Sucker's Progress* (New York: Dodd, Mead & Co., 1938), p. 205.

bank. The signal, which is made up by our signal committee (as differentiated from our vault committee and the 30 other committees we have humming away at First Mutual), can be a wastebasket overturned on a desk, or a cigarette burning in an ashtray, or a chair propped up against a desk—something simple, visual, prearranged, and, as I said, right off the old Warner Bros. lot.[29]

The issue here has structural significance. There necessarily occurs around any activity a cloud of events, often of very brief duration, whose relation to the main event is one of merely fortuitous co-occurrence, no further connection existing.[30] Scratching the nose, placement of hands, touching a particular piece of clothing, and other comfort movements are examples. Such of these incidentally co-occurring events that are easily subject to manipulation provide a good source of materials from which to fashion a secret code for transmitting strategic information. Understandably, then, when, as in bridge, teammates can use such a code to secretly convey information about their holdings to each other, we must expect that cheating will be common, and common, too, the suspicion, whether rightly or wrongly founded, that cheating is occurring; consequently, of course, there will be suspicion, rightly or wrongly, that one is suspected.[31]

VII

The complications so far considered in the tracking of experience are complicated still more when the activity that is in frame—the

29. "The Problem with Robbing Banks," by "Morgan Irving," as audited by Charles Sopkin, *New York Magazine*, September 10, 1973.

30. See the discussion of "connectedness" in "Normal Appearances" in *R.P.*, pp. 310–338.

31. A good example is the scandal at the 1965 World Bridge Championship Tournament in Buenos Aires when a British team, Terence Reese and Boris Schapiro, were accused of using finger signals produced through the manner in which the cards were held, the signals designating the number of hearts held when that suit was bid. The published discussion that followed argued that these scandals were always occurring, that participants believed that anyone who wanted to cheat by signaling information to his partner could easily do so, and that the only final solution would be to rearrange the evidential boundaries so that partners could not see each other during the bidding, and the bidding itself would be accomplished by a pushbutton code instead of voiced statements. See *The Observer* (London), May 30, 1965; *Life*, June 4, 1965; *San Francisco Chronicle*, May 25 and 27, 1965, and August 10, 1966.

officially attended activity—is itself a transformation of actual activity. Preliminary arguments are necessary.

The notion of evidential boundary has already been mentioned. In order to proceed, another concept must be introduced: *partici-pation status*. During informal talk between two individuals, it is likely to be apparent that both participants enjoy the same capac-ities and privileges: each is capable of listening and talking, and each has a right to do both. One might speak here of both partici-pants having full participation status. Relative to this reference point, one can immediately see some additional possibilities.

First, it is plain that one or both of the participants may suffer some physical incapacity in connection with speaking or hearing or that they may speak mutually unintelligible languages. So in the effective sense, participants of partial competency can be anticipated. An additional possibility must then be admitted, a special participation status, that of interpreter who can (and only can) relay messages between participants who would otherwise be cut off from each other.

Now recall that unbeknownst to participants, someone may be monitoring their activity aurally, visually, or both, and this moni-toring may occur by accident or design and through electronic or "natural" means. If the latter, then two possibilities. A ratified participant may secretly record or commit to memory whatever is happening; or someone within range who is treated and treats himself as being out of frame, a mere bystander to be dis-attended, may take improper advantage of his proximity to eaves-drop on the activity.

Next is toy status, namely, the existence of some object, human or not, that is treated as if in frame, an object to address acts to or remarks about, but out of frame (disattendable) in regard to its capacity to hear and talk. Note, this status may be relatively fixed, as with an infant, or momentary, as when a husband comments in passing about his wife as though she were not present even though she is.

Finally, one must allow for the fact that a participant may communicate to himself privily or, if more than one additional participant is present, to another, in a secret, collusive way, thereby establishing a self for himself different from the one that officially and openly applies.

It is apparent, then, that participation status, even in the context of informal conversation, can be considerably differentiated. When one looks at performer-audience interaction, matters get more complicated still.

When individuals are engaged in playing a sport or board game, repairing a car, or constructing a building, bystanders will often blatantly watch the proceedings and be suffered in this status of onlookers by those upon whom they are looking. (Something like a boxing ring can thus emerge naturally.) It is this onlooker status that becomes available whenever anyone has an accident or creates a scene; indeed, the creation of these rights of open looking constitutes one of the chief costs of getting into trouble in public. And, of course, certain sport contests are specifically organized to facilitate such watching. Note, this openness transforms tasks and games into performances, although, as suggested, not quite of the theatrical kind, since, on the surface at least, the rationale for these open activities lies entirely outside the enjoyment provided the viewers. There is a frame-relevant reason why performers in any kind of ring must tolerate onlookers whether they want to or not: for rules of eye aversion, rules relative to visual territory, pertain to individuals qua social persons, not individuals qua sport or game participants. Just as a gamesman has a right to stand outside his sporting deeds, sustaining all manner of side involvements at such times, just as he has a right to deeply involve himself and show rather open affect, so spectators may have a right to stare or applaud or cheer or boo wildly, for these attentions are to a self-dissociated realm of the sport, something that the player himself has a duty as well as a right to dissociate from his serious self. All of this is even more marked in board games and cards, where the characters in play are tokens of some kind; here a very open examination of the pieces in play is likely to be tolerated, even while a degree of avoidant respect is shown for the person of the player. Indeed, in games like bridge, in which concealment of one's own hand from opponents and partner is a basic requirement, "kibitzing" is usually tolerated, whereby a person who is not playing is allowed to "look" at one or more hands and to join in on the "postmortem" discussion. Should a player have to leave temporarily because of an emergency, a kibitzer may even be allowed to take over his hand. For, after all, bridge is a game between two two-handed teams, not persons. A committee could also be employed to decide a hand's play, as could a computer.[32]

Theatrical performances involve onlookers, too, but here they have a larger role. As with those who watch a sport, those who watch a play are disattended by the actor-in-character and yet they are fully privy to what is happening onstage in frame. However, as already considered, the staged interaction is opened up, slowed down, and focused so that the audience's peculiar form of eavesdropping is maximally facilitated, a fact that marks theatrical audiences off from other kinds. Theatrical audiences have only restricted rights to reply to the show they watch and are allowed only a restricted role, but unlike the onlookers at excavation sites, they do have *some* expectations in that regard.

The theatrical audience role of open eavesdropping is a major example of how, once experience is transformed for stage production, new positions can be taken up in regard to it. This is illustrated again in the special role of chorus,[33] "orator,"[34] or

---

32. Watchers of friendly amateur poker games may also be allowed to see a player's hole card, but in the higher reaches of the game this is not encouraged. Dissimulation of hidden values is a central feature of poker, and second-party looking can easily give the show away or subtly interfere with the player's deceptive expression. Also, pattern of play across all of an individual's hands in the game is felt to be important, and the kibitzer who can look at hole cards is in a favorable position to acquire this information without, as is the case of the opposing players, paying for it, which information the kibitzer could then use for his own gain should he ever play against the person about whom he has acquired it.

33. As Kenneth Macgowan and William Melnitz, *Golden Ages of the Theater* (Englewood Cliffs, N.J.: Prentice-Hall, 1959), suggest:

Properly understood, Murray pointed out, the chorus appears as an aid, not a hindrance, to the Greek playwright. The chorus was neither actor nor bystander. It was, rather, a kind of link with the audience, making the spectator feel a closer participation in the drama. The chorus was an instrument for the expression of complete and ultimate emotion over great or terrible deeds. It translated the feeling of the actor into a different medium. It brought to the audience emotions that the characters in a play sometimes could not completely feel, or emotions that could not be expressed in ordinary words. The chorus turned crude suffering into poetry, even into soothing mystery. [p. 16]

34. A statement of this role was provided by Samuel Chappuzeau in his *Theatre français*, published in 1673, when the role was apparently already on the decline:

The orator has two principal functions. It falls to him to address the audience and to compose the poster, and as there is a close connection between the two, nearly the same rules apply to both. At the end of the

other mediating, editorializing functions that can easily be built into the performance. The mediator—a specialized viewer who also participates as a staged character—can comment on whole aspects of the production, treating as an object of direct attention what the projected characters have to treat as something in which they are immersed. He is a footnote that talks. Prologues and epilogues can produce the same extensive bracketing. The subtitles in silent films accomplish a similar purpose. Puppetry provides another example of this reflexivity:

> The narrator is the voice of the puppets; he lays bare their thoughts and schemes. At the same time he is a guide to the audience, for whom he clarifies the complicated play of emotions in which the puppeteers with their charges are involved. He is of the stage yet beyond it, the actor and at the same time the commentator on life who points out the frailties of the human world revealed in microcosm by the puppets.[35]

Another example of this possibility of interposing an extra role between characters and onlookers is found in print and its editorial conventions. Given that the writer will employ punctuation marks and footnotes as part of the directional track, one finds that he also uses parentheses and brackets to comment in another voice—another role and another frame—on his own text.

---

play he addresses the audience in a speech which has for its aim the gaining of the good will of the spectators. He thanks them for their favorable attention; he announces the play to follow the one that has just been given; he invites the spectators by means of such praises as he showers on them to come to see it. . . . As a rule, his address is a short one and not premeditated. Sometimes, however, he plans his speech, when the King, the King's brother, or some prince of royal blood is present, or when he describes what happens in a machine-play. He also prepares his speech when he announces a new play that needs praising, or when he makes his farewell address in the name of the company on the Friday before Passion Week and at the re-opening of the theater after Easter, when the taste for playgoing has to be rekindled in the people. In his usual announcement the orator gives a preview of new plays to come in order to create anticipation. . . . [Cited in A. M. Nagler, *A Source Book in Theatrical History* (New York: Dover Publications, 1952), p. 183.]

The comparison here is with previews or "trailers" in movie houses and the master of ceremonies who makes a few business announcements before introducing the luncheon speaker.

35. A. C. Scott, *The Puppet Theatre of Japan* (Tokyo: Charles E. Tuttle Company, 1963), p. 42, cited in Hanck, "A Frame Analysis of the Puppet Theater."

Also, an editor or commentator may have recourse to another set of conventions for the purpose of introducing comments in his voice on the whole conglomeration of text and directional comments. Thus one finds abbreviations like "Ed.," which, when occurring before or after a footnote, cast the footnote out of the writer's frame and into another. Similarly the signs "[ ]" ordinarily mean that something is being included in a voice other than the writer's; and although the phrase "italics in the original" refers to something in the original, the phrase itself is in another (and in another's) voice. So, too, the sign "[*sic*]" means that a quotation has been reproduced exactly the way it appeared originally, and the apparent mistake (or usage) is in the original text, that someone not the author of the citation appreciates that the reader might have cause to think the citing is at fault when, in fact, the cited is. Ellipsis dots, of course, can mean something has been left out of the quoted text by the quoter, not the text author, and italics or quotation marks can mean that a voice different from the established one is intended.[36] And overlayed on all of

---

36. It is the object of conventions of this kind to be able to handle any need, and to distinguish consistently between laminations so that proper imputation of authorship will result. But although such metalanguage capacity can be approached, it cannot, apparently, be fully achieved. Thus, signs that ordinarily refer to interjections by a voice other than the one generating the text—signs such as "*sic*," "[ ]," ". . . ," present a problem when they are part of a text that is to be cited. So, too, when a writer quotes a bit of another writer's text which has in it a footnote, does the citing writer exclude the footnote superscript, or include it but exclude the actual footnote, or include both the superscript and the footnote? And if the latter, where is he to place this footnote so that it won't be read as *his* footnote? (The fact that scholars who would never think of changing a word or leaving a sentence out without duly noting the omission are ready to leave out footnotes attests nicely to the fact that the quoter seems to restrict himself to one voice and to being correct only about the materials occurring in that voice.) A similar question can be raised about the code employed to shift from one orthographic version of a text to another. Typewriter underlining is equivalent to italics in typeset, and this translation can be carried in either direction. But what do we do with underlining or boldface type in typeset that is to be represented in typescript?

Note, orthographic symbols for managing sentences (as opposed to comments about sentences) are themselves not fully worked out, and some symbols have multiple meanings (as do, for example, quotation marks) which are sometimes not resolved by the context. Thus, for example, splitting a word at the end of a line requires marking with a hyphen, but so does a hyphenated word which happens to break at the end of a line. Thus, there can be confusion as to which hyphen was meant.

these voices can be still other voices, ones sustained through special symbols which refer to aspects of the text but are meant never to be seen by readers. One set of these offstage marks allows copy editors and author to talk to each other about the text; another set allows proofreaders to talk to printers.[37] A page of typed manuscript text, then, can bear the writer's written-in corrections and marginal suggestions either to himself or to his editor, and in addition can bear comments and corrections by critical readers and by the copy editor. The draft that preceded this final typing could also have included directions to the typist and her queries to the writer. In all of this, type of writing instrument, color of ink, identifiability of hand, along with various partly developed symbol systems will be relied on to keep the voices separate. The object is not merely to tell who is saying what to whom. (That, after all, would be the issue also were six soft-spoken individuals to try to talk to and around one another on a dark night.) The object is to keep the frames separate. As confusing as the product may sometimes be, it is still the case that our adeptness at dealing with the mess seems to imply a remarkably well-developed capacity to accept the mutual presence of multiple voices, each talking on a different plane about different aspects of the same material.

Published texts of plays provide natural occasions for the utilization of multiple voices. First, clearly, is the directional track. For example, what is handled in a novel by the connective "John replied, 'No,'" and is managed in a play by having the actor playing John say, "No" (thereupon allowing sound source to serve as the connective), is managed in the play text by merely placing the name of the character on the left-hand side of the page, adding a punctuation mark such as a period or colon, and then beginning the speech. Also the author can add expression

---

37. These symbol systems are not by any means fully institutionalized, and many idiosyncrasies are found among printers, firms, editors, and the like. In an effort to standardize matters, journals and publishers sometimes print up a set of instructions detailing the symbols and illustrating their use. The editing and proofing of *these* statements provide special problems in editing and proofing, for although the symbols were selected in part so as to be easily distinguished from typewritten or typeset text, that easy differentiation breaks down when it is these symbols themselves that must form the text. This is a minor example of a very general frame issue considered at greater length later.

directions at the beginning of various speeches, provide staging advice at the beginning of the play and/or various acts and scenes, and preface the play with a long introduction designed solely for the printed version. In addition to these author's commentary voices, one still more removed may be taken up by an editor or translator who footnotes comments on parts of the text. Indeed, a playwright, in a voice other than the one employed in offering stage directions, may footnote comments about staging strategies employed in various productions, as Ionesco does in *Victims of Duty*.[38]

Out-of-frame print is to be compared with out-of-frame talk, seen most clearly, perhaps, in the facility with which an individual can, in dictating a letter to a stenographer, distinguish simply by use of paralinguistic cues what he means as text from what he means as comment on the text.

VIII

Re-created materials offer, then, participation statuses additional to the ones available in real, actual activity. More significant, I think, these transformations allow for special use of standard participation statuses and special use of evidential boundaries; similarly, such materials allow for the *staging* of out-of-frame channels and the use of these staged channels to carry events that ordinarily would be far beyond their capacity. Consequently, a staged strip of interaction can differ systematically and very radically from unstaged interaction, and yet, as one must see, be somehow substitutable for it.

---

38. [*While the* DETECTIVE'S *position remains unchanged, his recorded voice is heard coming from the opposite corner of the stage; during the ensuing monologue* CHOUBERT *stands quite still, arms hanging at his sides; his face expresses no emotion, but his body is occasionally shaken by shuddering despair.*][1]

    1. AUTHOR'S NOTE: During the actual performance the DETECTIVE raised his head and spoke directly. This seems the better solution.

        [Eugène Ionesco, *Victims of Duty*, in his *Three Plays*, trans. Donald Watson (New York: Grove Press, 1958), p. 136.]

Note that I must here employ the same sign, a superscript, for my footnoting and Ionesco's; if mine happened to be a "1" also, there would be a little doubt, perhaps, as to what is really going on.

Now look at the out-of-frame stage voice known as soliloquy: the convention by which an actor, alone on the stage, comes front and center and in the guise of his appointed character talks aloud—loud enough to be heard at the back of the auditorium—and thus makes the audience privy to his thoughts. The Western theatrical frame seems to allow for two slightly different kinds of soliloquy: one a kind of declamation or oratory, the sort of thing that a person in offstage life would never indulge in unless he was practicing a speech; and a second kind identifiable as musing, namely, the sort of talking to oneself that might occur in offstage life but here is done loudly enough to carry.

Individuals discovered in real-life soliloquies are likely to try to mask their lapse, for the frame of everyday interaction obliges the conversationally disengaged individual to keep his own counsel, and a soliloquy breaches this rule, much as would a truth blurted out or a too naked look. For the dramatist, however, a soliloquy allows the story line to be carried and orientation supplied, an easy means of providing continuity. The only requirement is that the evidential boundary be extended by convention so that instead of musing alone or silently, the individual addresses the whole house. And through this structural conceit his thoughts are opened up to the audience. Of course, the peculiarity about such flagrant exposure of self is balanced somewhat by the fact that those to whom the revelation is made are not themselves persons in ordinary participation status, but rather individuals restricted to the capacity of theatrical audience.

Soliloquies are to be contrasted with what is sometimes called direct (or extradramatic) address. This occurs when a character steps slightly out of frame, often in the direction of the stage line, and addresses a few remarks to the audience, these words designed as directed statements, not undirected declamations or musings. The intent may be to awaken the audience, expand on a moral point, explain an intricate twist in the plot, apologize for having to play two parts or provide a summary of what has happened or is about to happen. Direct address appears to have been common in medieval morality plays, the Western version of the audience not having yet become fully developed, and to have declined rather fully by the turn of the seventeenth century, by which time, in the West, plays had become relatively self-contained realms—this change constituting a good illustration of how framing practices vary over time.[39]

Take next the simple fact of physical barriers. In literal, informal interaction it is possible for individuals to be monitored accidentally, without benefit of bugs, when, for example, two persons discuss a strategic matter out of sight but not out of hearing of a relevant party—a next-booth phenomenon. But although this kind of overhearing is a distinct possibility, its likelihood is small compared, for example, to the possibility of finding that one has been caught out visually in the company of a particular other. But by the simple expedient of staging an appropriate barrier and scripting a reason why a particular person should be behind it while the right others are in front of it, overhearing can be arranged. And in plays such as *Much Ado about Nothing*, this possibility becomes a principal device.

Consider now asides and collusion. In unstaged interaction, as suggested, individuals can turn from their companions and give fleeting vent to their "real" feelings, through gesture and sotto

---

39. Anne Righter, *Shakespeare and the Idea of the Play* (London: Chatto & Windus, 1964), from whom I draw in these matters, argues the same change in Roman comedy with Terence demanding that the audience accept plays without prologues, as in life, whereas the earlier playwright Plautus (like Aristophanes) breaks the dramatic illusion in various ways, as the following nicely describes:

In addition, Plautus employs the device of the delayed prologue. Often, he launches his comedy as a perfectly self-contained play and then, having established a pretence of dramatic distance, breaks through it. Some character who has hitherto behaved as though there were no audience in sight oversteps the barrier between the stage world and reality "to do you the courtesy of outlining the plot of this play." Clearly, Plautus felt that information delivered directly and specifically to the audience in this manner had a better chance of being heeded than that offered less obviously in dialogue. Expository material would impress itself most vividly upon the spectators' memory if it could be combined with a sudden violation of dramatic illusion. Some of these violations are of the briefest kind, little jabs at the complacent inattention of the crowd. [pp. 47–48]

Chap. 2, pp. 43–65, of Righter provides a useful tracing of these changes in regard to direct address.

A somewhat similar shift seems to have occurred in the novel in modern times. In the nineteenth century, writers (for example, George Eliot) were at ease in changing frame and addressing their readers about the problems presented by a particular character or situation in the construction of a novel. Contemporary novelists occasionally do the same, but archly, that is, as a device one would not ordinarily employ.

voce comment, as though providing evidence through this behavior of a pressure-cooker conception of human nature. Similarly, one participant may engage another in collusive communication, being careful to shield his act from those who are cut off by it. So in the ordinary course of affairs, asides and collusion occur (more than at first one might think, as will be later argued), but these acts are carefully timed, shielded, and modulated to allow the impression to be maintained that all participants are giving themselves up equally to the proceedings.

Again, of course, theatrical framing allows these resources to be exploited in a quite special way. Since the audience must be able to see these acts if they are to be used in the production, they must be broad enough to carry to everyone in the hall, and this broad, of course, these gestures rarely are in offstage interaction. The only theatrical requirement is that this rule for characters be followed: any aside or collusion (as well as any direct address) not meant for oneself is not to be perceived to occur no matter how broad the act is. In brief, the concealment channel is scripted to carry more than it ordinarily could. It is understandable, then, that in a play like Congreve's *Double Dealer* it is possible for one character to give a soliloquy to the audience while another character, unbeknownst to the first, comes alongside him, overhears the remarks to the audience, and comments on them aloud in direct address to the audience, while being both unseen and unheard by the character giving the soliloquy. And it is understandable that stage characters can be wonderfully blind to obvious, noisy efforts of another character to sneak up behind them with evil or joking intent.

It is suggested, then, that in staged interaction, the barrier produced in offstage interaction by shielding or by volume control is here merely acted. The television shows that once brought long-lost relatives to surprise contestants were managed by means of another barrier, this time presumably real, the off-camera announcer filling in the audience so that they could be in the know. Quiz programs sometimes used the same split-screen effect, the announcer in "voice-over" telling the folks in TV land what the answer was while the contestant manfully strained at pretending to strain at recalling it. What one has here is a sort of electronic collusion.

Midway between staged collusion and broadcasting collusion is what occurs in talk shows and indeed is one of their mainstays. Events are allowed to develop that could be interpreted as casting a "guest" in a bad light or as breaching the moral standards sustained in public broadcasts. The emcee then utilizes this manufactured precariousness by engaging the audience in collusive looks, presumably out of view of the excolluded, be it the guest at whose expense the gesture is performed or those who guard the standards. Here the audience is led to half-believe that the collusion with itself is not a keying and not a fabrication but the real thing.

Wrestling (and roller derbies) provides another illustration of the same collusive lines manufactured with malice aforethought. The villain breaks the rules in order to mistreat the hero; the hero, after a suitable sequence of punishments, acquires rightful righteous indignation and vents anger back by means of improper acts of his own. But both villain and hero must break the rules out of sight of the referee and in sight of the viewers so that the latter, but not the former, will be in on what is happening. And this, of course, typically requires a high degree of cooperation between referee, offender, and offended in the matter of place and time.

No doubt the referee's blindness in wrestling is something that is carefully arranged in the scripted micro-ecology of the match. In baseball there is a more serious version. The pitcher may be caught by a TV camera as he gets ready to snap a throw to a baseman, his aim being to cut off a runner who has taken more than a safe lead off base. The angle of coverage can here give the TV audience a better chance at advance discovery than the runner himself. Similarly, the camera can catch a runner in the process of beginning to steal a base from behind the sight lines of the person (typically the pitcher) with the ball. In all of this a coalition between performer and audience is manufactured by the camera.[40]

Note now that in performances of all kinds the obligation to provide continuity for the audience, that is, constant guidance as to what is going on, accounts considerably for the manipulation of participation status and the enactment of channels. In the theater, for example, when only one person is onstage—a much

---

40. Suggested by Michael Wolff.

avoided possibility—then direct address, soliloquies, and dramatically meaningful gestures will have to be—and tend to be—relied upon.[41] When the setting contains only two persons, one is likely to be given the role of speaking straight and the other is likely to be scripted to engage in the responsive behavior already described—the half-suppressed off-angle self-communication, whereby some sort of alignment, often one to be taken as a "normal" person's response, is externalized. But now this disattended response is grossly exaggerated so as to be easily visible and audible to the audience, yet, of course, remaining undetected by the character who presumably called it forth. This exaggerated externalization seems to involve two elements, somewhat phased. The first is "registering," namely, the exhibition, often furtive, of the consequences for oneself of what one has just heard or witnessed. The second is "intention display," the portraying of what one is inclined now to do because of what has just happened.[42] Note, this sort of effect can be created even when

---

41. Continuity assurance on the cinematic stage when only one character is present has produced some rigidly stereotyped conventions. Our hero arriving at a sought address checks a slip of paper or does a head rise as the camera shifts to the house number plate or the name plaque. Watching a friend take leave, our hero shakes his head, as though summing up for himself his view of the departed.

42. Movies very often employ even greater expansiveness of intention display, but, as Balázs remarks, need not do so:

The film, especially the sound film, can separate the words of a character talking to others from the mute play of features by means of which, in the middle of such a conversation we are made to overhear a mute soliloquy and realize the difference between this soliloquy and the audible conversation. What a flesh-and-blood actor can show on the real stage is at most that his words are insincere and it is a mere convention that the partner in such a conversation is blind to what every spectator can see. But in the isolated close-up of the film we can see to the bottom of a soul by means of such tiny movements of facial muscles which even the most observant partner would never perceive. [Béla Balázs, *Theory of the Film,* trans. Edith Bone (New York: Roy Publishers, 1953), p. 63.]

It might be added that in both plays and movies when a character appears in a biographical disguise before others—a device as common in make-believe worlds as it is uncommon in the actual world—care is likely to be taken by the performer to give his disguise away continuously to the audience even while he appears to be sustaining it effectively before the other characters. Again, this duality of image is fostered in the interest of sustaining continuity, namely, a story line that can be followed continuously by the audience. Similarly, as Wayne C. Booth argues, if one char-

the two protagonists seem to be speaking directly to each other at close quarters. When three persons are present, then another resource becomes available—collusive communication—and its use tends to supplant the other two devices. So the work of maintaining continuity tends to shift from one device to another, depending on the number of characters in the scene. However, as long as the work gets done, the audience tends not to see that reliance has shifted from one mechanism to another.

The argument is that dramatic scriptings involving staged interaction allow the subordinate channels of interaction to be themselves staged and their ordinary functioning made a convenience of in the interests of dramatic continuity and similar effects. Now the whole matter must be complicated still further. The question is that of levels of organization, a question very familiar in analysis of sentence syntax but much less familiar in the analysis of other kinds of experience.

It is apparent that when large-scale deception occurs in face-to-face interaction, the deceivers are likely to rely considerably on the concealment channel. The organizational issues of when to begin the episode of interaction, how to manage its phases, and so forth, will have to be resolved secretly by the use of collusive communication and physical evidential boundaries. So a shift occurs in what the various tracks ordinarily would handle. Much the same can be said about live dramatic productions. For it would seem that what has so far been described as the expanded use of subordinate tracks in staged interaction applies *within* the drama that is presented. When one shifts up a level in organization, that is, when one examines the management of a whole stage production, then (as with fabrications) one finds that the concealment channel must carry directional cues, the prompter of course being a chief source. And indeed, this channel must also carry episoding arrangements: actors go on before they go on; they are poised and ready in the wings *before* their cue, much

___

acter is to lie to another, the playwright must first decide whether the audience is to know that lying is occurring; and if so (as is usually the case), then the lying must be done in a manner that makes evident to the audience that lying is going on (*The Rhetoric of Fiction* [Chicago: University of Chicago Press, 1961], p. 64). We onlookers thereby accept unblinkingly the strange notion of a wife lying to her husband by means of expression control that fools him but not us—we who have barely met the woman.

as would be true of the entrant of a confederate upon an episode of a con game.

For after all, the overall task in a stage performance concerns the performers who project characters, not these characters themselves. A character, note, cannot forget his lines. There isn't such a thing in natural interaction. All he could do would be to forget a name, or a date, or other items of the kind we forget— which forgetfulness, incidentally, can be scripted into a part. Similarly, a real person cannot fail to come in on time, simply because in ordinary life persons cannot fail this particular way. They can be, of course, and often are, late; but that is quite a different matter. Lateness can, for example, be accounted for, apologized for, and excused, and this remedial work does not have to be fitted into the script because there isn't one. Only individuals whose appearance at a given juncture has been built into the script which continues thereafter can miss their cues— and this means stage performers, participants in elaborate rituals, and fabricators such as con men.

Stage productions, then, involve modifications in that channeling of subordinate activity which is characteristic of ordinary offstage activity. But one cannot make sense of these modifications if they are treated all together. Two different levels or orders are involved, two different systems of reference, two different elements of the theatrical frame; one pertains to performers staging a production, the other to characters in a staged interaction. And matters must first be sorted along these lines before further analysis can be profitably attempted. The subtle look through which one performer secretly warns another that his wig has loosened is a real aside, the structural model for what the same individual *in character* may be obliged to enact through grossly pantomimed gestures as part of a scripted high sign.

IX

I have been suggesting that the very fact that a main line of activity can be carried on simultaneously with channels of out-of-frame doings provides a basis of flexibility in the organization of make-believe: for each out-of-frame channel can itself be performed and thereby used with considerable extension of initial capacity. Nor is that all. In the interests of satire or humor, subordinate channels can themselves become the focus of attention, part of the main story line, as when Hardy collusively communicates to Laurel in a hopelessly broad way, or old-time movies are depicted in which small-town messages are flashed on the screen in the overlay channel.

These facts should alert us to the expectation that framing does not so much introduce restrictions on what can be meaningful as it does open up variability. Differently put, persons seem to have a very fundamental capacity to accept changes in organizational premises which, once made, render a whole strip of activity different from what it is modeled on and yet somehow meaningful, in the sense that these systematic differences can be corrected for and kept from disorganizing perception, while at the same time involvement in the story line is maintained. Consider in this light some further differences between staged activity and its modeled-after counterpart.

It is a fact that stage style through the centuries and across various cultures varies greatly in the degree of realism of the stage props and also in the degree of consistency sought in the level of realism from one prop to another. (For example, clothing adjusted to the period of the play is itself a relatively modern conception.)[43] And certainly some items are likely to be literally realistic, such as cigarettes, and others not, such as walls and windows.[44] Yet this mélange causes no particular trouble.

---

43. As Macgowan and Melnitz suggest:

> It took the European theater about seventy-five years to accept completely the obvious idea—carried out by Macklin in 1773—that the costumes of a historical play should agree with the times and people it presented. Twentieth-century producers have done *Hamlet* and other old plays in modern dress and in modern scenery as daring experiments. "Modern dress," along with conventional scenery, was the general custom until the second half of the eighteenth century. And it was only between 1810 and 1850 that historical accuracy gradually became established. [*Golden Ages of the Theater*, pp. 109–110.]

4. And apparently so in non-Western stagecraft, too, as Gorelik notes in his discussion of classical Chinese drama:

> Extreme as this conventionalism may seem at first glance, upon reflection we find many illusory elements. When characters are represented as in a boat, there is no boat, but there is a swaying motion, and there is an oar for paddling. When a character is represented as on horseback, there is no horse, but the movements used in mounting an imaginary

Howsoever varied the realism of the various elements in a stage setting, at least it can be said that the characters on the stage remain at something of the same physical distance from the audience throughout the production. But, of course, even this is not the case in movies. Ever since Griffith freaked out his audience with a close-up, we have had the capacity to tolerate without loss of involvement great and rapid changes in angle of camera view and in closeness of focus, much as in ordinary life we come to use perspective to hold objects constant in size and shape regardless of distance from us or angle of vision. In the silent film we have subtitles in slow time (so that everyone can read them), covering only enough of the proceedings to ensure minimum continuity. The printed word itself tends here to be divided into two modes, "continuity titles," involving editorial mediating comment on the action in general (in comedies arch and ironic), and "spoken titles," bits of, and from, current dialogue. Yet moviegoers have no trouble at all in assembling material from these tracks into a single experience.[45]

In movies in general, and silent films in particular, the concealment track, as suggested, is much employed to carry the story line, the actors becoming to a considerable degree machines for externalizing silent feeling, silent not merely because there was

---

steed correspond closely to those used in reality. A beggar may wear silk rags: still they are rags as compared with the character of other costumes. There is differentiation in makeup and costume so that there are stage garments which approximate the armor of generals, the robes of monks or mandarins. Chairs and tables are used not only symbolically but in their proper character as chairs and tables. Fans, swords, bows and arrows, drums, flutes, tea-urns, are used naturally by the stage characters. It is impossible to draw a line showing which type of property is to be used symbolically, and which is to be used literally. In recent years under the influence of western drama the number of properties literally used has greatly increased, painted settings have been brought into the theatre, actresses are playing women's roles, which were formerly played by actors. [New Theatres for Old, p. 60.]

45. But of course there are limits to this flexibility, these themselves varying markedly in connection with "taste" and "sophistication," as Balázs unintentionally illustrates:

The film can evoke thoughts in the spectator, but must not project on to the screen ready-made thought-symbols, ideograms which have definite, known conventional meanings, like a question mark or exclamation point, a cross or swastika; for these would be merely a primitive picture-writing, hieroglyphs, that would be less convenient than our alphabet and certainly not art. [Theory of the Film, p. 129.]

no sound until the thirties, but also because if the various characters are to be kept in different information states, then "secret"
displays will be required behind the back of the hoodwinked. In
addition, and most radical of all as a means of reorganizing the
flow of experience, the actions and words conveyed to a character
are done portentously, with various versions of menace, know-
ingness, and the like, so that the audience can be told or reminded about what is "going on" even while "ignorance" is
maintained by some of the characters. Foretellings of impending
developments are also signaled in this way.[46] (It is as if the
characters portrayed come to half-recognize that they are in a
foretellable world—as indeed they uniquely are—and hence tacitly give significance to portents.)

Externalizations, of course, are not the only means of providing orientation in movies. No doubt the most important device is
the camera itself, which, by shifting from one point to another,
obliges the audience to follow along, leading it to examine that
part of the scene which the director has caused to be revelatory,
that is, which provides the next bit of information needed in
order to maintain the meaningfulness of the developing line of
action. (A less smoothly worked-out version of this can be seen in
TV panel shows in which a person may stop talking and go dead
before the camera has shifted from him, and another may attempt to come alive before the camera has got to him, thereby
throwing off the apparent naturalness of the flow of action.)

Another example of the framing devices employed to achieve
orientation in drama (and another example of the flexibility of
framing) is the techniques through which the social identity of
characters is effectively established and maintained. When an
American movie involves persons who are foreign, it is rare that
they are restricted to the language they would likely speak. Instead English is used but often with a corresponding "accent."
The accent stands for the foreignness.[47] (Frenchmen, Germans,

---

46. See the discussion of orientation in "Remedial Interchanges," in *R.P.*,
p. 132.

47. Also there are class arrangements. In American films, a "good" New
York or New England accent can readily be used as evidence of British
nationality. In English productions of Greek plays, Cockney comes to be
used for working-class Greeks, "received pronunciation" for the better
classes.

Russians, and Italians tend to get their own accents; nationals of lesser known, smaller countries often have to make do with a somewhat foreign foreign accent.) Now although it is imaginable that foreigners would use a version of English in talk with English-speaking characters, in which case a foreign accent would not abuse nature, the accent is also used in scenes in which two foreigners talk to each other out of the presence of the English-speaking characters. And in nature there would be no reason for this.[48] Yet apparently this arrangement causes the viewer no problem at all. Audiences systematically translate the accented speech into foreign speech. Interestingly, in comic books and other written materials, the same effect is sometimes obtained by using lettering reminiscent of the script employed in the language a foreign character would ordinarily be speaking. What one has here is something like the conventions that allow transposition from a typeset version to a typewritten version of the same text. The original text here is the foreign speaking of a foreign person; accent is the filmic transformation, and stylized type the comic-strip version of the same thing.

I am suggesting, then, that dramatic scriptings allow for the manipulation of framing conventions and that since these conventions cut very deeply into the organization of experience, almost anything can be managed in a way that is compatible with sustaining the involvement of the audience.

One can appreciate, then, how modern cinema and theater might work many changes and in each case manage to generate a calculus of action and reaction in which audiences could involve themselves. For example, in Thornton Wilder's *Our Town,* one finds a revival of the orator role, an editorialist who sits to the side of the stage and mediates between the play world and the audience. In the movie *Alfie* an updated version is provided: by means of superimposed photography (split screens, corner insets), the hero is made to step out of character while the action continues to be carried forward, and engage in direct address, in

---

48. *The French Connection*—an American movie—employs the neat trick of allowing two French characters, established as competent in English, to speak to each other in French while the foreign-film technique of subtitles is used to provide a translation, a nice example of how unnatural the provisions can be which yet serve to create a realistic, natural effect. A few earlier films used the same dodge.

character, to the audience, thereby projecting two realizations of the same character simultaneously. In Alan Ayckbourn's play *How the Other Half Loves*, two couples use the same set simultaneously as though they cannot see members of the other couple—although the female of one can telephone the male of the other—and again, the playwright can get away with it.

It is apparent, then, that much flexibility is possible in the conventions according to which characters of some kind in a drama of some kind can act toward one another and achieve through this action something that can engross audiences. Our capacity in this connection is even better illustrated by the devices audiences are prepared to accept in puppet plays:

> Hand puppets, for example, do all kinds of actions on stage that would be considered quite out of the ordinary if they were not defined as conventions. They enter and exit through the bottom of the stage; they pick up objects with both arms instead of with their hands; they may be animal puppets who speak and pick up objects with their mouths; they have mouths with lips that do not move when they speak or no mouths at all; they move their entire bodies whenever they move their heads; they beat the stage with their heads for emphasis or when extremely excited; they have no legs and don't sit down; they move across the stage without making any noise and may move at impossible speeds up and down or across stage; they may talk to each other in jumbled voices but still claim to perfectly understand each other; and they may not talk at all but pretend to communicate to other puppets or to a human cohort. Naively considered, any of the above actions by a puppet might be a cause for consternation and puzzlement for the audience. However, because these actions are stage conventions, their transformation from puzzling activities to meaningful and ordinary activities takes place prior to the play itself.[49]

---

49. Hanck, "A Frame Analysis of the Puppet Theater." Hanck adds:

Chinese shadow puppet shows illustrate a peculiarly interesting stage convention. Since shadow puppets are flat, they usually present a profile to the audience. This presents a unique problem for the puppeteer who must make his puppet face in the opposite direction for some reason. Convention allows the puppeteer to turn the character around by merely flipping the puppet over and quickly replacing it next to the screen. Members of the audience see the puppet's shadow briefly disappear and then reappear facing in the opposite direction. They are not bothered in the slightest by this maneuver. . . .

Another aspect of framing organization should be considered. If one examines the connectives in novels, it is perfectly plain that once a speaker has been identified, that identification will be sufficient until the next person speaks, at least in regard to text that can be read as a character's words. Apparently it is natural for us to read each identification across the variable amount of utterance that follows, stopping only when a new connective or nontalk is provided. Something similar is seen in silent movie subtitles, where a single subtitle is taken to apply to a whole strip of film.

In dialogue in novels, one very often finds something more than an alternation of utterances connected to speakers. Often the writer will record the effect on a character of the deed just performed by another character. As in movies, this response can take two forms. First, registerings or "takes." John, in reaction to Mary's comment, can be described as being startled, taken aback, staggered, visibly pleased, nonplussed, appeased, and so forth. Second, intention displays or (in a more realized form) "returns."

Upon examining dialogue, one finds that each character's response to the other's turn at holding the floor of action may involve (1) only a take; (2) only a return; or (3) a two-phased process, one that often starts with a take and then shifts into a return:

1. That stopped John in his tracks.
   Mary almost smiled.
2. "Why? Why now?" he pleaded.
   "What good is the reason?" his wife replied.
3. His face paled. His voice dropped. "Please don't." This time she did smile. "That won't work," she said, and left the room.

Whether a single-phased or double-phased action occurs, it tends to be read across the period when the character to whom it is attributed is acting, as if indeed that degree of complexity were sufficient to limn in something recognized as a full-fledged person. Now the point of all this is that although the result sounds perfectly natural, and very often "realistic," a *very* restrictive view of interaction is being presented. The response of each participant is fully oriented to the local, current scene, and a very simple, holistic reading is provided of his affective and behavioral response to the situation.[50] And this "situation" changes some-what with each participant's turn at having the floor, as might, for example, occur during a game of chess.

Another flexibility to consider bears upon the issue of skill. It is a remarkable feature of staging that although troupes differ very greatly in talent and scripts differ almost as much in "quality," it is yet the case that bad casts and bad scripts can still come alive for viewers. Indeed, in psychodrama persons without a script and without *any* qualifications as performers can yet stage an effective dramatic turn. Again what one sees here is evidence of the great capacity of audiences to adjust and calibrate in order to get on with getting involved.

In the same vein one can appreciate how patrons can be willing to attend plays of varying degrees of "seriousness" from drama to satire, to fantasy, to melodrama,[51] to burlesque, or to a

---

50. Viewing a character's elementary dramatic action as a take and/or a return read across the full period of his turn at bat allows one to see a parallel to the shows that wrestlers provide in their matches, except that in wrestling, takes will use the whole body instead of the face and hands, and returns will involve magnificent gladiatorlike blows instead of words and rapid stage crossing. The parallel is not accidental, since it is exhibition wrestling which supplies some of the terms that are useful in analyzing make-believe social interaction.

51. For example, Michael Booth, ed., *Hiss the Villain* (New York: Benjamin Blom, 1964):

In treatment of material, melodrama concentrates on externals; it stays on the surface and never explores the depths. This approach produces two of the form's most notable features: character stereotypes and rigid moral distinctions. The main character types constantly appearing in melodrama are the hero, heroine, villain, comic man, comic woman, old man, old woman, and character actor (usually comic). Other types appear from time to time, and a host of lesser characters are handled in various ways, but the general outlines remain the same for over a century. When they become blurred, and when the sharp divisions of morality are no longer observed, melodrama disappears as a separate form. The building can no longer stand on crumbling foundations.

One of the rules is that the hero and heroine must suffer distress, persecution, and separation, and that their suffering must continue unabated till a few moments before the final curtain, when they emerge united, happy, and triumphant. The heroine comes in for more persecution than the hero, especially as possession of her is frequently the villain's main object. In fact the hero is often of little use to her, either being in prison, or across the sea, or tied up in a cave, or without a weapon at inconvenient times. What intelligence, design, and thought

guying of any of these forms, and all this with little separation of time or playhouse to mark the difference. In fact, the same show can dip in and out of several forms and yet hold an audience, as for example, the *Get Smart* TV series, which was at once a spoof on spy shows and drama that relied on actual suspense. Indeed, this same staged content with no change in internal character can be treated seriously at one time and interpreted as a burlesque experience the next, evident, for example, in the revival during the sixties of the Batman serials filmed during the forties.[52] Changes in what is sometimes called level of sophistication are changes in framing, and these changes, ratified by an audience, can thoroughly transform the way in which the same production is received.[53]

X

The argument, then, is that we have a natural capacity to build up strips of engrossing, lively experience from the dramatic

---

there is in melodrama is resident in the villain and the comic man. [p. 10]

Booth provides a comment on the demise of this particular transformation:

The date of the decline of stage melodrama cannot be given precisely. It slowly withered away after the First War, and signs of disintegration were evident a good twenty or thirty years before. The question is confused by the fact that melodrama on tour lingered on long after it had ceased playing in cities, in some instances until years after the Second World War. Now, however, melodrama is only revived either as a form of burlesque or as a conscious archaism. As we have defined it, melodrama is no longer written. This is not to deny that there are melodramatic elements in modern plays, such as the thriller, but the pure form does not exist, and would not find audiences in its own spirit if it did. [p. 38]

52. See, for example, *Time*, November 26, 1965, a comment, incidentally, which was later reprinted as an advertisement for the replay of the Batman films (as in *San Francisco Chronicle*, "Date Book," December 9, 1965), an interesting rekeying in its own right.

53. The clearest case I know was the reshowing in the seventies of anti-drug films (such as *Reefer Madness*) made in the thirties and forties. In rerun houses in university and hippie neighborhoods, a perceptible scattering of patrons would quietly turn on and, amid quiet chuckles, passively watch a film depicting the destructive orgies claimed as a predictable consequence of succumbing to the weed.

interplay of characters who are governed by all manner of different participation statuses and all manner of modifications in regard to tracks or channels. In this connection, a note about behavior in mental hospitals might be added, since it is here that very obvious illustrations of variable participation statuses and other elements of frame can be found.

Consider the following:

1. the patient who is mute in all daily interactions and steps off the sidewalk to avoid confrontation with the staff, yet at the patient dance becomes verbally facile and behaviorally full of address;

2. the patient who stutters in ordinary talk but speaks clearly when engaged in taking another's part during psychodrama; (just as a stage actor who stutters may be free of this impediment when he declaims in an accent);

3. the patient who is hallucinatory and manneristic during ordinary conversation, but sanely and effectively takes a lead part in the hospital theatrical;

4. the patient who is too alienated to communicate as usual and is mute to all efforts at conversation, except that she will convey necessary messages in writing or in her ethnic speech;

5. the patient who acts out stories involving himself and persons not now present, yet in such a fashion that listeners feel he is acting toward them.

Given these bizarre forms of ward behavior, one must come to see that after all they are not so extraordinary, for what seem to be involved are merely atypical framing practices—practices which ought to be easy to adopt were there reason to do so, and which, once adopted, would generate a continuous array of insane behavior. Since realms are built up through the maintenance of these conventions, realms can be attacked by declining to sustain these conventions. A frame perspective, then, allows us to generate crazy behavior and to see that it is not all that crazy.

And when that is done, one can go on, as I shall try to do in the last two chapters, to look at what really goes on in ordinary interaction and what the commonsense "working world" of practical realities is.

8

The Anchoring
of Activity

I. *Introduction*

It has been argued that a strip of activity will be perceived by its participants in terms of the rules or premises of a primary framework, whether social or natural, and that activity so perceived provides the model for two basic kinds of transformation—keying and fabrication. It has also been argued that these frameworks are not merely a matter of mind but correspond in some sense to the way in which an aspect of the activity itself is organized— especially activity directly involving social agents. Organizational premises are involved, and these are something cognition somehow arrives at, not something cognition creates or generates. Given their understanding of what it is that is going on, individuals fit their actions to this understanding and ordinarily find that the ongoing world supports this fitting. These organizational premises—sustained both in the mind and in activity—I call the frame of the activity.

It was also suggested that activity interpreted by the application of particular rules and inducing fitting actions from the interpreter, activity, in short, that organizes matter for the interpreter, itself is located in a physical, biological, and social world. Fanciful words can speak about make-believe places, but these words can only be spoken *in* the real world. Even so with dreaming. When Coleridge dreamed his "Kubla Khan," he dreamed it *in* an undreaming world: he had to begin and terminate his dreaming in the "natural" flow of time; he had to use up a bed, a good portion of the night, and apparently some supplies of a medicinal kind in order to be carried away into his dream; and a sufficient control of the environment was assumed, pertaining to air, temperature, and noise level so that he could go on dreaming. (Think what has to be organized materially and correctly so that an astronaut in flight will be able to dream.) It is this intermeshing of framed activity in the everyday unstaged world that I want to consider in this chapter.

The relation of the frame to the environing world in which the framing occurs is complex. An illustration. Two men sit down at a game-equipped table and decide whether to play chess or checkers. In terms of the game-generated realm in which they will soon be lodged, the difference between chess and checkers is considerable; quite different dramas will unfold involving quite different game-generated characters. But should a stranger or employer or a janitor or policeman approach the two players, it will usually be quite sufficient to know that the men are playing a board game. The gearing of the game into the immediately surrounding workaday world is largely in terms of this relatively abstract categorization, for what are involved are such matters as the electric light, the room space, the time needed, the right of others to openly watch and under certain circumstances to interrupt the men and ask them to postpone the game or shift its physical location, the right of the players to phone their wives to say they will be delayed because of a game to finish. These and a host of other detailed ways in which what is going on must find a place in the rest of the ongoing world are relatively independent of *which* game is being played. By and large it is the mode of transformation, not what is thus transformed, that is geared into the world. And yet, of course, this independence is not complete. There are implications in the difference between chess and checkers that bear upon the world external to the playing of these games. For example, in America those seen playing chess tend to be regarded as possibly cultivated, an identification not secured by those seen playing checkers. Also, if but one set of each of the games is available, then the players who elect to play one of the games can force a next pair to play the other. And, of course, the players must come to whichever game they decide to play with prior knowledge of it. (They must enter also with a desire to play and a willingness to play each other, but these psychological prerequisites do not much differentiate between chess and checkers.) It should be repeated: a similar argument can be advanced in regard to any self-absorbing, fanciful activity.[1] A cup can be filled from any realm, but the handle belongs to the realm that qualifies as reality.

Observe that any discussion of the gearing of the playing of a game into its surround—any discussion of the rim of this frame —leads to apparent paradox. The understanding that players and nonplayers have of where the claims of the ongoing world leave off and where the claims of play take over is part of what the players bring to their playing from the outside world, and yet is a necessary constituent of play. The very points at which the internal activity leaves off and the external activity takes over— the rim of the frame itself—become generalized by the individual and taken into his framework of interpretation, thus becoming, recursively, an additional part of the frame. In general, then, the assumptions that cut an activity off from the external surround also mark the ways in which this activity is inevitably bound to the surrounding world.

This paradoxical issue is a harsh fact of life for those who we might think had other business. When two individuals come together to engage in one tossing of a coin, we might be brought

---

1. Simmel presents the case for works of art in "The Handle," in Georg Simmel et al., *Essays on Sociology, Philosophy and Aesthetics,* ed. Kurt H. Wolff (New York: Harper & Row, 1965):

Modern theories of art strongly emphasize that the essential task of painting and sculpture is the depiction of the spatial organization of things. Assenting readily to this, one may then easily fail to recognize that space within a painting is a structure altogether different from the real space we experience. Within actual space an object can be touched, whereas in a painting it can only be looked at; each portion of real space is experienced as part of an infinite expanse, but the space of a picture is experienced as a self-enclosed world; the real object interacts with everything that surges past or hovers around it, but the content of a work of art cuts off these threads, fusing only its own elements into a self-sufficient unity. Hence, the work of art leads its life beyond reality. To be sure, the work of art draws its content from reality; but from visions of reality it builds a sovereign realm. While the canvas and the pigment on it are parts of reality, the work of art constructed out of them exists in an ideal space which can no more come in contact with actual space than tones can touch smells. [p. 267]

to admit that enough light will have to be available to allow the gamblers to read the fall. But there is no need to think we might have to supply the gamblers with a snack and a bathroom. When the game is longer lasting, these latter services might have to be laid on, for wherever one's person goes, so, after a certain while, goes the role-irrelevant need for basic caterings. And the material equipment may come to require refurbishment. (Thus, in casinos, arrangements must be made to replace worn cards and to wash dirty chips.) But note that very often the services required by men and equipment—whatever the realm of activity sustained by what is thus kept in working order—are institutionally available, part of the fixed social plant. Indeed, the players and equipment used in quite different activities can employ the same service in a close interweaving of use. All this routine servicing allows individuals to take the matter for granted and to forget about the conditions that are being quietly satisfied. But there is a special set of activities calculated to remind us of the anchoring of our doings, namely, ones which draw us away for an extended time from socially institutionalized provisioning. Family camping trips, mountaineering expeditions, and armies in the field provide examples. Here the institutional plant must be carried along; logistics acquires a name and becomes a conscious problem, as much a part of the plans as the story line.[2]

The question of how a framed activity is embedded in ongoing reality appears to be closely tied to two others, namely, how an activity can be keyed and (especially) how it can be fabricated. William James himself gives us reason to inquire along these lines.

When James asked, "Under what circumstances do we think things real?" he assumed that somehow reality in itself was not enough and, instead, principles of convincingness were what

2. War games introduce a special twist. Since logistics is a major part of a military undertaking, the *practicing* of such a doing must include attention to supplies, medical treatment, communication channels, and all the other paraphernalia of a community. But since those engaging in the exercise will in fact be cut off somewhat from institutional services, it follows that real supplies, medical facilities, communication channels, and so forth will have to be assured, and, moreover, carefully kept from getting mixed up with the practice versions. Observe that the more the circumstances of the exercise give weight to logistics and the need to practice at it, the greater are likely to be the real logistics requirements.

really counted. (His answer, no doubt inadequate, does raise the question as to how it is that the world is tied together for us.) Now it might be thought that these principles could be fulfilled at times when what seemed to be going on was not in fact going on, and this is no doubt true. Immediately, then, a basic dilemma is produced. Whatever it is that generates sureness is precisely what will be employed by those who want to mislead us. For surely, although some evidence will be much more difficult than other evidence to fake, and therefore will be of special use as a test of what is really going on, the more it is relied upon for this reason the more reason there is to make the effort to fake it. In any case, it turns out that the study of how to uncover deception is also by and large the study of how to build up fabrications. The way in which strips of activity are geared into the world and the way in which deceptions can be fabricated turn out, paradoxically, to be much the same. In consequence one can learn how our sense of ordinary reality is produced by examining something that is easier to become conscious of, namely, how reality is mimicked and/or how it is faked.

II. *Episoding Conventions*

1. Activity framed in a particular way—especially collectively organized social activity—is often marked off from the ongoing flow of surrounding events by a special set of boundary markers or brackets of a conventionalized kind.[3] These occur before and

---

3. A clarification about usage is needed here. As employed in this book, brackets are not a heuristic device of mine but are claimed to be part of the organizational properties of actual experience—although, of course, some strips of experience seem to exhibit this feature much more clearly than do others, and it is society more than "nature" that seems to employ them. Those who write in the phenomenological tradition use brackets, I think, in a slightly different sense to refer not to natural boundaries of episodes of activity, but rather to the self-imposed boundaries the student can exploit in order to stop the stream of experience for the purposes of self-conscious examination, therewith holding back any preconceived notions about the elements or forces within that experience. (My term "strip" designates what would thus be cut off.) Husserl's view ought to be authoritative here, and a version is cited:

Thus *all sciences which relate to this natural world,* though they stand never so firm to me, though they fill me with wondering admiration, though I am far from any thought of objecting to them in the least

after the activity in time and may be circumscriptive in space; in brief, there are temporal and spatial brackets. These markers, like the wooden frame of a picture, are presumably neither part of the content of activity proper nor part of the world outside the activity but rather both inside and outside, a paradoxical condition already alluded to and not to be avoided just because it cannot easily be thought about clearly. One may speak, then, of opening and closing temporal brackets and bounding spatial brackets. The standard example is the set of devices that has come to be employed in Western dramaturgy: at the beginning, the lights dim, the bell rings, and the curtain rises; at the other end, the curtain falls and the lights go on. (These are Western signs, but the slot is more widely found. Chinese classical theater, for example, uses a wooden clapper called *ki*.)[4] And in the interim, the acted world is restricted to the physical arena bracketed by the boundaries of the stage.[5]

---

degree, *I disconnect them all, I make absolutely no use of their standards, I do not appropriate a single one of the propositions that enter into their systems, even though their evidential value is perfect, I take none of them, no one of them serves me for a foundation*—so long, that is, as it is understood, in the way these sciences themselves understand it, as a truth *concerning the realities* of this world. *I may accept it only after I have placed it in the bracket.* That means: only in the modified consciousness of the judgment as it appears in disconnexion, and *not as it figures within the science as its proposition, a proposition which claims to be valid and whose validity I recognize and make use of.* [Edmund Husserl, *Ideas: General Introduction to Pure Phenomenology,* trans. W. R. Boyce Gibson (London: George Allen & Unwin, 1952), p. 111.]

It might be added that although Husserl's dictum seems entirely desirable in the study of the established, effective sciences, application to the social sciences produces a certain amount of understandable hard feeling, since their practitioners themselves claim to be in the business of formulating sociological concepts, analyzing social presuppositions, and so forth. To bracket *their* doing is to claim, in effect, to do it better.

4. Shūtarō Miyake, *Kabuki Drama* (Tokyo: Japan Travel Bureau, 1964), p. 71.

5. Mary Douglas, *Purity and Danger* (London: Routledge & Kegan Paul, 1966), provides a version of the functioning of brackets:

For us, individually, everyday symbolic enactment does several things. It provides a focussing mechanism, a method of mnemonics and a control for experience. To deal with focussing first, a ritual provides a frame. The marked off time or place alerts a special kind of expectancy, just as the oft-repeated "Once upon a time" creates a mood receptive to fantastic tales. We can reflect on this framing function in small personal in-

There are other obvious examples. The gavel calling a meeting to order and adjourning it is a well-understood temporal bracket. The cinematic transformation of literal activity has, of course, distinctive spatial restrictions based upon the focal length of the lens:

> The normal human gaze, widely embracing the area in front of him, does not exist for the director. He sees and constructs only in that conditioned section of space that the camera can take in; and yet more—this space is, as it were, delimited by fast, fixed boundaries, and the very definite expression of these boundaries themselves inevitably conditions an inflexibility of composition in the spacial construction. It is obvious that an actor taken with a fairly close approximation of the camera will, in making a movement too wide in relation to the space he occupies, simply disappear from the view-field of the camera. If, for example, the actor sits with bended head, and must raise his head, at a given approximation of the camera, an error on his part of only an inch or two may leave only his chin visible to the spectator, the rest of him being outside the limits of the screen, or, technically, "cut off." This elementary example broadly emphasizes once again the necessity of an exact spacial calculation of every movement the director shoots. Naturally this necessity applies not only to close-ups. It may be a gross mistake to take instead of the whole of somebody, only two-thirds of him. To distribute the material shot and its movements in the rectangle of the picture in such a way that everything is clearly and sharply apprehensible, to construct every composition in such a way that the right-angled boundaries of the screen do not disturb

---

> stances, for the least action is capable of carrying significance. Framing and boxing limit experience, shut in desired themes or shut out intruding ones. [pp. 62–63]

Douglas then cites a statement by Marion Milner ("The Role of Illusion in Symbol Formation," in Melanie Klein et al., eds., *New Directions in Psychoanalysis* [London: Tavistock Publications, 1955]), which I extend from the original:

> I had already, when trying to study some of the psychological factors which facilitate or impede the painting of pictures, become interested in the part played by the frame. The frame marks off the different kind of reality that is within it from that which is outside it; but a temporal spatial frame also marks off the special kind of reality of a psychoanalytic session. And in psycho-analysis it is the existence of this frame that makes possible the full development of that creative illusion that analysts call the transference. [p. 86]

the composition found, but perfectly contain it—that is the achievement towards which film directors strive.[6]

Episoding conventions also mark the beginning of a "run," or series of performances, and the ending of it, giving rise to "opening night" and "closing night" behavior—good-luck telegrams, flowers, and the like. This higher-order bracketing does not seem to be much codified.[7]

No doubt keying signals provide the obvious examples of episoding practices. Bateson's discussion of the message "this is play" is an example. (The bracketing around fabrications is a more delicate matter, since it is in the nature of these designs that the fakery begins just before the dupe enters the scene and terminates just after he has left it—thus ensuring that he not see that reality has waited for him and that the fabricators have carefully arranged for him to mislocate the brackets.) Many sports and games, of course, have ceremonialized bracketing rules, in part to ensure "fairness," that is, an equal chance for all contestants, and these arrangements provide something of a model for bracketing conventions. Thus, the dropping of the puck in hockey, the kickoff in football, the quick handshake in wrestling, and glove touch in boxing.

2. Although the brackets I have mentioned are perhaps the most obvious ones, they bear primarily on recreational life, and should not be allowed to direct our attention from the places where bracketing does its everyday work. Mathematics, for example, employs the elegant and powerful device of simple typographic brackets—( )—which establish the boundaries of a strip of any length, all items in which are to be transformed in the same way and at the same time, and a place next to and on the outside of the left-hand bracket, the operator slot, in which any mathematical expression there inserted determines what the transformation will be. The number of lines deep that the brackets are is taken to signify the number of lines of mathematical symbols to be included in the bracketed reading. It is as though here all our human capacity to think and act in terms of

6. V. I. Pudovkin, *Film Technique and Film Acting*, trans. Ivor Montagu (New York: Bonanza Books, 1959), pp. 80–81.

7. For closing nights of jazz performers, see Ralph J. Gleason's column (headed on that occasion, "They Go Out Swinging"), *San Francisco Chronicle*, February 27, 1963.

frame were compressed and refined—a line drawing of a line drawing. Only less elegant, but even more important, are the bracketing practices employed in the syntactical organization of sentences, where sequential placement, punctuation marks, and part of speech determine what one or more words are to be bracketed together and what syntactic role is to be performed by the constituent unit thus formed. Note that in both mathematics and language (where brackets can take their "literal" form, as I am now illustrating), an operator and the bracketed material it transforms are themselves subject to bracketing as a whole and retransformation. This common theme is celebrated in the notations and operations of symbolic logic.

Bracketing becomes an obvious matter when the activity that is to occur is itself fragile or vulnerable in regard to definition and likely to produce framework tension. Thus, as already suggested, in the medical treatment of the naked female body and the art class treatment of the same object, devices seem likely to be used to make matters regarding perspective clear. In both cases the act of dressing and undressing is often given privacy and the naked body allowed to be suddenly produced and hidden by means of a robe, the taking off and putting on of which clearly marks the episoding of the exposure activity and presumably functions to stabilize the application of a natural framework under difficult circumstances. This episoding, of course, may be facilitated by a frontstage-backstage architecture:

> Backstage at a Strip hotel, where some of the most gorgeous girls in the world prance around—some half-clad, some unclad. The sight of a strange man in the wings and they scurry for cover. Girls who march around stage almost stark naked, blush and cover their bosoms as they pass from the stage to the dressing room. "After all, I don't really know you!" Odd to say, when these same creatures exhibit themselves to the ogles of hundreds of strangers nightly. "But it's different when you're not on stage. Well, it's so personal."[8]

Consider now the possibility that the bracket initiating a particular kind of activity may carry more significance than the bracket terminating it. For—as already suggested in regard to the notational system of mathematics—it is reasonable to assume that the beginning bracket not only will establish an episode but

---

8. Murray Hertz, *Las Vegas Sun*, September 14, 1961.

also will establish a slot for signals which will inform and define what sort of transformation is to be made of the materials within the episode. Certainly we make common use of the terms "introduction," "preface," "orienting remarks," and the like. Thus, in what must be the most famous prologue of all—Shakespeare's to *Henry V*—we obtain an explicit invocation of the theatrical frame. Whether the thirty-four lines are dramatically effective and actually do the work they set out to do is problematic; but they nevertheless provide a wonderfully explicit statement of the task of the theatrical frame and at the same time nicely illustrate the paradox that the preface is at once part of the dramatic world that follows and an outside comment on it.[9] Closing brackets seem to perform less work, perhaps reflecting the fact that it is probably much easier on the whole to terminate the influence of a frame than to establish it. However, epilogues do try to summarize what has occurred and ensure the proper framing of it. More important, consumers of commercially presented, vicarious experience will need to be sure that the ceasing of transmission marks the point when it is possible and proper to assess the full meaning of the drama that has been unfolding and not simply a point at which technical difficulties have occurred.

Two points might be made about the calibrative functions of episoding conventions. First, as suggested in the introduction, he who employs these devices often seems to rely on their power to reframe whatever comes after them (or before them in the case of epilogues) and seems to be somewhat on the hopeful side in this reliance. Thus, in giving a talk or lecture, the speaker remarks on how pleased he is to be present and how unworthy he is of the introduction received; he provides a little joke to show that the role that is about to be assumed has not driven its taker into an overelevated view of himself; and then he briefly locates the material to be covered in a wider context and defines the style of presentation, giving an apologetic account for it. When effective, this routine succeeds in prospectively recasting all that is to

---

9. One illustration of historical changes in framing practices is the decline in modern times of the prologue. Although we do have dramas that employ a prologuelike preliminary, an intended archaism (as in Wilder's *Our Town*) or a gimmick (as in Gelber's *The Connection*) may be involved. It is as if we had given up hope of being effective through this device.

come, adding to the whole an additional lamination, namely, the understanding that what is to be heard is merely *one* special measure of the talker, not an expression of all of which he is capable. (Indeed, some talks seem to function primarily as a means of display through which the speaker demonstrates what he can stand outside of, and through this provides a model for that particular kind of self-possession.) When the talk itself is ineffective—which is frequent—the audience finds that the speaker cannot easily be dissociated from the speech, and that his effort at framing the talk is something that lingers on inside the frame, disrupting the work it was meant to do. Similarly, the possibility that closing words can recast all that has gone before, adding a lamination to it, can induce a speaker to try to add to his accomplishment in this way, sometimes with the consequence that he further undermines it.

Second, insofar as "opening remarks" can set the stage and frame what follows, there is a reason why "getting the first word in" might be considered strategically significant. An illustration:

> Our only close brush with the law came once when we were making our getaway, three of us in the front seat of the car, and the back seat loaded with stuff [stolen goods]. Suddenly we saw a police car round the corner, coming toward us, and it went on past us. They were just cruising. But then in the rear-view mirror, we saw them make a U-turn, and we knew they were going to flash us to stop. They had spotted us, in passing, as Negroes, and they knew that Negroes had no business in the area at that hour.
>
> It was a close situation. There was a lot of robbery going on; we weren't the only gang working, we knew, not by any means. But I knew that the white man is rare who will ever consider that a Negro can outsmart him. Before their light began flashing, I told Rudy to stop. I did what I'd done once before—got out and flagged them, walking toward them. When they stopped, I was at their car. I asked them, bumbling my words like a confused Negro, if they could tell me how to get to a Roxbury address. They told me, and we, and they, went on about our respective businesses.[10]

3. Now consider that episoding conventions cover the prescribed means available by which an individual who is about to become active in a particular role or part and enter an activity

---

10. *The Autobiography of Malcolm X* (New York: Grove Press, 1966), pp. 144–145.

can give evidence that he is doing so. Comments on how speakers assume the speaker role have already been made. In the case of hypnotic trance—or at least what some take to be hypnotic trance—devices for beginning and terminating the episode are also devices for symbolizing the passage of the subject into a hypnotized character and his being brought back "to himself." The transformation from man to spirit in voodoo possession provides a very marked example of this taking on of character:

> The explanation of mystic trance given by disciples of Voodoo is simple: a *loa* [spirit] moves into the head of an individual having first driven out "the good big angel" (*gros bon ange*)—one of the two souls that everyone carries in himself. This eviction of the soul is responsible for the tremblings and convulsions which characterize the opening stages of trance. . . .
> The symptoms of the opening phase of trance are clearly psychopathological. They conform exactly, in their main features, to the stock clinical conception of hysteria. People possessed start by giving an impression of having lost control of their motor system. Shaken by spasmodic convulsions, they pitch forward, as though projected by a spring, turn frantically round and round, stiffen and stay still with body bent forward, sway, stagger, save themselves, again lose balance, only to fall finally in a state of semi-consciousness. Sometimes such attacks are sudden, sometimes they are heralded by preliminary signs: a vacant or anguished expression, mild tremblings, panting breath or drops of sweat on the brow; the face becomes tense or suffering.
> In certain cases trance is preceded by a sleepy condition. The possessed cannot keep his eyes open and seems overcome with a vague languor. This does not last long: it suddenly gives place to a rough awakening accompanied by convulsive movements.[11]

---

11. Alfred Métraux, *Voodoo in Haiti,* trans. Hugo Charteris (New York: Oxford University Press, 1959), pp. 120–121. Métraux qualifies the description thus:

> This preliminary phase can soon end. People who are used to possession pass quickly through the whole range of nervous symptoms. They quake, stagger, make a few mechanical movements, and then, suddenly —there they are: in full trance. Even as much preamble as this may be dispensed with when a ceremony is in full swing and demands instantaneous entries on the part of the gods. [p. 121]

He also inadvertently provides an example of how the disciplinary language into which a doubted interpretation is reframed might itself be doubted by those in another discipline.

Interestingly, since the theater is supposed to make onlookers directly privy to events on the stage, as if by magic, the taking on of a part is precisely what the characters will not show, for, after all, they are already supposed to be themselves. (As suggested, the pause a star may give in response to the applause that may greet his first appearance represents a momentary abeyance of the character he will play, not its establishment.)

4. As one finds with all other elements of framing, differences regarding episoding conventions are found not only across cultures but also within a society through time. Change in the theatrical frame over time in Western society is a general case in point, and change in its episoding conventions a particular example. It is said that the introduction of gaslight in London theaters in 1817 and the introduction of electric spark lighters for gas in the 1860s made it technically possible to dim and extinguish lights in the auditorium, thereby providing a signal for the beginning and ending of action within the theatrical frame.[12] Changes are also recorded regarding use of a curtain to mark beginnings and endings of scenes:

> Elaborate devices for quickly changing scenes bring up a point that has been curiously neglected. Until the last quarter of the nineteenth century, scene changing was done in full view of the audience. It was part of the entertainment. People enjoyed watching one scene magically dissolve into another. The idea persisted in the transformation scenes of extravaganzas and pantomimes not so many decades ago. Then why did the Roman theater have a curtain, and the renaissance and restoration theaters, too? It was there merely to hide the first setting and to close the play. Until about 1800 in England there was no "act curtain": the audience knew that the act was over when all the players left the stage. And in England until 1881 there was no curtain to hide changes of scene during an act; then Henry Irving introduced the so-called "scene curtain" to hide 135 stagehands, property men, and gas men who were involved with large pieces in *The Corsican Brothers*.[13]

5. The beginning and ending temporal brackets so far considered ought sometimes to be called the "external" ones because

12. Kenneth Macgowan and William Melnitz, *Golden Ages of the Theater* (Englewood Cliffs, N.J.: Prentice-Hall, 1959), p. 113.

13. *Ibid.*, p. 31. On the history of the use of the curtain in Roman drama, see W. Beare, *The Roman Stage* (London: Methuen & Co., 1964), Appendix E, "The Roman Stage Curtain," pp. 267–274.

in many activities internal ones occur, that is, brackets which mark brief pauses within an ongoing activity, the pauses to be held as time-out-of-frame. Again the classic example is the moments between scenes or acts in a play; the break between quarters, rounds, innings, and halves might be taken as other examples.

Internal brackets themselves vary considerably in structure. There are brackets that are built into an ongoing activity in advance, scheduled to mark a temporary pause—a temporary time-out—for all but a specialized few participants, as in the seventh-inning stretch and the second-act intermission. And, in contrast, there are unscheduled brackets that particular individuals may be allowed to employ, demonstrating a right to hold up the proceedings momentarily to accommodate what is defined as sudden personal need. Between scheduled, collectively applied internal brackets and unscheduled, individually employed ones, intermediate forms can be expected, and, what is more, a history of transition from one to another; the institutionalization in modern times of the office coffee break (and in Britain, a most advanced nation in this regard, "elevenses") is a case in point.

Activities vary according to the sorts of internal brackets they allow. Tennis interaction involves more time-out than time-in, although as in many sports, once the ball is in play, time-out cannot easily be arranged. Sexual interaction is practically all time-in, nature herself often being accorded the sole right to establish rest periods between acts.

Apart from these differences across various activities, there are no doubt differences from one culture to another. Gregory Bateson provides an instance in point:

> The formal techniques of social influence—oratory and the like—are almost totally lacking in Balinese culture. To demand the continued attention of an individual or to exert emotional influence upon a group are alike distasteful and virtually impossible; because in such circumstances the attention of the victim rapidly wanders. Even such continued speech as would, in most cultures, be used for the telling of stories does not occur in Bali. The narrator will, typically, pause after a sentence or two, and wait for some member of the audience to ask him a concrete question about some detail of the plot. He will then answer the question and so

resume his narration. This procedure apparently breaks the cumu-
lative tension by irrelevant interaction.[14]

The relation between bracketing conventions and role cycles is
worth considering. Taking any particular organized occasion of
social activity as a point of reference, what appear to be its
external brackets take their character (in part) from the presence of internal ones. But from a different point of view—a
wider, more inclusive one—these external brackets can be seen
as internal ones, too. Thus the good-bye ritual that terminates a
day at the office can be seen as an external bracket from the point
of view of that particular day's work, but it can also be viewed as
an internal bracket relative to a more abiding undertaking,
namely, the continuing performance of the work role, a performance that is interrupted at the end of each weekday, on week-
ends, and at holidays. In a similar vein, each performance of a
play can be seen from someone's perspective as part of a continuous whole—a "run"—and thus the opening and closing curtains
are merely internal brackets, except, of course, on opening and
closing nights.

6. The distinction here recommended between external and
internal brackets can serve only as a beginning; a series of
structural issues is actually involved and must be addressed.
First, in many social affairs, such as an evening's theatrical
performance, the bracketing process is associated with the readying and orienting of the participants, and a certain amount of
standardized preperformance and postperformance activity results, necessitating a distinction that Kenneth Pike has clarified,
one between "game" and "spectacle," that is, between a dramatic
play or contest or wedding or trial and the social occasion or
affair in which these proceedings are encased.[15] (An exaggerated example can be found in the instruction and warm-up given
a studio audience by talk show impresarios before the final taping
occurs.) Thus, time-out from the formalized undertaking in progress—that is, the "inner" events—is not necessarily time-out

14. Gregory Bateson, "Bali: The Value System of a Steady State," in
Meyer Fortes, ed., *Social Structure: Studies Presented to A. R. Radcliffe-
Brown* (Oxford: Oxford University Press, 1949), p. 41.

15. Kenneth L. Pike, *Language in Relation to a Unified Theory of the
Structure of Human Behavior* (Glendale, Calif.: Summer Institute of Linguistics, 1954), pt. 1, pp. 44–45.

from the social affair in which the proceedings are located.
Indeed, to take the theatrical case, it is when the audience has
not quite yet begun onlooking, or has ceased temporarily to be
active in that capacity, or has just finished with onlooking, that
its capacity as theatergoer will dominate activity. Observe that
the shift from spectacle to game—from encasing events to encased events—typically involves a change in frame, the encased
or inner events hopefully generating a realm that is more narrowly organized than that represented by everyday life. In any
case, in a precise examination of formal social proceedings, one
would expect to find that the formalized starting and stopping
brackets were themselves bracketed by informal ones pertaining
to the social occasion in which the proceedings were housed.[16]

---

16. A structurally interesting issue arises when the inner, official activity
is not itself formalized. Some students of parties would hold that "things"
don't start with the advent of the first guest, and, in many cases, may never
start at all, never, as once was said, get off the floor. Indeed, the understanding that late arrivals may overlap with early leavers implies that no
precise formal proceedings will be involved, and that perhaps no particular
inner proceedings are demanded. It is easy to identify beginning sequences
such as (1) hosts ready to receive; (2) first arrival (if single or couple),
allowing for partial assimilation to host-helper role; (3) second arrivals
providing the first arrivals with nonhosts to talk to, and, incidentally, with
the obligation to talk to persons they might not otherwise spend time with;
(4) arrival of sufficient number so that clusters can form, allowing some
expression of choice. Terminal phases can also be discriminated. But the
midgame is hard to define. However, F. Scott Fitzgerald, a student of the
form, takes Kenneth Pike's position:

The bar is in full swing, and floating rounds of cocktails permeate the
garden outside, until the air is alive with chatter and laughter, and
casual innuendo and introductions forgotten on the spot, and enthusiastic meetings between women who never knew each other's names.

The lights grow brighter as the earth lurches away from the sun, and
now the orchestra is playing yellow cocktail music, and the opera of
voices pitches a key higher. Laughter is easier minute by minute, spilled
with prodigality, tipped out at a cheerful word. The groups change more
swiftly, swell with new arrivals, dissolve and form in the same breath;
already there are wanderers, confident girls who weave here and there
among the stouter and more stable, become for a sharp, joyous moment
the center of a group, and then, excited with triumph, glide on through
the sea-change of faces and voices and color under the constantly changing light.

Suddenly one of these gypsies, in trembling opal, seizes a cocktail out
of the air, dumps it down for courage and, moving her hands like Frisco,
dances out alone on the canvas platform. A momentary hush; the
orchestra leader varies his rhythm obligingly for her, and there is a burst

The difference, then, between spectacle and game (to use Pike's terms) complicates the matter of brackets, leading to the possibility of sharply different perceptions, depending on whether the outer or inner realms are of chief concern. One illustration is provided: the announcer's role in chamber concerts.

As a spectacle, as a social affair, a chamber concert is likely to begin considerably before the musicians walk onstage. If the concert is to be broadcasted, something of the same format will be maintained. The announcer, then, will need something to say during the time between the point when radio broadcasting begins and the point at which the musicians start playing (as he will during intermission also). He can provide "relevant" commentary or a spoken version of what is going on in the hall. But provide something he must. For broadcasters have the reasonable belief that "dead air" cannot be excused. (Framing is the reason; without continuity of sound, current listeners may think something has happened to their radio or the station, and potential listeners may feel nothing is going on at that point on the dial.) However, announcers cannot fix very closely the moment the musicians will choose to come onstage and, after that, the moment they will choose to begin to play. So the announcer must come prepared with a variable script, one he can cut or lengthen to suit the need. Should the musicians for whatever reason delay beginning to play for a long time, the announcer can become

---

of chatter as the erroneous news goes around that she is Gilda Gray's understudy from the *Follies*. The party has begun. [*The Great Gatsby* (New York: Charles Scribner's Sons, 1925), pp. 40–41.]

If, following Fitzgerald, one can say that a party "begins" when a contagion of feeling has been accomplished which moves participants out of themselves together and in a pleasant direction, then one could argue that social parties and bridge parties can both ensure that a spectacle will occur; but only the latter can give any assurance that within these brackets an inner activity will take place. What characterizes a social party, in fact, in contrast to organized social occasions with a formalized core, is the precariousness of getting the inner activity going. A teacher in a classroom, a clerk in a court, a chairman at a club meeting, can more or less command a shift from preproceedings small talk to the business at hand, but a host cannot call a party to order. (But observe, although these leaders can often decide on the time to close the official proceedings, they may have appreciably less power to terminate the postproceedings and close out the spectacle.) For one study of the shift from preproceedings to proceedings see Roy Turner, "Some Formal Properties of Therapy Talk," in David Sudnow, ed., *Studies in Social Interaction* (New York: The Free Press, 1972), pp. 367–396.

hard pressed, forced to repeat many times what he has already said but know this is preferable to saying nothing at all. Now (and the point of all this), when the musicians begin to tune their instruments, producing audible sound, the announcer can, if he wants, pass the audience to the stage microphone. For although the players certainly aren't yet making music, they are audibly making what the social occasion demands, namely, signs that a social affair is properly under way and that in due course the inner events will begin. The sound that serves an instrumental function for its maker can be heard as a waste product by the audience; but for the announcer, these scrapings can be consciously appreciated for what they are: part of the substance of the social occasion. It might be added that tuning up is a sign that the music—the inner event—is very soon to begin. The pointed hush that occurs immediately after the tuning, the moment when the musicians settle before their scores and align their attention in immediate readiness for the closely coordinated activity that will follow, is a second and final sign. Together these two events seem to clearly serve as a beginning bracket—but, of course, the beginning of the music, not the beginning of the occasion.

Here it can be observed, then, that one of the things we mean by the lay term "formality" is a social affair in which there is a great distance in time and character between the outer, informal beginnings and the inner, formal ones, and by implication much protection of the innermost show. An extreme in this regard is provided by the annual Sumo tournaments in Japan: a day's activity may begin at 2:30 P.M., end at 5:30 P.M., and feature twenty fights, each of which lasts about ten seconds; the rest of the time is taken up with ritual practices surrounding the actual wrestling.[17] The ceremony preceding a Spanish bullfight provides another example.

It is to be expected that significant changes occur over time in the preproceedings and postproceedings, and these changes will tell us something about the changing status of the activity in the society at large. Take hangings, for example:

> The increasing time taken by the processions to cover the three
> miles from Newgate to Tyburn and the unruly behaviour of the

---

17. One report is available by William Chapin, *San Francisco Chronicle*, February 1, 1963.

crowds led to the decision by the Sheriffs to end this procession, although such was the weight of tradition that they had grave doubts about their right to do so. In 1783 they ordered that executions should take place in front of Newgate prison so that the condemned would only have to walk a short distance to the scaffold. The first execution was carried out at Newgate on December 3rd, when 10 men were hanged. One old tradition, the Tyburn procession, disappeared, but another was instituted. It became the custom for the Governor to entertain to breakfast afterwards certain officials and people of distinction he had invited to the execution. Invitations soon became laconic—"We hang at eight and breakfast at nine."[18]

Today the whole show is on the wane and staged very infrequently; where and when it still occurs, viewers are officials, and the preproceedings and postproceedings are cut short. No one admits to the possibility of having a good time.

7. The relation between spectacle and game, between social affair and inner doings, requires further examination. It is apparent that this dual arrangement functions as a buffer, allowing flexibility with respect to time; once the spectacle has begun, participants seem to be able to wait more comfortably for the "real" events, that is, the realm of being that is hopefully to be generated, a realm, incidentally, that is often anything but "real." (Something of the same design allows a waitress to pacify customers by taking their orders—or, even less, by placing water on their tables—for dinner can begin considerably before eating does.) And this wait can be adjusted to performance contingencies; it can be cut rather short or appreciably extended, for in a sense it is time without time, serving at the convenience of the inner events. But of course, only within limits. If "things" begin too quickly, there may be complaint, and if waiting is too long, there certainly will be. So we find that the very flexibility of the buffer can be given formal limits. Thus, time-out in various sports may be limited by various rulings, so that while the time itself is out of play, belonging to the spectacle, not the game, the limits are part of the inner proceedings.

All of this obliges us to make conceptual distinctions of a bothersome kind. External brackets which begin and end matters must themselves be seen to be of two kinds; those pertaining to

18. Justin Atholl, *Shadow of the Gallows* (London: John Long, 1954), p. 51.

the spectacle and those pertaining to the inner official events. And internal brackets, as we must now come to see, can have an even greater complexity.

The question of internal brackets can be approached by looking at the way in which time[19] is handled in dramatic scriptings.

Here the start can be traditional. There is considerable material on the influence of Aristotle in establishing for tragedy the rule that a unity in regard to time—twenty-four hours—was to be observed, and respectful observance during the seventeenth century in France can be contrasted with the license that came after the Revolution.[20] So direct discussion is available concerning the fact that although each act is played in accordance with "real" time and "natural" progression,[21] the periods that are to be taken

---

19. A treatment is available by Richard Schechner in "Approaches," in his *Public Domain* (Indianapolis: Bobbs-Merrill Co., 1969), pp. 74–81. See also Elizabeth Burns, *Theatricality: A Study of Convention in the Theatre and in Social Life* (London: Longman Group, 1972; New York: Harper & Row, 1973), chap. 6, "Rhetorical Conventions: Space, Setting and Time," pp. 66–97.

20. Here see, for example, W. L. Wiley, *The Formal French* (Cambridge: Harvard University Press, 1967), pp. 112–119. Wiley adds these further suggestions:

> Tragedy was not only rigidly encased by the unities in France, but also by other limitations that the French regarded as necessary to the genre. Among these would be the avoidance of deeds of violence on stage, the exclusion of any scenes of low comedy (there had been comic relief in the mystery plays), and of any language that was not properly elevated and dignified. [p. 119]

21. Here film again has different framing conventions. Movies allow a behavioral course of action within a scene to be shown through various times—usually shorter than real but sometimes longer—simply because bits of film can be edited out or edited into the flow of what is eventually seen, and a variable number of "frames" can be filmed per second. This manipulation works, of course, because the viewer can be relied on to make all kinds of inferences from sequences of brief shots. Pudovkin provides an early statement of this play-film difference, along with useful comments on the *history* of the difference, in this case the emergence of shooting and editing techniques that departed from the prior practice of merely photographing stage plays (*Film Technique*, pp. 52–57). Béla Balázs also provides a comment:

> The film may have shown a race of a thousand yards in a short sequence lasting five seconds and then give the struggle on the last hundred yards, in twenty rapidly changing close-ups, between competitors running neck and neck, panting, now gaining, now losing a few inches until at last they reach the goal. These twenty shots may last, say, forty seconds, that is, longer in *real* time than the sequence showing the first nine hundred

as having occurred between acts can vary somewhat—can in fact have claimedly simultaneous ("meantime") beginnings—providing only that a backward direction is not employed.[22] And, of course, the dramatist will be able to select his own starting point, whether past, present, or future. In all of this, appreciable explication is provided concerning the rule with respect to time in the theatrical frame.

Modern Western drama, of course, allows for a distance between acts of the playwright's choosing. Scene changes in film allow a similar license, but the matter apparently must be handled "convincingly":

> On the stage as much time as the author pleases may elapse between the acts, while the curtain is down. There are plays in which a century elapses between two acts. But film scenes are not separated from each other by curtains or intervals. Nevertheless the lapse of time must be conveyed, a time-perspective given. How is this done?
>
> If the film wants to make us feel that time has elapsed between two scenes, it interpolates between these two scenes another scene enacted in some other place. When we return to the former place, time has elapsed.[23]

The fade-out has come to be associated with the passage of time:

> Fading out a picture can also convey the passing of time. If we see a ship slowly disappear from view on the edge of the horizon, a certain passage of time is expressed by the rhythm of the picture. But if in addition to this, the picture is also faded out, then to the

---

yards of the race. Nevertheless we feel it to be shorter, our time-perspective will tell us that we have seen only a short minute, magnified as though under a time-microscope. [*Theory of the Film,* trans. Edith Bone (New York: Roy Publishers, 1953), p. 130.]

22. There is an interesting comparison here with the conventions sustained in the cartoon-strip frame. As Boris A. Uspensky suggests in "Study of Point of View: Spatial and Temporal Form" (a preprint from his *The Poetics of Composition: Structure of the Artistic Text and the Typology of Compositional Form,* trans. Valentina Zavarin and Susan Wittig [Berkeley: University of California Press, 1974]), here each individual "frame" provides a brief moment of the narrative frozen in time, and the sequential shift from one frame to the succeeding one cuts out a variable amount of narrative time from view (p. 16). The time progression from frame to frame is somewhat like that from scene to scene in a play, except that in the latter case greater time leaps seem common.

23. Balázs, *Theory of the Film,* p. 121.

feeling of time-lapse caused by the disappearance of the ship in the distance is added a feeling of further and scarcely assessable time-lapse. For now the shot shows two movements: movement of the ship and movement of the camera diaphragm. Two times: real time of the ship's disappearance and filmic time produced by the fade-out.[24]

And even space can serve that function:

> The film produces a most interesting link between time effect and space effect; so interesting, indeed, that it merits a closer analysis. Here is a fact corroborated by every experience: as has already been said, the film inserts a lapse of time between two scenes by means of cutting in a scene enacted in a different place. The experience is that the farther away the site of the inserted scene is from the site of the scenes between which it is inserted, the more time we will feel to have elapsed. If something happens in a room, then something else in the anteroom opening into it and then something in the same room a second time, we will feel that only a few minutes have elapsed and the scene in the room can go on straight away. We feel no jolt in time. But if the scene inserted between two scenes enacted in the same room leads us to Africa or Australia, then the same scene cannot be simply continued in the same room, because the spectator will feel that much time must have elapsed, even if the real duration of the interpolated distant scene is by no means longer than that of the similarly interpolated anteroom scene mentioned before.[25]

Now, by shifting back to the live stage, the point of all this can be seen. The opening and closing curtain are, one could say, the game-external brackets; for it seems these curtains do not cut off the spectacle from the environing world but rather the game from the spectacle. So, too, in its way, does the intermission curtain. It does not return theatergoers to the world beyond the social occasion, but instead brings the audience back from the inner events to the spectacle. (Indeed, that is why it is possible for the intermission to be the reason for attending.) The intermission curtain, then, would have to be called a game-internal bracket. But scene breaks on the stage or fade-outs in a movie are not designed to make *that* sort of transition, but one at a different level, one that occurs *within* the fictive world being sustained, the realm of the inner events. The beginnings and endings of dramatic episodes are being marked, not the beginnings and endings of dramatic action as such. If forced to it, one could speak here of inner brackets.

And then one could go on to the final embarrassment, namely, that a single marker, such as a curtain drop, can apparently function as a bracket relative to different orders of activity all at the same time. Thus, when the intermission curtain comes down, dramatic activity is temporarily suspended *and* a dramatic episode is brought to an end.

8. A final point. It is possible not merely to say that official proceedings are likely to be encased in a social occasion of some kind, but also that these casings can be relatively uniform compared to the variability of what is managed inside them. The "introductory remarks" which bridge between social occasion and the business at hand tend to be provided by a well-known personage after bringing the audience to attention, and this is so whether a political speaker is to be featured or a vaudeville act or a judge on the bench or a town meeting. And the same closing applause can bring a great range of offerings to an end.

III. *Appearance Formulas*

1. As suggested earlier, whenever an individual participates in an episode of activity, a distinction will be drawn between what is called the person, individual, or player, namely, he who participates, and the particular role, capacity, or function he realizes during that participation. And a connection between these two elements will be understood. In short, there will be a *person-role formula*. The nature of a particular frame will, of course, be linked to the nature of the person-role formula it sustains. One can never expect complete freedom between individual and role and never complete constraint. But no matter where on this continuum a particular formula is located, the formula itself will express the sense in which the framed activity is geared into the continuing world.

In formulating a separation of some kind between person and role, one should in no way precommit oneself to notions about the "essential" nature of each. There is a tendency to assume that although role is a "purely" social matter, the engine that projects it—the person or individual—is somehow more than social, more real, more biological, deeper, more genuine. This lamentable bias should not be allowed to spoil our thinking. The player and the capacity in which he plays should be seen initially as equally problematic and equally open to a possible social accounting.

Nor should images of biology and "animal substratum" confuse us here. Thus, the social role of mother is securely relevant to matters biological, as securely, it would seem, as the creatures of fashion who one year believe that their fundamental nature obliges them to become mothers and the next (and I think more warranted) that a political doctrine of destiny is serving to keep women in their subordinate place. Moreover, what is individual or person in one context is role or capacity in another. Just as one can speak of women who are or are not mothers, so one can speak of presidents who are or are not women. Consider now some elements in the person-role formula:

a. Casting: Given a role to be performed, what limitations are established concerning who can qualify for playing it? The answer is nearly coextensive with sociology, and no great effort can be made to provide an answer here. Obviously, there exist what might be called social factors, preferred or ancillary qualifications required of the person who takes the role, these organized in our system of age grading, sex typing, class and ethnic stratification. For example, in the sixties, the Vatican ruled that Sister Marie Bernadette of the University of Detroit could not take a part—any part—in a college production[26] but granted permission for Sister Michael Therese to become a pilot to further the work of the Church in Kenya;[27] in both cases, the sisters made news, and the news pertained to the person-role formula. Note that a double perspective ought to be applied here. Just as a role may call for a player who has certain "incidental" social qualifications, so a player may feel obliged to restrict his choice of role because of public expectations regarding someone with his profile of social attributes.[28]

26. *San Francisco Chronicle,* March 16, 1966.

27. *Ibid.,* March 17, 1966.

28. The TV series *What's My Line?* featured a set of "experts" who put general questions to guests who provided a yes-no reply. The object was to see who could guess the informant's occupation and how quickly. The

Just as there are social factors in casting, so there are also "technical" ones, these, incidentally, often serving as a rationalization for purely social considerations. Every adult role requires some competencies and capacities that cannot be acquired on the job, as it were, but must be brought to the scene by the person who would participate in it. Again a selectivity, and hence a connection, is implied between person and role.

b. In addition to casting issues, the matter of broadly applied and broadly restricting social standards must be considered. These pertain to physical conditions of work as they affect health, comfort, and safety, and to allowances for the performer's other role obligations.[29] Such standards also apply differentially, as in the case of child labor laws and maternity leave; for example, a child can accept the role of stage actor, but should the show go on tour or otherwise require a large block of time, the law requires that some arrangement be made for continuous special schooling. It is hardly my intent to doubt the desirability of these various standards; I want only to point out that they function to restrict the claims that a role can have upon a performer and indirectly constrain choice of person for function.

c. Consider next the matter of "responsibility." When an individual performs a deed while actively engaged in a particular role and performs the deed by virtue of the role, what liability for the act does he carry away with him to times and places in which he is no longer active in that particular role? When, for example, an individual performs a harsh act under command of a properly constituted superordinate, what relief from responsibility can he claim by virtue of having acted "under orders"?

No doubt a central frame issue regarding responsibility has to

---

audience was let in on the answer off-camera. Cosmological tensions were thus invoked, for each guest was selected on the basis of not looking like the sort of person who did his sort of work, selected, in effect, to contradict accepted person-role formulas. Of course, the format allowed for additional sources of amusement, for example, questions put in ignorance, which, in the light of the informant's actual occupation, would carry an additional and risqué meaning for the audience. This show demonstrated that appearances can be misread and innocent meanings undermined by risqué potential readings. But more significantly, I think, it demonstrated that a costly extensive operation must be sustained if such framing troubles are to be induced on schedule.

29. See *E.*, pp. 141–142.

do with our understanding of the rights of an individual to be relieved of it should some impairment to will and rationality be demonstrable, a question already touched on in regard to actor transforms. A person who commits a crime while not "himself," while drugged, intoxicated, or impassioned, is ordinarily not held *as* responsible for his act as one who performs in a clear-headed fashion; but he is not merely held responsible for being drugged, drunk, or impassioned. Punishment is likely to occur, usually in a reduced form but sometimes heavier than would be meted out to "normal" actors.

The question of responsibility and defects of competency raises the question, of course, of mental disorder. As already suggested, Western cosmology has no happily accepted formula here. When an institutionalized mental patient commits a crime, he is usually not held legally responsible for his act; when caught he is not brought to trial and sent to jail. But he is returned to the hospital. He is held responsible for being crazy, apart from the acts he commits while in that state. And indeed when he does arrive back at the institution he is very likely to be made to feel some consequences for the trouble he has caused.

The matter of psychotic delusions by uncommitted persons on the "outside" introduces much more delicate issues. The Mc-Naghten Rules (the answers delivered in 1843 by the chief justices of Britain in response to questions put them by the Lords in connection with the acquittal of one Daniel McNaghten of a murder on grounds of insanity) are relevant in this regard, and the fourth especially so:

> (4) If a person under an insane delusion as to existing facts, commits an offense in consequence thereof, is he thereby excused?[30]

> To the fourth question the answer must of course depend on the nature of the delusion: but making the same assumption as we did before, namely, that he labours under such partial delusion only, and is not in other respects insane, we think he must be considered in the same situation as to responsibility as if the facts with respect to which the delusion exists were real. For example, if under the influence of his delusion he supposes another man to be in the act of attempting to take away his life, and he kills that man, as he

---

30. Richard C. Donnelly, Joseph Goldstein, and Richard D. Schwartz, *Criminal Law* (New York: The Free Press, 1962), p. 735.

supposes, in self-defense, he would be exempt from punishment. If his delusion was that the deceased had inflicted a serious injury on his character and fortune, and he killed him in revenge for such supposed injury, he would be liable to punishment.[31]

There are nice judgments here regarding the anchoring of deeds in the wider world. The justices in effect argued that a deluded individual was indeed in another realm, an imagined one, but granted that he was still obliged to act in that realm according to the laws of the real land, as if these laws were to be carried into that realm. And if this seems a rather fanciful judgment, there are students who suggest that no one has much improved on it.[32]

d. A final consideration pertains to out-of-frame behavior. During the performance of any particular role, the performer will apparently have some right to sustain or fall back upon a self that is separate from the one relevantly projected. Role gives way to person. For example, as already considered, no matter how formal the occasion, he is likely to have some legitimate right to squirm, scratch, sniffle, cough, and otherwise seek comfort and repair minor disarray to his costume. These deviations from role exhibited during role performance can be extended by a kind of fiction to cover brief leave-taking, as when an individual excuses himself for a moment to answer the telephone or go to the bathroom. Rights to this kind of out-of-frame behavior can properly be seen as one expression of the limits placed upon the claims of role. May it be repeated that here I make no assumption about the inevitable biological substratum of the human actor, at least in the analysis of this sort of behavior. Recent fashion allowed considerable right to almost everyone to dress with relative "comfort," an expression of the belief that man should not be pressed too far into the formalities of a role. We have learned to accept premiers banging lecterns with their shoes and presidents exposing their operations. But, of course, behind this license is a fashion and a local cultural understanding; turn back our own society a few generations and one finds individuals willing to bear silently, and as a matter of course, a considerable formality of dress and bearing along with the accompanying discomfort.

---

31. *Ibid.,* p. 737.

32. For example, see Sidney Gendin, "III. Insanity and Criminal Responsibility," *American Philosophical Quarterly,* X (1973): 99–110.

The across-the-role right to a minimum of creature comfort is not the only basis of out-of-frame behavior. Two others might be mentioned. First, when an individual finds himself obliged to engage momentarily in activity that is quite unsuitable for him, activity that cannot easily be seen as consonant with what he brings to his roles and takes away from them, he may playfully guy his action, transforming what he does into unseriousness, into playfulness, so that the whole scene is conducted out of role. Here we have a means, then, of regaining a looseness of connection between person and role, but it is a looseness that must be sought and can be found because of the usual inflexibilities between person and role.

Second, when an individual is obliged to treat himself, and accept being treated, purely as a physical object in accordance with the constraints imposed by a natural framework, as when he submits to the handling of a physician, barber, or cosmetician, a little joke is likely to be allowed him (one that expresses frame tension), and, more important, *complete* assimilation to object status may be something that those who are handling him will themselves deplore. In brief, individuals who are expected to make themselves available as objects are not expected to do so with abandon and ease. A pertinent example may be taken from a report on the gynecological examination:

> Some patients fail to know when to display their private parts unashamedly to others and when to conceal them like anyone else. A patient may make an "inappropriate" show of modesty, thus not granting the staff the right to view what medical personnel have the right to view and others do not. But if patients act as though they literally accept the medical definition this also constitutes a threat. If a patient insists on acting as if the exposure of her breasts, buttocks, and pelvic area are no different from exposure of her arm or leg, she is "immodest." The medical definition is supposed to be in force only as necessary to facilitate specific medical tasks.[33]

---

33. Joan P. Emerson, "Behavior in Private Places: Sustaining Definitions of Reality in Gynecological Examinations," in Hans Peter Dreitzel, ed., *Recent Sociology No.* 2 (New York: Macmillan, 1970), p. 87. As Emerson illustrates, "In a gynecological examination the reality sustained is not the medical definition alone, but a dissonance of themes and counterthemes" (p. 91). Here, see also the section titled "A Simultaneous Multiplicity of Selves," in "Role Distance," *E.*, pp. 132–143.

Nor in allowing physicians to see them without clothing do patients necessarily allow themselves to be seen in no costume. For example, patients often decline, or attempt to decline, to give up their false teeth when facing surgery or delivery—as if one's teeth were part of the base formula for all presentations.

2. I have cited ways in which restrictions apply to variability between person and role and thus ways in which role is not independent of the apparently irrelevant features of those engaged in projecting it: casting practices, wider cultural standards, "personal" responsibility, and out-of-role rights. In all cases these understandings pertain to our occupational and domestic life in its everyday, ordinary occurrence. The formula that results should be contrasted—as a whole—to the formula we apply to keyings and fabrications, for what then becomes at issue is not roles or capacities but transformed versions of the whole, namely, parts or characters. And instead of a person-role formula we have something like a *role-character formula*. To consider this latter formula, however, some special care must be taken in the matter of organizational level.

An easy beginning is provided by the stage in its various forms, including cinematic. If one looks at stage acting as an occupational role, one can expect to find circumstances in which an individual will be prohibited from becoming so occupied. An example in the case of a nun was already given. An even more standard case is that of using women as players:

> In many ways the theaters and the shows of Spain resembled those of England from 1580 to 1640. In many ways they did not. In London, boys always played women's parts until after the Restoration in 1660. As we have seen from Rojas' description of the Spanish-companies, both boys and women appeared on the rude provincial stages. In Madrid, actresses were not licensed to appear in the public theaters until 1587.[34]

---

34. Macgowan and Melnitz, *Golden Ages of the Theater*, p. 52. Note, these restrictions apply to the theatrical frame. Analysis of frame leads us to appreciate that when the key is shifted slightly, a different set of restrictions may apply. Amateur theatricals, which allow an individual to project a character without first becoming a professional actor, no doubt allow for some liberty in casting that professional theater does not, so that household, school, and college plays have had access to high-born players at times when commercial productions did not. It was thus in a Cambridge production of Orton's *Erpingham Camp* that Prince Charles could dress as a padre and receive a custard pie full in the face (*Life*, December 13, 1968). Sim-

The question here is not *what* parts or characters women were allowed to play, but whether they would be allowed to play *any* part, that is, to participate (except as audience) in the theatrical frame, to be persons with a role in the theater. But given a social category's right to perform, the question of the particular parts members are allowed to perform still remains. In short, there is a question of both role rights and character rights, the right to participate in the application of a particular frame and the right to participate in a particular way in such an application. For if a particular part is felt to slightly raise or lower the stage actor playing it (and hence to a degree the person who has the role of stage actor) and to reflect, therefore, on both him and the other stage parts he might play, then total flexibility will not be possible. An historical example is the Spanish religious play, the *auto sacramental*—performed in part in church—providing as it does an example of shifts in framing rules:

> In 1473 a church council issued a decree against the presentation of monsters, masks, bawdy figures, and "lewd verses, which interfere with the divine offices." There were probably many more decrees, but the ribaldries persisted—in the street shows if not in the churches. The seventeenth and eighteenth centuries saw the

---

ilarly, as orientation to frame might cause us to expect, plays produced for charity have had access to players who would ordinarily eschew the boards; and stage productions which aren't quite plays might well employ a person-role formula quite different from that which regulates the legitimate stage. One example of the latter:

> The last form of theatrical entertainment that was developed in the time of Elizabeth and perfected under the first two Stuart kings is the "masque." Its roots are in the court shows of the Italian Renaissance. On Twelfth Night in 1512 young Henry VIII "with xi other wer disguised, after the manner of Italie, called a maske, a thynge not seen afore in Englande." There had been "disguisings" and ballroom pageantry before this, but now for the first time royalty took part in the entertainment. Henry's daughter Elizabeth also enjoyed the masque—a name borrowed from France—and her shows, like her father's, were mainly pantomime. . . .
>
> Some of the masques were given at the Inns of Court, but most of them in the royal palaces. . . . Courtiers as well as trained singers and dancers took part in them. Prince Henry "walked on" in the silent title-role of *The Masque of Oberon*, and Charles I and his queen played parts in some of these spectacles. James I's Queen Anne loved masques even more than the theater, and blacked her face to play one of twelve Negresses in *The Masque of Blackness*. [Macgowan and Melnitz, *Golden Ages of the Theater*, p. 88.]

attacks increase. Laymen as well as priests inveighed against professional players in *autos*. An anonymous writer objected because an actress played the Mother of God, "and . . . having finished this part, the same actress appears in an *entremes,* representing an innkeeper's wife . . . , simply by putting on a bonnet or tucking up a skirt," and dances while she sings an indecent song. "He who played the part of the Savior in a beard takes it off and comes out and sings and dances 'Here Comes Molly.'" Priests echoed such attacks on the players. It was abominable that "the woman who represents the lewdness of Venus, as well in plays [in the theaters] as in her private life, should represent the purity of the Sovereign Virgin." Such attacks persisted until at last, in 1765, Charles III prohibited by royal decree the performance of all *autos sacramentales.*[35]

A 1973 example is provided by Marilyn Chambers, uncontroversially pictured as the mother on Ivory Snow boxes until disclosure of her stardom in hard-core pornographic films.

It is apparent, then, that one must be careful in considering activity such as the theater to specify whether one is concerned with an occupation per se or any particular biographical guise that the occupation requires the individual to adopt on a particular occasion, and that restrictions in regard to the latter are not in the fullest sense necessarily restrictions in regard to the former.

It is, of course, a feature of the stage in modern times that an almost ideally loose connection exists between stage actor and part. Once an individual accepts being a stage actor, he is very little held responsible for the part he plays on any occasion, except as this reflects upon his status in his calling and adds or detracts from his vulnerability to typecasting. The basic thrust is for the stage actor to accept any part. But of course, we demand a continuity in regard to sex,[36] age, race,[37] and (to a lesser degree) social class. Further, there is the disinclination of actors to portray homosexuals, as already mentioned. The very recent change in this connection need not be seen necessarily to reflect

---

35. *Ibid.,* pp. 45–46. Ellipses and brackets in the original.

36. An exception: early radio tended to use women as a voice source for children's parts.

37. Interestingly, the use of black store dummies, recently established in the U.S.A. and Britain, is to date still markedly resisted in South Africa. See "Clothes Dummies Stir South Africa," *The New York Times,* January 4, 1970.

increased social acceptance of this social role (although presumably that is involved); for what is immediately at issue is a change in framing conventions, in this case an extension of the power of dramatic scriptings to insulate performers from their parts.

An obvious limit also exists in regard to roles in sexual interaction. And here one must attend to the complexities involved in the question of changing frame conventions. A "daring" act on stage or screen strikes at two matters: what producers can get away with staging and what actors can stage without becoming personally contaminated. The recent legalization of hard-core pornographic films would seem to reflect more change in the former than in the latter. When, in Gerard Damiano's *The Devil in Miss Jones,* the heroine slices her wrists in a tub and commits suicide, there is no question of the actress, Georgina Spelvin, being thereafter identified as someone who has acted this deeply reidentifying deed. The suicide is merely called for in the part; any actor in character is prepared to commit it. But the acts which Miss Jones commits while waiting for her assignment in hell, while certainly called for in the script, are not ones that Miss Spelvin will be able to easily dissociate herself from. At least currently. Yet, of course, the open acceptance (and even the seeking) of notoriety can itself be a move in the direction of legitimation, and the current willingness of players with conventional reputations to accept some contamination no doubt is both cause and expression of a change in framing conventions. Nor is established professional reputation the only means through which the insulating capacity of the theatrical frame can be strengthened. In 1973 a part-time actress, a 14-year-old, middle-class, suburban ninth-grader played the possessed child in the movie *The Exorcist. Newsweek* reported: "Her face and body a ghoulish wreck of blood, pus and welts, she screams the most obscene language ever heard on screen, kicks a doctor in the groin, brutally attacks her mother, masturbates with a crucifix and spews vomit at the priests who come to exorcise the demon." The magazine then went on to suggest that the young actress as well as her family were able to take the movie-making in stride, protected by levelheadedness and respectability.[38] (But here,

---

38. January 21, 1974.

perhaps, the fact that the movie character is not herself performing these acts, being merely a vehicle for the devil, provides insulating distance for the actress who is merely a vehicle for the character.) Note that a willingness to breach the theatrical or cinematic frame nonetheless should not be seen as part of the make-believe world; such an act is as real and serious as any other morally risky business.[39]

The difference between the legitimate and cinematic stage regarding the role-character formula is interesting:

> The work of finding the necessary actors, the selection of persons with vividly expressive externalities conforming to the requirements made by the scenario is one of the hardest tasks of the director. It must be remembered that, as I have already said, one cannot "play a part" on the film; one must possess a sum of real qualities, externally clearly expressed, in order to attain a given effect on the spectator. . . . In order to make concretely clear this inevitable necessity to use, as acting material, persons possessing in reality the properties of the image required, I shall instance at random the following example.
>
> Let us suppose that we require for a production an old man. In

---

39. Of which a sense is given in the following. In 1968, the innocence-typed actress Susannah York played a five-minute lesbian lovemaking scene in *The Killing of Sister George*, which, for its time, somewhat breached the limits of the cinematic frame. The following is cited from an interview conducted by Nora Ephron with Miss York:

Do you feel you were taken advantage of?

"No. It was something Bob [Aldrich, the director] evolved. He was as frightened as any of us. I was very frightened. You can't do a scene like that—at least I can't—without trust. Unless you are drunk—and I wasn't drunk. But over a period of two or three days, you don't stay at the same level of trust. I worried horribly. It was a difficult period. Difficult for me and difficult for Coral [Browne]. I think that there's very little that's more vulnerable than being an actor. You're a writer, but it's your book. If you're a painter, it's your painting. But if you're an actor, it's *you*—it's your face, your skin, your body. Well, they can have all that. They can take your body and your face. But nobody can invade your thoughts. And what worried me, what terrified me, was the fear that this was the moment that I was not going to be mine anymore. It's like the Arab who so dreads to be photographed because he feels someone is taking his soul. I thought I might be giving too much away. I thought that scene would be the thing that might be able to chip my soul away. The sheer fact of being undressed, of having to expose yourself. . . . Whatever your rational mind says, you can't help feeling violated." [*The New York Times*, December 29, 1968.]

the Theatre the problem would be perfectly simple. A comparatively young man could paint wrinkles on his face, and so make on
the spectator, from the stage, the external impression of an old
man. In the film this is unthinkable. Why? Just because a real,
living wrinkle is a deepening, a groove in the face. And when an
old man with a real wrinkle turns his head, light plays on this
wrinkle. A real wrinkle is not only a dark stripe, it is a shadow
from the groove, and a different position of the face in relation to
light will always give a different pattern of light and shade. . . .
    In the Theatre, make-up of this kind is possible because the light
on the stage is conditionally constant and throws no shadows.
    By this example it may in some wise be judged to what degree
the actor we seek must resemble his prescribed appearance in the
scenario. It may be said, in fine, that in most cases the film actor
plays himself, and the work of the director consists not in compelling him to create something that is not in him, but in showing, as
expressively and vividly as possible, what is in him, by using his
real characteristics.[40]

An average film lasts an hour and a half. In this hour and a half
there pass before the spectator sometimes dozens of faces that he
may remember, surrounding the heroes of the film, and these faces
must be especially carefully selected and shown. Often the entire
expression and value of an incident, though it may centre round
the hero, depends from these characters of second rank who surround him. These characters may be shown to the spectator for no
more than six or seven seconds. Therefore they must impress him
clearly and vividly. . . . To find a person such that the spectator,
after seeing him for six seconds, shall say of him, "That man is a
rogue, or good-natured, or a fool"—this is the task that presents
itself to the director in the selection of his human material.[41]

Whatever the differences in role-character formula between
various types of stage, and whatever the currently sustained
limits, the whole set of arrangements provides something of a
model for unconnectedness between character and its projector.
Other keyings and fabrications seem to provide similar but reduced versions of the same theme.
    Take again the issue of reputation, but this time as a constraint

_____
40. Pudovkin, *Film Technique*, pp. 107–108. Pudovkin here, I think, gets
a little carried away. The job is not to find someone who fits the part but
someone whose offstage appearance gives a quick onstage impression of the
characteristics sought. The characteristics themselves, at either offstage or
onstage level, may be entirely in the value judgments of the observer's eye.
    41. *Ibid.*, p. 113.

on how an individual might throw himself into simulations off the stage. For example, he who plays a suitable practical joke can be free of enduring implications of having organized reality in this manner; but, of course, that is what we mean by suitable. He who perpetrates an overelaborate or costly or harmful or tactless practical joke, that is, an improper one, acquires a reputation for so doing. Similarly, he who simulates insanity or homosexuality to avoid the draft may sometimes succeed, but if so, sometimes because investigating psychiatrists take the view that anyone who would stage such a show must be a poor mental risk—by which interpretation psychiatry steps in to bolster our notion concerning limits of simulation. But, of course, no easy history can be written here.

A related factor is associated with the dignity of office, causing incumbents to feel that certain carryings-on, however unserious, are not appropriate for them. In 1967 the governor of the State of California could allow the following during his initiation into the Los Angeles Club as an honorary member:

> As part of the ceremony the 57-year-old Governor sat blind-folded on a wooden hobby-horse before an audience of 600, with his right hand in a plate of scrambled eggs, while a club official recited a long series of comical incidents in the former actor's life—to each of which he had to reply: "I admit it."[42]

Were he to be elected president, however, that sort of initiation might be considered a little inappropriate, even though initiations as such, at least in America, have institutionalized crazy, unseemly behavior, reminding us that one of the things we mean by insane behavior is participation in an activity that would ordinarily be thought to be beneath the dignity of a person of a given type.[43] The mayor of New York City saw fit to act thus:

> Though Lindsay's vaunted equanimity has also suffered, he recovered his good humor long enough to supply a surprise postscript

---

42. *The New York Times*, July 27, 1967.
43. *Life*, October 23, 1970, contains a picture of a businessman on Milwaukee's South Side sitting in an aluminum rocker barefooted, wearing a tee shirt, pants rolled up, corncob pipe in mouth, with a bucket, fishing in a manhole, local police smiling, since, after all, it was known that he was engaged in an American Legion initiation. Because initiations provide institutionalized license to be out of frame, their social limits are much different from ordinary social limits on framing.

to the annual musical lampoon staged by political reporters. Always a show business buff, Lindsay donned straw hat, white gloves and cane for a soft-shoe song-and-dance routine with a professional partner. "Maybe," he quipped, "I can save this show yet."[44]

Again, were Lindsay to have been elected president, this sort of good sportsmanship might no longer have been allowed him. Although American presidents can with goodwill be audience to satirical skits of their administration, especially when produced by the Press Club of Washington, D.C., their taking to the stage is restricted, the limits of which were nicely pressed politically when President and Mrs. Johnson joined Pearl Bailey and Cab Calloway for an almost arm-in-arm singing of "Hello, Lyndon" during the Washington, D.C., appearance of the black cast production of *Hello, Dolly,* this apparently being the first time an American president ever appeared in a stage production.[45] This is not to say, of course, that rules for being a person in high office can't change and haven't, of which more later.

Consider now the question of biographical disguise. When an individual is operating within a particular key or construction, and by virtue of this takes on a part or character—a whole fictive personal identity, not merely a role—what responsibility does he bear for his acts, that is, what claims can be made upon him as a person by virtue of his conduct as a character?

When "under" what is presumed to be hypnosis, or when acting in his sleep, the individual is not held responsible for the actions of the character he portrays while thus enthralled. Among believers, when a man is mounted, that is, possessed, by a *loa,* a similar looseness between rider and mount is said to occur:

> The individual in a state of trance is in no way responsible for his deeds or words. He has ceased to exist as a person. Someone possessed can express with impunity thoughts which he would hesitate to utter aloud in normal circumstances.[46]

Interestingly, here one finds the claim that a person emerging from trance has access to no memory of what happened during

---

44. *Time,* March 18, 1966.
45. *Life,* December 8, 1967. Nixon appeared in the 1968 campaign on Rowan and Martin's *Laugh In,* where he said, "Sock it to me." It is said that Nixon performed this skit only after a written agreement forbade its use after the election.
46. Métraux, *Voodoo in Haiti,* p. 132.

possession. Mediums, it seems, claim the same dissociation between their person and the character they take on.

However, this looseness between an individual and his disguise does not seem typical. There are internal constraints deriving from his sense of shame and propriety. Undercover police apparently feel it appropriate to assume almost any disguise, for their "real" status protects them from being permanently identified with the guise they temporarily take on. Nonetheless, there are certain guises the police are loathe to fall into, especially those requiring the practice of homosexual acts.

Moreover, internal constraints can receive the sanction of official agencies, so that whatever the personal sensibility of the performer, he will nonetheless be discouraged from certain disguises even though allowed to engage in others. The following news release regarding limits on strategic monitoring provides an example:

> New York (AP)—Attorney General Ramsey Clark has issued an order prohibiting FBI agents from posing as newsmen in future investigations.
>
> Clark disclosed the order in a letter dated July 8 to Bill Small, CBS News bureau chief in Washington. The contents of the letter were released yesterday.
>
> Small had complained on behalf of three networks that FBI agents had posed as television newsmen June 17 during an alleged draftcard burning incident in Washington staged by female members of the New England Committee for Nonviolent Action.
>
> ABC News correspondent Irv Chapman reported at the time that the FBI agents presumably posed as newsmen in order to gather evidence on film for later prosecutions. Chapman charged in a newscast that the FBI agents "thus compromise our profession."[47]

Laws against impersonating members of the opposite sex are another example, and of special interest here because specification of the scope of these statutes forces a close consideration of frame, as a footnote in a book on arrests suggests:

> In 1958, the disorderly persons ordinance [in Detroit] was amended to make it unlawful for "any member of the male sex to appear in or upon any street, alley, highway, sidewalk, bridge, viaduct, tunnel, path, parkway, or other public way or place, or in,

---

47. *San Francisco Chronicle,* July 11, 1968.

upon or about any private premises frequented by or open to the public, in the dress of the opposite sex: Provided, however, that this section shall not apply to any person while legally giving, conducting, producing, presenting, offering or participating in any entertainment, exhibition or performance." Detroit City Ordinances, chap 223, S 8-D, as amended July 29, 1958.[48]

Here implied is a suggestion concerning the significance of our framing conceptions, for behind formal legal restrictions one can sometimes find some basic presuppositions about persons.

3. Return, then, to the theater and reconsider person, role, and character. As suggested, when we say that a particular stage actor is too old for a part or when we automatically cast for a part within the same sex, we are implying that some of what we will see as part-appropriate behavior in the stage actor's part is "natural" to him, that is, part of his offstage behavior, and that this unacted appropriateness is just as much demanded as the lines in the text. And so Sartre, in his preface to Genet's *The Maids*, provides us with this appealing argument:

> Genet says in *Our Lady of the Flowers:* "If I were to have a play put on in which women had roles, I would demand that these roles be performed by adolescent boys, and I would bring this to the attention of the spectators by means of a placard which would remain nailed to the right or left of the sets during the entire performance." One might be tempted to explain this demand by Genet's taste for young boys. Nevertheless, this is not the essential reason. The truth of the matter is that Genet wishes from the very start to *strike at the root of the apparent.* No doubt an actress can play Solange, but what might be called the "de-realizing" would not be radical, since there would be no need for her to play at being a woman. The softness of her flesh, the languid grace of her movements and the silvery tone of her voice are natural endowments. They constitute the substance that she would mold as she saw fit, so as to give it the appearance of Solange. Genet wishes this feminine stuff itself to become an appearance, the result of a make-believe. It is not Solange who is to be a theatrical illusion, but rather *the woman Solange.*[49]

48. Wayne R. LaFave, *Arrest* (Boston: Little, Brown and Company, 1965), p. 469.

49. Jean-Paul Sartre, Introduction to Jean Genet, *The Maids and Death-watch*, trans. Bernard Frechtman (New York: Grove Press, 1954), pp. 8–9.

Apparently Sartre's position, then, is that a woman taking the part (as was indeed the case during the play's first production) could "naturally" act like a woman, would in fact "be" a woman, which being would be beyond the threatrical frame, something unsuppressible by it. But, of course, behaving like a woman on or off the stage is a socially defined portraiture, no more "natural" and inevitable than the occupational role of maid. And what Sartre is telling us about is not nature—whatever that might be—but about his unexplicated preconceptions concerning the limits of the theatrical frame.

A further point. Given what has been said about role-character formulas, it is understandable that "typecasting" will occur, that is, that a stage actor who is "well suited" for a part (or type of part) and performs it frequently can become identified with it, and not only be restrictively accorded that kind of character onstage but also come to be seen offstage as characterizable by this part he usually projects. (Indeed, if one views matters comparatively, it can be seen that Western understandings about typecasting tendencies provide only one possibility. In Japan, for example, apparently there are lineages that have been associated with the stage for centuries and have managed to become nationally recognized as possessing a sort of mandate for certain kinds of parts; and here offstage identification with onstage part can be very great—especially in the case of males who specialize in female parts.) What might not be seen is what has been found all along in this study to be characteristic of framing processes, namely, the possibility of these very processes being themselves treated as a subject matter for reframing. Thus, in the professional wrestling business, performers are accorded a character as "villain" or as "clean wrestler," and once a wrestler seems to catch on with the public in one of these parts, care will be taken that each match conforms to and affirms the typecasting. The result of this practice is not only that each particular match is faked, but also that the carry-over from one match to another is itself carefully facilitated and managed, thereby increasing the value of the performing properties. In short, qualities that transcend particular performances can themselves be sustained by appropriate performance. A better example still is the Standwells, an acting troupe of five puppets that has appeared for eleven consecutive seasons in Manhattan in a wide range of plays.[50] Although two men animate the five puppets, each of the five is felt to have a distinctive personality, and this determines the choice of part and style of performance, with each of the five shining through in a characteristic way all the parts "he" or "she" plays. Fan mail, telephone messages, and the like, are addressed not to the characters performed in particular plays but to the "performers" behind these various characters in happy disregard of what everyone knows, namely, that behind all the "performers" are the same two men. What one has here, then, is the keying of the limitations of framing.

A final comment. There is an understanding in our society (as probably in all others) that a given individual can perform different roles in different settings without much embarrassment to the fact that it is a single, selfsame individual at work. (Thus my easy use above of the phrase "the same two men.") Indeed, it is a basic assumption of any particular role performance that the performer has a continuing biography, a single continuing personal identity, beyond that performance, albeit one that is compatible and consistent with the role in question. A shoe salesman can wait on a relative, and although this breakdown in usual "audience segregation" may be a little embarrassing, the difficulty can usually be dispelled by a joke or a reduction in price. For after all, the relative is not likely to be surprised by who it is who is found there, having probably selected that shop for that reason.[51] Very specifically, then, in taking on a role, the individual does not take on a personal, biographical identity—a part or a character—but merely a bit of social categorization, that is, social identity, and only through this a bit of his personal one. However, should an individual fake a role, impersonating a doctor, a newspaperman, or a person of the other sex, then this acquisition of a false social role also implies acquisition of a false personage or individuality, and in just the degree that the role in question would ordinarily imply an anchoring in the biography of the performer.

---

50. See the review in *Time*, "Mini Music Hall," January 4, 1971.
51. Argued in *E.*, esp. p. 141.

IV. *Resource Continuity*

Whatever goes on within an interpreted and organized stream of activity draws on material that comes from the world and in some traceable continuation of substance must go back into the world. Chess pieces must be taken from their box at the start of the game and returned thereto when the game is over. Even if the players and the pieces go up in smoke during play, the smoke can be shown to be an identifiable physical transformation of what had been. (If Irene Worth, playing Celia in *The Cocktail Party*, had really been eaten by ants, she couldn't return each night for a curtain call; but even if Miss Worth *were* eaten by ants—a fate some audiences devoutly hoped for—her fillings and her buckles would presumably remain and they could be identified as *her* fillings and buckles.) Each artifact and person involved in a framed activity has a continuing biography, that is, a traceable life (or the remains of one) before and after the event, and each biography ensures a continuity of absolute distinguishableness, that is, selfsameness.[52] Thus, when amateurs are done with the props that transformed the stage into a Victorian scene and the audience of the last showing has left, there will still be the chore

---

52. How much of this continuity is demonstrable is not the issue, just so long as *some* is, for some, if valid, is all that is needed. Thus, in some branches of art, authentication can come to turn upon matters not much related to what might be thought of as the meritorious element in art. Nelson Goodman, *Languages of Art* (Indianapolis: Bobbs-Merrill Co., 1967), footnotes a useful comment:

> To be original a print must be from a certain plate but need not be printed by the artist. Furthermore, in the case of a woodcut, the artist sometimes only draws upon the block, leaving the cutting to someone else—Holbein's blocks, for example, were usually cut by Lutzelberger. Authenticity in an autographic art always depends upon the object's having the requisite, sometimes rather complicated, history of production, but that history does not always include ultimate execution by the original artist. [p. 119]

In the case of sculpture, the production discontinuity is clear enough in, for example, a *surmoulage,* an unauthorized casting from an original piece. However, if a dozen casts are authorized by the artist from his original mold, these are all authentic; the thirteenth, taken by someone at the shop where the original mold is stored but without the authorization of the artist, is a fake, but the thread which establishes this fact has to do with the history of decisions, not the merit of works of art.

of returning the borrowed pieces to the good people of the neigh-
borhood who lent them.

The fact of resource continuity can be given a science gloss by
reference to the basic laws of physics dealing with the conservation of matter, the thesis here being that these principles apply
no matter what else happens. The relevant social implication is
that we all live in a world that we assume, by and large, has a
permanent residual character. Once an event happens we can
assume that a permanent tracing will be left of it, and that with
sufficient research and interrogation, a record of the event could
be uncovered. The residue is not lacking, only the reason. When
there is a reason, as in the checking out of a claimed historical
document, then retrieval can become extremely impressive.[53]
And a fundamental disorientation in the world takes place when
the individual believes an event has occurred and then finds that
he cannot prove this to others. Stories of *The Lady Vanishes*
genre exploit this theme.

The assumption of resource continuity underlies our notion of
faking and impersonation, the first pertaining to material objects,
the second to human ones. There is, of course, a vast literature
detailing efforts in both directions and means of detecting these
efforts.[54]

One interesting expression of resource continuity is what was
called "style," namely, the maintenance of expressive identifiability. Thus, when an individual engages in a strip of activity, the
fact that it is he and not someone else who is so engaged will be
exhibited through the "expressive" aspects of his behavior. His
performance of a standard social routine is necessarily a rendition of it. Style here refers to a transformation, a systematic
modification of a strip of activity by virtue of particular features
of the performers. A very general matter seems to be involved.

---

53. A useful general source is Robin W. Winks, ed., *The Historian as
Detective* (New York: Harper & Row, 1970).

54. An analytically impressive treatment of faking in art can be found
in Goodman, *Languages of Art*, pp. 99–123, who, incidentally, also
provides comments on the issue of resource continuity:

The general answer to our somewhat slippery second problem of authenticity can be summarized in a few words. A forgery of a work of art
is an object falsely purporting to have the history of production requisite
for the (or an) original of the work. [p. 122]

There is the style of a particular actor, a particular theatrical troupe, a particular theatrical period. There is the linguistic style of a language community, which means, for example, that when a translation is attempted from one language to another, lexical and grammatical constraints will not be the only ones that a nice effort must satisfy.[55] There are culturally distinctive styles of pictorialization:

> For a Fifth-Dynasty Egyptian the straightforward way of representing something is not the same as for an eighteenth-century Japanese; and neither way is the same as for an early twentieth-century Englishman. Each would to some extent have to learn how to read a picture in either of the other styles. This relativity is obscured by our tendency to omit specifying a frame of reference when it is our own.[56]

And also of motion pictures. The Navaho, put to making amateur movies as an experiment, apparently take different shots than we more recent Americans do and put together excerpts from footage into sequences different from the ones we fall into employing—in brief, a difference in "narrative style."[57] There is the style of a particular chess player and the style, say, of Soviet players as opposed to American ones. There are national styles of diplomacy or at least tendencies in that direction.[58] A gang of thieves can

55. See the discussion of language as style in Dell Hymes, "Toward Linguistic Competence" (unpublished paper, 1973).

56. Goodman, *Languages of Art*, p. 37.

57. Sol Worth and John Adair, in a useful study, *Through Navaho Eyes* (Bloomington: Indiana University Press, 1972), esp. chap. 9, "Narrative Style," and chap. 10, "Sequencing Film Events."

58. See, for example, Fred Charles Iklé, *How Nations Negotiate* (New York: Harper & Row, 1964):

> Western diplomats differ of course in their training and cultural traditions. These differences may find some reflection in their methods of negotiation, but usually they are not pervasive enough to produce a distinctly recognizable negotiation style. More important are the differences in government structure determining the domestic constraints under which each negotiator must operate. These, however, vary from issue to issue. An example of a somewhat more constant national characteristic is the high sensitivity of American diplomats to public opinion, which might derive both from cultural factors and the particular features of American political life. French diplomats are prone to elaborate historical-philosophical themes as a background to their negotiating strategies, perhaps because their education puts such stress on the composition of synthesizing essays. German and American negotiators at times place a

have a style, a characteristic *modus operandi*. There is a poker style for males and one for females.[59] Indeed, all our so-called diffuse social roles can be seen partly as styles, namely, the *manner* of doing things that is "appropriate" to a given age, sex, class, and so forth.

One can think of style as a keying, an open transformation of something modeled after something else (or after a transformation of something else). But there would have to be qualifications. Style often seems to involve a very minor keying or at least the kind of transformation that allows us to feel that an activity styled in one way is very little different in its consequences from the same activity styled in another way—which is not true of all keyings. Further, keying is, by definition, an openly admitted transformation. Style strikes us as false if it is intentionally aimed at, and, in the case of a criminal's *modus operandi,* it may be exhibited in spite of the efforts of the producer to disguise the authorship of his production.

Style, of course, is much used as an identificatory device with respect to both persons and their products. When, therefore, identification is required, style can become a central issue. Note also that style can be systematically faked. More common, it is mimicked for purposes of play: satires and takeoffs are the standard examples. Also, in forming an image of another, we may draw on such aspects of his style as we can formulate and use (along with style we impute but do not really uncover) as a nub around which to build an identificatory picture. So style is something the actor brings to his act and also something we are very ready to think we have perceived.

Style, then, can be seen as a property of any particular activity, a property that the producer of the activity brings to all such productions, the property itself somehow continuing in him. But, of course, other properties will exhibit a similar continuity. An individual who is to play Hamlet must learn the part, but he need not be taught theatrical English unless he is a high school Prince; presumably his occupational role as a professional actor guarantees that he already knows how to speak in that manner and can

---

greater emphasis on legal aspects than the diplomats of most other Western countries, probably because of the important role that lawyers play in the conduct of foreign policy in Bonn and Washington. [pp. 225–226]

59. T. Uesugi and W. Vinache, "Strategy in a Feminine Game," *Sociometry,* XXVI (1963): 75–78.

bring this capacity (alas) to any character he is obliged to project. And when becoming a professional and learning theatrical English, presumably he does not have to learn English—or at least not all of it—since presumably he brings *that* capacity to any role he takes on, whether that of professional actor, lawyer, or outright thief. Furthermore, after having once performed Hamlet in a run, he presumably can take on the part at a later date without having to spend as much time learning the lines; his memory will help him here at least to some degree. And he who casts plays may well take this presence of memory in players as a relevant matter to consider. And memory, of course, is a feature of the resource that an individual brings to a role. Thus, for government and business, personnel with access to strategic information constitute a special problem. As employees, they can quit, be fired, or retire; however, when termination occurs, they cannot turn in their memory with their key, continuing thus to constitute a concern to management.[60] A recent case here has been the apparent concern of the office of the presidency that former maids, cooks, chauffeurs, aides, and cabinet ministers appear to be increasingly inclined to sell their memoirs, thereby defaming *and* scooping the chief officer himself.[61]

Obviously, then, an activity does not totally remake the individuals it makes use of. This is so even—as earlier suggested—in the case of those undertakings that are designed to divest individuals of their social baggage upon entering and to afford them maximal involvement in the here and now—namely, games like chess and bridge. Thus, if the contestants aren't first matched for level of skill, there is poor chance that spontaneous engrossment

---

60. For which a legal protection may be attempted. Thus in Allen Dulles, *The Craft of Intelligence* (New York: New American Library, Signet Books, 1965):

The practical difficulties which a career in intelligence imposes upon a man and his family stem partly from the conditions of secrecy under which all covert intelligence work must be done. Every employee signs an oath which binds him not to divulge anything he learns or does in the course of his employment to any unauthorized person, and this is binding even after he may have left government employment. [p. 168]

In Britain, the Official Secrets Act has a similar function, being a remarkable device for putting the interests of the state above any understanding that might be had concerning the disjunction appropriate between person and role.

61. See, for example, the article by Hugh Sidey, "Memoirs Come to Market," *Life*, February 13, 1970.

in the game will develop. Further, although a game like bridge enforces a random deal of cards and radically incomplete communication between partners, still it is the case that persons who have played as partners to each other for a long time are greatly advantaged. In all of this, once again it can be seen that as long as activity contains materials of any kind, including individuals, a range of connections will link the activity to the ongoing world, a world from which the activity's resources came and to which these resources will be returned.

V. *Unconnectedness*

Consider now a relationship of activity to context that at first might seem to be no relationship at all: the assumption that every activity will occur in an environment of closely occurring other events that are to be taken as unconnected and unrelated to the event in question—a matter of chance, indifference, and the like. Even when an actor utilizes features of the immediate environment on the open assumption that these features will be there to be used, he will be able to assume that in many particulars what he uses is present for reasons indifferent to his own.[62] In sum, one relation we have to our immediate surround is that some of its elements have no relation to us.

As mentioned in the first chapter, we employ a series of terms to designate the belief that mutually proximate activities *could* have little connection with each other. The terms "luck" and "accident" can be taken to designate unanticipated occurrences that impinge for good or ill upon us. The term "negligence" refers to unplanned impingements that work ill, that should have been perceived in advance as something to avoid, and for which we are held somewhat responsible. The term "coincidence" sometimes refers to the contact of two parties with prior relations to each other who had not anticipated a coming together at this time. And finally, the term "happenstance" can refer to comings together that were in no way planned, the parties thereafter coming into a relationship because of the contact.

---

62. Considered in more detail in "Normal Appearances" in *R.P.*, pp. 310–328.

Unconnectedness obtains through space at any one particular time, and over time, in depth, as it were. The second dimension links consideration of unconnectedness to the notion of resource continuity, since any tracing backwards in time of a particular element in a situation is likely to lead to sources outside those directly involved in the current activity. A chair, in theory, can be traced to the tree from which its wood came, but the tree did not grow so that that particular chair could be made. And presumably the chair was not bought at a particular store so that a particular business meeting could be provided with seating for its participants. On the other hand, if a chair is to be bugged, then indeed tracing it back in time will soon lead to evidence that unconnectedness has broken down.

A final point is to be added. In the previous chapter, consideration was given to the process of disattention and to the capacity of participants in an activity to deal with a range of events in these terms. It should be evident now that participants can afford to accord this treatment to these events because of the assumed unconnectedness of the events to the matter at hand. Given the absence of any designed link between the disattended event and the activity in progress, participants need only predict the course of the event and allow for it; and with that done, the event can indeed be safely disattended.

VI. *The Human Being*

It is hardly possible to talk about the anchoring of doings in the world without seeming to support the notion that a person's acts are in part an expression and outcome of his perduring self, and that this self will be present behind the particular roles he plays at any particular moment. After all, from any and all of our dealings with an individual we acquire a sense of his personality, his character, his quality as a human being. We come to expect that all his acts will exhibit the same style, be stamped in a unique way. If every strip of activity is enmeshed and anchored in its environing world so that it necessarily bears the marks of what produced it, then surely it is reasonable to say that each utterance or physical doing that the individual contributes to a current situation will be rooted in his biographical, personal identity. Behind current role, the person himself will peek out. Indeed, this is a common way of framing our perception of another. So three cheers for the self. Now let us try to reduce the clatter.

Start with a simple case. A popular radio comedy series features a small, permanent cast of players, each of whom, as the series progresses and settles down to an effective formula, acquires a colorful personality, a cast identity all his own. Each becomes as familiar and human as living individuals need to be for us. It is these radio personages who are given particular parts to play in the skits which make up each week's show. The accent and mode of speaking each cast personality has developed and become identified with is each week partly submerged in the character he is obliged that week to play. Part of the humor of the show will be to see how the personality we know so well must bend himself to the particularities of a particular part, yet will be constitutionally unable to bend very far. Parts but not "casting" will often be announced in advance, so that the first spoken word will tell listeners "who" is going to do that part and what strains on credulity are to be joyfully expected. Broad comedy will be achieved when such a personality finds that he has been saddled with a part that is too uncongenial for him and finds a comic reason to drop his mask and petulantly revert back to his true self—if only for a moment—before he regains his self-control and disappears again into the appointed part.

Now it happens that knowing followers of the show come to appreciate that the personality sustained by each player across his several parts may itself be somewhat put on, or at least tailored to increase its power as a typification of a possible way of being. And, in fact, closer examination of the show credits proves that something not unlike the Standwell puppet show is involved, for it turns out that the whole show is put on by three or four actual performers, each of whom plays two or more members of the cast. And the accents that show through a character's accents are themselves put on. Once again we are reminded that a sense of the humanity of a performer is somehow generated by discrepancy between role and character, which discrepancy itself can be manufactured for the effect it produces. If such is true of role-character contrasts, what about person-role contrasts?

Look now at fiction—the novel and the short story. As suggested, the writer can choose how openly intrusive he will be; he can obviously speak through a particular character and, if he wants, provide a running comment in an impersonal voice that can only be his "own." Just as the manner in which his characters saying what they say will convey their personality, so the manner in which he handles the author's task will—so it seems—convey his personality and beliefs. And an important part of what the reader gets out of his reading is the experience of contact with the writer. For the latter turns out to be (and indeed must be or he would not be much read) a person of fine spirit, broad knowledgeability, and deep moral feeling, who incidentally implies that the reader is just the sort to appreciate such quality, else the author would not be writing in the first place. Here the theatrical frame is different from the fictional one, since in plays the writer must work through his characters entirely, and their virtues tend to be attributed to them, not to him.[63] All of this is also true, perhaps to a lesser degree, of nonfiction writers.[64]

But this sense of the author can only be a facilitated delusion. With only the text to draw on, at best a partial picture can be adduced, for there will be a great deal about the writer that never gets into his print. But more to the point, whatever does get in is not some sort of spontaneous unschooled expression. After all, the writer and his editors have the text to work on at their leisure.

---

63. As Patrick Cruttwell remarks in a useful paper, "Makers and Persons," *Hudson Review*, XII (Spring 1959–Winter 1960):

> . . . the drama's characters must be self-explanatory in their actions and their sayings—whereas in the novel, or the narrative poem, the opportunity is always there for the writer to comment and explain and tell the reader how such and such a character or episode ought to be taken: and that is where, in narrative, the personal usually enters. [p. 495]

64. Cruttwell extends the argument to personal journals, even those not written (apparently) with publication in mind (*ibid.*, pp. 487–489). In a very useful article Walter Gibson, "Authors, Speakers, Readers, and Mock Readers," *College English*, XI (1950): 265–269, took up the case in regard to book reviewing, suggesting how much of that literary form consists of using the works of others as a target of response which will confirm for the reader that he has found a brilliant, many-sided critic who appreciates that the reader is the appropriate recipient for this response. Writing, then, breeds a presumed (Gibson calls him mock) writer who, in fact, is likely to be vastly different from the actual writer, and a presumed reader, who on the same grounds is likely to be vastly different from the actual one. The posturing of the writer, Gibson argues, calls out a posturing from the reader —a mutually affirmed affectation.

Lapses in taste and knowledgeability can be corrected. Spelling errors, grammatical mistakes, repetitiveness, bad puns, "too" frequent use of particular words, and other mannerisms can be caught in time. Phrases can be turned, tuned, and tempered. If in one draft he seems to be striving for an effect, then in the next draft he can strive to remove this impression. False notes must be caught during rehearsal and played again right. Indeed, it is apparent that if this polishing has not been done, critics will be quick to note the fact disapprovingly. So the quality of mind and feeling the writer's writing implies he has is no less a labored artifact than the quality of self a playwright's words generate for one of his characters. Yet although we readers are prepared to see that the characters an author presents to us are fictional, along with their personal qualities, this very mindfulness on our part seems to lead us to assume that what we sense to be the writer is the real thing; we respond to what we sense is spontaneous, to what we sense is uncalculated, to what is therefore organically characteristic of the way the writer is as a person. Which means that the work a writer does ends up being work through which he cuts a figure, and that the materials provided him in fictional plots, topics of public interest, and the efforts of other writers become disguises for some sort of exhibitionism. That he who might write this last sentence would still take some editorial care over it does not deny what it says.[65]

---

65. Which is but to mimic Gibson. In extracting the pretensions contained in quoted bits of two book reviews he presents—and I think effectively—a statement in one paragraph followed then by a next paragraph which applies to the first paragraph the analysis that paragraph recommends. To wit:

It will surprise no one to learn that the first passage was taken from a recent issue of *Partisan Review*, and that the second is from the *New Yorker*. Perhaps it is fair to say that the mock reader addressed by these speakers represents ideal audiences of the two periodicals. In any case it seems plain that the job of an editor is largely the definition of his magazine's mock reader and that an editorial "policy" is a decision or prediction as to the role or roles in which one's customers would like to imagine themselves. Likewise, a man fingering the piles at a magazine stand is concerned with the corollary question, Who do I want to pretend I am today?

(The mock reader of this article numbers among his many impressive accomplishments the fact of having participated at various times as mock reader of both the *New Yorker* and the *Partisan Review*.) [*Ibid.*, p. 267.]

The argument, then, is that in fiction and even nonfictional writing, the sort of person the author is emerges from the writing, but that this is an artifact of writing—certainly so in part—and not a result of some organic expressive carry-over from actor to actions. It should also be apparent that the channel through which this projection is accomplished is not the one that carries the story line; rather the writer in effect relies on the subordinated channels, namely, aspects of discourse that need not be directly attended. So the fact that impressions of the author are somehow indirectly delivered, there to be sensed, certainly not something for the author to lay claim to directly, is a feature of the channeling of communication as much as it is a feature of man.

Now turn to real face-to-face interaction among persons. Again one finds that a discrimination is made between the individual as a continuing selfsame entity and the role he happens to be playing at the moment. It is, in addition, this difference that carries the burden of conveying personality.[66] And this "role distance" will be carried largely in the subordinate tracks. But although this stylistic carry-over from personal identity to current role can be treated as another aspect of the sense in which an individual's behavior is grounded or anchored in something beyond itself, I do not think this should be the first place to look for an accounting.

Perhaps the lead can be given to us again by looking at written productions. Follow Gibson's argument:

> Most teachers agree that the attitudes expressed by the "lover" in the love sonnet are not to be crudely confused with whatever attitudes the sonneteer himself may or may not have manifested in real life. Historical techniques are available for a description of the sonneteer, but the literary teacher's final concern must be with the speaker, that voice or disguise through which someone (whom we may well call "the poet") communicates with us. It is this speaker who is "real" in the sense most useful to the study of literature, for the speaker is made of language alone, and his entire self lies on the page before us in evidence.[67]

As with sonneteers, so with makers or writers of fiction. Obviously, the author cannot be identified with a particular character in his story if for no other reason than he has managed to pro-

66. Argued in "Role Distance," *E.*, p. 152.
67. Gibson, "Authors, Speakers," p. 265.

duce more than one character, and each of these presumably has its own claim to reflect a little of him. But just as we obtain an impression of each character, so we obtain an impression, or rather glean an impression, of the author. And just as we rely on what is said and done by or in regard to a particular character for our impression of that character, so we tend to rely on the whole content of the fictional work itself to gain an impression of the author. Of course, the reputation of the writer may well precede our response to a given particular product, but this prior preparation is not in one sense necessary. For the kind of conclusion we come to can be arrived at solely from what the printed world makes available to us. We learn about the *writer* from literary gossip, published and unpublished; we learn about the *author* from his books.[68]

And so it is during actual dealings between actual persons. Again there will be a response to the role that each presents as his mantle for the moment. Again something will glitter or smolder or otherwise make itself apparent beyond the covering that is officially worn. And again, the sense of otherness that is created, the sense of the person beyond the role, is, or certainly can be, a product of what becomes locally available. Again, of course, externally established information will be brought to bear. But again, this is not necessary for the *kind* of response that is produced. A sense of the person *can* be generated locally. And this discrepancy between person and role, this interstice through which a self peers, this human effect, need no more depend upon the world beyond the current situation than does the role itself. Whatever a participant "really is," is not really the issue. His fellow participants are not likely to discover this if indeed it is discoverable. What is important is the sense he provides them through his dealings with them of what sort of person he is behind the role he is in. In Gibson's terms, they are concerned

---

68. Book dedication is a possible exception, for here there is a sense in which the writer exploits the authorial channel to convey—nay, to broadcast—a personal message in a voice different from the one he will immediately take up. A Durkheimian twist. As if the self-demanding labor of doing the book gave the writer the privilege and obligation to show publicly that he has a separate, private life and is committed to it, while at the same time those who make up this life have a right to be so recognized. One is reminded of the presence of hand-held wives when husbands accept success or defeat in their effort to win an election.

with the poet, not the sonneteer. They are concerned with the author, not the writer. They are concerned with something that is generated in the contrasting streams of his immediate behavior. What they discover from their gleanings will apparently point to what this fellow is like beyond the current situation. But every situation he is in will provide his others with such an image. That is what situations can do for us. That is a reason why we find them (as we find novels) engrossing. But that is no reason to think that all these gleanings about himself that an individual makes available, all these pointings from his current situation to the way he is in his other occasions, have anything very much in common. Gleanings about an individual point beyond the situation to what presumably will be found in all other gleanings of him, but one cannot say that they point in the same direction, for it is their very nature to make themselves felt as pointing in a same direction.

The function of a striking remark, ironic, witty, or learned, is not to disclose or conceal the perduring nature of its maker, for a remark (or a novel) can hardly do that; its function is to generate the notion that an interactant brings a personage along with him, a poet or an author of whom such sentiments can be characteristic. And of poets and authors and personages they certainly can be.

You will note that the characters a playwright designs have a local setting, visible to us, in which to stride, lounge, and bubble. They are given things to say and do so that they can be directed to say and do them with particular style. What results is the creative mystery of the dramatic arts. For somehow or other stage characters known to be stage characters can end up giving the realest possible impression of possessing real personal qualities, indeed quite striking ones. But why shouldn't a stage scene be sufficient for the production of these effects? Those materials are just what we employ to create ours.

So once again one is faced with the recursive character of framing. The resources we use in a particular scene necessarily have some continuity, an existence before the scene occurs and an existence that continues on after the scene is over. But just as this is part of reality, so conceptions that this is so become part of reality, too, and thus have an additional effect. There is no "objective" reason why a flag or any other piece of ritual equipment should not be treated as sacred while it is functioning within a ceremony but be treated in an everyday way while being manufactured or, after being in use, while in storage awaiting the next ceremonial occasion. And that, by and large, is what occurs. But close examination will disclose that although flags and the like are treated in a relatively matter-of-fact way when not in ritual use, some small circumspection will continue to be displayed.[69] And *this* continuity of character is not forced upon us by the continuity of material things but by our *conceptions* about the continuity of spiritual ones. Sacred relics, mementos, souvenirs, and locks of hair do sustain a physical continuity with what it is they commemorate; but it is our cultural beliefs about resource continuity which give to these relics some sentimental value, give them their personality. Just as it is these beliefs that give us ours.

---

69. In the case of national flags, this examination need not be very close. Nation-states are our really sacred entities, and most members of this club lay down a "flag etiquette" to deal with offstage handling and "flag desecration" statutes to deal with violations of the rules. Here, see Sasha R. Weitman, "National Flags: A Sociological Overview," *Semiotica,* VIII (1973): 337. A close study of offstage management of sacred religious objects is available in Samuel Heilman, *"Kehillat Kidesh:* Deciphering a Modern Orthodox Jewish Synagogue" (Ph.D. diss., Department of Sociology, University of Pennsylvania, 1973), esp. pp. 101–115.

9

Ordinary Troubles

From the perspective of discreditability, two basic framing possibilities have been considered. In the first, all participants share an understanding of what it is that is going on and what it is that everyone is about; and in this view about what is taking place they are effectively correct. Involved may be the simple application of a primary framework or various keyings thereof—in brief, "straight" activity. New facts cannot be a risk, and literal discrediting is not imaginable.[1] The second possibility involves a construction of some kind—an outer one—leading to deception. It is this sort of frame that is subject to a special vulnerability—disruption due to discrediting. A structural feature is that participants are divided into two groups, those in the know and those taken in, and each will have a different view of what it is that is going on. Since the fabricators will be involved in the work of sustaining the show, the show can last for a long time; certainly there have been constructions that contained their dupes for a lifetime. One final complication: as earlier considered, an indi-

---

1. In the case of an exploitive fabrication lodged within a keying or a benign fabrication, as in the play within the play, a certain amount of care is required in analysis. The inner fabrication is subject to discrediting—indeed, typically of a violent kind—but the resulting collapse is itself part of an admittedly make-believe world and so is an admittedly enacted version. It is the characters that are thrown off balance and go out of play, not the stage actors or theatergoers. What one has here, in short, is a transformed discrediting, not a real-life one.

vidual can apparently deceive himself, as when he dreams, becomes paranoid, and so forth—or at least he can act so that people think he is deceiving himself.

Involvement in straight activity is here contrasted to deception and delusion. The contrast directs attention away from another set of possibilities already mentioned, ones that occur with no one's intent or help and yet prevent the individual from lodging himself in straight activity. In brief, *illusion*. Here, as in the case of fabrications, the individual's situation can collapse, disintegrate, go up in smoke, but although a definition of the situation is discredited, persons aren't, unless it is the definer himself who feels he was acting with less care and discrimination than is required in daily living. For here no person's presentations can be seen as motivated by an intent to deceive. So here one has a special category of situations, "misframings," with innocence borrowed from straight activity and collapsibility borrowed from fabrications. That is what this chapter deals with.

I. *Ambiguity*

It is perfectly possible for individuals, especially one at a time and briefly, to be in doubt about what it is that is going on. Reference here is not to *any* kind of doubt (as when, for example, in flipping a coin, an individual does not know whether the outcome will be heads or tails, or when, in glancing at his watch in the dark, he does not know whether the time is 2:10 or 3:10). Nor to those ingenious drawings designed to be perceptually unstable, giving now a picture of a rabbit, now a duck, or now that of an urn, now two human profiles (depending on figure and ground), for these can be unambiguously seen as drawings which produce optical illusions. The concern, rather, is the special doubt that can arise over the definition of the situation, a doubt that can properly be called a puzzlement, because some expectation is present that the world ought not to be opaque in this regard. And insofar as the individual is moved to engage in action of some kind—a very usual possibility—the ambiguity will be translated into felt uncertainty and hesitancy. Note, ambiguity as here defined is itself of two kinds: one, where there is question as to what could possibly be going on; the other as to which one of two or more clearly possible things is going on. A difference between vagueness and uncertainty.

In our own society we often give over to specialists the task of clearing up an ambiguity of frame. When a man dies during a bar fight, we call in a medical examiner to determine whether the death was caused by a blow or, for example, a ruptured aneurysm, something that locates the death in the physiological frame instead of a social one.[2]

Varieties of ambiguity can be distinguished according to the element in framing to which ambiguity attaches.

First are ambiguities regarding primary frameworks.[3] Hearing

---

2. Marshall Houts, *Where Death Delights* (New York: Coward-McCann, 1967), p. 193. Cause of death is something we attempt to be clear about, and the framework of frameworks in this connection is well worked out. Death can come, we feel, from accident, suicide, homicide, natural causes, or war. (In the West we allow for one exceptional method, but this restricted largely to adventure fiction, namely, heroic certain self-sacrifice in a small group setting, as when a weak survivor slips over the side of an overweighted lifeboat and is said to give his life, not take it.) When one of these understandings is selected, questions may arise, sometimes quite pointed, concerning the possibility that one of the other causes really qualifies. This doubt, however, need not imply doubt concerning the distinctions among basic causes or their exhaustiveness. Nor does it imply that the framework is just another arbitrarily designed typification. From the perspective of the workings of society, this classification is not merely *a* construct; it is a good one. The social organization of our whole society supports these distinctions and is consonant with them; they are as real as the society that sustains them and as objective and factually grounded as any other aspect of our social system. Similarly, other obvious ambiguities are resolvable to a small number of frame-relevantly different possibilities, each of which draws its character from a different part of the social organization. Thus, when a hotel guest re-enters his room and finds someone in it, the person is almost certainly to be someone in the guest's party, a housekeeper, a hotel official, a stranger who has mistaken rooms, or a thief. A returning guest may be momentarily puzzled concerning "who" is in his room, but this puzzlement occurs within a narrow matrix of likely possibilities, most of which are quickly called to mind. These possibilities, incidentally, also provide a choice of covers an intruder can use to dissemble his "real" reason for being present, a reason which usually is nicely covered by the same matrix.

3. John Austin, *Sense and Sensibilia* (Oxford: Oxford University Press, 1962), has a version worth noting:

Sometimes the plain man would prefer to say that his senses were deceived rather than that he was deceived by his senses—the quickness of the hand deceives the eye, &c. But there is actually a great multiplicity of cases here, at least at the edges of which it is no doubt uncertain (and it would be typically scholastic to try to decide) just which are and which are not cases where the metaphor of being "deceived by the

something at the door, the individual for a moment may not know whether a purely natural event is involved, say, the brushing of a branch against the door by the wind, or a social one, namely, a knock. Feeling something touch his back, the individual for a moment may not know whether he has accidentally come up against a building or a fence, or whether an old friend is greeting him, a stranger is attempting to draw his attention to something, a gun is being stuck in his ribs, or a neural twinge has occurred. Finding that the voice at the other end of the line has suddenly stopped, he may not know whether the person at that end has been cut off by a technical defect, has dropped in his tracks with a heart attack, has accidentally depressed the cradle, has had it purposely depressed by an armed robber, or has terminated the talk because he thought it was over, or because he was angry, and so forth.[4] With the lights failing all over New York, the individual does not know whether there has been a technical failure, an enemy attack, or sabotage.[5] A driver wiggling his hand out the window can cause other drivers to be uncertain for a moment as to whether he means to signal a turn or greet a friend. In all of these cases what is ambiguous is the meaning of an event, but what is at stake is the question of what framework of understanding to apply and, once selected, to go on applying, and the potential frameworks available often differ quite radically one from the other. Observe that ambiguous events of the kind here considered are often immensely distracting. Little offstage sounds can draw acute attention to themselves as if they had physically overridden legitimate foci of attention. The reason, of course, is that these ambiguities have to be resolved, lest the individual be forced to

---

senses" would naturally be employed. But surely even the plainest of men would want to distinguish (a) cases where the *sense-organ* is deranged or abnormal or in some way or other not functioning properly; (b) cases where the medium—or more generally, the conditions—of perception are in some way abnormal or off-colour; and (c) cases where a wrong inference is made or a wrong construction is put on things, e.g. on some sound that he hears. [p. 13]

4. And, of course, a function of verbal listener cues such as "um-hmm," "wow," is to use the only channel available—the auditory—to dispel the possibility of these other interpretations.

5. See A. M. Rosenthal and Arthur Gelb, eds., *The Night the Lights Went Out* (New York: New American Library, Signet Books, 1965), and the cover story in *Time*, November 19, 1965.

remain in doubt about the entire nature of the happenings around him.

Ambiguities in regard to primary frameworks typically seem very short-lived and for a good reason: because these frameworks are fundamental to the organization of activity, because a whole tissue of organization derives from each, any point of doubt will usually be resolved quickly by information from a multitude of extraneous sources. Indeed, it seems a characteristic of human life that any activity we become involved in carries at least this much orderliness. On the other hand, it seems also the case that very brief ambiguities at the level of the primary perspective will be relatively common. Certainly ambiguities which involve allied frameworks occur. He who unpacks after a house move, not finding an article in the box it was thought to have been packed in, can feel that it must be in another box, or that it was stolen by the movers, or that it got misdirected to other users of the van, or that it was not packed in the first place; and these accounts of differing depth of difference from one another can jostle and vie for his belief.

Just as ambiguity can arise in regard to primary frameworks, so it can arise in regard to transformation—although here we might be more likely to speak of uncertainty instead of vagueness. Sometimes keying is at issue. (When a phone is heard ringing, is it the "real" one in the house or the one located in the drama now in progress on television?) More often, it seems, a question of fabrication is involved. As already argued, here is a version of ambiguity that would seem to occur in every society, namely, suspicion. Is the person before us what he appears to be? And is the scene involving him to be trusted at its face value? Out-and-out disbelief of persons and appearances may not be common. But *doubts* about the straightness of an event seem everywhere a possibility, especially momentary doubts fleetingly entertained concerning another's "real" beliefs or intent in connection with a passing matter.

Momentary doubts very commonly occur in regard to the possibility of benign fabrication—leg-pulls, put-ons, and the like. Thus if the President decides to "keep in touch" by phoning without warning various persons around the country, especially media people who have treated his decisions favorably, then it can be predicted that recipients, upon being told the White House is calling, will at the very least suspect that they are being put on.[6] However, unseriousness need not be involved. Indeed, some occupations, such as that of the police, seem especially to predispose their incumbents to suspect serious accounts presented to them.[7] So, too, the citizenry has come to suspect any event which creates newspaper publicity for its doers, the suspicion being that the act was performed in order to get publicity, not in spite of it. Thus, when an interior decorator is found half-naked, crucified to a cross in Hampstead Heath, one response is that a radical religious sect must be involved; but this response is likely to be (as it was) tested against another (and in consequence found incorrect), the other being that a publicity stunt is what was really going on.[8]

An important source of suspicion concerning fabrication derives from what are called accidents, since these events typically lend some credence to the possibility that a guided doing was really involved in the disguise of fortuitousness. Thus, when two Syrian pilots land their jet fighters on a northern Israeli airstrip, an uncertainty as to the event is created until it can be proven that they are not deserters, merely poor navigators.[9]

---

6. See the *Life* report by Hugh Sidey, " 'This Is the White House Calling,' " April 2, 1971. Correspondingly, individuals with "good" reasons for phoning a celebrity often feel they are in for trouble convincing the operator that their request is not a put-on.

7. See, for example, James Q. Wilson, *Varieties of Police Behavior* (Cambridge: Harvard University Press, 1968):

> Thus, the tendency of the patrolman to be and act suspicious arises not simply from the danger inherent in his function but from his doubts as to the "legitimacy" of the victim. Middle-class victims who have suffered a street attack (a mugging, for example) are generally considered most legitimate; middle-class victims of burglary are seen as somewhat less legitimate (it *could* be an effort to make a fraudulent insurance claim); lower-class victims of theft are still less legitimate (they may have stolen the item in the first place); lower-class victims of assaults are the least legitimate (they probably brought it on themselves). [p. 27]

The doubts here expressed are doubts concerning frame, more specifically, transformation: the question is whether a righteously indignant complaint voiced to the police is a genuine expression of the complainant's feelings or a simulation for various purposes of gain.

8. Reported in the *San Francisco Chronicle*, August 30, 1968. Apparently the team involved hoped to sell pictures of the event.

9. Reported in a release from *The New York Times* in the *San Francisco Chronicle*, August 14, 1968.

There are, then, ambiguities with respect to frameworks and transformations. A third source of doubt occurs in regard to anchoring of the frame, especially the biographical identification of the ingredients in the scene, including, importantly, the human ingredients. The most familiar example, perhaps, is what unfolds when an individual answers the phone and is greeted by a strange voice that addresses him warmly by name while awaiting recognition. Something similar occurs when one comes across a friend who has almost been forgotten.

Frame analysis, then, recommends an analytical basis for discriminating sources of ambiguity. It also leads us to ask about the circumstances under which an ambiguity can persist through time. One answer, to be further considered later: when the intent of an actor forms an important part of a scene, and he is no longer alive to provide this information. Self-inflicted death can provide the circumstances, especially when the victim is too young to qualify socially as competent to consider the consequences of his acts, the issue being whether full-fledged suicide was involved, or a serious gesture, or a playful gesture, or a pure accident.[10] The sudden disappearance of an individual also leaves matters fully up in the air until he can be found. Incidentally, this latter source of ambiguity is very much limited by the retrieval machinery we have for persons, this making it very difficult for them to disappear from everyone's view, although disappearance from the view of family and friends is not so uncommon.[11] When it appears that an individual has suffered

---

10. For example, the case of an eight-year-old boy found hanging by a necktie in his bedroom closet (reported in the *San Francisco Chronicle*, February 25, 1966), and the fourth-grader who, being "sent to the cloakroom for punishment was found dead thirty minutes later, hanging from a coat hook by his shirt collar" (*ibid.*, November 15, 1967).

11. One newspaper example from the *San Francisco Sunday Examiner and Chronicle*, January 30, 1966.

Ridgefield (Conn.)—(AP)—The father of 19 year old Fred Grossfeld closed the doors of his haberdashery shop yesterday to begin a full time search for his son.

The father, Israel Grossfeld said:

"If it takes all my life, this is my number one job—to find the boy, nothing else."

Young Grossfeld, an honor student at Massachusetts Institute of Technology, has been missing for 50 days. He vanished from the campus after a late evening bridge game.

foul play, it is important to discover his remains, unsettling as this may be, not merely so that they can be given a decent burial, but so that issues of frame can be decently put to rest.

II. *Errors in Framing*

The various kinds of ambiguity, including vagueness and uncertainty, have their counterpart in error, that is, in beliefs, uninduced and erroneous, as to how events at hand are to be framed. Instead of merely stopping short to try to figure out what is happening, the individual actually lodges himself in certitude and/or action on the basis of wrong premises. He "misframes" events. Of course, ambiguities can, when wrongly resolved, lead to error, just as the discovery of error can be prefaced by a moment of doubt.

Some errors involve the actor in nothing more than misperception, as when he takes to be a bird in flight what is really a kite on a string. But typically, it seems, a misreading leads to at least the incipient formulation and execution of action. However, the distinction between perception and action is not relevant here. To repeat, the issue is that an individual may not merely be in error—as when he adds a column of figures wrong—but that certain of these errors prove to be a matter of "misframing," and consequently involve him in systematically sustained, generative error, the breeding of wrongly oriented behavior. For if we can perceive a fact by virtue of a framework within which it is formulated, if *"To experience an object amounts to being confronted with a certain order of existence,"*[12] then the mispercep-

---

Since then, the grieved parents have been sending out notices with pictures of the youth, who is of medium height and who wears dark-framed glasses.

Mrs. Grossfeld said yesterday she and her husband feel their son "may be a victim of foul play, or may have been kidnapped by foreign agents."

"He has a brilliant mind, and this may be the reason why he may have been kidnapped," she said.

Grossfeld also suggested another possibility—"something may have gone wrong with Fred's mind."

"I feel he is alive," Grossfeld said, "so I'm going everywhere I can and see anybody who can be helpful."

12. Aron Gurwitsch, *The Field of Consciousness* (Pittsburgh: Duquesne University Press, 1964), p. 381.

tion of a fact can involve the importation of a perspective that is itself radically inapplicable, which will itself establish a set, a whole grammar of expectations, that will not work. The actor will then find himself using not the wrong word but the wrong language. And in fact, this metaphor is also an actual example. If, as Wittgenstein suggested, "To understand a sentence means to understand a language,"[13] then it would seem that speaking a sentence presupposes a whole language and tacitly seeks to import its use. A person who is bilingual in English and German and in the company of others who are similarly competent can hear a sound he takes for "nine" and believe he is involved in talk utilizing English and its numbers, when in actuality a negation has occurred, namely, *nein,* and German is being spoken—a question of hearing the right sound but responding in the wrong frame.[14]

Consider now, as was done with ambiguities, errors typified according to their bearing on frame.

1. First, error with respect to primary framework. The organizational import of primary framework, and our deep commitment to being right about what it is that is going on at this level, is exhibited by the embarrassment and chagrin individuals manifest upon discovery that they have been schematically wrong. Thus, a student nurse attempting to straw-feed a patient whose face is bandaged can become upset when she learns that the reason for his apparent lack of thirst is that all along he has been dead and therefore systematically a different kind of object than she had thought.[15] A person leaving a shop and offering an apology for tripping over the clerk's foot can be peculiarly chagrined when he looks down and finds that it is the carpet he has tripped over, an

---

13. Ludwig Wittgenstein, *Philosophical Investigations,* trans. G. E. M. Anscombe (Oxford: Basil Blackwell, 1958), pt. 1, sec. 199.

14. The example derives from Yehoshua Bar-Hillel, "Indexical Expressions," *Mind,* n.s., LIII (1954): 370. The "indexicality" or laconicity of ordinary talk, which Bar-Hillel thoroughly documents, provides a guarantee that ambiguity and error will always be possible. (The issue of homonyms and metaphor will be considered later.)

15. David Sudnow, *Passing On* (Englewood Cliffs, N.J.: Prentice-Hall, 1967), p. 87. He also tells us: "The student nurse who was told the patient she had just injected was already dead cried nervously and trembled for several minutes; she was given a half-hour off to recover from her distress" (p. 88).

entity not to be addressed socially. And the following can become a newsworthy, apocryphal tale:

> Chicago (UPI)—"Help me, help me, please help me," cried a voice from the basement of a North Side school.
>
> "Come to the door," called policeman William Diaz, who had been summoned to the scene by worried residents. "Nobody will hurt you, you're safe."
>
> Nobody came. Diaz broke the door down. There sat a Myna bird, pet of a school janitor.
>
> Diaz said the bird was unhappy at being found out. When it saw Diaz, the bird switched tactics and began berating the policeman in shrill four-letter words.[16]

In all these cases, embarrassment is eminently understandable. If it is the case that there is a structural logic to every activity, involving a fine mesh of presuppositions, then, as suggested, any involvement on the basis of a wrong framework or even an error in regard to any particular element in the frame of an activity will lodge the actor in a diffusely inappropriate relationship to events.

Questions regarding frame become acute in circumstances in which we feel a natural framework alone ought perhaps to override social ones. Thus, in many cases a decision must be made whether to respond to an individual's behavior as though it were a full-fledged guided doing or to treat it as a symptom of some kind, a decision as to whether to assess action within a deterministic perspective or a voluntaristic one. The social significance of this framing dilemma should not deter us from seeing that in selecting between a reduced responsibility and full responsibility perspective, a simple misframing is possible:

> The way Dave Niles reported it on KNBR, this guy is lying face down on Powell St., with traffic backed up for blocks. A Little Old Lady climbs down from a stalled cable car and begins giving him artificial respiration—whereupon he swivels his head and says: "Look lady, I don't know what game you're playing, but I'm trying to fix this cable!"[17]

Misframing can also occur when differing bases for reducing responsibility can be applied. Thus, severe lobar or walking

---

16. *The Evening Bulletin* (Philadelphia), June 22, 1970.
17. Herb Caen, *San Francisco Chronicle,* November 29, 1967.

pneumonia causes a subject to "go into periods of delirium. He acts insane: his conduct exactly mimics that of a person who is 'out of his mind,' or drunk to the point of passing out."[18] Epileptic seizures can also produce an appearance of drunkenness, and the resulting misunderstandings constitute one of the contingencies of this family of disorders.[19] And the following report:

> Suddenly the half-empty tram came to a screeching and clanging halt.
>
> The motorman rushed to the back of the car, bending over the limp form of a middle-aged, matronly woman who had collapsed in her seat. Seconds later the frightened man relaxed.
>
> "I guess she's drunk," he told a few other passengers who had gathered around. This diagnosis of the woman's condition made sense to everyone in the car. There was the apparent smell of alcohol on her breath, and when the motorman tried to lift her out of the seat she started vomiting and tried to say something in a slurred voice.[20]

Four hours later, in the drunk cell of the nearest police station, the woman, a teetotaler given to using mouthwash, died of a cerebral hemorrhage, with no trace of alcohol in her bloodstream.

2. In addition to error in regard to primary frameworks, there is also error with respect to key. These "miskeyings" are common and often reported in the press:

> London—One man in the crowd gripped his walking stick when he saw three men racing down a busy street near Trafalgar Square yesterday, [followed by] policemen.
>
> He knew where his duty lay if cops were chasing robbers.
>
> He raised his stick, cracked one man over the head and vanished from the scene. His only desire was to be an unsung hero.
>
> The injured man was taken to a hospital to have his gashed head stitched.
>
> Last night, nursing his aching head, 30-year-old actor Michael McStay bemoaned the fact that the movie sequence had proved too realistic.

---

18. Houts, *Where Death Delights,* p. 261.

19. E. Henrich and L. Kriegel, eds., *Experiments in Survival* (New York: Association for the Aid of Crippled Children, 1961), p. 101.

20. *San Francisco Chronicle,* December 17, 1964.

"I suppose this is an occupational hazard," he said, "but I do think he owes me a drink."[21]

A very common source of miskeying is provided by those occasions when something ominous occurs and participants insist for a moment that playfulness is at work, in part because it is just such events that are performed as a joke:

A blonde teller at Civic Federal Savings and Loan Association was so surprised that she laughed when a gunman pointed a .45 caliber automatic at her shortly after noon yesterday.

"It isn't funny," the sharply dressed bandit told 25-year-old Carol Gilbert. "Get all your dough out."

Miss Gilbert, who told police she had been hoping the whole thing was a joke, then handed over $3500 in $5, $10 and $20 bills which the husky holdup man stuffed into a brown attache case he was carrying.[22]

Or:

Van Nuys—Kenneth A. Lindstrand, a 32-year-old salesman, went to a Halloween costume party at a luxurious apartment in this Los Angeles suburb early Sunday morning.

Lindstrand, who lived across the street, was one of the few not in costume. He danced several dances and left. When he came back, a man with a gun was chasing him.

---

21. *San Francisco Chronicle*, May 23, 1966. It is actors who err, not necessarily persons, as a story reported in *The Times* (London), August 5, 1970, illustrates:

An Alsation dog which savaged a child to death may have mistaken the baby for its squeaky rubber toy, it was stated yesterday at the Southwark inquest on Kathleen Howard, aged three weeks.

The child's grandfather, Mr. George Howard, of Stanstead Road, Forest Hill, London, said the dog had a toy dachshund. "It used to squeak like a baby when he bit it. But it got on our nerves and I took the squeaker out. I think he mistook the baby for his toy."

. . . .

The baby's mother, Mrs. Kathleen Howard, aged 19, wept as she said, "It was the first time Kathleen had been in the garden."

A police sergeant said the toy dog had been bitten on the chest, and this was where the baby had been bitten.

. . . .

A verdict of Accidental death was recorded.

22. *San Francisco Chronicle*, May 18, 1966. Similar short-lived miskeying is exhibited by individuals who are about to be mugged. See Robert Lejeune and Nicholas Alex, "On Being Mugged: The Event and Its Aftermath," *Urban Life and Culture*, II (1973): 265.

Everyone laughed.

"It looked like a toy," said another guest, Bruce Cane. "I saw the flashes."

Lindstrand fell and the guests watched and laughed as he writhed on the floor for several minutes.

His assailant fled, virtually unnoticed.

Finally one of the guests went up and tried Lindstrand's pulse. He shouted, "He has no pulse. This man is dead."

Detectives questioned everyone, but said they had no clue to the identity of the killer.[23]

As might be expected, the one effort in the annals of modern American crime to rob a casino led to a miskeying. The setting is the Mounds Club in Lake County outside Cleveland, 1947:

At 12:15 A.M. the second show of the evening began in the green and yellow dining room. A big crowd was on hand. The attraction was Mary Healy and Peter Lind Hayes.

Miss Healy, staging an impersonation of Hildegarde, was dragging Hayes from a ringside table when a masked man wearing a green GI fatigue uniform entered from the kitchen.

The masked man was carrying a machine-pistol, and he fired a volley into the ceiling. The audience roared with laughter at this "realistic" bit of play-acting. Miss Healy, realizing the shooting wasn't part of the act, ran into the rest room and remained there.

Three more hooded men entered. One wore a gray hat and appeared to be the leader. The audience applauded, still assuming it was part of the entertainment that made the loss of their money less painful. Another volley into the ceiling ended the laughter.[24]

Interestingly, devices exist, such as firecrackers, which function as institutionalized sources of imitations of serious sounds and, by virtue of this, also provide a basis for wrongly imputed unseriousness; King Hassan of Morocco, celebrating his forty-second

---

23. *San Francisco Chronicle*, October 31, 1967. It might be noted that a favorite set piece of murder mysteries on the screen is to have the climactic scene occur in a circus or fun fair or costume ball, so that the hero can be chased in a context in which his plight and the ominousness of his pursuers will be miskeyed by the revelers who will see the dramatic pursuit as a costumed, innocent affair.

24. Hank Messick, *The Silent Syndicate* (New York: Macmillan, 1967), pp. 230–231. Apparently within six months the comedians who staged this show were permanently removed from nature's Equity.

birthday at a palace festivity, was host to an example, the cause being an attempted coup d'état:

> "All of a sudden popping sounds were heard," Ambassador Rockwell said, "and most of us thought they were firecrackers. But a man staggered through the open doors onto the patio bleeding profusely from his legs."[25]

In referring to these last-mentioned errors as "miskeyings," an overly general term was used. Guests at the Mounds Club, at the Van Nuys apartment, and at King Hassan's could be said to have "upkeyed" their experience, for they attributed more laminations to events than were really there to be found. This designation allows us to anticipate the opposite kind of error—"downkeyed response"—and examples such as the following:

> Robert Christopher vowed yesterday that he will never play with toys again.
>
> Christopher is 23.
>
> He was sitting in a car waiting for a friend Friday afternoon, when his eye caught a toy tommy gun lying on the seat. He idly picked up the olive-green gun, stuck it out the window and pulled the trigger.
>
> Rat-a-tat-tat.
>
> Unfortunately for Christopher, the car was parked outside the downtown Palo Alto office of Lytton Savings & Loan Association.
>
> A company official heard the "firing," looked out and saw the gun.
>
> Within minutes, six policemen converged on the car. One of them cautiously approached the open window and demanded: "Hand it over."
>
> Christopher did.[26]

In these cases someone attempting to be unserious finds that matters get out of hand because others treat his joke in the wrong way, neglecting to key the strip of activity that is involved. Playfulness can come a cropper independently of belief, however, when physical events transpire to lend literalness to play, if only retrospectively. I cite examples of these fateful pranks:

> Frank N. Hicks, 28, was feeling frisky early yesterday and decided to play a little game of Russian roulette with his wife, Barbara, 27.

---

25. *The New York Times,* July 12, 1971.
26. *San Francisco Chronicle,* July 18, 1965.

They were in bed in their apartment at 3112 14th Avenue, Oakland, when Hicks reached into the cabinet drawer, pulled out a .38 caliber revolver and checked the cartridge cylinder.

Teasingly he pointed the gun at Mrs. Hicks, and pulled the trigger.

It clicked.

Then he checked the gun chamber again and placed the weapon at his right temple. He pulled the trigger, the gun was fired and a bullet entered his head.

"No one was more astonished than he," Mrs. Hicks sobbed hysterically. "He died with an absolutely bewildered look on his face."

Relatives said Hicks had been "in and out" of the Army for 11 years.[27]

Blandford, England—A 17-year-old student from an exclusive boys' school was found near a railway track yesterday bound and gagged, with both feet severed.

Police said he apparently had been tied to the track and struck by a train.

Authorities raised the possibility that the youth was the victim of a school hazing incident.

Stephen Hargreaves told workmen who found him, "They tied me up." He could say no more. He was reported in fair condition in the Salisbury Royal Infirmary.[28]

You will note that in considering upkeyed and downkeyed response, I have so far looked mainly at open joking, joking of the kind that is designed to be seen from the start as such, the point being that it wasn't seen when it was supposed to be, or was seen when in fact no joking was occurring. There is an easy transition here to a consideration of fabrications in the creation of error, starting first with mild teasing and other benign fabrications and going on from there to the exploitative kind. However, I mean to exclude the relation an individual has to a world that intendedly contains him; to be effectively deceived by others is to be wrong about what is going on, but that wrongness is not what has here been called error. To be excluded also is what happens when an individual believes he is duping others when, in fact, they are managing matters so that he does not discover that he has been discovered, and that it is he, not they, who is contained.

---

27. *San Francisco Chronicle*, August 10, 1966.
28. *Ibid.*, September 25, 1964.

Error with respect to fabrication might be said to occur when an individual believes an attempt is being made to take him in when, in fact, no such attempt is present.

I would like to add that arms and explosive devices figure largely in misframing stories because these instrumentalities have a special framing power, that of transforming ordinary activity into what, retrospectively, comes to be seen as an ill-fated taking of things for granted, in short, erroneousness.[29]

The miskeyings so far cited involve gross movement and bustle, but frame analysis is to be understood to apply to experience of any kind, including the merely cerebral. Take, for example, the famous framing issue explored by logicians under the title "use and mention." In statements, names are used in order to refer to, that is, mention, objects, and are obviously not these objects themselves. The objects about which logicians and grammarians make statements, however, *are* names and the statements that can be constructed out of them. Now, in order to be clear that a name is being mentioned and not what it denotes, a framing device of some kind is used, such as quotation marks or a colon followed by insetting or boldface type or (as here employed in connection with "colon") the spelling out of a symbol. In this way, presumably, one can clearly leave the world of objects for the more laminated one of verbal keyings of those objects.

In commenting on the need in logic to consistently distinguish use and mention, Quine writes:

> Quotation is the more graphic and convenient method, but it has a certain anomalous feature which calls for special caution: from the standpoint of logical analysis each whole quotation must be regarded as a single word or sign, whose parts count for no more than serifs or syllables. A quotation is not a *description*, but a *hieroglyph;* it designates its object not by describing it in terms of

---

29. Other circumstances have the power of "derealizing" ordinary reality, of transforming ordinary activity into something that is not serious, or at least not real. This structural irony occurs, for example, when someone upon whom the individual's day-to-day plans depend suddenly dies while away at work, or bolts for it, leaving the individual to proceed under what will turn out to be false assumptions. Hence the hospital practice of letting the immediate next of kin know about a death as soon as possible after it happens. This not only saves the bereaved from learning about the news from the wrong person and in the wrong way, but it also saves them from playing out strips of what would have to have come to be seen as false reality, a hollow show. Here see Sudnow, *Passing On,* chap. 6, "Extensions Outside the Hospital," pp. 153–168.

other objects, but by picturing it. The meaning of the whole does not depend upon the meanings of the constituent words.[30]

He then goes on to argue that some of the notations of logic apply at the level of mention, serving as (logical) connectives between what it is the connected statements are about, whereas other symbols serve solely (or ought to) as a means of saying something about statements as such, each such statement to be taken as a token of a form, a "name" of a statement, in brief, a keying of the statement. Then, in an editorial aside, he suggests that miskeying has been common in these matters:

> Frege seems to have been the first logician to recognize the importance of scrupulous use of quotation marks for avoidance of confusion between use and mention of expressions (cf. Grundesetze, vol. 1, p. 4); but unfortunately his counsel and good example in this regard went unheeded by other logicians for some thirty years.[31]

And understandably. For perhaps it will always be possible to find circumstances in which frame clarity regarding use and mention breaks down. For example, when a writer wants to suggest that a word (or phrase) he is using is not one that he himself would ordinarily use, he sets it off in quotation marks, framing it so that it will be taken as a usage, not literally a word in use. However, whether or not to take personal responsibility for a term is sometimes a matter of taste and sensibility, not syntax—a question of the figure a writer wants to cut.

3. In addition to errors with respect to frameworks, keying, and fabrication, there are errors with respect to biographical identification of materials in the scene—a framing issue because in many activities unmistaken identification (in either social or personal terms) is systematically presupposed in the building up

---

30. Willard Quine, *Mathematical Logic,* rev. ed. (Cambridge, Mass.: Harvard University Press, 1965), p. 26.

31. *Ibid.* Some actual examples of this unheeding are cited by Rudolf Carnap, *The Logical Syntax of Language,* trans. Amethe Smeaton (London: Kegan Paul, Trench, Trubner & Co., 1937), pp. 158–159. John R. Searle, in *Speech Acts* (Cambridge: Cambridge University Press, 1970), pp. 73–76, argues that some logicians have here been unreasonably scrupulous, confusing matters by their attempts at clarification. The implication, then, is that framing practices are not complete enough to provide everywhere the basis for informed agreement. But it can also be taken that where a difference of opinion is found, this difference can itself be debated—and with some clarity—in print.

of the interaction that follows.[32] The classic case here, no doubt
is that of imprisonment on grounds of mistaken identity:

> Roanoke, Va.—A man sentenced to 15 years in jail for bank
> robbery was freed yesterday in a dramatic courtroom scene after a
> former policeman confessed to the crime.
>
> John Edward Marsh, 29, was convicted by a Federal Court jury
> here last April of the $14,000 robbery of the Commercial and
> Savings Bank branch in Winchester, Va. He has been held in jail
> since November 9, when he was arrested by the FBI in Reno.
>
> The conviction was based mainly on the identification of Marsh
> by the bank's manager, Roxy R. Hockman, and its teller, Caroline
> Hickerson. Yesterday they took the stand in the same courtroom
> and admitted they made a mistake.
>
> It took a surprise confession June 7 by Charles A. Lauritzen, 40,
> a Fairfax, Va., building contractor and a policeman for seven years
> in Montgomery county, Md., to reopen the case.
>
> . . . .
>
> Judge Dalton said Marsh could receive compensation for his
> false conviction.
>
> "It now appears that we erred," said Judge Dalton, in his closing
> statement. "We have certainly moved as quickly as we can to
> correct the error."[33]

Mere misidentification of physical objects can also have the effect
of lodging actors in a complex stream of unsoundly framed
activity:

> Fresno—A five-man crew, hired to move the old parsonage of
> the Church of God to a new location, had spent a busy day getting
> it ready.
>
> They disconnected all the wiring and plumbing, then jacked up
> the building for the cross-town haul. They were just about to start
> the journey when the Rev. Doyle R. Zachary came up, took one
> look and screamed:
>
> "Stop! This is the Church of Christ. The Church of God is across
> the street."[34]

---

32. Thus the playwright's comic device of having a character appear in
a "false" guise unbeknownst to the other characters but known, of course,
to the onlookers. In this easy way the playwright can build up a fully
collapsible world.

33. *San Francisco Chronicle,* June 23, 1966.

34. *Ibid.,* July 23, 1965.

4. In an earlier chapter it was suggested that any strip of activity could be seen as organized into tracks, a main track or story line and ancillary tracks of various kinds. One of the strong arguments for this tracking hypothesis is that distinctive errors, that is, misframings, can occur in the management of each of the several tracks.

Take first the disattend track:

> Paterson, N.J. (UPI)—Three masked bandits set up an ambush in the rectory of a Roman Catholic Church yesterday. While a funeral was going on next door, they staged a $511,000 hold-up of a bank armored truck that stopped to pick up Sunday church collections.
>
> The bandits, who also stole $1,100 from the church while they were waiting for the truck to arrive, tied and gagged four priests and a sexton. One of the priests tried to run but was brought down by a flying tackle.
>
> Another priest on the second floor of the rectory heard one of the bound victims trying to scream an alarm through the gag of tape pasted over his mouth. But he ignored it, he said, because the priest screaming "always sang" in a loud voice.[35]

The point here is that singing of the type described is what is usually read out of a scene as not relevantly occurring.

Misframing regarding the directional track also occurs, the actor treating directional material as part of the main text:

> On being informed by her postmaster that she need no longer include "R.F.D. 2" in her address, a Westport matron we know informed Bonwit Teller, among others, of the fact. Her next bill from Bonwit was addressed to:
> > Mrs. Hillary Jones
> > Eliminate R.F.D. 2
> > Westport, Conn.[36]

Secretaries provide other examples when, in taking shorthand, they record as part of the text what was meant as comment on it, an error that is (as already suggested) surprisingly infrequent given the subtlety of the cue which differentiates the on-record and off-record streams.

Finally, misframing occurs in regard to what would ordinarily

---

35. *Ibid.*, December 22, 1964.
36. In a "Talk of the Town" column, *The New Yorker*.

be sustained outside the purview of some of the participants, errors involving inadvertent exposure, a failure to maintain evidential boundaries. A reminder of this possibility is "exposure fantasy," namely, anxieties about appearing in public unknowingly clothed incompletely. This type of misframing—involving the concealment track—is of special concern in the staging of performances. In radio broadcasting, for example, there are off-mike bloopers, words addressed on the incorrect assumption that the nearby mike is "dead." In television there are, correspondingly, off-camera bloopers, acts performed on the incorrect assumption that the actors are out of range of the camera or that the camera in range is off. In both cases broadcasting equipment demonstrates its power to transform unstaged acts into ones that are, perforce, staged. And, of course, when a staged show *is* intendedly in progress, someone may mistakenly treat the show as a rehearsal or as untransformed activity, in either case introducing openly what would ordinarily be concealed from the audience:

> During a "live" telecast of the *Kraft Theatre*, the dramatic excitement of the most suspenseful moment of the play was reached when above the actors' voices was heard, *"Who ordered the ham on rye?"* The luncheonette delivery boy had walked right into the studio unobserved.[37]

Observe that directional cues designed (in the manner of a promoter's hints) to be concealed from those to whom a presentation is made can also be misframed:

> Many advertising agencies mark their scripts to show which points to emphasize. Listen to this nervous novice announcer as he does his first commercial:

> "Collins Bread is slow baked. Punch this, that means make this sincere. Every inch of each loaf is evenly browned, making for deliciously wholesome super digestible bread. When your grocer asks you, emphasize this. Be sure you say Collins Bread."[38]

> Bess Meyerson, former Miss America, and co-MC on *The Big Payoff*, popular network TV program, was interviewing a contestant on the program. She was handed a note from one of the

37. Kermit Schafer, *Prize Bloopers* (Greenwich, Conn.: Fawcett Publications, Gold Medal Books, 1965), p. 53.

38. Kermit Schafer, *Pardon My Blooper* (Greenwich, Conn.: Fawcett Publications, Crest Books, 1959), p. 113.

members of the production staff, which told her that the contestant was London bound, so as to get this added color into her interview. Believing that this note was an added reminder of the contestant's name, she introduced him thusly: "Ladies and gentlemen, I would like you to meet Mr. London Bound."[39]

As in the case of ambiguities, then, misframings can be distinguished according to the element in framing that is at issue. And again one can ask about the conditions under which long-term misframing might be possible. Presumably errors are less common than ambiguities, even short-lived errors, if only because the action the individual introduces on false assumptions is likely in itself to create contradictions and add to the likelihood of his detecting that (and how) he has gone wrong. Nonetheless, lengthy error is possible, even in regard to primary framework:

> Santa Barbara—For six months, the sofa in their rented apartment did seem a bit lumpy.
> And it was such a strange lump—it would apparently shift its position every so often even when nobody was on the sofa.
> Then yesterday, Manuel A. Valencia and his family found that the lump had suddenly disappeared.
> The reason was as close as the family refrigerator. There, curled under the humming machinery, the Valencias found a 20-pound, 7-foot-long boa constrictor.
>
> . . . .
>
> Zoo officials speculated that the apparently abandoned boa might have come out at night to feed on mice in the apartment. The meal may have made the snake so lazy that it didn't mind being sat on during the day.
> And reptile experts noted that one really enormous meal—fed the boa as long as six months ago—could have kept the boa content in the sofa for that long a period.
> Meanwhile, the Valencias were staying temporarily with relatives.[40]

III. *Accounts and Disputes*

1. It is reported that what is horseplay and larking for inner-city adolescents can be seen as vandalism and thievery by officials

---

39. *Ibid.*, p. 62.
40. *San Francisco Chronicle*, December 13, 1967.

and victims. Now although eventually one of these sides to the argument may establish a definition that convinces the other side (or at least dominates coercive forces sufficiently to induce a show of respect), an appreciable period can elapse when there is no immediate potential agreement, when, in fact, there is no way in theory to bring everyone involved into the same frame.[41] Under these circumstances one can expect that the parties with opposing versions of events may openly dispute with each other over how to define what has been or is happening. A frame dispute results.

But these are exceptional grounds for frame disputes. More common are the brief arguments arising from soon to be admitted error apparently made in good faith by one or both of the parties.

Still another basis for disputes must be mentioned, this one of a different order from the other two. Here a more extended comment is required.

At the beginning of this study, muffings and other such accidents were mentioned as some of the troubles that can arise in regard to frame. It was also suggested that chance could throw into apparent connection what were, in fact, independent streams of action and events. So, too, in later chapters, it was argued that the individual might come wrongly to suspect that he is being deceived in some way and, in consequence, to doubt some of the world around him. And in this chapter ambiguity and error have been presented as further sources of frame failure. These are all cases, note, when the ordinary flow of framed activity fails for ordinary reasons, and the individual finds himself cut off, at least momentarily, from confirmatory involvement in his world.

When these failures of framing occur, he who has thus failed to soundly lodge himself in the ordinary flow of activity may admit his failure and give misframing as an excuse and thus account for his ineptness or apparent guilt or his unwarranted suspicion. So, too, others may give such accounts to reduce their own culpability for contributing to his now admitted misalignment. And these accountings may be disputed or at least doubted

---

41. The famous example from Frank Tannenbaum, *Crime and the Community* (New York: Columbia University Press, 1938), p. 19.

by those to whom they are directed. So again a frame debate results, but this time of a higher order; for the parties now agree as to how matters ought to have been perceived, differing only in their views as to why they weren't.

As a means of dealing with frame disputes (of whatever order) one finds that judicial bodies of various kinds will be authorized to hear the arguments on both sides and pass judgment. As Pike suggests:

> In our culture there are, furthermore, specific legal procedures which are used in an attempt to differentiate between events which are physically similar but emically different, with sharply different cultural penalties: Was the man carrying a pistol when he robbed the house? Did the driver run through a red light when he hit the man? Was the violence premeditated or the result of sudden anger? Was the author of it insane or was he deliberately cruel? Was the prisoner really trying to escape, or did the guard misunderstand, or pretend to do so, or even stage the event under orders? Nonlegal activity similarly attempts to apply criteria to determine such matters: Is this explanation the real reason, or is it just an excuse to mask laziness or irresponsibility or viciousness? Was the plate really cracked?[42]

2. Frame disputes, especially those of higher-order, raise some fundamental issues. If pleas about misframing can be introduced to prove actual innocence, then such pleas can also be introduced as a means of avoiding actual responsibility for an act, a way, in short, to beat the rap. And certainly he who makes frame excuses can be suspected of using a dodge, whether he has or not. (After all, that is what makes higher-order frame disputes possible.) And, of course, he can suspect—correctly or incorrectly—that a skeptical view of his account will be taken, whether such a view is warranted or unwarranted. Finally, others believing his version may nonetheless act as if they don't (just as they can act as if they do when they don't), and he can correctly or incorrectly suspect this. These possibilities are endemic to framing, constituting a fundamental feature, a fundamental slippage, in the organization of experience. (Thus, if an individual's account is suspected, two distinctly different matters can be in doubt: the

----

42. Kenneth L. Pike, *Language in Relation to a Unified Theory of the Structure of Human Behavior* (Glendale, Calif.: Summer Institute of Linguistics, 1954), pt. 1, p. 13.

facts as he presents them, and whether he himself believes in
what he presents. For we recognize that there is a possibility in
the world of innocent misguidedness.) It follows, then, that
frame disputes of higher order can hardly be considered without
also attending to the play of doubts from which such disputes
emerge.

There is, then, a "breeding" character to an individual's misframing of events. Not only is he likely to go on to a whole series
of erroneous acts, but when he comes to account for his actions,
the explanations themselves will create doubt in others, and doubt
in himself about the possibility of not being doubted. And one can
expect that when it incorrectly appears that the individual has
misframed events, he may despair of being believed and even
refrain from attempting to set matters straight. For example,
were a supernatural event actually to occur, the observer might
well decide to forget the whole thing. So because of the very
nature of framing, events have an essentially loose character,
subject to doubt, a looseness that affects both the actor and his
claims and the witness and his. And probably the play of doubts
is found in some degree in every society.

An implication is that innocence is not to be seen simply as a
quality of an actor's soul; it is the relationship in which he stands
to events generated by the misframing of his acts by others.

3. As with ambiguities and misframings, frame disputes can
be directed to different elements in framing. For example, there
are disputes addressed to questions of primary frameworks, illustrated, as earlier suggested, every time someone claims the intervention of supernatural forces:

> Acayucan, Mexico—About 1000 enraged farmers ran their
> parish priest out of town Sunday because he refused to accept their
> claim that a miracle had occurred.
>
> Police said an ancient tree which had been lying on its side for
> five years was found standing upright after a recent thunderstorm.
>
> Convinced they had witnessed a miracle, the farmers began
> praying in front of the tree. They asked their priest to build a
> chapel beneath the tree and celebrate Mass.
>
> When the priest refused, the villagers threatened to lynch him
> and drove him from town.[43]

---

43. *San Francisco Chronicle*, July 26, 1966.

Similarly, there are disputes—not uncommonly heated—in the matter of whether or not to see a particular act as a symptom of some kind, to be viewed in a natural framework, or as a culpable guided doing. Theories of crime, for example, provide no agreement on this matter, tending to fall into two camps, depending on which analysis is put forward.[44] Obviously, viewing a criminal as sick leads to one remedial ideal, viewing him within a moralistic framework, another. Indeed, there are criminal offenses that one jurisdiction will see primarily as expressions of psychological disorder and another jurisdiction as a question of responsible bad behavior. (And moreover, if there is institutionalized machinery for dealing with cases defined in both of the two ways, and if, in addition, there are professionals occupationally committed to the two different approaches, then an institutional basis for frame disputes is to be found.) And so—to take a homely example—a person caught with unbought goods in a shopping bag can claim forgetfulness due to worry and pain, which can then lead the jury to consider whether the defendant would seem to be the sort of person who would steal.[45] And the following, which is something of an exemplary case:

> The Army of the United States has rubbed out a decade of disgrace and restored a degree of dignity to the life of one of its war heroes, The Chronicle learned last night.
>
> For Victor M. Hungerford Jr., this means the removal from his Army records of the blot of a dishonorable discharge, restoration of the rank of major, honorable retirement for physical disability, and back retirement pay that will total about $50,000.

---

44. See, for example, Walter B. Miller, "Ideology and Criminal Justice Policy: Some Current Issues," *Journal of Criminal Law and Criminology*, LXIV (1973): 141–162.

45. An example is the shoplifting trial of Hedy Lamarr reported in *San Francisco Chronicle*, April 26 and 27, 1966. In the analysis of deviancy it is sometimes argued that the issue is not so much what an individual has done, but rather the perspective brought to bear upon the deed by those empowered to act in regard to it. When alternative perspectives are examined in detail, however, it becomes apparent that judgment about the case will consist of making a choice among available perspectives or frames and sometimes using one as mitigation or exacerbation of the applicability of another. The framework of frameworks can be taken as given, and the creative element in the labeling process restricted to that of pressing the applicability of a particular primary framework or a particular transformation.

It was in July, 1954, that Hungerford's once brilliant military career came to an inglorious end.

He was arrested on charges of desertion and writing bad checks and in mid-1955 court-martialed and sentenced to serve a one-year term at the Army's prison at Lompoc.

The dishonorable discharge was stamped on his records when he finished serving the sentence.

It might never have been removed except for the fact that Hungerford continued his habit of writing bad checks and eventually, in 1959, was sent to State prison.

Before being confined in a specific prison, however, Hungerford went to the State Medical Facility at Vacaville for routine examination.

It was there that he told of the terribly painful headaches he had been suffering since July 16, 1950, when he was knocked unconscious by a Communist tank shell blast while leading a charge against the enemy in Korea.

It was the same story almost of blinding pain he had previously told Army hospital, and, later, Veterans Administration hospital doctors on numerous occasions.

They maintained the headaches were of his own making, the result of not being able to conform to peacetime military life.

State doctors, however, decided to look into Hungerford's complaints of pain more carefully.

On December 5, 1959, a neurosurgeon operated on Hungerford's brain. He knew what he was seeking. X-rays had shown an area of possibly injury.

The X-rays proved correct. The operation disclosed Hungerford had suffered major brain damage due to a head injury that could have been caused by a severe concussion such as a shell blast.

. . . .

Early this year, Hungerford decided to gamble on his belief the U.S. Army will admit a mistake. He petitioned, through the law office of Melvin M. Belli, to have the Army re-examine his case.

It proved a slow and sometimes agonizing process; three months of hospitalization while Army doctors checked and re-checked the findings of the 1959 brain operation through many series of X-rays; appearances before an Army physical evaluation board where he was questioned and re-questioned.[46]

Observe here how a dramatic news story confirms our framework of framings even while it reports its misapplication.

---

46. Reported by Paul Avery, *ibid.*, November 23, 1964.

4. Behind courtroom debates and other kinds of frame disputes, one can often find "compromising circumstances," namely, circumstances in which the events at hand give ordinary observers innocently incorrect impressions of the forces at work, impressions which serve to defame some of those involved in the activity, setting the stage for the presentation of explanations and excuses. Slapstick comedy, of course, makes much use of the theme of compromising circumstances, the Laurel and Hardy films being particularly excruciating in this regard. A domestic example might be cited:

> *Dear Abby:* This problem is not mine, it's my sister's. She lives in a housing project where all the neighbors are very friendly.
>
> One day a neighbor knocked on her door and said his wife was out of town and he needed someone to massage his back. He had one of those portable electric massagers.
>
> My sister said she'd be glad to help him, so she invited him in and gave him a bottle of beer, as it was hot out.
>
> He took off his shirt and she started massaging his back when they heard her husband coming. The neighbor got panicky and hid in the closet, leaving his shirt behind. When my brother-in-law saw the shirt and the beer bottle, he went into a rage and started searching the house. When he found the man in the closet, he roughed him up and threw my sister out of the house. Like a fool she went back to him the next day. He is still mad at her and hasn't been a husband to her in over six months. She keeps asking me for advice. I can't help her. Can you?[47]

Of course individuals ordinarily act so that easily induced misunderstandings are avoided in advance: he who might misunderstand exercises tentativeness in his approach to one who might be misunderstood, who in turn externalizes in his own bodily behavior information that is designed to keep the record straight. To be sure, the following can occur:

> At New Montgy. and Howard yesterday morn [four days before Christmas], Howard Young noticed a woman rummaging in a trash can and said gently to her: "Kinda rough this season—would a dollar help?" She: "Mind your own damn business—I threw my Christmas cards in here by accident."[48]

---

47. *Ibid.*, August 29, 1965.
48. Herb Caen, *ibid.*, December 22, 1964.

But ordinarily it doesn't simply because passersby typically keep on passing by, whatever their assessment of the situation of another, and a person who has a respectable reason for looking into trash barrels either forgoes the act or does it in a manner that replies in advance to any misimputations which might be evoked. So, too, institutionalized means of social control function to keep frames of interpretation easy to apply. (Thus, if a chess player wants to make sure that he will be seen as trying to physically adjust a piece in its square instead of thinking out a move by tentatively shifting a piece, he can draw on the phrase *J'adoube,* thereby formally dispelling all ambiguity.) To repeat, for us the important point here is not that misunderstandings occur but rather that they occur so infrequently, and behind this the fact that persons ordinarily take precautions in advance to make sure of this infrequency. And so discretion and good sense generate a world in which framing works as a means of interpretation—by design if not by nature.

Behind compromising circumstances is to be found something more general, namely, incidental connectedness—as when an innocent person coming on the scene of a crime takes up the implement that was employed and is then apprehended with his fingerprints where it is misleading for fingerprints to be. A guided doing is thus attributed when only "alongsidedness" ought to be. Understandably, books for police on investigative methods always seem to cite at least a few examples of environments of events which induce framing errors. One example might be given:

> Another incident which magnifies the danger of drawing speedy conclusions before investigating thoroughly, happened early one Sunday morning on a main street in a small city. The officer involved was walking along the sidewalk and noticed a man and woman apparently in a mild argument standing on the sidewalk at a bus stop about a block away. It was in the business area, and these two people and the officer were the only ones on the street at that hour. The officer turned his attention away from the couple for a moment to inspect a store window. Immediately, he heard the smashing of glass and a dull thud. He looked up. The woman was lying on the sidewalk and the man was bending over her holding a broken whiskey bottle by the neck in his right hand. The officer rushed to the scene. The woman was dead. The man was overanx-

ious to prove that he had done nothing. The street was quiet except for these three people. The man stuck to his story that they were talking and suddenly the bottle smashed and he caught the neck of the bottle in his hand. Apparently the bottle had been nearly full of whiskey. . . . The man was charged with murder, but the officer kept working on the case. . . . Five days later he uncovered the true facts. A group of store clerks had finished dressing the store window about midnight Saturday night and had gone to a little room on the roof of the seven story building to play cards the rest of the night. They had several bottles and some way this one had been placed in the open window. Unknown to them it had been pushed or had fallen out, and they had never missed it. Even when the account of the murder was in the paper they did not associate the facts because no one had missed the bottle.[49]

5. Frame debates often arise in connection with claims of inadvertence—claims that although it might appear the suspect had been engaged in blameworthy action, he has not been engaged in any action at all, at least in that regard, merely an innocent loss of control. Thus, for example, an officer of the law provided the following explanation of the shooting that occurred when he had given chase to a car driven by a black and had finally caught up to the car and stopped it:

> Los Angeles—Policeman Jerold M. Bova testified yesterday that he was knocked off his feet by Leonard Deadwyler's lurching car, and as he "instinctively grabbed" for support his service revolver "unintentionally fired" and killed Deadwyler.[50]

Two passengers in the car provide the following story (weakened by their being accused of being drunk at the time):

> Mrs. Deadwyler and Ferguson both testified that Deadwyler was rushing her to General Hospital when police stopped them. The pregnant Mrs. Deadwyler had suffered kidney pains which she thought were labor pains and that brought about the hurried drive toward the hospital.
>
> Mrs. Deadwyler and Ferguson both testified that their car was halted and then a policeman stuck his revolver in the passenger window and shot Deadwyler.[51]

---

49. Captain Juby E. Towler, *Practical Police Knowledge* (Springfield, Ill.: Charles C. Thomas, 1960), pp. 112–113.
50. *San Francisco Chronicle*, May 26, 1966.
51. *Ibid.*

Or, if not an innocent loss of control, then an inadvertent conjunction of events gives a guided doing an entirely unexpected consequence, as when a man out deer hunting with rifle and telescopic sights shoots to the right of his companion and cuts him down with one shot through the head.[52] And if not this, then the argument that misidentification was involved—a human, excusable weakness, not an immoral intent:

> Canterbury, England—A man who pocketed a fortune teller's crystal ball explained in court yesterday that he mistook it for a glass of beer.
>
> Malcolm Cammiade, 21, said he had been drinking in a tavern and was looking for the toilet when he fell through a curtain into the consulting room of 75-year-old clairvoyant Madame du Barry.
>
> "I put my drink down and later picked up the ball because I thought it was my glass," he told the court which gave him a conditional discharge.[53]

Claims to innocence, whether grounded in unconnectedness or inadvertence, raise a special problem regarding frame limits, namely, how far can the plea of essential innocence be pressed— apart, that is, from the issue of how far it can be pressed convincingly. The answer (as the last illustration suggests) seems to be: very far indeed. After all, the scene of any crime can have persons "who were merely passing by." When a female thief is apprehended and a $1,350 diamond and emerald pin complete with price tag is found in her bra, and in her panties a $1,300 diamond ring, two men's wristwatches, a gold and diamond bracelet, a pearl bracelet, and an empty ring box, she can deny knowing anything about a jewel theft, and by implication how the jewels got there, except that she remembers drinking and dining with a man.[54] Of course, our storyteller was not believed, but the point for us is that she found it worthwhile to concoct this account in such damning circumstances, thus providing indirect evidence for us that *any* connection between a person and an event can be denied by him on grounds that although it looks as though an apparent link is present, this is not the case.

6. Interesting disputes over frame occur in connection with

52. *Ibid.*, December 2, 1967.
53. *Ibid.*, December 21, 1967.
54. *Ibid.*, October 21, 1965.

claims regarding keying, claims that although the events at hand
may look like untransformed activity, they are really keyed, or at
least were meant to be. Of course, whether the claim is valid or
not, an effort can be made to avoid the responsibility and blame
which attaches to the literal activity. Take, for example, the
Berrigan-Kissinger episode:

> The priest was asked [during a courtroom interview] if he had
> planned to kidnap Kissinger and blow up heating tunnels, as the
> government charges.
>
> "There was no planning," he replied. "There was a discussion.
> We were trying to determine as millions of other people do,
> whether the political kidnappings in Quebec and in Uruguay were
> possible in the United States."
>
> . . . .
>
> "Millions of people have these kind of ideas at sometime or
> other. It doesn't mean they would act or want to act, but why
> shouldn't they think about it and maybe discuss it and even in-
> vestigate it."[55]

Of all the claimed keyings through which responsibility can be
relieved, the plea that one was only joking seems to be the most
important. It appears in every context and must be one of the
most widely employed dodges in the history of man. And once
again extreme examples provide a comment on the limits of
framing. I cite the Valachi papers, the specific issue here being
the need to squirm out of a bungled hit:

> Apparently Genovese and Miranda had some second thoughts
> about the whole thing and ended up assigning the contract to Cosa
> Nostra professionals. A ludicrous sequence of events followed
> which doubles Valachi over with laughter every time he thinks
> about it. When Rupolo heard that Boccia had been murdered, he
> proceeded with phase two of the original plot. He and Gallo at-
> tended a movie in Brooklyn one night, and as they walked down
> the street afterward, he took out a pistol, put it against Gallo's
> head, and pulled the trigger. The pistol misfired. Rupolo quickly
> tried again. Still nothing. When Gallo demanded to know what was
> going on, Rupolo lamely passed it off as a joke and said that the
> pistol was not loaded. The two continued on to a friend's house,
> where Rupolo examined the pistol, discovered that the firing pin
> was rusty and oiled it. Upon leaving the house, they walked to-

---

55. *The Evening Bulletin* (Philadelphia), January 24, 1972.

gether for several blocks and then Rupolo took another crack at
Gallo. This time the pistol went off, but all Rupolo managed to do
was wound him. Rupolo, identified by Gallo as his would-be assas-
sin, was sentenced to nine to twenty years in prison.[56]

Interestingly, the individual offering the unserious reading
may himself be the victim, one who is prepared to defend a
friendly assailant against third parties by supporting his plea of
innocence. And such an interpretation may be offered even
though no solidarity is sustained between victim and offender,
the point being that no other reading seems palatable:

> *Dear Abby:* I have a girl friend. She is 15 (so am I) and we are
> always over at each other's houses. When I first met her father, I
> thought he was neat because he was so friendly. But he got to
> doing things I knew weren't right. Like putting his hands on me,
> and trying to kiss me. He never did this in front of anyone else. I
> tried to avoid him, but he'd send his daughter out of the room to
> get something for him. I pretended I thought his actions were all in
> fun, but deep down I was scared to death. I hate to quit seeing my
> friend, and if I tell my mother about this she will have his scalp.
> What should I do.[57]

A further point. If an individual can claim unseriousness in
order to avoid penalty for an act he has committed, the claim
being made after the fact, then certainly at times the individual
may from the beginning arrange his actions so that if he is called
to account he can argue for its unseriousness. In brief, action can
be styled to carry its own excuse in advance of an actual call for
it. Certainly action can be *thought* to be so styled, and a case
made for this interpretation, whether or not in fact such styling
has occurred. A domestic example:

> *Dear Abby:* My mother is in love with her new son-in-law. Well,
> "in love" may be a little strong, but she seems to have trouble
> keeping her hands off him. "Boobie" (as she calls him) doesn't
> know how bad it looks. He is 33, mother is 48 (but looks 30), and
> the whole thing is pretty nauseating. Mother is either sitting on his
> lap, scratching his back, giving him a neck rub, or begging him to
> dance with her.

---

56. Peter Maas, *The Valachi Papers* (New York: Bantam Books, 1969),
p. 156.
57. *San Francisco Chronicle*, February 15, 1966.

My sister (Boobie's wife) thinks it's lovely that her husband and mother get along so well. This could be serious as mother is a swinging divorcee and the plot seems to thicken all the time. What can we do, short of telling Sis to open her eyes and hold on to her husband?[58]

A standard technique for communicating through safe hints follows something of the same design: the individual acts so that some others who can be trusted not to entrap him can read his action in one way, the way that will further the business he is intent on, while other others who might take exception can at any time be put off with a claim that playfulness was meant.[59]

Claims regarding open joking (where a keying is involved) are not much different from claims regarding playful deception (where a benign fabrication is involved). An example of the latter involving a husband-wife team is cited:

Jack F. Wilson, 23, was a loyal husband. And yesterday his wife Terry, a 20-year-old girl with reddish brown hair, was restored to him.

. . . .

The curious case came to light when Roger Perkins of East Palo Alto, a friend of Mrs. Wilson's first husband, went to the district attorney's office in San Jose and threw a hand-written contract on a deputy's desk.

The single paragraph document, in Mrs. Wilson's writing, said Perkins was entitled to half the proceeds of the sale of the family home and half the insurance Mrs. Wilson would collect from her husband's death.

Horace Boydston, a special investigator from the District Attorney's office, was sent immediately to the Wilson home. He posed as the prospective killer and reported back to his superiors that Mrs. Wilson was indeed ready to go through with the plan.

But Mrs. Wilson's husband, a warehouseman at Winthrop Laboratories in Menlo Park and a part-time auto racer, promptly hired a lawyer for his wife.

---

58. *Ibid.*, November 20, 1967.
59. As some sort of extreme test of the power of the unserious definition of the situation, an individual may initiate an admission of exactly what he is suspected of, the assumption apparently being that it is commonly believed that no one would invite by way of unserious admission the very thing he must avoid being accused of. (The strategic limitations of misdirection by candor are considered in *S.I.*, pp. 57–70.)

And the defense convinced the jury the whole thing was all a hoax and that, at the appropriate time, Mrs. Wilson had planned to call Perkins' bluff.[60]

Note that claims regarding unseriousness in either of its forms seem anything but suitable for presentation to the law; nonetheless, these tacks are frequently employed in that capacity, whether honestly or not. Thus, from a study of eavesdropping:

> Mason admitted that a man without integrity doing this kind of work could use his equipment for blackmail purposes. As an example of this he told of how a young lady in Los Angeles invited a director of a private Hollywood school to her apartment, after she had secreted a recording machine under her couch. She recorded his amorous intentions and later began to blackmail him. The school director, however, went to the police department and the district attorney's office, and the young lady was arrested. However, she was acquitted when she demurely testified that the recording had been a joke and that she had actually expected the school director to marry her.[61]

7. Just as an individual can argue (with warrant or not) nonintent or unseriousness for his act, the aim being to reconstitute its meaning and reduce his responsibility for it, so also he can retrospectively claim benign fabrication of the nonjoking kind, such as experimentation, vital testing, and the like. So also he can claim to have been "framed," arguing that others have intentionally arranged for events to occur which place him in a false, bad light. Fabrication is claimed, but this time not benign and not produced by the person seeking exoneration. That a few actual frame-ups can be pointed to (some involving spectacular reconstituting of the world around the victim) opens up the possibility, howsoever small, that claims to having been framed are valid, and that whatsoever the evidence, wicked engineering produced it:

> London—A young American was convicted yesterday of stealing more than $60,000 from the Moscow Narodny Bank in London and sentenced to three years in prison by an Old Bailey court jury.
> The jury rejected the story of Brian Christopher Terrell, 23, of

---

60. *San Francisco Chronicle*, August 22, 1964.
61. Samuel Dash, et al., *The Eavesdroppers* (New Brunswick, N.J.: Rutgers University Press, 1959), pp. 190–191.

Houston, Tex., that he had acquired nearly $70,000 for spying for the Soviet Union and the United States. He had claimed the theft charges were trumped up by the Russians when they found out he was a double agent.[62]

Consider also that persons other than the actor can dispute whether an act is straight or a fabrication. Thus, for example, the issue of whether a suicide attempt is real or a gesture, that is, done to produce demise or to produce a response from others and in such a manner as to avoid much chance of the real thing occurring. A frame dispute results:

> At least five youths tried to commit suicide at the Spofford Juvenile Center in the Bronx during a 10-day period earlier this month.
> Reporting on the situation in a statement yesterday, City Councilman Robert I. Postel asked:
> "Are these suicide attempts not proof enough of barbaric conditions at Spofford and the dire need for reform there? Or must we wait for the death of a child to shock us into action?"
> Wallace Nottage, deputy director of probation in charge of institutional services, acknowledged in an interview that "we've had a rash" of such cases. However, he said there was "some question of the sincerity" of the youths, adding that the youngsters apparently believed suicide attempts would get them removed from the detention center.[63]

If one starts with bodies, not attempts, then a basis for debate is still available. The nicest of points can be involved. The very circumstances which ordinarily confirm that a real effort was to be made to commit suicide will be just those circumstances that someone will manufacture whose overriding intent is to demonstrate to himself and others that he is serious, although he isn't— he thought.[64]

---

62. *San Francisco Chronicle*, June 1, 1965.

63. Reported by Grace Lichtenstein, *The New York Times*, November 22, 1970.

64. There is an argument that suicide itself is totally a question of what the relevant parties make of it, and that any effort to find out in any particular case (effective or ineffective) what was "really" going on is foredoomed. It is clear, surely, that civil agencies can make mistakes, and certainly public policy can lead to defining deaths as accidental which are not and to defining as gestures what are serious efforts. Certainly there are ways in which a troubled person can increase the level of his risk-taking

8. The accounts and debates I have been considering mainly pertain to the issue of what framework or transformation ought to be applied or what, if any, misframing was involved. Most of these debates leave undisputed the framework of framing arrangements available in the community. The Acayucan priest who refused to support the local farmers in their belief that a miracle had taken place would probably still allow that miracles *had* taken place and might do so in the future. However, a deeper issue can arise, the question of our cosmology itself. For after all, the position could be pressed upon our Acayucan farmers that no spirit interference in the natural world has ever taken place or ever will. Similarly, when an object from outer space falls on our land, and some would see the possibility of minded agents and their products, the geologist who is called in can recommend that this object was unguided because everything from outer space is untouched by humanlike hand. So, too, a legal scholar can argue that although a brain lesion can be held to have some general effects upon conduct, it cannot be shown alone to account for a specific social practice, such as forging checks, nor can its presence completely rule out the sense in which such activity constitutes a guided doing.

Disputes regarding cosmology, even more, it seems, than debates which assume common beliefs about cosmology, lead to adjudication by specialists acting in a semiofficial capacity. Usually, of course, these custodians of our cosmology put things to

---

which might lead a student to call this suicidal behavior stretched over time. And since intent is involved, only the intender can ultimately know. Further, clear-cut intent can certainly hold sway at one moment and weaken at the next and pass through these changes quickly. Also, very effective concerted efforts to commit the act may be associated with minor efforts to hedge the bet. But to question the intent of a suicide on the grounds that solid purposefulness dissolves with microscopic analysis into a loose webbing of different undemonstrable aims is to question every act, since every act is understood in relation to assumed intent of the actor. *That* sort of questioning is interesting, for it leads to a reassessment of the whole of social life, if only incidentally to a critique of traditional views regarding suicide. However, in the particular story cited (and in the view taken in this book), the councilman and the probation officer still have a dispute that might well be resolvable in the folk terms they establish. The very fact that claimed intent is routinely used as a cover and that those who might "rightfully" claim an intent worry about being disbelieved is an argument in its favor—and in any case, an indisputable subject matter in its own right. A useful statement of the opposing argument is available in Jack D. Douglas, *The Social Meaning of Suicide* (Princeton, N.J.: Princeton University Press, 1970).

rest, affirming a "natural" explanation, one that allows us to continue on without having to alter any of our primary frameworks or their relationships. Understandably, these guardians of our cognitive order will be subject to a certain amount of deference.[65] And here one can see a connection between everyday events and final, official courts of appeal in law, science, and the arts. These institutions, in short, are not merely concerned with maintaining standards; they are also concerned with maintaining clarity with respect to framing. An example is the following "landmark" decision:

> Washington, D.C.—The District of Columbia's highest court ruled yesterday that a chronic alcoholic cannot be convicted of the crime of public drunkenness.
>
> In an 8-to-0 decision, the United States Court of Appeals for the District of Columbia said that proof of chronic alcoholism is a defense to a drunkenness charge because the defendant "has lost the power of self-control in the use of intoxicating beverages."
>
> Since such a defendant lacks the necessary criminal intent to be guilty of a crime, he cannot be punished under the criminal law, the court ruled.[66]

Another case in point concerns "personal expression." In America, the constitutional right of free speech is restricted only in contexts in which clear and immediate harm might result therefrom, as were an individual to jokingly cry "fire" in a crowded auditorium. But how interpret the case of an individual ritually burning his draft card at a public meeting as an expression of his attitude toward the war? Is he expressing resistance to the war or is he engaging in resistance to the war?[67] A judge is required to decide the issue, even though, in deciding, he cannot win everyone's consent that he has the authority to so decide. In recent times, it might be added, two debates regarding primary

---

65. Thus Edward Shils, "Charisma, Order and Status," *American Sociological Review*, XXX (1965) argues:

> The disposition to attribute charisma is intimately related to the need for order. The attribution of charismatic qualities occurs in the presence of order-creating, order-disclosing, order-discovering power as such; it is a response to greater ordering power. [p. 204]

Hence the respect shown for judges, legislators, lawyers, physicians, scientists, and artists.

66. *San Francisco Chronicle*, April 1, 1966.

67. A report is given by Loudon Wainwright in *Life*, March 4, 1966.

frameworks have made news; one involves the declining concern of the Catholic Church to press the possibility of miracles, and the other, which apparently went beyond official adjudication to secret military inquiry, involves the possibility of unidentified flying objects, namely, space vehicles guided by a hand *like* man's.

IV. *Clearing the Frame*

When an individual finds himself in doubt or in error about what it is that is going on, a correct reading is usually soon established. In some cases he himself will sharply orient to an examination of the setting so as to pick up information that will settle matters; and, of course, he can make direct requests for information. Often, too, others will provide accounts and other interventions so as to keep his interpretations stable and correct. (When the sound goes off the TV the puzzled watcher may soon be greeted by a message: "The audio part of the signal is not coming through; do not adjust your sets, the fault is in the transmission.") When the individual is contained by others or by himself, his consequent misalignment to the facts is likely to last longer than in the case of simple misframings, sometimes a lifetime. But here, too, a "seeing through" may occur and perhaps eventually is likely to occur. In all these cases, one can say that the individual's relation to the frame is "cleared."

Perspective must here be specified. An organized deception provides a clear relation to frame for the organizer but not for those who are contained. By the term "clear frame" I shall refer to the arrangement which occurs when *all* participants in the activity have a clear relation to the frame, and a distinction will be intended between clearing one's own relation to the frame and participating in a frame that is clear, that is, clear for all participants. To say that a frame is clear is not only to say that each participant has a workably correct view of what is going on, but also, usually, a tolerably correct view of the others' views, which includes their view of his view.[68]

---

68. In these latter connections one can expect some problems, since a nicely working consensus can involve a shading into doubt in the recursive edges of the relationship. Examined in detail, any simple agreement shows

The information that clears a frame can stem from various sources. In the face of ambiguities or incongruities, the puzzled or suspicious individual himself will sharply orient to his surround and maintain vigilance until matters become clear, sometimes making open requests for facts in order to settle the issue. With immense frequency, individuals who feel they may be (or have been) misunderstood will provide accounts, explanations, and other interventions in order to clarify the situation. A fabricator may himself give the show away intentionally, at a strategic moment (as when Mr. Funt says, "Smile, you're on *Candid Camera*," or the fireman says, "Surprise, I'm Officer Green of the Police Department, and I have a search warrant for your house"), or inadvertently or because he suspects he is about to be caught in some part of his act and wants to preserve an appearance of honesty at no cost other than that of a disclosure that is about to occur anyway. In the case of dreams, the dreamer, by awakening, terminates his own delusion. And, of course, third parties may intercede, as when a wife of an errant husband receives a phone call that is opened with the phrase, "This is a friend calling. . . ." Sometimes official action is involved in clearing the frame:

> Chicago—For ten days Claire Stelmaszek, 34, remained silent throughout her arrest and detention, the shocked disapproval of her friends and neighbors and the taunting and harassment of her children.
>
> But yesterday there was generous praise from high officials for the courageous mother's action in helping to break up a mobster-run gambling operation.
>
> Police revealed that Mrs. Stelmaszek, mother of four and operator of a tavern on the South Side, pretended to cooperate with gangsters to help police.

---

points of ambiguity. Two motorists in a minor collision on an icy road can each frame the event as an entirely accidental, faultless one, which, in terms of alternative interpretations, it may certainly be. So the frame is clear. But if they do not get out of their cars to chat about the matter, they will not know that they are in agreement, nor, of course, will they be able to know that each knows the other knows of the agreement. (Similarly, they will not be able to know how they disagree and that they agree or disagree about how they disagree.) Communication, especially face-to-face communication, seems to collapse these layerings or at least to give a sense that they have been.

Three crime syndicate hoodlums tried for two months to install crooked dice tables in a room behind her tavern before Mrs. Stelmaszek went to police.

Seeing a chance to learn more about crime syndicate techniques for invading legitimate business, police asked Mrs. Stelmaszek to play along with the hoodlums.

Police planted recording devices in the tavern and taped threats made by the mobsters and details concerning the rigged gambling operation, which the gang began running May 10.

When police moved in, they arrested Mrs. Stelmaszek along with 18 other persons. This was done in order to keep her role a secret. She was released on bond.

"When neighbors started harassing her, we offered then and there to tell the world her part even though the longer we could keep it a secret, the better it would be," said police lieutenant Edward Berry.

Mrs. Stelmaszek decided to remain silent.

"The hardest thing she had to endure was not being able to tell her children," said Berry. "Kids can be cruel but these never lost faith in their mother."

Her teen-age youngsters were ridiculed by classmates because of their mother's arrest, he said.

The truth about Mrs. Stelmaszek was told after she testified before the Grand Jury.[69]

These various sources of information are, of course, merely that. Evidence that becomes available must be used mentally to provide a subjective, cognitive reorganization before a frame is cleared. Clifford Beers provides a useful statement regarding a subjectively instigated delamination, the shift being from a world in which all elements were merely designed to give an impression and were false, to a world in which things were more nearly what they appeared to be:

In the afternoon, as usual, the patients were taken out of doors, I among them. I wandered about the lawn, and cast frequent and expectant glances toward the gate, through which I believed my anticipated visitor would soon pass. In less than an hour he ap-

---

69. *San Francisco Chronicle,* May 20, 1965. Interestingly, the piece is subtitled "Chicago Heroine." The entire operation is a nice example of the contingencies faced by those who would make a living from crime. Had this "self-enactment" and set-up occurred in connection with left-wing political action, some readers would have had doubts concerning the heroism.

peared. I first caught sight of him about three hundred feet away, and, impelled more by curiosity than hope, I advanced to meet him. "I wonder what the lie will be this time," was the gist of my thoughts.

The person approaching me was indeed the counterpart of my brother as I remembered him. Yet he was no more my brother than he had been at any time during the preceding two years. He was still a detective. Such he was when I shook his hand. As soon as that ceremony was over he drew forth a leather pocket-book. I instantly recognized it as one I myself had carried for several years prior to the time I was taken ill in 1900. It was from this that he took my recent letter.

"Here's my passport," said he.

"It's a good thing you brought it," said I coolly, as I glanced at it and again shook his hand—this time the hand of my own brother.

"Don't you want to read it?" he asked.

"There is no need of that," was my reply. "I am convinced."

. . . .

This was the culminating moment of my gradual re-adjustment. The molecules of my mental magnet had at least turned in the direction of right thinking. In a word, my mind had found itself. . . . The very instant I caught sight of my letter in the hands of my brother, all was changed. The thousands of false impressions recorded during the seven hundred and ninety-eight days of my depressed state seemed at once to correct themselves. Untruth became Truth. My old world was again mine. That gigantic web woven by an indefatigable yet tired imagination, I immediately recognized as a snare of delusions, in which I had all but hopelessly entangled myself.[70]

One must expect a somewhat similar experience of frame correction when an individual suddenly concludes *incorrectly* that he now has matters straight; for certainly he can suddenly feel he no longer has reason to suspect everyone around him when indeed he ought.

It is apparent that when an individual sees through a fabrication, the frame as a whole is not necessarily, not even likely to be, cleared. As already suggested, one of the oldest strategic moves in the world is for the discoverer to continue on as if he were still fooled, thereby reversing the frame and obtaining a wide range of

---

70. Clifford Whittingham Beers, *A Mind That Found Itself* (New York: Longmans, Green & Co., 1908), pp. 78–79.

advantage.[71] So the clarity he obtains for himself he removes
from those who had been tricking him. And should the discoverer
confront the fabricators with evidence, admission again is not
necessary or even likely; protestations, accounts, and counter-
accusations are likely to be introduced, at least temporarily,
resulting in a frame dispute. Indeed, wise legal counsel recommends that an apparent culprit never under any circumstances
admit to the accusations made against him. (Thus benign fabrications can be contrastively defined by the fact that here discovery and confrontation *does* lead to admission and a general
clearing of the frame.) One should expect to find, then, that
when a denouncement occurs, a functional equivalence may be
sought out as a substitute for an admission or confession that is
due but cannot be obtained. As already illustrated, frame debates
held in courtrooms and other places for official hearings seem to
offer such an arrangement, the decision of the judging in effect
clearing the frame for everyone. In the classical detective story
the calling together of all the involved parties and an official or
two sets a similar scene, but here the detective's confronting
analysis is confirmed in effect by the sudden effort of the suddenly unmasked villain to bolt or fight.

Clearing the frame is associated with two minor possibilities
that might be mentioned. The first of these involves unnecessary
confession and unnecessary self-exposure. An individual can feel
that his masquerade is surely over and participate in clearing the
frame, only to find out that his secret had not in fact been
known:

> Blabbe—A car was weaving down 19th avenue and made an
> illegal left turn onto Irving avenue, so a police patrol car stopped it
> about 6:15 P.M. last night.
> Driver Leonard Soforo, 22, who said he's a movie sound engi-
> neer, startled officers by walking back, getting into the patrol car
> and saying, "Okay, you've got me."
> He then confessed, officers Pete Tasseff and Al Holder said, to
> growing marijuana in his apartment, smoking it, and using LSD,
> the hallucinatory drug.

---

71. See *S.I.*, pp. 54–55. There is a significant difference between discovery of foul play and mere suspicion. In the latter case there is often felt to
be no good reason for holding fire; direct confrontation often occurs, the
accuser feeling that there is a chance that a satisfactory account will be
offered.

Sure enough, [in] Soforo's apartment at 85A Coleridge street officers found two small marijuana plants—and a small jar filled with a liquid that Soforo said was LSD.[72]

The second process to consider is, in a way, the opposite of the first. An individual can believe that he has discovered the other's construction and openly expose him, with a mind to clearing the frame for everyone, only to discover that the other's show of innocence was not merely a show, and that the exposer is exposed at wrongly exposing—a would-be unmasker. Thus, when the late Joseph Valachi was to appear as a grand jury witness in Queens County courthouse, New York, and was being protected by twenty U.S. marshals and three hundred city police:

A touch of humor was added to the proceedings by a prospective juror found wandering the courthouse with a violin case under his arm. The violin case long was used by underworld executioners to conceal deadly weapons.

The man, Nicholas D'Amico, was stopped half a dozen times and forced to prove that he really was carrying a violin. As a musician, he explained, he treasures the instrument and always carries it with him.[73]

Interrogators commit the same gaffe when they tell the subject they know for a fact that he did a certain act when indeed he knows he didn't, and knows thereby that their protestations of playing straight with him and knowing about him are false.

V

It is plain, then, that our framing of events can lead to ambiguity, error, and frame disputes. (It should be just as plain that an individual may project these responses as a cover for some other relation to the facts; that twist one should always expect in matters of frame.) We do come to be sharply in the wrong but— as argued throughout—only exceptionally. Our very considerable capacity for perceptual discrimination in regard to matters of frame seems to be what saves us—along, of course, with the care our others take to behave definitively. This discriminatory capacity has already been illustrated and extolled in the earlier con-

72. *San Francisco Chronicle,* June 8, 1964.
73. *Ibid.,* October 17, 1963.

sideration of "transformational depth." One further example
might be given, that of the careful discrimination individuals can
make between unstaged activity and its staging, even when an
intimate jumbling of the two seems to be involved. The report is
on the filming of *The Strawberry Statement* in Stockton, California, where off-duty policemen and firemen apparently performed as on-duty policemen and firemen, student rioters as
student rioters, television cameramen "there to cover the filming"
were photographed as television cameramen, and real, on-duty
police were in the Stockton City Hall (used as a stage university)
to guard city property. And in that mixed role context, the following clarity was reported:

> For instance, on the evening I was there, one of the extras, who
> happened also to be the president of the U. of P. [University of the
> Pacific] Black Student Union, was haranguing his fellow students
> in the City Hall lobby between takes. He pointed out that they were
> working overtime, but were not being paid accordingly. He sug-
> gested that they refuse to perform. A low-level M-G-M functionary,
> unsuccessful in his attempts to shut him up, became considerably
> agitated and finally called upon a real, live white policeman
> present to arrest the black. The cop, having satisfied himself that
> this was not part of the movie, moved to comply.
>
> The sound of a bullhorn intruded, "All right, National Guard
> and police: once you enter the building—no yelling, no shouting,
> just turn around and come out again." A whistle blew; sirens
> wailed; 700 kids jumped up and started chanting. The policeman
> shrugged and walked off camera.
>
> The scene went very well, I guess. . . .
>
> One of the actors had stepped on a piece of glass. Two people
> were attending him. One was wiping the blood off his foot. One
> was applying more blood to his chin.[74]

------

74. James Kunen, "Son of Strawberry Statement," *New York Magazine*,
January 12, 1970, p. 47.

10

Breaking Frame

I

Thus far, the individual considered is someone who has perceptions, frame-accurate as one possibility, deceived, deluded, or
illusionary as the other; he also takes action, both verbal and
physical, on the basis of these perceptions. And it has been
argued that the individual's framing of activity establishes its
meaningfulness for him.

Frame, however, organizes more than meaning; it also organizes involvement. During any spate of activity, participants will
ordinarily not only obtain a sense of what is going on but will also
(in some degree) become spontaneously engrossed, caught up,
enthralled.

All frames involve expectations of a normative kind as to how
deeply and fully the individual is to be carried into the activity
organized by the frames. Of course, frames differ quite widely in
the involvement prescribed for participants sustaining them.
Some, like traffic systems, are properly sustained as an off-and-on
focus of attention whose claim upon the participant is deep only
when there is sudden trouble to avoid. Other frames, like that in
which sexual intercourse is understood, prescribe involvement
that is literally and figuratively embracing. In all cases, however,
understood limits will be established, a definition concerning
what is insufficient involvement and what is too much. The

various sets of materials with which the individual works and plays will differ according to how effective they are in grasping and holding his attention; some, like board and card games, seem to be specifically designed to provide "engrossables," establishing a standard in this regard against which other sets of materials can be judged—including the sets that the world of everyday provides us.

Involvement is a psychobiological process in which the subject becomes at least partly unaware of the direction of his feelings and his cognitive attention. That is what engrossment means. It follows that if a particular focus of attention is to be maintained, it cannot be maintained intendedly (at least wholly so), since such an intention would introduce a different focus of attention, that of maintaining a particular one. Our conduct, when analyzed, must prove to support the official focus of attention, but not because we are attempting to do so. Here, then, it is proper involvement that generates proper conduct. And broadly correct identification of an activity in which we participate is often not enough. For example, as a European, an individual can know correctly that the performance in progress is Indian music—he can even know that a sarod and tabla are being played—and yet be, and give evidence of being, uncomfortably out of the world that listening ought to have established for him. He cannot follow along, he cannot get into the music; and so the unpleasant constraint of sitting out an experience while sitting in it.

Involvement is an interlocking obligation. Should one participant fail to maintain prescribed attention, other participants are likely to become alive to this fact and perforce involved in considering what the delict means and what should be done about it—and *this* involvement necessarily removes them from what they themselves should be involved in. So one person's impropriety can create improprieties on the part of others. And whether the individual maintains too little or too much involvement, he will have reason to manage the show of this involvement in order to minimize its disruptive effect on other participants.[1]

To say that there are limits of license to sustain much or little involvement should not hide from us the fact that some deviation

---

1. Discussed further in "Alienation from Interaction," in *I.R.*, pp. 113–136.

from the norm is tolerated. And if effective cover is maintained, a great deal of deviation can be got away with. Indeed, that deviation is an element in almost all fabrications.

It should be stressed that the matter of being carried away into something—in a word, engrossment—does not provide us with a means of distinguishing strips of untransformed activity from transformed ones: a reader's involvement in an episode in a novel is in the relevant sense the same as his involvement in a strip of "actual" experience. When James and Schutz spoke of something being "real after its fashion" and of "multiple realities," it was potential for inducing engrossment that they really had in mind.[2]

II

Given that the frame applied to an activity is expected to enable us to come to terms with all events in that activity (informing and regulating many of them), it is understandable that the unmanageable might occur, an occurrence which cannot be effectively ignored and to which the frame cannot be applied, with resulting bewilderment and chagrin on the part of the participants. In brief, a break can occur in the applicability of the frame, a break in its governance. Various examples were considered in early chapters.

Now it is apparent that the human body is one of those things that can disrupt the organization of activity and break the frame, as when an individual appears in clothes that are unbuttoned or unsuitable or a guest slips on a rug or a child knocks over a vase.

---

2. As William James footnotes it:

It thus comes about that we can say such things as that Ivanhoe did not *really* marry Rebecca, as Thackeray *falsely* makes him do. The real Ivanhoe-world is the one which Scott wrote down for us. *In that world* Ivanhoe does *not* marry Rebecca. The objects within that world are knit together by perfectly definite relations, which can be affirmed or denied. Whilst absorbed in the novel, we turn our backs on all other worlds, and, for the time, the Ivanhoe-world remains our absolute reality. [*Principles of Psychology*, vol. 2 (New York: Dover, 1950), pp. 292–293.]

(As earlier suggested, James hedged his bet, going on to say that: "When we wake from the spell, however, we find a still more real world, which reduces Ivanhoe, and all things connected with him, to the fictive status, and relegates them to one of the sub-universes. . . .")

It is also plain that when an individual misframes events, his subsequent action will break the frame but can itself be quite calm and self-possessed. Consider, too, that in sustaining fabrications, the individual has a special predicament. He cannot rely on an unmanaged relationship between his own behavior and the scene in which it occurs, since the mutual consistency which ordinarily comes without apparent effort must now be consciously achieved and consciously sustained. Not only can there be a break in such a frame entirely apart from the conduct of participants, but also the calm and considered action of a fabricator can constitute a slip, breaking the frame that was being sustained for the dupes. He need not become improperly involved emotionally but merely act so as to discredit the cognitive assumptions of the scene that is being sustained.

Another set of circumstances that allows for unruffled frame breaking involves scripted stage performances. These activities are expected to involve the watcher, carry him away, until he half-believes that the relation between character and the staged scene is the ordinary one—one that sustains a mutual compatibility without special effort on the part of the actor. But obviously this mutual support is a carefully designed one, planned and scripted well in advance, worked out in every detail, and, of course, subject to misfiring. Thus, a performer can find not only that the scene itself has suddenly failed to sustain his show, but also that now the script he himself is attempting to follow leads him to further discredit the realm he has been fostering. So again one has an individual breaking frame without the requirement of improper involvement. (In unstaged life we need but carry off an action, in performances a whole scene.) Similarly, puppeteers must face the prospect of a wire or string breaking or becoming entangled with a puppet in action, a piece of a puppet falling off, a marionette inadvertently being caused to walk a couple of inches off the ground or move its mouth out of synch with a backstage voice or answer to the wrong name. And if the voice producers use a "swazzle" in order to effect a change in tone, there is the prospect of inadvertently swallowing it.[3] So, too, political speakers can find themselves driven too fast or too slowly by the teleprompter. Radio announcers must face reading

---

3. I draw throughout here on Gerold L. Hanck, "A Frame Analysis of the Puppet Theater" (unpublished paper, University of Pennsylvania, 1970).

a misworded script and thus being catapulted into space on an impossible sentence or impossible thought, or, because time has become short, find themselves speeding up their delivery until all pretense of ordinary speaking is discredited. In "live" radio shows, sound effects have sometimes failed, as in the following:

GANGSTER: "Okay you rat, I've got you covered and now I'm going to drill ya."
(*Complete silence*)
GANGSTER: (Realizing that the sound effects man has run into trouble) "On second thought I'm going to slit your throat."
Two shots—The sound man had located his trouble.[4]

In all of this one sees that the human body, like any other part of a current scene, can fail to sustain the frame in which it finds itself. However, the difficulties to be considered now involve a special part of the body, the part that carries facial expression. For here there are special contingencies to deal with. Facial expression is capable of extremely rapid changes and extremely delicate shadings. It can be exquisitely responsive to the passing moment and is required to be. (Indeed, one could speak of a facial frame, for the face will ordinarily be ordered in keeping with the framed activity in progress.) It is through this expression—more constantly than any other—that the individual is obliged to demonstrate appropriate involvement in and regard for the scene at hand. Yet necessarily this field of expression is a labile, unstable thing. It can be deformed by any perceivable wind. It is this screen of responsiveness that must be examined functionally.

When an individual participates in a definition of the situation, circumstances can cause him suddenly to let go of the grasp the frame has upon him, even though the activity itself may continue. This disengagement takes two forms.

In one, leave is taken in an authorized manner, with the establishment of an official time-out through the use of internal brackets; or there is exercise of a personal right of distraction, as when a speaker pauses for a moment to take a drink of water. Not uncommonly, one who thus withdraws reestablishes appropriate involvement on his return. In any case, what witnesses

---

4. Kermit Schafer, *Pardon My Blooper* (Greenwich, Conn.: Fawcett Publications, Crest Books, 1959), p. 9.

allow for here is the rights of a person to be something beyond the role he is currently projecting, which something has needs of its own, in this case to leave the frame. An orderly retreat.

The second kind of disengagement is the one that bears upon facial expression and involves a disruption of the portraying of appropriate, respectful involvement. No authorization is available for the withdrawal, and typically the actor cannot easily insert himself back into appropriate involvement, back into control by the frame. And his precipitous departure from effective participation can disrupt the proper involvement of other participants. Note, again, the multiplying effect. Whatever can cause an individual to break frame has produced in him the behavior which can cause others to also, thereby giving them a reason in addition to his own for improper involvement. Consider now the breaking of facial frame.

1. There is the central possibility that the individual will capsize as an interactant, and in this mode of self-removal fail to assemble himself—at least temporarily—for much of any other kind of organized role. Thus, in all societies, seemingly, an individual can find himself dissolving into laughter or tears or anger, or running from an event in panic and terror, in a word, "flooding out."[5] (Left open here is the fact that any number of the participants in an activity, from one to all, may flood out at the same time, and that a circular process can be involved, either damping the disruption or exacerbating it.) Indeed, there is even a popular understanding that the varieties are to be considered together:

> Some months ago I stepped out of my car, jammed my purse and two large books in the crook of my left arm, heard the satisfying slam of the door as I pushed it closed with my right hand and discovered with a shock of pain that my thumb was still inside. I should like to report that intelligent presence of mind directed me to drop the purse and books and quickly open the door with my left hand. But it didn't. I clung to the impediment as if I were cemented to it and screamed like a wounded cougar for my companion, who was several yards away, to come to my rescue. Thus did intense pain cause me to make an ass of myself and cease to function rationally.

> Fear, another unpleasant state of mind, often has a similar debilitating effect on mankind's thinking process. Who hasn't

---

5. See "Fun in Games," in E., pp. 55–61.

heard harrowing tales of the panicky flyer who freezes to the stick and renders himself incapable of pulling out of a fatal dive? Or of the terrified driver who cannot lift his foot from the accelerator when collision with a speeding train is suddenly imminent?

When Juan Marichal and John Roseboro triggered last Sunday's celebrated rumble at Candlestick [Park] they were not, of course, motivated by pain or fear. But they were in the grip of an equally mind-shattering emotion—Rage!

Except for the fluky circumstance of a bat in Marichal's hand, when long smoldering tempers flared out of control, the issue over the Dodger's beanballing of the Giant would have been settled by flailing fists alone. For Marichal is neither vicious nor cowardly. But in the heat of their blazing fury, Juan "froze to the stick."

Fortunately, the potentially lethal situation—Roseboro, usurping a pitcher's prerogative, senselessly throwing a baseball at Marichal's head, Juan senselessly retaliating by swatting Johnny with the infamous bat—resolved itself into a kind of Homeric Punch and Judy show. Neither man was seriously injured.[6]

Most common, no doubt, is the flooding out that represents an unsuccessful effort to suppress laughter, sometimes called "breaking (or cracking) up." A Herb Caen story illustrates:

The [Bach Aria] Group, which includes [tenor Jan] Peerce, Soprano Eileen Farrell, two other fine singers and a chamber group, gives sedate, even austere recitals—everybody dressed in black, sitting primly in straight-backed chairs onstage and being very, very dignified, as befits Bach.

Before one recital Peerce was backstage warming up his remarkable vocal cords and hitting one high C after another, as Miss Farrell listened in wonderment. At last she asked, "How do you do it, Jan? How do you hit those high ones so effortlessly?" "Easy, Eileen," he smiled. "I just imagine I'm being goosed by an ice-cream cone."

A few minutes later the Bach Aria Group filed onstage—serious and proper—and took its seats. As Peerce started to arise for his first solo, Miss Farrell whispered something, whereupon he fell back, helplessly convulsed with laughter; in this instance the show did NOT go on and the delicate mood was never restored. What she had whispered was: "What flavor?"[7]

6. Doris Kurry in *San Francisco Chronicle*, August 28, 1965.
7. *San Francisco Chronicle*, November 8, 1964.

Observe that when an individual floods out, he will often make a ritualistic effort to conceal what has become of him, the most common form being to cover the face with the hands—an instrumentally futile act that apparently has a fairly wide cross-cultural distribution.[8]

Now the question: What standard circumstances make for flooding out? Some suggestions are possible. One: When individuals are obliged to enact a role they think is intrinsically not themselves, especially one that is felt to be too formal, and yet no strong sanction is present to inhibit a frame break. Gerald Suttles thus writes of slum youth:

> When street workers attempt to introduce explicit roles, like president or secretary, the boys tend to think them very funny. Apparently, the incongruity of someone "playing his part" is too much for them and "breaks them up." Thus, when elected to an office most boys find it almost impossible to keep a "straight face."[9]

Similarly, it is reported that on naval destroyers the first time a neophyte goes through the ritual in changing watches with a buddy, he is likely to break up.[10] The participant observer confronts a similar problem; in responding to utterances and actions that are totally unbelievable by "modern" standards, the ethnographer must try to act as if he has not been jarred out of conversational involvement, although often he will have been. During formal sociable occasions guests face a similar issue, especially if any degree of solemnity must be consistently maintained. So, too, those involved in sustaining a benign fabrication, such as a practical joke, are vulnerable to giving the show away by failing to conceal suppressed laughter, and indeed children contest to see who can make whom break up, and who can best maintain a fixed bodily and facial pose.[11] Stage performers can

---

8. One bit of photographic evidence is provided by Irenäus Eibl-Eibesfeldt, *Love and Hate* (New York: Holt, Rinehart & Winston, 1971), pp. 50–51.

9. Gerald D. Suttles, *The Social Order of the Slum* (Chicago: University of Chicago Press, 1968), pp. 185–186.

10. David L. Cook, "Public Order in the U.S. Navy" (unpublished paper, University of Pennsylvania, 1969).

11. In unpublished lectures, Harvey Sacks presents a useful description of the children's game "Button, Button, Who's Got the Button?" and argues for the role of such straight-face contests in socializing the young into being competent adult dissemblers.

experience a similar fate, illustrated, for example, in Joan Mac-Intosh's comments regarding one of her parts in the Schechner production *Dionysus in 69*:

> The first speech as Dionysus is the hardest part of the play for me. To emerge vulnerable and naked and address the audience and say I am a god. Absurd and untrue. I didn't believe and therefore the audience didn't believe. Eyes glazed, body mobilized and defensive. Rehearsed with RS. Told him I felt like a fraud, doing that. He said expose that, deal with that anguish and fraud—don't cover it up and be phony. Very hard to do. I am always afraid that something will happen that I can't control. But I've found that when I'm honest, laughter and joy are liberated in me. The absurdity of telling 250 people that I am a god makes me laugh and the audience laughs with me and gradually the strength comes and the self-mockery fades away.[12]

Obviously, in these examples one deals with the limits of a frame, in particular the limits of its capacity to hold the actor to the transformation he is obliged to maintain.

Individuals attempting to maintain "normal appearances" under hazardous and fateful conditions, whether engaged in a benign or exploitive deception, have a problem, too; restraining themselves from flooding into defensive behavior can generate what is seen as furtiveness, a flooding out that gives the show away.

It is interesting that flooding often occurs when an individual must accept restraints on bodily behavior over an appreciable portion of his body (as when he must keep immobile for a fitting, a portrait, a stiff costume, or a narrow tunnel); laughter and joking are the common result. Unable to sustain the minor adjustments through which a viable alignment is ordinarily maintained the individual guys his whole situation, making a ludicrous character of his current self so that he can preserve something else as the performer.[13] Similarly, when the indi-

---

12. Richard Schechner, ed., *Dionysus in 69: The Performance Group* (New York: Doubleday & Company, 1970), unpaginated.

13. An unfunny version is found in the camisole, wet pack, and straight jacket used in mental hospitals with the actively disordered, confinement here producing a flooding into rage, this adding to the uncontrollable that is being controlled. Exhaustion can result—of the self as well as the body. It had been suggested that this medical device shows a certain want of empathy between those who authorize its use and those upon whom it is

vidual is forced to consider himself in some future, alien guise, joking can also result, as a legal scholar suggests:

> The ceremony surrounding the execution of the will tries to be noble and solemn. In the office of a large law firm, the ceremony is likely to be brief, brisk, and accurate; nonetheless, many clients will giggle in an embarrassed way, and make some self-conscious joke touching on their close mortality.[14]

Note that in these jocularities a very subtle shift can occur: the individual begins to engage in stagelike behavior and shifts from projecting a role to projecting a whole fictive personal identity, for it seems that whole persons can be better guyed than role performances.

Just as there are situations which engender breaking up, so there are those which put participants at risk of other kinds of flooding and generate for some of those involved (and sometimes for all) a sense of the precariousness of the frame:

> Speed is the basis of the humanity which governs an execution by hanging, not merely speed in producing death (and nothing can be speedier than instantaneous death) but speed in the necessary preliminaries. This speed also makes for technical efficiency, as it reduces the time during which a prisoner may fully realize what is happening and collapse, and probably explains why Mr. Pierrepoint has had experience of such few faints. A prisoner who faints or a prisoner who fights inevitably spoils the smooth execution drill and the possibility must haunt officials, but as Mr. Pierrepoint told the Commission, "99 out of every 100 go calmly." For the lack of hysteria considerable reliance is placed on the chaplain. "I think the chaplains do a wonderful job and I think they get them calm enough for that short space of time," as one witness put it.[15]

---

used, the more so because of the argument sometimes put forward, namely, that patients who are disturbed may obtain profound relief from constraint, indeed, may be seeking it.

14. Lawrence M. Friedman, "The Law of the Living, the Law of the Dead: Property, Succession, and Society," *Wisconsin Law Review*, CCCXL (1966): 373–374.

15. Justin Atholl, *Shadow of the Gallows* (London: John Long, 1954), p. 127. The point about a hanging, of course, is that it is a ceremonialized act occurring on a stage, and as long as the condemned can see that he is indeed the lead performer, he will have a keying of the facts that he and the audience can live with—an orderly, attenuated version of reality, one that he and they are likely to be able to manage without too much flooding out, a harness, as it were, for feelings which might otherwise race on re-

Here, of course, one sees the limits a particular group of persons has for keyings of various kinds. For example, when, in 1965, Christian Dior brought his *haute couture* collection to Warsaw, the Polish-speaking narrators were greeted with laughter at various points, the dress and the comments apparently being too far out of reality for the audience to take seriously, that is, as the particular keying found in modeling displays.[16] Or the following:

> Vienna—The actors stood motionless on the stage of Vienna's Stadt theater An der Wein, where Beethoven's "Fidelio" and many other famed works were performed for the first time.
>
> "Vietnam," one member of the cast of the avant-garde American Living Theater Company shouted as the work progressed Monday night. "Washington, D.C.," shouted another. "Stop the war." "Feed the poor." "Freedom now."
>
> The actors distributed toilet paper, blew their noses and started to spit.
>
> It was all part of a work called "The Mysteries" by the controversial company headed by American Julian Beck and his wife Judith Malina.
>
> It proved too much for some in the audience. About 30 tuxedo-wearing playgoers stormed the stage to prove, as one man put it, that "this can be done by anyone."
>
> Fist fights between the audience and the players broke out. There were screams and only after the curtain fell was order restored.[17]

Memoirs of a first visit to the theater and hence the first effort to maintain a theatrical frame provide another illustration of capacity limits, but this time on an individual basis:

---

grettably. Interestingly, such ceremonialization of killing is sometimes contrasted to the way in which savages might behave, although I think it would be hard to find a more savage practice than ours—that of bestowing praise upon a man for holding himself to those forms that ensure an orderly, self-contained style to his execution. Thus, he (like soldiers in the field) is being asked to approve and uphold the action which takes his life, in effect setting the first above the second. *That* sort of line is fine for those who write or preach or legislate in one or another of the names given to society. But to accept death politely or bravely is to set considerably more weight on moral doctrine than is required of those who formulate it.

16. *San Francisco Chronicle*, December 9, 1965.

17. *Ibid.*, December 1, 1965.

"Which is the theater?" asked my father (he too was going to this kind of fête for the very first time). He was shown the curtain. We sat down as well, therefore, and pinned our eyes on this curtain. Written at the top of the canvas in large capitals was "Schiller's *The Brigands,* a most entertaining play," and just below, "No matter what you see, do not be disturbed. It's all imaginary."

"What does 'imaginary' mean?" I asked my father.

"Hot air," he answered.

My father had his own problems. He turned to ask his neighbor who these brigands were, but too late.

Three raps were heard, and the curtain opened. I stared in goggle eyed amazement. A paradise had unfolded before me: male and female angels came and went, dressed in gaudy costumes, with plumes, with gold, their cheeks colored white and orange. They raised their voices and shouted, but I did not understand; they became angry, but I did not know why. Then two hulking giants suddenly made their entrance. It seems they were brothers, and they began to argue and hurl insults and pursue each other with intent to kill.

My father pricked up his ears and listened, grumbling with dissatisfaction. He squirmed on his chair; he was sitting on hot coals. Drawing out his handkerchief, he wiped away the sweat which had begun to flow from his brow. But when he finally realized that the two gangling beanstalks were brothers at odds, he jumped to his feet in a frenzy.

"What kind of buffoonery is this?" he said in a loud voice. "Let's go home!"

He grabbed my arm and we left, overturning two or three chairs in our haste.[18]

As might be expected, these framing capacities can change over time, and not always in a direction one might favor, as Harold Nicolson suggests in connection with Roman pastimes:

Their cruelty, both to human beings and to animals, became increasingly atrocious. In the days of the Republic a circus-audience had been shocked by a massacre of elephants which Pompey staged. From southern Morocco he imported Gaetulian toughs, who had been trained to throw javelins at the animals, aiming at their eyes. The ensuing butchery was incompetent and slow; the blood cascaded down the legs of the elephants, who

---

18. Nikos Kazantzakis, *Report to Greco* (New York: Simon and Schuster, 1965), pp. 76–77.

raised their trunks and trumpeted in pain. The spectators rose in
their seats and clamoured that the show be broken off. Cicero,
commenting on this episode, remarked that the unpleasant spectacle had aroused a curious sense of pity, "as if the animals possessed something in common with human beings." In imperial
times the nerves of the circus audiences became less sensitive.
They much enjoyed watching naked men and women being slowly
mauled by beasts.[19]

It should be apparent that when an individual discovers that he
has misframed events and is lodged into cognition and action on
false assumptions, he is quite likely to flood out, breaking from
the unsupportable frame he had been sustaining. Similarly, when
individuals observe or witness another, whether as authorized
onlookers or as persons providing proper civil inattention, this
witnessing presumably involves tacit framing assumptions;
should the witnessed person fail to maintain sustainable activity,
his observers are likely to be caught up short, too, and may well
break frame facially. Thus one can account for Bergson's accounting of humor: *"The attitudes, gestures and movements of
the human body are laughable in exact proportion as that body
reminds us of a mere machine."*[20] So, too, when the individual
hears himself for the first time on tape[21] or sees himself for the
first time on film,[22] he is likely to break up, that is, flood out in
laughter. He cannot take the role of other or of onlooker, because
it is he himself who is talking, and yet, of course, it isn't, for he
himself has been displaced. Another example bears these notions
out, serving as a kind of natural experiment:

Governor Grant Sawyer of Nevada laughingly weathered what
he said was one of the most flabbergasting moments of his political
career here yesterday.

19. Harold Nicolson, *Good Behaviour* (London: Constable & Co., 1955),
p. 82.
20. Henri Bergson, *Laughter*, trans. Cloudesley Brereton and Fred Rothwell (London: Macmillan & Co., 1911), p. 29.
21. Paul Ekman of the University of California at San Francisco has
taken film in New Guinea of Stone Age people hearing (for the first time
for anyone in their society) audio tapes of themselves and breaking up in
response. He should not be forgiven.
22. It has been suggested (by John Carey) that individuals in our culture are more likely to break up on hearing themselves than upon seeing
themselves, presumably because we all get used to looking at ourselves in
mirrors.

The youthful governor, scheduled as the principal speaker at a Las Vegas "Salute to San Francisco" luncheon, walked belatedly into the crowded Mural Room of the St. Francis Hotel just as the master of ceremonies had finished reading Sawyer's speech to the assembled guests.

Amid gales of laughter, he was duly introduced by his stand-in, Julian Moore, senior vice president of Frontier Fidelity Savings and Loan of Las Vegas.

Still unaware that his speech had already been delivered, the governor stepped forward to the microphone.

Moore stepped down, and as he did, whispered to the governor.

"You've already read my speech?" Governor Sawyer said incredulously into the mike.

"This creates a rather perplexing problem," he said to his roaring audience.[23]

In these duplications of self, the individual finds that the role he was about to play is unnecessary and the one his image is playing is ungeared to himself, so that neither of these selves can sustain, and be sustained in, what is to follow. The fun involved in watching mimics—later to be considered—presumably has the same basis.

2. I have considered at length the single possibility that an individual can be overthrown as an interactant and find himself sustaining no particular role. By keeping the system of reference clear, another possibility can be seen: that an individual who is presumably outside a framed activity, a mere uninvolved bystander, but one who is actually involved covertly, can suddenly lose control of his appearance of disinvolvement in the activity and openly flood into it.[24] An illustration is provided in the biography of an American diplomat in Russia, in which the writer comments on his farewell with the tail assigned to him in Moscow:

A number of our friends were on the platforms to bid us farewell and there were several tearful partings (the Russian vacuation demand). I have always loathed departures of this sort and it was with a certain amount of relief that I saw the porters closing the train doors. At this moment I looked out across the platform and there stood my shadow, propped up against a pillar. He was gazing

---

23. *San Francisco Chronicle*, October 16, 1965.
24. Discussed in "Fun in Games," in *E.*, pp. 63–64.

intently at me, hands in the pockets of his mackintosh and his head hunched on his shoulders. He looked absolutely miserable and it occurred to me that perhaps he was not looking forward to a change of job after all; he might get landed with somebody very much more difficult and less accommodating than myself. As the train jerked and slowly moved, on a sudden impulse I leant out of the carriage window, looked straight at him and gave him a cheerful wave. To my astonishment he took both hands from his pockets, waved them in the air and grinned from ear to ear, revealing a mouth crammed full of gold teeth. It was even more laughable when, in the middle of this demonstration, he realized what he was doing, wiped the grin off his face and stuck his hands back in his raincoat pockets.[25]

3. The suggestion, then, is that when an individual breaks frame, disorganized flooding out and "flooding in" are possible. There is another possibility: the individual's behavior can retain role organization but in a shifted key. Thus, the individual's experience within a particular frame can itself produce a mounting cycle of response in him, a surging of feeling, which sweeps him into decreased or increased distance from the initial activity, thereby adding or subtracting a lamination from the frame of his response. What one has here is not merely upkeyed or downkeyed response, but the circumstances which generate these transformations starting from appropriate definitions—circumstances which show us the limits of the capacity of a key to order the beliefs and feelings of its users.

a. Downkeying: Perhaps the most obvious example of the process of downkeying occurs in regard to playfulness that gets, as they say, out of hand, as when mock acts become real ones. An ethologist studying children's play provides an illustration:

> Sometimes the fleeing involved seems to "turn real." A child fleeing for a long time without chasing back, going faster and faster, may raise its eyebrows and stop smiling and its laugh changes and becomes a more continuous vocalization, a tremulous scream.[26]

25. John Whitwell, *British Agent* (London: William Kimber & Co., 1966), pp. 138–139.

26. N. G. Blurton-Jones, "An Ethological Study of Some Aspects of Social Behaviour of Children in Nursery School," in Desmond Morris, ed., *Primate Ethology* (London: George Weidenfeld & Nicolson, 1967), p. 359.

Similarly, during professional boxing matches, the fight may get
"out of control," and someone may get slugged more frequently,
more savagely, than is consistent with the boxing frame or,
incidentally, the recipient's life.[27] Professional wrestling exhibitions have even become downkeyed in this way, with the astonishing consequences that wrestlers have found themselves
looking at blood, real blood, their own.[28] And spectators at these
sports can, in getting carried away, get too far carried away, until
the mask on expression is dropped and overt participation
occurs:

> Istanbul—A soccer match exploded into violent fighting between
> rival fans yesterday, killing at least 39 persons and leaving some
> 600 others injured, Turkish police said.
>
> Witnesses said the fans fought with knives, pieces of chain,
> rocks and clubs. Some were shoved off balconies.
>
> Spectators tried to flee the stadium and trampled many near the
> exits.
>
> Witnesses said the rioting started when Kayseri scored a goal in
> the 20th minute of play in the match against Sivas in the central
> Anatolian town of Kayseri.
>
> Sivas fans became so angry at the score that they rushed into
> stands occupied by Kayseri rooters and the tragic struggle was on.
> Fighting raged for several hours.[29]

Participants in a meeting can similarly break frame and downkey
from restrained verbal dispute to the more direct kind:

> New York—Maritime union leader Jesse M. Calhoon, 41, sur-
> rendered to police yesterday on a complaint by a shipping company
> executive that Calhoon jumped on a conference table and kicked
> him in the head during a contract bargaining session.[30]

Individuals who attempt to practice speed reading report a similar experience: they start out reading fast, paying little heed to

---

27. A good example was the fatal welterweight fight between Emile
Griffith and Benny (Kid) Paret, March 24, 1962. See, for example, *San
Francisco Chronicle*, March 26 and 27, 1962. Apparently Paret was hit
rather too avidly twenty-two times after he had gone limp against the ropes.
(Note the frame-relevant fact that a good example can be a bad event.)

28. One is reported in *Life*, December 2, 1957.

29. *San Francisco Chronicle*, September 18, 1967.

30. *Ibid.*, June 6, 1965. That skilled negotiators may simulate a frame
break at the strategic moment is certainly a possibility, just the kind that
the analysis of frame allows us to anticipate.

what they are reading, but after a few moments find themselves
becoming involved in the text and, of course, slowing up in speed.
Proofreaders can be similarly affected. Incidentally, students of
interaction often have the same problem: they start attending to
a particular element of the scene but soon find that they have
been drawn into ordinary involvement and are no longer attending to the special focus of observation they had set themselves. In
Nevada casinos a shill ordinarily finds it all too easy to maintain
obligatory distance from the game itself, but sometimes, in response to a particular combination of cards, he may find himself
actually concerned about what the next card will be, such as
would a bona fide player. So, too, in the conduct of military exercises, the umpire can have as one of his tasks "focusing the
attention of all participants on the training aspects of maneuver
play rather than in the achievement of a fictitious 'victory' or
'defeat,' guiding, where necessary, the development of situations
to avoid the latter tendency.[31] Similarly, when a linguist asks his
inner-city informants to illustrate ritual insults called "sounds,"
there can be a gradual shift from illustration to doing.[32] So, too,
announcers at "live" events, who are supposed to provide a
running commentary with considerable emotional distance between their reporting and what it is they are reporting on, can
sometimes get carried away and exhibit direct spectator involvement—or at least more directly than announcers properly do:

> (*Noise of crowds*)
> "Got twenty-eight seconds to go—there's the snap back from center
> —looks like a pass—it is a pass."
> (*Screams*)
> "There he goes—he's up to ten, up to twenty, to thirty—he does
> it—"
> (*Screams*)
> "He's going wild, he's going, going—look at that son of a bitch
> run!"[33]

---

31. Department of the Army Field Manual (FM 105–5), *Maneuver Con-*
trol (Washington, D.C.: Department of the Army, 1967), p. 95.

32. Reported in lectures at the University of Pennsylvania by William
Labov.

33. Quoted in Schafer, *Pardon My Blooper*, p. 106. The most famous case
in American broadcasting occurred during the arrival of the Graf Zeppelin
Hindenburg when the announcer, Herb Norrison, in the middle of his

Perhaps the best-known examples of downkeying are those associated by fact or legend with dramatic scriptings. There are stories of performers who became so engrossed in the character being portrayed that they shifted from the theatrical key to the real thing:

> Newcastle-on-Tyne, England, Oct. 2—Orson Welles banged Desdemona's head so hard on the bed in the murder scene from "Othello" here last night that members of the audience began murmuring protests.
>
> Mr. Welles said after the performance that he guessed he just got caught up too realistically in the spirit of the play.
>
> Said Gundrun Muir, who played Desdemona: "It was in a good cause."[34]

> Soprano Anna Moffo threw herself into her role of Lucia Monday night in Detroit. She had completed her death scene in the touring Metropolitan Opera's "Lucia di Lammermoor" and was taking a curtain call when she collapsed in a faint. A psychiatrist who examined her said she so immersed herself in the role that she thought she had died. The singer recovered quickly.[35]

Nor need passion be involved. A simple break in cognitive tension seems sometimes to occur, as a blooper suggests:

> The TV play was *Abe Lincoln in Illinois* . . . in which Raymond Massey starred. The actors on stage were bidding farewell to the president . . . when one of them called out . . . "G'bye Mister Massey."[36]

If actors in live performances are vulnerable to downkeying, then audiences ought to be vulnerable, too. Contemporary reports are not hard to find:

> New York, March 12—A young typist, apparently upset at a scene in the Broadway play, "Look Back in Anger," leaped across the footlights during last night's performance and attacked the leading man.
>
> Crying "He left me, he left me," Joyce Geller, 25, began striking British actor Kenneth Haigh, who portrays an adulterer in the play.

---

speech, was witness to the sudden ignition and explosion of the balloon. Apparently he was fired for flooding into direct response, a sanction less likely to occur nowadays.

34. *New York Herald Tribune*, Paris ed., October 3, 1951.
35. *San Francisco Chronicle*, May 23, 1962.
36. Schafer, *Pardon My Blooper*, p. 58. Ellipses in the original.

"Why do you treat this girl this way?" she cried.

Haigh warded off her blows as a fellow actor came to his aid. The two herded her toward the wings and actress Vivienne Drummond called for the curtain.

Miss Geller, who later said she identified her own life with the scene, said the sadistic treatment meted out by Haigh was too much for her.

She calmed down backstage and apologized and was released without charge.[37]

Similarly, it is reported "that during a puppet performance before a group of Virginia mountaineers, a drunken member of the audience fired his rifle at one of the puppets playing the devil."[38] On a different time scale, one finds that characters in radio and TV serials come gradually to acquire reality for some members of the audience, who record these peculiar beliefs by writing letters of advice, admonition, support, and so forth to the station.[39]

An important kind of downkeying is found in everyday actual behavior. In Western society, at least, each language community has a corpus of expressions containing informalities, slang, curse words, blasphemies, and the like, which are, in the main, defined as appropriate only among age and sex equals and of these, especially among the companionably related. Language competence involves the ability to closely assess the formality and delicacy of a scene or setting and to censor one's language from minute to minute accordingly. There is, then, a sort of sliding key available to every speaker. When this control is weakened (seen as occurring through anger, fatigue, inebriation, or surprise), momentary downkeying can occur involving what is taken as more "direct" expression. For example, when police in Philadelphia (as in most other American cities) talk on the air from their cars to the station dispatcher, they are obliged to use a somewhat stilted language involving formalities, code terms, and legalistic expressions. However:

---

37. *San Francisco News,* March 13, 1958.

38. Hanck, "A Frame Analysis of the Puppet Theater," citing Paul McPharlin, *The Puppet Theatre in America* (New York: Harper & Brothers, 1949), p. 204.

39. The British version is described in some detail in Arthur Koestler, *The Act of Creation* (New York: Dell Publishing Co., 1967), pp. 302–303.

One night an officer was describing [to the dispatcher] a suspect who had escaped his custody. He was out of breath and racing through his report wildly, finally losing control of his temper. "The nigger prick is cut on the head because I jacked him good," he said. The dispatcher cut him off and began to rebroadcast the description, concluding with the words, "The suspect may have a laceration on the back of his head inflicted by the officer in pursuit."[40]

Downkeying apparently often occurs during activity involving rekeyings. Thus, in 1966, when the comic strip *Batman* was brought to TV as an ostensible form of "camp" (followed by *Superman, The Green Hornet,* and *Tarzan*), viewers found themselves oscillating back and forth between seeing the events satirically and becoming "genuinely" involved.

As must be expected in all matters dealing with frame, downkeying is often portrayed in commercial fantasies, thus providing us with the frame complexity of a transformed downkeying. When TV viewers were slipping into seriously watching *Batman,* magazine cartoons were depicting the fact.[41] But here, no doubt, the most famous example is the one that Cervantes bequeathed. His hero starts out to watch a puppet show, adds a few scholarly points to the interpreter's narration, and then, upon being gradually caught up, forgets himself, draws his sword and rescues Don Gaiferos from the Moorish puppets, not calming down until the little theater has been destroyed, for which he is quick to provide cash compensation.[42] Hollywood has its own classic in this connection: the "discovery kiss." The heroine submits for various

---

40. Jonathan Rubinstein, *City Police* (New York: Farrar, Straus & Giroux, 1973), p. 86.

41. For example, *The New Yorker,* March 12, 1966.

42. Miguel de Cervantes Saavedra, *Don Quixote,* trans. Samuel Putnam (New York: Viking Press, 1949), pt. 2, chap. 26. See also Alfred Schutz, *Collected Papers* (The Hague: Martinus Nijhoff, 1962), 2:149–150. Nor was Cervantes the first to key downkeyings:

Like Don Quixote at the puppet-show, Jonson's poor gull in *Bartholomew Fair* (1614) and Nell the citizen's wife of *The Knight of the Burning Pestle* (1607) begin by being aware that what they watch is only a dance of shadows—and then forget. Simon, in Middleton's *Mayor of Quinborough* (1616–1620?) loses patience with an actor who will not confide his purse to him for safekeeping, and the foolish Morion in the anonymous *Valiant Welshman* (1610<>1615), watching a masque, falls in love with the Fairy Queen. [Anne Righter, *Shakespeare and the Idea of the Play* (London: Chatto & Windus, 1964), p. 83.]

good or bad reasons to a kiss from the hero, expecting to get through it as painlessly as possible, only to find, halfway through, that real emotion and relatedness have suddenly occurred, presumably in response to the special potency which the hero has in this regard. And radio provides us with Welles' *War of the Worlds*, wherein radio actors in the part of radio announcers enact breaking down in the face of what they see, no doubt influenced by the record of the real thing produced by the burning of the *Hindenburg*.[43]

In considering examples of downkeying, I used the behavior of excessively involved members of the audience as a source of examples. But indeed, ordinary audiences exhibit a degree of downkeying, too. The process at the beginning of a play whereby the spontaneous involvement of the onlooker is induced and he finds himself dissolving into a make-believe world is much like the downkeyings properly so named, except the onlooker doesn't lose himself completely, and this balance is precisely what the arrangement between stage actors and audience calls for. Something similar can occur in story reading to an audience. At the beginning of the telling the listeners will firmly discriminate two "I's": the one that refers to the reader and the one that refers to the character in the story from whose point of view events are told. As the reading proceeds, however, and the audience falls under its spell, merging can occur between these two "I's" until it is half taken that the reader and the narrating character are one and the same.[44] It might even be worthwhile to extend the

---

43. Some members of the audience for Welles' show are almost as famous as the performers themselves because of the vigorousness of their response. However, apparently most of those who misframed the event did so from the very beginning of their listening (which apparently had often begun well along in the show), and so one would say their response was downkeyed but did not exhibit the process of downkeying.

44. There are circumstances in which a reader may be obliged to follow Brecht and purposely check this downkeying process. I once listened to a man read his wife's paper at a professional meeting, the cause being her suddenly required presence elsewhere. When he came to the first "I" in the text, he read it, stopped, and added parenthetically "that is, my wife" (or words to that effect), reminding the audience of the laminations involved. Interestingly, a minute later, on having to deal with the next "I" in the text, he only changed intonation somewhat and raised the little finger of his left hand (the latter easily visible because it had been grasping the top edge of the lectern), as though now, in the light of his prior carefulness, dissociable signs would be enough to affirm the appropriate frame, namely, one in

argument to containments of the full-fledged exploitive variety. When a skeptical dupe puts aside his suspicions and fully credits what was designed to deceive him, then once again the process of literalizing what isn't real has occurred, but this time it is in regard to fabrications, not keyings. But, of course, here the delamination, although not prescribed, is something devoutly sought by the fabricators.

b. The contrast to downkeying is upkeying: a shift from a given distance from literal reality to a greater distance, an unauthorized increase in lamination of the frame. For example, in gambling games when stakes are pitched low in relation to the "gamble" of the players, betting sometimes degenerates; larger and larger amounts are bet based on worse and worse risks, to the accompaniment of increasing laughter. So, too, break-in dealers start a morning's practice at training school making modest bets with house-supplied silver but soon find themselves shifting from practice to "as-if" games, and from there to higher and higher bets with greater and greater risks until the whole session of mock dealer and mock player collapses in laughter. In this break-in dealers are like other learners, for it seems everywhere easy for those engaged in practicing to drift into guying what they ought to be doing. (It is as if making jokes at such a time can derogate the activity which is being practiced while not directly threatening the occasions of its serious execution, and that such possibilities are too good to be missed.) And this situationally engendered playfulness can mount in rate and broadness until the participants break from the constraints of the practicing activity and flood into a horseplayed version of the task at hand.

In the ordinary course of events, obligations, especially to superordinates, prevent an individual from upkeying a spate of activity and treating it as more distant from untransformed reality than it was meant to be. Even stage actors are protected somewhat in this way from audiences treating a stage production lightly. However, in the case of nonlive entertainment, such as movies, only an onlooker's obligations to other members of the

which he was a substitute speaker, more like another member of the audience than like the author. In this case, note, an audio tape of the talk would not provide a record of the work done by the raised finger, and a traditional paralinguistic description and analysis might not be much better.

audience who might be taking the show "seriously" prevent up-keying. Thus a British movie review of a melodramatic John Wayne movie:

> I am not going to tell you what happens, nor shall I discourse upon the acting, about which there is little profitable to say. But I do feel bound to comment on the laughter. Now laughter in a theatre has an ugly sound, when aroused by something that is not meant to be funny. It is ugliest, of course, in the living theatre, where there are flesh and blood actors to be hurt by it, but even in the cinema it is uncomfortable and embarrassing, and many a good film has been spoilt for some by the laughter of others in the wrong places.
>
> The trouble with such laughter is that once it has begun it's hard to stop. The first giggle will set off a dozen more. That was the case when I saw "Legend of the Lost," at a public performance, not a special show for critics. As the toothsome Miss Loren snatched the Tuareg hood away from her face, the audience let out a roar of laughter from which the film never recovered. They laughed when Mr. Brazzi gazed upon his father's bones and observed "I knew he was dead—they murdered him—but to see him like this!" They howled when he pawed by moonlight at the sleeping Miss Loren and she responded with the drowsy question, "What is it, Paul? Do you want to talk to me?" They rocked in their seats when the adventurers discovered a ruined city and one said "It's Roman" and the other "Are you sure?" and the first came back with "Look at the architecture." The sad thing is that the ruins were quite genuine (the company had found their way to Leptis Magna), but by this time the audience was in no mood for believing anything.[45]

Of course, with neither actors present *nor* an audience of strangers, license to upkey can be considerable, and it is to be expected that, for example, private film showings and TV plays will be vulnerable to an upkeying response from various quarters:

> A most important and unanticipated finding which we repeat-edly observed while studying the television-viewing behavior of 40 lower-class Negro families in Chicago was the jocular quality of their interaction with the medium performer, with the accompany-ing fact that they seemed to carry on a continuous joking dialogue

---

45. C. A. Lejeune, in her film column in *The Observer* (London), Janu-ary 26, 1958.

with the television persona. The lower-class Negro television spectator in these cases tended to personalize the media relationship to
a great extent and to inject himself actively into the ongoing interaction between media performers, either as a third party or as an
actual interacting participant. The kinds of repartee developed in
these relationships—the spectator would chide the performer, ca-
jole him, answer his questions directly, warn him of impending
dangers, compliment him, and so on—were executed lightly,
humorously, and freely, in a highly personal manner. Because
most media spectators maintain identifications of a serious nature
with media performers, it was the very frivolity and joviality
characterizing the responses of those lower-class Negro viewers
which sensitized us to other factors. It was precisely because these
relationships were couched in such jocular terms that they were
suspect: the understanding that humor often conceals basic hostil-
ities directed our inquiry.[46]

This concept of pseudo-jovial skepticism necessarily assumes
that the spectators participating in the media relationship tend to
translate the relation into a concrete, reciprocal, personal encounter. . . . Although the lower-class Negro responds to the medium
and its presentation, he does not seem to take it seriously—he is
"putting the medium on" and he seems to believe that the medium
is reciprocally "putting him on."[47]

---

46. Alan F. Blum, "Lower-Class Negro Television Spectators: The Concept of Pseudo-Jovial Skepticism," in Arthur B. Shostak and William Gomberg, eds., *Blue-Collar World* (Englewood Cliffs, N.J.: Prentice-Hall, 1964),
pp. 431–432. Blum goes on to say:

The media relationship tends to engender its own world—its own
reality, events, roles, and identities—but one which is predominantly a
white cosmos, and not easily accessible to Negroes. When the Negro
viewer is invited to project himself into a role, an identity, an event, or
a setting which he knows from experience to be restricted to whites, he
must mobilize a remarkable single-mindedness in order to blot out the
view of external reality which contradicts the norms of the relationship
in which he is involved. As an interaction, the media relationship generates its own schema of interpretation, and this interpretation is derived
from the perspectives of spokesmen for a white society. At every point in
the encounter, the media performer's interaction, his simulation of sociability and intimacy, his attractiveness and appeal, must be reassessed.
The Negro spectator cannot internalize the goals of the interaction because he is incapable, even if he desires, of mobilizing a complete identification with the reality of the media context. [p. 433]

47. *Ibid.*, p. 432. Upkeying expressed in self-sustained dialogues has a
parallel in the upkeying device of the "restructure-ending" of folk humor,
such as "between the sheets."

4. All social activity seems vulnerable to flooding out and key shifting on the part of its participants, but scripted dramatic presentations and presented contests seem especially vulnerable in this regard, owing, perhaps, to the complex frame structure of these undertakings. One might expect, then, that there will be types of frame break that are specific to these social arrangements.

a. For example, take the line ordinarily maintained between a stage area and an audience region. "Direct address," that is, literal interchange, is officially restricted to established junctures just outside of the performance brackets. And this arrangement is, of course, vulnerable:

> Forest Hills, N.Y., Sept. 2 (AP)—Earl Cochell, of Los Angeles, was suspended yesterday by the Lawn Tennis Association for ungentlemanly conduct in his match on Wednesday with Gardner Mulloy, of Miami, Fla., in the National Tennis Championships.
> . . .
> Cochell, 29, won the first set from Mulloy and fell behind in the second when he lost his service. Apparently believing the set lost, he began hitting the ball left-handed and clowning generally.
> Spectators complained.
> Cochell shouted back at them, and finally walked over to the umpire's chair. He tried to grab the microphone, but an official refused to let him do so.
> Cochell, however, managed to make himself heard without the microphone.[48]

> The 38-year-old Minneapolis-born [Cornell] MacNeil, a former resident of Cliffside Park, N.J., now living in Rome, had been enthusiastically applauded in Parma's theater last night.
> But Saturday night, with Verdi's "Un Ballo in Maschera" (masquerade ball) on the program, spectators heckled MacNeil and his two Italian co-stars, tenor Flavino Labo and soprano Luisa Maragkiano, through the first two acts.
> In the third act, as MacNeil started an aria, a burst of catcalls stopped him and the orchestra cold.
> He turned to the audience and shouted: "Basta, cretini" (enough, idiots). Then he walked off the stage.
> Spectators plunged toward the stage. Many made their way back stage. Police rushed into the theater. There was a scuffle when

---

48. An Associated Press release, September 3, 1950.

MacNeil came out of his dressing room to face irate spectators gathered there.[49]

So there can be a kind of "flooding through." One further illustration may be provided, separated only by space, time, and content from the first mentioned:

> The privilege [of extending formal invitations to notables] was exercised to a varying degree and less and less as the years passed. But the execution of Henry Wainwright in 1872 the Lord Mayor and Sheriff sent invitations to sixty friends. Wainwright, brought to the gallows, turned deathly pale as he saw the unexpected crowd which had assembled. Then he recovered and spat out, "Come to see a man die, have you, you curs?" One of the invited spectators told Henry Irving that the effect was that "I have felt sick and mean and ashamed of myself ever since."[50]

b. Another example of frame breaks specific to performances: performers can flood out or downkey at that point of temporal juncture when the performance is about to begin or about to terminate. The result is a botching of the process of taking on a role (or a character) or putting it off. In a word, bracket-breaks. One example from a presented contest performance:

> Last night's scheduled 12-rounder at Oakland Auditorium for the California heavyweight championship never came off.
>
> Instead, a minor riot erupted in the ring when challenger Willie Richardson repeatedly attacked champion Roger Rischer with kicks to the groin just prior to the referee's instructions, and was disqualified and suspended indefinitely.
>
> The San Jose heavyweight, who had been knocked out by Rischer there on November 2, suddenly ran from his corner as the fighters were called to the center of the ring and kicked his opponent without any warning.
>
> Despite attempts by his surprised handlers and referee Vern Bybee to restrain him, Richardson stalked Rischer, who retreated into a corner, holding his groin in obvious pain.
>
> The tableau in the ring at first appeared to us to be a staged performance, and even Rischer later said he thought it was "a gag." But when the berserk Richardson broke loose and attempted to kick Rischer again, it became evident to everybody that it was the real

---

49. *San Francisco Chronicle*, December 28, 1964.
50. Atholl, *Shadow of the Gallows*, pp. 86–87.

thing, and many of the crowd of approximately 1400 started to encircle the ring.

Rischer's version was that, "Richardson knew he was in for the worst beating of his life, and he went apart at the seams, like a wet soda cracker. He panicked, lost control of himself. Maybe if I was in his shoes, as scared as he was, I'd have done the same thing."[51]

c. Just as there are frame breaks specific to performances, so there are acts that are frame breaks *except* during performances. Explication is required.

Earlier it was suggested that portrayed characters on stage simulate interaction apparently oblivious to the fact that an audience is openly watching. Just as the actors have a right and obligation to sustain this fiction during the in-frame period, so during the same time the onlookers can act as if its appreciative sounds were not being heard by the characters onstage. A member of the audience can break into tears or laughter, that is, flood out, without this counting as a *real* break in frame, providing only that the expression is sympathetic to the intent of the play. Indeed, at rock concerts all manner of ecstatic moans may be permissible. The audience has much license to act this way because, given the fiction of insulation between characters and audience, these lettings go are part of a discounted reality, an offstage one, and can as much be treated as not really going on as can the staged action be treated as what is actually taking place. Even unsympathetic expressions from the audience can be effectively managed, providing only that no recognition from the stage is given them—an overlooking that is easily accomplished because, to repeat, everything the audience does *during* the show is meant to be out of frame relative to the domain of action sustained by the characters. But, of course, if a member of the audience makes the actors crack up, then a real frame break occurs:

> "Here's Love," at the Curran, was five minutes into its second act Tues. night when a man in the third row suddenly leaped to his feet and positively hollered: "Migawd, I'm in the wrong theater!" The show stopped cold, cast convulsed, as he inched over to the aisle and ran out to "Camelot," at the next-door Geary.[52]

---

51. Reported by Jack Fiske, *San Francisco Chronicle*, February 11, 1965.
52. Herb Caen, *San Francisco Chronicle*, November 6, 1964.

Here, I think, it might be useful to consider a special kind of watcher, the kind radio and TV broadcasts employ: the live studio audience. The audiences at quiz shows, interview programs, talk shows, and other "participation" programs enjoy the same rights possessed by play audiences, namely, to watch and to react as though from behind a one-way soundproof mirror. But these rights are extended. Any time a guest or cast member makes a minor verbal slip, thereby placing himself or others in a questionable light, the audience is likely to burst out laughing, as though breaking frame, as though all obligation of tact has ceased. For the slip can be defined as a comic turn, a brief venture in projecting an unserious self, and this self is expendable, just as the laughter it evokes can be defined as appreciative and out of frame.

The same rule of open laughter applies to (or rather against) a member of the audience, who, for some reason, is given a hearing, and during this acts in a way that is out of keeping with the standards presumably sustained in broadcasting. (Correspondingly, the audience sometimes laughs out of duty to show that an effort to provide the sort of sally which would cause out-of-frame witnesses to break up has not failed of its aim, that indeed nothing serious has occurred.) The apparent willingness of the official host to engage particular members of the audience, either to provoke a response or to reply to one, is not here a serious breaking of frame; for the target of the host's action has become, by virtue of being a target, a temporary member of the cast, a temporary stage performer.[53] If a performer—audience-recruited or official—did take umbrage at the open laughter caused by his conduct, he would likely be seen as the poorest of poor sports, someone utterly without a sense of humor. For he could take umbrage only in the capacity of a participant in literal,

---

53. An actor's decision to exchange words directly with a member of the audience during a legitimate stage play is a very serious one, for the character he has been appointed to portray must be entirely set aside if he is to do so, and at such a time the fundamental point of the whole show is to sustain the domain of existence wherein the projected characters have their being. As one shifts downward (if the expression be allowed) to TV talk shows, the performer appears more and more in his own guise and the audience has more and more right to try to break through (or more and more obligation to suffer the performer's breaking through to them). The correlation of these changes is understandable. The shift is from staging an alien character to staging an unserious version of oneself.

offstage interaction, a place where tactful considerateness is owed him, and that would imply a misframing of the unserious self his conduct was taken to express. (The deep obligation of temporary performers, then, is not to be correct but to take in good humor the response their lapse calls forth; and *that* obligation they almost invariably sustain.) It is thus that all of these shows have the character of being continuously reestablished as a scene for comic turns; and it is thus that should a host or official guest desire to say something "serious," something to be heard as equivalent to what might be said in literal interaction, then special quotation marks will be introduced, as though to temporarily allow for something out of frame to be said.[54]

One confirmation of this general argument regarding audience license might be cited, one that comes from a peculiar direction. As already considered, amateur and professional sports share an interesting feature: they can be looked in on. They are "open" activities. A private person about to tee off or ski down a slope must submit to watchers (if any care to watch), just as much as do those who perform professionally for spectators. Yet if the same individual were reading on a park bench, or talking to a friend while walking down the street, he would be protected from being stared at, at least in this particular way; for staring is seen as an invasion of territoriality, an impertinence, a hostile act. Why the difference?

The answer, I think, is that engaging in a sport places the individual in a frame in which the serious side of selves is not to be involved and in which the special realm of the game takes the place of workaday affairs. Given this realm, the participant's serious self and the serious selves of watchers are out of frame, not present, not to be seen. Given that watchers aren't in the frame, the player has an obligation to sustain the fiction and act as if they are not there, much as does an actor who is on stage.[55]

---

54. Described in Helen Hogan, "Some Bracketing Devices Used on Television Talk Shows" (unpublished paper, University of Pennsylvania, 1970).

55. Professionals in team sports often exhibit a full and deadly intent and display much passion, as do their fans. So one could say that for them the game was very serious indeed—and no wonder considering the income and prestige involved. But another interpretation can be argued. Lifelong occupational careers can be committed to professional sports, but nonetheless the whole of a sporting occasion is institutionally defined as part of unserious, recreational life. Passions that transport the participant have there-

(Note the enclosed manner in which two tennis players exchange niceties while totally neglecting the gallery watching.)

It was suggested that the members of an audience often have a right to cry or laugh out of frame, because it can be assumed that characters and audience are not fully in the same domain, that a looseness of this kind obtains. Where else does this looseness occur?

When we engage in unstaged, actual interaction with individuals of radically reduced status, we sometimes assume the right to break up easily at what we come to see as their antics. The treatment of small children is a case in point. Flooding out into laughter or smiles at what a child attempts to do and fails or attempts to do and does with characteristic childlike style seems a common response, one based upon adult license to treat children as merely qualified to begin to hold the conversational stage: we start by carefully extending them a show of full conversational rights, but as soon as the charitable impulse is spent, we pounce on any deviation as grounds for breaking up and thus relax from the care that had to be extended to sustain the social fiction of equal participation. The children become performers, and we become licensed members of an audience. Breaking up at the antics of foreigners as they assault our language provides another example. But perhaps the most apt example of all comes from royalty, who, more than any others, must forbear their lessers, the least of these being natives:

> Kota Kinabalu, Malaysia—(UPI)—A marksman with the deadly blowgun from the Murut Indian tribe today blew his chance to impress the British royal family visiting this Borneo capital.
>
> At the request of Prince Philip, the native took up his blowgun to demonstrate his expertise.
>
> "Darling, do be careful. It's poisonous," Queen Elizabeth told her husband. Local officials accompanying the touring royal couple and their daughter, Princess Anne, scurried to clear a range and find a cardboard box for a target.
>
> The tribesman, clad only in a loin cloth, took aim and blew mightily into the long blowgun. Nothing.
>
> "Maybe it's stuck," said Prince Philip.

---

fore not carried away his serious self. From this derives the *license* to act fully involved; the *reasons* for full involvement are another matter and certainly have to do with the palpable rewards that professionals obtain.

The tribesman banged one end of the blowgun against the ground trying to loosen the poison dart.

He lifted the pipe again, and again blew mightily. The dart still did not emerge.

The warrior gave up in disgust and stalked off. The Royal family burst out in laughter.[56]

5. It has been argued that when the individual breaks frame, he does so by becoming interactionally disorganized or by shifting key. One might reason that the individual could also break from behavior in one primary framework (whether transformed or not) to conduct implying a radically different framework. Thus, motorists *sometimes* become angry enough to chase after another driver or a pedestrian with intent to injure; hockey players will sometimes forget to style their aggressions as part of the instrumental movements of the game and use their sticks frankly as clubs; pitchers in baseball have on occasion broken into similar candor.

But this argument is not fully convincing. For it seems that behind many apparent shifts in primary frameworks there is really a shift of another kind, from suppressed and inhibited response within a frame to a "more direct," that is, less laminated reaction within the same terms. When a very hungry person suddenly exhibits naked voraciousness in his approach to food, when stimulated sexual interest turns to rape, when uneasy walking to an exit turns to a panicky race, when polite exchange of insults turns to all-out verbal attack—when any of these releases occur—something like a downkeying has taken place, a downkeying in which the appearance of reserve is discredited.

One example. In 1947 during an American visit (the story goes) Saudi Arabia's crown prince, Emir Saud, visited Hollywood, an event which apparently gave a prankster, one Jim Moran, an opportunity. On the evening the real prince left, Moran, with the help of a few friends costumed as retainers, appeared at Ciro's Restaurant at a table the party had reserved:

During a lull in the proceedings the Prince spoke sharply to one of the servants, who bowed low and then walked to the bandstand. In a thick accent he told Jerry Wald that His Royal Highness would enjoy hearing *Begin the Beguine*. No sooner said than done. The

56. *The Evening Bulletin* (Philadelphia), February 28, 1972.

orchestra played the number and when it was over, the Crown
Prince nodded his appreciation. Then from his belt he took a goatskin pouch and opened it and spread the jewels out on the table,
poking through them, looking for a particular one. He settled on a
stone (the thirty-dollar amethyst) that looked like a whopping
diamond. He handed it to the servant, muttering something, and
the servant went again to the bandstand and presented the gem to
Mr. Wald. A loud buzzing of conversation passed through the
room—everyone had witnessed every detail of the drama.
. . . .

   At last the Crown Prince decided it was time to leave. He
clapped his hands together. One of the servants adjusted his robes.
He and his companions stood up. The dance floor was clear, so the
royal party started across it, toward the entrance. All eyes in the
place were on them. Suddenly there was a rattling clatter—the
goatskin pouch had fallen open and all those jewels had spilled on
the glistening floor. The royal party paused, and the servants
started to bend down and pick up the jewels. But His Royal Highness barked a command, waved his hand imperiously, and the four
Arabians continued toward the door, leaving the jewels. They had
bounced and scattered in all directions and now, almost instantly,
Ciro's turned into a mad scramble. Down on the floor went some of
the greatest names in Hollywood, both male and female. Chairs
and tables were knocked over and some of the waiters joined in the
scramble.

   The Crown Prince and his people didn't even turn around to
look. They marched out of the place, got into their limousine, and
departed allegro. Mission accomplished.[57]

Two points can be made here. First, the scramble (if such there
was) can be seen as an abrupt change in framework for the non-
Arabian guests, the shift being from nightclub table talk to a
naked rush for what appeared to be valuables. But if one assumes
that the sight of the jewels on the table earlier in the evening had
excited desires then amply held in check, then what came to
occur with the breaking of the bag was a downkeying of these
earlier desires—a downkeying into open, direct action.
   The second point has to do with the fact that popular writings

---

57. H. Allen Smith, "Some Shots That Found Their Marks," in Alexander
Klein, ed., *The Double Dealers* (Philadelphia: J. B. Lippincott Co., 1958),
pp. 53–54, reprinted from Smith's *The Compleat Practical Joker* (New
York: Doubleday & Company, 1953).

(some of which have been cited in this study) and apocryphal tales managed within the oral tradition seem to be full of heroes or villains breaking frame. Indeed, few moral tales cannot be climaxed and validated by reference to an extreme frame break which purportedly occurred as the consequence of the doings under consideration. So whether or not such topplings occur commonly in everyday life, it is the case that the imagery of these explosive displays provides an important element in the way we picture interpersonal dealings.

This secondary utilization being the case, and given the convoluted character of the framing process, one can expect rekeyings of these keyed breaks. For example, when Don Adams of *Get Smart* had as his "guest" Don Rickles, and the script apparently called for the two, dressed in spy-black, to hang from their hands, they apparently had trouble staying in frame during filming and apparently repeatedly broke into laughter. The film clip was saved, and when the two appeared as "guests" on Johnny Carson's show (July 12, 1968) the clip was shown. The seeing of a cinematic record of what was apparently a very real frame break provided the basis for the three stars onstage to break up, and the sight of a filmed version of a rehearsal flood and a living version of the performer's flood caused the Carson studio audience itself to flood out. Of course, the audience in TV land was involved in watching a televised *taped* showing of a flood-out response to a movie clip of a flooding out and were thus located one lamination further away from the original events than were the performers and audience in the studio. Observe that the original frame break was probably the most "spontaneous," unscheduled one of all— certainly we could call it an "actual," "real," "literal" frame break—and yet, of course, a vision of Don Rickles and Don Adams as spies stretched against a wall is (even in our funny age) quite unreal.

11

The Manufacture of Negative Experience

I

When an individual is lodged in a stream of framed activity, he sustains some check upon his immediate, spontaneous involvement in it. This will vary in degree with boredom at one end (including the kind that is a defensive response to a compelling preoccupation), nearly full engrossment at the other. Along with affective reserve (in whatever degree it is found), there is likely to be a measure of cognitive reserve also, a wisp of doubt concerning framework and transformations, a slight readiness to accept the possible need to reframe what is occurring; and this reserve, as well as the emotional kind, varies.

When, for whatever reason, the individual breaks frame and perceives he has done so, the nature of his engrossment and belief suddenly changes. Such reservations as he had about the ongoing activity are suddenly disrupted, and, momentarily at least, he is likely to become intensively involved with his predicament; he becomes unreservedly engrossed both in his failure to sustain appropriate behavior and in the cause of this failure. Whatever distance and reserve he had in regard to prior events he loses, at least temporarily, along with some of whatever conscious control he had over what was occurring. He is thrust immediately into his predicament without the usual defenses. Expecting to take up a position in a well-framed realm, he finds that no particular frame is immediately applicable, or the frame that he thought was applicable no longer seems to be, or he cannot bind himself within the frame that does apparently apply. He loses command over the formulation of viable response. He flounders. Experience—the meld of what the current scene brings to him and what he brings to it—meant to settle into a form even while it is beginning, finds no form and is therefore no experience. Reality anomically flutters. He has a "negative experience"—negative in the sense that it takes its character from what it is not, and what it is not is an organized and organizationally affirmed response.

Here mark that in the matter of frame analysis, face-to-faceness is not a technical limitation; assessments are involved, but these can be based either on indirect means or on direct perception of scenes in which the perceiver is alone. When involvement is considered, however, face-to-faceness becomes much more a delimiting factor. And when the focus is upon negative experiences, one finds oneself almost exclusively considering occasions when two or more persons are in one another's immediate presence: in brief, "social situations." For it seems a fact that the arrangement in which an individual's sense of knowing what is going on is most often threatened is one in which other individuals are immediately present. The major exception—the one that will much concern us now—is provided in the strips of depicted social situations presented commercially in movies, TV, and print; but these make-believes are social, too, merely once removed from the viewer, who may, of course, be solitarily viewing.

With frame breaks, then, there is typically a face-to-face phenomenon to look at—the context for negative experience. Once examined, however, it becomes plain that this disorganization can itself have a place in a wider organization.

When a person floods out he does preserve himself from having to ratify fully what it is that has caused him embarrassment. He stops the flow of action, knocks the board over, and brings a halt to the defaming events, if only temporarily. He shields himself from having to ratify and acknowledge what it is that has occurred.[1] He opts out and thereby preserves the possibility of later opting in. Moreover, in thus ostensibly giving up all

---

1. See "Embarrassment and Social Organization," in *I.R.*, pp. 110–112.

control over his situation he does demonstrate that he can act honestly and feelingly and is, in a way, to be trusted, for if it is apparent that at the moment he can work no design, he can hardly work an evil one. And in addition to rendering himself (it is thought) free of guile and out of control, he also exposes himself as someone who has been bested, someone for whom matters were too much. This, of course, can be an aggressive gain for those who have caused him to lose his control and a vicariously aggressive one for those watching the process.

There are other organizational aspects to interactional disorganization. If someone has the job of making sure that most participants are intensely involved in what is occurring, he may well be obliged to push things to the point at which a few persons become quite carried away. What is fully involving for some will be overinvolving for a few. Indeed, that a few cannot keep themselves in control can be a sign that the many are fully engrossed. Thus, for example, in the management of rock concerts, the aim of those in charge may be to repeatedly bring members of the audience to such a pitch that they almost tear down the walls of the occasion, then to allow a falling back until another surge is engineered.[2] So, also, if a torture show in a circus is to carry away most of the audience into the horror of it all, a few members of the audience may have to be carried away far enough to throw up.[3] Similarly, if "vertigo" rides in fairgrounds are to be effective in creating pleasurable fear for some—what Roger Caillois calls *une sorte de panique voluptueuse*—then a few are likely to be seriously frightened, that is, find the experience to be "too much for them." It therefore follows that, in organized recreation at least, the flooding out of some persons is not a sign of the disorganization of the others, but rather an incidental by-product of effective management.

Now a central point about the organizational role of disorganization. As already remarked, individuals merely observing another—"onlooking" him—follow along in frame terms with some sort of blend of affective sympathy and cognitive set. When

---

2. Recommended by Ralph Gleason, a student of the form. See his "Twisters' Audience Grabs the Show," *San Francisco Chronicle*, January 29, 1962.

3. See, for example, Dan Mannix, *Memoirs of a Sword Swallower* (New York: Ballantine Books, 1964), pp. 140–141.

he who is observed becomes upset, those watching are likely to become a little concerned, too. But what is too much for him may well be, with the reduction of distance, just enough to ensure their involvement in events, events containing an individual in trouble with respect to frame. They may be dislodged from their prior involvement, as is he who has broken frame, but in its place they have the collapsing individual to become involved in. (It is plain, thus, from a thousand different examples that passive participation is not as passive as one might have thought. If the onlookers laugh when the clown suddenly finds himself falling like a stone it is because they had all along been projecting their musculature and sensibilities sympathetically into his walk and now find that their leaning into his anticipated conduct, into the anticipated guidedness of his doings, their framed prediction of what is to come, is disordered. In this sense watching is doing.) Moreover, no fellow participant is caught up short because these onlookers have been caught up short, for after all, they are not officially participating in the scene before them. So their flooding out has no multiplying consequence. They get a free ride. Of course, for both the person who has broken frame and the observer the dislodgment may be quite momentary; but (it can be argued) even a moment's release from the prior frame may allow everyone psychologically to fit back into the frame and be more at ease than before.

Of interest here is the quiz show scandals in the late fifties.[4] The producers of the show, aiming to involve the audience intensively, sought contestants whose character and behavior seemed likely to ensure this. Given the effort involved in finding the "right" candidate, it became natural to school him in that kind of behavior which would best stimulate audience involvement, a task, incidentally, best accomplished if the actual issue of guessing answers did not intrude. So in the answer booth the candidate sweated out recall to the point of nearly breaking the facial frame for seemly behavior, in this way convincing the audience that a "real" contest was in progress, and at the same time providing them with a stimulus to involvement.

---

4. See, for example, "TV Quiz Business Is Itself Quizzed about Fix Charges," *Life*, September 15, 1958; "Quiz Scandal (Cont.)," *Time*, September 8, 1958; Jack Gould, "Quiz for TV: How Much Fakery," *The New York Times Magazine*, October 25, 1959.

An interesting illustration of the role of frame breaks as a means of inducing involvement for those who watch is found in a practice central to drama, namely, the fictional production of differential information states. One faction of characters in the play, "unbeknownst" to the other, enfolds it in a deception. The fabricators may, of course, be taken in themselves, in one or another of the various forms of multiple containment. The audience typically is in on some of the secrets but rarely all. In the last act the frame is cleared. That moment brings shock, chagrin, and surprise to the contained characters. But to the audience it brings involvement. (An added source of involvement, as will be later seen, is that the audience can feel it is behind the scenes, even behind two sets of scenes.) Something similar is found in novels and other such commercial make-believe. In these scenarios, comic heroes routinely find themselves forced to sustain a precarious fabrication which is soon destroyed, and villains routinely attempt to sustain a serious deceit, only to be found out and totally discredited. Comic and villain are both capsized to their chagrin but not to the readers'; the latter are merely ensured of having something to be engrossed in.

An individual who floods out, then, can be a source of involvement for others, not merely a form of disorganization in his own right. But this is only half the story. Something more than the capsizing of an individual can be involved in frame breaking.

If the whole frame can be shaken, rendered problematic, then this, too, can ensure that prior involvements—and prior distances—can be broken up and that, whatever else happens, a dramatic change can occur in what it is that is being experienced. What then *is* experienced is hard, of course, to specify in a positive way; but it can be said what isn't experienced, namely, easy acceptance of the prior conception of what was going on. So one deals again with negative experiences.

Another issue. It appears that minor frame breaks can readily be allowed, if for no other reason than the fact that they seem to ensure the continuity and viability of the established frame. Indeed, the disattend track specifically permits the occurrence of many out-of-frame acts, provided only that they are "properly" muted, that is, within the disattend capacity of the frame. The concealment track allows for a similar release. Thus, collusive exchanges between friends at stiffish gatherings can be at once a means of breaking frame and a means of staying within it. Indeed, every setting has its moments when participants may momentarily break frame. The following example from a paper on the required role behavior of artists' models is to be understood in terms of the obligation of students to avoid catching the eye of the model when she is posed nude before them.

> If, as actually must occur, she inadvertently indulges in behavior that does not support this "model as aesthetic object" performance, such as yawning, scratching, etc., actions that indicate that this is, in truth, an inhabited body that performs all the usual physical functions, she may neutralize these revelations by ignoring them; or, she may form a "we're all human" collusion with persons in the audience by a conspiratorial smile.[5]

It is just such a release that a performer may attempt to introduce publicly in response to heckling or to some other untoward event which taxes the capacity for disattendance of audience and performer. He risks an admitted break in frame in the hope of quickly reestablishing the initial definition of the situation but now with less to forcibly disattend. (And it is the possibility of this and other bits of ad hoc engineering that distinguishes the legitimate stage entertainer from his movie counterpart; the latter is stuck with his performance and can do nothing to correct for restiveness in the audience.) Thus, even participants in a presented contest or match may find it desirable (although not necessarily effective) to attempt to cope with a gross distraction by ratifying it momentarily. What can happen (and has) should a small girl trundle onto a tennis court during a tournament match before a large gallery is therefore understandable: stopped in his play by an extraneous event that can hardly be disattended, the closest player bows low and proffers the girl his racket.

II

Given the various functions of negative experience, one should anticipate that intentional effort will be made to produce these states. I want now to review some locations of negative experi-

---

5. V. M. Frederickson, " 'The Modeling Situation': A Structural Analysis" (unpublished paper, University of California, Berkeley, 1962).

ences, always keeping in mind that in many cases it will not be possible to say in positive terms what it is that is produced, only what it is that is undercut and disorganized.

1. Encounters: Negative experiences have a place in the organization of unstaged, actual verbal interaction but perhaps not a major one.

a. First is teasing and taunting: one individual attempts through verbal and physical acts to push the recipient of his efforts a little beyond the latter's limits of self-control, often for the benefit of fellow participants.[6] Here the status of the butt as a full-fledged participant is temporarily abrogated (very often with his partial collaboration) to provide, in effect, a source of easy involvement for those who watch. The "dozens" and "sounding" are examples; so also, in a way, are traditional leg-pulls, fool's errands, and the like, for even as the butt in these designs is induced into a fabricated world, those witnessing the induction are getting ready to participate in the chagrin they expect him to experience when the frame is cleared. Trick questions employed by the young are perhaps the most elementary examples: the answer that is set up will, when it is given, transform the question and answer retrospectively into another frame of meaning, resulting in the licensing of an action against the subject which he ordinarily would never have encouraged.[7] So, too, the practice of acting as if a joking statement had been taken seriously or a serious statement heard as a joke, thus lodging the butt in an effort to clear up the frame, only to find that the frame is suddenly cleared, but he, the butt, has not cleared it.[8]

---

6. In our society, females are thought to continue later in life than males to provide blushes and other floodings in response to teasing.

7. A selection is provided in Iona and Peter Opie, *The Lore and Language of Schoolchildren* (London: Oxford University Press, 1967), pp. 57–72.

8. Although teasing generally has a simple three-role structure—butt, teaser, witness to the flooding—and although informal conversation is its usual locus, more complicated frames are possible. Thus, two actors in character onstage can teasingly try to break each other up by means of sotto voce quips that are entirely out of (staged) character. Friends in the audience have similarly teased performers. I knew a Vegas dealer who reported that when he had a quarrel with the dancer he had been living with, he would kiss her good-bye and suck her front tooth plate out. She would then be forced to dance while keeping her mouth carefully shut. He would sit up front and make faces to break her up so that the hole in the front of her face would be exposed.

There are, then, verbal devices individuals can employ to produce a frame that can be broken or break one that has already been established, all for the moment of negative experience that results.

b. Second is a special type of stressful persuasion which relies upon causing a subject to facially flood out. A practice in police interrogation, psychotherapy, and small-group political indoctrination involves dwelling on what is ordinarily disattended or undivulged, to the point at which the subject "loses control of the situation," control of information and of relationships, becoming subject to self-exposure and new relationship formation.[9] Persons engaged in quick courtship can draw on similar devices, especially that of inducing the provision of autobiographical material ordinarily withheld from new acquaintances, again the consequence being that the informant is removed from his prior framework of social distances.

A special comment is warranted here about psychotherapy. From a nonbeliever's point of view, the value of psychotherapy seems open to all kinds of doubt, but there is no doubt that troubled persons often find it somehow worthwhile to initiate the relationship and come to their sessions regularly, paying considerably for the privilege. During therapy they seem willing to tolerate, if not espouse, the interpretation of events invoked in various direct and indirect ways by the therapist. What accounts for this enthrallment, especially since the persons enthralled are typically the kind who have experienced a certain difficulty in relating to others?

The medical answer is that the person seeking help is sane enough to know that he has a medical problem and that a physician should be appealed to for treatment. An alternative answer is that the conventions for conducting a therapeutic session breach the frame of ordinary face-to-face dealings at just those points at which an interactant would otherwise be protected from influence and relationship formation; thus the patient is trapped into a special relationship.[10] As follows:

1. The client's informational preserve can be penetrated by the therapist beyond the point at which the client might penetrate

---

9. See *S.I.*, pp. 34–35.

10. I have profited here from an early effort of Roy Turner to apply frame analysis to psychotherapy.

it himself. (The secrecy defense against relationships is thus breached. This license, however, is not reciprocal.)

2. Client behavior which would ordinarily be treated as outside the main track, such as initiatory and terminal rituals, tone of voice, blushings, silences, slips, spurts of anger and the like (being person rights relative to role) are to be treated as proper subject matter for the therapist to address.[11]

3. The reprisal principle of ordinary social intercourse is held in abeyance by the therapist, a wide range of "acting-out" behavior being tolerated by him in support of the doctrine that the client's behavior is directed not at the therapist but at significant figures into which the therapist is projectively transformed, in short, that the behavior is not quite literal, although the client may be unaware of this.

4. The client is encouraged to break the decency rule and the modesty rule prevailing in ordinary interaction. Not only taboo fantasies, but also petty, egocentric daily reactions are given the focus of attention as worthy of extended consideration. Also, the therapist recommends versions of the client's version of the therapist which would ordinarily be considered immodest and improper for a professional to support. But while the client's self is thus placed in the very center of affairs, inflated sufficiently to fill the whole stage, it is the therapist's vocabulary drawn from doctrines of "personal dynamics" (albeit in a respectfully lay version) that the client is led to employ in these considerations.

5. As part of the obligation to free-associate, the client must be

---

11. The beginning of this practice is documented by Brill in his Introduction to the Modern Library publication of Freud. (After finding Paris disappointing, Brill took advice and went to the clinic of psychiatry at Zurich [The Burghölzli Clinic, recently introduced to Freud's writings by the director, Eugen Bleuler, 1907–1908]):

I was fortunate enough to arrive there at the beginning of a new era in psychiatry shortly after Professor Bleuler had recognized the value of Freud's theories and urged his assistants to learn and test them in the hospital. Professor Bleuler was the first orthodox psychiatrist to open his clinic to psychoanalysis. . . .

. . . .

In the hospital the spirit of Freud hovered over everything. Our conversation at meals was frequently punctuated with the word "complex," the special meaning of which was created at that time. No one could make a slip of any kind without immediately being called on to evoke free associations to explain it. It did not matter that women were present —wives and female voluntary interns—who might have curbed the frankness usually produced by free associations. The women were just as keen to discover the concealed mechanisms as their husbands. [*The Basic Writings of Sigmund Freud*, ed. and trans. A. A. Brill (New York: Modern Library, 1938), pp. 25–27.]

ready to consider his relationship to any and all his intimate others, divulging what would ordinarily be the preserve of these relationships, and in consequence, betraying them; so, too, with organizations, groups, and other structures.

6. The client's negative response to the application of these rules and the reservation this creates regarding the session and the therapist is itself a legitimate matter for considering ("analysis of the negative transference"), and so the protective distance this alienation ordinarily provides is itself expropriated, becoming a matter for consideration, not a basis for an unstated stand.

The suggestion, then, is that teasing and intensive persuasion are examples of the use of negative experience within conversationlike encounters. One other example should be mentioned: what Gregory Bateson has made well known under the title "double-bind."[12] The argument has it that "schizophrenogenic" individuals communicate to loved ones in a manner that provides contradictory instructions, leading to a disorganizing interpretation of the communicator's intent, feelings, and so forth. Whatever the case with schizophrenics (whatever, if anything distinctive, they might be), it seems that self-negating statements and actions are very commonly found at certain junctures in personal dealings. These actions—performed, it is said, "in bad faith"—allow the double-binder to decline an overture or the satisfying of a presented need, even while the importuner is given some evidence that the denial is not permanent, perhaps not even a denial at all, and in consequence is tacitly led to keep himself ready for a relationship but not presumptuous regarding it. The double-binder at a later date will then be in a position to determine retroactively what it was he meant to establish about the relationship all along. The method is to employ careful ambiguities or a tone that can be claimed to signal either a joking unseriousness or a face-value intent, that is, a keying or an untransformed statement, and thereafter any tendency on the

12. As in, for example, Gregory Bateson et al., "Toward a Theory of Schizophrenia," *Behavioral Science*, I (1956): 251–264; Gregory Bateson, "Minimal Requirements for a Theory of Schizophrenia," *AMA Archives of General Psychiatry*, II (1960): 477–491. See also L. C. Wynne et al., "Pseudo-Mutuality in the Family Relations of Schizophrenics," *Psychiatry*, XXI (1958): 205–220; Harold F. Searles, "The Effort to Drive the Other Person Crazy: An Element in the Aetiology and Psychotherapy of Schizophrenia," in his *Collected Papers on Schizophrenia and Related Subjects* (New York: International Universities Press, 1965), pp. 254–283.

recipient's part to elect one of the interpretations is checked by an act that gives strength to the alternative reading. A technique, in effect, for keeping someone on the hook. Note, considerateness motivated by tact often double-binds a little and generates negative experience, for it allows the recipient to see himself in a relatively favorable light, even while he may privately question the candor and genuineness of the other's response—which response may well have been phrased so as not to preclude these questionings.

III

Although negative experiences have some bearing on what occurs within offstage, face-to-face encounters, the central locus, I believe, of this sort of experience is to be found in pure performances—for example, exhibition sports, such as wrestling and roller derby, and dramatic scriptings, whether live, taped, photographed, written, or drawn. Although spontaneous, easy involvement is a crucial feature of ordinary encounters, there can yet be many good reasons for continuing along in one in spite of disaffection. But in the case of pure performances, engrossment is not merely an indicator of how well things are going, but by definition is also the main issue: the performer is charged with inducing it, and the audience expects to enjoy it. Therefore, in these shows any device that recaptures attention, or at least demonstrates that the uninvolving events in progress are not the real performance, has a special value. Here, note, a particular kind of frame break will largely figure, the kind that therapists and interrogators exploit when they verbally and calmly draw attention away from the anticipated story line to the framing mechanisms presupposed in its maintenance; in brief, self-referencing *reflexive* frame breaks. For although a performer can run out of lively traditional materials, he cannot want for one particular out-of-frame resource—his own current effort to stage a production.

In considering the organization of negative experience in pure performances, one element of frames at a time can be examined.

1. *The Brackets:* Given that contests and dramatic scriptings typically have clear-cut brackets—both temporal and spatial—

producers can generate negative experience for the audience by doing violence to these boundaries. Initial interpretations of what it is that is occurring can thus be built up and discredited, and such reservations and distances that had been generated can be involvingly breached.

Begin by looking at what Pirandello does with temporal brackets. (Since he appears to have set the pattern for so much of contemporary exploitation of frame, I propose to draw on him at length.) *Tonight We Improvise* is the model: [13]

> *Punctually at the hour designated for the performance, the* LIGHTS *in the theatre go down and the* FOOTLIGHTS *on stage softly come up.*
>
> *The audience, unexpectedly plunged into darkness, is at first attentive. Then, not hearing the buzzer that usually announces the parting of the curtains, they begin to rustle about in their seats. And all the more because on stage, through the closed* CURTAINS, *confused and excited voices are heard—as though the actors were protesting about something, and someone else, reprimanding them, was trying to restore order and silence the uproar.*

A GENTLEMAN FROM THE ORCHESTRA: (*Looks around and loudly asks.*) What's happening up there?
ANOTHER FROM THE BALCONY: Sounds like a fight.
A THIRD FROM A BOX: Maybe it's all part of the show.[14]

---

13. Pirandello uses three main formats for raising the issue of appearance and reality, the issue of frame. In one, illustrated by *Henry IV* and *The Rules of the Game*, the traditional respect for projected characters is sustained. In the second, *Six Characters in Search of an Author*, the conventional performer-character formula is attacked, but the attack stops at the stage line. In the third, this line between onstage and auditorium is breached in various ways.

14. Luigi Pirandello, *Tonight We Improvise* (London: Samuel French, 1932), pp. 7–8 (first performed 1930). Of course, the trick is not new, as Anne Righter tells us:

> Jonson's *Love Restored* (1612) begins with the arrival of Masquerado before the King to announce that there will be no masque. The various altercations which follow pretend to be unrehearsed, events accidentally overheard by the spectators. It is the old device of French farce, of Lyndsay's banns for the *Thrie Estaits*, or the servants' dialogue which begins *Fulgens and Lucres*. The play denies its own nature; it pretends to share the reality of its audience. [*Shakespeare and the Idea of the Play* (London Chatto & Windus, 1964), pp. 204–205.]

Jarry, Apollinaire, the Surrealists, and the Dadaists also made much use of French tricks before or contemporaneously with Pirandello, as did, of course, Brecht.

(*But the* CURTAINS *do not part. The* BUZZER *instead is heard still again. To this, from the back of the theatre, the irritated voice of the director,* DR. HINKFUSS, *is heard replying. He violently pulls open the door at the back and angrily hurries down the aisle that divides in two the rows of the orchestra.*)

DR. HINKFUSS: *Why* the *buzzer? Why* the *buzzer?* Who ordered it rung? I'll order it, I alone, when it's time to. (*These words are shouted by* DR. HINKFUSS *as he comes down the aisle and climbs the three steps that join stage to orchestra. . . .*) I am deeply grieved by the momentary confusion the audience must have noticed going on behind the curtains just now, and I must ask their indulgence— though perhaps after all I might be said to wish it all to be taken as a sort of involuntary prologue—

THE GENTLEMAN FROM THE ORCHESTRA: (*Delightedly interrupting.*) Ah, there! Didn't I say so myself?
DR. HINKFUSS: (*With cold severity*) What is it that the gentleman wishes to observe? . . .
THE GENTLEMAN FROM THE ORCHESTRA: That those noises on stage were all part of the show.[15]

Shifting from the legitimate stage to radio, one finds, of course, the famous box of tricks employed by Orson Welles in his *War of the Worlds*, including a bracketing device: a weather report was given and then the audience was taken to "Ramon Raquello and his orchestra in the Meridian Room of the Park Plaza in New York," during which a series of station interruptions brought the story into being. Thus, Welles caught his first listeners not yet ready to bring the theatrical frame to what they were listening to. They were presumably waiting for the Welles show to begin.[16] Contemporary novelists employ a similar device: by using a false prefatory publisher's note, or the kind of preface suitable for documentary, case record, biography, or autobiography, the writer can induce a wrong set on the part of the reader, a deceptive frame that will eventually be cleared, ensuring an active negative experience during the process. A book review by Whitney Balliett provides some examples:

---

15. Pirandello, *Tonight We Improvise*, pp. 8–9.
16. An LP of the broadcast is available. The basic report is Hadley Cantril, *The Invasion from Mars* (Princeton, N.J.: Princeton University Press, 1940).

The non-novel is a dodge, a masquerade, an act of feigned shyness. It may be written in diary form or as a series of letters or as a tale told by a narrator over port and biscuits. It may be a "memoir," discovered after its "author's" death and edited by a "friend." It may be a prolonged dream or nightmare, or it may be told through the dishevelled senses of an idiot or a madman. It may, like Nabokov's "Pale Fire"—surely the most fancy-footed non-novel ever written—be a poem surrounded by extensive footnotes. No matter which mask the non-novel dons, its evasiveness and assembling paradoxically call twice as much attention to its author. Such is certainly true of "Appendix A" (Macmillan), an elaborately arranged non-novel by the poet Hayden Carruth. The charade begins with a "publisher's note":

> Although this document was written in fulfillment of a prior contractual obligation, it would not have come to the attention of the publishers if it had not been through the agency of persons acting in what may best be described as a semiofficial capacity. It is now, in fact, part of a subdepartmental dossier in the files of a state bureau of public health. No illegality, or any improbity whatever, is attached to its publication, but considerations of private sensibility nevertheless dictate that no further identification be made. The reasons for publishing it in this uncorrected state will be, we hope, evident to those who read it. Publication has been arranged with the author's knowledge, and by the kind permission of Mr. Geoffrey Whicher Carruth, Crossington, Ohio.[17]

---

17. Whitney Balliett, in *The New Yorker*, January 4, 1964. Another case in point is the use of the diary device in Alberto Moravia's *The Lie*. It might be added that if some readers are to discover this sort of put-on slowly, which seems to be the optimal arrangement, other readers are very likely to be totally taken in:

> Grove Press has been getting complaints from booksellers and readers over Stephen Schneck's "The Nightclerk." Grove rushes to all concerned this explanation: " 'The Nightclerk' is an unusual book, so unusual that it starts on page 9, in the middle of a sentence. That is the way the author wrote it—and so this is the way we publish it. Your copies have not been incorrectly bound!" [*San Francisco Chronicle*, November 1, 1965.]

In the social science literature the few efforts at satire (such as Edgar Borgatta's "Sidesteps Toward a Nonspecial Theory," *Psychological Review*, LXI [1954]: 343–352) all seemed to have generated requests for reprints by scholars who took the writing seriously.

A nice line is to be drawn between novelists who expect their readers to discover the fabrication, or at least to entertain appreciable doubt, and those free-lance psychologists and psychiatrists who present case-history

Another example, this time from a musical performance, is Karlheinz Stockhausen's *Hymnen;* it begins with taped sounds of static—a classic nonperformance sound—which later, retrospectively, turns out to have been the beginning of the piece.

A model here is George MacDonald Fraser's *Flashman: From the Flashman Papers, 1839–1842,* a "biography" which is halfway between a corrective hoax and a satire. The inside jacket material sets a prefatory tone that is consistently maintained, and a considerable time is ordinarily necessary before the reader's suspicions are formed and hardened:

> Soldier, lover, duelist, imposter, coward, and hero (worthy of a full four inches in *Who's Who*), Harry Flashman had his inglorious beginnings in literature as the drunken bully expelled from Rugby School in *Tom Brown's School Days*. From then onward, however, the whereabouts of this Victorian rake remained cloaked in secrecy. Fortuitously, in 1965, at a sale of household furniture in England, one of the great literary finds of the century was unearthed. There, stored in a tea chest and carefully wrapped in oilskin covers, lay a great mass of manuscript known as the Flashman Papers.
>
> Written in old age by the arch-cad himself, these personal memoirs—now arranged and edited by George MacDonald Fraser —follow Flashman's early career from his expulsion from Rugby through his service with Lord Cardigan's hussars to his ignoble participation in the historic retreat from Kabul.[18]

Terminal brackets can be exploited, too, of course. Thus in the performance of Schadrin's Concerto for Orchestra No. 1, the piece apparently ends, the conductor turns to take a bow, the

---

books on fashionable deviancy, with the fictional, or at best composite, character of the subjects very inconspicuously noted, the rest of the text leading the reader to falsely assume he is learning about particular persons. A good example is Theodore Isaac Rubin's *In the Life* (New York: Macmillan, 1961).

18. *Flashman: From the Flashman Papers, 1839–1842,* edited and arranged by George MacDonald Fraser (New York: World Publishing Company, 1969). I here cite the work according to its avowed title, but, in fact, editorial conventions do not cover the case. Straight citation makes me help with the joke; quotation marks, which have as one of their editorial meanings that the enclosed identity is self-claimed and not to be credited, would warn the reader properly but constitute an incorrect citation. Interestingly, some of the reviewers gave a straight notice to the book, some gave the joke away, and some carried on in the put-on vein.

orchestra rises, and then the pianist begins the real ending, which the rest of the orchestra soon helps to complete. In the Dadaist Daumal's play *En Gggarrded,* a voice from the audience is scripted to be heard *after* the curtain comes down.[19]

2. *The Character-audience line:* Here to be considered is the exploitation of "direct address."[20] A performer who has taken, or will take, on a character cuts across the footlights before or after curtain call to say something purportedly outside the script to the audience directly in what appears to be open communication out of character. Similarly, there can be an effort to simulate a breaking through by an actor purporting to *be* the director or the playwright, not merely *in* the character of the director or playwright. Acceptance of what he says about the script is thus obtained at the cost of increased distance from what is now taken to be the script itself. From this it should be plain that novelists may attempt a similar technique, as when they switch from a conventional mode of presentation to some sort of direct address. John Barth provides an example:

> The reader! You dogged, uninsultable, print-oriented bastard, it's you I'm addressing, who else, from inside this monstrous fiction.

---

19. Reported in Gary Alan Fine, "Audience and Actor" (unpublished paper, University of Pennsylvania, 1970).

20. Direct address in pre-Shakespearean drama in the West was implanted in a specialized role, that of clown or fool. As suggested, later drama was characterized by the curtailment of this mode of action, not the invention of it. Indeed, even Greek plays (especially the comedies) used direct address. The Greeks also used frame breaks. Aristophanes' *Peace* provides an example in connection with the practice of hoisting a player up above the setting for a grand aerial effect:

TRYGAEUS (*exposing himself*): I am fitted with a rudder in case of need, and my Naxos beetle will serve me as a boat.
LITTLE DAUGHTER: And what harbour will you put in at?
TRYGAEUS: Why, is there not the harbour of Cantharus at the Piraeus?
LITTLE DAUGHTER: Take care not to knock against anything and so fall off into space; once a cripple, you would be a fit subject for Euripides, who would put you into a tragedy.
TRYGAEUS (*as the Machine hoists him higher*): I'll see to it. Good-bye! (*To the Athenians*) You, for love of whom I brave these dangers, do ye neither fart nor crap for the space of three days, for, if, while cleaving the air, my steed should scent anything, he would fling me head foremost from the summit of my hopes.
[Whitney J. Oates and Eugene O'Neill, Jr., eds., *The Complete Greek Drama,* vol. 2 (New York: Random House, 1938), pp. 675–676.]

You've read me this far, then? Even this far? For what discredit-able motive? How is it you don't go to a movie, watch TV, stare at a wall, play tennis with a friend, make amorous advances to the person who comes to your mind when I speak of amorous ad-vances? Can nothing surfeit, saturate you, turn you off? Where's your shame?[21]

Nightclub routines of the Don Rickles variety employ the same principle in the form of audience insults, that is, direct address-ing of a member of the audience; this is done outside the periods, if any, conventionally established for this purpose or at a level of intimacy and derogation inappropriate for overheard talk.[22] In effect, the recipient of the frame-breaking remark is forced into the role of performer, forced sometimes to project a character. He, in consequence, floods out, and this provides a source of involvement for the remaining members of the audience.

So, too, the impression can be created that a member of the audience is directly addressing the characters or the production, as when stooges are planted in the audience and scripted to disrupt on cue. Again Pirandello provides examples, although more popular ones could be drawn on, such as Olsen and John-son's production of *Hellzapoppin*.

Scripted breaching of the performer-audience line is a feature of many different kinds of performance: even the circus can provide an example, as a recent student of the life suggests:

> In the development of a given act we can identify progressive phases very close to the pattern of successive transformations that take place in folktales. . . .
> This is always true of any basic act. But there are more sophisti-cated patterns in which we see at work a transformation or a series

---

21. John Barth, *Lost in the Fun House* (New York: Doubleday & Com-pany, 1968), p. 127.
22. To a latecomer, for example: "Sit down, you dumb broad, or we'll bid on you." The *unscripted* version of this frame break has apparently oc-curred from time to time in the musical world. An article on bad manners of audiences in *Time*, January 21, 1966, provides examples:

> Classical Guitarist Andrés Segovia recently stopped a performance in Chicago, whipped out an enormous handkerchief, and honked and wheezed along with the audience. Jascha Heifetz prefers the withering glare or, if things get too bad, departure. The late Sir Thomas Beecham was even less subtle, once whirled on the podium and roared: "Shut up, you fools!"

of transformations by inversion as are often found in folktales. For instance, as the speaker announces a girl acrobat, a drunken sailor causes a disturbance in the audience, starts an argument with the speaker, ends up in the ring (where he can hardly stand), claims that a sailor knows better than the girl how to climb a rope, scares away the circus people called for help by the speaker, and begins the ascent towards the trapeze. Up there, he behaves as a man who has never touched a trapeze in his life—and if he does not fall down it seems to be due to mere luck. Then suddenly he makes a beautiful one-foot balance, gets rid of his sailor outfit and is introduced as the greatest equilibrist in the world—the acrobatics start and the act is carried out according to the usual pattern.[23]

3. *The Role-character formula:* Here is one of the most common forms of intentionally generated negative experience. The individual, in the guise of the character he is performing, comments on himself as performer or upon his fellow performers, or in other ways draws attention to what he ought not to be able to draw attention to—the role-character formula. A reflexive frame break—a mixing of levels of being—results.

Perhaps the central figure here is the fool:

> The fool actor can in this way call reality into question, or even dissolve it, because of the queer nature of the reality he has for us as a person. (As we have seen, his role as a fool actor tends again and again to collapse, with the result that he simply presents what

---

23. Paul A. R. Bouissac, "The Circus as a Multimedia Language," *Language Sciences,* no. 11 (August 1970), p. 6. The parallel here is to the competency surprise employed in movies, as when a character played by Don Ameche tries to persuade a character played by Sonja Henie that it is safe to follow him out on the ice. American movies, unlike European ones, can also feature second-language competency in these upset surprises, although no doubt casting is easier if the concealed competence is to involve tap dancing, singing, judo, and other American arts. Of course, in the right circumstances, of which an example was provided in the life of Samuel Taylor Coleridge, writing will do, too:

> Thence he proceeded to Jesus Coll., Camb., in 1791 where he read much but desultorily, and got into debt. The troubles arising thence and also, apparently, a disappointment in love, led to his going to London and enlisting in the 15th Dragoons under the name of Silas Tomkyn Comberbacke. He could not, however, be taught to ride, and through some Latin lines written by him on a stable door, his real condition was discovered, his friends communicated with, and his release accomplished, his brothers buying him off. [John W. Cousin, *A Short Biographical Dictionary of English Literature* (New York: E. P. Dutton & Co., 1933), p. 89.]

he is in a way more immediate than that of formal drama.) As a person he is sometimes *too much there,* the clod who gets in the way of nonfools as he asserts himself, coarsely indifferent to the conventions of either reality or the imitation of it. He is also sometimes too *little* there. He is often "not all there" with respect to intelligence or sanity. . . .[24]

An obvious example of role-character breaching is the use made by TV and film of "typecasting." As is well known, an actor often becomes identified with the parts he has played, even while these parts are selected in confirmation of prior effective castings. Near the end of his career, when his typecasting has become maximally established, he will sometimes lend himself to comic turns in which he plays a takeoff on "himself," an incongruous part for someone of his own typecasting to perform.[25]

One current version of this turning upon oneself is illustrated in children's TV shows wherein becostumed chimpanzees play cut-down versions of popular television offerings, inducing the audience to teeter on the edge of becoming involved in what approaches fairly closely an ordinary production.[26] Another standard version is the mime nightclub act employing gesture dubbing: a recording is presented of a well-known voice whose owner is identified with well-known physiognomic features, and on the stage the performer mimes the words, thus managing to attach an impossible body to the voice or an impossible voice to the body.[27] (There is a parallel in private fun in the practice of

---

24. William Willeford, *The Fool and His Scepter* (Evanston, Ill.: Northwestern University Press, 1969), p. 56.

25. There is also a serious version of the same attack. Thus in the movie *I Walk the Line,* Gregory Peck begins the part of sheriff, playing the morally solid hero he, Gregory Peck, has become for his public. Gradually the sheriff becomes disorganized by a passion for someone improper to his age station. The effect of his downfall draws on the prior stereotype established by and for Peck in his previous films. Here see the review by Jacob Brackman, "Films," *Esquire,* January 1970, pp. 44 and 162.

26. Reviewed in *Life,* October 2, 1970. A comparison could be made to comedy which features a man in ape's clothing, but not aptly. Fake apes are meant to fool other characters in the plot, both persons and "real" apes, and build up to an explosive comic disclosure. Real apes dressed in human garb are not meant to take anyone in but rather to provide a humorous inversion of the cosmological line dividing us from them.

27. The harlequin-hermaphrodite theme in clown shows, comic movies, homosexual bar shows, and the like is another case in point. Here see Willeford, *The Fool,* pp. 179–187. A static version is provided in cut-out

"taking off" someone.) In these cases a character gets built up and tumbled continuously, resulting in a corresponding flooding out of the audience. (Beatrice Lillie employed a like device in her famous routine of performing, in a long formal gown, a well-known aria sung "straight" and almost passably, and then, when the audience had begun to wonder how to take this, lifting up her skirts and roller-skating off the stage, a retrospective collapse of role following in her wake.) Something similar seemed to be achieved in those old-fashioned party games in which a blind-folded person was led to do something that seemed to him reasonable but for the seeing others clearly out of character, a forced clowning based upon automatically generated, unwittingly inappropriate acts.[28]

An elegant example of role-character breaching is to be found in sophisticated ventriloquist shows. As in the case of the Piran-dello device of having a character expand on the mechanism by which a performer is changed into a character, the dummy is caused to develop a character in the interaction with the ventrilo-quist and is then made to turn upon himself as merely a poor dummy, discussing with the audience the unreality of his person-ality—something that ought not to be possible for a real dummy —thereby acquiring a special status in the teeth of his actual one, or at least undercutting the established reservation the audience has in regard to the part before them. Thus, dummy to audience:

> "He's pretty good, isn't he? He isn't moving his mouth."
> "No ventriloquist can say potato without moving his lips, can he?"
> (Then repeats this louder and louder in what amounts to a folk presentation of Epimenides' paradox.)[29]

---

photography at fun fairs, a subject posing his head above the neck of a plasterboard figure radically different in social identity from his own.

28. Herb Caen, *San Francisco Chronicle*, April 8, 1966, suggests a public example:

Funniest sight on Postreet the other afternoon: a terribly haughty-look-ing girl, about eight months pregnant swinging snootily down the street, unaware that somebody had pinned to the back of her coat a note read-ing: "I only LOOK smart!"

29. It is interesting to note that although characters in movies, plays, nightclub routines, comic strips, and ventriloquist shows all have been caused by their writers to break frame reflexively and address the audience on the illusionary nature of character status, rarely has a figure in a novel

Although it is certainly possible to find role-character play in a variety of scripted presentations, the legitimate theater, of course, provides the major source. For example, in his play, *We Bombed in New Haven,* Joseph Heller apparently tries to make his political point by reflexive frame breaks, tries, that is, to increase the immediacy of his argument by chivying the audience's situation, as in the following attack on the role-character formula:

HENDERSON: Then how can he be dead and buried?

STARKEY: He wasn't real. I'm not real. I'm pretending, and I'm sure that all of you—(*To the audience, altering the details of his speech to correspond to his actual experience as an actor*)—and all of you out there, have seen me act many, many times before in many different roles. As you know, I've been doing very, very well lately. I've had much bigger parts than this one. I've also made lots more money. But I do like to be involved in serious, important things, when I can find some time between my movies. And that's why I consented to play this part of a captain, for a little while. (*To the men*) Do you understand? (*Bailey and Fisher applaud deadpan. Starkey, missing their sarcasm, is pleased*)

BAILEY: That's the hardest part you ever played.

STARKEY: A captain?

BAILEY: No. An actor. (*The men guffaw*)[30]

And he manages to find an aspect of a white actor that is a functional equivalent of the one Genet found (in *The Blacks*) in a black actor:

STARKEY (*To the audience*): Now, none of this, of course, is really happening. It's a show, a play in a theater, and I'm not really a captain. I'm an actor. (*His voice rises with emotion, as though to drown out the noise of a plane that passes very close and recedes steadily into the distance*) I'm _____ _____ (*He mentions his real name*) You all know that. Do you think that I _____ _____ (*Repeats his real name*) would actually let my son go off to a war and be killed . . . and just stand here talking to you and do nothing? (*An edge of hysteria and grief comes into his voice, as*

---

been caused to do this. Yet there is no reason why a character could not be developed in a novel and then, once lodged, turn upon the reader and talk to him about the illusion that has been created.

30. Joseph Heller, *We Bombed in New Haven* (New York: Dell Publishing Co., 1970), pp. 94–95.

though he knows what is to follow) Of course not! There is no war taking place. (*In the distance, there is the sound of a single, great explosion, and Starkey whimpers and seems on the verge of weeping as he shouts out insistently*) There is no war taking place here now! (*He sags a moment, then continues desperately*) There has never been a war. There never will be a war. Nobody has been killed here tonight. It's only . . . make-believe . . . it's a story . . . a charade . . . a show.[31]

4. *Spectacle-game:* If one examines the devices that showmen employ to attack brackets it becomes plain that what is entailed is a violation of the conventional arrangement between social occasion and the main proceedings, the inner realm, which the occasion can encase. The bridge ordinarily available for crossing from one sphere to the other—houselights, prologue, preface, tuning up—is simply absorbed into the inner doings, forcing the audience to drink out of the handle of their cup. Similarly, an attack on any other specific element of the frame can be extended to a whole episode of framed activity, threatening thereby to flood the game into the spectacle and mingle performer with onlooker, character with theatergoer. For example, once a character begins to address the issue of the performer who is sustaining him, it is a small step to extending the syntactical breach by addressing directly the whole matter of the show under presentation.

The so-called theater of the absurd provides many examples of this totalistic attack—in fact, so many that one might better call it the theater of frames. Thus Genet in his interesting play *The Blacks:*

ARCHIBALD: Be quiet. (*to the audience*): This evening we shall perform for you. But in order that you may remain comfortably settled in your seats in the presence of the drama that is already unfolding here, in order that you be assured that there is no danger of such a drama's worming its way into your precious lives, we shall even have the decency—a decency learned from you—to make communication impossible. We shall increase the distance that separates us—a distance that is basic—by our pomp, our manners, our insolence—for we are also actors. When my speech is over, every-

---

31. *Ibid.*, pp. 218–219. Pirandello uses the "real-name-trick" also; Welles, in the Mars broadcast, increased realism by using real place names for the landing site, university laboratory, etc.

thing here—(*he stamps his foot in a gesture of rage*) here!—will take place in the delicate world of reprobation.[32]

ARCHIBALD: To us, too. They tell us that we're grown-up children. In that case, what's left for us? The theater! We'll play at being reflected in it, and we'll see ourselves—big black narcissists—slowly disappearing into its waters.[33]

ARCHIBALD: You think you love her. You're a Negro and a performer. Neither of whom will know love. Now, this evening—but this evening only—we cease to be performers, since we are Negroes. On this stage, we're like guilty prisoners who play at being guilty.[34]

It should be noted that when a character comments on a whole episode of activity *in frame terms,* he acquires a peculiar reality through the same words by which he undermines the one that was just performed.

Thus in N. F. Simpson's *A Resounding Tinkle,* the second scene opens with a performer in the character of the author coming before the front of the undrawn curtain and engaging in a lengthy disquisition beginning:

I agree. A pretty epileptic start. We're going to see what we can do in the next scene about pulling the thing together. Because this

---

32. Jean Genet, *The Blacks: A Clown Show,* trans. Bernard Frechtman (New York: Grove Press, 1960), p. 22.

33. *Ibid.,* pp. 46–47.

34. *Ibid.,* p. 47. As suggested, Genet can have his characters point to their color and contrast it with that of the audience, and this color, of course, is a feature also of the performer underneath the character. So the dramatic frame is pierced by a sliver of reality and the audience is made to see that for us color status (as with age and gender) can cut deeper than the difference between character and performer. Gelber, in *The Connection,* must fake fixing, so his performers are merely acting, although the music performed is real and is played by real musicians who are billed under their own names. (But, of course, the term "real" gets tricky here. Real music happens to be itself entirely suited for performance before an audience and is thus, incidentally, well suited to unsettling of this kind. So real here isn't quite real. Someone not a professional musician who took the role of one and played music on the stage would still have to be able to really play music. If a play has a part for a juggler and the character taking this part illustrates his art on the stage, he must really be proficient in juggling to do so. But if a character merely talks about playing music or juggling as being his profession, then nothing "real" happens except the competent use of English speech. In any case, note that although the color of actors is "real," the relevance of this, and thus its reality, is purely social; it is thinkable that someday "color" will mean only complexion.)

isn't at all of course how I wrote the play. You must have realized that.[35]

And before that the characters have commented on the play:

MR. PARADOCK. My lines seem to be coming to me in bits. Or what seem to be bits. This is like some unspecified milk of paradise.
MRS. PARADOCK. What you can't remember you can make up.
MR. PARADOCK. And what I can't make up can go unsaid.
MRS. PARADOCK. No one minds with this kind of play. No one notices. You can be eight sheets in the wind or whatever it is practically from the word Go and the more the merrier from the author down. Or up. So don't for God's sake start having any qualms over remembering your lines or anybody else's lines. Just put it down to the ambrosia. Let ambrosia look after it.[36]

Here the critical reservations of the audience are taken right into the play—expropriated—leaving them without the usual defense against a play, unsure about the feelings they are supposed to have, and unsure about their judgment that they are watching a bad play. Beckett uses a similar device: his characters comment in passing on the task they must perform, namely, putting on a play.[37] Jack Gelber's *The Connection* provides another set of standard efforts to attack a theatrically framed episode. The play opens with real musicians practicing onstage and characters in the guise of the play's director and author entering from the audience aisles, talking as if things had not yet begun. And throughout there are comments such as the following:

JIM [producer]: Stop it kids. We haven't begun yet. I'm not finished. Turn those lights down.[38]

JIM: This word magician here has invented me for the sole purpose of explaining that I and this entire evening on stage are merely a fiction. And don't be fooled by anything anyone else tells you. Except the jazz. As I've said, we do stand by the authenticity of that improvised art. But as for the rest it has no basis in naturalism. None. Not a bit. Absol——[39]

35. (London: Faber & Faber, 1968), p. 29.
36. *Ibid.*, p. 11.
37. See the discussion in Hugh Kenner, *Samuel Beckett* (New York: Grove Press, 1961), "Life in the Box," pp. 133–165.
38. Jack Gelber, *The Connection* (New York: Grove Press, 1960), p. 18.
39. *Ibid.*, p. 19.

JIM: Why don't we do the whole play in the dark? There's an idea for you, Jaybird.[40]

JAY BIRD: (*Enters from the audience*) Cut it! Cut it! You are murdering the play. What are you doing? Let's go over it again. You're to give the whole plot in the first act. So far not one of you has carried out his dramatic assignment.[41]

ERNIE: Stop it. Shit! Shit! I don't trust any of you. Yes, I've tied everything into nice small packages for you. You can go home and say that Ernie really knows. Boy, he really can rip things apart. Shit. Do you hear? I don't trust one son of a bitch here or in the audience. Why? Because I really don't believe any of you understand what this is about. You're stupid. Why are you here? Because you want to see someone suffer. You want to laugh at me? You don't want to know me. And these people? Sam doesn't care about me or my music when it comes right down to it. . . . Where's Cowboy? Where is he? That bastard better come back. It's no use. No use. I want my money. Where is my pay? We're supposed to be paid. Jaybird, where's my pay? I'll kill you. Do you hear?[42]

The intermission—that is, the internal brackets—is itself exploited:

JIM: Huh? Good people, do not be intimidated by any of these boys during the intermission. No matter what they tell you they will be turned on a scientifically accurate amount of heroin in the next act. And that is their payment for the performance, excluding the money made on the movie. Also, we are selling some Turkish delight [and whatever else that is sold] in the lobby. Now . . . anyone in the audience for a smoke?
(*Lights slowly fade.*)[43]

---

40. *Ibid.*, p. 21.
41. *Ibid.*, p. 33.
42. *Ibid.*, pp. 47–48.
43. *Ibid.*, pp. 53–54. There are also many efforts by less well-known dramatists to disrupt the self-enclosed coherence of the inner realm of a play. The following excerpt from a review by Kenneth Tynan illustrates:

The setting looks like a fragment of eroded rampart, or a magnified slice of stale and curling toast. On to it there wander two actors, casually deploring the play in which they are to appear. . . . They resent having to repeat the same inconsequential snatches of dialogue night after night. "If there were a point," Mr. Foster remarks, "all this would be beside it."
They are joined by a blonde actress whose interest in the production is peripheral at best, since no one has told her what to do. . . . With the

Movies also occasionally feature a violation of the realm of being that movies themselves try to establish. For example, there is the gimmick of having a character comment on the brief "personal" appearance of a well-known star, referring to him by his "actual" name. Sophisticated producers have drawn on the Brecht pattern of drawing attention periodically to the fictive character of the whole, so that the audience isn't allowed too long a period for holding one set of laminations. A film critic thusly describes Lester's *How I Won the War:*

> For instance, a blimpish colonel gives the lieutenant a gung-ho speech in a dugout. When the camera pulls back at the end of his exhortation, the dugout—suddenly—is on stage, and the curtain descends as the colonel finishes roundly. (Lester does not leave it there. The audience in that theater is sparse and the applause is slack.) A number of incidents are swiftly replayed in different settings as in a spoof of *Marienbad.* The music yawns scoffingly: whenever we cut back to these bedraggled desert rats, we get a swell of grandiose Oriental goo on the sound track in *Lawrence of Arabia* style. And we are continually reminded that the whole thing is a film. When one of the men is hysterical, another soldier turns to the audience and says angrily, "Take that camera out of here," and we flash to a shot of two cockney biddies in a cinema watching the awful scene comfily. At the end, as the war is finishing, two soldiers discuss what they are going to do next and think they may get work in a film that is going to be made about Vietnam. (There is a marked difference here from the "film-consciousness" of *Persona.* In the latter, Bergman reminds us that we and he are involved in a film. But Lester tells us that we, he, *and the actors* know that it's a film.)[44]

Godard makes much use of frame-discrediting breaks, too. A statement is available in a useful essay on the director by Susan Sontag:

---

advent of the author (a restless, high-voltage performance by Michael Bryant) and the actor engaged for the hermit's role, things get really perplexing. Mr. Foster conducts a running dispute with Mr. Bryant, arguing—among other things—that it is useless to argue with one's author, since he can always win. [Review of James Saunders' *Next Time I'll Sing to You* (an "anti-play"), in *The Observer Week End Review* (London), January 27, 1963.]

44. Stanley Kauffmann, "Looking at Films," in *New American Review,* no. 2 (New York: New American Library, 1968), p. 167.

Such procedures tend, of course, to reinforce the self-reflexive and self-referring aspect of Godard's films, for the ultimate narrative presence is simply the fact of cinema itself; from which it follows that, for the sake of truth, the cinematic medium must be made to manifest itself before the spectator. Godard's methods for doing this range from the frequent ploy of having an actor make rapid playful asides to the camera (i.e., to the audience) in mid-action, to the use of a bad take—Anna Karina fumbles a line, asks if it's all right, then repeats the line—in *A Woman Is a Woman*. *Les Carabiniers* only gets underway after we hear first some coughing and shuffling and an instruction by someone, perhaps the composer or a sound technician, on the set. In *La Chinoise*, Godard makes the point about its being a movie by, among other devices, flashing the clapper board on the screen from time to time, and by briefly cutting to Raoul Coutard, the cameraman on this as on most of Godard's films, seated behind his apparatus.[45]

---

45. Susan Sontag, "Godard," in her *Styles of Radical Will* (New York: Dell Publishing Co., Delta Books, 1970), pp. 169–170. That what one has here is simply a managed device is clearly expressed by Sontag in the lines that continue:

> But then one immediately imagines some underling holding another clapper while that scene was shot, and someone else who had to be there behind another camera to photograph Coutard. It's impossible ever to penetrate behind the final veil and experience cinema unmediated by cinema. [p. 170]

Sontag only fails to note that this evidence of bad faith holds not merely for Godard and not merely for tricky filmmakers but for anyone in any frame who tries to convey something about the character of the frame he is employing; the posture he thereby assumes inevitably denies awareness of the frame in which *that* posture is struck. (And this holds as well for one whose intent is to direct attention to this effect.) The actor describing himself acting necessarily engages in an act he cannot include in the description; he can appear to succeed in the try but cannot then describe the trying; he can try to describe trying to describe himself describing, but then there is another try that characterizes him and escapes his description. And if in an effort to manifest whatever good faith is possible under the circumstances, he candidly allows that it is impossible for him to really capture the posture required to posture, then this allowance, too, cannot incorporate the posture which produced it.

Here, perhaps, is the deeper reason why the term "sincere" has a contradictory application, referring both to someone who can intentionally give the impression that he is without guile and reserve (as a stage actor in character might) and to someone who *is* without guile and reserve. For any expression which conveys that the actor is a straight shooter, a simple, open man, must itself be a bit of effective expression, something that may provide valid evidence of straightforwardness, but need not, as stage actors acclaimed for their sincerity demonstrate.

Trintignant, with a script by Robbe-Grillet, provides a further example in a film called *Trans-Europ-Express:*

> Screenwriter Alain Robbe-Grillet gets onto the Paris-Antwerp express with his wife and a friend. A guy skulks through the station, onto the train, glumphs into their compartment, abruptly gets up and vanishes as if being trailed.
>
> "That was Trintignant," one of the trio remarks, using the actor's real name. "I wonder what he's doing here?"
>
> Robbe-Grillet turns to his friend: "Let's make a movie about the Trans-Europ-Express and the drug traffic."
>
> And off they go, the camera following Jean-Louis Trintignant to Antwerp, around Antwerp, and back to Paris, while the camera cuts occasionally to the Robbe-Grillet trio still on the Antwerp-bound train discussing how the film is developing.[46]

Just as a frame-directed remark can function as an attack upon a particular transformation, so remarks can be designed to provide a sequence of possible shifts, the negative experience deriving from simulated multiple frame clearances. Here once again Pirandello is the master:

> THE CHARACTER ACTRESS: And just what should I do then? *Pretend* to hit you? I haven't a written part to play. My lines come from here (*She makes a gesture from the stomach up.*) and I do not stand on ceremony, understand? You'll grab at me, and I'll let you have it.

---

46. Walter F. Naedele, *The Evening Bulletin* (Philadelphia), October 10, 1968. These effects should be distinguished from the frame-consistent effort to make a movie about the making of a movie. Thus, François Truffaut's *Day for Night* makes much point of extending the focus of the ultimate camera so that we can see the placement of "lights" and "cameras" in the "production" of many of the scenes in the film within the film, along with sync slate and retakes. But the in-frame effort of the "director" to draw the necessary effort from the "actors" and the "production crew," and the personal entanglements of these participants with one another is never breached. We are shown how snow is produced for a scene but not how the scene was produced in which snow is shown being produced. More important, the film within the film is shown only in bits and pieces, a realistic enough device, but one that incidentally assures that we will not get caught up in the inner show. That the actual director of the actual film also plays a part in the film, that this part is that of director, and that this director represents Truffaut, is merely a minor conceit; he could equally have selected someone else to play himself, or used a fictive instead of autobiographical model, or (as Welles was wont to do) use himself to play the character of someone other than a director of movies. (Nor was every frame-containable complication exploited. The film within the film was a domestic drama; it could have been about the making of a film.)

DR. HINKFUSS [the "director"]: Ladies and gentlemen, ladies and gentlemen, not here in front of the audience, please.

THE CHARACTER ACTRESS: We're already in our parts, Dr. Hinkfuss.

. . . .

DR. HINKFUSS: But does it seem possible to you to have it done this way? In a chaos before the curtain and outside of the scenery?

THE CHARACTER ACTRESS: It does not matter. It does not matter.

DR. HINKFUSS: What do you mean it does not matter? Just what do you expect the audience to think?

THE LEADING ACTOR: They'll get it. They'll get it all the better this way. Leave it all up to us. We're all in character already.

THE CHARACTER ACTRESS: Everything will seem—you must believe it —much easier and more natural this way. None of the problems and restraints of a set place and action. We'll not forget to do everything you've planned for this evening. . . .

. . . .

THE CHARACTER ACTRESS: Just look at him [the Leading Character] whistle, look at him! (*Then, coming out of character, to* DR. HINK-FUSS) Everything's going like clockwork, isn't it?

DR. HINKFUSS: (*With a wicked little gleam in his eye, finding here a way to get out of his predicament and save his battered prestige.*) As the audience must already have guessed, this rebellion against my orders among the actors was faked, agreed on in advance between them and me, in order to make the performance seem more authentic. (*At this underhanded getaway, the* ACTORS *stop and stare at him suddenly, like so many mannequins, in various poses of astonishment.* DR. HINKFUSS *notices it at once. He turns and looks at them and then points them out to the audience.*) Faked, too, this astonishment.

THE LEADING ACTOR: (*Trembling with indignation.*) A dirty trick! The audience must not believe a word of it. My protest was not in any way faked. (*He pushes back the green curtain as at first and strides off angrily.*)

DR. HINKFUSS: (*At once, confidently to the audience.*) Acting, acting, all acting, even this outburst.[47]

As already suggested, it would be a mistake to think that only modern playwrights—beginning, say, with the Dadaists—resort to an attack on the arrangement under which a dramatized realm is sustained, with a view to the production of negative experience. The Florentine theater of the seventeenth century instructs in that connection:

---

47. Pirandello, *Tonight We Improvise*, pp. 18–20.

We possess a detailed description of this scenic prank in a letter by the eyewitness Massimiliano Montecuculi to the Duke of Modena, a better and more reliable account, on the whole, than Chantelou's much later one of Bernini's own somewhat faded reminiscences. "When the curtain had fallen, one saw on the stage a flock of people partly real and partly only feigned, who had been so well distributed that they seemed almost to represent those on the other side, who had come in great number to see the comedy." Chantelou supplemented this account by asserting that the crowd on the stage was seated in a "second auditorium" and that there were, in fact, "two theaters." And now Bernini proceeded to strengthen the sense of illusion by inserting two middlemen, themselves spectators of a kind, who saw what the audience beheld, and proclaimed the reality of the two rival theaters. "Upon the scene there were two braggarts [played, so Chantelou asserts, by Bernini himself and his brother] who pretended to draw, paper and pencil in hand, one with his face toward the real, the other toward the fictitious audience." After working in silence for some time, they fell into conversation and came to realize that the group that each of them beheld was deemed illusory by the other; it being their unavowed intent to impair the spectator's awareness of himself and to involve him in a presumably delightful confusion of realities. Then, the time having come for making the best of this theatrical paradox, the two braggarts decided "that they would pull a curtain across the scene and that each would arrange a performance for his own audience alone," of which one, the above-mentioned comedy, was in fact submitted to the real spectators. But Chantelou narrates that "it was interrupted at times by the laughter of those on the other side, as if something very pleasant had been seen and heard" and that, with the second theater out of sight, the sense of reality was now seemingly unimpeachable. At the end the two braggarts reappeared and asked each other how they had fared, whereupon the impresario of the fictitious stage asserted—and thereby rendered the confusion complete—that he had never shown anything more than the audience itself preparing to leave "with their carriages and horses and accompanied by a great number of lights and torches," a scene which, according to Chantelou, was in fact, exhibited on the stage in the midst of flats or periacts representing the Piazza di San Pietro.[48]

---

48. Richard Bernheimer, "Theatrum Mundi," *The Art Bulletin*, XXXVIII (1956): 243. Cited in part in Righter, *Shakespeare and the Idea of the Play*, pp. 206–207.

It is this sort of stage trickery that provides the best background for understanding such modern theater of frames as Tom Stoppard's *The Real Inspector Hound* (1968), in which the outer stage contains two actors in the character of critics watching a play on an inner stage, some of the "performers" of which are "known" to them personally; gradually the critics are drawn into the play as mistakenly identified protagonists, starting with a telephone call within the inner play which proves to be for one of the critics, who, in accepting the call, crosses over into the inner-stage world, after which the two worlds, outer stage and inner stage, begin to interpenetrate increasingly to the open dismay of the critics.[49]

An obvious method of violating the arrangement between spectacle and game is for managers of a performance occasion to bring together an audience in the conventional way and then follow through with some of the forms of the promised activity but without a traditional performance. The "happening," an emptied entertainment performance current for a couple of years in the sixties, is one example;[50] straight-faced concerts of John Cage's aleatory music are another, wherein all the conventions of a concert are duplicated except for the music content which can appear to the audience to be designed to pointedly assure randomness, that is, avowed mere noise. The creator here is said to have a didactic interest: an audience is presumably made conscious of its own restrictive conventions when it is forced to

---

49. Note that although the Stoppard play is almost entirely a conceit around the notion of a line between character and performer, and character and audience, still, as in Pirandello's *Six Characters*, the play is kept within some of the bounds of the classical form, the real audience-character line scrupulously preserved. But although Stoppard's play presents a play within a play, it is of a radically different order from, say, the one in *Hamlet*. For there is nothing fanciful in the *Hamlet* play within a play. The King's situation and the doctored play-within-a-play merge in a thinkable way, howsoever remote from actual possibility. The two teams in the Stoppard play do not have a realistic basis of merging, and some liberties must be taken (such as open misidentification) to make the whole thing work out. Because *Hamlet* and *The Real Inspector Hound* are merely plays, we tend to lump everything that occurs within them as having the same unreality, when, in fact, some interesting frame differences are to be found.

50. It is hard now to believe that happenings happened. See, for example, Michael Kirby, ed., *Happenings* (New York: E. P. Dutton & Co., 1966).

sustain its side of the bargain, readying itself for the performance proper, only to find that delivery is not made, this failure itself being the intent of the performance. (Actual performances of this kind often do succeed, of course, in driving the audience up and down various keys in their effort to arrive at a viable interpretation of what is being done to them.) In any case, these occasions provide natural experiments in what happens when a spectacle occurs without its game, a social occasion without the inner activity that presumably occasioned it.

Interestingly, the didactic practice of forcing patrons to look at the presuppositions of the activity they are patronizing—including the distinction between social occasions and inner proceedings—was beautifully realized by the psychoanalyst, W. R. Bion, from whose report on group psychotherapy at Tavistock Clinic I cannot forbear to quote at length:

> Early in 1948 the Professional Committee of the Tavistock Clinic asked me to take therapeutic groups, employing my own technique.
>
> . . . .
>
> At the appointed time members of the group begin to arrive; individuals engage each other in conversation for a short time, and then, when a certain number has collected, a silence falls on the group. After a while desultory conversation breaks out again, and then another silence falls. It becomes clear to me that I am, in some sense, the focus of attention in the group. Furthermore, I am aware of feeling uneasily that I am expected to do something. At this point I confide my anxieties to the group, remarking that, however mistaken my attitude might be, I feel just this.
>
> I soon find that my confidence is not very well received. Indeed, there is some indignation that I should express such feelings without seeming to appreciate that the group is entitled to expect something from me. I do not dispute this, but content myself with pointing out that clearly the group cannot be getting from me what they feel they are entitled to expect. I wonder what these expectations are, and what has aroused them.
>
> The friendliness of the group, though sorely tested, enables them to give me some information. Most members have been told that I would "take" the group; some say that I have a reputation for knowing a lot about groups; some feel that I ought to explain what we are going to do; some thought it was to be a kind of seminar, or perhaps a lecture. When I draw attention to the fact that these ideas seem to me to be based on hearsay, there seems to be a

feeling that I am attempting to deny my eminence as a "taker" of groups. I feel, and say, that it is evident that the group had certain good expectations and beliefs about myself, and are sadly disappointed to find they are not true. The group is persuaded that the expectations are true, and that my behaviour is provocatively and deliberately disappointing—as much as to say, I could behave differently if I wanted to, and am only behaving like this out of spite. I point out that it is hard for the group to admit that this could be my way of taking groups, or even that I should be allowed to take them in such a way.[51]

Group psychotherapy seems to be hardly a performance and therefore quite distant from the legitimate stage, but the device here being considered for generating negative experience could carry us further away still. Take academic lecturing. College students in social psychology classes must often forbear an instructor who gives firsthand illustrations by "analyzing" the tittering of his class to his jokes, thereby expropriating the listener's critical response. One example might be cited here, the ending of a valuable paper by Elizabeth Bott, "Psychoanalysis and Ceremony," first presented as an address to a professional association:

> Even in the lecture situation in which we find ourselves, it seems to me there is a ceremonial component. There is some dramatisation of roles, though it is not nearly so complex as in the kava ceremony. There is not much sense of continuity with the unique past history of British society, but there *does* seem to be symbolic expression of unspoken thoughts. I would gather from your presence and your attentiveness that you are here because of sympathetic interest in the subject, but it would be surprising if interest and curiosity were not accompanied by criticism, doubt, and at least some measure of hostility both towards the subject and towards the speakers. Similarly, the speakers experience a complex

---

51. W. R. Bion, *Experiences in Groups* (London: Tavistock Publications, 1961), pp. 29–30. It is interesting that although Bion was wonderfully naughty about denying what, after all, were rather legitimate expectations of the clients who came to his meetings, his publication of the record of this experience is conventional in every degree, following all rules, all expectations of orthography, grammar, etc., and very effectively so. When cut-ups *do* attempt to carry their approach into the orthography of their books (as did, for example, Spike Milligan, John Lennon, Jerry Rubin, and Abbie Hoffman), this irreverence has to be at least as closely edited and proofed as the text of any conventional book.

mixture of feelings. The conventional arrangements of lectures like these—the raised platform, the physical distance between speaker and audience, the loudspeakers, the chairman, the introductions, the applause, the questions—all these are partly necessary for purely practical reasons, but they also provide a setting that both expresses contradictory feelings and keeps them under control.[52]

Recently, of course, there has been an appreciable development of this attack on the lecture frame. In several of the social sciences, instructors have come to occasionally turn their classes into arenas for the display of "group processes," the understanding being that live demonstrations are better than organized lecturing on related topics. In the manner of group psychotherapy, various roles (or "games") can be defined, the instructor directing attention to actual illustrations. The social organization of classroom activity can thus be uncovered, as well, perhaps, as features of discussion groups in general; the trouble is, of course, that that is *all* that can be done. Every topic becomes reduced to one. And incidentally, a lecture does not have to be prepared, nor need criticism of what occurs be treated at face value, since it becomes a topic of consideration, too.[53]

Or, to depart still further from stage performances, take art works of the variety called *trompe l'oeil,* as when an object is painted very realistically and in full scale, or a simulation of the back of a painting is painted, or a package with string torn to reveal a painting, the consequence being that the viewer sees that all along there were frame limits to the subject matter he had expected painters to choose. So, too, pop art products like Roy Lichtenstein's much-mentioned painting titled *"Masterpiece,"* containing male and female comic-strip characters, the latter saying (following statement-balloon conventions), "Why, Brad Darling, this painting is a *Masterpiece!* My, soon you'll have all of *New York* clamoring for your work." Or what for a time was apparently called "the new realism" in art, involving the attach-

52. In J. D. Sutherland, ed., *The Psychoanalytic Approach* (London: Institute of Psychoanalysis by Bailliere, Tindall and Cassell, 1968), p. 76.

53. A self-reported specimen is provided in the opening thirteen pages of "A Curtain Raiser: Transcending the Totalitarian Classroom," in Michael Rossman, *On Learning and Social Change* (New York: Random House, 1972).

ment of domestic artifacts to canvas without regard to the
boundary—the brackets—which usually cuts the artist's statement off from the room in which it is hung.

And by way of a respected frame cartoonist like Saul Steinberg,
one can arrive at comic strips which allow a character to chip up
the bracket line around the cartoon, or talk back to the cartoonist
who has become a figure in the cartoon, or draw characters like
himself who are also drawing characters like him. Indeed, even
quite unfashionable comic strips commonly exhibit Pirandello-
like effects (as in the example which follows), but sophistication
is not ordinarily credited to them:

(2/7/72)   JEFF: In this comic strip you are the straight man
                       and I'm the fall guy—
              MUTT   (jumping up and down with anger on the
                       ice): I AM NOT A STRAIGHT MAN! I AM NOT
                       AN ACTOR. I'M A HUMAN—
              (Mutt falls right through the ice.)
              JEFF   (to a standing block of Mutt-ice): O.K.
                       you're the fall guy. But you look like a
                       straight man to me.
(2/8/72)   (Now walking home from the iced pond.)
              MUTT: This ain't show biz! This is a comic strip!
                       We don't have a straight man and a fall
                       guy. I'm not.
              JEFF: Well, what are we?
              MUTT: We are just two ordinary blood and flesh
                       human beings doing things that ordinary
                       people do!
              JEFF: You mean we are not MAKE BELIEVE, we
                       are REAL PEOPLE?
              MUTT: Well, in a sense YES! We are just as real as
                       Santa Claus.
              JEFF   (in audience or off-partner address): Merry
                       Mutt and Jeff Day![54]

Later we will have to see that in the matter of unaccredited frame
sophistication, ordinary conversation qualifies even more than
ordinary cartoons.

---

54. *The Evening Bulletin* (Philadelphia), February 7 and 8, 1972. Observe that cartoonists, like playwrights and group therapists, can employ
characters who declaim an analysis of the frame as a means of generating
a complete performance. (Peter Handke's play *Offending the Audience* is
a good example—as good as the frame analysis it provides.) Painters,
sculptors, and musicians are less favorably placed in this connection.

IV

The manufacture of negative experience during performances directs attention once again to an important structural feature of framed activities: tracking. Whereas the subordinate tracks are typically taken for granted or carefully kept out of other people's minds, their existence is made an intentional subject for consideration in the cognitive playfulness under discussion. This has already been illustrated in regard to the disattend track. However, illustrations could also have been drawn from the other subordinate tracks.

Take talk shows, for example. Comments ordinarily reserved for collusive communication, that is, for the concealment track, can be provided relatively openly in the form of loud, conspiratorial asides to a confederate, the asides being glaringly obvious to the excolluded. Or self-collusion can be used, this taking the form of widely gesticulated responses employing third-person address in reference to persons who are immediately present. More obviously, backstage maneuverings among characters on the stage can be exposed physically in a sort of cross-sectional view of a fabrication. And, of course, the mechanics of regulating the flow of talk so as to give the appearance of spontaneity can be archly exposed—including use of cue cards, teleprompter, timing signals, and the like.

A favorite exploitation of the directional track is to fake editorial comments. The convention of print, of course, is that howsoever doubtful the body of a text is, and whatsoever its realm status—whether biography, documentary, avowed make-believe, poetry—the footnoted editorial comments will be impeccable in regard to literalness and reliability. (After all, comments about, say, two different versions of a text are openly about *texts* and therefore can be literally true whether the text be a scientific paper or a children's fairy tale.) Now just as an editorial preface can be used to induce temporary deception, so editorial comments in passing can serve the same function. Nabokov's *Pale Fire* is a model in both editorial connections. An epic poem is presented between traditional literary scholarship brackets which allow the poem to be inundated by offstage comments formulated as part of an exegetical key. These comments, quite properly, are restricted to a long forward, an extended commentary, and a glossary-index. (Of course, although we are quite ready to see that what looks like an epic poem is really a parody or insane ramblings, we are much less ready to see that out-of-frame comments on the parody or insanity are themselves a parody or an insanity.) Jorge Luis Borges similarly exploits the device, providing scholarly editorial footnotes to fictive texts in short stories such as "The Garden of Forking Paths," "Pierre Menard, Author of Quixote," and "The Zahir."[55] So, too, do mystery story writers: a documentary or biographical air can be enhanced by using foreign, local, or argot terms and then footnoting an explanation, as if there were some split between editor or compiler and source of textual material—as if, in fact, the editor could slightly undercut the text in the interests of the reader and exactitude. But since the footnoter *is* the writer, and since his fictional characters say whatever he decides they will say, and do this in a context he can manipulate at will in an authorial voice, an exegetical footnote is hardly necessary, except to trick the reader into giving greater realness to the story and knowledgeability to the teller than might be generated by a conventional format.[56] Mark that the exploitation of multiple voices to enhance the apparent authenticity of a text is to be distinguished from the outright guying or satirizing of multiple voice conventions as an end in itself. *That* frame possibility is canonized in the second chapter of Part II of *Finnegans Wake*. For example:

---

55. The three stories are available in translation in his *Labyrinths* (New York: New Directions, 1964). Borges, of course, more than any other modern short story writer, has exploited matters of frame, and is to his form what Pirandello is to his. Dreams, visions, and cautionary tales lose all capacity to keep their subjects in their proper frame place; these figures step out and "real" protagonists step in.

56. For example, Len Deighton in *The Billion Dollar Brain* (New York: G. P. Putnam & Sons, 1966), uses the term *abgeschaltet* on p. 221 and footnotes it thus: "Jargon: *Abgeschaltet* means lit., switched off, unused. To 'surface' someone is to announce their capture or defection. This is often long after it happens." Also he uses the word "friend" and footnotes his usage:

Stok used the word *droog*. While a *tovarich* can be anyone with whom you come into contact even if you hate him, a *droog* is someone who has a special closeness and for whom you might possibly do something against the national interest. [p. 283]

Here are the cottage and the bungalow for the cobbeler and the brandnewburgher:[2]

2. A viking vernacular expression still used in the Summerhill district for a jerryhatted man of forty who puts two fingers into his boiling soupplate and licks them in turn to find out if there is enough mushroom catsup in the mutton broth.

Now one further use of the directional track to generate negative experience. The issue is "connectives." It was argued that connectives are part of the organizational requirements of experience and ordinarily do their work unnoticed, part of the directional track. As suggested, it is in special circumstances that awareness of connectives arises. For example, when a would-be novelist first learns his craft, he must consciously attend to providing connectives without undue repetition or stereotyping. But, of course, jokesters can draw on connectives as a resource. Thus, in the Grove Press edition (1965) of Ionesco's *The Bald Soprano*, pictures of the heads of the figures are used as connectives instead of using the traditional technique of the figure's name followed by a period or colon.[57] In the BBC's *Goon Show* (1952–1960)—a fine source of frame-breaking fun and games now available in typescript[58]—a principal "member" of the troupe, "Bluebottle" (one of the personages played by Peter Sellers), employed the device of saying aloud with an offstage voice what would ordinarily be the parenthetical offstage author's directions for each speech.[59] One episode carried this device one

57. After a page or two of adjustment by the reader, this device serves as well as conventional connectives. The layout of the whole edition is indeed an experimentation with various means of *illustrating* the figures and actions of the play along with the printing of lines.

58. *The Goon Show Scripts*, written and selected by Spike Milligan (London: Woburn Press, 1972).

59. As might be expected, printing a version of this practice creates frame ambiguities. Thus, from the *Goon Show* text:

SEAGOON: Well done, little thrice-adolescent hybrid. Lead me to President Fred's headquarters and this quarter of liquorice all-sorts is yours.

BLUEBOTTLE: Oooh! Licorish! Thinks. I must be careful how many of these I eat. Right, Captain, quick—jump into this cardboard bootbox. Hurriedly wraps up captain in brown paper parcel labelled "Explosives" and stuffs him through headquarters letter box. Jumps on to passing dustcart and

step further: the participants in a dialogue read aloud narrative-like connectives (such as "he said") for each other's turn at talk.[60]

V

Of all the performances that draw on negative experiences none is so accessible to analysis, I believe, as televised wrestling matches (called "exhibitions"). Obviously, the aim of these shows is to involve the audience; just as obviously, frame attacks are employed as a major means of doing so. Wrestling exhibitions, then, can serve as material upon which the analysis so far recommended can be illustrated.[61]

Traditionally, wrestling matches (like boxing matches) were models in the matter of temporal brackets. Conventionally these brackets were marked by ceremony, and ordinarily it would have been unthinkable for a protagonist to begin fighting before the bracketed beginning had occurred or continue after the ending had been established. But, of course, this is exactly what TV wrestlers do.

Traditionally, boxers and wrestlers were in direct address with the audience before and after the match but not in between.[62] Wrestling exhibitions, of course, also attack this assumption, by having both protagonists, but especially the heavy, not only shout and gesture to the audience but also threaten it at times.

---

exits left to buy bowler before price goes up. Thinks—
that wasn't a very big part for Bluebottle.

[*Ibid.*, p. 121.]

60. In *The Bald Soprano*, Ionesco carries framing play to something like a final conclusion by having his characters say the lines meant for other characters, thereby making us aware that "proper" attribution is at once something that is a constraint upon strip construction and something that is quite taken for granted.

61. An interesting dramaturgic treatment of wrestling is available in a statement by Roland Barthes, written in the early fifties and reprinted in his *Mythologies*, trans. Annette Lavers (New York: Hill & Wang, 1972), pp. 15–28.

62. Hockey, baseball, and tennis have even more stringent rules about performer-audience communications, since in many cases etiquette requires that players make no acknowledgment of opening or closing applause, nor of boos and catcalls. These sounds are simply defined as part of a frame the players are not in. (At the same time, as suggested, verbal communication *between* opponents may be quite acceptable and has at times closely adhered to ideals of courtesy and gallantry.)

Further, in "real" sports, the umpire inhabits the directional channel, his job being to bring editorial control, to punctuate the proceedings, but otherwise to be, in effect, invisible. In traditional wrestling and boxing there were occasions when the umpire's directives were not followed for a moment, but this occurred in the heat of the unminding fighter's attack and was excusable on those grounds. In TV wrestling, the umpire's ruling is not merely flouted, so that he must continuously come close to disqualifying the villain, but the umpire himself may be directly attacked—a monstrous infraction of framing rules—as though a sentence were to disregard its own punctuation marks.

Traditionally in wrestling, internal brackets were elegantly sustained, there functioning to ensure everyone that the opponents were contenders oriented to a contest, not beasts oriented to the kill. If a match had more than one fall, the wrestlers properly went out of frame when a fall was signaled and readied themselves for the signal to begin again. (A bodily portrayal was involved, an externalization, displaying a relaxation of intent— very pretty to behold.) A cautionary tap would also cause a wrestler exerting an improper hold to release his grip and "break free." These internal brackets, of course, are among the first things to go in show wrestling, although an understanding of what would have traditionally occurred is helpful in appreciating the antics of offense.

So, too, the spatial brackets. Traditionally when one wrestler was pushed off the mat, a tap on the shoulder of the advantaged man given by the referee would break the game, and the men would reassemble in proper array well within the mat boundary (the disadvantaged man on all fours and the other free to take a hold). Should a wrestler happen to fall out of the ring—a rare occurrence—the contestants would immediately go out of frame, and the courtesies of the street, not the ring, would come into force. Clearly, the bodily movements employed by a wrestler in returning to a restarting point were in a different frame from those by which he got holds or countered the opponent's attempts to do so. (The first, for example, were never rushed; the second, very often.) In exhibition wrestling, the ropes and elevated stage remain as points of understanding but now in part because they give meaning to violations, and violations abound. Wrestlers routinely step or crawl outside the ropes to force a stopping of the match. They are routinely thrown out of the ring into the audience or escape imminent doom through the same route. Once outside the ropes (and even the ring) they take up afresh their quarrel with the audience, the umpire, and the opponent, the last sometimes joining the ousted enemy in order to continue the fight.[63]

As already suggested, the story line itself depends on issues of frame. Typically the contestants start out staying within the rules, except that often an elaborate point is made (especially by the villain-to-be) of doing so. Then character differentiation into heavy and hero begins. Foretold by the differential reputation and appearnce of the two men, the differentiation begins to be established through the heavy-to-be's beginning to break the rules. He starts to make moves that are illegal, persists in these so that more than verbal admonishment is required by the referee, and when he finally desists he sneaks in a postterminal dollop. He threatens the audience, haggles with the referee, and shamelessly pleads for mercy when he is disadvantaged. He slaps the hero and steps on him in imperial acts of contempt that radically reframe fighting moves into purely ritual ones. The hero, weakened by punishing illegal attacks, inflamed by insulting gestures, abused by countless infractions of the rules, falters. Finally he is flagrantly sinned against once too often. His righteous indignation boils over, releasing new strength, and now, having earned the moral right to take the laws of wrestling into his own hands, he becomes downkeyed into a wild beast who roars for the kill, strikes back illegally, and wins the match. And what has been faked is not a demonstration of wrestling skill (there is *very* little attempt to do that) but, sometimes magnificently and sometimes cathartically, the violation of a traditional frame.

---

63. "Tag matches" allow official action across the boundary provided by the ropes and seem to have been designed with frame breaking in mind. Interestingly, roller derby contests follow much the same script as wrestling in regard to story line and frame breaking, although the surface appearance is dissimilar. One difference is that, as in hockey, aggressions are—at least initially—styled as modifications of playing activity, and when open fighting breaks out, a full shift in apparent primary framework has occurred; in wrestling, the shift from technical application of grips and counters is rather quickly made in the direction of a no-holds-barred style, and the shift from that to "unrestrained" open fighting (as when a wrestler follows his opponent out of the ring) is but a downshifting in key. Another difference is that it is possible that roller derby fans interpret the fights they watch as being less faked than the ones wrestling fans watch.

VI

One can, then, look at negative experience by examining the variety of scenes in which it occurs and the variety of structural devices which generate it. Behind these differences, however, a common theme is found. After the Becks almost strip in the Living Theater and urge the audience to participate, the theatrical frame is still there; after you get half-frightened on the ferris wheel, you still, after all, arrive safely and reestablish for yourself that the ride was without risk; after a girl blushes prettily or hides her face or lightly hits at her tormentor, the bounds of polite conversation are reestablished as they were before. So the Becks are engaged in only theater, and circuses in only providing rides, and interactants only in conversational fun. So, too, when Brecht periodically reminds his viewers that what they are involved in is but dramatistic make-believe or Godard introduces protagonists by showing the cut-board and the cameraman—but not, of course, the cut-board and cameraman behind the ones shown. Walter Kerr's argument seems to apply:

> Lights fade up [on the play *Riot*] on marching figures, phantom warnings of the guerrilla forces that are to descend upon America shortly. The figures, stop, stomp, splay outward on the open floor, advance toward those who are watching, thrust their bayonets in a 1-2-3 rhythm directly at us. Lights out. But—this time—there are titters. The intention has been to give us the actual feeling of steel at our throats. (We know perfectly well that it's there on the streets.) But the nature of the theater has intervened. What we know, in the theater, is that this steel (if it is steel and not just wood or rubber) is going to poke thus at our throats. It's going to stop short of penetration, there is simply nothing actual about it, and all an audience can do, given the threat that is not a threat, is giggle.
>
> Similarly, another face-in, this one during a furious debate over the problem of rat control, reveals a trash can in a pool of light capped by two real rats, nibbling away. At this point the women in the audience—some of them, anyway—should scream. They don't. The rats are there, they are apparently free and could invade the audience at any moment, we are confronted with facts. Confronted with this sort of fact in the theater, we instantly derail ourselves with questions: How has the director managed the effect, are the rats drugged to make them secure, and so on?

The real thing, in the theater, instantly becomes the wrong thing, the false thing, just as in "Big Time Buck White" the moment a debater actually collars a member of the audience and hurls him violently up the aisle, you know—for certain, now—that the man being manhandled is a plant. He can be nothing else. The management certainly isn't risking law suits by thrashing the daylights out of genuine customers. The nearer the action comes to seeming an actual confrontation, the bigger and more transparent is the lie being told.

Direct theater, theater that abandons art for the actual, thus has an automatic cut-off valve built into it, a moment when it turns into artifice, after all. Mightn't it, then, have been better as honest artifice—as art—to begin with?[64]

But, of course, underlying this falseness is the possibility of real effect, albeit merely a frame-relevant one. If indeed an audience can be jarred from protective psychological distance by threats to frame, then one can expect that once breaches of this kind have been discovered and employed, other producers of like performances will follow suit and repeat the tricks. Presumably, then, the effect will become blunted and conventionalized, leading, perhaps, to a permanent change in the conventions for a frame. The exposure of breasts in film is a recent example.

And here a general statement might be attempted concerning dramatic scriptings and presented contests. It seems that howsoever venerable the tradition of exploiting frame breaks for entertainment or instruction, we are today experiencing a special leaning in this connection, a fashion reflected in a whole range of practices.

Legitimate stage productions in the sixties seemed to consist very largely of the theater of frames; the content differed, but the devices were all the same. Insult comedy became widely popular. TV emceeing, as in the talk shows, became trickier, with much explicit reference to backstage elements of the show (censorship, sponsors) and much joking point made of mistakes, errors of timing, and slips, in fact exactly what ordinarily would have been studiously disattended; and flooding out by performers seemed to be actively encouraged and made much of.[65] Indeed,

---

64. In his useful article, "We Who Get Slapped," *The New York Times*, December 29, 1968.

65. See Helen Hogan, "Some Bracketing Devices Used on Television Talk Shows" (unpublished paper, University of Pennsylvania, 1970).

the special contingencies of televising a show were exploited, as when sound effects were purposely transmitted out of sync, or mock-up stage props made to collapse, or actors openly vied for the small center of the screen, or gestures "meant" to be off-mike or off-camera were picked up.

Sports contests have been witness to the same trend, elegantly illustrated by the antics of Lee Trevino, the golf champion who uses competitive golf as a backdrop for a performance that contains a full array of cracks, flood-outs, audience-directed comments, and other hijinks.[66] Bo Belinsky, Joe Namath, and the dramatically gifted Rumanian tennis star, Ilie Nastase are other representatives of the new school.[67]

Finally, speaker style (whether political, civic, or academic) has changed, with greater stress on "directness" or sincerity, that is, the appearance of a nonspeaking manner, and greater license taken in regard to performer needs; thus, when President Nixon dropped a medal in the act of pinning it on a hero, he enacted a laughing flood-out complete with hand hiding his face. Soviet leader Leonid Brezhnev recently followed the same line:

> Brezhnev last year accidentally spilled his drink on Secretary of State William P. Rogers. And in the State Department on Wednesday, Brezhnev spilled some on himself.
>
> The onlookers waited to see whether they should laugh or look the other way. When it became obvious that Brezhnev thought the incident funny—and so did the President—the audience laughed, and then applauded.[68]

Presumably the assumption here is that everyone knows that those who perform rituals are only human and need not be much ashamed of making an unintentional mistake—an obvious locker-room fact that heads of state only a short time ago would not have considered publicly acknowledging. In sum, it now seems

---

66. See "Lee Trevino: Cantinflas of the Country Clubs," *Time*, July 19, 1971.

67. See Welles Twombly, "Here Comes Nasty," *The New York Times Magazine*, October 22, 1972.

68. Lawrence M. O'Rourke, *The Evening Bulletin* (Philadelphia), June 22, 1973. I might add that the decision by a politician as to how to play these moments (or indeed, whether to create them intentionally so the decision will be available) is a delicate one requiring fine tuning to prevailing understandings. To ask, in the face of all this, that the laughs and face-hides be "spontaneous" and "genuine" is to ask too much.

almost a fashion to exploit the mechanics of staging a character or role, the intent being to generate spontaneous involvement through a comic presentation of reflexive frame breaks.

VII

1. I have so far considered negative experiences which are intentionally generated by persons who are more or less in charge of the proceedings or by persons who figure as the chief performers of a show. Of course, not all proceedings are ones which have directors or central performers, and so not all are well designed to be transformed into a source of negative experience. And few proceedings are so well designed for manipulation as those which present two-person contests to spectators, for these are just the performances in which one person figures very large in the determination of events; if he chooses to deviate from the norms, his action will hardly be disattendable. It is in a boxing match that a Maxie Baer can threaten to transform everything into unseriousness by dancing circles around a Canero and patting him on the rump. It is in tennis singles that the following threat to frame can occur:

> The Most Bizarre lawn tennis match I have ever seen took place in the French championships here at Stade Roland Garros today. In a cat-and-mouse encounter the Russian No 1 Thomas Lejus toyed with unranked American Bill Hoogs for three hours before putting over the winning shot for victory by 6–3, 6–3, 4–6, 8–10, 9–7. Previously Russia's Anna Dimitrieva had given the impression of not trying as she lost to Fay Toyne (Australia) by 6–8, 3–6. Both incidents no doubt were inspired by the fact that South African opponents awaited the winners.
>
> Twice last year in Britain Russians withdrew from matches rather than play against South Africans because of their country's racial policies. Today Lejus said he had been troubled with "sore feet."
>
> When the Russian had led by 5 love in the fourth set all appeared set for a routine win. But gradually he began to lose his lead and soon it was apparent that he was not bent on victory.
>
> His tactics were the same throughout the fourth and fifth sets. Lejus double-faulted as he reached match point and hit out whenever it seemed likely he might win. Finally, on his fifth match point

the Russian, looking towards his officials in the stand and apparently receiving permission from them to end the charade, set down an untouchable service ace.[69]

One can go on to argue that the reason those with performance power do not create more havoc than they do is not because skill would be required but because ordinarily they do not have reason for disrupting what is, after all, their own show. So in the case of the negative experiences considered so far, nothing happens; no basic relationships are disturbed. However, it is apparent that those presumably not in charge of the activity can intentionally attempt to create negative experiences for those in presumed control. And often they can succeed, at least for a moment.

Perhaps the proper beginning here is with the young, with those who are suffered as participants in a social occasion, who, as is said, "test the limits," that is, initiate a minor situational delinquency and then progressively increase its scope until adults must intercede to protect the affair they expect to continue to be involved in. Often this testing will involve cooperation between two offenders in teasing or roughhousing which mounts progressively until more disturbance is caused the occasion-at-large than can be carried in the disattend track. Sometimes the offenders will create the circumstances in which an accident is likely, one that abruptly throws one of them out of interactional kilter. In these various ways the situation is attacked, and the relationship between the periphery of the occasion and the central activity is threatened. Here, may I add, the great mythic model is the running of the bulls at Pamplona during the second week in July. Channeling the movement of the bulls through the town is itself a difficult task, the bullish performers uneasily limiting themselves to their pathlike stage, easily lunging into the spectators on either side. But in addition, the young bloods of and in the town have the right and perhaps the obligation to get into the act and taunt the bulls into breaking out of course, breaking frame; and he who succeeds in this disruption may receive punishment simultaneous with praise, as though fathers, schoolteachers, and police had all suddenly combined and gone wild.

The standard and minimum audience frame break is heckling —a form of conduct easier to find than to analyze. Sometimes

---

69. Tony Mottram in *The Observer* (London), May 23, 1965.

heckling is treated by performers as if it were not occurring, part of the disattend track, something that adds tension to the occasion but no abrupt shift in its definition. On these occasions a particularly apt heckle will be required if the audience is to follow the heckler in breaking frame with a laugh—aptness here meaning that the improper remark reconstitutes a lengthy strip of a performer's or character's activity, or transforms this activity into the first move of a two-move interchange of which the remark turns out to be the second move, one that enunciates an adage that is all too true.

Here it is seen again that sheer volume of disturbance from an audience is not what disturbs. Rock concerts featuring groaning auditors who totally obliterate sound from the stage have already been mentioned as a case in point. A loud remark made to a comedian which he can reply to lightly or treat as not to be specifically answered can easily cause less danger to the theatrical undertaking than might a quietly uttered statement by a member of the audience to someone onstage in the manner of direct address. For it is the latter, not the former, that breaks frame. No matter how small and picayune an event, one ought to be able to imagine a context in which it has the power to become all too meaningful and to threaten a frame. In the right scenario a cat can do considerably more than look at a king:

> Driven by a snorting, angry bull to the safety of the sturdy wooden barrier, the toreros in the plaza de toros in Seville, Spain had left the toro in sole command of the arena. As they stood there ignominiously, a white cat defied both the bull and all the ritual of bullfighting by entering the bull ring from the stands. While the bullfighters gaped, the cat circled the arena. At the end of its promenade, when the cat disappeared behind the barrier, the crowd thundered out applause that it usually bestows on only the bravest of bullfighters.[70]

2. To say that frame breaking can be employed from below in mild attack upon the occasion is to open one door; but, of course, as in all matters of frame analysis, that door merely leads us to another. For a dramatic scripting, let alone a talk show, can be established in which not only heckling is to be expected, but also direct response of the performers to these lapses. There can be,

---

70. The caption of a full-page picture of the event in *Life*, June 6, 1955.

then, a keying of a frame break, one in which the audience for
the show and the performers are one. Take, for example, melodrama at the Old Bowery in the community of the same name at
the turn of the century and the histrionic effects of one Count
Johannes:

> When he struck the Old Bowery a little later, its patrons had al-
> ready heard of him and were waiting zestfully—a full house. The
> management, knowing its customers, had stretched a net across
> the stage, but not high enough to shield the Count from the plung-
> ing fire of the galleries. As soon as the Count got going on "Angels
> and ministers of grace defend us," the gallery let him have
> it—carrots, eggs and tomatoes. The Count plowed right ahead,
> evidently used to bombardments. But the ghost wasn't—when a
> carrot popped him in the eye, the spooky majesty of Denmark
> gathered up an armful of ammunition from the stage and rushed
> before the net to return fire with fire with pretty accurate results.
>
> From then on every scene was climaxed with another bombard-
> ment. The Count kept his end up all through, particularly by
> raising Cain when his leading lady—an actress named Avonia
> Fairbanks, who was almost as big a clown, conscious or uncon-
> scious, as he was—came in for the audience's attentions. "Get thee
> to a nunnery," says he to Ophelia, and a patron in a stage-box chips
> in with "Don't you pay no attention to him, honey," so the Count
> steps out of character to bawl the patron out—result, more eggs,
> tomatoes, carrots and general hullabaloo. Cabbages were flying
> toward the end. During the graveyard scene, the Count picked up a
> cabbage instead of Yorick's skull, held it out toward the audience
> and amended Shakespeare for the customers: "Alas, poor cabbage-
> head," he said, "gaze upon thy brothers out there!" That drew fish-
> heads, riper eggs and more cabbages.[71]

VIII

One finds, then, frame breaks that come from below but leave the
superordinates—typically performers—in charge, indeed may ul-

---

71. William A. Brady, *Showman* (New York: E. P. Dutton & Co., 1937),
pp. 20–21. Obviously there is a delicate definitional issue here. Theatrical
traditions differ widely in terms of volubility of audience response permitted during a performance. But I think that the frame associated with
melodrama was not merely one which allowed great license to audience
response; to some degree at least, audience and performers together participated in a send-up of ordinary theatrical frames.

timately function to ensure this. But, of course, something more ambitious may be involved, namely, the discomfiting and discrediting of an adversary by violating the rules of the frame for interaction he is helping to sustain. These actions do not tell us about the organizational role of frame breaks but rather about the vulnerabilities of framed experience. Yet by reason of their form and content, they warrant treatment here. Observe that a special kind of trouble is at issue. It is situational—or at least it could remain so. The effort is to disrupt ease and order in social occasions, this to be done by means which do not have a directly continued consequence beyond the situation in which the attack occurs. After the act only the negative experience need remain. (The effort of those in charge to reestablish order and sovereignty can, of course, lead to very substantive consequences on all sides—to matters getting out of hand—and this seems sometimes to be the intent of the attackers.) One might refer here to "social sabotage." Practitioners have recorded a few examples, but so far there has been no organized analysis, hence no *principled application*, merely hit-or-miss, fallen-upon bright ideas.

Social sabotage always raises a double question. Given the individual or individuals who are sabotaged, whom, if anyone, are they treated as representing? Given the individual or individuals who perform the mischief, whom, if anyone, do they see themselves representing? Some attacks from below seem to have a private character: an individual acting more or less on his own behalf attempts to create a negative experience for someone who only vaguely represents a shadowy ultimate opponent. Abbie Hoffman provides us with an example: "I enjoy blowing people's minds. You know, walking up to somebody and saying, 'Would you hold this dollar for me while I go in that store and steal something?' "[72] At other times, politics more directly enters the action: the targets are public offices, and the disrupters more clearly act in the interests of an actual or potential collectivity, not simply "for themselves." Here, too, Hoffman can provide a text:

> We appeared at Brooklyn College and announced, "The classroom environment is free," unscrewed desk tops and transformed them into guns, passed out incense and art, wrote Black Board on

72. *Revolution for the Hell of It* (New York: Dial Press, 1968), p. 62.

the door, switched off the lights and continued in the darkness, announcing that the security guard was one of us, freeing him through the destruction of his identity, and in general doing whatever spontaneously came to mind. Our message is always: Do what you want. Take chances. Extend your boundaries. Break the rules. Protest is anything you can get away with.[73]

In thinking about social sabotage, it becomes clear that sheer volume of commotion and furor is not what signifies, but again, it is frame relevance that counts. Thus, the mere *presence* of certain kinds of witnesses can have a severe deflationary effect. For example, note the subtle power of the action taken by the Female Moral Reform Society in New York in 1834 in the war against prostitution and, by implication, the war against the double system of sexual morals:

> The Society's three missionaries visited the female wards of the almshouse, the city hospital and jails, leading prayer meetings, distributing Bibles and tracts. A greater proportion of their time, however, was spent in a more controversial manner, systematically visiting—or, to be more accurate, descending upon—brothels, praying with and exhorting both the inmates and their patrons. The missionaries were especially fond of arriving early Sunday morning—catching women and customers as they awoke on the traditionally sacred day. The missionaries would announce their arrival by a vigorous reading of Bible passages, followed by prayer and hymns. At other times they would station themselves across the street from known brothels to observe and note the identity of customers. They soon found their simple presence had an important deterring effect, many men, with doggedly innocent expressions, pausing momentarily and then hastily walking past. Closed coaches, they also reported, were observed to circle suspiciously for upwards of an hour until, the missionary remaining, they drove away.[74]

The action of the Female Moral Reform Society raises the issue of the history of social sabotage; examples of such activity can be found in any period, but the examples that immediately precede the contemporary practice can perhaps be identified as the active history of the form.

---

73. *Ibid.*, p. 157.
74. From Carroll Smith-Rosenberg's interesting paper "Beauty, the Beast and the Militant Woman: A Case Study in Sex Roles and Social Stress in Jacksonian America," *American Quarterly*, XXII (1971): 568–569.

Our practicing of social sabotage seems to have a precursive expression in the work of the surrealists—especially André Breton.[75] Take, for example, Breton on moviegoing:

> I understand, moreover, quite poorly, I *follow* too vaguely. Sometimes this does bother me, and then I question those sitting near me. Nevertheless, certain movie theaters in the tenth arrondissement seem to me to be places particularly intended for me, as during the period when, with Jacques Vaché we would settle down to dinner in the orchestra of the former Théâter des Folies-Dramatiques, opening cans, slicing bread, uncorking bottles, and talking in ordinary tones, as if around a table, to the great amazement of the spectators, who dared not say a word.[76]

Military use of these arts can be found in the "psychological warfare" schemes dreamed up by various government agencies during World War II. After the war, academic social psychologists contributed using, of course, an experimental frame. And then came shows like *Candid Camera.* (Historically speaking, Mr. Hoffman didn't invent himself; he just made certain modifications and improvements.) Some of the "dirty tricks" techniques the two major American political parties employed against each other during the 1968 and 1972 campaigns were fruits of the same tree.[77]

Of the various forms of social sabotage, the one of chief concern here is what is sometimes called "confrontation": an open frontal attack upon the ground rules of a social occasion—the frame of official action—this followed by a pointed refusal to accept the authority of those who consequently attempt to restore order.

Confrontations can occur during unstaged talk, although not

---

75. Suggested by Michael Delaney in an unpublished paper, University of Pennsylvania, 1970.

76. From his *Nadja,* trans. Richard Howard (New York: Grove Press, 1960), p. 37; first published 1928.

77. Apparently an innovator here was one Dick Tuck. *Time* (August 13, 1973) reports:

"There was an absent-minded professor who knew I was in politics and forgot the rest," says Tuck. "He asked me to advance a Nixon visit." With that opportunity, Tuck's career of pranksterism was launched. He hired a big auditorium, invited only a handful of people and introduced the candidate with a long-winded, soporific speech. Finally turning to Nixon, Tuck asked him to speak on the International Monetary Fund.

as readily as might be thought. The more vulnerable the dominant participant to deviant subordinate response, the more selection apparently there is in regard to subordinates. With the most inflexible of personages—royalty, unpopular presidents—care may be immense. The audience Pope Paul recently gave to sixty hippish youths provides an exceptional case in point:

> As if this [critical reaction by the right-wing press] were not enough, the Pope also came in for criticism from the musicians. "If you have the power to ban the contraceptive pill," demanded John Bedson, a shaggy drummer from Liverpool, "why don't you halt conscription? Why don't you order all Catholics not to take part in war? Why don't you abolish the Italian army?"
>
> "It is not within our power," replied His startled Holiness.[78]

Another is reported by a student of black youth:

> In the summer of 1966 I studied a Federal program designed to help lower-class youths find jobs. The program was known as TIDE. It was run by the California Department of Employment, and classes were held five days a week in the Youth Opportunities Center of West Oakland.
>
> . . . .
>
> Actual employers, usually those representing companies that hired people only for unskilled labor, came to TIDE to demonstrate to the men what a good interview would be like. They did *not* come to interview men for real jobs. It was sort of a helpful-hints-for-successful-interviews session. Usually one of the more socially mobile youths was chosen to play the role of job applicant. The entire interview situation was played through. Some employers even went so far as to have the "applicant" go outside and knock on the door to begin the interview. The students thought this was both odd and funny, and one said to the employer: "Man, you've already *seen* the cat. How come you making him walk out and then walk back in?"
>
> The employer put on a real act, beginning the interview with the usual small talk.
>
> "I see from your application that you played football in high school."
>
> "Yeah."
>
> "Did you like it?"
>
> "Yeah."

---

78. *Ibid.*, April 26, 1971.

At this point, the men got impatient: "Man, the cat's here to get a job, not talk about football!"

. . . .

Sometimes during these mock interviews, the very nature of the work being considered was put-down. During one mock interview for a truck-driving job, some of the men asked the employer about openings for salesmen. Others asked him about executive positions. At one point the employer was asked point-blank how much he was paid, and what his experience was. They had turned the tables and were enjoying the opportunity to interview the interviewer. Regardless of a potential employer's status, the young men treated him as they would their peers. On one tour of a factory, the students were escorted by the vice-president in charge of hiring. To the TIDE participants, he was just another guide. After he had informed the students of the large number of unskilled positions available, they asked him if he would hire some of them, on the spot. He replied that this was just a tour and that he was in no position to hire anyone immediately. One youth looked at him and said: "Then you're just wasting our time, aren't you?"[79]

Formal ceremonials are guarded, too (if only because of the vested interest of the central figures), and it is rare that the worst that can happen to them does. However, the dedication of the giant free-form fountain on the Embaracadero Plaza in San Francisco is a model exception:

The sun shone, a rock band played, and dignitaries assembled on a platform at the fountain top. . . . A crowd of several hundred people collected in the plaza below. Suddenly there was a ripple, a movement, a collective rush to the pool. For there, stomping about waist-deep in the water, was the vandal of the night before: black sweater and beard, dark hair hanging below his shoulders, and a new can of red paint, with which he was vigorously stenciling another *Québec Libres* [painted over from the night before] on the fountain. He was, as it turned out, none other than the artist himself, Armand Vaillancourt.

On the platform [Thomas] Hoving and the civic dignitaries droned out their general platitudes while Vaillancourt waded to and fro beneath them, imprinting more *Québec Libres* on his fountain. Now and then, he advanced to the mikes and cameras at the pool's rim to explain in loud broken English his rage at "com-

---

79. David Wellman, "The *Wrong* Way to Find Jobs for Negroes," *Transaction*, April 1968, p. 12.

promises," which, he claimed, [landscape architect] Halprin and the Redevelopment Agency had pressed on him. Defacement? "I am not defacing my sculpture." Did he repudiate it? "No, no. It's a joy to make a free statement. This fountain is dedicated to all freedom. Free Quebec! Free East Pakistan! Free Viet Nam! Free the whole world!"

"If our artist is in the audience," said [Redevelopment Agency's Executive Director] Herman, with apparently some ironic intent, "will he please raise his hand so that we may applaud him?" From poolside, his feet still dangling in the water, the maestro put his hand to his mouth and uttered a piercing Indian war cry.[80]

There are interesting issues here. A ceremony, like a conversation, has a disattend track. Action in that track must be disattended or formally terminated. But every social affair or occasion locates an activity specific to it which cannot be handled in either of the two mentioned ways. Simply put, a formal occasion cannot ignore or terminate what it is that is designated the official focus of attention. It follows that every celebration of a person gives power to that person to misbehave unmanageably. (Furthermore, in the cited example, since some locals saw the fountain as being a defacement anyway, how could one tell where the artist's sculpturing left off and his commenting began—surely an anomic circumstance.)

During live dramatic productions, attacks from the floor can openly reject the official transformation. Again one sees that the force of the attack is tied to the status of the attacker, specifically the relevance of his status for the show in progress:

Interrupting the "Mock Trial for Huey Newton," Black Panther Chairman Bobby Seale took the stage Sunday afternoon to criticize the performance of "political theatrics" by the Afro-American Students Union.

A satirical portrayal of the Newton trial, the structural improvisation was called "a lot of bullshit" by Seale. Challenging the black students engaged in the drama, Seale told them, "You think you can sit up here in the big walls of the University of California, but there's black people in the black community who's dying!"

Held in Wheeler Auditorium, the whole room was a simulated courtroom. The "Mock Trial" was a fictional interpretation of the issues underlying the Huey P. Newton murder case. Although most

80. *Time*, May 3, 1971.

of the characters in the play were cast as whites they were portrayed by black students in the AASU, who wore white greasepaint on their faces.

Explaining that Huey Newton's mother had objected to the proposed play, Seale said that any Panthers in the play would be suspended.

However, Leslie Perry, who played the prosecuting attorney and directed the play, held, "I have made no mistake and I'm ready to die for it." The audience—over two-thirds of whom were white—felt the tightening tension. One white girl in the front shouted out "Shut up!", while a black man on one side exclaimed, "Mr. Seale, you're wrong!"

Trying to gain control of the situation, the courtroom judge, played by Judge Haywood, banged his gavel and announced, "Those interested in continuing this debate, please step outside. This trial will continue with no further disturbances."

Before the courtroom had calmed down, one of the black actors wearing a pig mask (signifying that he was a policeman) tore off his mask and helmet and disgustedly threw them on the floor.[81]

The contrast in character between attacks from above that are designed to be manageable and attacks from below that are not is nicely illustrated in the Becks-Schechner incident, as reported by Tom Prideaux:

> The actors gathered on stage just before curtain time—except there wasn't any curtain. Since Brooklyn's big Academy of Music was full, some of the audience was allowed to join them on the edge of the set—except there wasn't any set. . . .
>
> The show, called *Paradise Now,* was one of the new works put on by the Living Theater, a gifted band of young American rebels who had gone to jail and been virtually exiled in Europe rather than compromise their belief in freedom, uncensored drama and utopian brotherly love. Their *Paradise Now* began as one by one the 37 actors came from the stage into the aisles, halting in front of the spectators and chanting, "I'm not allowed to travel without a passport."
>
> . . . .
>
> Then the actors changed their attack. They began shouting, "You can't live if you don't have money."
>
> . . . .
>
> I returned to my seat just as the actors took up a new chant. "I am not allowed to take my clothes off," they announced and started

---

81. Debbie Heintz, in *The Daily Californian,* May 28, 1968.

to undress in the aisles. By this time I felt I had done my bit for actor-audience sociability, but still I turned to my friend Richard Schechner, editor and critic of the *Drama Review*, who was sitting directly across the aisle, and made a gesture as if to loosen my tie.

It ignited Schechner, "All right, let's take our clothes off," he said grinning under a large mustache. Then with a speed and purposefulness that would have honored a warrior preparing for battle, he shucked off his apparel. Every stitch of it. Shorts, shoes, even socks.

Too cowardly to follow, I watched with dumb amazement, as did several hundred other people close enough to see. Totally disrobed, Schechner stood up, made a quick formal bow to the audience and sank back into his seat. His girl friend laid a protective hand on his knee.

Under normal conditions had Mr. Schechner done such a thing —which, of course, he wouldn't have—he would have outraged the audience and probably been arrested for indecent exposure. But at *Paradise Now,* it was the appropriate, brotherly thing to do. To my surprise, though, the actors in the aisles, who were busy undressing down to minimal bikinis and jock-straps, gaped at Schechner with alarm and hostility.[82]

---

82. Tom Prideaux, "The Man Who Dared to Enter Paradise," *Life*, November 22, 1968. Frame analysis, note, allows for care in the examination of deviant theatrical events. Thus, in some of the Living Theater productions, the practice of the cast was to carry the show out into the streets at the end of the performance when the actors were like unto nude. This act broke the frame boundary not between characters and onlookers, but between performers and theatergoers as a single group, and the world outside the theater building. Although presumably more or less scripted, these overflowings constitute actual, not theatrical, confrontations between the troupe and those in charge of order in the streets. One of these jurisdictional incidents early in the Becks' season was reported by William Borders (*The New York Times*, September 28, 1968):

New Haven, Sept. 27—Julian Beck, his wife, Judith Malina, and eight others were arrested early this morning after the Becks' Living Theater ended a performance at Yale University by leading the audience outside in dress the police considered indecent.

. . . .

"The police misunderstood the significance of the event," said Robert Brustein, dean of the Yale Drama School. James F. Ahern, New Haven Chief of Police, replied: "As far as we're concerned, art stops at the door of the theater, and then we apply community standards."

. . . .

As a finale, the 34 members of the Beck company walked through the

The frame implications here are interesting. A downkeying is involved, a member of the audience providing a literal response to what is (although almost not) a theatrical presentation. And a vulnerability of the performance is exposed to us, this being the point at which a downkeying is dramatically facilitated. Mr. Schechner's clinically precise attack can be matched from the life of the infamous rake Sir Francis Dashwood, who came to found *the* Hell Fire Club, and whose life surely could have stood as an inspiration for the fictional hero of negative experience, Terry Southern's Magic Christian:

> He [Sir Francis] had gone, conventionally, on the Grand Tour, but had taken pains to make it as unconventional as possible. . . . In Rome he played a joke which might well have had serious consequences for him. On Good Friday, in the Sistine Chapel, the penitents scourged themselves, gently, to the accompaniment of feigned cries of pain. Sir Francis joined the queue, received a miniature scourge, entered the chapel and concealed himself behind a pillar, until the penitents had stripped to the waist. He then drew from its place of concealment beneath his coat, a large horse-whip, with which he proceeded to lay about right and left until the church echoed with screams of agony and terrified cries of *"il diavolo!"*[83]

It might be added (for such as do seek justice) that what Schechner did to the Becks' *Paradise Now* others did to Schechner's *Dionysus in 69:*

> The people in the audience, experiencing a total sensory immersion, were surprised by loud screams and bites and scratches. This transformation was not altogether sudden, but passed through a

---

aisles of the Yale theater leading several hundred members of the audience onto York Street, in the heart of the campus.

Half a block away, as bystanders sang "America the Beautiful," the police stopped the parade and arrested Mr. and Mrs. Beck, three members of the company, one Yale undergraduate and four others who had been in the audience.

. . . .

"We're breaking down the barriers that exist between art and life, barriers that keep most men outside the gates of paradise," he explained, as he stood with supporters and co-defendants outside the Criminal Court.

83. Burgo Partridge, *A History of Orgies* (New York: Bonanza Books, 1960), p. 148.

phase familiar to lovers when the stimulation intensifies and strokes become clawings and nibbles bites. Often, pandemonium filled the room, with the screams of the audience joining our own. Pentheus was tracked down, mortally wounded by being gouged in the gut. He dragged himself back to the death ritual.

But these events, effective as they were, could not be maintained. With increasing frequency, audiences gawked, talked, or wanted to make out with the performers. Sometimes this was pleasant, but on more than one occasion a nasty situation unfolded in the darkened room. The performers refused to continue with the caress. One girl put it very bluntly: "I didn't join the Group to fuck some old man under a tower."[84]

Temporal and physical brackets exhibit an interesting vulnerability to attacks from below. Obviously true of the theater, less obvious but also true of the social space occurring within an organization. For everywhere brackets tend to become specialized —ritualized in the ethological sense—for the organizational work they do, thereby providing something the disruption of which can spread disorganization throughout a strip of activity. For example, in many schools, class periods begin and end with the help of a bell which sounds throughout the establishment, so that activity is pulsed by means of an electrically timed marker. And this machine, of course, establishes a model for simulation, allowing for Abbie Hoffman's recommendation: "Make war on bells in school. Bring alarm clocks to class and have them ring on the half hour instead of the hour."[85]

Recently attacks from below have occurred in one of our most sacred state and national shrines, the judicial setting. Negative experiences have been generated by confrontations with the trial frame, the ultimate purpose presumably being to cast some discredit on the operation of the law. In a useful introduction to a volume on the "Chicago Trials," Dwight MacDonald provides a text:

In old-style political trials, from the pre-revolutionary trial in which Peter Zenger was successfully defended against His Majesty's

---

84. Richard Schechner, ed., *Dionysus in 69: The Performance Group* (New York: Doubleday & Company, 1970), unpaginated.
85. Hoffman, *Revolution*, p. 158. See also Rossman, *On Learning and Social Change*, throughout.

prosecutors on a charge of publishing seditious matter, to the recent trial of Dr. Spock et al., in Boston, both sides, in dress and behavior, accepted the conventions of the ruling establishment. The lawyers sat down when the judge told them to and didn't ask for permission to bring birthday cakes into court, the defendants wore business suits and neckties (or socks and tie wigs) and not purple pants, Indian headbands, or—as Abbie and Jerry did at one point—judicial robes, nor did they laugh or make abusive or witty remarks—and the spectators didn't shout "Right on!" or "Oink!" or, indeed, anything at all. Repression reigned. The defense behaved as if they shared the values and life style of the Court, even when they didn't, as in the big IWW trial in 1918 under the Espionage Act.[86]

In the new-style courtroom tactics, either the lawyers share the alienation and often the hair style of their clients, or there are no lawyers. Also, as in the Living Theatre and other avant-garde dramatic presentations, the audience gets into the act; the spectators raise their voices, or, worse, their laughter, at crucial moments despite all those beefy marshals. And the defendants, hitherto passive except when they had their meagre moment on the witness stand—"Please answer the question, yes or no"—feel free to make critical comments on the drama when the spirit moves them. The Chicago trial is the richest specimen of the new free-form trial to date, owing to the ingenious tactics of the defense (and the Judge's collaboration). . . .[87]

Interestingly, the availability of police and TV cameras allowed these showmen a tremendous scope for creativity, making it possible for them to transform nonperformance social occasions into embroilments containing persons in dispute and an audience.[88]

---

86. Mark L. Levine et al., eds., *The Tales of Hoffman* (New York: Bantam Books, 1970), p. xviii. See also Ronald P. Sokol, "The Political Trial: Courtroom as Stage, History as Critic," *New Literary History,* II (1971): 495–516.

87. Levine, *Tales of Hoffman,* p. xx.

88. See the useful review by Elenore Lester, "Is Abbie Hoffman the Will Shakespeare of the 1970's?" *The New York Times,* October 11, 1970, and Hoffman, *Revolution.* Another authority argues the following:

Have you ever seen a boring demonstration on TV? Just being on TV makes it exciting. Even picket lines look breathtaking. Television creates myths bigger than reality.

Demonstrations last hours, and most of that time nothing happens. After the demonstration we rush home for the six o'clock news. The

It is to be noted that in these several examples of attacking the frame of a public occasion from below, the involvement generated in the physically present audience—even the TV audience—may well have been troubled, sometimes deeply; yet when the whole experience is enclosed in yet another insulating key, that of news report to magazine readers, mere interest is the likely result. Again an example of the rule: what is too much in an activity is just enough in its reporting—although not necessarily enough to serve as the text for a conventional dramatic production.[89]

One need only combine the efforts of playwrights to embroil the audience and the efforts of the disaffected to embroil agents of social control in a newsworthy show, and the contemporary attack on public frames becomes evident, as one of the attackers suggests:

> Jokes and plays are not "real"—that is, as Bentley points out, "In farce, as in drama, one is permitted the outrage but spared the consequences." It used to be that way. Today's theatre is mixing really with "reality"—from the confrontational aesthetics of Grotowski, to the regulated audience participation of TPG [The Performance Group], and on to the massed acting-out of *Paradise*

---

drama review. TV packs all the action into two minutes—a commercial for the revolution. [Jerry Rubin, *Do It!* (New York: Simon and Schuster, 1970), p. 106.]

89. For example, Lester, "Abbie Hoffman":

The superiority of Theater of the Apocalypse to traditional propaganda drama is that it demonstrates rather than preaches; it creates vignettes of reality, which force people to take sides. Traditional propaganda drama is created for and by the already convinced. It comforts believers by sanctimoniously preaching to non-believers who simply don't turn up. But willy-nilly, like it or not, everybody is plugged in to Theater of the Apocalypse.

A recent Off Broadway play, "Conspiracy '70," was a perfect example of how weak old-fashioned propaganda theater is compared with Theater of the Apocalypse. The production was a replay of excerpts from the Chicago Seven conspiracy trial, immediately violating Abbie's excellent cardinal rule of not telling people what they already know. In order to add interest to the thoroughly publicized trial material, the director was forced to introduce a clumsy load of theatrical gadgetry—heavily caricatured acting, a painful and unconvincing elaboration of the not-too-mind-blowing idea that the trial had an "Alice in Wonderland" flavor. A fatuous aura of holiness was cast on the defendants and their witnesses, and the judge was a weak attempt at creating a commedia dell' arte buffoon.

What infinitely better theater the actual trial was!

Now. Conversely, the political actions of young radicals are sometimes hard to distinguish from guerrilla theatre. Putting the lemon pie in Colonel Akst's face or even taking a building and demanding amnesty are not "real" acts. They are authentic and meaningful. They trail consequences. But they are also self-contained (as art is) and make-believe. They lack the finality of, say, an armed attack. Radical actions are often codes—compact messages falling somewhere between war and speech. They stake out a new area not mapped by either traditional politics or aesthetics.[90]

90. Richard Schechner, "Speculations on Radicalism, Sexuality, and Performance," *Tulane Drama Review*, XIV (1969): 106.

12

The Vulnerabilities of Experience

I

In the last chapter some threats to one side of experience were considered, the side having to do with engrossment. The discussion began with benign breaks in frame clearly engineered in the interests of entertainment and ended with a consideration of serious efforts from below to disorganize a social occasion and deeply embarrass those in charge of it. These latter possibilities, of course, point not to the organizational role of frame breaks but to the vulnerability of framed experience. Now I want to try to bring together and extend what has been said about the vulnerabilities of the other side of experience—the purely cognitive sense of what it is that is going on.

Assume that the sense of any strip of activity is linked to the frame of the experience and that there are weaknesses inherent in this very framing process. It follows, then, that whatever the vulnerabilities of framing, so, too, will our sense of what is going on be found vulnerable. Of course, the vulnerabilities of the organization of our experience are not necessarily the vulnerabilities of our life in society; a few decades ago, a man could receive what everyone defined as a fair trial, be sentenced to hang, and in due course be so dispatched with no questions rising in anyone's mind about what was really going on.

These matters, of course, have already been indirectly addressed in the previous chapter. Many of the techniques used to induce negative experience work by virtue of ensuring that incorrect assumptions are initially made. So benign deceits and temporary vulnerabilities have been considered. In many cases only a slight shift in emphasis will be required and the vulnerabilities of framing will be at issue.

The conventional approach to these matters is largely concerned with the question of when to doubt a claimant and what can be done about checking up on claims. My concern, rather, is to learn about the way we take it that our world hangs together, and for this, artful means for deceiving are as instructive as artful means for nosing out deception, and perhaps more widely reported.

Take what has been for centuries in our society the popular ideal of small-time falsity—in traditional criminal argot, the short con. A pre-Xerox example: The mark happens into an inventor who has a small machine that turns out twenty-dollar bills. The mark is allowed to buy the machine, but when he takes it home and turns the crank only paper comes out. Here a printing machine was used as a model in accordance with which a totally false machine was pasted up, fabricated, constructed. Traditional teachings about how to survive in the wicked city provide a set of protections against such fraud. This compendium of folk advice about how to avoid getting bilked contains within it our understanding of how a little episode of experience is grounded in the ongoing world, and, by implication, what the nature of that world is. Central, of course, is the notion that if a strip of activity is allowed to proceed long enough, or if the biography of the materials from which it is constructed is checked out, the truth will out.

II

My interests, then, are special, but my assumption follows the common one: that our interpretive frameworks are more or less adequate. Some apparent exceptions support this argument.

It is obvious that a given appearance can on different occasions have different meanings. He who cleans off his dinner plate can be seen as starved, polite, gluttonous, or frugal. But usually the context, as we say, rules out wrong interpretations and rules in the right one. (Indeed, context can be defined as immediately available events which are compatible with one frame understanding and incompatible with others.) And when the context might not suffice, participants take care to act out requisite evidence, here, as it were, helping nature to be herself. Even when something *does* occur that is deeply ambiguous or erroneously defined and is destined to remain so for all time, still it is felt that were the effort spent, the "facts" could be uncovered and matters set right. The unexplained is not the inexplicable.

Now consider wordplay. It is apparent that words, even sequences of them, can have more than one meaning. For the obvious possibility exists that in addition to its intended sense, a spoken word may have an homonymous or metaphorical (when the intent was literal) or literal (when the intent was metaphorical) reading. If there is some reason to respond to the word as though in passing, out of the context of nonverbal relevancies that would ordinarily rule out alternatives, then appreciable misunderstanding can result, for each alternative meaning will be part of—and thus introduce—a diffusely different texture of meaning. But ordinarily what the participants bring (and are known to bring) of their past involvements to the current one, as well as the context of gestures, other words, and objects in the current environment, combine to rule out all effectively different meanings. And ordinarily these bases of specification are consistently effective because the speaker has premonitored his formulations, ensuring that alternate meanings can be ruled out. (Indeed, speakers are obliged to censor and qualify their statements according to the company and the setting, which requires them to test out the meanings of their upcoming choice of words while there is still time to do something [smoothly] about improper selections, as well as incorrect or misleading ones.) Even more so in writing. In fact, when a writer is obliged to rely entirely on his own surrounding text as the specifying context which his readers will have for checking out their interpretations, he (and they) can yet do so with assurances. Nonambiguous writing is surely not a result of nature but the grammatical understanding that ambiguity of meaning is not permissible, this supported by training and the rather general practice of checking over one's words in draft form so that such ambiguities as have escaped censorship can be "picked up."[1]

However, it *is* possible for a speaker or a writer to orient to these correctives and for a time, at least, nullify them, thus creating playful optical illusion. Puns are one form. Another is the ingenious ambiguities through which generative grammarians illustrate the limits of mere immediate constituent phrase structure analysis and recommend appealing to deep structure, to underlying strings or "sentence kernels" as a technique for systematic disambiguation. Riddles are still another, these turning on the construction of a question for which there is no apparent answer, the one the riddler comes to give being apt by virtue of its power to reconstitute the meaning of the question, thus opening up the possibility of itself as the answer. So, too, in a more elaborate way, do short stories with trick endings function: they are carefully written to induce an obvious interpretation and to affirm this interpretation through details until the very last sentence, when the reader is provided with that statement which recasts the whole of the story retrospectively in a radically different light. Witticisms, as Bergson and others have suggested, follow the same design, except that the wit has to find the transforming word or phrase for a statement which was not itself constructed to allow for this reframing:

A : He's always running after a joke.
B : I'll back the joke.

Or, to take an example of what can be done with the actor-character formula:

HIGH SCHOOL INTERVIEWER : Do you think Romeo and Juliet were sexually intimate?
JOHN BARRYMORE : Well, in the Chicago company they were.

But, clearly, the fact that the riddler has to prearrange the words that will be transformed, and that the wit must patiently

---

1. Leonard Bloomfield, *Language* (New York: Henry Holt & Company, 1946), pp. 148 ff., presents the interesting argument that where metaphorical or multiple meanings of terms are available, one will be primary, and this primary meaning will be employed unless something in the context denies it; then a secondary meaning will be sought out. Neglected here seems to be the obvious fact suggested above that we intendedly organize what we write so that ambiguity is ruled out.

wait until a phrase spoken by another allows for this transformation, attests more to the safety in words than to their vulnerability.[2] Wordplay seems to celebrate the power of the context to
disqualify all but one reading, more than it disconfirms the
workings of this force. In any case, one deals here with something quite different from a mere fabrication; for the dupe does
not discover that he has been told a lie, but that the obvious
reading he had been giving to what is being told him is wrong,
what is right proving—quite unlike a lie—to have been openly
within reach all along.

Next examine the special jumbling of the world provided in
the genre of radio comedy represented by the *Goon Show*. Here
fingers aimed shoot "real" bullets, the Gas Board sends a courier
on its waterproof bicycle across the Atlantic to quickly collect a
bill, Wurlitzers are raced at Daytona Beach, oceans are drained,
the telephones abruptly ring anywhere so that mentioned persons
can reply to what they could not have heard. But of course, these
liberties can be taken with the organization of the world because
of the liberties already taken by serious radio. Because radio
audiences allow themselves to depend on a few sounds to establish and sustain the context of broadcasted action—the context
including place, weather, time, company, occasion, and undertaking—they necessarily set themselves up for frame foolery. For
sound effects can be used to instantly flesh out and realize all
kinds of puns and multiple meanings. (Threatened by the
enemy, our hero can quickly eat an apple, thus providing himself
with the First Apple Corps, the sound of thousands of marching
boots followed closely after the sound of munching.) And since
readers of newspaper and cinema cartoons depend in a similar
way on simple line drawings, their world, too, can easily be made
to connect and disconnect itself in impossible ways—the Max
Fleischer Studio version of Betty Boop in *Snow White* being a
very notable example.

---

2. The misunderstandings made possible by homonymy, improper punctuation, and the like raise the interesting issue of how long a text can be
and still allow an ordinary reader or listener to misconstrue radically what
is being meant. And how can words be arranged so as to prolong "un-
naturally" the span of verbal material over which an erroneous response is
likely? Underlying these questions is the important fact that as increasing
information is obtained the chance of gross interpretive error decreases,
simply because pieces of valid information tend to confirm each other, and
the more pieces, the more likely an effectively unassailable interpretation.

A further exception that proves the rule regarding our capacity to correctly interpret the world: the comedies of Shakespeare. Through ignorance and misperception characters start off on misguided courses of action. They employ biographical disguises to further their designs. Hidden hearing and seeing places allow them to become secretly privy to the deceptions of others. All of this enables the characters to sustain spectacular misalignments to the world across the events of many scenes and several acts. They can start off (or be started off) on the wrong foot and continue (or be continued) in that direction. One could argue, then, that the comedies provide a showcase for the world's stock of real confusions. But I think the better lesson is that in order to generate these sustained distances from the facts, these comic situations, one has to have constant recourse to the ridiculous devices that Shakespeare was forced to employ. Ordinarily the world does not allow such cockeyed situations to develop; to get them to develop the playwright must introduce a fun house full of trick devices. So the Comedies provide evidence of the sobriety of the world, not its drunkenness.

III

Facts, it is claimed, are not merely a matter of opinion; given the various interconnections among events, an illusion or delusion or deception is by and large just that, whether or not the subject becomes alive to the matter. I have also implied that error in regard to frame is not likely to be long-lasting.

With these words in lukewarm support of the certitudes of social life, consider now its dubiousness. Consider first some general sources of vulnerability to which our framing practices expose us. And may I add that it is just such sources (and the more specific ones that will be examined thereafter) that tend to be left unaddressed and unanalyzed when one takes a skeptical view of *all* realms of being, including all social realities.

1. A grounding statement can be drawn from what has already been considered. It is apparent that every individual must face at various times ambiguities regarding frame and suspicion regarding the role of the individuals in a frame; furthermore, he can expect to misframe events on various occasions. Similarly,

occasionally he will be a victim of deception and delusion and discover that these fabrications of reality have occurred. Indeed, in everyday life people engage in a multitude of minor doctorings of the world—as when, for example, they arrange to turn up "accidentally" at a place where they are likely to run into someone they secretly want to see; or provide a tactful lead into a question they want someone else to raise; or ask a question as part of a "natural" series of questions so that it will appear that their interest is in the series, and hence general, and that they have no special and thus revealing interest in the particular question motivating the whole display.

Consider too that in theory it should be possible to misframe *any* short strip of activity. The right misleading circumstances are all that is required and an illusion, an error in framing, will result. Nor doubt that it will always be possible to be deceived concerning what is going on. Here intent, immorality, and resources are all that will ever be needed. Material evidence can always be manufactured and given an appropriate biography in order to provide a false grounding for events. A conspiratorial social net can be produced involving multiple witnesses and doubly false unconnectedness: the unconnectedness of the witnesses to one another (and hence, presumably, the impossibility of prior agreement concerning what to avow) and the unconnectedness of the witnesses to what they happen to witness (and hence the assumption that they have nothing to gain by deceiving). In fact, to repeat, whatever we use as a means of checking up on claims provides a detailed recipe for those inclined to cook up reality; whatever makes it hard for fabricators to function also makes it easy.

2. Turn now to a more specific vulnerability: the relevance of certain kinds of power. When the overall treatment of an individual hinges on judgments of his competence, and when his protestations regarding judgment can themselves be discounted, then misframing can be common and long-lasting. Actor transforms are involved:

> Nampa (Idaho)—(UPI)—A man with an intelligence quotient of 135 has been found among residents of Idaho's State School for the mentally retarded it was revealed yesterday.
>
> Dr. John Marks, school superintendent, said the man, not identified, has been in the school for 30 years. He was admitted as an

infant when his parents thought him to be mentally retarded. Marks said a recent stepped-up testing program revealed the man was not mentally retarded—only deaf.

"He spends his time studying and doing calculus problems in his mind as he has for years and nobody knew it," Marks said.

Despite the man's high IQ, Marks said that 30 years in an institution has left the patient socially inadequate.

Marks said the patient will receive special training to prepare him for work outside.[3]

Indeed, wherever organizational machinery provides that the life an individual is about to lead will be determined by an assessment of him of some kind, functioning as a sorting device, then fateful errors are possible.

The power to enforce a course of conduct seems necessarily related to vulnerabilities of framing. Take the following example:

Frankfort, Ky.—Kentucky's highest court ruled yesterday that if a woman falsely tells a man she is pregnant to induce marriage, it is grounds for annulment.

. . . .

The appeals court said the couple had engaged in premarital relations and the woman said she was pregnant and threatened the man with expulsion from college and court action if he would not marry her.

After being married a week, the man discovered the woman was not pregnant.[4]

The interesting point here is not that the individual may begin to build up a new and in some sense false life because of a fateful fact about which he has been deceitfully misinformed, or that the courts in this instance set a legal limit to fabrication, but rather the hint given about what it is that can create life situations and hence what it is that can be discredited in them.

A man who holds up a liquor store with a revolver that the counterman can see is inoperative is discredited in his efforts; but

---

3. *San Francisco Sunday Examiner and Chronicle*, October 1, 1967.

4. *San Francisco Chronicle*, September 23, 1967. The dissenting opinion was given by Judge Earl Osborne, who said, "It is regrettable that this court should see fit to further weaken the institution of marriage in a time when it needs all the support and strength that could be mustered upon its behalf." It probably does.

that this is so should lead us to see that a gun, seen as one that is likely to be properly functioning and seen to be properly handled by someone seen as capable of that sort of thing, has the power to terminate the previous scene and to initiate by force an entirely new scene. At work, I think, is the possibility that every definition of the situation, every continued application of a wonted frame, seems to presuppose and bank on an array of motivational forces, and through certain extreme measures any such balance seems to be disruptable. To be able to alter this balance sharply at will is to exert power: that is one meaning of the term.[5]

A gun, having this power, can give to its holder an expectation that he can radically restructure what is to occur and carry off a scene that overrides the existing one. Should his intent or capacity (which may mean his perceived suitability for the role) be given no credit, then indeed a fiasco can occur, an open failure to carry off not only the goods, but also the scene:

> The Bicycle Bandit Caper was apparently solved last night by Oakland police with the arrest of two free-wheeling juvenile desperadoes.
>
> . . . .
>
> According to Inspector Gil Zweigle, the 17-year-old—armed with a .32 caliber revolver furnished by the younger suspect [16]—paid a Sunday night visit alone to LePage's, a candy store at 6675 Foothill boulevard, Oakland.
>
> Wearing a mask made of rags, the would-be bandit confronted owner Norbert LePage, 57, and demanded the Valentine's Day eve receipts.
>
> LePage, his nerves worn to a frazzle after a busy day, replied simply: "Get the hell out of here!"
>
> The budding bandit gulped.
>
> "But I've got a gun," he stammered.
>
> Not intimidated one whit, LePage started hurling candy boxes in the suspect's path. One-pounders, five-pounders—gift wrapped, Valentine-shaped—loaded with a choice assortment of "caramels, nuts and fruits."
>
> Before beating an empty-handed retreat, the juvenile squeezed

---

5. The suggestion, then, is that guns do not have this effect because they are glorified in the movies; rather, they are glorified in the movies because they can have this effect. And we often first interpret a real pointed gun as a joke, perhaps because jokes are soon over and allow us to continue on with our serious realities intact.

off a single shot that went wild in the confusion of the candy assault.

LePage, following the fleeing youngster out the front door, launched another volley of candy before the youngster jumped on a beat-up bicycle with a high racer seat and took off into the night.[6]

3. There is also the notion to address that certain beliefs— religious ones being the most famous example—can be quite effectively held by very large populations quite in the face of "evidence." Religious beliefs are likely to touch on a million matters, and be supported by a religious establishment which sometimes can become vastly ramified and extremely long-lived. Yet across different societies, widely different beliefs will prevail on religious questions, and not much basis can be adduced for choosing among them.[7] To speak in this connection of correct and incorrect framing or to distinguish easily between illusion and self-delusion is a little optimistic.

IV

There are, then, some general vulnerabilities in our framing of experience. One is thus encouraged to consider the specific conditions under which illusion, delusion, and deception are easily produced, and, whether easily produced or not, the practical means for inducing these frame-related vulnerabilities.

1. Given the assumption about the interconnectedness of literal events in the real world, it follows that much of what is precarious about framing must turn upon a limitation of information regarding these connections. To wit: activities which must be predicated on a small amount of information are especially vulnerable to misguided framing. A question then: Where does

---

6. *Ibid.*, February 17, 1966. The language employed in the news story is closely selected to affirm the note of fun the piece is meant to generate—at the expense, of course, of the holdup man. One must bear in mind how the scene could have gone had the youth been junior marksman champion of his state, his specialty shooting from the hip, and his weapon a .22 target pistol. In a movie, of course, the storekeeper would have started to take away the reality that the boy had started out to invoke and then would have this taking away taken away.

7. Peter Berger and Thomas Luckmann, *The Social Construction of Reality* (Garden City, N.Y.: Doubleday & Company, Anchor Books, 1966), p. 119.

one find situations in which reduced information must be relied upon?

a. As already suggested, when an event occurs but once and in apparent isolation from other events—as when a "strange" noise is heard in the distance—then, of course, vulnerability to wrong framing, especially to misframing, is great. This conclusion raises another question, namely, what are the conditions under which isolation of events occurs? One answer, interestingly, is natural disasters, for an event of this kind is often associated with a sudden effect which is visible or audible or otherwise sensible at great remove from the center of the event itself. Hence those who experience a disaster first in terms of a distal sign must deal with a sensation that has little context or continuity as a source of corroborative or corrective details, at least right away. Thus a student of disasters who interviewed locals after a mine had suffered a "bump," that is, an underground upheaval, reports:

> The five off-shift miners who did not interpret the tremor as a bump [seven did] attributed it to a variety of causes, including a bomb:
>
> I thought some kids had put a bomb under Jim Brown's house. I said, "What in the hell is that?" And my friend said, "I don't know." Then a neighbor came out and she hollered, "What was that?", and I said, "I don't know."
>
> The other four attributed the shock to various phenomena: "I thought a stool had fallen," "I thought a transfer truck had hit the house," "I thought it was the kids upstairs," "My first thought was that the furnace had blown up."[8]

On the occasion of another bump, the student reports: "The shock was variously perceived [by those not correctly identifying it] as a 'jet plane breaking the sound barrier,' 'blasting,' 'a tank exploding,' 'a truck had hit the side of the garage,' 'thunder.' "[9] He also comments:

> The tendency to interpret new cues within a framework of normal expectations has been reported in virtually every disaster studied. This has meant, for instance, that the roar of an approaching

8. Rex A. Lucas, "The Influence of Kinship upon Perception of an Ambiguous Stimulus," *American Sociological Review*, XXXI (1966): 230.
9. *Ibid.*, pp. 235–236.

tornado was interpreted as a train, and flood water in the living room was attributed to a broken pipe.[10]

b. Issues which turn on events that occurred in the distant past are especially vulnerable; for it seems obviously true that the longer in the past an event took place, the less can ready evidence about it be collected, and the more must reliance be placed on whatever can be dredged up. Indeed, the term "evidence" implies reliance on fewer of the facts than are available for establishing the character of ordinary current events. (That is not to say that trained historians cannot manage prodigies of research in which a claim regarding a past event is credited or discredited by tracing down and uncovering a whole tissue of cooccurring events. These prodigies merely attest again to the interconnectedness of events and the biographical residue that all events leave.)[11]

c. Information concerning an event must sometimes be taken entirely from what is relayed through an individual, he being the sole available channel. These are the circumstances, of course, which produce the "cry wolf" myth warning us, among other things, against the vulnerability of told worlds. Note, any narrowing of even this channel, as in telephone and telegraphic communication, further increases vulnerability.

d. An individual who relays an occurrence through himself is, of course, in a position to edit what he relays, indeed, can hardly fail to do so very appreciably. The same is true of recording devices, audio and visual, except that in the latter cases a greater impression of presenting the whole flow of activity seems to be given. Paradoxically, then, what we have come to call documentary (tape, stills, or film) is exactly what should be suspect relative to standards of documentation. For one, the recording of an unexpected or dangerous event presupposes the prior presence of recording equipment and an environment stable enough to manage this equipment.[12] Behind the hero taking chances

10. *Ibid.*, pp. 231–232. Lucas is concerned to show in this paper that persons with kin who can be directly affected by a disaster are much more likely to form a disaster-connected account than are those not connected in this way to the trouble.

11. For an example, see Arthur Pierce Middleton and Douglas Adair, "The Mystery of the Horn Papers," *William and Mary Quarterly*, 3d ser., IV (1947): 409–443, excerpted in Robin W. Winks, ed., *The Historian as Detective* (New York: Harper & Row, 1970).

12. An example. In 1966 the California Peace Officers Association in

may be a cameraman who can manage these difficulties and a camera as well. In any case, the angle from which he *does* shoot is limited to angles from which he *can* shoot, and so a bias. This but repeats what was already suggested: A protagonist who muses aloud about what he has been through is not musing about what it is like to agree to muse before recording equipment. A writer who candidly and directly writes on the trouble he takes or doesn't take to produce what he is now producing cannot comment on what it is like writing a comment of that kind, unless, of course, he acts so as to generate something behind the comment on the comment that is itself not commented upon. Further, the more telling a film is as "caught footage" the more worthwhile it will have been for the producers to ensure the occurrence that is then recorded.[13] And all of this is true apart from the obvious opportunity that all recording gives to its producers to edit what is presented but not present information about where the editing has occurred.[14]

A central example of the questionability of documentary is, I

conjunction with the Golden State Film Productions produced a documentary called *Sudden Birth* to be shown to paraprofessionals to help train them to cope with emergency births. The film showed a Berkeley police officer delivering a child in a car, following voice-over directions provided in lay language. In fact, a real birth was filmed, the arrangements having been made long in advance. The car, cut in two in order to allow for camera work, was not quite in the highway, however, but had been set up in a building on the Alta Bates hospital grounds. And the patrolman was actually the mother's obstetrician in full Berkeley police colors. (See *Berkeley Daily Gazette*, February 28, 1966.)

13. An illustration is the movie *Gimme Shelter*, produced by the Maysles on the Altamont concert. It does not disclose the manner in which the concert came to be so that a movie could be made of it. And when it shows Mick Jagger looking at the footage of the concert, it does not provide documentation of rehearsing and arrangements for *that* footage. See Pauline Kael, "Beyond Pirandello," *The New Yorker*, December 19, 1970, in which she discusses this and other framing issues.

14. Indeed, there is a "New Journalism" which employs the style of documentary reporting to get at the "spirit" of an occasion. To this end, "verbatim" dialogue and gestures are painted in to fit the needs of what is being depicted, and the reader is left with no visible means of determining how to frame what he reads—fact, fiction, or fraud. See, for example, F. W. Dupee, "Truman Capote's Score," *The New York Review of Books*, VI (February 3, 1966). Norman Mailer has carried matters one step forward by use of "suppositional biography," through which any actual person can be got to do, think, or feel anything by means of a special bracketing device: "Who is to say but that. . . ."

think, our nightly TV news coverage.[15] It would seem reasonable
to assume that the purpose of the networks is to get a crew to
where the news occurs and then let the film itself tell the whole
story, the only concern and constraint being the drive to do just
this better than competitors. Viewers, then, can feel that they are
rather directly witness to the major events of their day, separated
only by space and a very brief time. But it can be argued that
viewers are not so much involved in current events as they are in
a special type of entertainment, the raw materials for which are
provided by the recorded sight and sounds of happenings. The
issue is not merely that the network has its own slant to maintain
and that it must also comply with government regulations and
satisfy the tastes of affiliated stations. Nor that some of the
happenings that are reported occurred just so recordings could be
made of them. The issue is that the recordings themselves are put
together in accordance with the constraints and aims of show
manufacture. There is actually very little coverage, since each
network has only a handful of crews in a handful of cities. Of the
film shot for a story that the central office has decided on, only a
very small part will eventually be used and that in patches. Part
of the sound is likely to come from a library of cans, and the film
shown is likely to contain shots filmed at different times and at
different places and to include strips specifically designed long
beforehand as dateless fillers. (Indeed, persons gathering the raw
footage are likely to be under obligation to take some shots that
will not date themselves.) Only the commentator's lead-in and
lead-out are assuredly current. Unanticipatable events aren't
much usable because of the difficulty of getting a crew to the site
on time and the low quality of the film that otherwise becomes
available; so it is scheduled events or long-lasting ones that can
be used. And although it is persons in the field who do the shooting, it is a committee in the central office that does the editing.
The shots themselves may have been given a sense of objectivity
in part by the camera's compliance with our cultural tastes for
this condition: head-on, eye-level placement of the camera relative to the subject matter,[16] and a range equivalent to impersonal talking distance.[17]

---

15. I draw here from the very useful book by Edward Jay Epstein, *News
from Nowhere* (New York: Random House, 1973).

16. Gaye Tuchman, "The Technology of Objectivity: Doing 'Objective'
TV News Film," *Urban Life and Culture*, II (1973): 7.

17. *Ibid.*, pp. 15–20.

e. The editing license that documentary making enjoys is somewhat limited by the fact that often a sequence of actual events occurring through a brief period of time is what is being documented, and often this strip of action will have occurred in the not too distant past. However, there are many circumstances in which an individual is concerned to provide himself or others with an interpretive verbal analysis of the developing character of an organization or person, and he has special access to events which can be presented as evidence. On these occasions of diagnostic assessment, unlimited license seems to obtain, allowing the formation of any desired picture whatsoever.

For example, whenever the current doing of an associate leads us to find in his past a set of acts which together can be read as evidence of his character or personality, evidence that makes of the current act something that, after all, was only to be expected, then we are off in a frame-treacherous game where any picture can be painted, and, incidentally, many strong motives exist for engaging in this artwork. The extreme here occurs when we come to review the actions and attitudes of someone we know well, our purpose being to determine whether his previous apparent sanity can now be seen to disguise and portend a current episode, or whether his past apparent insanity can now be seen to reflect simply and sanely upon the company he had been forced to keep. But that is only the extreme. Less dramatic imputations abound; for example, whether an associate has all along been sincere or insincere, trustworthy or untrustworthy, level-headed or impulsive, and so forth. The divination of moral character by adducing indicators from the past is one of the major preoccupations of everyday life. And the treacherous feature is that "a case can be made," and at the same time there is no foolproof way of determining whether it is made correctly. In these circumstances any novel current event can provide the pretext for a review of the facts and the "discovery" of a pattern that was there all the time but only now appreciated.

2. I have considered briefly some circumstances in which reduced information is found and hence frame vulnerability. Consider now another basis for vulnerability: marketable information.

In certain enterprises, success can hinge on maintaining effective guard over access to information and (by implication) effective check on the loyalty of those before whom the guard must be dropped. A variety of organizations are vulnerable in this connection: governmental offices guarding intelligence of political value to enemies; executive offices guarding information which will have consequence for the market value of the company's product; research organizations guarding industrial secrets valuable to competitors; and finally, criminal confederates, launched in the planning of a crime, whose information on plans has value as something to sell or trade to the police.

Those who manage the interests of such organizations are particularly dependent, then, on information control, especially when opponents know that vital information is being guarded and who it is that is guarding it. Now it is a special feature of information that it can be obtained and transmitted without this action necessarily leaving much of a trace; for example, nothing of a material kind need be removed or even permanently shifted. A disloyal person with access to a secret is therefore in a position to chance the sale of the information on the grounds that the theft will be discovered only when the information thus obtained comes to be used, and that this delay may increase his chances of avoiding identification as the culprit and otherwise ease his situation. Obviously, then, those with marketable information to protect are very vulnerable to shows of loyalty that conceal subversive intent.

3. There are activities which depend for their resolution upon chance outcomes. Gambling games and lotteries are examples. If the decision machine is "fixed" then the whole enterprise is transformed into a construction, a fabrication, the players not in on the fix being persons who are thoroughly contained. Now it is a feature of chance that its proper operation can never be demonstrated—at least in regard to runs of practical length. Only doctored outcomes can. It follows that whenever an individual must rely on the operation of a decision machine which purportedly grinds out random decisions, he will have no way of knowing whether or not he is being cheated. Not knowing this, he will be in a vulnerable world, at least to the degree to which the game is fateful or engrossing. The issue is not that he might lose his bets—that is a different kind of vulnerability—but that he can (and properly) come to feel that he doesn't know what is really going on.

4. Zero-sum games of strategy,[18] that is, assessment games, provide a special case in the study of the vulnerability of framed experience.[19] When a set of individuals plays at a game, a realm can be generated for them, a complete psychological habitat. In the case of assessment games, this plane of being has special features. An overriding purpose is provided (to best the opposition in some way), and this purpose thrusts the participants into fully interdependent actions, such that a move on one participant's part can have overriding consequences for him and for the other players. Certain clearly defined elements become determinative: resources (some visible, some concealed, often taking the form of game characters of particular value), tactical intent, matrix of possible moves, gaming ability,[20] and finally "expression," namely, events that could "leak" information about a player's situation. All these factors taken together provide the player with a meaningful field of action and the bases and reasons for making moves.

Each player, then, must assess what is going on with the opponent and act accordingly. But, of course, the opponent is concerned to misdirect this assessment so he himself can defeat the assessor. The assessor, knowing this, must see that the picture he obtains of the opponent's situation may be one that has been specifically designed to produce a false impression. The participant, then, by virtue of the structure of the game, is forced to determine a considerable part of his own situation on the basis of the events and material immediately associated with the opponent, and all of this he is right to feel may be organized to misdirect this assessment—in brief, to contain him.

---

18. "Mixed-motive" games involving partial coordination provide much the same conditions.

19. Popular pastimes vary considerably in the extent to which they realize the conditions for pure assessment games. Poker, for example, does not depend entirely on bluffing or "sucking in," and bridge obliges the player to disclose information about his holdings through bidding and the rule of following suit. In these cases, it is only particular plays that can be fully analyzed in game theoretical terms.

20. Where physical skill is at issue in a game, the stage is set for that very special form of modesty by which a player conceals his competence until well into play, the better to guard against the reflection that an unexpectedly brilliant opponent would have on him or to induce favorable initial terms. The nice statement here is Ned Polsky's "The Hustler," in his *Hustlers, Beats and Others* (Chicago: Aldine Publishing Company, 1967), pp. 41–116.

Assessment games are to be seen, then, as arrangements for instituting and embodying the specific vulnerabilities of framing. A reason why these games seem at the very least to be tolerable, and at the most to be utterly engrossing, is to be found in the realm of being generated by the game. The whole domain is considered to be cut off from the ongoing world, an "artificial" universe, neither make-believe nor real. This is so regardless of the amount of the bet that may be attached to the outcome. Action itself is divided up into relatively autonomous "hands" or "deals." During one of these subunits, the individual may find himself bluffing, in the next being bluffed, in another bluffing and being bluffed, and so forth. As soon as one of these mini-episodes is played out, another follows immediately. Anxiety about what reading to put on the opponent's apparent situation (and anxiety about the reading he is placing on one's own) is on the whole restricted to a particular episode. Often no anxiety whatsoever attaches to the context as a whole, namely, that an artificial domain is being sustained by happy mutual consent. This understanding is itself not problematic—except, of course, where cheating is suspected or enough heat is generated to cause participants to break frame and flee or fight. So anxiety about the opponent's intent, reading, and resources, hence anxiety about what is really going on, is kept within the bounds of a particular round, doubly a matter of merely a game. This I believe to be one of the deeper reasons why bettors can tolerate such great losses and wins without becoming quite beside themselves; after all, in games it is not "themselves" that they could get beside.

Assessment games introduce an optical-illusion element into the actor's situation. He does not know whether things are as they seem or their opposite; what it is that is going on flips in and out of perspective much like a gestalt illusion. In nongame situations, situations in which matters are defined as serious and real, the actor can maximize the gamy element through the way he construes and conceptualizes the situation (as, for example, game-theory-oriented advisers on international relations sometimes do), but the situation is likely to have some elements which cannot readily be assimilated to this design. One exception, however, can be found: episodes of negotiation. In bargaining, to take one example, the buyer projects indifference about acquiring the object, disagreement (whether gently or forcibly expressed, depending on local rules) concerning the claimed value of the object, inadequacy of resources, and sometimes access to the same thing elsewhere on better terms. The seller projects an argument regarding the high value of the object, its scarcity (and the likelihood that it will soon be lost to another customer), his unconcern to sell, and his obligation to get the asking price by virtue of a set of inflexible constraints over which he has no control, such as the cost to him. Thus, each party attempts to contain the other,[21] and what occurs, in fact, is a competition of containment. Much the same argument can be made regarding the character of threats and promises during arbitration and contract negotiations.

This view of bargaining and other negotiations adds nothing new to these topics but does, I think, relate them to the more general issue of frame. To suspect a bluff is not merely to withdraw belief from a given threat; it is to radically reconstitute one's frame (or decline to allow its reconstitution), for the threatened event ceases to determine the sense one has of one's situation, and what then does define the world is a fact of a quite different order, namely, that attempted containment is in progress. The specific outcomes threatened become collapsed into no more than another illustration of deception.

5. It is easy to appreciate that one person's expression of feeling about another is vulnerable to all the doubts and suspicions and misframings to which isolated, single events are subject. An academic example might be cited:

> Let us suppose the individual to be richly praised. What transformations can convert such positive evidence into the opposite?

---

21. That a fabrication or containment (or an attempt) is involved is nicely illustrated in the following report below the picture of a bust:

> This plaster bust, bought by New York's Metropolitan Museum of Art at an auction for $225, may be worth $500,000. Museum director James Rorimer said that the bust appears to be an original by either Leonardo da Vinci or his teacher, Andrea del Verrochio. Museum officials kept their interest in the bust a secret until after the sale by inspecting it only when no one was looking and by sending a minor clerk to do the bidding. [*San Francisco Chronicle*, October 27, 1965.]

A version of sophisticated bargaining is described in Fuad I. Khuri, "The Etiquette of Bargaining in the Middle East," *American Anthropologist*, LXX (1968): 698–706.

First, the sincerity of the judge may be questioned. He cannot really believe what he is saying and indeed he is using exaggerated praise to mock me. Second, he praised only this work because he knows that everything else which I have done is trash, and he is praising this work because there is nothing else to praise. Third, he may be sincere, but he is probably a fool to be taken in like this— and he is thereby exposing me all the more to the ridicule of those who can evaluate properly. Fourth, this is a temporary lapse of judgment. When he comes to his senses and sees through me, he will have all the more contempt for me. Fifth, the judges have incomplete information. They do not really have all the evidence which they would need to see the worthlessness of the work of the self. Sixth, this is a fluke. It is truly praiseworthy, and the judges are not mistaken but it was a lucky, unrepresentative accident, which will probably never occur again. Seventh, others are trying to control me, holding out a carrot of praise. If I eat this I am hooked, and I will thenceforth have to work for their praise and to avoid their censure. Eighth, they are exposing how hungry I am for praise and thereby exposing my inferiority and my feelings of humiliation, even though they do not intend to do this. Ninth, they are seducing me into striving for something more which I cannot possibly achieve. Ultimately this praise will prove my complete undoing by seducing me into striving for the impossible and thereby destroying myself. Tenth, he is acting as though he alone is the only judge of my work, as though I am incapable of correctly judging its worth and so I must forever be dependent upon his or their judgment.

So may genuine respect be transformed in the monopolistic humiliation equation.[22]

We seem less ready to see, however, that formal relations might be less subject to the play of doubts than are intimate ones. It is that possibility I want to consider now.

It is apparent that two persons who are much together have an opportunity to create something of a privately shared world for themselves. Each supplies the other with details of prerelation personal biography, and they begin to develop a new phase of their biography jointly. In addition, each is in a position to influence greatly the opinion the other has of matters, the more so the more the pair is cut off from other sources of influence. (Hence the possibility of *folie à deux* and the apparent clinical fact that

22. Silvan Tomkins, *Affect-Imagery-Consciousness* (New York: Springer Publishing Co., 1963), vol. 2, pp. 442–443.

when the leader is withdrawn, the delusion of the follower collapses rather quickly.) Moreover, the affection, loyalty, and respect of a first party for a second is something that comes, it is believed, from within the first, something he alone is privy to, and something he conveys, indicates, or expresses through signs over many of which—after all—he might have considerable control. In sum, the relationship between our first and second parties will be for the second a significant part of the world, and the faking of this is within the control of the first, known by the second to be so, and known by the first to be so known. Observe, fakery will not require elaborate sets, extensive equipment, or outside help; words and touches and glances are all that are required, and of these the fabricator ordinarily already has an ample supply.

It is understandable, then, that two quite intimately related individuals can each spend a considerable amount of time in private thought trying to piece out what the other really "meant" by doing a particular thing and what the implications of this meaning are for the state of the relationship. And although, as suggested, this doubting will often occur between persons not intimately related, the state of uncertainty and suspicion that thus develops is not likely to be chronic, simply because other sources of information and other events ordinarily will become available; also, other matters of importance will soon take over. In the case of intimates, such as marital pairs, however, the "real" feelings of other for self become central and continuous as an issue, and therefore doubts in this connection can quite effectively undermine the individual's everyday world. And often this doubt will be well grounded. It is here that Laing has a useful comment:

> Interpersonal life is conducted in a nexus of persons, in which each person is guessing, assuming, inferring, believing, trusting or suspecting, generally, being happy or tormented by his phantasy of the other's experience, motives, and intentions. And one has phantasies not only about what the other himself experiences and intends, but about his phantasies about one's own experience and intentions, and about his phantasies about one's phantasies about his phantasies about one's experience, etc.[23]

---

23. R. D. Laing, *The Self and Others* (Chicago: Quadrangle Books, 1962), from an appendix, "A Shorthand for Dyadic Perspectives," p. 171.

More than the issue of divining true feelings is involved. Persons who are intimately related and much together sustain joint undertakings made up almost wholly of the personal contributions of each. Should one of them come to suspect the other of falseness or insincerity, then he will also come to suspect that the ordinary events involving him are fabrications. Again, such fabrication is easily within the capacity of the other, since his own actions are mainly involved. Here is the real democracy of dyads. Large-scale organizations can ordinarily be totally subverted only by the few individuals who either manage them or have access to their secrets; an ordinary participant who is treacherous can fake his involvement but often not much else. But in the case of close-knit dyads, all participants are in key roles and perfectly placed for subversion.

The power of one member of a twosome to fabricate the everyday world of another is sometimes seated in households and the equipment these establishments contain; differently put, if one party is to become suspicious of another, then households provide a good scene for it. For example, the fact that a wife may be stationed in the house during the workday and yet have many just reasons for being absent at any one moment—say, because of shopping, errands, visiting female friends, attending meetings, and so forth—provides favorable circumstances in which a suspicious husband can wonder what his wife is really doing away from the house, and in which a wife who correctly or incorrectly thinks she is suspected can be concerned about the impression she is creating when indeed she is away from the house for a "perfectly good" reason. Nor do I mean to imply that the household is primarily a place only for ungrounded suspicions. The fact that the housewife's time is "unaccountable" in the sense that no supervisor is immediately there for her to answer to[24] does in fact allow her to lead a secret life should she want to, and, what is more, a very extensive one. It is this fact that enabled a suburban minister to organize twelve of the housewives in his church to keep a running tail on Syndicate gambling operations in his community unbeknownst to almost everyone, guilty and innocent.[25] It is this fact, plus the basic assumption that household

24. Suggestive comments on the matter of accountability and illicit activity are provided in an unpublished paper by Arthur Stinchcombe.

25. Reverend Albert Fay Hill, *The North Avenue Irregulars* (New York: Pocket Books, 1970).

goods can be guarded by the respect shown to physically marked conventional boundaries, which allowed a housewife to achieve the following, and store the achievement in her house:

Detroit—(UPI)—More than $200,000 worth of jewelry, watches, rare coins, stock certificates, guns and other small items lay neatly piled in the attic.

Alongside was a stack of 25 pillowcases—the mark of the "pillowcase burglar."

"I'm glad it's all over," Mrs. Helen Ann Haynes was quoted by police as saying as she led them to the attic of her West Side home.

The 26-year-old housewife admitted that she was responsible for some 150 to 200 Detroit-area burglaries in the past eight months. Downstairs, police found more stacks of carefully washed and pressed pillowcases.

Mrs. Haynes told police a girl friend talked her into breaking into the home of another woman against whom the girl friend wanted revenge. The friend got cold feet and Mrs. Haynes began her career alone late last year, she told police.

She tripped up when she tried to use a stolen credit card and a store clerk became suspicious. As she fled the store, Mrs. Haynes left behind a stolen check, the credit card and the registration to her husband's truck.

Arraigned on a charge of breaking and entering, Mrs. Haynes was at a loss to explain why she did it, police said.[26]

The equipment in households itself provides opportunities for grounded and ungrounded suspicion:

Dear Abby: My husband is trying to make me, and other people, think I am insane. He takes things out of my drawers, hides them, and then after I have searched the house for days, he puts them back in their original places and tries to tell me they were there all the time. He sets all the clocks ahead, and then sets them back until I am so confused I don't know what time it is! He calls me vile names and accuses me of terrible things like going with other men. . . .[27]

---

26. *The Evening Bulletin* (Philadelphia), July 22, 1970. Mrs. Haynes either has an extraordinary natural talent for this line of work or she reflects severely on the stereotype of risk and skill associated with professionals.

27. *San Francisco Chronicle,* February 7, 1966.

The literary version, of course, is to be found in *Gaslight*.[28]

Just as one individual in a relationship will be vulnerable to being contained by the other, so he will be vulnerable to being informed by the other that this is the case, even though it may not have been; and whether such information is true or false, it may not be retractable:

> *Dear Abby:* After nearly 20 years of marriage my husband has asked me for a divorce. He says he needs a wife, not a house-keeper.
>
> Two years ago, in the middle of a heated argument I told my husband that his love-making did nothing for me—that I had only been putting on an act.
>
> Abby, it wasn't exactly the truth. I only said it to hurt him. He hasn't touched me or kissed me since that day.
>
> I would do anything to have my husband back the way he was. I have a fine home, wonderful children, and I don't want a divorce. Please tell me what to do.[29]

A final comment. Our understanding of people seems to be linked to a tacit theory of expression or indication. We assume that there are such things as relationships, feelings, attitudes, character, and the like, and that various acts and postures some-how intentionally or unintentionally provide direct evidence con-cerning these things. But the position can be taken that in the main what exists are doctrines regarding expression, gestural equipment for providing displays, and stable motives for encour-aging certain imputations. It could then be granted that certainly feelings, relationships, and attributes can be faked and that indications can be provided in absence of their proper referent. And further, that it is important to distinguish these fakeries from the real thing. But what is real in each case, it could be argued, is merely a differently grounded—usually more stable and more acceptable—motive for maintaining a particular ap-pearance. And insofar as this is the case—insofar, for example, as a personal relationship can be defined as a coalition between two players to provide each other with expressions of the exis-tence of a desirable bond—then, of course, two-person worlds are

---

28. Originally Patrick Hamilton's play *Angel Street*, filmed under the title *Gaslight* and later (1966) adapted as a novel by William Drummond—a considerable framing career.

29. *San Francisco Chronicle*, October 6, 1967.

vulnerable indeed. The *indication* that each party provides the other that nothing whatsoever could break them apart is itself the substance, not the shadow, and should the motives of either or both change in this matter of supporting a particular appearance and encouraging a particular imputation, then the displays themselves can be very quickly altered.

V

There are, then, weak points in social life where participants become more than usually vulnerable to deception and illusion, to a wrong relation to the facts and a misalignment to experience. Consider now some other vulnerabilities, this time ones directly generated by the special opportunities that framing provides for those who would deceive.

1. *Back-up designs:* When an individual comes to question the activity he is involved in, comes to wonder whether or not he has mistaken the primary framework or key or is being duped or deluded, he seeks for confirmatory evidence. The more he suspects his situation, the more will he seek out bits of evidence he presumes to be foolproof. He thus becomes particularly vulnerable to the faking of this evidence, since he will be trustful of it and very dependent on it. There is a variety of these designs:[30] the practice of arranging for what appear to be independent witnesses; the display of "telltales," those minor acts or objects which provide careful observers with incidental clues (they think); the scattering of faked evidence in depth so that a texture of support is available for the erroneous interpretation; the arranging of "vital tests";[31] the creation of cover, that is, good (but

---

30. Considered at length in *S.I.*, pp. 19–28, 58–70.
31. Of which an example might be given:

These undercover police agents were principally used in the investigation of illegal narcotics sales. The agent's most difficult task was becoming acquainted with drug peddlers in a way that would encourage their having trust in him. This was accomplished in one case by having the agent frequent a bar known to be used by drug peddlers. One evening a police raiding squad attacked the bar and lined the customers up against the wall. When the sergeant in charge of the raid spotted the agent, he slapped him in the face and, calling him by his assumed name, demanded to see his criminal registration card. After pretending to review

fake) reasons for being someplace or doing something;[32] finally,
the use of faked newspapers and broadcasts, these being sources
of information thought to be especially independent of any particular agency.[33]

An obvious question, of course, is just how extensive and
prolonged backup design can be.[34] Virtuoso efforts are a popular
theme in modern fiction and drama (beginning, say, with the
romances of John Buchan and ending with TV serials such as
Mission Impossible), some being organized precisely around this
theme.[35] This should remind us of the great and troubled inter-

---

the card, the sergeant told the agent he knew he was a drug addict and
warned him to keep out of his district. The agent was assured of a warm
welcome by the drug peddlers after the raiding officers left. [Samuel
Dash et al., *The Eavesdroppers* (New Brunswick, N.J.: Rutgers University Press, 1959), p. 254.]

32. Cover can be built backwards in time so that when independent
sources are asked corroborative questions about the suspect's past, safe
answers will result. For example, the following is reported of a French
physician who helped maintain Allied intelligence on German fortification
on the Normandy coast:

Coldly, clinically, he planned his Resistance. His practice would give him
access to the entire area where agents were lacking, but he must think
always as a doctor, not as an agent. . . . He would not risk visiting any
sector of the coast unless a professional call provided him with an alibi.
The call would be logged in advance in his daybook, and the pharmacist's
records would serve as a double check that he had called and prescribed
medicine. The immunity of the battered black Gladstone bag holding
instruments and stethoscope would be a useful cover for his sector map.
[Richard Collier, *10,000 Eyes* (New York: Pyramid Books, 1959), pp.
183–184.]

33. For example:

Then the captain—who was also an intelligence agent—cabled Warsaw.
He explained how he had Adam in his grip, and he proposed that the
youth could be recruited to work for Polish intelligence if Warsaw acted
swiftly. Within a few days the captain was able to hand Adam some
clippings—made in Warsaw—which he told Adam had come from local
German newspapers. They related the shooting incident in impeccable
German type and described the missing man who was wanted for murder
—Adam Kozicki. [Pawel Monat, *Spy in the U.S.* (New York: Berkley
Publishing Corporation, Berkley Medallion Books, 1963), p. 177.]

34. See the comments in *R.P.*, pp. 318–319, and *S.I.*, pp. 61–62.

35. In these entertainments, there are two basic ways in which the hero
can become anomically related to the world. First, a whole sphere may be
fabricated around him, almost everything being false except himself. The
movie *36 Hours* (direction and screenplay by George Seaton) is an example; the TV serial *The Prisoner* (later adapted for paperback by Thomas

est produced by historically verified occasions when considerable conspiratorial collusion was managed in order to wrongly convict innocent parties—the Dreyfus Affair and, in the United States, the Becker-Rosenthal case[36] being examples. And these efforts,

---

M. Disch and Ace Books, 1969) is another, and one that seems to pointedly exploit almost every frame possibility one can think of. The second method is to provide the hero with a vital event that is fated to be disbelieved by the ordinary citizenry, who—given his need to warn the world—will have the effect of encapsulating him in skeptical responses wherever he goes, transforming the path he cuts in the normal world into a swath of unreality.

This second method of anomizing an individual's relation to the world is sufficiently used in commercial fantasies to have acquired a formula of sorts. The hero, heretofore part of innocent well-framed society, gets accidentally caught up in a secretly conducted conflict because he is mistaken for someone he isn't, or happens to witness a vital event, or is there when a participant in the conflict needs immediate help. He then finds himself with a bit of information which proves that a secret design is at work, but of course he finds that no one believes him, either because of honest skepticism on their parts or because they have been systematically bribed or otherwise induced to conceal what they themselves know about the machinations. The hero's problem is to get others to believe him before he fails to evade the network that is out to get him. Eventually he manages to convince (he thinks) two persons or at least obtain sympathy from them. One of these will prove to be the first of a growing group of honest folk who have come to be convinced; the other will be an agent of the enemy who becomes doubly dangerous because he has become a confidant. Eventually, of course, the hero is vindicated, that is, his reading of events becomes the credited one; he wins the hand of the heroine and, more to the point, reestablishes the world as a place where there is an absolute continuity of resources and infinitely confirmed connectedness and unconnectedness.

Whether the first or second method is used, these commercial fantasies provide an obvious source of comment on our conception of the way the world is made up, and an obvious reminder of the questions students of worlds ought to be asking. For example, the film *Bunny Lake Is Missing* (from a novel of the same name by Evelyn Piper) turns on the fact that a young mother visiting London finds that her child has disappeared from a school and that no one will believe that indeed she had a child to lose. The cosmological issue, then, is how to arrange to cast into doubt a woman's claim that she has lost a child. How much of the world has to be intentionally altered through bribes, threats, etc.? How much of the difficulty can be attributed to misunderstanding, a desire of witnesses "not to get involved," and so forth? How much to the fact that the claimant may not seem to be reliable? In short, how much would the world have to be reordered to allow for such a grotesque disordering?

36. Andy Logan, *Against the Evidence: The Becker-Rosenthal Affair* (New York: McCall Books, 1970). A more current case is the eventually successful effort of Ronald Ridenhour to disclose the atrocities at Songmy. (Here see the report by Christopher Lydon, "'Pinkville' Gadfly," *The New*

being known about, in turn create the possibility of conspiracies being claimed when none exists, or none that we can be sure of.[37] In any case, behind the various kinds of interest in conspiracy, I think, there is to be detected a sense of the acute dependency we all have on the world not tolerating any extensive and protracted manufacture of spurious reality or even doubts as to which of opposing views is correct.

2. *Bracket use:* It seems generally true that much social activity is episoded by brackets, and that there will be a kind of backstage period before the activity begins and after it is over. Individuals are not merely out of role at these times, but they are unguarded in ways they won't be as soon as the activity proper begins.

Thus it is understandable that he who would contain another may be advised to work his design on the moments *before* the scheduled activity, since then the dupe will be least wary. And the purpose here can be deeper than that of merely producing an entertaining negative experience.

Take, for example, experimental hoaxing. In order, in a study of "racial attitudes," to learn about interviewer bias, the following method was employed: A class was given a nine-item attitude scale adopted from *The Authoritarian Personality:*

> The scales were administered to the entire class, both male and female, and Ss were led to believe that the test administration constituted a complete study. . . .
>
> At a later date, a person other than the administrator of the attitude scale approached the students in class and requested volunteers for an experiment. Since participation in psychological experiments is required of all students in general psychology, these Ss are not "free volunteers." Appointments were then made for the male Ss and these Ss were instructed to report individually to a specified room in the Psychology Building at the scheduled hour.
>
> When the S arrived for his appointment, he found another student (actually an experimental assistant) already seated in the room. As soon as S was seated, E entered and explained that the

York Times, November 29, 1969.) To understand how these conspiracies could be managed is also to understand how conspiracies can be claimed where none exists or where no final proof is established.

37. See, for example, Jim Garrison, *A Heritage of Stone* (New York: G. P. Putnam's Sons, 1970); Edward Jay Epstein, *Counterplot* (New York: Viking Press, 1969).

previous S had not yet finished, and then departed. On a signal, another assistant, with a petition, entered from another door, explained the purpose of the petition and requested the assistant to sign. The assistant signed or refused according to a prearranged sequence. The petition-bearer then requested the S to sign the petition, and recorded his response. . . . The S was then requested by E to accompany him to the experimental room, where he was given a Semantic Differential form to complete. Since the purpose of the task was to make the actual experimental condition seem realistic, the Semantic Differential was discarded after S left the room.

Within the framework of the above procedure, half of the Ss encountered a Negro waiting his turn in the waiting room, while half shared the waiting room with a white assistant. . . .

The petition employed in this study contained a proposal to extend the library hours on Saturday evening until eight o'clock. This was chosen because it represented an issue on which there should not be strong approval or disapproval.[38]

The same technique is recommended to interrogators in the form of the two-character approach, whereby one interrogator, playing the heavy, establishes a frame which the other interrogator, playing the sympathizer, can be outside of:

After Interrogator B (the unfriendly one) has been in the interrogation room for a short while, Interrogator A (the friendly one) re-enters and scolds B for his unfriendly conduct. A asks B to leave, and B goes out of the door with a pretended feeling of disgust toward both the subject and A. A then resumes his friendly, sympathetic approach.

This technique has been effectively applied by using a detective as the friendly interrogator and a police captain as the unfriendly one. As the captain leaves the room after playing his unfriendly role, the detective may say, "Joe, I'm glad you didn't tell him a damn thing. He treats everybody that way—persons like you, as well as men like me within his own department. I'd like to show him up by having you tell me the truth. It's time he learns a lesson or two about decent human behavior.[39]

---

38. Philip Himelstein and James C. Moore, "Racial Attitudes and the Action of Negro- and White-Background Figures as Factors in Petition Signing," *Journal of Social Psychology*, LXI (1963): 268–269. This experiment follows a pattern laid down by a prior set of experimenters and is not to be seen as extraordinary in regard to the hoodwinking of subjects.

39. Fred E. Inbau and John E. Reid, *Criminal Interrogation and Confessions* (Baltimore: Williams & Wilkins Co., 1962), pp. 58–59.

Thus the change from one interrogator to the other can be seen by the subject as a shift from one drama to another, when, in fact, a single show is being played which starts before he thinks it does and fits into a whole in a manner he is blind to.

In preopening play, international politics have recently been unpleasantly creative. Letter bombs are the example. Although we assume a message may cause unease, we do (or did) not assume that the envelope it comes in is a problem, too. Problems are supposed to start in a reading, not when getting down to it.

The beginning bracket, then, can serve to deceive but, of course, so, too, can the ending bracket. When an activity arouses acute wariness and suspicion among participants, its apparent termination may very effectively restore ease and trust, sometimes at the cost of the parties concerned:

> True tale, new racket gimmick, or one of those strange stories that pops up every now and then and makes the rounds? Goes like this:
>
> A Northeast resident found his car stolen one morning. Two days later, it was returned, with a note on the front seat saying: Sorry, car had to be taken but was needed for an emergency . . . leaving two tickets for a sports event "to make up for the inconvenience."
>
> The car owner was delighted, took his wife to the sports event with the free ducats, returned to find their home completely ransacked.[40]

Another example is the practice of staking out a possible stake-out, as when an agent, distrustful of a meet he has set up with a potential contact, has the meeting place covered in advance by two of his men who will remain in place *after* the meeting to see if any evidence of surveillance appears after the agent has left— the assumption being that "plants" in the vicinity will take care to maintain cover during the meeting but will feel safe in breaking cover after the meeting.[41]

There is also a form of deception derived from interchanging beginning and ending brackets. Thus, a standard device in mind-reading exhibitions is the sequence misdirection, in which the

---

40. *The Evening Bulletin* (Philadelphia), January 25, 1972.

41. A case of contained containment. See Alexander Orlov, *Handbook of Intelligence and Guerrilla Warfare* (Ann Arbor: University of Michigan Press, 1963), p. 118.

mentalist mind-reads a series of sealed messages from the audience, starting first with a message which his sole confederate in the audience will confirm having sealed in the first envelope. This envelope, opened and read aloud by the mentalist after he has made his first divination, will naturally confirm the telepathy. But actually the confederate's envelope is placed at the end and the mentalist is seeing in the first envelope what he will then divine as being in the second; and when he opens *that* envelope to confirm his reading, he will acquire the message he divines as being in the next envelope, and so on. Thus, what the audience takes as mind-reading followed by a confirmatory disclosure of the written message is really a mind-reading *following* a confirmatory disclosure.[42]

A final point about brackets. When the individual leaves a scene of stress, one in which his view of justice is not sustained, he can seek out a class of persons who seem particularly unconnected with the difficulty and who are committed to a framing of events that he feels will support him. Confidants and lovers are examples. Officials of the law and perhaps physicians and clergy also qualify, for these persons seem to symbolize society's support of fair-mindedness and truth; they stand for independent judgment, and if nothing else, at least will not connive with the agencies complained about. It follows that when these latter sources of support, selected in part because of their assured unconnectedness with the trouble, prove to be in league with it, the individual is very likely to feel acute vulnerability. This sort of thing occurs when someone in police authority proves to be in league with the criminals against whom a citizen secretly brings a complaint. With intelligence agents it is said to occur commonly, perhaps never so fully as in the work of the pre–World War I *chief* of Austrian intelligence, Colonel Alfred Redl, who had been turned by the Russians upon their discovery and exploitation of the Colonel's special sexual tastes:

For ten years Redl, an Austrian, had been Russia's chief agent in Austria. Not only had he sold the Russians all his country's secrets in return for protection of his social secret and money to indulge it,

---

42. This reading I derive from Marcello Truzzi. See his discussion of the "one-ahead technique" in "Unfunded Research No. 3," *Subterannean Sociology Newsletter,* II (January 1968): 7.

but he had actually betrayed to them his *own* agents operating at *his* direction against Russia. Again, in an equally grotesque twist, when a tremendously important Russian plan for attacking Germany and Austro-Hungary was offered to Redl by a defecting Russian unaware of Redl's own treachery, Redl drew up fake plans that seemed to smack of some vague Russian treachery and showed them to his own Government. Meanwhile he returned the real plans to Russia and betrayed the defector. For this he received a handsome bonus from the grateful Russians.[43]

Perhaps no great moral issue is involved in the fate of this particular would-be informant, compared, say, to the slaughter that the Serbian army inflicted a little later on the Austrian forces by virtue of being privy to the complete details of the Austrian plans for the Balkan action early in World War I—an advantage also due to Redl's disloyalty. Nonetheless, this informant's vulnerability provides us with an instructive extreme. The highest intelligence officer of a nation is in some way a court of last appeal, and a court of last appeal is in some way the guardian of reality. (And he speaks with a foreign-office accent.) If the final person in authority secretly sells you out to his nation's enemies and is therefore the opposite of what he seems to be, then what can be trusted to be as it appears to be? It might be added that the highest political office in a state seems to bring its incumbent into a special relationship to realities. He is taken as representing them. Should it prove, then, that he is being deceived or is deceiving, his reputation is not the only thing that suffers; the reputation of realities suffers, too.

3. *Tracking deceptions:* Given that attention is designed to focus upon the main track, the story line, of any particular activity and to treat in sharply different ways matters that occur in the subordinate ones, it is apparent that the intentional manipulation of tracking can effectively render a frame vulnerable. Here, especially, what can be said about the generation of negative experience can also be said about the vulnerabilities of realms of activity.

---

43. Allison Ind, *A History of Modern Espionage* (London: Hodder & Stoughton, 1965), pp. 60–61. This example was culled and used before the Watergate investigations in Washington, D.C., in 1973 established the American political scene as a new competitive source for intrigue stories of this kind.

For one, on the assumption that background features of an activity will not be attended, those who would conceal, disrupt, and engage in other improprieties can exploit these areas. Thus, animal droppings have been used as antipersonnel mines, the assumption being that the ground will be seen but not seen.[44] A somewhat similar exploitation of the physical frame of activity is described in prisoner-of-war-camp literature:

> We established communications with the camp and among ourselves. With the aid of pencil butts dropped in the courtyard where we walked, notes were later written on pieces of lavatory paper, and left to be picked up by officers. The first Red Cross parcels had just arrived. We asked for food in our notes and were soon receiving it: chocolate, sugar, Ovo-sport, cheese!
>
> We would enter the courtyard carrying our towels as sweatrags. After a turn or two we would notice an inconspicuous pile of swept-up dust. This was the food done up in a small round parcel. A towel would be dropped carelessly in the corner over the rubbish and left until the end of the half-hour's exercise. The towel and the parcel would then be recovered in one movement and nonchalantly carried back to the cells to be divided later and left in the lavatory.[45]

As already argued, what would ordinarily be disattended provides a good cover for a collusive message system. Again, prisoner-of-war experience provides an example. The situation is that of secretly digging an escape tunnel:

> The routine was simple enough; one man worked at the wall-face, another man sat on a box inside the room with his eye glued to the keyhole of the door looking along the passage, a third man read a book, or otherwise behaved innocently, seated on the stone steps at the only entrance to the building a few yards away from the passage, a fourth man lounged, or exercised, in the farthest courtyard. After a couple of hours the two men outside and the two men inside would change places. Warning of the approach of any German was passed by noncommittal signals, such as the blowing of a nose, along the line, depending on the direction from which he appeared. The man on the wall-face would immediately stop work on receipt of the signal.[46]

44. See "Normal Appearances" in *R.P.*, p. 292.

45. P. R. Reid, *Escape from Colditz* (New York: Berkley Publishing Corp., 1956), pp. 48–49.

46. *Ibid.*, p. 17.

One further example of vulnerability due to the manipulation of tracking can be suggested: what might be called informant's folly. I refer to the individual's assumption that although the text of his remarks or behavior may be recorded and discussed, the out-of-frame elements carried in the subordinate channels will not. But of course they often are. The folly derives from the fact that although the informant may suspect and fear this reporting in depth and although he may attempt to control his conduct accordingly, he can rarely succeed in doing so.[47] For if the individual acts at all, it seems he must channel his stream of behavior into a main track, the content of which is meant to be openly attended, and a set of subordinate tracks which carry material meant to manage and be managed by the proceedings, not be the proceedings. It will therefore always be possible for interviewers to record behavioral detail the subject thought was part of the not-for-comment element of his behavior. Thus, for example, in a magazine article report on the food at New York's late Le Pavillon, the writer records the following observations on the great Henri Soulé's successor:

> Shorn of my usual restaurant anonymity (having interviewed Mr. Levin for other articles), I suffered, bringing out the best—the best table, the best captain—and the worst in Stuart [Levin] as trilingually he nimbled from French to English to Yiddish. Stuart as Jackie Mason kibitzing his own Alliance Française performance as an elegant maître d'hôtel. He reared in exaggerated indignation as I described the goujonnette de sole as "rather resembling Mrs. Paul's fish sticks." "What do you mean, Mrs. Paul's?" he scolded, poking my shoulder. "Here we serve Mrs. Schwartz's." He slapped his forehead with the flat of his hand . . . moaning that I was probably recording every word of his "shtick."[48]

---

47. *R.P.*, p. 303.

48. Gael Greene, "Exorcising the Ghost at Le Pavillon," *New York Magazine*, September 21, 1970, p. 65. The history of changes in the respect shown for "no comment" is hard to piece out. One change is due to recent interest in nonverbal behavior, which amounts to a change not in what a recipient receives but what he is prepared to report on, an extension sometimes associated with the "new journalism." Another influence is the style of profiling in evidence in *Esquire* magazine in the sixties, especially in efforts to squeeze an article out of recluses like Howard Hughes. (By close textual comment on the various ways of being told that no interview is to be given, an importuning reporter can generate enough material for an article.) The New York literary scene during the same period moved in the

Mr. Levin's predicament bears close examination; it nicely illustrates the frame complexity of social interaction. As suggested, when an individual knowingly provides a report for purposes of relay, he falls into the assumption that he can interlard his comments not only with directional cues which will go unreported, but also with off-the-record asides of various kinds. Ironically, the very fact that the interviewer is not merely a mechanical relay but someone to whom a relationship of sorts must be extended and expressively confirmed assures this double stream of behavior on the subject's part, for he will owe the interviewer an orientation and address that is not owed the interviewer's ultimate market audience. (Observe that in any kind of talk, the phrase "this is off the record" or its functional equivalent is always a possibility, for an invisible audience which the speaker at the moment may not want to address is always thinkable.) Further, should the subject suspect that his off-mike behavior may be reported, he is very likely to give some expression to this feeling, and *that* expression he assumes will not be reported. Thus, it is almost inevitable that an on-the-record action will generate a component of behavior not meant to be recorded, and if recorded, then not meant to be explicitly addressed.[49] We embroider our discourse with multiple voices (or "registers"), and some of these, being wholly responsive to the site in which the discourse actually occurs, are doomed to be out of place if witnessed away from their original setting.

4. *Insider's folly:* When a construction is discredited—whether by discovery, confession, or informing—and a frame apparently cleared, the plight of the discovered persons tends to be accepted with little reservation, very often with less reservation than was sustained in regard to the initial frame itself. And

---

same direction, especially in terms of the practices of Mailer and Baldwin and the lesser lights who made contact with them. A meeting would occur at a party, in a bar, or on the phone, and soon one of the participants (sometimes two) would publish a close record of the style the other(s) employed in managing the interaction. See, as a specimen, Seymour Krim, "Ubiquitous Mailer vs. Monolithic Me," in his *Shake It for the World, Smartass* (New York: Dell Publishing Co., Delta Books, 1971), pp. 125–151.

49. Therefore, the response "no comment" becomes a comment that reporters can record in expressive detail and hence is very much a comment. A linguist I know tries to employ a real no-comment act by telling reporters that he will call them right back. *That* they do not report, at least not yet.

this acceptance tends to be given by all parties to the uncovering, the duped, the dupers, and the informants. It also seems that when an individual becomes involved in containing others, his critical reservation in regard to the venture itself and to his co-conspirators is appreciably reduced. In regard, then, both to clearing frames and constructing false ones, there will be a special basis for a firm belief in what it is that is going on. This being so, there is also a special way of inducing misguided belief. That is insider's folly.

The most familiar exploitation of insider's folly is found in the theatrical device of the play within a play, in which the intent (as with other devices for manufacturing negative experience) is to con the audience out of nothing more than the intensity of its involvement and its willingness to make believe. As suggested, the characters onstage are divided into two sets, one set serving as an audience and the other set as individuals staging characters. Since the character-staged characters—the characters of the play within the play—are merely dramaturgic constructs, those watching them onstage as an audience must be something other than mere fictions themselves. And so they are; they are traps for inducing involvement and belief. And it is, of course, Shakespeare who provides the advanced lessons on how to exploit this possibility, exceeding here ventriloquists, cartoonists, and other sophisticated tricksters who make use of reflexive frame breaks:

> O, what a rogue and peasant slave am I!
> Is it not monstrous, that this player here,
> But in a fiction, in a dream of passion,
> Could force his soul so to his own conceit,
> That, from her working, all his visage wann'd;
> Tears in his eyes, distraction in's aspect,
> A broken voice, and his whole function suiting
> With forms to his conceit? and all for nothing!
> For Hecuba!
> What's Hecuba to him, or he to Hecuba,
> That he should weep for her? What would he do,
> Had he the motive and the cue for passion
> That I have? He would drown the stage with tears. . . .[50]

---

50. *Hamlet*, Act II, Scene II. A trapping into belief is, of course, only one function of the play within the play. As Elizabeth Burns, *Theatricality: A Study of Convention in the Theatre and in Social Life* (London: Longmans

A further point about the play within a play. The performers-to-be of the inner play are seen going through last-minute preparations before the curtain within a curtain goes up. The paying audience thus gets to see both sides of a stage line. In consequence, they are hardly carried away by the play within the play—although Pirandello, just to flex his muscles, sometimes induces this. But again, they find that in being eased out of belief in the play within the play, they are automatically eased into belief concerning the play that contains the play within the play. The more clearly they see that the play within the play merely involves performed characters, the more fully they accept that it is performers who are putting on these characters. But, of course, it is not performers who are putting on these characters; it is characters who are putting on these characters. In brief, a glimpse behind the scenes can be a device for inducing the belief that you are seeing the backstage of *something*. Obviously, once you've got the staging area and the backstage you've got the whole thing and can feel secure in your frame anchorage. And the moment you feel secure, of course, is the moment you can be diddled.[51]

Turn now from theatrical entertainment to the exploitation of insider's folly in literal life. The clearest case in point is found in

---

Group, 1972; New York: Harper & Row, 1973), p. 44, suggests, there are others: provision of an interlude, a means of presaging what is to come, a device for furthering the action, and so forth. See also pp. 48–49.

51. Recently TV commercials have attempted to do so. For example, an obviously professional actor completes a commercial pitch and, with the camera still on him, turns in obvious relief from his task, now to take real pleasure in consuming the product he had been advertising.

This is, of course, but one example of the way in which TV and radio commercials are coming to exploit framing devices to give an appearance of naturalness that (it is hoped) will override the reserve auditors have developed. Thus, use is currently being made of children's voices, presumably because these seem unschooled; street noises, and other effects to give the impression of interviews with unpaid respondents; false starts, filled pauses, byplays, and overlapping speech to simulate actual conversation; and, following Welles, the interception of a firm's jingle commercials to give news of its new product, alternating occasionally with interception by a public interest spot, this presumably keeping the faith of the auditor alive.

The more that auditors withdraw to minor expressive details as a test of genuineness, the more that advertisers chase after them. What results is a sort of interaction pollution, a disorder that is also spread by the public relations consultants of political figures, and, more modestly, by microsociology.

swindles. It is a central feature of con games that the mark must be led to think he is joining in a swindle of someone else. Con men often rationalize this technique by saying that the sucker has larceny in his heart, but what he has there is beside the point. The question is one of belief, not heart. It happens to be that while committing an illegal act we can feel we are putting something over on somebody else, and it is the latter alignment, not the presumed illegality, that induces belief.

In primitive versions of the con, the mark's newfound fellow conspirators and the presumptive dupes are cut from much the same cloth—mere strangers about town. In more sophisticated versions, a nice role differentiation is obtained:

> A 67-year-old woman told police this afternoon she had lost $4500 of her savings to a ring of flim-flam artists.
>
> . . . .
>
> She said that two women got the other $1500 last Tuesday after approaching her at 29th st. and Ridge av. with a package of "money" they had "found" and offered to share with her if she put up cash to show "good faith."
>
> Detective Thomas McCusker said the two women accompanied Mrs. House to the Philadelphia Saving Fund Society branch office at 7th and Walnut sts., where she withdrew the $1500 and gave it to them. They promised to bring a share of the "found" money to her home later.
>
> Mrs. House, McCusker said, was still waiting today when two men came to her home, identified themselves as detectives and offered to catch the women who had her money. But they said they needed some money to further their investigation.
>
> They all went to the PSFS branch at 7th and Walnut where Mrs. House withdrew another $1500, McCusker said. Then the men learned she also had an account at the PSFS branch at Broad and Oxford sts. They convinced her she should keep her money in one bank.
>
> The three went to Broad and Oxford, where she withdrew $1500, and then returned to 7th and Walnut sts. The two men, who carried the money for her, handed her an envelope and told her to go in and deposit it.
>
> When Mrs. House opened the envelope she found it empty. The men had disappeared.[52]

---

52. *The Evening Bulletin* (Philadelphia), May 5, 1969. The same paper reports the same ruse ("Widow Is Swindled Second Time in Three Weeks")

A second example of this design provides for "bank officials" to phone a depositor and enlist his help in trapping a "dishonest" teller. The depositor is to contribute by pretending to withdraw his savings. These funds, presumably having been marked, will then be taken by the officials to serve as evidence against the teller. And taken the funds sometimes are.[53] Again, observe that nothing very elaborate need be employed in this design, merely some verbal formula which allows the mark to perform what he would otherwise be leery of doing, his misguided trust deriving from the fact that he has been led to think that he is not engaging in actual banking transactions but merely participating in a staged plot. Similarly, he who warns of the danger of a misdeed occurring is likely to be held ouside the range of those considered to be possible misdoers, for the commentator on a situation tends to be defined as someone beyond and outside of what he comments on. All of which he can exploit, as the following example from the mid-nineteenth century suggests:

> These latter gentry [fake auctioneers] commonly called Peter Funks, were themselves a source of great annoyance to the municipal authorities during the 1840's and 1850's, and many unsuccessful attempts were made to stop the sales of shoddy and worthless merchandise by which they robbed thousands of countrymen every year. Once, in 1854, Mayor Westervelt hired a large number of men to parade Broadway bearing signs inscribed, "Beware of Mock Auctions," but the Peter Funks met this attack by placing similar signs in their own windows.[54]

Another version of this sort of con is found in the role of *agent provocateur*, the current manifestation of which can be

---

in the same city, May 30, 1973. These double actions expose a charming structural feature of any first swindle, namely, that the swindler's associates will always be able to approach the victim with the kind of knowledge of the theft *and the thieves* that is the very core of the effective detective's role. All that is needed is the victim's home address and cool. The difficult work has already been done by the first swindler.

53. A series of attempts at this dodge is reported in the *San Francisco Chronicle*, February 27, 1965.

54. Herbert Asbury, *Sucker's Progress* (New York: Dodd, Mead & Co., 1938), p. 182. The Boston Strangler employed the tack of asking the lady who answered the door whether she had seen a prowler looking through her window and if her husband would help him look for the man— in this way obtaining the requisite information and a rationale for knocking all at the same time. See Gerold Frank, *The Boston Strangler* (New York: New American Library, 1966), p. 335.

observed in the police and government contributions to radical politics—now much publicized. As already suggested, the agent actively engages in minor offenses and in planning major ones, which not only gives him something to inform on later, but also establishes his own cover by enabling him to share in the solidarity and mutual trust generated by those who conspire—a case of building a trap and a rabbit to fall into it.[55]

I have cited what might be thought of as the classic examples of insider's folly. The list can be extended with less acclaimed forms. In intelligence work there is the so-called reserve story, namely, a cover tale an agent can provide the moment his initial cover story is broken and he seems beyond any further fabrication.[56] In countries where tax dodging is a high art, businessmen reportedly may keep three sets of books: one to record actual business, one to give right off to the tax collector, and a third to

---

55. Of course, a standard structural possibility and a very old story, support indeed for formal sociology. For example, when the 1917 Provisional Government in Russia held a commission investigation of the operation of the Okhrana, the following apparently came to light:

The Okhrana bosses protested that they had never countenanced "provocation," and that what the Commission called *agents provocateurs* were merely "secret collaborators." The police chiefs insisted that these operatives had been used exclusively as collectors of political intelligence, and had not been instructed to take active part in revolutionary work. Former Okhranniks were, however, forced to admit that it had been difficult for any secret collaborator long to maintain a completely passive posture within his revolutionary group, owing to the need to preserve cover by making at least some show of activity. For many years, accordingly, Okhrana agents had organized assassinations, fomented strikes and printed stirring calls to bloody revolution. Moreover, since a bonus was paid to Okhranniks who unearthed illegal printing presses, it was not uncommon for a police official to found such a press himself—and on police money—as a preliminary to "detecting" it and claiming the customary reward, also from police funds. In these and other ways the Okhrana had systematically undermined the very legality which it was charged to uphold. . . . Fantastic as were the absurdities promoted during the Empire's dying spasms by political police provocation run riot, the Okhrana was in essence merely using a routine technique of detection as employed all over the world by civil police forces in the investigation of common crime. [Ronald Hingley, *The Russian Secret Police* (New York: Simon and Schuster, 1970), p. 113.]

Mr. Hingley has perhaps proven hasty in describing the working of the Okhrana as especially absurd and fantastic.

56. See Oreste Pinto, *Spy-Catcher* (New York: Harper & Brothers, 1952), pp. 42–43.

give him after he has forced an admission that what he first saw was doctored.[57] And of one of the most domesticated of male occupations—milkman—one learns that disclosure about the staleness of the company's products may be made to the housewife in order to give her a sense of having broken through to a valid source of product information.[58]

Just as well-plotted flooding out can induce involvement from watchers (as did the "announcer" in the *War of the Worlds* broadcast), so also it can induce belief that the person who has broken frame is no longer in a position to dissimulate, else he would not have collapsed in the first place. Thus the strategy an individual can employ of acting as if he has lost his temper and control during arbitration and collective bargaining proceedings. (Interrogation teams made up of a soft and a heavy induce a version of insider's folly, too.) Perhaps an implication of formal social occasions can also be raised here: when people are to be brought together in full social regalia, stiff with pomp, moments offstage are inevitably manufactured, and a subset of participants will have been able to stand on no ceremony in regard to one another, thus inducing the belief that although the formal occasion will involve or has involved falsity, this one does not.

5. *False connectives*: It has been argued that a fundamental feature of experience is that deeds and words come to us connected to their source, and that ordinarily this connection is something we can take for granted, something that the context of action will always provide, something that ensures the anchoring of activity. Interestingly, although the violation of this feature of experience is often attempted in play—as when an individual momentarily disguises his voice in calling to a friend—the serious possibilities seem to be very little exploited, the "pranks" employed in the 1968 and 1972 presidential campaigns being a major exception.[59] The issue is not new, of course, for those

57. From an article on tax dodges in Spain in the *San Francisco Chronicle*, February 20, 1966.

58. Otis E. Bigus, "The Milkman and His Customer: A Cultivated Relationship," *Urban Life and Culture*, I (1972), esp. "Contrived Disclosure," pp. 149–151.

59. Apparently one or both parties employed designs of the following sort: food and drink invitations to rallies that had never been planned; limousine delivery of apparently invited guests to fund-raising dinners where attendance was closed to those who so arrived; obstreperous, ex-

involved in the action and lore of revolutionary movements. In that sphere, when one party suffers an atrocity, possibly leading to public sympathy and to condemnation of the presumed perpetrators, the question is traditionally raised as to whether the victim may have engineered it, especially since the victim is itself an organization of factions whose interests might be seen as not identical. What is less appreciated is how extensively ordinary life depends upon unguarded security in regard to connectives and how very vulnerable we are to violations thereof, and, in turn, to the development of diffuse anxiousness in this connection. There is the possibility here for the Balkinization of life.

6. *Frame traps:* When an individual is misunderstood and others misframe his words and actions, he is likely, of course, to provide a corrective account. In this way matters get set straight. So, too, when an individual errs for other reasons in defining the world, contrary evidence is likely soon to appear. And realignment can come when deception is revealed, whether through discovery by the deceived, admission by the deceiver, or disclosure by third parties. All these operations help clear the frame. What I want to suggest here is that the world can be arranged (whether by intent or default) so that incorrect views, however induced, are confirmed by each bit of new evidence or each effort to correct matters, so that, indeed, the individual finds that he is trapped and nothing can get through.

The notion of a frame trap is conventionalized in the interrogation joke, "Have you stopped beating your wife?" More instructive, I think, is the following story purportedly depicting the framing practice of a Restoration rogue and sharper by the name of Major Clancy. The episode is cited at length:

> One day Clancy went into a woolen-draper's shop in St. Paul's Churchyard, takes up so many yards of cloth to make new liveries, has it carry'd into a coach, tells the draper he has not money enough about him, but send one of his prentices along with him, and he would pay him. The Major rides away, a prentice follows the coach, he knows not whither; but instead of going to his

---

tremist support of a candidate by persons whom the opposition hired for their improprieties; display of in-party dissensus by placard-bearing persons not in the party; inopportune publicity releases from nonexistent organizations named in honor of the opposition's extreme wing; use of newsmen's credentials as a cover for spying; fomenting of intraparty bad feeling by use of forged signatures, stolen letterheads, and faked press releases.

lodgings, goes into a barber's house, into one of his upper rooms, to be trim'd; and being shav'd, gives the barber 5 shillings, saying to him, do not think that I give you so much money for your pains you took in triming me; no, for I have a greater charge to give you, in which I must entreat your care and diligence, for which you shall be well rewarded; that is, as soon as I am gone, you must call up a young youth that waits on me, he's a little bashful, and you'll hardly persuade him to confess his infirmity, till you force him; therefore lock him in with as much privacy as you can, and search him, and if you find things be amiss which I suspect you will, pray apply such medicines for his recovery as you think most expedient, and I will pay you well for your trouble. The Barber-Surgeon promises to be mindful of the lad, and so soon as the Major went into the coach, he bid the young man go along with the barber, and he would do his business: The prentice makes a handsome leg and bow, and goes along with the barber, who leads him into a private room, locks the door, begins to preach to the boy, in telling him what a pure stick of wood he was, to follow whoring so early: The lad thought the fellow mad, and blush'd to hear him: Come, come, (says the barber) your pretended modesty must not serve your turn, your master has told me your tricks, I must see how you are. The lad thought the devil had possest the fellow, ask'd him what the matter was, or what he would be at; that he came for his master's money for cloth. The barber reply'd, I must follow your master's orders; I am to search you for the pox, and as I am hir'd to cure you, I will do my duty. The lad vow'd and swore he had no pox, that his master liv'd in St. Paul's Churchyard, and sent him with the gentleman he had shav'd for money for his cloth. All this would not serve the barber's turn, but he must be true to his trust, and will search, so that the dispute ended in some cuffs betwixt 'em; but in the end, the barber being too hard for his patient, forc'd down his breeches, and search'd him, whom he found to be as clear and sound as any creature could be. The barber satisfy'd himself that he had done his part; but the poor lad much troubled for this abuse, goes home to his master, tells him the whole story, how that instead of money, he had a good threshing bout, and a long encounter with a barber, who search'd him for the pox; but the master not knowing how to help himself, could not choose but smile at the passage, and contentedly sat himself down with his loss.[60]

---

60. Theophilus Lucas, *Lives of the Gamesters* (1714), reprinted in *Games and Gamesters of the Restoration* (London: George Routledge and Sons, 1930), pp. 135–136.

This case, no doubt apocryphal, illustrates the way in which corrective remonstrances themselves confirm the recipients in their misreading of the events. The accusation of insanity functions in something of the same way, transforming remonstrances into symptoms. More delicately, an analysand's disagreement with the interpretation provided (whether openly or tacitly) by the therapist can be read by the latter as resistance, a psychic condition which has the miraculous power of transforming verbal disagreement with the therapist into evidence that the therapist is right.[61] Indeed, everyday conduct tends in the same direction: routinely, the character we impute to another allows us to discount his criticisms and other professions of belief, transforming these expressions into "what can only be expected" of someone of that character. Thus are interpretive vocabularies self-sealing. In these cases, truly, we deal with the myth of the girl who spoke toads; every account releases a further example of what it tries to explain away.

The manufacture of negative experience in the several arts, considered at length in the last chapter, provides material on frame trapping. Two assumptions seem to be required. First, for each of the arts, critics can point to a time a decade or so ago when what is now considered fully acceptable and meritorious was violently rejected as not art at all. Contemporary patrons of the arts are aware of these now embarrassing assessments. Second, one's turning up at the social occasion of a performance is likely to involve a commitment of resources and anticipations of a particular kind of experience. Given these two assumptions, it can be argued that patrons open themselves up to a special predicament: exposure to what seems to be nonsense under circumstances such that they cannot be very sure of the correctness of their resentment and must expose themselves to themselves if they become sure. Having committed themselves to the spectacle, they are stuck with a game the only meaning of which may be

---

61. Fiction provides set pieces written around the theme of frame traps, and there is even an interesting paper on how one might arrange for two therapists to be treated by each other, each under-the impression that he was treating, not being treated. See Hellmuth Kaiser, "Emergency: Seven Dialogues Reflecting the Essence of Psychotherapy in an Extreme Adventure," *Psychiatry*, XXV (1962): 97–118.

instructional, namely, that this is the way one can get stuck with anything.

John Simon raises the question in a review of Peter Handke's "play" *The Ride across Lake Constance:* "When is a play not a play but a fraud? When, in fact, is any so-called work of art not a work of art but a piece of trickery, a hoax, a nonsensical game, a fraud?"[62] The answer, I think, is another question. Given that aleatory music and the paintings of Andy Warhol are often taken seriously, how would one fill a concert hall or a canvas (or in the case of Handke, an auditorium) in order to convince everyone that they were being taken in, conned, deceived? And might this task not be, almost by definition, impossible to accomplish?

The transformation of experience referred to as a test or trial is the source of another kind of frame trap. Any theory of how matters in the real world ought to go or what ought to happen can be preserved in the face of disconfirmations simply by seeing the unfulfilling events as a test of the actor, a means employed by higher authorities to make sure that he is worthy of what will indeed befall him. It was God who tested Job by causing his world to go awry on the prediction that Job would not lose faith, and after the proof was in, of course, the world did go as Job deserved; but once the game has been played in this way, there is no reason why any Job shouldn't see personal disaster as really a personal test. In any case, that, apparently, is how Mrs. Keetch and her world-enders were able to interpret the failure of their predictions—as merely a "drill," a "dry run," a test to see if they were worthy, ready, and able.[63] And if a test can be at work, then other hidden powers can make a convenience of the world, too, at least Cervantes so suggests after a lance has been broken on a windmill:

> "God help us!" exclaimed Sancho, "did I not tell your Grace to look well, that those were nothing but windmills, a fact which no one could fail to see unless he had other mills of another sort in his head?"
>
> "Be quiet, friend Sancho," said Don Quixote. "Such are the fortunes of war, which more than any other are subject to constant

---

62. John Simon, "Fraud by Audience Participation," *New York Magazine,* January 31, 1972.

63. Leon Festinger, Henry W. Riecken, and Stanley Schachter, *When Prophecy Fails* (New York: Harper & Row, 1964), pp. 148, 153.

change. What is more, when I come to think of it, I am sure that this must be the work of that magician Freston, the one who has thus changed the giants into windmills in order to deprive me of the glory of overcoming them, so great is the enmity that he bears me, but in the end his evil arts shall not prevail against this trusty sword of mine."[64]

One sees here that actions and events, not merely words, can be trapped out of contact with reality. Other illustrations can be provided. For example, under certain conditions attackers and defenders engage in much the same course of action, and in these circumstances it will be easy for one of them to misinterpret the actions of the other and, perforce, continue to do so, since each conformance to the task of defending will give the impression of attack:

> It seemed for a time today that police had picked up a good suspect in the recent series of armored car robberies.
> An armored car driver alertly noticed a car trailing the vehicle today, and was able to notify the police in Malden.
> Police swooped down on the man, and took him into custody.
> First reports said he had weapons in his car.
> If so, he undoubtedly had a license for them.
> It turned out, police said, that he was a private detective hired by the armored car service to keep an eye on things.[65]

Indeed, two defenders can both misread the other's action and both find themselves with a ready-made opposite number:

> A restaurant owner and a deputy sheriff—each thinking the other was a burglar—engaged in an early morning shoot-out in East Palo Alto yesterday.
> Deputy Eugene Boklund, 27, suffered minor wounds in the arm while restaurant owner Henry C. Mora, 52, escaped uninjured.
> The two men arrived at Mora's restaurant on Ralmer street almost simultaneously when a burglar alarm sounded.
> Mora, thinking Boklund was the burglar, shouted at him to lie down. Traffic drowned out Mora's voice and Boklund failed to comply.
> This brought a salvo from Mora's shotgun and answering shots from the deputy's revolver.

---

64. Miguel de Cervantes Saavedra, *Don Quixote*, trans. Samuel Putnam (New York: Viking Press, 1949), pt. 1, pp. 63–64.

65. *Boston Traveler*, October 24, 1966.

The gunfight ended when two more deputies arrived and disarmed both of the combatants.[66]

Again, observe that more than misframing is involved here; what occurs is action that will be misinterpreted called forth by other action that has been misinterpreted, such that after the interaction starts, each response is doomed to confirm the misunderstanding.

Cries and signals of alarm, being specialized means for warning of danger, assure that nothing is up when they do not sound and thus, of course, introduce frame problems of their own. Because he has an alarm system, an individual can withdraw wariness from occasions when no alarm sounds; doing this, he becomes vulnerable in a new way. But the availability of alarm signals creates still deeper framing problems. The "cry wolf" theme contains the point: if an alarm is to be something the individual has the power to give whenever he feels the need has arisen, then it must be something he is empowered to sound in jest; and once an alarm is seen as something that might be sounded in jest, no real alarm can be sounded but that it might be similarly seen. And the key of unseriousness need not be the only trap; any other transformation will also do:

> About $250,000 worth of jewels were stolen from the vault of a diamond shop at 58 West 47th Street early yesterday morning while a burglar alarm sounded and apparently while a special Holmes Protective Association guard sat outside the vault.
>
> The guard, who had been posted there at 4:07 A.M. because of the ringing of the alarm for the second time in an hour, remained at his post until about 8 A.M., when someone arrived from next door and said: "Hey, the police are here. You've been robbed."
>
> . . . .
>
> The first sign that anything was wrong came at 3:15 A.M., when the burglar alarm sounded. Holmes men responded but could see nothing amiss because the vault door was closed.
>
> What they couldn't see was a two-foot square hole through the eight-inch plaster and concrete brick wall separating the vault from the Villa Nova Restaurant. . . .
>
> When the alarm sounded a second time just after 4 A.M., the Holmes patrol investigated again. Deciding the system was defec-

---

66. *San Francisco Chronicle*, March 17, 1965.

tive, they telephoned a repair man and posted a guard in front of the shop.[67]

A significant source of frame traps is grounded in suspicion and normal appearances. That the individual checks up on the world around him by appealing to signs of innocence, to indicators of innocuousness, can be assumed, as can also the fact that those who might harm him will disguise or cover their threat with precisely these signs. When the individual himself becomes suspicious, he is led, then, to suspect those indicators which ordinarily pacify him. And the more those who are misunderstood by him attempt to demonstrate that they mean him no harm, the more they must employ signs which are precisely the ones that are now suspected.[68]

VI

I have so far considered some of the circumstances in which an individual's notion of what is going on can become shaky, and, in reverse, what an individual can do to undermine the frame employed by another. My intent has not been to compile tips on how to hoodwink but to learn about framing. With that in mind, I would like to raise some further issues concerning frame and its own vulnerabilities.

1. Consider the license that novelists and playwrights employ in regard to keys and constructions. They seem very prone to fall into the use of twists and gimmicks. They employ frame tricks. And no wonder. Once a strip of depicted experience is set up, it is easy, by means of a line or two, to add a whole new border to the experience, including one that defends the creator against criticism. So there is much to be gained—a whole new viewing of what has been put together—merely by means of a twist. (The one price is that repeated viewings may not be encouraged, since once a particular viewer knows what is "really" going on, he himself may find little amusement in going through the whole

---

67. Thomas F. Brady, *The New York Times*, April 5, 1969.

68. An organized version—organized in the sense that the trap is inevitable—is the so-called prisoner's dilemma game: given the payoff matrix and disallowance of communication, no tacit agreement can be reached by the prisoners allowing each to admit during his interrogation that which would lead to a reasonable payoff.

disclosure again.) All of this I think reflects a basic framing vulnerability of everyday activity also.

As already considered at length, persons who have become acutely suspicious of their surroundings direct our attention to the vulnerability of experience, for what seems perfectly natural can be suspected on precisely those grounds. The concern a fully paranoid person has about the merely apparent innocence of his surround is not something he invents; it is in the nature of framing and of the scenes around one that this sort of transformation is possible, and all that the ill person brings to the case is insufficient reason for his suspicions. It also follows that we all have had a taste of what it is that makes him ill.

2. It is important now to observe that the possibility that a given strip of experience will have an unapparent transformation (in the sense of a construction) provides the framework for properly understanding the concern we have for fleeting expressions. We give weight to an individual's signs of guilt or signs of being barely able to suppress laughter or signs of embarrassment and furtiveness; and this we do not merely because of the possible impropriety of these expressions themselves. For these signs are evidence that someone in our world is insecurely in it, perhaps because he is in another or fears that we are. These fleeting expressions are important, then, because they suggest that what we take to be actually going on might not be, that we might be wrong about its laminations. And as this holds for our perception of him, so it holds, we know, for his perception of us.

To be "natural," then, is not merely to seem at ease, but to be acting in such a way as to convince others that the apparent frame is in fact the actual one. That is what is meant, functionally speaking, by sincerity and spontaneity. When we deal with an incompetent person and find it difficult not to smile, or deal with a mad one and find it difficult not to show fear, or deal with the police and find it difficult not to show guilt, what we are tending to give away is not a person, ourselves, but a frame, one that we had been maintaining. These affects and responses are only incidentally of persons; they are primarily about frames, and it is only in frame terms that one can make sense of the concern shown in regard to them. Very often, then, to suspect something is to question more than one event; it is to question the frame of

events. For the suspect event can readily be seen as an exception
not to an otherwise innocuous situation but to the success that
has otherwise been achieved in sustaining constructions, benign
and otherwise. Suspicion, then, would seem to be a universal and
basic structural possibility in social life, and its analysis a best
way of beginning to appreciate the framed character of our
realms of meaning, including our realities.

3. An allied concern must now be raised. Just as it is possible
for the "true" facts to leak out from behind the effort of an actor
to disguise or conceal them, leading to doubts or discreditings he
would have liked to prevent, so it is possible for him to use hints
and double meanings to convey information collusively in a half-
open fashion. By carefully selecting his terms and carefully
guiding intonation and stress, the actor can use a word, a phrase,
or a sentence to say something that he can disclaim having said
should the need arise. All of this, of course, is perfectly well
known; now one should see that it is only to be expected—given
the unavoidable flexibility provided by framing practices. One
should also expect that if intended hinting can occur through an
innocuous screen and be appreciated as such by a recipient, then
it should also be possible for a recipient to read intended double
meanings when only single ones exist, and, correspondingly, for
an actor to fear that hinted meanings will be read into his behavior without warrant. Perhaps the conduct of those defined as
mental patients provided the obvious examples:

In the course of an hour with a 24-year-old schizophrenic
woman I became assailed with feelings of confusion and unreality,
when she, a luxuriantly delusional person, was reading to me from
an instruction book concerning the Japanese game of "Go." She
appeared to find some hidden meaning in almost every word and
even in almost every syllable, looking at me significantly, with a
sarcastic smile, very frequently, as though convinced that I was
aware of the secret meanings which she found in all this. The
realization came to me, with a temporarily quite disintegrating
impact, of how threatened, mistrustful, and isolated this woman
was. What she was doing with me compares very closely with her
mother's taking her to movies, during her childhood, and repeatedly commanding her, "Now *think!*" which the patient took—
correctly I believe—as the mother's command for the daughter to
perceive the same secret, special meanings in the course of the

movie which the mother, an actively psychotic person throughout the girl's upbringing, found in it.[69]

And observe again that in these ideas of reference, actions and objects seem to be even more vulnerable to rereading than are words. For the individual may not only wrongly see a connection to himself in a matter taken in its own right, but also wrongly read its shape or sound as carrying a coded message for him— and nothing seems so gross and stolid as to foreclose its contours being treated as a sign vehicle. The spells of overconnectedness that August Strindberg apparently suffered provide examples:

> He attempted to gather and to sustain himself by lonely walks through the streets of the Montparnasse section. In the course of these walks he found meaning everywhere. To repeat his words, "Things that would previously have lacked significance now attracted my attention." Flowers in the Luxembourg Gardens seemed to nod at him, sometimes in greeting, sometimes in warning. Clouds in the shape of animals foretold ominous events. Statues looked at him trying to tell him something. Scraps of paper in the gutter carried words that he tried to piece together into a message. Books which he found in sidewalk bookstalls seemed to have been specially "placed" there for him. The design of a leather cover of one seemed to contain a prophecy for him and when he opened the book a sliver of wood pointed to a particular sentence. Twigs on the ground took the shape of the initials of a man who he feared was pursuing him intent on murder. Seemingly unrelated items in the newspaper were connected to his inner preoccupations. Urgent personal meanings were everywhere.[70]

4. Still another vulnerability due to framing should be mentioned. In everyday life the understanding seems to be that the participant is likely to be spontaneously involved (in various degrees) in a scene of activity or, by virtue of having fabricated the scene, outside of it completely. But other possibilities exist. For example, an individual can become misaligned to events in

---

69. Harold Searles, *Collected Papers on Schizophrenia and Related Subjects* (New York: New York University Press, 1965), pp. 274–275.

70. From Donald L. Burnham, "Strindberg's Inferno and Sullivan's 'Extravasation of Meaning,'" *Contemporary Psychoanalysis*, IX (1973): 191–192. Useful illustrations of breakdowns in unconnectedness can be found throughout Clifford Whittingham Beers, *A Mind That Found Itself* (New York: Longmans, Green & Co., 1908), esp. pp. 22–23, 24–26, 52, 54–55, 64, 70–72.

such a fashion that he sees as a single, managed scene something that he himself is not managing, not fabricating, and that others are spontaneously involved in. In this manner, the individual may establish for himself a place that is psychologically outside the world of the others around him.

Perhaps the most striking example of this vulnerability of frame is found during revolutionary religious or political excitements or at times when apocalyptic cognitive beliefs about the world unseat their believers. Take, for example, a member of the end-of-the-world cult studied by Festinger and his colleagues, one Bob Eastman, "an undergraduate majoring in educational administration":

> Eastman attended every meeting of the Seekers and spent a great deal of time at the Armstrong home. He gave up smoking, drinking, swearing, and "other rough habits" and soon developed into one of the most apt and serious students of the movement. . . .
>
> He had learned "who he was in the Bible" and had given considerable thought to the problem of finding his soulmate. He was thoroughly conversant with the prediction of the flood, could cite it from memory, and believed it completely. Furthermore, he had reordered his life in expectation of it. Not only had he forsworn earthly pleasures in order to raise the density of his vibrations, but he was, as he said on several occasions, "giving up all earthly ties," and asserted often in December that he was "ready to go any time." He continued to attend his classes, but did so merely, he said, in order to preserve an outward appearance of normality and thus not arouse the panic in his college mates that might ensue if he were to quit completely. He had given up studying for courses and was devoting all his spare time to "the lessons," although he fully expected to fail in one or more courses.
>
> He sold some property he valued a great deal in order to get money to pay off debts. He spent his Thanksgiving vacation in Steel City "winding up his affairs" and "saying goodbye" to his parents and friends. He did not sell his car, since he thought it might be useful transportation for him and other believers during the last days. . . .[71]

----

71. Festinger, Riecken, and Schachter, *When Prophecy Fails*, p. 78. Young men who have been conscripted and are awaiting their draft call similarly wind up their affairs and go through the motions of some of the day's routines, all the while committed elsewhere, but this latter bracketing is, of course, somewhat sanctioned by the community.

A newspaper account gives us another example:

> A San Francisco car salesman, convinced that the world would end any moment literally threw his worldly goods—$220 in cash—to the winds late yesterday.
>
> Officers said Milton Edwin Hays, Jr., who identified himself as Jehovah, tossed two $100 bills and a $20 bill into the air at Vista Point.
>
> Witnesses said a middle-aged woman and two teen-agers picked up the bills and drove away from Vista Point with them.
>
> A little later Hays was stopped for speeding and running a stop sign on the Sausalito turn-off north of the Golden Gate Bridge.
>
> California Highway Patrolman Newton Prince said that the lanky driver said:
>
> "I have divine knowledge that the world will end today. I am casting my worldly goods upon the waters. I am going to meet my Maker."[72]

—which provides a modest, modern version of a statement made in the First Letter of Paul to the Corinthians (7:29–31):

> The time we live in will not last long. While it lasts, married men should be as if they had no wives; mourners should be as if they had nothing to grieve them, the joyful as if they did not rejoice; buyers must not count on keeping what they buy, nor those who use the world's wealth on using it to the full. For the whole frame of this world is passing away.[73]

On a slightly lesser scale we have overheated beliefs about political conspiracies and the "real" meaning of various political events; the interpretation of the French Revolution as the plot of a small group of Freemasons is one example.[74]

Utter fancifulness of a religious or political kind is not a requisite for the bracketing under question. Thus, during the Cuban missile crisis, some Americans headed away from urban centers and presumably urban life, just as they did during various periods of publicity regarding fallout and other sources of radiation; and gainsaying them is not all that easy, perhaps not even to be recommended. For it is not the logic of their account which is

---

72. *San Francisco Chronicle*, August 27, 1965.

73. *The New English Bible* (London: Oxford University Press, 1961), p. 288, for which suggestion I am grateful to John Lofland.

74. See Edward Shils, "The Fascination of Secrecy: The Conspiratorial Conception of Society," in *The Torment of Secrecy* (Glencoe, Ill.: The Free Press, 1956), pp. 27–33.

particularly bad, but rather their willingness to put brackets around the whole of their civil life and take unified action in regard to what has thus been framed. What is our ground becomes their figure.

Nor need one limit the topic to crises of a potential or actual public kind. Consider the disaffections that can occur regarding smaller realities, such as domestic life, and the consequent bracketing of something that ordinarily would encompass daily domestic actions:

> *Dear Abby:* My husband and I have enjoyed your column for a long time. Perhaps it is the only thing we have in common. After six years of married life with a fine M.D. specialist, I have had it. My problem is not how to make this marriage work, but how to work myself out of it with the least possible hurt to my husband and our two dear, innocent children, both under 5 years of age. Since my husband and I are no longer in communication in any important way (physically or mentally), there is nothing left. He's kind and generous, but possessive and dull. He is hard working and a good provider, but he's neither interesting nor fun. I have tried everything, from vacations for two to new hobbies, to bring back that old feeling, but I have failed. I am bored and miserable. My husband thinks everything is just fine, but I can no longer live this dull life as though we were 50 instead of 35. How can I make him understand it is all over for me before I see a lawyer?[75]

It should be plain now that framing bears upon the psychiatric problems of depression and mania. Although we are prepared to see that an individual will play many of his scenes in a style inimitably characteristic of him, we also demand that he vary considerably from scene to scene in terms of what by way of affect he manifests in it. Depression and mania, in part, are what we impute to someone who apparently declines to follow these affect rules, someone who insists on playing different scenes as though they generated the same emotional response. A framing account accounts for some of this: he who sees as part of the same scene what others see as part of different ones, he who places brackets around a long strip of activity, locating in the same frame what others have divided up for changes in framing,

---

75. *San Francisco Chronicle*, March 17, 1966. A novelistic exercise in the role of scenic brackets is provided in Joan Didion's *Play It as It Lays*, which deals with the domestic use of staging-a-scene terms by characters who are professionally connected with Hollywood.

is someone who can give an impression of mania or depression. But, in part, what is wrong is not his affect but his framing.

VII

Now a final consideration bearing on frame and its vulnerabilities. Given an orientation to frame analysis, how could one go about disorganizing the world? Anybody's world? If there is a cognitive organization to the world we are in such that correctives to error, deception, and delusion often emerge, how can these correctives be best offset?

One answer, perhaps, is to be found by reexamining the issue of transformation. For, as urged already, the hardest reality is subject to systematic alteration, provided only that a keying of some kind can occur. Turn matters on their head, then, and ask: If one wants to end up with a vulnerability in the world, especially the everyday world, let us see how an activity could be keyed and then create this keying. From here one is led to appreciate that to transform an activity a way must be found in which the activity can be, bit by bit, systematically altered. And to do this what is needed is an infrastructure of some kind, that is, a patterning of activity, a structural formula that is repeated throughout the course of the activity. Once this continuously repeated design is found, something about it can be changed or altered, which, when accomplished, will have a generative effect, systematically transforming all instances of the class, and, incidentally, systematically undermining the prior meaning of the acts.

The mischief here considered has the special quality that it is entirely within the compass of one individual, and he need not have recourse to extensive physical equipment. The only condition is that others in the situation must continue interacting with him in some way.

As a beginning, take, for example, physical and cultural handicaps associated with the apparatus of communication: features such as lisps, hairlips, drools, facial tics, wall-eyedness, a "common accent," and the like. A defect of this order has effect at the infrastructural level, a calibrative effect, in that each word or glance during face-to-face interaction creates anew the problem, grinds out, as it were, generates another sin. The breath of such behavior smells. That, of course, is exactly what transformation accomplishes; it introduces a systematic item-by-item transposition of an otherwise ordinary strip of activity. But in the above examples one deals with involuntary transformations—self-setting frame traps, as it were. It is what occurs when the message "This is play" is given, except that here the individual whose conduct is redefined is not someone who wanted the transformation applied. Now the question is, what sorts of transformation of an individual's own conduct can he *voluntarily* employ that will have the effect of throwing off the response of others, disallowing what they would ordinarily bring to the situation?

Perhaps the mildest and most common example is what might be called "speech enterprise," that is, an individual's apparently self-conscious transformation of speech pattern in the direction of what he takes to be refinement—to be distinguished, of course, from "talking posh," that is, the use of what is taken to be upper-class speech for the *avowed* purpose of mere play. The example is worth consideration.

The "accent" of a speaker is employed by others as a device to ground him in his social origins and identify him in a manner that can be taken to apply beyond the occasion of contact, a feature of him before the interaction and after it. If someone tries to fake an accent, so that it isn't "real," we expect this will show through, especially if the interaction is lengthy; and typically, of course, it does.

"Real" accent consists of phonological features of speech at the infrastructural level, that is, it attaches not to words and phrases as such but to consonants and vowels, and clusters of same, out of which words themselves are made, as well as to matters such as intonation contour by which classes of phrases and sentences are syntactically managed. Through a phonetic analysis of an individual's speech, it is possible to show just where his distinctive accent is located, that is, upon which particular elements of sound and phrasing. A formula can then be developed to describe this accent, and it is a formula that can generate an infinite number of accented words and phrases. Were it possible for an individual to learn this formula viscerally in order to apply it to his own speech production, he would be able to generate the accent "naturally," from within, as it were, and never give himself away no matter how lengthy his discourse; this is what some linguistically sophisticated copyists approach. The consequence, of course, is the generation of a palpable change in identity.

Now let us shift from the behavioral style that an individual incidentally brings to many of his face-to-face situations to features of face-to-face interaction itself; for that is the fruitful direction it seems, if one would learn how to "anomicize" the world. It is known that on every occasion when two or more persons are in one another's immediate physical presence, a complex set of norms will regulate the commingling. These norms pertain to the management of units of participation, situated and ego-centric territoriality, display of relationships, and the like. And if talk occurs, then of course norms will apply regarding organization of turns at talking and initiation and termination of the encounter in which the exchange takes place. Note these various forms are *constantly* coming up for affirmation whenever individuals are in one another's presence. It follows, therefore, that any consistent breaching of these rules—whether unintentional or intentional, whether due to "incompetence" or not—will have a generative effect, unseating all the interaction the rule breaker engages in. This is known from the tricks that have been played by experimenters (Stand "too" close in talk and see what happens), small boys (Keep pace with an old lady one sidewalk square away and see what she does), and interrogators (Take away his belt and shoes laces so he must present himself sloppily whenever he is brought to a session).

When more generalizations have accumulated concerning face-to-face interaction, there will be greater resources to draw upon for intentionally unhinging the frame of ordinary events. Ironically, this application of microsociology may be among its most effective ones.

13

The Frame Analysis of Talk

I

The strips of activity so far employed as examples, depictions, mock-ups, typifications, and cases—representative, common, pure, exceptional, extreme, limiting—featured speaking as a possibility, a likelihood, and occasionally even a requisite. So in a sense, the analysis of these strips was also the analysis of the act of saying things. And just as these strips are subject to transformations—to keyings and fabrications—so also are spoken statements. As a blow can be administered in jest, so a command can be issued unseriously as a joke. As thoroughly as a money-reproducing machine can be a deception, so also can an avowal. Just as the individual can flood out of an instrumental physical activity (upon failing, for example, to thread a needle), so he can flood out and break frame through the manner in which he manages the production of words—indeed, that sort of sputtering flood is the most obvious kind.

A case in point is the role of words as a source of misframing for their recipient. It is true that context helps to rule out unintended meanings and suppress misunderstanding, but the immediate surround could not have this power apart from the sophistication—the cultural competence—of interpreters. And so a source of verbal framing error is found in what we take to be cultural incompetency, typified, for example, in the lore of "cute mistakes" perpetrated by unknowing children:

Horace Stoneham's [owner of the San Francisco Giants] three-yr-old grandson, Peter, just started nursery school at Stuart Hall on B'way, and is coming along fine. "What's one and one?" the teacher asked. "A ball and a strike," replied Peter.[1]

The issue here cuts deeper, I think, than might appear. Examine the following:

Ah tourists: This one walked into Delmas & Delmas at Ghirardelli Square, looked at a jade bracelet, and asked Mgr. Henry Murray: "How much?" Henry: "One fifty." Tourist, laying down a dollar bill and two quarters: "I'll take it!" (Oh no you won't).[2]

Exposed here is a "simple" misunderstanding, one that leads to a misguided, unsustainable act, soon to be discredited. However, it can be that the tourist's consequent embarrassment was due in part to exposure—exposure as someone who presumed a knowledge of jewels he now appears not to possess. And this in turn suggests that the correct interpretation of any statement may have as one of its implications the saving of the interpreter from exposure as someone who presumes competence—cultural as well as linguistic—he does not have.[3]

A further point about the tourist and the jade. Had the manager stated the price in full without ellipses, the customer, presumably, could easily have mustered a response that terminated interest and at the same time sustained the impression that he was somewhat knowledgeable, somewhat used to the finer world of costly jade. It must be seen, then, that the correct interpretation of events allows the interpreter to employ the routine defenses—many perceivable as rather shabby—which ordinarily save him from making untenable, discrediting moves.

In sum, then, spoken statements provide examples of most of the framings that have been considered in this study: fabrications, keyings, frame breaks, misframing, and, of course, frame

---

1. Herb Caen, *San Francisco Chronicle,* September 25, 1967. From this point it is but a step to intentional misframing as a source of snappy comebacks. With this step, under the name of "bisociation," Arthur Koestler (*The Act of Creation* [New York: Dell Publishing Co., 1967], esp. pp. 32–38) makes an interesting attempt to cover the world.

2. *San Francisco Chronicle,* June 26, 1968.

3. A nice distinction here seems to be made by the citizenry. Is it a lack of learnedness in linguistic skills that is expressed or is it ignorance of some specialized, technical field? He who uses a word "wrongly," especially a big word, weakens his tacit claim to well-educatedness; he who hands his garage mechanic a wrong tool following a named request is not seen as being deficient in the linguistic arts, only in the manly ones.

disputes. But our being able to tag examples of these forms does not tell us anything that is distinctive to utterances. Nor is the situation improved if one turns, as I now do, to a special type of speaking, the informal kind we call conversation, chatting, or talk, the kind that assumes an easy exchange of speaker-hearer role and involves a small number of participants engaged in a consummatory moment or more of enjoyable idling, whether this be the official purpose of the participants or a momentary diversion.[4] Again one finds frame breaks,[5] frame disputes,[6] and the

---

4. The issue here is sometimes drawn in terms of a contrast between formal and informal interaction, although that distinction conceals the fact that during the most formal and official of occasions, occasions when an individual speaks for a prestigious organization and provides information others will need in coordinating their acts, he may still, nonetheless, intersperse project-relevant statements with informalities of all kinds—greetings, joshings, irony, and the like.

5. As suggested, gender role stereotypes in our society establish differential license regarding minor flooding out during informal talk. Among males one presumably finds sudden flaring of anger, total belief, total resolve, and the like; females are supposed to dip momentarily out of talk with a blush of pleasure, embarrassment, or hurt feelings. In any case, as will be argued, informal talk almost by definition does not involve a single, preestablished agenda with elaborate differentiation of parts to be played, and so a sudden frame break by one participant need not create ramified disorganization. Indeed, the capsized participant can be used as a temporary target of attention and coddled back into composure simply because what would otherwise have occurred can be postponed or even forgone without dire organizational consequences.

Note, if these mini frame breaks can occur in actual informal interaction, they can be expected to occur in dramatic presentations, the cinema being a showplace for such expressions. Thus, for example, Béla Balázs:

In the early days of the silent film Griffith showed a scene of this character. The hero of the film is a Chinese merchant. Lillian Gish, playing a beggar-girl who is being pursued by enemies, collapses at his door. The Chinese merchant finds her, carries her into his house and looks after the sick girl. The girl slowly recovers, but her face remains stone-like in its sorrow. "Can't you smile?" the Chinese asks the frightened child who is only just beginning to trust him. "I'll try," says Lillian Gish, picks up a mirror and goes through the motions of a smile, aiding her face muscles with her fingers. The result is a painful, even horrible mask which the girl now turns toward the Chinese merchant. But his kindly friendly eyes bring a real smile to her face. The face itself does not change; but a warm emotion lights it up from inside and an intangible nuance turns the grimace into a real expression. [*Theory of the Film,* trans. Edith Bone (New York: Roy Publishers, 1953), p. 65.]

6. A relevant statement is provided in Joan P. Emerson, "Negotiating the

like; and again the distinctive features of the activity remain hidden. True, one learns what I think is a significant fact, namely, that talk is like a structural midden, a refuse heap in which bits and oddments of all the ways of framing activity in the culture are to be found. (The structurally different techniques for inducing negative experience seem all to be employed, if only in a fleeting form, and this without the benefit of any instruction from Pirandello.) But what can be said about the midden beyond acknowledging the communicative competence we must have to produce it and to survive in what we have produced?

II

Apart from ambiguities, misunderstandings, and other characteristically brief confusions, the strips of activity considered in earlier chapters have mainly had a protracted identity of organization. Activities such as stage plays, planned con operations, experiments, and rehearsals, once begun, tend to foreclose other frame possibilities and require sustaining a definition of the situation in the face of diversions. Once initiated, these activities must find a palpable place in the ongoing world, and the ongoing world must find a palpable place for them. And although these framings are subject to a multitude of different transformations —the warrant for a frame analysis in the first place—these reconstitutings themselves have real consequences, especially

---

Serious Import of Humor," *Sociometry*, XXXII (1969): 169–181. Emerson suggests:

> While it is understood that persons have some leeway in joking about topics which they could not introduce in serious discourse, the line between acceptable and unacceptable content is ambiguous. So it must be negotiated in each particular exchange. Anyone making a joke cannot be sure that the other will find his move acceptable and anyone listening to a joke may find he is offended. [p. 170]

> When a person responds seriously to the topic of a joke, he immediately opens negotiations about how the original joke is to be defined and who is responsible for introducing the topic into the serious conversation. By making it ambiguous whether he has understood that a joke was intended, the transposer leaves room for the joker later to make explicit that a joke was intended and thus partially to discount the serious discussion. After a few exchanges the joker may try in retrospect to restore the humorous definition to his remark. [p. 176]

when at the rim of the frame, and must take up a real place in the world.

Consider now the various ways in which utterances—whether formal or informal—are anchored in the surrounding, ongoing world. Physical resources, such as energy and air, are used in the production of speaking, a trivial consideration no doubt, except for those in economy space capsules, a keying of whose situation in this regard can be found in the last act of *Aïda*. Also, physical sound waves are produced, and although these are quickly dissipated, recording is possible, sufficient to cause leery talkers to hold their conversations in funny places. More significant is the fact that if face-to-face talk is to occur, participants must be in such sight and sound of one another as is required for the management of this kind of communication system; and this means that the nonparticipating setting of objects, persons, and sounds that might have interfered has been accommodated to or has been accommodating. But again, this interconnection with the surrounding world pertains to the using of vocal equipment, not so much to the messages exchanged thereby.

The organization of whatever *is* meaningfully said will have to satisfy the rules of a language, competence in which a participant will have to bring with him to his moments of talking and listening, just as he will have to bring the requisite acoustical equipment. This competence is closely linked with another, one that specifically bears on the actual social situation in which it is exercised, for there will be required use of "indexical expressions," for example, those of time, place, and person, which are responsive to this setting—the one in which the speaking is occurring—as opposed to the setting that is spoken about. Further, the participants will be bound by norms of good manners: through frequency and length of turns at talk, through topics avoided, through circumspection in regard to references about self, through attention offered eagerly or begrudgingly—through all these means, rank and social relationship will be given their due.

But all of this, it should be admitted, somewhat misses the point; it avoids the serious functions of talk and hence the serious sense in which it might be argued that utterances take up a place in the world. For, of course, individuals act upon what is said to them, and these actions in turn become inextricably part of the ongoing world. Obviously, the coordination of most social activity, let alone close teamwork, assumes that self-believed, if not correct, statements are possible and even likely and that promises and threats are to be relied on.[7]

Here one finds a difference between conversational talk and much of what has so far been considered. Much of informal talk seems not to be closely geared into extensive social projects, but rather occurs as a means by which the actor handles himself during passing moments; and these handlings of self are very often somewhat optional, involving quite fleeting strips of activity only loosely interconnected to surrounding events. Although any conversational move is appreciably determined by the preceding moves of other participants, and appreciably determines the moves that follow, still much looseness is found; for at each juncture a whole range of actions seems available to the individual, and his particular selection is a matter of free choice—at least at a given level of analysis. A boxing match or a poker game can drift into unseriousness, but once this has occurred, returning to propriety is often neither automatic nor easy. In contrast, the chatter accompanying extended projects seems to fit itself to interstices, precisely where brief decoupled acts can be performed inconsequentially. And there seems to be a necessity here; for a central function of talk is to provide the talker with some means of taking up a self-saving alignment to what is happening around him even while he forgoes any immediate effort to redirect the situation.

There is varied support for this looseness argument. Unlike scripted interaction in plays, it is rare in "natural" conversation that the best answer is provided on the spot, rare that witty repartee occurs, even though this will often be the aim. Indeed, when during informal talk a reply is provided that is as good as the one that could be later thought up, then a *memorable* event has occurred. So the standards participants are alive to are ones they can rarely realize. Moreover, finding himself with a conversational slot to fill, the individual will often find that all he can

---

7. It is much believed that should a speaker depart too frequently from reliable reporting of what he knows, he will acquire a reputation for this—one which allows others to calibrate all that he says in the direction of doubting it. It is such a norm, presumably, which transforms words into deed equivalents. But in fact, as will be argued, there are structural reasons why this norm quite commonly can't be applied.

muster up is a grunt or nod. Timed and toned correctly, such a passing over of an opportunity for speech will be organizationally quite satisfactory, equivalent syntactically, in fact, to an extended utterance, and often gladly suffered, since it means that the other participants will wait less long between turns at bat. (After all, conversation often seems to involve an arrangement through which each participant is allowed to half-tune himself out during the time when the other participants must be allowed their turn to talk.) Moreover, the speaker often finds cause for minor reflexive frame breaks, turning to his own just finished verbal behavior as something to which he now directs exegetical or apologetic asides. Such self-generated, self-referential, inwardly spiraling grounds for response are necessarily somewhat cut off from the ongoing *inter*action, for here the actor all on his own provides at one moment the response to which he himself reacts at the next.

So one is left with the notion that in a significant sense talk can be loosely tied to the surround in which it occurs. By implication, then, talk is more vulnerable than most activity to keying and fabrication (whether or not this vulnerability is exploited), for this looseness is precisely what transformations require. And one should anticipate that although there are moments when the individual is obliged to speak in a straightforward, responsible way—or lie seriously—on many occasions (as suggested in regard to talk shows) unseriousness and kidding will seem so standard a feature that special brackets will have to be introduced should he want to say something in a relatively serious way: "Kidding aside," "Now, I'm really serious about this," and other such tags become necessary as a means of momentarily downkeying the flow of words. And (as will be considered later) if the speaker's doing is loosely geared into the world, the hearer's interpretive response is even more so.

The argument is that informal speech—talk or conversation—is more loosely connected to the world than other kinds of utterances. All speaking, it could be argued, tends to be loosely geared to the world; talk is merely looser.

Consider in this connection, then, the belief the speaker has in what he says. When an individual speaks—formally or informally—sometimes what he seems to be doing is voicing an opinion, expressing a wish, desire, or inclination, conveying his attitude, and the like. These attestations of the existence of what are taken to be inner states have a relevant feature; they can be as little established as disconfirmed. For here, definitive evidence would be hard to imagine, let alone acquire. And even in those cases in which it appears that the individual's later conduct will bear out his current claims regarding inner states or disconfirm them, no one usually bothers collating the result and confronting him with it. Differently put, the interconnectedness of the world here doesn't help us very much, for little is altered (except, perhaps, the management of turns at talking and other factors in the organization of conversation) by many of the attestations the individual makes about his feelings on a matter. So license abounds. The individual is just not much obliged to be very consistent in his "expression" of beliefs, attitudes, intents, and so forth.

More important, the expression of claims regarding inner states is not what takes up most of the individual's speaking time. Nor is much time actually spent in giving orders, announcing decisions, declining requests, making offers, and the like. And when any of these possibilities do occur, they often do so indirectly, operating through something else; they are an effect that is produced, but an effect that tells us little about the details of the strip of activity that produces it. A question put can be answered affirmatively by a nod, a monosyllabic word, an adage, or an anecdote, but this performative function tells us little about the structure of adages or anecdotes. It can often be correctly said of a strip of speech that it carries the burden of saying yes or no or maybe or watch your step; but what is the shape and character of these vehicles which carry our burdens?

As will be considered in detail in what is to follow, what the individual spends most of his spoken moments doing is providing evidence for the fairness or unfairness of his current situation and other grounds for sympathy, approval, exoneration, understanding, or amusement. And what his listeners are primarily obliged to do is to show some kind of audience appreciation. They are to be stirred not to take action but to exhibit signs that they have been stirred.

For what a speaker does usually is to present for his listeners a version of what happened to him. In an important sense, even if his purpose is to present the cold facts as he sees them, the

means he employs may be intrinsically theatrical, not because he
necessarily exaggerates or follows a script, but because he may
have to engage in something that is a dramatization—the use of
such arts as he possesses to reproduce a scene, to *replay* it. He
runs off a tape of a past experience. At issue here is not the fact
that words are necessarily some sort of transformation of what it
is to which they refer—although that has significance in the
study of frames. Obviously when to the question "How did you
buy your car?" the answer is "Cash," this word merely designates
money and is not itself money. But that is not the concern here.
At issue is the fact that when that question about the car is asked,
the answer can well be something that starts with: "Well, my
father-in-law knows this guy who just bought a dealership. So we
went over there one Sunday and he was just cataloging the old
stock. And we asked him if. . . ." And although this functions as
an answer (as would the word "cash"), it is on the face of it an
invitation to sit through a narrative, to follow along empathetically as a tale unfolds.

I repeat. A tale or anecdote, that is, a replaying, is not merely
any reporting of a past event. In the fullest sense, it is such a
statement couched from the personal perspective of an actual or
potential participant who is located so that some temporal, dramatic development of the reported event proceeds from that
starting point. A replaying will therefore, incidentally, be something that listeners can empathetically insert themselves into,
vicariously reexperiencing what took place. A replaying, in brief,
recounts a personal experience, not merely reports on an event.

The replayed character of much informal talk can easily be
missed because the realm status of brief utterances can blindly be
taken for granted. The recounting of a lengthy incident by a
practiced raconteur can easily be seen to qualify, but linguists
have been less ready to appreciate the replayed character of
sentence-long stories contributed by persons on the run, persons,
furthermore, with no special claim on listeners. Yet if long stories
are examples of replayed experience, so are quite short ones.
Thus, a past event:

"There was a boat there but a big wave came and carried it away."

Or a conditional one:

"That boat there; one big wave and it could be carried away."

Or a future one (providing, thus, what might be called "pre-plays"):

"That boat there; one big wave and it will be carried away."

Or, indeed, an event that is *currently* in progress:

"That boat there! A big wave is carrying it away."

These examples apart, it is apparent that an actual person can figure in the event, including, of course, the speaker himself.

"I was in that boat; a big wave came and I was carried away."

In fact, as implied, most brief replayings seem to feature a protagonist—usually the speaker.

The question of recounting storylike events—the question of replaying—can easily be confused with another framing issue, one that occasions the linguistic term "embedding." A brief comment is required.

Among the events that an individual may report are utterances themselves, whether self-imputed or imputed to another:

"I told John, 'No.'"

"John told me, 'No.'"

These reported utterances may contain still other utterances, at about which point linguists tend to use the term "embedding":

"John said that Mary said, 'No.'"

Now it appears not only that the verb "to say" (and its equivalents) can generate this kind of insetting, but also that there is a large class of these possibilities, a class of "laminator" verbs. For example:

"John wrote [saw, hinted, felt, dreamed] that Mary wrote [saw, hinted, felt, dreamed] that the boat had been carried away."

And that these verbs may engage in multiple embedding with one another:

"John wrote that Mary said that Harry felt that the boat would be carried away."

Given the possibility that a statement made by one person can be about a statement made by another (or by that person himself), one can anticipate that some of these reported utterances will have a storylike structure and thus qualify as replayings :

> "John answered me, 'The boat was there a moment ago; a big wave carried it away.' "

Opening up the possibility of multiply embedded replayings :

> "John told me that Mary wrote that the boat was there one moment and got carried away the next."

One reason why replayings and embeddings are easy to confuse can now be recommended. In a suitable context, reference to an individual whose past statement is about to be reported appears to establish the personal perspective and temporal starting point of an anecdote, such that *any* quoted statement which follows can somewhat serve as the concluding part of a temporally developed two-part story, in this way providing a replaying of sorts.[8]

In sum, talking is likely to involve the reporting of an event—past, current, conditional, or future, containing a human figure or not—and this reporting need not be, but commonly is, presented as something to reexperience, to dwell on, to savor, whatever the eventual action the presenter hopes his little show will induce the audience to undertake.

III

If, for the edification of listeners, a speaker is to report on experience, if, that is, he is to play the tape of a past strip, a current strip, a future strip, or a possible strip, then these listeners must in some way be ignorant of what is to be unfolded and must be desirous of knowing the ending. *We have been ready to see that this issue of information state is crucial in the telling of a riddle but less than ready to see that any presentation of a strip of experience falls flat if some sort of suspense cannot be maintained.* For, indeed, suspense is to the audience of replayings

---

8. The term "replaying" is sticky in another way. When an individual says something and obtains the reply, "What did you say?" he may take it (or, more likely, act as though he were taking it) that a repetition is required and oblige. The result will be a recycled statement that could nicely be called a replay but not nicely called that here.

what being lodged in unforetellable unfoldings is for participants in real life.

In staged productions, as already considered, it is quite clear that the performers all know all the secrets and outcomes, and yet the character each projects will act as if he did not know some of the relevant matters, and furthermore, he will be treated seriously in this by the other characters and by the audience. It bears repeating that the willingness of the audience to "suspend disbelief" involves a willingness to be led through the discovery of outcomes by those who, in some sense or other, must already have discovered them. No one stops to say: "But this is nonsense. The person taking the character of the King knows that the Prince is going to have at the King; why doesn't he do something about it?" In novelistic strips of fictive reality, the author, of course, knows what all the characters will come to know (and what the readers will come to know), but no live performer—unless the editorially involved are to be so seen—stands to the author's book as an actor stands to a play he is doing. Here again the action of a particular character at a particular moment in the story abso-lutely requires that he be ignorant of outcomes the author is already privy to, else the character's ensuing actions make no sense at all; and again the readership accepts in good spirit this strange assumption.

These implications of structured suspense come to be just as marked when conversational replayings of strips of activity are examined. For in these presentations not only must the listener be ignorant of the outcome until the outcome is revealed, but also the protagonists in the strip must themselves be ignorant—often differentially—as are characters in a stage play. The listeners thus must put themselves in the hands of the teller and suspend the fact that the teller knows what is to occur and that the indi-viduals in the story, including the teller in his "I" form, will have come to know and therefore must (in some sense) now know. Interestingly, listeners can appreciate that the speaker has told the same tale several times before, without this discrediting the teller's spontaneous involvement in his task, his savoring the unfolding of his own storytelling. It is only if listeners themselves have already heard the story, especially if they have heard it from the same teller on another occasion, that the savoring by the teller will seem false and inappropriate. In short, the teller's proper relation to his tale, his telling it as if this is the first time *he* has told it, is generated not by him, but by his having a first-time relation to his current listeners. The genuineness and spontaneity he can bring to his telling is generated by his current listeners' experiencing of genuine suspense; he borrows spontaneity from them. Effective performance requires first hearings, not first tellings.

The element of suspense is sufficiently important that often speakers make a special effort to establish the prospective hearer in this set. Thus the very common use of ritualistic hedges ("tickets," as Harvey Sacks calls them), as when a speaker-to-be or a speaker-to-continue uses passing words or gestures to establish the listener's permission to go ahead: "Do you know what I think?" "Do you know what happened?" "Listen to me," "Did you hear what happened to Mary Jane?" and so forth. If on these occasions permission to go ahead is given or at least not specifically withheld (the strong form here being the reply: "You already told me about it"), then the importuning speaker continues on with something that is unfolded, something that makes dramatic sense to listen to only if the assumption is made that the listener does not know the outcome, has an interest in knowing it, and will soon be told.

All in all, then, I am suggesting that often what talkers undertake to do is not to provide information to a recipient but to present dramas to an audience. Indeed, it seems that we spend most of our time not engaged in giving information but in giving shows. And observe, this theatricality is not based on mere displays of feelings or faked exhibitions of spontaneity or anything else by way of the huffing and puffing we might derogate by calling theatrical. The parallel between stage and conversation is much, much deeper than that. The point is that ordinarily when an individual says something, he is not saying it as a bald statement of fact on his own behalf. He is recounting. He is running through a strip of already determined events for the engagement of his listeners. And this is likely to mean that he must take them back into the information state—the horizon—he had at the time of the episode but no longer has. (No wonder, then, his license to suddenly switch from past tense to present tense, as in: "Then he refused to back the car up. I get in mine, I give him a push. Then he really got sore.")[9] Our readiness, then, as members of a theater audience to allow stage characters to interact on the basis of an ignorance of outcomes which the performers know all about should not be so very startling, for everyone engages in this suspension of knowledge in everyday, unstaged interaction. Of course, off the stage, we performers will often be concerned to convince listeners that what we recount for them is a true story, a concern playwrights usually don't have. But both we and they employ preformed "unreelable" strips—they because they have a script, we because we have a version of something that has happened or will happen—*and this complete knowability of the sequence-to-be is exactly what literal experience does not have, especially in regard to interaction between individuals*.

Although it should now be clear that both staged strips and personally recounted strips have a common feature—preformulation—there are relevant differences in the kind of preformulation that is found. Obviously a playwright can take his story line anywhere he wants it to go; on the other hand, an honest speaker presumably exercises some respect for the way he thinks things actually went or (in the case of preplayings) the way they are likely to go or could go. But there is a less obvious and more interesting difference.

The prefabricated character of ordinary informal talk occurs primarily during any particular participant's replaying of a particular strip of his experience. Often he will run the entire tape off during one turn at talk. Sometimes he will sustain his story across several consecutive turns, the interposing talk of others largely taking the form of encouragement, demonstrations of attentiveness, and other "back channel" effects. As already remarked, the connection between such a turn at bat (whether involving one turn at talk or several consecutive ones) and other contributions (whether his own or others') can be relatively loose; and if not loose, then an appearance of looseness will often be carefully maintained.

Of course, there is mutual determinacy between any two adja-

9. Suggested in Boris A. Uspensky, "Study of Point of View: Spatial and Temporal Form," a preprint from his *The Poetics of Composition: Structure of the Artistic Text and the Typology of Compositional Form,* trans. Valentina Zavarin and Susan Wittig (Berkeley: University of California Press, 1974), p. 16.

cent turns at talk and from one talker's turn to his next, but this determinacy is ordinarily not much subject to awareness, being one the analyst of talk must himself uncover. True also, an illustrative story by one participant provides a ticket another participant can use to allow the matching of that experience with a story from his own repertoire; but this opportunity can also be passed over without disorganizing the conversation.

Plays and other such strips present a different picture. As in unstaged conversation, the content of a particular turn at talk will be preformulated. But in addition, there is across-turn scripting. Every statement—save perhaps the first—made by a character can be one that was "set up" by the prior speaker; indeed, a climactic terminal speech may have been what much of the whole play was designed from the beginning to make possible; for it is perfectly practical for a playwright to start writing with an ending in mind and then seek for the kind of beginning and midgame which can "naturally" lead up to the destined closing. In any case, the writing of a play inevitably involves considerable extensive forward and backward scripting, now finding a statement to follow from a prior one, now finding a prior one for a statement that has already been scripted as one that is to come later.

The question now is: How much setting up occurs in talk, that is, how much do we design a reply now (or an initiating statement) so that the likely response to it will provide us with the condition we need in order to make as a natural next move the move we had been concerned all along to make? Ideally, conversation or talk is to have none of this. Actually, as already remarked, one-step setting up is common; we fish for compliments, "steer" a conversation, introduce a topic likely to lead in a usable direction, and the like. But this "playing the world backwards" is limited. More extensive efforts are very much taboo, whether this means frequent one-step buildups or multiple-step efforts.[10] Indeed, more than taboo is involved, for it is in the

---

10. N. K. Linton, "The Witness and Cross-Examination," *Berkeley Journal of Sociology*, X (1965), argues that it is a feature of trial interrogation that the witness must face the threat that current apparently innocuous questions are being put in order to obtain the answers that are needed as the basis for the embarrassing questions which the interrogator had from the beginning been scheming to put. Linton suggests that informal conversation exhibiting this feature can be felt to be improperly like interrogation (p. 9).

nature of literal strips of ordinary, unstaged activity that not much more than one link in an action-response sequence can be firmly preestablished. It is just this structural looseness of actual strips of workaday activity that makes of them something different from a ritual and renders extensive prefabrication something that must necessarily be precarious and problematic, something that works out better in fiction than in fact.

IV

The argument that much of talk consists of replayings and that these make no sense unless some form of storyteller's suspense can be maintained shows the close relevance of frame—indeed, the close relevance of dramaturgy—for the organization of talk. Now we must see that a quite different line of analysis leads to the same conclusion.

Begin with the traditional informational perspective tacitly employed by linguists that the individual is an agency to whom questions, requests, commands, and declarations can be addressed who will then reply. This reply will draw on the facts as he sees them, the facts stored and hidden in his head. He may elect to reply frankly and fully or to withhold information or to lie knowingly. The process of replying will itself carry some expressive involuntary overtones which provide the observant recipient with additional information—gleaned, not transmitted. (This channel, of course, the informant can purposely exploit, if he is able, and a recipient can try to uncover this deception if *he* is able.) Here, then, is what might be called the "black box" model of the interactant.[11]

---

11. No doubt we all become considerably attached to the black box model, one indication of which is found in the anxieties expressed by some "disturbed" people. Victor Tausk's famous paper, "On the Origin of the 'Influencing Machine' in Schizophrenia," *Psychoanalytical Quarterly*, II (1933): 519–556, provides a useful statement:

Attention may be called now to a symptom in schizophrenia, which I have named "loss of ego boundaries." This symptom is the complaint that "everyone" knows the patient's thoughts, that his thoughts are not enclosed in his own head, but are spread throughout the world and occur simultaneously in the heads of all persons. The patient seems no longer to realize that he is a separate psychical entity, an ego with individual boundaries. A sixteen-year-old patient in the Wagner-Jauregg Clinic indulged in gay laughter whenever she was asked for her thoughts.

These simple assumptions underlie a considerable amount of our understanding about the functioning of the individual. Because he can provide relevant information he feels is valid, he can be used as part of cooperative teams. Because he can decline to provide information when there is a need for it, and even decline to admit that he is so doing, and because he can provide information he knows is false, he can be used as a fabricator. In these two major ways he can make a contribution to an extensive project involving the close and continuous meshing of contributions from various actors.

But again, this utilitarianlike approach to speech ill equips us for what individuals actually do during speaking.

The key to the issue is to be found, I think, in the relation of the speaker to himself as someone about whom he is speaking. It is understood from theater and from misrepresentations that the individual can act out a character not his "own," at least not his own in one sense of the term. But these concessions leave relatively intact the basic notion that in daily life the individual ordinarily speaks for himself, speaks, as it were, in his "own" character. However, when one examines speech, especially the informal variety, this traditional view proves inadequate.

When a speaker employs conventional brackets to warn us that what he is saying is meant to be taken in jest, or as mere repeating of words said by someone else, then it is clear that he means to stand in a relation of reduced personal responsibility for what he is saying. He splits himself off from the content of his words by expressing that their speaker is not he himself or not he himself in a serious way. Later I will consider the less obvious and more common forms of this reduced responsibility. The point now is that traditional approaches to speech fail to provide an adequately central place for these reductions of responsibility.

Reconsider now the basic assumption that the human actor

Catamnesis revealed that for a long while when being questioned, she had believed I had been jesting; she knew that I must be familiar with her thoughts since they occurred at the same time in my own head. [p. 535]

Tausk's general position is that some patients imagine a machine run by an unsympathetic agent which can displace executive control and secrecy ordinarily attaching to voluntary acts. However little this sort of symptom tells us about illness, it tells us much about everyday, deep-seated assumptions concerning normal competence and the frame of everyday activity.

stores information in his skull and that these materials are hidden from view by skin and bone; his facial features are the evidential boundary he employs during face-to-face interaction. Except, then, for leakage due to involuntary emotional expression, the actor is able (and often willing) to play an information game, selectively withholding from interrogators what they would like to know.

This model of the actor is useful for some purposes but does not, of course, fit nicely with what seems to be assumed in the various interaction systems reviewed in earlier chapters. Allow a summary. In card games a split exists between what is told and what is concealed, but this split is accomplished not by the nature of man but by the arrangement of cards and the various rules requiring, say, that suits be followed if possible. In TV wrestling, the camera angle and alignment of the players puts the hero, the villain, and the audience in one information net and the referee in another—he being the one from whom infractions must be "hidden." In silent movies (and to a lesser extent in talkies) the inward emotional response of especially the leading character is kept from some of the other characters but given to the audience through registerings—looks, signs, gestures—so that the audience can follow along with the story line. Broadly expressed intention displays also contribute. In Restoration drama the hidden mind of a character is leaked to the audience through soliloquies and asides, in addition to registerings and intention displays, that is, the gesticulation of takes and returns. In novels the author simply assumes the astonishing right to report on the secret thoughts of his characters, even though in actual life God alone is a second party to these materials.[12] In marionette shows which feature animals, a human mediator may be empowered to receive whispers from the characters and to relay this information to the audience—the audience and characters being established as not being able to communicate directly. In comic strips, inner thoughts of the cartoon characters are made available to us through balloon readouts, but the characters themselves cannot read each other's ballooned thoughts.

---

12. Of course, as suggested, the novelist is making some other assumptions, too, for example, the right to generate a perspective from a given point in time and place, from a particular degree of omniscience, from the constant or intermittent perspective of one or more narrators, and so forth.

So although it might be taken that the individual in unstaged, face-to-face conversation plays his cards behind his face, so to speak, in other interaction arrangements other natural boundaries are employed; in retrospect, then, the traditional black box model is but one possible arrangement for the management of information. With this broadened view, one should be prepared to see that in fact the traditional model is a simplification even for ordinary conversation, for the insides of the actor's head are exposed in ways other than through voluntary statements or involuntary leakage.

The most obvious issue, and one that requires the least alteration of the traditional approach, is "collusion." When three or more persons sustain a state of talk, collusion of the classical kind maintained by means of collusive communication can occur. But self-collusion can also occur, with the individual half-openly speaking to himself on matters he is also apparently concealing from the others present. Moreover, as in silent films, a certain amount of "registering" occurs: while one character performs a deed, another tends to register visibly his response to it.[13] And, as in the movies, the doer acts as if he cannot see the response he is evoking; yet in fact he is likely to be at least dimly aware of what is being displayed. In the case of such genteelisms as jokingly covering one's face with one's hand to reveal the concealment of a mock smile or mock gasp of surprise, the purported stimulus for the response must more than dimly see what is happening. Thus, even in talk between two persons alone together, an arrangement designed for an audience may prevail. In addition, then, to collusion with others there is collusion with self.

Further, it is plain that sarcasm, irony, innuendo, and other members of that family are to be found, all of which—to repeat

---

13. In movies the audience is to read the registering character as behaving in a natural only-human way, not noteworthy in itself. Actually, it is a nice question as to which came first in regard to this practice, the movies or us. Observe that although talking movies could easily employ vocal registering in addition to the visual kind, the tendency seems to be to rely on the latter, perhaps because of the tradition established in silent films. Of course, talkies use background music to portray the inner feelings of a character (as Lee Ann Draud has reminded me), and silent movies sometimes used live piano accompaniment for the same purpose, but here, so to speak, the character provides only the text, not the transcription.

—allow a speaker to address remarks to a recipient which the latter will understand quite well, be known to understand, know that he is known to understand; and yet neither participant will be able to hold the other responsible for what has been understood. Here we have the controlled, systematic use of the multiple meanings of words and phrases in order to conceal speech behind speech, thereby effecting collusive communication between the very persons who are excolluded.[14]

Finally, there is the complicity of behavior found in simple fun. Obviously, when one participant teases the other or "pulls his leg" or "puts him on" or "kids" him, the efficacy of the sally will depend upon the recipient's being contained for a moment before the frame is jokingly cleared. Less obviously, a recipient of such treatment may know that he is being fooled with, know that it is perhaps known that he knows, and still act out a figure who is unknowingly being misled, a person who will shortly be surprised when he comes to learn the actual facts—all this the better to make the sport possible. (In a similar manner, an individual can vociferously act angry, embarrassed, nonplussed, and so forth, doing so out of a higher duty, albeit with a tinge of unseriousness, to provide body to the interaction.)

In sum, then, the individual systematically handles information as though he were something other than merely a black box. The traditional model of the actor whose facial features are his evidential boundary does not fit the facts but instead somehow overrationalizes man. Indeed, given the individual's tendency to split himself up into different parts, a part that is keeping a secret from a part of someone who is present and a part that divulges or shares the secret with various subsets of persons present (this often being done, as suggested, with the half-knowledge of the presumably excolluded participants), it becomes apparent that something akin to theater is going on, but, to repeat, not merely in the obvious pejorative sense. *The dramatic effect of veiled*

---

14. A simpler version of this controlled use of ambiguity is found in public political speeches wherein the speaker addresses special publics by means of second meanings that are not discernible (he hopes) to the larger audience. This technique in turn is to be distinguished from another framing possibility: a speaker's use of special voice and kinesic markers to *openly* direct his words temporarily to a special public.

statements and gestural asides is understandable only if it can be assumed that the character a recipient projects is unaware of what has been conveyed about him even while he as performer clearly appreciates what is happening. It is as though the special possibilities of theatrical production and the special possibilities of three-person talk are to be collapsed back into two-person talk, there to serve as an underlying structure, each of the two participants allowing himself to be pressed into use as a multiple entity for want of numerically adequate personnel. And in those situations in which the black box model fits the actor's behavior, one can say that he has guided his conduct so as to ensure this fit, sustaining a human nature to fit the frame.

V

So by examining two matters—replayings and information management—we can come to see that the traditional model of the individual actor does not quite fit what goes on in ordinary speaking, especially the informal, conversational kind. To find the fit it will be necessary to move beyond the ideas that are fundamental to traditional sociological analysis, which breaks up the individual into multiple roles but does not suggest that further decimation is required. Suggestions concerning this reorientation have been made throughout; here finally they must be brought together and clarified.

Start with a feature of strips of experience that has already been discussed: connectives. The meaningful organization of interaction obviously depends on correctly connecting acts to their *source*. Ordinarily, in spoken interaction these devices are routinely effective, although when a teacher screeches, "Who said that?" there is a suggestion that they have failed.

The first point to note about connectives and sources is that, like everything else, they are subject to transformation, especially keying. When I say:

> When we were in third grade we had this terrible teacher. He was really shortsighted. Well, we'd sit back of the room and put him on. We'd give these wrong answers purposely. And he'd screech, "Who said that?"

it is I who am the source of a little story which has embedded in it a statement attributed to another,[15] the form being that of direct quotation.[16] So the teacher is a keyed—or, as we might say, "imputed" or "embedded"—source and the connective employed ("he would screech") is one designed to manage attribution to such sources. Indeed, in first discussing connectives, it was this kind that I drew on.

The second point to consider is one that ought to allow us—eventually—to see the treacherousness of the first. When an individual—call him John—makes an ordinary avowal in an ordinary, natural conversation, it appears that he is its source in two different senses. He is the *principal* or *originator*, the party (in this case an individual) who is held responsible for having willfully taken up the position to which the meaning of the utterance attests. And he is the *emitter* of the statement, being himself the current, actual sounding box from which the transmission of articulated sound comes. When, however, John answers Mary's phone call and as a favor to her turns to Harry and says, "Mary wants to know if you can come there tonight," then John would seem to be no longer functioning in a dual capacity. He is the

---

15. That statement itself conceals the contract it depends on, a tacit agreement which I am relying on as much as anyone else. For after all, I am not making a statement orally to you but rather providing a printed transformation of it addressed not to yourself but to anyone who happens to read on this page. So the explication in the text above is itself something that occurs in quotation marks, except these marks bracket the whole book. It seems that expository books of all kinds are presented as though their content were being spoken by the writer to a particular recipient—"dear reader"—when in fact a print keying of that sort of communication is involved. Further, were I to compare in print an interchange culled from the printed text of a play and a genuine interchange overheard on the street, each transcription would unambiguously *refer* to something, in the first case a bit of text, in the second a bit of past actual behavior; but in addition, the transcription of the text would rather fully *present* what was in the text, whereas the transcription of the actual interchange would present only a sketch of what had happened, the sketchiness of which being quietly left an open question. As for the status of this footnote (and, in turn, the comment on this footnote, and comment on the comment), I fall back on the argument employed in the preface concerning the capacity of ordinary language.

16. Charles Fillmore ("Pragmatics and the Description of Discourse," [unpublished paper]) suggests that in English, in addition to direct quotation and indirect quotation, embedding may occur in the form of "represented" speech, as in Fillmore's example: "Could he please try it again? he asked his mother."

emitter of an invitation, but Mary is its responsible origin, even though, as we say, she did not convey it "in person." It would, observe, be easy to think of the invitation being given on behalf of Mary and her roommate, in which case it would become apparent that principal is a party which can contain more than one member.

A little trouble is caused by the word "emitter" itself. When John answers the phone and says, "Hello," Mary may learn from John's "tone of voice" whether her call is inopportune or not. Were it the door John was answering, something could also be learned from his bodily behavior, something which might well affirm or deny or qualify the words he there and then employs. One might say, then, that John does not merely emit his own statements, he *animates* them.

When John as a favor conveys a message from Mary to Harry his voice is likely to carry a neutral tone and *relatively* little by way of accompanying gesture. Indeed, there are special paralinguistic stylings for this kind of transmission. However, if John is irked at Mary and knows Harry will be, too, he may cover the phone speaker with his hand and mimic some of the "expressive" features of Mary's way of speaking, that is, her style, thereby conveying the speaking as well as what was spoken. And in fact, it seems that whenever an individual during ordinary talk directly quotes someone who is absent, the quoted strip will carry paralinguistic and kinesic efforts to mark the quoted person's age, sex, class, and so forth, these efforts serving to vivify the presentation. And this whether or not mimicry is intended. So as with statements John makes in his own name, one can say that he not merely emits Mary's message; he animates it.

Once it has been seen that source involves two functions—principal and animator—and that these can be carried by different individuals, it is time to become even more careful. For it appears that each of the two elements plays its role in a different lamination of the frame, and if this is not kept in mind, the concept of source will inevitably breed deep confusion. The point about the telephone call is not that John and Mary are different persons, but that responsibility pertains to the internal meaning of a statement (or act), while animation refers to something else, namely, the process of transmission. It follows, then, that if John, after hanging up on Mary, were to turn to Harry and say:

"I want to know whether you'd like to come over to Mary's with me tonight," the principal and the animator here, too, would turn out to be not quite the same. Here "I" designates an entity to which responsibilty can be attached, and although this particular pronoun is distinctive in that it refers to something that can be identified with the animator,[17] it need not refer to him in his animating capacity. The thing doing the animation, of course, is a relatively identifiable organism which is not functioning as a sign referring to something else; it is not functioning referentially but physically. (Analytically speaking, the animator is more akin to the ink with which the word "I" is printed than to the referent of that word.)

Observe that this difference in level between animator and principal applies in the embedded case of reported talk. John's citing of Mary's statement implies a double-sided role for Mary; she is an imputed animator of her own statement, and in turn this statement of hers ("Tell Harry I want to know if he'd like to come over tonight") contains a connective, "I want," for embedded statements attributed to an imputed principal.

Let me repeat. Although certainly the pronoun, "I," refers to the speaker, and although certainly the speaker is a specific biographical entity, that does not mean that the whole of this entity in all of its facets is to be included on each occasion of its being cited. For he who is a speaker might be considered a whole set of somewhat different things, bound together in part because of our cultural beliefs regarding identity. Thus, the referent of "I" in the statements: "I feel a chill," "I will take responsibility," and "I was born on a Tuesday" shifts, although in no easily describable way.[18] More apparent is the difference in "I" when one says

---

17. "I" and the singular distancing "we" (distancing because the respondent will presumably use indirect address in return, i.e., "Does the General desire to leave now?") seem to refer to the speaker from the speaker's point of view and are therefore to be distinguished from Orientalisms that don't, such as, "This unworthy barbarian would like three gallons of gas," and from the Western versions "the author . . . ," "your reporter . . . ," "this observer . . . ," and so forth. The regal "We," of course, must be distinguished from the usual plural referent "we" (which varies itself in interesting ways), and from the parental "we," considered later, which may mean "you."

18. A line of argument identified with Ludwig Wittgenstein. Here see his *Philosophical Investigations,* trans. G. E. M. Anscombe (Oxford: Basil Blackwell, 1958), pt. 2, sec. 403–410. Indeed, speakers have a whole

"I'm sorry" in response to having interrupted another's already
begun statement and in reply to the establishment of blame for a
wrong done two years ago.[19]

Given the difference between animator and principal, given the
fact that an individual routinely replays bits of past experience,
the conveying of which locates "I" in different laminations, and
given that the "I" in any of these positions can itself refer to
different shadings of the self, one can begin to see the work done
by the first-person pronoun and the work that one must do to
understand this work. When an individual utters the statement,
"I feel I have to tell you I was upset that night and told Mary
everything," three standard entities are implied. There is the
animator (a fully situated transmitting machine); there is the
"addressing self," the one the speaker refers to as currently
responsible and accessible to the listener, the self that the
speaker has come to be up to and as of this moment, the self,
incidentally, that is to be taken as closely geared to its possessor's
capacity as animator; and there is the self-as-protagonist, the
principal of the embedded, reported action, this latter person
being someone the speaker may feel is no longer like the he in
whose name he is now speaking.[20]

---

array of expressions, some purely gestural, to use when referring to an own
past action that is blameworthy or praiseworthy, thereby ensuring that the
"I" who is currently before his recipients is to be distinguished from the "I"
responsible for the action in question.

19. Another example. At medical conferences one can hear this during
question period: "Could I follow that up? Last year I saw a 45-year-old
obese male with. . . ." The questioner here draws on his clinical experience, a reservoir which physicians tend to treat impersonally as an almost
official corpus, reference to which does not involve personal immodesty.
A physician attached to a well-known clinic could just as well say, "Last
year we saw a. . . ." The ease of changing the second "I" (in the first
doctor's report) in contrast to the practical impossibility of changing the
first "I" argues strongly for there being a difference in referent.

20. Here the matter of multiple me's is but raised, opening up questions,
not answering them. For example, I have heard in 1973 a radio announcer
provide the names of the musicians he had been playing over the last hour
and then say, "And the announcer was yours truly, Don Smith." Here, in
the absence of apparent embedding, three slightly different entities are still
involved: the individual who had been announcing over the last hour, the
individual who was presently animating an announcement, and the perduring personage behind them both who will receive payments from the
station and tax notices forwarded on from his last address. Had the announcer said, "Your announcer was Don Smith," listeners may have con-

Nor need the speaker work through these standard entities. Take this bit of melodrama:

"There is no excuse. You are right to hate me. I am coming to do so myself."

Warmly animated, this utterance is something of a paradox. After all, anyone who identifies himself with the standards against which the culprit is being judged (and is found wanting) can't himself be all bad—and isn't, and in the very degree that he himself feelingly believes he is. A self-deprecator is, in a measure, just that, and in just that measure is not the self that is deprecated. He secretes a new self in the process of attesting to the appraisal he is coming to have of himself.

If this argument about source deepens the notions of reportings, replayings, and embeddings, it is still the case that my consideration so far has been narrow. As suggested, in contemporary American middle-class conversation, direct and indirect quotation tends to employ first-person singular and third-person singular as embedded source, and to use connectives to distinguish the quoted strip from the strip in which it is actually,

---

cluded that the person presently talking was someone other than Don Smith. Had he said, "Your announcer is Don Smith," listeners may have concluded that although the person talking now is Don Smith, the person who had been doing the show was not. (Interestingly, the announcer seemed a little bashful about using such an old-fashioned phrase as "yours truly" but seemed to imply that he could find no other way to get across what he wanted to say.)

Of course, there are occasions when only the immediate present appears to be in question and only two of an individual's possible selves seem to figure, himself as animator of the words spoken, and himself as originator of the current deeds his words describe. Thus, the bomb defuser who talks his doings into a microphone: "Now I am unscrewing the base; now I have it off; I see two leads . . . ," so that should he go wrong, the next defuser will know from the tape why. In these circumstances a second party watching the work through binoculars could generate the same running report, the only transformation required being the accommodation of a different personal pronoun. But although the latter reporting is a common enough type of arrangement—as, for example, when a golf tournament is being broadcasted—the former appears to require very special circumstances indeed. A customer trying on shoes and a surgeon working in a visually restricted field can both provide first-person running commentaries, but these are likely to be closely interspersed with self-references that pertain to less situated aspects of the self.

The semantic and syntactic issues of multiple selfing illustrated here have been very little explored.

currently being presented. In many cultures, however, somewhat different framing practices are found. In folk communities, for example, much use seems to be made of adages, sayings, little homilies, and the like, and here the imputed principal is not an individual but something like the wisdom of the people. Further, in many cultures a speaker can cite the opinion of mythical creatures, spiritual forces, and so forth. And in some languages —American Indian languages provide examples—the source of a reported action is established not by a pronoun-verb link but by a verb suffix.[21]

A still further extension of these framing notions is necessary. Although our own society may not be one wherein the telling of long stories is much cultivated as a competency, there are other peoples who seem to make more of this art. In any case, as suggested, a continuum can be claimed between a one-line replay of a past event told to a friend in passing and a full rendition of the happening as told in stretched-out form by a practiced raconteur to a roomful of appreciative listeners. (Admittedly, of course, listeners become in the process transformed into an audience.) From animators who claim to be replaying a strip of past happenings, it is an easy step to teachers who read a story from a book at hand to their pupils, whether the story is purported history, fiction, or avowed fairy tale. Again the statements and actions of protagonists will be cited, but this time not ones from the teller's own past experience. And from there, starting with readings done onstage, it is an easy step to full-fledged theater. At least in certain respects, then, a common field of analysis is to be found in the organization of little tales told in passing and the organization of commercially presented dramatic scriptings.

With this broadened view, examine the fact that animation can be done at varying distances. A puppeteer works his strings a yard away from the doll that he brings to life. A ventriloquist works his puppet close by so that it can be manipulated from behind and appear to be the actual emitter of sound. A chess player is within easy reach of his pieces, his men, his figures. A stage performer works closer still, since he manipulates his own

---

21. As apparently in Wintu and Tonkawa, in which latter connection, see Harry Hoijer et al., *Linguistic Structures of Native America*, Viking Fund Publication in Anthropology No. 6 (New York: Viking Press, 1946), esp. p. 310, for which reference I am indebted to Joel Sherzer.

limbs and his own lips—as, to a degree, we also do in quoting someone during ordinary talk. Where we work in everyday life when speaking for ourselves remains to be considered.

All of which forces us to a further refinement. When an actress takes on the stage part of Celia Coplestone, she animates a make-believe person, a stage character. By using much the same physical configuration—her own body—she can, appropriately attired, project entities of other realm status; a historical personage, a goddess, a zombie, a vampire, a fleshy mechanical woman. And, of course, if an actress does her voicing from behind the scenes, she can animate configurations not her own: a ghost, a stuffed animal, a loquacious chair, and so forth. These various configurations which an actress (or actor) can animate need a generic title: call them *figures*. And don't exclude what our actress animates when speaking in real offstage life on her own behalf. The term "character" might have done as well as figure except that it carries a bias for the human form.

One more refinement. In ordinary conversation, he who takes up a position, he who is responsible for what he says or does—in the sense of being the principal or originator—is likely also to be the person who decided on what position he was to take. But, of course, there are lots of interaction systems in which the job of assessing the situation and diagnosing what ought to be done in the circumstances is given over in part or in whole to a specialist of some kind. Thus, the person in whose name a stock is bought need not be the person who decided what stock it was best for him to buy. So some sort of strategist's function must be allowed.

The compliment of basic terms is now nearly complete: principal, strategist, animator, and figure. An individual engaging in ordinary talk *can* function simultaneously in all four capacities. Whenever transformations are involved, however, the functions will cease to coincide. In *The Cocktail Party*, Celia Coplestone is the make-believe originator of her remarks and the make-believe animator; but, of course, the actual animator (during the first run) was Irene Worth. And as for the actual originator—there really isn't one. Eliot is the author of the play and therefore dreamed up Celia's lines. But he is not socially responsible for taking up the position Celia takes up, only responsible for writing an avowedly make-believe script, a play. Authoring a remark and making it are quite different matters.

VI

It is plain that students of myth and folk tales might have a need to identify the various unnatural agencies that people their stories. It is apparent, too, that the legitimate stage can provide a setting for these arcane figures, for live actors can animate all manner of phantasms. But surely students of ordinary, real talk could limit themselves to more substantial matters; talkers, after all, provide parts for themselves in response to other persons much like themselves. But once we allow that much of talk involves replayings, we are forced to forgo solidity. For obviously, although it will never be that a two-headed green man from Mars will debate with the ghost of Andrew Jackson, it is structurally just as easy during real talk to replay a purported scene between these two as it is to replay a conversation which occurred that morning with the postman. All that is required for the former is that one observe the framing rules which dictate that a dependent clause peopled with, say, dream characters, does not draw on pronouns and proper names which refer to individuals in their capacity as characters who are not of the dream world.[22] To begin to deal with the frame structure of talk, then, it is necessary to attempt to catalog the kinds of figures utilized in our culture, along with the connectives employed in each case.

1. *Natural figures:* I refer here to live, physical, flesh and blood bodies—animal or human—each with an ongoing personal identity. Our concern will be mainly with conversationally competent ones—adults who are able to hear, speak, and be spoken to, and inclined in those directions. These entities can be current actual animators and originators, the only figures to physically emit on their own what is attributed to them. Competent natural figures, while speaking, will naturally be speaking in a particular capacity, that is, playing a particular role. But in spite of this, each such speaker sustains a single personal, that is, biographical identity, typically visibly so. (In comedies, as suggested, a charac-

---

22. Here see the suggestive paper by George Lakoff, "Counterparts, or the Problem of Reference in Transformational Grammar," mimeographed (Bloomington, Ind.: Indiana University Linguistics Club, 1968). A formalization is presented by David K. Lewis, "Counterpart Theory and Quantified Modal Logic," *Journal of Philosophy*, LXV (1968): 113–126.

ter can successfully appear in a disguise before someone he knows, and Sherlock Holmes used to carry it off, but an attempt to do this in actual interaction is not recommended.)

The connectives, as already suggested, are apparent: direction finding through hearing, perception of lip movements and their synchronization with what is spoken. No doubt there is a host of second-best devices, allowable when the best ones aren't available. And obvious problems exist. As suggested, during the verbal interaction between natural figures appearing on TV, a next speaker must not only get the attention of last speaker, but must also be sure that the camera will shift, lest the audience not be able to tell who is talking. Telephone conversation presents even greater problems. We can tell whether or not a voice comes from a natural figure.[23] We can tell more or less whether the natural figure who had just been talking is the one doing so now, i.e., same-voice identification. And there will be a number of voices that we can "recognize." But, obviously, in those cases in which sound alone must be relied upon, the connecting of voice with speaker necessarily remains precarious. The three kinds of playful obscuration are encouraged: imitating a particular other, imitating a well-known social category, and the mere obscuring of one's own (and otherwise known) personal identity.

2. *Staged figures:* Include here fictive or biographically derived characters on the legitimate stage, screen, radio, and cartoon page. Something like a natural shape is retained, and the connectives employed approximate the ones used with competent natural figures. A staged figure is the animator and principal of acts and statements but not literally, for the whole action is encompassed in a strip of activity that is itself a make-believe—often, incidentally, the product of several hands. (In the case of the theater, for example, playwright, producer, director, performers all contribute.) So while one or more individuals can be held responsible for the overall dramatic effect, no one is responsible for literally averring a character's statements or literally executing his acts.

Natural figures stand for themselves; being real, they can be

---

23. With the exception that recent efforts to write sentence speaking programs for voicing machines have produced a passable human imitation—and no doubt wonderful improvements are to be expected shortly in this technology.

imagined to be. This imaginable realness is not a possibility for all staged figures. Some are thinkable as real (although admittedly not real in this particular representation), others not; and this line is differently drawn by persons of different culture. (A child can believe that there are real angels, although the one presented on the stage is merely a portrayal; the child's parent may be less sanguine about what exists up there.) So one might speak of natural staged figures and unnatural ones. The unnatural varieties can be fitted to a wide array of configurations: human animating forms, animals, papier-mâché mock-ups, wooden frames, and even, in the case of ghosts, empty spaces.

As suggested, the connectives employed with staged figures are similar to the ones employed with natural ones. However, when the actual animator does not use his own body, certain adjustments are required. Mechanical mouth movements may be employed, as well as mechanical and electrical means of locating the emission source close to the place where it "ought" to be. Further, in the case of invisible spirits and the like, connection may have to depend on the body orientation of a staged figure qualified to hear and/or see, and on what can be deduced from this character's apparent involvement in dialogue. Attribution is also possible by displaying the guided movement of objects under no visible guide.

Unnatural staged figures, even more than natural ones, are likely to be managed by allowing them a wide variety of differential participation statuses. As suggested, once the realm of the literally real is left, great license is to be expected. For example, it is common to have spirits onstage performed by persons visible to the audience, whom the audience is meant to see, but who ostensibly cannot be seen by all or some of the staged figures. It is also possible to have spirits-in-effect who are in all matters invisible to the audience (for good reason) but ostensibly visible or audible or both to selected characters in the play.[24]

---

24. Attention to frame makes it clear that these figures have a realm status different from the ghost of Hamlet's father. *That* gentleman is meant to be unrestrictively real, merely reticent. And all these figures are to be distinguished from spirits, made palpable or not, which are intended to be treated as mere figments of a character's imagination. To neglect these fundamental differences merely because nothing real is involved in any case is to neglect a mode of analysis that *does* in other circumstances bear upon literally real events.

The cartoon world presents an even more complicated arrangement of participation statuses and warrants extended comment. Some of the figures are able to speak with each other. Typically this speaking is made available to the audience through dialogue print (as in printed plays) in the local language—in this case, English. In this way we can listen in not only on human cartoon figures but also on animal figures of various species. Incidentally, animals are often allowed to talk within and across species, sometimes beyond our own ken, in which case evidence of talk may come from undecipherable script. Here the cartoonist must necessarily "claim" a unique competence—more than merely phonetic—since the transcription is not in any recognized code. Some animal figures (like Charles Schulz's Snoopy) can understand the talk of some species of these figures and can relay this to us through direct address ballooned in our own language. (A comparison here is with TV dragon shows in which an adult is stationed outside of the immediate stage and serves as a relay, explaining to the audience what the animals have confided to him.)

Further, inner thoughts—or rather thought-feelings—are typically defined as being transcribable into standard sentences in the reader's local tongue, being made available in balloons—certainly an interesting arrangement.[25] These balloons, as suggested, cannot be read by the figures in the cartoon world. (I suppose a figure cannot even read its own balloon.)

Finally, there is *expression speech*. It is not commonly appreciated, but adults engage considerably in a very special kind of "communication" with animals, prelinguistic children, and furniture that has been accidentally bumped up against. Feelings of love, anger, approval, disapproval, promise, threat, and admoni-

---

25. On the face of it, emotional responses to what is currently happening ought not to take the form of sentences, and thus presenting them would seem to constitute a considerable license. And so in realistically inclined novels—most famously in *Ulysses*—one finds the "stream of consciousness" or "interior monologue" as a device to give the impression of real subjectivity through broken sentences and other typographical designs. But here sophistication may be naïve. It can be argued that although puppies may be made out of feelings, we are made out of sentences, our innermost self consisting of unvoiced verbal expression. Novelists and cartoonists can get inside the minds of their figures without causing us surprise because that's what our mind is—a thing designed for others to get inside of, a box of sentences.

tion are verbally expressed, along with an appropriate paralinguistic coloring. Typically the sentences are quite short and do
not form part of an extended burst. The speaker, necessarily a
linguistically competent person, appears to assume that the atti-
tudinal gist of his remark will somehow be understood by the
recipient, but not literally, that is, not lexically. (I believe that
with animals, if not with children, this is often a reasonable
assumption.) The speaker uses conventional sentences because
somehow that is the outward form in which feeling and response
can most easily be managed. Finally, quite unlike talking aloud to
oneself, expression speech is done openly, without blushes or
excuses, in the very close presence of second parties, whether
fellow conversationalists or passing strangers. Thus, somewhat
striking examples such as the following:

> A middle-class woman leaves her car in the bank parking lot to
> make a deposit. As she gets out of the car she says to her poodle,
> who is in the front seat: "Mommy will be right back."

> A middle-class woman comes to her door in angry response to her
> dog's scratchings: "I told you not to do that."

remind us that almost everyone who calls a dog uses sentences
such as: "Come here, Ladd."

Cartoonists make extensive use of expression speech by extending it in two ways. First, statements made in this frame are
allowed to be more discursive than would seem to occur in
nature—defining nature here as the place where unstaged interaction occurs involving natural figures as animators and principals. Second, although the cartoon figures who use this speech
assume that it cannot, of course, be literally understood by the
recipient, often the latter does indeed understand the statement
"literally" but does not let the speaker know that his actual language is being understood. (Snoopy, a rather special figure, is in
addition given the capacity to read English, presumably both
written and typed, which capacity *is* recognized by the natural
cartoon figures.) What is remarkable here is that cartoonists who
employ this device of literally understood expression speech seem
to have hit upon it independently and do not seem to be overly
conscious of the arrangement they are using. (As might be
expected, occasionally a cartoonist slips up and inadvertently
allows a user of expression speech to act as if he "knew" that his

statements were being literally understood.) Here again there is a parallel to puppet and TV dragon shows which feature a staged figure as mediator. For this figure may appear to be unable to literally talk to the animals or be talked to by them, having instead to rely on his apparent heightened responsiveness as a target of their emotional displays, the significance of which he then communicates to the audience.

3. *Printed figures:* I refer to figures in fiction and biography constructed out of words, not out of live performers or (as in cartoons) out of pictures. The models here can be natural or unnatural ones. The writer himself can divulge the content of the heads and hearts of these figures to the readership. Some of the connective devices have already been considered; others involve typographical signals such as capital letters, paragraph indenting, and the like.

4. *Cited figures:* Natural figures have the capacity to tell of the doings—past, current, possible, or future—of other figures, including, necessarily, "themselves." These cited doings may, of course, involve statements embedded in the teller's discourse through direct and indirect quotation. A transformation of activity is clearly involved, often a replaying or preplaying of a strip of experience—a playing of a tape. And the figures acclaimedly responsible for the reported action or words are cited ones, the referent of "I" being by far the most common.[26]

---

26. Some of the transformation rules can be formulated. For example, Fillmore, "Pragmatics," suggests that in indirect quotation ("reported speech") indexical and referencing expressions are changed so that they are adequate to the orientation needs of the recipient of the report, not the recipient of the original statement. Thus, an astronaut could say to a fellow member of the landing crew, "My wife said I'd never get here," and assume that it would be understood that his wife had not literally said "here," since only men on the moon could say that. She, presumably, had said "moon" or "there" or "it." Similarly, she would have said "you'll," not "I'd." Often the "back shifting" of verbs will also be required. Recently attention has also been given to some of the limits placed upon translation (that is, reframing), from direct to indirect discourse. I cite from the useful article by V. N. Vološinov, "Reported Speech," in Ladislav Matejka and Krystyna Pomorska, eds., *Readings in Russian Poetics: Formalist and Structuralist Views* (Cambridge: M.I.T. Press, 1971):

The analytical tendency of indirect discourse is manifested by the fact that all the emotive-affective features of speech, in so far as they are expressed, not in the content but in the form of a message, do not pass intact into indirect discourse. They are translated from form into con-

Now, obviously, just as natural figures can provide these tapes, so also staged and printed ones can. Further, a cited figure can himself cite another's words or actions, giving us multiple embeddings, as already illustrated. (The limit on the number of successive embeddings compatible with understanding no doubt differs from group to group and presents an interesting issue in the frame organization of experience.)[27] What a cited figure ought

---

tent, and only in that shape do they enter into the construction of indirect discourse or are shifted to the main clause as a commentary modifying the *verbum dicendi*.

Thus, for example, the direct utterance, "Well done! What an achievement!" cannot be registered in indirect discourse as, "He said that well done and what an achievement." Rather, we expect:

He said that that had been done very well and was a real achievement.

or:

He said delightedly that that had been done well and was a real achievement.

All the various ellipses, omissions, and so on, possible in direct discourse on emotive-affective grounds, are not tolerated by the analyzing tendencies of indirect discourse and can enter indirect discourse only if developed and filled out. [p. 161]

A further example. If an individual wants to say, "I wouldn't dream of going," as a direct quotation of what he said to himself, he must, to avoid implication of indirect quotation, say, "I said to myself, 'You wouldn't dream of going.'"

Again note that our competence here in managing transformations is far ahead of our capacity to explicate the practices involved. What, for example, allows a Bulova full-page advertisement to picture a frying pan with a diamond watch in it and a card saying "I love you" under the explanatory title: "For all the cold gray mornings that she made your breakfast," besides, that is, commercial sexism?

27. Multiple embedding limits in the discourse of natural figures is a problem considered in linguistics without reference to the cognate issue of layering limits in multiple containment, but I think the same fundamental question is involved. Also, as suggested, linguists tend to confuse reportings in general with a special class thereof, replayings, and to neglect the fact that embedding can be accomplished through a whole class of devices, not merely by reporting on an utterance. Thus, from the point of view of the complexity of a natural figure's discourse, it does not matter whether the innermost event is a physical deed or an utterance; what matters is that the secondmost inner layer contain a "laminator" verb, for although a cited figure can report on, think of, dream about, or see another figure doing something, he cannot do another's doing.

Interestingly, extremes in layering are often treated as the province of logicians and the playful intellectual sophistication for which their choice of illustrations tells us they are known. In fact, competence in these matters occurs in quite surprising places, such as the informal talk of preadolescent urban black girls, reminding us again that sociolinguistic competence is not

not to do, however, is to refer to the animation process which is producing him. But, as considered at length earlier, what ought not to be done is exactly what does get done in order to generate negative experience.

These remarks about cited figures follow the linguistic treatment of embedding. But one must go on to look at a kind of insetting which has not been so considered. I refer to the extremely common practice of "autobiographical address," whereby an assertion, request, or whatever is prefaced by a self-reference:

> In my opinion . . .
> If you ask me . . .
> I've always felt that . . .
> In my experience . . .

What follows the self-referential connective is to be placed in parentheses, a voice slightly different from the one the speaker had been using, one which presumably allows the speaker and his listeners to align themselves together over against the figure to whom the remarks are to be attributed.[28] I might add, parenthetically, that often users of this distancing device give the impression that they are sidestepping the modesty rule in conversation, as though the injunction against speakers using the floor for self-aggrandizement does not apply since a figure not quite the speaker is being put forward. (The reader might observe that my using the tag, "I might add, parenthetically . . ." in the previous sentence did not prevent me from using that sentence in discussing what it turns out it also embodied.) Observe that the

---

a product of formal schooling or social advantage. Here see Charles and Marjorie Goodwin, "The Construction of Accusations in the 'He-Said-She-Said,'" in C. Laughlin et al., eds., *Theory on the Fringe: Structure and Evolution in Human Society* (New York: The Free Press, forthcoming). A formalized glimpse in group theory terms of the permutational possibilities in three-person talk is provided by Kenneth L. Pike and Ivan Lowe, "Pronominal Reference in English Conversation and Discourse: A Group Theoretical Treatment," *Folia Linguistica*, III (1969): 68–106. Who speaks to whom, about whom, and in what grammatical case generates a considerable number of differently organized strips, each of which can then embed a second strip drawn from an equally large class, and so forth. (For this reference and other help, I am grateful to John Fought.)

28. Basil Bernstein, in "Social Class, Linguistic Codes and Grammatical Elements," *Language and Speech*, V (1962), argues that (in England) these initial tags are more common to middle-class than to working-class speech (pp. 224, 237).

storyteller's hedge ("Did you hear . . ."), already mentioned, serves in a similar way: specifically, as a means of stimulating a request to talk and hence a compliance that can more easily be segregated from the self than an outright insistence on talking could be. In short, a wide variety of statements can be cast in the self-distancing reporting form, however uncongenial this framing might at first appear.[29]

Now a statement is necessary about the limitations of framing frame analysis in print, and, therefore, the limitations of the arguments presented so far concerning the capacity of ordinary language to do what one wants to get done. In his discussion of embedding, Vološinov writes as follows:

> A reported message, however, is not just a theme of speech: it has the capacity of entering on its own, so to speak, into speech, into its syntactic makeup, as an integral unit of the construction. In so doing, it retains its own constructional and semantic autonomy while leaving the speech texture of the context incorporating it perfectly intact.[30]

He then (as I have) gives examples. But, of course, although these examples refer to embeddings occurring in speech, they can be presented to the reader only as printed transcriptions thereof. Now, if it is the case that the syntax of reported speech is respon-

---

29. It might, of course, be claimed that every statement uttered by an individual carries at least an implied or tacit connective, such as "I aver that," and that every utterance can therefore be construed as a reporting on of sorts. Presumably a query as to who made any last statement could then recover the connective, as in the answer, "I said that." However, even were this doubtful claim granted, there would remain the task of accounting for why individuals use an explicit connective at certain points in their talk, obtruding an "I think that," or an "I feel that," even though an implied reporting (along with an implied distance from what is reported) might be claimed to be already present. In support of tacit connectives, see the very interesting argument by John Robert Ross ("On Declarative Sentences," in Roderick A. Jacobs and Peter S. Rosenbaum, eds., *Readings in English Transformational Grammar* [Waltham, Mass.: Ginn & Company, 1970], pp. 222–272) that every unadorned declarative sentence is to be analyzed as an embedded dependent clause of a "performative" clause containing "I" as the deleted noun phrase, "say" as the deleted verb in the verb phrase, and "you" as the deleted indirect object, the claim being that only by appealing to this deleted higher clause in the deep structure can certain surface constraints on the use of reflexive pronouns (and certain other locutions) be accounted for by grammatical rules.

30. Vološinov, "Reported Speech," p. 149.

sive to the context *in* which the report is made (as opposed merely to the context *about* which the report is made), and if it is the case (as Vološinov himself nicely states) that some statements made in direct quotation cannot quite be made in indirect quotation, then why should one not assume that the rules for embedding a statement in talk will be somewhat different from the rules for embedding the "same" statement in written discourse? And if that is the case, how would one illustrate the difference in print? A classroom would certainly suffice, but would a book? Could it be that every frame is a trap which systematically undermines the possibility of conveying—at least with any ease—certain matters that are handily conveyed in another?

One illustration of this sort of problem will be attempted, bearing in mind that an illustration might not be possible, certainly not easy, to convey without the mode of conveyance obscuring the matter.

In live theater, statements are heard to come directly from the human sounding boxes onstage. No question of embedding arises unless a character chooses to repeat what he or someone else said, intending that his utterance be heard by the other character as a report on a statement, not the statement itself. The transcription of such an event in the *printed text* of the play is clear enough:

JOHN: "No, I will not!"
MARY (turning to Harry): "John said, 'No, he will not.'"

The transformation of this bit of dialogue for the novel version of the play is also without issue:

John answered, "No, I will not!"
Mary turned to Harry, "John said, 'No, he will not.'"

But if I want to discuss interchanges of this type in print, a problem arises, one suggesting that the traditional distinction between "use" and "mention" cannot always be easily sustained. In natural conversation, as in stage plays, utterances come "directly" from human sounding boxes, from live participants. But how are these utterances transcribed for printed presentation in a discussion, say, of interchanges? In the frame of this book, the printed statement:

"I said that John said, 'No.' "

presents "No" as an embedded utterance. But what about the following?

John said, "No."

Are we to take it that for convenience I have deleted the connective "I say that" but that this tacit preface is there to be recovered if interpretation requires? And that in effect, this second "No" is an embedding-by-implication? Or, contrariwise, do I mean the reader to understand that the printed sentence, "John said, 'No' " is to be used as a stand-in for a bit of live dialogue coming from a live sounding box, and that further worry about the line would only confuse use with mention? And this issue, note, is different from the allied one already considered, namely, whether or not every *spoken* statement is to be understood as tacitly deleting a connective, such as "I aver that."

And if the written word cannot be used to deal with all the differences between the spoken word and it, is one not to expect that there will be other such embarrassments? Thus, he who is born deaf in a deaf household may use manual sign language to tell a story whose difference from a speaking person's version may never be fully available as something that can be talked (or written) about.[31]

5. *Mockeries and say-fors:* Four types of figures have been discriminated: natural, staged, printed, and cited. Now the last, a much neglected class of doings through which an individual acts out—typically in a mannered voice—someone not himself, someone who may or may not be present. He puts words and gestures in another's mouth. However, serious impersonation is not involved, since no effort is made to take anyone in, nor is theater involved, since the strip of animation is typically quite brief and unconnected to the efforts of other performers. At the center is the process of projecting an image of someone not oneself while preventing viewers from forgetting even for a moment that an alien animator is at work.[32] Neither the animator nor the figure

---

31. Following here the argument of Aaron Cicourel. See, for example, his "Gestural Sign Language and the Study of Non-Verbal Communication" (unpublished paper).

32. There seems no final reason why an individual should not take off on himself, and presumably this occurs, but not commonly.

he projects are thus allowed to hold the stage, allowed a full hold on the imagination of the viewers. Note, these little turns do not provide merely another variety of cited figure. Connectives of the kind used in discourse are not employed, since something closer to stage acting than to reporting is occurring.

Somewhat formal examples of this process of "say-foring" are found in patter songs, nightclublike entertainments wherein a performer gesturally follows a recorded voice which ultimately had derived from a body very much different from his own. Somewhat less formal are theatricallike "turns," whereby a performer off or onstage does a takeoff on a well-known personage and is accorded a special performer's status while so doing. Song performers also sustain a not-self of this order, except that no specific other is the attributed figure, and some affinity is presumed between the singer and the figure in whose name the singer sings.[33]

Say-fors can thus be accomplished by individuals who are themselves in the role of stage performer. The significant point about these projections, however, is that they are available to individuals who are ostensibly engaged off the stage in routine conversational interaction. Thus the practice of projecting mimicked words into the mouths of figures that are present—babies, pets,[34] fellow participants, and the like. Similarly, the license taken with persons absent, marked in some cultures by the presence of a special term and by appreciated competencies.[35]

---

33. I mean here merely to raise the issue of the relation of a singer to the "person" from whose point of view the lyrics are uttered, that is, the "I" of the song words. The relation is complex and one of the wonders of popular culture. The remarkable point is that every day millions of auditors hear songs in which the singer is in a complicated relation to the figure projected in the song, but no one except a few students seems concerned about the matter. Faint intellectual stirrings are to be seen in the occasionally indulged impiety of cutting off the TV sound and watching the singer's gestures in isolation from such meaningfulness as the words provide. Disclosed thereby is a small repertoire of hand-arm gestures—some five or six—which prove to be almost all the singer needs to create an apparently varied flow of self-accompanying gesture.

34. Erving Goffman, "Communication Conduct in an Island Community" (Ph.D. diss., Department of Sociology, University of Chicago, 1953), pp. 153–154.

35. Among Shetlanders of a decade ago "taking off" was a well-developed recreational art. Particular members of the community were widely known for being good at doing other particular members, much as comedians get

Also "voices" (or "registers"), these being stereotyped accents employed by individuals during informal talk to say something that can be attributed to a figure other than the speaker, the figure being categorically, not biographically, defined. Baby talk, ethnic and racial accents, national accents, and gender role expressions are examples. Although baby talk is sometimes used between consenting adults as part of affectionate styling (now perhaps mostly found on TV) and very often used to children as a means of dispelling the fear they might have in dealing with adults, another function is at issue here: its use as a mock-up in which a speaking adult acts out a response that a nonspeaking child might make if he could (or would) talk. A similar form of ventriloquism is used to animate pussy cats, teddy bears, and other lovable objects.[36] Of course, "expression speech" is often

known for their James Stewart or Marlon Brando. Claudia Mitchell-Kernan in her study of contemporary black English provides another example and a useful description:

> *Marking* is essentially a mode of characterization. The marker attempts to report not only what was said, but the way it was said, in order to offer implicit comment on the speaker's background, personality, or intent. Rather than introducing personality or character traits in some summary form, such information is conveyed by reproducing or sometimes inserting aspects of speech ranging from phonological features to particular content which carry expressive value. The meaning in the message of the marker is signalled and revealed by his reproduction of such things as phonological or grammatical peculiarities, his preservation of mispronounced words or provincial idioms, dialectical pronunciation and, most particularly, paralinguistic mimicry. [Claudia Mitchell-Kernan, "Signifying and Marking: Two Afro-American Speech Acts," in John Gumperz and Dell Hymes, eds., *Directions in Sociolinguistics: The Ethnography of Communication* (New York: Holt, Rinehart & Winston, 1972), p. 176.]

36. The syntactical form of these throwings-of-voice can be obscure. Thus, a mistress to her cat: "Jezebel says she doesn't like soap, does she?" Only the nonlexical features of this statement identify it as a means of putting words in the cat's mouth. The interchange could then be completed by the mistress saying in expression speech, "We won't hurt baby, will we?"

Note in the above that the cat's owner uses two devices characteristic of talk with incompetent lovables: the "parental plural," which tends to erase the line between self and other, and suppression of pronouns in favor of proper names and kin titles, these phrased from the perspective of the lovable. As a consequence of these two changes, the *written* version of an utterance can be frame ambiguous in a rather spectacular way, either words spoken *to* an incompetent lovable or words spoken *in the name of* an incompetent. Thus: "Daddy will spank us if we do that" can be translated back into: "I will spank you if you do that" or (said for the child): "You will spank me if I do that."

added before or after say-fors in order to simulate a completed interchange.

VII

Connectives were defined as those devices which tell us who is saying or doing whatever is being said or done. Now on first blush it might be thought that that is all there is to reporting strips containing figures, namely, connecting up words and acts properly to their imputed makers. But it was argued that more than that is involved. In repeating another's words, the speaker also is licensed to repeat something of the expressive stream in which these words presumably did or will occur. Speaker is allowed within limits to mimic the figure, to copy its expressions. So the direct quote is marked not only with a connective, but also with an altered expressive accompaniment; in fact, it will often be possible for a listener to come in late after the connective has done its work and disappeared, and still be able to detect that the speaker is not speaking in his own name but rather is projecting a figure not himself who is speaking. Further, it appears that there are rules of mimicry, that is, limits, varying from culture to culture and within a speech community from one category of speaker to another, concerning how much copying is appropriate. Incidentally, here one finds a difference between direct and indirect quotation, the latter apparently allowing for less mimicry than the former.

Along with mimicry conventions, censorship conventions ought to be considered. Take, for example, lecturing on literature, say, the modern English novel. The speaker has a right—nay, the obligation—to quote a strip or two of the original. He reads aloud to illustrate and to support his arguments. Critics who publish their analyses do likewise. Now, given the time, place, and audience (and the manliness of some current fiction), the speaker may well find that he must forbear reading some passages because of considerations of taste. The point is that wherever a commentator draws this line, it will be differently drawn from the one he employs in guiding speech which he himself is currently producing in his own name. Typically a speaker exerts stricter standards regarding what he himself says at the moment than in regard to what will be seen after all as someone else's words, words which the speaker is merely animating.

Mimicry norms and censorship norms are both part of the limits associated with the lecture frame, reminding us that certain materials cannot be cited effectively, and that citation itself —like the transformation from direct to indirect quotation—has limitations. There are other examples. As already suggested, in regard to the task of reading another's paper, there seems to be a set of discourse elements such as "I" which introduce the threat of downkeying and must be corrected accordingly. Another example. Jokes and puns have the property of being self-contained and insertable into anyone's discourse. Credit seems to go to any teller instead of the creator—when indeed there can be said to be one—allowing an individual to say where he got the material without thereby destroying the reputation for wit (or the lack of it) he might earn by giving tellings. It follows that when a lecturer takes jokes or puns as his topic of discussion, and naturally provides illustrations, he may feel that his examples are constantly slipping out of their frame status as mere examples, and that consequently he cannot fully insulate himself from the reputation that real tellings would ordinarily earn him. In such circumstances, the speaker may follow an illustration with a very marked, wry expression, as if to shore up the illustration frame— a correction not required by other materials he might cite.

Now it appears that, like lecturers, conversationalists are also guided by norms when reporting another's words, limits which can, incidentally, be more strict than those a lecturer recognizes in citing.

Given this frame perspective, what problems specific to informal talk can be addressed?

1. In the replaying of old experience, what are the limits of the size of the cast that can be managed by the speaker and by the audience? And how long a tape can a speaker play during any one presentation? (Here, of course, the issue arises as to when and how a shift is made from mere participant in a conversation—with the right, of course, to play various short tapes—to the specialized and functionally differentiated role of raconteur and storyteller.)

2. What are the vertical limits of embedding, that is, how far can a speaker go and expect to be followed in having a cited

figure quote someone who in turn draws on a cited figure, and so on?

3. Given our working assumption that natural figures will accompany their talk with a complex expressive overlay of feeling, gesture, and accent, how much of this is properly to be mimicked when a speaker is "doing" someone other than himself? For example, if a speaker quotes a person of the other sex, how far can gender expression be mimicked without the mimic becoming suspect?

4. Censorship rules: In quoting another's use of curse words and other taboo utterances some license is provided beyond what the speaker can employ on his own behalf, but where does this license stop?

VIII

The notion of information state and that of connective provide some of the bases individuals require in order to present strips of reexperience. The concepts of principal, animator, and figure provide further bases. Now a final term is needed.

As suggested, in ordinary interaction a figure can also be the animator and the principal of the remarks issuing from him. In stage plays the three functions are separated. For although a staged character may act as if he is the animator and originator of what he says, this is merely part of the dramatic fiction; the ultimate animator will be the actor, and there will be no ultimate principal, strictly speaking. Clear enough, even in the case of a playwright who takes a part in his own play. Now what about plays and stories that are read aloud by a reader to a listener? If the reader is a professional one, the various characters in the text will be mimicked quite consistently. Each will be given its own voice. And the teller will reserve still another voice—presumably one close to his "own"—for nondialogue parts of the text, including, ideally, connectives and stage directions. (He may omit some of the connectives in the text because his special voice for each character will provide sufficient connective, his omission serving to increase the theatricality of what he is doing. And he is likely to fail occasionally to restrict a particular voice precisely to the bracketed strip over which it properly applies, resulting in "smeared" connectives.)

Obviously here the organization of the experience must be kept clearly in mind or analysis will falter. The reader is the actual animator of the whole story, the voicing machine. But embedded in this story are characters who, at their own level, can be engaged in originating and animating stories. These will be transformed originations and transformed animations, but originations and animations nonetheless.

When one shifts to the silent reading of novels and plays by ordinary readers, the question of who literally animates the lines becomes a little cloudy. Indeed, it seems that the reader here is the actual animator of the words, and that he has an audience of one, himself.

Which brings us to the final term that is needed—"audience." As already noted in discussing the theatrical frame, in our society the audience is a recipient in a special way, having very limited obligations: to pay the fee, sit more or less quietly, show interest and appreciation during the performance, and clap at the end of it. What is said onstage is not said *to* them, but *for* them; appreciation, not action, is their proper response. It is the other characters in the production who must respond, and, of course, their response is in character and hence not "actual." And note that the appreciation is not simply for the performer, but somehow has a diffuse target involving, in addition to the performer, the character he stages, the producer, the director, the playwright, and the entire dramatic effect. (There is reason after the curtain falls for the whole circus to come back on to take a bow collectively.) All of this, of course, can also be said when we respond appreciatively to a novel or to a play that we ourselves are reading.

Face-to-face informal talk can now be addressed. Because here there are few listeners, each will be obliged to show that he has received the message, understands it, and does not feel the speaker is drastically out of line. In all of this the traditional terms of communication analysis are reasonable—more so than when applied to large audiences, since numbers themselves reduce the communication obligation of any one recipient. But in addition, and often primarily, the listener's job is to show appreciation, not merely for the speaker but also for the whole scene (along with its protagonists) that is being presented. Here, to repeat, the classic linguistic forms of assertion, question, command, exclamation, and so forth are simply wide of the mark. On the face of it, what is going on is not that sort of thing. One might say that often sympathy is being sought, not appreciation, and this is so, except that sympathy itself can be its own end, a final action, a measure in full of what the speaker will obtain from his listeners.

During a stage play, the onlookers are radically cut off from the statements and actions made at any point by a character. Unlike the characters on the stage, onlookers can only respond through the back channel, disattendably expressing in a modulated way that they have been stirred by what is being unfolded before them—stirred in spite of the fact that they know tomorrow night the same show will be given for another audience. So, too, during actual conversation. It is not the shout of responsive action that talk mostly needs and seeks to get but murmurings—the clucks and tsks and aspirated breaths, the goshes and gollies and wows—which testify that the listener has been stirred, stirred by what is being replayed for him.

IX

Starting with the traditional notion of the individual as self-identified with the figure he cuts during ordinary interaction, I have argued some frame-relevant grounds for loosening the bond: that playfulness and other keyings may be involved which sharply reduce personal responsibility; that often what the individual presents is not himself but a story containing a protagonist who may happen also to be himself; that the individual's presumably inward state can be shared around selectively, much as a stage performer manages to externalize the inner feelings of the character he enacts.

But these theatricalities in the relation between animator and animatings are only one side of the special license that framing rules provide the participant. There is another and quite different side, namely, the right of the individual to dissociate himself from the imperfections (and perfections) of his current role performance, and this by virtue of a claim that role as such has limited claims. The difference between these two sides to license is syntactical and very deep, yet, unless the issue of frame is carefully addressed, easily overlooked. It is the difference, for example, between expertly mimicking a figure who happens to be scripted to muff an act and muffing an effort which happens to be that of mimicking a figure. The first draws on the standard license to separate oneself from the figures one animates, the second on one's capacity to withdraw responsibility for one's own activity. It is this second type of protective distance I want to consider now. So the issue is not who the individual is attempting to project but rather how he manages the contingencies of any such projection.

The first matter to examine is suppressible diversions. Here, for example, are fleeting facial frame breaks: aways, flooding out into smiles and laughter, into bursts of anger and vituperation, into blushings. And breaks more fleeting still: comfort actions, such as scratching the face, rubbing the nose, coughing, shifting in the seat. Here also are small bits of business styled to be treated by others as out of frame: side-involving byplays, temporary leave-taking to attend to private projects, reading of mail, and so forth. Here fuguelike, dissociated side involvements sustained as part of the self that is out of frame: doodling, nail biting, finger sucking; various forms of intake, such as smoking, munching, chewing. Finally, there are acts designed by the individual to keep his front in order, performed as though open use were being made of the concealment channel: checking tie and collar, straightening hair, putting skirt in order, and so forth.

Through all of these acts, the individual is seen marking the limit to which his current role can hold him—an open admission and assertion that the individual qua animator is larger (or at least other) than any of the current roles he is obliged to project, and openly and avowedly so. It is as if others participating were voluntarily to be allowed a backstage glimpse, and this on the assumption that they don't quite rate a perfect performance.

A second matter to consider is the management of excuses and apologies. When the individual visibly muffs a task, he can, of course, act as if nothing wrong has occurred, obliging the witnesses to act accordingly. Indeed, this is the tack usually taken in the most formal of occasions, for anything else will itself be another delict. Alternatively, however, he can stop his doing in midflow for a moment to offer an excuse or apology. Interestingly, this sort of endeavor is often classified as a form of politeness and hence a type of formality; but in fact, it is anything but that. For to provide this sort of remedy for trouble is to demand of the others involved that they suddenly accept the actor on a different footing, that of a human being who can make mistakes in his carrying out of a specialized role.

When a physical task had been involved and is now over, a shift to verbal excuse-making is often not disruptive, nor when the excuse precedes the effort to be excused. A simple matter of retrospective or prospective reframing is involved, this fitting into natural junctures in the activity. However, when the failure pertains to the performance of talk, then matters are more complicated. Excuse-making can here supplant the very doing the failing at which it was meant to excuse.

One example—this one not of informal talk. News broadcasters on national prime time read their lines in a close to faultless manner, effectively maintaining the sense that something other than mere reading is occurring. When a word is flubbed, these performers tend to recover themselves with minimal reference to the mistake, either blandly repeating the spoiled strip as if no repetition were involved or proceeding as if neither notice nor correction were required. In contrast, announcers on new special-interest local stations not only make an appreciable number of mistakes but also exercise considerable liberty in dealing with the trouble. They give open voice to apologies, self-castigations, exasperation, and may even let the audience into their confidence concerning the trouble they have always had with various words, phrases, languages, and pronunciations. In this way, they show that they themselves are alive to how announcing ought to go, but in thus attempting to save the self some more of the program is lost. And the audience finds that it has been invited to participate in the situation of announcers instead of the situations they have been instructed to announce. Observe that since one utterance an individual makes must here address itself to another one he has made (or will make), a difference in voice across the whole of the editorial aside will have to be evident, and so it usually is—this being a characteristic feature of reflexive frame breaks.

As with excuses, so also with "false starts" and voiced (or "filled") pauses, of which "uhhh" is the basic example. These latter sounds can be found throughout the broadcast talk of those not accustomed to talking before a microphone. These audibles provide continuity, showing that the speaker is still in the business of completing a reply even though he cannot immediately muster up the right words to effect this.[37] But the very provision of this continuity requires that the audience patiently tolerate the holdup, according the mind of the performer time to function, time to mobilize itself for the role that was meant to be in progress.

In performing a role, then, the individual is likely to take minor liberties, ducking out for a moment to stretch or apologize. These fleeting derelictions are but shadows of acts, very easily unseen; certainly sociology has managed for long to ignore them. That a stage performer must disavail himself of these lapses when presenting a character (except when they are scripted) should quicken our interest in them and lead one to appreciate more clearly that although the social world is built up out of roles sustained by persons, these persons have, and are seen to have a right to have, a wider being than any current role allows. These very small acts celebrate very large issues.

X

A summary now of the arguments about talk and the application of frame analytical terms to this sort of interaction.

Talk appears as a rapidly shifting stream of differently framed strips, including short-run fabrications (typically benign) and keyings of various sorts. Transformation cues are involved, specifying whether a variation from the typical is to be employed, and if so, what kind. When such variation is intended, bracket cues

---

37. There is now an appreciable psycholinguistic literature on the hesitation phenomenon. See, for example, Frieda Goldman-Eisler, "A Comparative Study of Two Hesitation Phenomena," *Language and Speech*, IV, pt. 1 (1961): 18–26; H. Maclay and C. E. Osgood, "Hesitation Phenomena in Spontaneous English Speech," *Word*, XV (1959): 19–37; Donald S. Boomer, "Hesitation and Grammatical Encoding," *Language and Speech*, VIII (1965): 148–158. On the whole, this work is methodologically neat and tidy. However, it fails to give much attention to the central sociological issue of the rights an individual has to be hesitant and the role he is in while hesitating. So clean have these students kept their house that nothing much is left in it.

will also be given, establishing where this transformation is to
begin and where it is to end—that is, across what past strip or
upcoming strip the reconstituting is to apply—the cues themselves being placed to function prospectively or retrospectively.
(Asking a personal question in a typically laconic form and
receiving an angry reply, the asker can retreat by disputing the
framing, claiming that he had really meant his question literally
or as a joke.) A brief strip keyed or fabricated in one way follows
immediately a brief strip transformed in another, all of these
mingled with strips that carry "zero transformation," being as
literal as typically found in the circumstances. And these transformations can be quite subtle, the special intent of the speaker
causing his remarks to be cast so that their literal content is not
quite what is at issue. As Grice suggests, when a question is put,
the recipient may be meant to recognize that the open intent
of the asker is to be reminded about something that is on the tip
of his tongue, or that the open intent is to test the recipient's
knowledge or obtain an admitted confession from him, and so
forth.[38] (The asker here is not seeking an answer to his question
but an answer to his questioning; if he succeeds, the literal response will only be the inner lamination, a something that has
been upkeyed.) Indeed, even within a single brief utterance, use
of metaphor will require (and will obtain) momentary shifts out
of and back to literal interpretation.[39] The speaker can add fur-

---

38. H. P. Grice, "Utterer's Meaning and Intentions," *Philosophical Review*, LXXVIII (1969): 166–167.

39. Nor, apparently, only in Western talk, as Ethel Albert illustrates regarding a Central African people:

In addition to idioms, i.e., locutions that are incomprehensible if taken
literally, there are in Rundi discourse a number of stylistic conventions
that make statements misleading if taken literally. Speaking of a revolutionary . . . it is conventional to say, "Nobody knows who he is; nobody
knows his family." The speaker knows perfectly well and will go on to
tell in great detail the history of the patrilineage in question, its alliances,
successes and failures, and ultimate destruction. The conventional introduction is a negative value judgment. If anyone says of a man, "He has
no children, there will be nobody to bury him," this must not be taken
literally, especially if it is said in the presence of the man's sons. It means
that some of his sons have died, i.e., "He fathered many, but many have
died." In a somewhat lighter vein, the statement, "I went to X's house but
there was no beer," means in fact that only a few quarts were downed,
but either the total available supply was small or the number of visitors
great, or the reception was not friendly enough, so there was no point in

ther variety by reporting statements made by others than himself, who may themselves be quoted as quoting. And when he
does cite himself, when he does use "I," this I is likely to be different in some respects from the speaker himself-at-the-moment,
thus ensuring that he will be speaking with reduced weight and
in a special frame, parenthesizing himself from the cited figure
in his own reporting of his own experience. Finally, the whole
will be punctuated with a multitude of minor reflexive frame
breaks, some apparently "spontaneous," others quite mannered,
in either case serving to shift attention from what the speaker has
said to the way he said it, thus transforming the doing of talk
into a subject matter for it. No group in our society seems unable
to produce such choppy, streaming lines of change in frame;
and no competent person seems to be incapable of easily picking
up the frame-relevant cues and ordering his experiencing of another's behavior by means of them. And if a participant in a conversation did not constantly apply adjustments for frame, he
would find himself listening in on a meaningless jumble of words
and, with every word he injected, increasing the babble.

The argument is that the response we often seek is not an
answer to a question or a compliance with a request but an
appreciation of a show put on. It is tempting to find another
argument behind that one: for many reasons we seem to feel
safer if we can put some distance between ourselves as animators
and ourselves as figures to whom final responsibility for words
and deeds is imputed. Perhaps the accommodative pattern of face-
to-face interaction requires us to shift doings out of the close
circle of conversational co-participants, leaving only what can be
much more easily accommodated, namely, a review of action, not
action itself—a review the response to which is appreciation, not
counteraction, a review employing a protagonist who is often
called "I" but is thereby dissociated just a little from the person

---

staying on, one's thirst would not be quenched. The name traditionally
given to an eleventh or twelfth child is *bujana*, "Hundreds," signifying
that the family is a large one. Stylized exaggeration is also common in
practical contexts, notably in economic or political negotiations, claims
for damages, and in praises—a generous person may be called *mwami*,
king, or Imana, God. [" 'Rhetoric,' 'Logic,' and 'Poetics' in Burundi:
Culture Patterning of Speech Behavior," *American Anthropologist*,
Special Publication, LXVI, pt. 2 (1964): 51.]

who thus refers to himself. Whatever the reason, the life of talk consists principally of reliving.

Individuals presumably can engage in naked performative utterances, as when a bridge player takes his turn by saying: "Three clubs." But as with vacuums, nature abhors a performative utterance. Individuals can instead conjure up a scene that has already occurred or will perhaps occur. They can in particular quote another person or even themselves. They can utter words clownishly as if the person speaking them were a stereotypical member of a class, nation, planet, race, sex, region, occupation, or a character from *Alice in Wonderland,* or a Chinese sage, or a person under the influence of alcohol, God, or passion. They parenthesize their remarks with all manner of hedges, reservations, and other reductions in weight, accomplishing this often by introducing an otherwise unnecessary self-reference. And even while engaged in these performances they can in other voices make apologetic asides about these doings, breaking their own frame to do so.

And so it is that when an individual appears in person before his familiars and joins with them in talk—surely the place where we ought to see him in the round, acting for himself, in his own name and in his own way—he frames himself from view. To say that he assumes a role and presents himself through it is already a bias in the direction of wholeness and authenticity. What he does is to present a one-man show. He animates. That much is his own, his doing of the moment. But this capacity to present is largely used in the name of principals other than he-himself-at-the-moment to enliven figures other than himself-at-the-moment. Certainly beliefs, concerns, feelings, attitudes, are "expressed"; "inner states" are documented. But these displays are not some privileged access to the biological innards of the speaker, for they are properly to be attributed to a figure animated, not the animator.

Nor does looseness stop there. If in truth the informal statements of a speaker are appreciably cut off from the environing world, then surely the interpretive activity of the listener is even more free to float. For in perceiving, however accurately, what the speaker means to evoke, the listener can decline to be stirred, and can instead upkey what he hears, dissolving it into a single whole, construing the utterance for the sense in which it is merely a disguise for self-promotion, or a tired effort at flattery, or but another telling of a story he has often heard the speaker tell before, or an interesting effort at faking a prestigious accent. (Reductionist analysis begins, apparently, at home.) Thus, overlaid on the quickly changing frames of a speaker's talk may be another lattice of frame changes, this set introduced by the hearer—if sometimes only for himself. Adding perversity to polymorphousness.

Certainly it is possible during a game of bridge for a player to take his turn at bidding by saying, "Three clubs," and his turn at playing a card by doing just and only that. Certainly such use of talk might be satisfactory for bridge. But as for talk, examine the frame structure of the following conversation taped during an actual friendly bridge game.[40] A hand is in play:

MARILYN: Did uh,

.

.

.

MARILYN: —Helen tell you what I was gonna come over after,
MARIE: *Dih*—eh—*She* never told you hel*lo* the other day. *You* were talking to her, and I was sitting in the other office and Frank Rom*a*no was standing there and I said "*Th*at's my *fri*end,
SARAH: ((clears throat))
MARIE: —on the phone there" and he said, ·hh "*He*len, tell her Marie said hel*lo*." And Helen was so busy yakking to you she never, she did hang up without saying it.
MARILYN: Oh.   Uh huh.
MARIE: But she ⌐kept—
MARILYN: ⌊hhmh!
MARIE: Cause I heard her talking to you a couple times. Something about the,

.

.

.

.

.

---

40. Taped and used by permission of the players. The taping was done by Arvilla Payne. The tape transcription was done by Gail Jefferson, who has somewhat simplified her usual orthography and has capitalized game-relevant statements where she felt she safely could. To give some sense of time-without-talk when, presumably, the game alone was in progress, she has provided time-equivalent dots.

MARIE: —the bill, or whatever it was, and uh,

      .

      .

MARILYN: Did they tell you what I, requested,

MARIE: No.

MARILYN: Hho hunh hunh! huh—They *di*(h)⌐dn't?

MARIE: ⌊*They* didn't—elaborate any I just⌐knew you were talking to 'em.

MARILYN: ⌊Hoh! hhhhhhhhhhhh Well one day I
was getting all their tickets for them y'know and
they're, "Well we're c-calling our good friend Marilyn
again and⌐blah blah⌐blah" and changing,

EILEEN: ⌊Mm.

MARIE: ⌊Yeah, they call—

MARIE: You're, their⌐good friend Marilyn.

EILEEN: ⌊THAT WAS MY LAST⌐CHANCE TO
MAKE IT, HMHH

MARILYN: ⌊Yeah.

MARILYN: ⌐So I says "Okay,"

SARAH: ⊦((clears throat))

EILEEN: ⌊THE, FINESSE'D WORK,

SARAH: IF THE FINESSE⌐WOULD WORK, YEAH.

MARILYN: ⌊I says "no(h)w I'm gonna ask
⌐*you*(h) to be a good friend.

SARAH: ⌊MNUH, ·HHHHHHH
HHHHHHHHHHH WELL THAT'S IT SHE HAD
ALL THE CARDS HHHH

XI

In the last decade there has been an impressive rise in the
number of man-hours spent in the world watching television.
Some small part of what is watched involves rather undramatic
use of language, pictures, and diagrams, as when the weather is
forecast, a government ruling reported, or a commercial product
displayed. A large portion of TV time, however, is devoted to
drama or comedy involving movie reruns or movielike scripts.
And, more surprisingly, there has been a great increase in documentary watching. News coverage seems increasingly oriented to
"actualities." Actual scenes of newsworthy events are presented,
and interviews of participants are given when these persons can

be assumed to be still in the quick of their involvement and still able, merely by answering questions, to exude the reality of their concern. ("Were your mother's clothes burning when you saw her trying to get out of the building?") No doubt all of this makes for the better informing of the public. But also what is involved is the transformation of political or tragic events into raw materials for scriptings, the replaying of which provides viewers with an opportunity for vicarious participation. Events which have no actual bearing on our lives, or very considerable eventual bearing on our lives, can easily be used as a resource for plot materials. Apparently, a way to smother real events is to give them live coverage.

So various arguments of a socially responsible kind could be made about the dramatization of the world and our consequent inoculation against everything. There is another point, however. I do not think that suddenly we have been turned into passive viewers demanding that the world present itself to us so that we can be temporarily enthralled by a show and that behind this orientation in life there are advertisers and politicians arranging for the profitable delivery of vicarious, secondhand experience. I believe we were ready for the enthrallment all the time. (And ready, too, for such apparently bizarre embedding effects as sports announcers produce when they employ "instant replays"—sometimes at slow speed—to improve on the natural ratio of exciting to nonexciting periods.) For there is one thing that is similar to the warm hours we now spend wrapped in television. It is the time we are prepared to spend recounting our own experience or waiting an imminent turn to do so. True, we seem to have forgone some of this personal activity in favor of the work of professionals. But what we have given up thereby is not the world but a more traditional way of incorporating its incorporation of us.

XII

The argument so far has been that the frame structure of the theater and the frame structure of talk, especially the "informal" kind, have deep-seated similarities. This leads us in conclusion to look once again at the actual content of plays and to compare it with what occurs in real life.

1. Take it that the crucial feature of the theater, at least as far as popular opinion would have it, is that what goes on there is not real. It's make-believe. It really doesn't happen. And, of course, in the sense meant, it doesn't, although the events depicted in a biographical drama may have once occurred, and the performance itself, *relative to its rehearsals,* can properly be called real. Even ceremonials have greater actual consequence.

But this nasty fact of life in the theater forces one to ask the same question of the individual's own sphere. How real is it?

The traditional answer plays it both ways. Certainly the individual is involved in real, literal-minded projects of action and is an object of such action also. (I, too, believe him to be.) On the other hand, it is known, although perhaps not sufficiently appreciated, that the individual spends a considerable amount of time bathing his wounds in fantasy, imagining the worst things that might befall him, daydreaming about matters sexual, monetary, and so forth. He also rehearses what he will say when the time comes and privately formulates what he should have said after it has come and gone. Not being able to get others to speak the lines he wanted to hear from them, he scripts and commands these performances on the small stage located in his head.

A point to be made here is that this traditional balance between doings and dreamings leans much too far, I think, in the direction of doings. What it misses is that when the individual is not engaged in private fantasy but engaged in routine talk throughout the day, much of this talk fails to qualify as straightforward activity; it turns out to be just as much removed from actual worlds as is the stage. Instead of stating a view outright, the individual tends to attribute it to a character who happens to be himself, but one he has been careful to withdraw from in one regard or another. And when a moment to idle becomes free or can be stolen, he seems much inclined to use the opportunity to tell little anecdotes, re-create little strips, play little tapes, in which he figures as protagonist in the tale as well as the teller of it. Just as in the theater, these sallies are to be appreciated by an audience, not acted on by a teammate—at least on the face of it.

Of course, one can argue that the idling circles in which these recountings are given contain well-selected participants, and, moreover, that the right to play favorite tapes is never equally distributed. One can therefore move from the study of talk to a study of clique structure, friendship networks, the arrangement between the sexes, the class politics of sociability, and other aspects of the infrastructure of social organization. But there is also a truth in saying that a social function of this infrastructure is to provide each of us with sympathizers who will stand by while we recycle remains of our old experience. We are the vehicles of society; but we are also overheated engines prone to keep firing even though the ignition is turned off.

2. If the fact that theatrical action is not real is its first feature, then its second is that the unreality it presents is of a distinctly dramatic kind. After all, a playwright could try to fill the stage with a simulation of just the sort of thing that fills up everyday life, and although this could certainly pass as an experiment or put-on, and on that basis enjoy a short run, it would do so exactly because it was *not* theater.[41] (Or else, for example, anyone with a tape recorder and transcribing typist would be a playwright.) So what is theatrical about what occurs onstage is not (or not merely) its unreality, but rather the *kind* of unreality that it presents. That is our problem now.

The beginning of an answer is found, I believe, in attending to what it is the theatrical frame can bracket, that is, what can be stuffed inside the actual space and time in which the dramatist and his cast must do their presentation. Setting aside for a moment the issue that what goes on up there is not "really" happening, one can ask: What is there in real life that *could* be available to invisible witnesses if one were able to arrange for them to view a stage-size bite of this reality across the two hours of real time available to a playwright, the viewing, of course, to be from that distance from the stage that is established by ordinary theatrical practice? Or, contrariwise, what by its very nature can't be pressed into these confines?

First, it is perfectly plain that some events can quite comfortably occur in their original form within the "real" space-time of a

---

41. A parallel can be drawn to the cinema in connection with what is ordinarily taken to be very obvious: the appeal of pornographic film. These films directly violate the norms of the cinematic frame regarding sexual exposure. It is assumed that they show what they do in spite of the policing of films; it could almost as well be argued that they present what they do *because* it breaks the cinematic frame, generating thereby an appreciable negative experience.

stage presentation, were one to use this setting for real, not theatrical, life. A cigarette can be lit or put out or even smoked; a drink can be mixed and consumed; a greeting performed in its entirety; a telephone answered; a magazine leafed through. Such events, one could say, are "directly" presentable, their whole course manageable within the space-time available. I set aside for a moment the difficulty of using the term "directly" with any precision,[42] and the fact—also true of events in real, literal life—that indicators must be relied on which are less than and often considerably different from what they are taken to signify. To say, then, that some events can be directly presented throughout their whole span onstage is not to say anything about how *fully* they are witnessed or through what indicators. The dying of a man onstage or in real life can be indicated by the collapse of a surgical balloon, by a falling away of his head on his chest, or by the fluttering away of a rose petal from between his fingers; but in any of these cases, the dying itself is seen as something that could there and then occur.

Second, it is also plain that some events are not the kind that could (in the sense described) directly appear on a stage, either because they are long since over, such as the unkind cut that Brutus gave Caesar; or because they take too long, such as the maturing of an individual; or because they could not be encompassed in so small a space, such as is true of a boat race; or because of combinations thereof, such as the industrial revolution.

If these recalcitrant events are to form part of a play, they must appear on the stage indirectly. Dramaturgy offers various techniques. Peripheral indicators can be employed, a small local fact serving as evidence of a larger whole, as when the sound of battle comes in through the drawing room window, or no answer is obtained from the phone, this signifying that the dirty work has already occurred at the distant crossroads. Verbal reports can be provided, either in the form of special prologues which set the scene or, more covertly, by having a character appear to answer or put a question to another character, when in fact the intent is to provide onlookers with required information. (Whatever the

---

42. On the complications of this word see John Austin, *Sense and Sensibilia* (Oxford: Oxford University Press, 1962), pp. 14–19.

excuse, a character need only provide a spoken report of an event and, except for quite technical facts, there it is.) Note, the occurrence onstage of a verbal quarrel is not merely a verbal means of providing indirect evidence of bad relations; it constitutes a direct presentation of an event. It would be a report about a verbal quarrel that would be indirect, although it would provide a direct presentation of a reporting of a quarrel.

In addition to use of prologue (or epilogue) forms and the "incidental" introduction of information, there are other, trickier devices for expanding what may be included onstage. For example, the dramatist may choose to collapse real time between scenes or acts, achieving this by presenting the same characters successively aged. Thus, a character can appear young in the first act, middle-aged in the second, and old in the third, thereby bringing to the stage an aging process that actually takes decades to accomplish.[43]

It should be apparent that directly presented events will, on the whole, be livelier to the sense of the onlooker than indirectly presented ones. After all, it is likely that directly presented events can be conveyed by many indicators in many sensory channels, whereas indirectly presented ones must often rely on narrow indicators, on a few signs, not streams of them.

Now the question can be put: What sort of things do playwrights fill their stages with? Or, more pointedly, what sort of material do onlookers find interesting and involving?

Apparently events occurring outside the stage which at the same time do not immediately affect the characters are of little interest, although, of course, some have to be described in the interests of establishing the context of the action. The industrial revolution as such, however interesting a thing in its own right, won't help much.

Nor can one appeal to *any* kind of directly presentable event. As suggested, there are a host of task performances, such as washing dishes, and a host of side involvements, such as smoking a whole cigarette, that could be shown in their entirety. It would also be possible to script the characters to engage in just the sort

---

43. The cinema can draw on a wider range of devices; in early films, for example, seasons were shown quickly going by, pages of a calendar turned by breezes, and so forth.

of small talk that might actually occur in real life in just such a space-time as the stage. Just as obviously, these events in themselves have little interest; when they are present on the stage, they are meant to be seen as incidental acts that convey realism and ordinariness or to link up significant passages or, more importantly, to serve as vehicles for covertly freighting with special significance. So one can find acts which are fully portrayable but of no interest; indeed, there is no reason why the stage figures themselves in their projected, acted existence should be interested in these activities either.

This last fact could mislead us. It would be possible to stage a bridge game from start to finish with nominal stakes, and the characters in the staged realm could be conceived of as becoming intensely interested, caught up, carried away. After all, they would have the special realm of the game to enter. But the onlookers, what about their position? They, too, could get caught up in the game, providing some device were available for displaying the hands and the play of tricks, but then there would be no reason for their going to the theater. They would be better advised to watch match point play at the local bridge hotel; the admission would be cheaper, the bridge better.

But the answer, I think, is close by. The dramatist provides a gamelike activity for the audience to get caught up in, for after all, if the audience fails to get involved, the play necessarily and irrevocably fails, and games are good assurers of involvement. In the game the playwright provides us, however, the scripted characters do not engage one another in the narrow capacity of game partners and opponents who then deal with one another at still further remove through the figures available in a deck of cards or a box of chess pieces. The world onstage is more perverse than that. For in the gamelike activity the dramatist presents, the cards and pieces are themselves personlike figures. And the moves taken and plays made are those in which something of long-standing, fateful significance for the life situation of the protagonist is determined. Note, it is not any kind of fatefulness that is dealt with, only the kind that could have a *directly* perceptible occurrence and *directly* perceptible culmination, that is, a crisis, a turning point, a realization, a coming to a head within the real space-time available to the dramatist.[44] (This can, of course, include talk, providing the talk involves confessions, disclosures, fallings out, comings together, and so forth, all of which can be actually fateful in real life, in spite of taking place through mere words.) There is thus established the suspense characteristic of games, the necessity to look to the moment to find out what is going to happen, in short, the eventfulness of a contest, but in connection with individual life situations. Of course, to accomplish these realizations, it will be necessary to provide background information about the characters, including their pasts, their prospects, and their personalities. But this will be done by indirect means, and, in any case, what is provided is merely the base for action, the deck of cards, as it were, the hands that are dealt, and not the play. The play is the *dramatic* element, the presentable determination of fate.

And, of course, it is with such events that plays are packed, until the boards groan with an amount of fateful eventuating that an ordinary two hours of life is very unlikely to have. Thus one finds disclosures, accidents, fights, initial admissions of love, firings and hirings, agreements to marry and divorce, plottings, captures and apprehendings, meetings after long absences, reception of good and bad news, and so forth. Babies are conceived, born, and their sex disclosed. Faces are slapped, blows struck, shots fired, tears shed, cries uttered, embracings occur, and as the lights are dimmed, romance is consummated. Knowledge is obtained that money has suddenly been acquired or lost. Characters die off at an appreciable rate of every known cause. News is produced and the response to the news depicted—that Celia Coplestone got eaten by ants.

All in all, then, the argument is that drama is not only fictive, make-believe, "unreal," but also that it is inordinately filled with

---

44. There is a parallel here between the materials playwrights can use and materials effective in unstaged conversation. Individuals who engage in games of chance, including the stock market, seem remarkably prone to replaying hands, races, and transactions to friends and acquaintances. But although they sometimes manage to get hearers it is much harder to get anyone to really listen. Interpersonal doings, however, are much more effective as materials for recounting. That sort of interplay persons seem willing to listen to. Instead, then, of saying that individuals are always willing to listen to gossip, one might better say that gossip is what individuals are always willing to listen to.

fateful eventfulness—with turning points, redirections, expo-
sures, major decisions—specifically that eventfulness that bears
on the presumed life course of the stage figures. And here is a
further unreality to the stage. Each of these fateful events or
turning points is something conceived of as such by members of
our culture. We feel that loss of a job, the gaining of a husband,
the disclosure of a tainted past, and so forth are the sorts of
things which do provide structuring to life, a key to the individual's "situation." Playwrights, after all, must start from where
their audience starts: the belief that individual lives do indeed
have a structure and course, and that the determinative forces
can be identified. And this belief, this cultural lore, is only that.
The citizenry could well sustain these conceptions uniformly, and
yet, in some sense, a poor naturalistic description might be
involved. If in fact personalities and lives are characterizable,
popular lore may support the wrong characterization or at best
focus on a small, arbitrary selection of the actual possibilities.
One could, in fact, argue that popularly recognized life-course
themes do not merely make scripted presentation possible but are
conceived of *in order* to make these entertainments possible.
Human nature and life crises are what we need to make life
stageable. How else account for how well-adapted life appears to
be for theatrical presentation?

Behind the possibility of staging drama, then, are two quite
fundamental assumptions made in our culture about individuals:
that individuals have long-term developing careers, situations,
personalities, and so forth, which provide a means of characterizing them; and that these central, long-term strands can demon-
strably become broken, spliced, twisted, and appreciably
strengthened during a social situation, replicas of which occasions can therefore be fitted onto a stage.

When one turns to the sort of stories and posturings that
individuals provide during informal talk, minor contrasts with the
stage become apparent. As suggested, individuals offstage by and
large don't express themselves well, not usually being in a position to get their associates to feed them the right line at the right
time. Also a playwright is presumably concerned to entertain and
inspire; natural figures seem more concerned to establish warrant and justification for their position. Such is the extent of the
difference. The accountings that individuals provide of their lives,

the strips of experience that they replay or preplay, are not somehow a sure reflection of life, merely now once removed; or at least these tapes are not likely to be. For ordinarily an individual's view of his past actions and future prospects, his recounting of why he did what he did and how he proposes to act in the future, will have a demonstrable linkage only to picayune and minor events. The moment he provides a statement which has some general import, some overviewing of his life and times, he is off into the game of providing a picture of the central features and themes of life. And his view of these structurings—even when they pertain to himself—would seem to be just as dramatic, just as biased in the direction of the eventful, just as much a response to our cultural stereotypes about the mainsprings of our motivation, as are those conceptions which are presented on the stage, or, of course, in any other of the channels for commercial vicarious experience. What is presented on the stage did not happen that way in fact—except (to a degree) in the case of biography. But what is presented by the individual concerning himself and his world is so much an abstraction, a self-defensive argument, a careful selection from a multitude of facts, that the best that can be done with this sort of thing is to say that it is a lay dramatist's scenario employing himself as a character and a somewhat supportable reading of the past.

One further argument. Although a stage drama involves figures who are personlike, not cardlike or checkerlike, the gamelike character of these scriptings is enhanced (as already suggested) by the tendency of the dramatist to work with a closed resource, that is, a set of characters that makes an early appearance and that provides a sufficient and necessary source for what will prove to occur. As with a game, the audience can look to the interplay of these known resources for all relevant outcomes. In this way the audience can be given a sense of commanding witness of the whole of the relevant world, a sense that what turns out to happen could theoretically have been divined from the initial array of figures and forces, as in a riddle. As with a game, no early interaction will turn out to be irrelevant for what proves to materialize later. And as in a game, the action of any one character is interdependent in a massive, not merely incidental, way upon the action of the other characters. (But unlike games of chance, plays—at least modern, unmelodramatic ones

—do not allow chance a major role.) To have plotted a play is to be able to present innocently now what will prove to have been a necessary preliminary shortly. To write the ending of a play is to show what all the preceding events were leading up to, which events can truly be shown to have been leading up to something because that is the main reason why they were put there in the first place. Now, patently, ordinary life—especially urban life—is not organized in that fashion. New characters and forces are always a possibility and can enter the story line at late points without the earlier events having been designed with this entrance in mind. Crucial turning points occur for apparently incidental reasons, the consequences of acts often being out of all proportion to their causes. Instead of well-plotted developments, one finds something closer to a Brownian movement. However, in actual, informal talk, tales told about experience can (and tend to) be organized from the beginning in terms of what will prove to be the outcome. What is developed in the tale can be phrased as having resulted totally from the interplay of figures within the tale, all of which interplay, and only which, is needed to accomplish this development. Tales, like plays, demonstrate a full interdependence of human action and fate—a meaningfulness— that is characteristic of games of strategy but not necessarily characteristic of life.

So it can be argued that although individual projects and undertakings literally do occur, the individual's presented tales about these projects would seem to be more akin to drama than to facts. And since natural figures do not have a cast of trained actors at their disposal or much time to polish a script, since they merely have their own amateur capacity at recounting events, there is rarely any question as to which is more lifelike, the stage or what it is that private persons present to those whom they can get to listen.

14

Conclusions

1. This study began with the observation that we (and a considerable number of theys) have the capacity and inclination to use concrete, actual activity—activity that is meaningful in its own right—as a model upon which to work transformations for fun, deception, experiment, rehearsal, dream, fantasy, ritual, demonstration, analysis, and charity. These lively shadows of events are geared into the ongoing world but not in quite the close way that is true of ordinary, literal activity.

Here, then, is a warrant for taking ordinary activity seriously, a portion of the paramount reality. For even as it is shown that we can become engrossed in fictive planes of being, giving to each in its turn the accent of reality, so it can be shown that the resulting experiences are derivative and insecure when placed up against the real thing. James and even Schutz can be read in this way. But if that is comfort, it comes too easy.

First, we often use "real" simply as a contrast term. When we decide that something is unreal, the reality it isn't need not itself be very real, indeed, can just as well be a dramatization of events as the events themselves—or a rehearsal of the dramatization, or a painting of the rehearsal, or a reproduction of the painting. Any of these latter can serve as the original of which something is a mere mock-up, leading one to think that what is sovereign is relationship, not substance. (A valuable watercolor stored—for safekeeping—in a portfolio of reproduced masters is, in that context, a fake reproduction.)

Second, any more or less protracted strip of everyday, literal activity seen as such by all its participants is likely to contain differently framed episodes, these having different realm statuses. A man finishes giving instructions to his postman, greets a passing couple, gets into his car, and drives off. Certainly this strip is the sort of thing that writers from James on have had in mind as everyday reality. But plainly, the traffic system is a relatively narrow role domain, impersonal yet closely geared into the ongoing world; greetings are part of the ritual order in which the individual can figure as a representative of himself, a realm of action that is geared into the world but in a special and restricted way. Instruction giving belongs to the realm of occupational roles, but it is unlikely that the exchange will have occurred without a bordering of small talk cast in still another domain. The physical competence exhibited in giving over and receiving a letter (or opening and closing a car door) pertains to still another order, the bodily management of physical objects close at hand. Moreover, once our man goes on his way, driving can become routine, and his mind is likely to leave the road and dart for moments into fantasy. Suddenly finding himself in a tight spot, he may simultaneously engage in physically adroit evasion *and* prayer, melding the "rational" and the "irrational" as smoothly as any primitive and as characteristically. (Note that all these differently framed activities could be subsumed under the term "role"—for example, the role of suburbanite—but that would provide a hopelessly gross conceptualization for our purposes.)

Of course, this entire stratified strip of overlapped framings could certainly be transformed as a whole for presentation on the screen, and it would there be systematically different by one lamination, giving to the whole a different realm status from the original. But what the cinematic version would be a copy of, that is, an unreal instance of, would itself be something that was not homogeneous with respect to reality, itself something shot through with various framings and their various realms.

And by the same argument, a movie showing could itself be seen as part of the ordinary working world. It is easily possible to imagine the circumstances in which an individual attended the movies and became involved in its offering as one phase of an evening's outing—a round that might include eating, talking, and other actualities. Granting this, one can imagine the circumstances in which the moviegoer might compare the reality of the evening's round with watching a TV drama in which such an evening was depicted. Contrariwise, in court, establishing an alibi, our individual could avow that he really had gone to the movies on a particular evening in question, and that doing so was for him an ordinary, uneventful, everyday thing to do, when, in fact, he had really been doing something else.

2. But there are deeper issues. In arguing that everyday activity provides an original against which copies of various kinds can be struck, the assumption was that the model was something that could be actual and, when it was, would be more closely enmeshed in the ongoing world than anything modeled after it. However, in many cases, what the individual does in serious life, he does in relationship to cultural standards established for the doing and for the social role that is built up out of such doings. Some of these standards are addressed to the maximally approved, some to the maximally disapproved. The associated lore itself draws from the moral traditions of the community as found in folk tales, characters in novels, advertisements, myth, movie stars and their famous roles, the Bible, and other sources of exemplary representation. So everyday life, real enough in itself, often seems to be a laminated adumbration of a pattern or model that is itself a typification of quite uncertain realm status.[1] (A famous face who models a famous-name dress provides in her movements a keying, a mock-up, of an everyday person walking about in everyday dress, something, in short, modeled *after* actual wearings; but obviously she is also a model *for* everyday appearance-while-dressed, which appearance is, as it were, always a bridesmaid but never a bride.) Life may not be an imitation of art, but ordinary conduct, in a sense, is an imitation of the proprieties, a gesture at the exemplary forms, and the primal realization of these ideals belongs more to make-believe than to reality.

---

1. See Alfred Schutz, "Symbol, Reality and Society," *Collected Papers*, vol. 1 (The Hague: Martinus Nijhoff, 1962), p. 328. Here again I am grateful to Richard Grathoff.

Moreover, what people understand to be the organization of their experience, they buttress, and perforce, self-fulfillingly. They develop a corpus of cautionary tales, games, riddles, experiments, newsy stories, and other scenarios which elegantly confirm a frame-relevant view of the workings of the world. (The young especially are caused to dwell on these manufactured clarities, and it comes to pass that they will later have a natural way to figure the scenes around them.) And the human nature that fits with this view of viewing does so in part because its possessors have learned to comport themselves so as to render this analysis true of them. Indeed, in countless ways and ceaselessly, social life takes up and freezes into itself the understandings we have of it. (And since my analysis of frames admittedly merges with the one that subjects themselves employ, mine, in that degree, must function as another supportive fantasy.)

II

1. In looking at strips of everyday, actual doings involving flesh-and-blood individuals in face-to-face dealings with one another, it is tempting and easy to draw a clear contrast to copies presented in fictive realms of being. The copies can be seen as mere transformations of an original, and everything uncovered about the organization of fictive scenes can be seen to apply only to copies, not to the actual world. Frame analysis would then become the study of everything but ordinary behavior.

However, although this approach might be the most congenial, it is not the most profitable. For actual activity is not merely to be contrasted with something obviously unreal, such as dreams, but also to sports, games, ritual, experimentation, practicing, and other arrangements, including deception, and these activities are not all that fanciful. Furthermore, each of these alternatives to the everyday is different from the others in a different way. Also, of course, everyday activity itself contains quickly changing frames, many of which generate events which depart considerably from anything that might be called literal. Finally, the variables and elements of organization found in nonliteral realms of being, albeit manifest and utilized in distinctive ways in each of these realms, are also found in the organization of actual experience, again in a version distinctive to it.

The argument, then, is that strips of activity, including the figures which people them, must be treated as a single problem for analysis. Realms of being are the proper objects here for study; and here, the everyday is not a special domain to be placed in contrast to the others, but merely another realm.

Realms and arrangements other than the ordinary can, of course, be a subject matter of interest in their own right. Here, however, another use is claimed for them. The first object of social analysis ought, I think, to be ordinary, actual behavior—its structure and its organization. However, the student, as well as his subjects, tends to take the framework of everyday life for granted; he remains unaware of what guides him and them. Comparative analysis of realms of being provides one way to disrupt this unselfconsciousness. Realms of being other than the ordinary provide natural experiments in which a property of ordinary activity is displayed or contrasted in a clarified and clarifying way. The design in accordance with which everyday experience is put together can be seen as a special variation on general themes, as ways of doing things that can be done in other ways. Seeing these differences (and similarities) means seeing. What is implicit and concealed can thus be unpacked, unraveled, revealed. For example, on the stage and on radio we have come to expect that a performer will externalize the inner state of the character he is projecting so that continuity of story line can be assured, so that, indeed, the audience will know at every moment what is going on. But precisely the same sort of intention choreography can be found in daily life, most evidently when an individual finds he must do something that might be misconstrued as blameworthy by strangers who are merely exercising their right to glance at him before glancing away.

2. As a paradigm case, take three or four flesh-and-blood individuals performing an actual task in one another's immediate presence—in short, an everyday strip of activity. What can frame analysis find to say about the scene and its participants?

First, the tracks or channels of activity. Assume that there is a main activity, a story line, and that an evidential boundary exists in regard to it. Assume at least four subordinate tracks, one sustaining disattended events, one directional, one overlaid communication, and one matters for concealment.

Second, the laminations. The strip under question presumably has none. Neither a keying is present nor a deception. Certainly such straightforwardness is possible. But one should see that it is not likely for a very long period of time. And often effort will have had to be exerted to ensure even this. The absence of laminations is to be seen, then, as something worth seeing.

Third, the question of participation status. A two-person chat sustained in a sequestered place implies, on first analysis, a full sharing of ratified participation status and, overlaid, an exchange of speaker and recipient roles.

But expand on these possibilities. Add a third participant, and allowance must be made for the speaker addressing the participants as a whole or singling out a particular other, in which latter case one is forced to distinguish between addressed and unaddressed recipients. (Then it can be seen that an unaddressed recipient, especially a chronic one, may stand back somewhat from ordinary participation and view the speaker and his addressee as a single whole, to be watched as might be a tennis match or a colloquy onstage.) With a third participant the possibility has also been created for a two-person collusive net and a distinction between colluders and excolluded. Add, instead, a third person who is a nonparticipating stranger and one has the bystander role whose performer is cut off from the others by civil inattention. Script the two-person arrangement or either of the three-person arrangements and perform it on a stage and one then has, in addition, the performer-audience roles.

Simple enough. But now see that these expanded possibilities can be drawn upon in order to quicken our sense of what can enfold within an actual, fully sequestered, two-person talk. As already considered at length, the possibility of collusive communication can occur in two-person talk, in the form of either self-collusion through which one participant performs gestural asides during the other's turn at talk, or (as it were) collusive collusive communication, involving both participants playing both colluder and excolluded roles. Also one participant can style the externalization of his response so that the other is encouraged to perceive it but act as if he hasn't, thereby encouraging the latter to contribute two ways of functioning, not one, in effect expanding the two-person arrangement into something more complicated. And when a speaker replays a strip of experience for the delectation of his listener, the latter (and the speaker to a degree) may stand back and function not unlike an audience; the listener *and* the speaker can show appreciation for what the speaker presents before them.

In brief, arrangements which articulate multiperson interaction may be folded back into two-person talk, there to be given a structural role. And as spoken narrative forces simultaneously occurring events into a temporal sequence, and as cartoon strips force temporally sequenced events into a spatial sequence, so living interaction may itself be somewhat coerced by those sustaining it so that sequencing is more marked than it might otherwise be and timing of turns more nicely determined by a hidden effort to allow clear scorekeeping. It is thus that a child who falls and scrapes his knee may wait until he crosses the street to his parent before bursting into tears that are as hot and fresh as these things get. It is thus that an adult may puncture a conversation with a burst of laughter,[2] a spurt of anger, a sudden interruption, a downward look of chagrin and embarrassment—or any other genuine flooding out—and somehow manage in effect to time this rupture so that it neatly occurs at a juncture in the other's talk that would best allow an unseen audience an unimpaired view, a completed hearing, of what it is that called forth this response. And here instead of our following the usual practice of "sequentializing" what is actually concurrent, we allow ourselves to see as overlapping what has actually been managed sequentially—thereby deeply enlisting framing practices in the general conspiracy to sustain beliefs about our human nature, in this case, that behind our civil niceties something undisciplined, something animallike, can there be found.

3. Given this perspective, one can turn to the central but very crude concept of participant (or player or individual), for again the comparative approach allows us to address assumptions about ordinary activity that would otherwise remain implicit. And one can begin to see, for example, that the body itself and how it functions in a frame is an issue that warrants systematic treatment.

Start with a board game such as chess. The dramatic focus is two opposing sets of figurines destined to move against each

2. Here see Gail Jefferson, "Notes on the Sequential Organization of Laughter" (unpublished paper, 1974).

other in regulated ways. Behind this interaction of moves are two players, each of whom stands to gain or lose by the outcome, each of whom diagnoses what moves his side should make, and each of whom physically manipulates—animates—the pieces on his side.

It should be obvious how differently from this chess can be arranged and yet be, overall, the same game. The figures may be actual persons on a courtyard square. The diagnostic, cognitive function may be performed by a committee or a computer. The manipulation may be performed by third parties in response to voiced commands, or by an electrical arrangement, or by the figure itself in the case of courtyard matches. When the game is played only "for fun," then each of the two parties exercising the cognitive function presumably gains or loses whatever is going by way of psychic stakes. But if there is money at stake, or national pride, or team score, then, of course, parties other than the two mentioned can directly participate as principals, that is, as backers, partners, and so forth. So, as already suggested, the following functions: figures, strategists, animators, principals.

Two points should be mentioned about chess. Although the several functions discussed can be performed by different entities, our very notion of player assumes that a full overlay will be present and that this needs no thinking about. Second, the role of the human body is here very limited. It is the pieces that cut the swath. Ordinarily a body is used only to maneuver the pieces, and this operation is ordinarily seen as unproblematic, routine, of no consequence. A polite request with instructions and one's own move can be physically made by the opponent. It is the cognitive function that is problematic.

Take now a brawling street fight between two men. Again it is possible to define each fighter in terms of multiple functions, for example, the principal or party with something at stake and the strategist who decides which moves to make. Easier than before, one can see that these functions could be segregated. (Professionalize the fight and a trainer-coach will share in the cognitive function, and backers, if not owners, will share in the gain or loss.) But in addition there is a rather obvious yet instructive contrast to chess. Instead of chess pieces as the figures, the human body serves that function. And whereas a chess piece draws its attributes, its powers, from the rules which tell us how it may move, and is in that sense unproblematic, a human (or animal) fighter draws its powers—strength, technique, exertion —from within, and it is these powers, perhaps even more than the cognitive ones, that are at issue.

When one turns to organized, equipment sports like tennis, fencing, or hockey, again one or more bodies per side figure as figures, except that here each body employs an extension thereof —a stick, club, bat, or whatever. These devices are used in an extremely efficient, instrumental way, which only very long practice can ensure, so that, incidentally, the plane within which the body operates becomes restricted in the matter of how exertion is channeled. Furthermore, the effort and skill involved make no sense unless one agrees on the special and peculiar goals of the game, the precisely defined measurements of the equipment (along with the obligation to restrict oneself to their use, and this within the rules), and mere markings as outer boundaries of the field of play. The actions induced in sports contests have thus an arbitrary, artificial character.

The dance might now be mentioned. Here the choreographer seems to claim much of the strategic function. Again, of course, the body figures largely, but this time in no way as a utilitarian task performance. The purpose is the depiction of some overall design, including bodily mimed feeling and bodily symbolized fate, and although muscle and bone and training and stamina are certainly required, and problematically so, all this is exerted for pictographic ends. Boxers, of course, can display grace and economy of movement, as can tennis players, but this must be a by-product, at most a marginal concern, the main one being physical, describable in terms of a state to be accomplished in whatever way seems most effective at the time—within the rules, that is.

When one turns to ceremony and ritual, another combination of elements is found. On the face of it, no decisionmaking function is operative, the whole having been scripted by tradition, lore, and protocol. Again the figures involved are bodies, but although some practice may be required in performance of the ritual, proper execution can easily become routine and unproblematic. And again, utilitarian procedures are not involved; the controlling, open intent is a kind of symbolization, a special kind of rounded, well-formulated representation.

Imagine now a high school debate. Two teams are involved, each with two or more players. What is put at play is verbally presented arguments, these judged on standards of content and delivery. The delivery itself is certainly a problematic and important feature, and certainly control of voice, monitoring of speech, and other physical acts are involved. But the body as a whole has dropped out. The individual is expected to debate on his feet, but if he needs a wheelchair he can still participate fully.

Now look at everyday activity, especially that involving face-to-face talk. It might be thought that as in a high school debate only arguments and competence to express matters verbally will be in play. But that is much too narrow a view. Verbal commitments are made which have real consequence in the future. Signaling is facilitated through which close collaboration in physical tasks becomes possible. Interpersonal rituals are performed.

And as a by-product of his doings, the doer provides gleanings of, for example, his personality, social status, health, intent, and alignment to others present. Therefore, in the case of most strips of ordinary, unstaged activity, it seems perfectly possible to show that although the bodily behavior of the actor is learned and conventional, that indeed a set piece is being run through, the action is nonetheless perceived as direct and untransformed. Ordinary body movements are seen not as a copy, as in the case of the faked emotional displays of con men, or as a symbolization, as in the openly enacted emotional displays of some native mourners, but, to repeat, as a direct symptom, expression, or instance of the doer's being—his intent, will, mood, situation, character. This "directness" is a distinctive feature of the frame of everyday activity, and ultimately one must look to frames, not bodies, to obtain some understanding of it.

Ordinary behavior, then, is taken as a direct instance of, or a symptom of, underlying qualities and therefore has an expressive element, but symbolization—say, in Susanne Langer's sense of the term—is not taken to be centrally involved. Yet, of course, postures are struck and appearance is tailored, and this is a symbolizing action more akin to what is found in the dance than what is generated in other frames. And furthermore, behind expression and symbolization will often be found some threat, distant or close, of physical force, and some inclination, encouraged or not, to direct sexual contact, both of which imply still other roles for the body. Moreover, it is characteristic of everyday interaction that the immediate source of these emanations from the self will continuously shift: now the eyes, now the hand, now the voice, now the legs, now the upper trunk.

One can see, then, that in everyday interaction, the body figures in a limited but nonetheless very complicated way, and this one sees by checking back to the role it plays in other frames of activity.

4. Consider now the human nature said to ground the behavior of he who participates in ordinary doings. Again approach this comparatively, starting this time with the emotional self-response displayed by figures in various frames.

In stage and movie performances it is apparent that a well-trained and highly committed actor will be willing to take the part of an emotionally effusive character or an extremely self-contained one, depending only on what the script calls for. In the former case, he will be willing (in character) to break down under assorted pressures, flaunt his problems and feelings, beg for mercy, cry, groan, curse, and generally carry on in a manner he might well find quite unsuitable in real life—because of both the manners of his social group and his own particular version of them. Furthermore, on the stage he is willing to emote before a much larger number of people than would witness these outpourings in ordinary life were he there to indulge them; and moreover this larger group looks right at him instead of tactfully disattending.

In presented contests, again it is often the case that a more expansive display of emotion, especially chagrin, is allowed than in the sportsman's everyday life. (Indeed, each sport seems to provide a conventionalized use of its own equipment for this purpose, as when a baseball bat is thrown to the ground after a strikeout, or a tennis ball is hit into the backwire after a return has been muffed.) But these outbursts tend to be located just after the taking of a move, try, or turn, for at that moment the individual has ceased to be active in his player capacity, and what he does bears on that realm no more than does the applause or boos from the onlookers—which response he can elect to disattend. If a ballplayer throws down his bat during a pitch, he is a faulty player; if he throws it down after he has struck out, he is merely commenting on himself as a player during a moment of time-out in the play, a time when the players on the field are not in play either. So although the graphically displayed anguish of a golfer who misses an easy putt *looks* to be like the emotional volubility of a stage actor's performance of an excitable character, the difference is syntactical, bearing on the structure of experience.

A musician during a performance presents still another picture. He (like a conductor) is allowed to follow the physical act of performing with a parallel and supportive show of effortful disarray, for after all, he is modeling sounds, not comportment. But should he make a mistake, his preferred strategy is disattendance. If he is part of an ensemble, any stopping on his part to engage in chagrin, anger, embarrassment, and so forth would throw the whole into further disarray—even if he himself is temporarily not playing. If he is performing solo or with accompaniment he can make a point of stopping everything and beginning the troublesome passage again, but he can do this only once or twice a performance, and when he does he must be very sure to treat the whole contretemps as something manageable with distance and a twinkle so that it is not his full, literal self that has entered into the failure but only an expendable version of it. And what the twinkle says is that he knows the audience will be willing to collaborate in his momentary frame break, that they won't worry about his being really out of control or that he might think that they think that his little intransigence is disrespectful. Observe that what here calls for a virtuoso frame break, a performance that has to be exquisitely styled if it is to come off, is a commonplace achievement in everyday interaction. For there no audience is present with lofty expectations, and very often no one but the flubber himself is held up by his emotional self-response to the flubbing.

Now look again at the performance of popular songs. The story line typically involves some drama of the heart. As suggested, the story is typically told in first-person singular. As in stage productions, the animator and the figure are seen as technically different, but in the case of popular singing, some inner bond unites the two. In fact, the more the animator's life (as the audience knows it) qualifies for the plight that is being sung about, the more "effective" is the result. "Sincerity" here means singing as though the lyrics were true of oneself. In any case, singers routinely trot out the most alarming emotional expression without the lengthy buildup that a stage play provides. Thirty seconds and there it is—instant affect. As a singer, an individual wears his heart in his throat; as an everyday interactant he is likely to less expose himself. As one can say that it is only qua singer that he emotes on call, so one can say that it is only qua conversationalist that he doesn't. Neither comment tells us about persons as such; both tell us about figures in frames.

The notion of emotional self-response is one part of "emotional expression." Another has to do with unintentional self-disclosure. The doctrine associated with the frame of everyday actual behavior is that the actor has incomplete control over his emotional expression. He may attempt to suppress this source of information about himself or falsify it, but in this (we presume) he can never be fully successful. Thus, he can willfully tell an outright, boldface lie, but can hardly fail to show some expression of guilt, hesitation, or qualification in his manner. It is felt that his nature itself ensures this. He who can be utterly false in his address to others can be thought to be "psychopathic" or, God forgive us, "sociopathic," and in any case if we strap wires to him, the polygraph—our cosmological defense in depth—will show that he really doesn't contradict human nature.

In sum, as natural persons we are supposed to be epidermally bounded containers. Inside there are information and affect states. This content is directly indexed through open expression and the involuntary cues always consequent upon suppression. Yet when the individual engages in bluff games such as poker, one finds that he either blocks off almost all expression or attempts the most flagrant, expressively ramified deceptions—the kind which would give him a very bad reputation were he to attempt unsuccessfully such a display in his actual, literal activity.[3]

---

3. A nice case is provided by the game "So Long Sucker," in which the rules and playing are organized so that subsets of players must form working coalitions, and each player, if he is to win, must betray his coalition and join another, which, too, he must betray, and so on. Apparently the game doesn't usually get finished because of the refusal of players to continue. Until the game blows up, however, one obtains a remarkable expressive show of assurances by each player that he will remain loyal to the coalition he is about to enter, when indeed all along he knows this will not be possible. See M. Hausner, J. F. Nash, L. S. Shapley, and M. Shubik, "So Long Sucker, a Four-Person Game," in Martin Shubik, ed., *Game Theory and Related Approaches to Social Behavior* (New York: John Wiley & Sons, 1964), pp. 359–361.

An answer is apparent. Incapacity to perfectly contrive expression is not an inheritance of our animal or divine nature but the obligatory limits definitionally associated with a particular frame —in this case, the frame of everyday behavior. When the frame is shifted, say, to bluff games, and this frame gives the player the assurance that his dissembling will be seen as "not serious" and not improper, then magnificently convincing displays occur, designed to attest to holdings and intentions the claimant in fact does not possess. In brief, we all have the capacity to be utterly unblushing, provided only a frame can be arranged in which lying will be seen as part of a game and proper to it. And the same virtuosity can be elicited when the deceiver knows that what he is participating in is really an experiment, or in the best interests of an obviously misguided recipient, or as an illustration of how someone else carried on. It appears, then, that "normal honesty" is a rule regarding the frame of ordinary literal interaction, which rule, in turn, is a particular phrasing of a more general structural theme, namely, that the party at play has something to conceal, has special capacity and incapacity for doing so, and labors under rulings regarding how he is to comport himself in this regard.

5. And at the heart of it? The individual comes to doings as someone of particular biographical identity even while he appears in the trappings of a particular social role. The manner in which the role is performed will allow for some "expression" of personal identity, of matters that can be attributed to something that is more embracing and enduring than the current role performance and even the role itself, something, in short, that is characteristic not of the role but of the person—his personality, his perduring moral character, his animal nature, and so forth. However, this license of departure from prescribed role is itself something that varies quite remarkably, depending on the "formality" of the occasion, the laminations that are being sustained, and the dissociation currently fashionable between the figure that is projected and the human engine which animates it. There is a relation between persons and role. But the relationship answers to the interactive system—to the frame—in which the role is performed and the self of the performer is glimpsed. Self, then, is not an entity half-concealed behind events, but a changeable formula for managing oneself during them. Just as the current situation prescribes the official guise behind which we will con-

ceal ourselves, so it provides for where and how we will show
through, the culture itself prescribing what sort of entity we must
believe ourselves to be in order to have something to show
through in this manner.

Take your auctioneer. He proves to be a "character." He is not
in awe of what has been entrusted to him. He comments wryly on
one or two of the articles he is obliged to knock down, showing he
is slightly cynical about the sellers, the buyers, and what is being
sold. He emcees, he editorializes, he wheedles and teases. He
upbraids the assembly for bids not forthcoming. He declines to let
well enough alone; he ever so slightly puts the whole enterprise
on. (None of this, admittedly, prevents him from seriously tout-
ing the major items and may, in fact, provide a basis for his
credibility here.) So this auctioneer seems a special fellow, except
that in auctioneering a tradition, as well as the opportunity, exists
for this sort of thing, and many of those who take on the role also
take on the irreverent personal style encouraged in this particular
business endeavor. So, too, your air stewardess. She can serve
coffee with no more than a distracted half smile on making the
offer and a facial flick when withdrawing the pot, wrapping the
service in no more ritual than is available at every counter in
America. But instead I have seen the following:

> Speaking lightheartedly as if announcing a novel possibility, and
> gesturing with the pot, the stewardess asks a middle-aged male in
> an aisle seat if he wants coffee. He nods yes. Apparently knowing
> she was nearing the end of a run, she sneaks a peek over the edge
> of the pot and gives a warning *moue*, reducing her age to the point
> at which it would be appropriate for the passengers in sight to take
> up her perspective on events in neglect of their own. She pours,
> finds the cup is just filled, shakes the pot with a mock serious effort
> to free the last drop, jokingly breaks frame with a conspiratorial
> adult laugh, thrusts the pot a shade in the direction of the female
> passenger who is next in line, withdraws it covetously while raising
> her face and tightening her mouth in mock hauteur, and says
> aloud, "I gotta go back for more."

The feeling the man might have had that, after all, he had
come in for the dregs on his turn, and of his seatmate, that, after
all, she had just missed an unpostponed turn, have been stirred,
faced, and reframed as the required backdrop for what is to be
taken in good humor, a girlish effort to push a slightly ludicrous

adult role down a hill. A coalition against seriousness is induced so that remonstrances against the taste and temperature of the coffee can just as well be invoked by the server as by the served. Obviously she is a good kid, the sort who enjoys her work, is full of life, and loves people. She has a nice personality. Except she did not invent this way of no-contesting a transaction, nor, probably, could she ham it up in less favorable circumstances. Her age, sex, and appearance supply one part of the mix, her job the other. All the girls in her training class were encouraged to warm the world in the same way, and many succeed in flight in doing so. Thus, auctioneering and stewarding provide more than roles; they provide particular ways of not merely performing them, particular ways of keying literal events. In sum, whenever we are issued a uniform, we are likely to be issued a skin. It is in the nature of a frame that it establishes the line for its own reframing.

6. And "oneself," this palpable thing of flesh and bone? A set of functions characteristically superimposed in ordinary, literal doings but separated in all manner of ways in other realms of being. So, too, the persons we have dealings with. And if these functions—functions such as principal, strategist, animator, figure—are separated in extraordinary realms of being, why shouldn't analyses be able to separate them in ordinary reality? As Merleau-Ponty, for example, has tried:

> It is not sufficiently noted that the other is never present face to face. Even when, in the heat of discussion, I directly confront my adversary, it is not in that violent face with its grimace, or even in that voice traveling toward me, that the intention which reaches me is to be found. The adversary is never quite localized; his voice, his gesticulations, his twitches, are only effects, a sort of stage effect, a ceremony. Their producer is so well masked that I am quite surprised when my own responses carry over. This marvelous megaphone becomes embarrassed, gives a few sighs, a few tremors, some *signs of intelligence*. One must believe that there was someone over there. But where? Not in that overstrained voice, not in that face lined like any well-worn object. Certainly not *behind* that setup: I know quite well that back there there is only "darkness crammed with organs." The other's body is in front of me—but as far as it is concerned, it leads a singular existence, *between* I who think and that body, or rather near me, by my side. The other's body is a kind of replica of myself, a wandering double

which haunts my surroundings more than it appears in them. The other's body is the unexpected response I get from elsewhere, as if by a miracle things began to tell my thoughts, or as though they would be thinking and speaking always for me, since they are things and I am myself. The other, in my eyes, is thus always on the margin of what I see and hear, he is this side of me, he is beside or behind me, but he is not in that place which my look flattens and empties of any "interior."[4]

—only neglecting to apply to these references to self the analysis they allow him to apply to other.

4. Maurice Merleau-Ponty, *The Prose of the World* ed. Claude Lefort, trans. John O'Neill (Evanston, Ill.: Northwestern University Press, 1973), pp. 133–134.

Index